POLITICAL RADICALISM
IN LATE IMPERIAL
VIENNA

Karl Lueger, 1844–1910
Mayor of Vienna, 1897–1910

Photo from the collection of the Bildarchiv of
the Österreichische Nationalbibliothek.

JOHN W. BOYER

POLITICAL RADICALISM
IN LATE IMPERIAL
VIENNA

ORIGINS OF THE
CHRISTIAN SOCIAL MOVEMENT
1848–1897

THE UNIVERSITY OF CHICAGO PRESS
Chicago and London

The University of Chicago Press, Chicago 60637
The University of Chicago Press, Ltd., London
© 1981 by The University of Chicago
All rights reserved. Published 1981
Printed in the United States of America
85 84 83 82 81   5 4 3 2 1

Library of Congress Cataloging in Publication Data

Boyer, John W
   Political radicalism in late imperial Vienna.

   Bibliography: p.
   Includes index.
   1. Vienna—Politics and government.   2. Radicalism
—Austria—Vienna.   3. Socialism, Christian—Austria—
Vienna.   4. Lueger, Karl, 1844–1910.   I. Title.
DB854.B68   943.6′1304   80-17302
ISBN 0-226-06957-5

John W. Boyer is an associate professor of Central
European history at the University of Chicago and
editor of the *Journal of Modern History*.

For Barbara

Contents

Preface

The political history of Central European cities in the nineteenth century is as yet a largely unexplored area. In part this reflects the relative calm and political homogeneity which characterized much of the local and municipal political life in Prussian cities under the three-class franchise system. Where significant conflict did occur and municipal politics became something more than a conventional mode of providing for and legitimating local administration, this was usually the result of fringe protest movements which did not endanger the core control exercised by the German Liberal parties (in the Rhineland, the Center party, but on the basis of an even narrower franchise). In Berlin, for example, the efforts of Stöcker in the 1880s and the Social Democrats in the 1880s and 1890s to destroy Liberal hegemony provided much noise and political turmoil, but left control of the city's administration firmly in the hands of the Progressive-Liberal party. In contrast to the often violent confrontations on the national level in Imperial German politics, urban politics had a self-satisfied, closed aura which tended to infect all who came in contact with it—witness the effect of the Berlin communal activity of the SPD on Eduard Bernstein.

The political history of the Hapsburg lands offers, in contrast, two major examples of intense urban conflict in the later nineteenth century which, although both began on the local, municipal level, had far-reaching implications for the evolution of a non-Liberal, social interest party system on the national level after 1890. In Prague, the conflict between the embattled German community with its proud local traditions and the Czech majority offered a prime example of the force of ethnic and linguistic loyalties as major determinants of bourgeois political action. In Vienna, a larger and more cosmopolitan city in which nationalism was not a major political variable, the conflict initiated in the 1880s by the artisan *Bürgertum* led by 1895 to the destruction of that city's German Liberal tradition as well. Nationalism on the one hand, class and social interest group aggrandizement on the other—in each case the result was the isolation of the German Liberals within one of the major political cultures of the Hapsburg Empire.

This book is the history of this process of political revolution in late Imperial Vienna. Nowhere else in Central Europe in the nineteenth century did an explicit non-Liberal political movement with a powerful command of bourgeois loyalties take control of a major urban administration. Rarely was a party with such pronounced bourgeois social interests so successful in violating and denigrating Liberal political pieties, while using and adapting the very technical and organizational resources of urban politics which the Liberals had themselves created. The study of Viennese Christian Socialism is thus a study in the continuities of radical political change.

The interpretation of the Christian Social party presented here suggests that its history is best understood in terms of the coalition of social and occupational groups, all of them sharing and affirming traditional ideals of the Austrian Bürgertum, which came together in a consecutive, four-stage movement to destroy Viennese Liberalism by 1896. The artisans between 1880 and 1886, the priests and Democrats between 1886 and 1890, the *Beamten* and teachers between 1890 and 1894, and finally the property owners in the crucial years of 1895–96—these were the four stages in the internal destruction of the local Liberal tradition. Liberalism was not so much destroyed from without as it was undermined from within by social groups who (with the notable exception of the lower clergy) had formerly belonged to its most loyal and trustworthy cadres. Each stage was crucial to the success of the movement as a whole. Each occupational and political group contributed vital elements to the general success of the party by 1896.

One conventional description of the Christian Social party has been that of a political Catholic movement. Those historians who view the pre-war party from the perspective and historiography of the First Republic, when the party's intelligentsia came largely from clerical circles, have naturally chosen to emphasize the Catholic nature of the movement.[1] Unlike the Center party in Germany, however, Viennese Christian Socialism could not rely on religion alone to provide the self-identity and group loyalty which any successful political movement must generate in its voters. Although its popular religion played a powerful subsidiary role in political-cultural terms (not the least of which was its ability to defuse the utility of Liberal anticlericalism as a viable issue after 1885), the Christian Socials cannot be understood as a formal political Catholic movement. To do so is to read the history of the First Republic back into the more diffuse and less ideologized political culture of the late Imperial period. Similar attempts to view the party in terms of its antisemitism alone hardly encompass the rich secular interests and social traditionalism which underpinned the party's electoral recruitment.[2] Antisemitism was an exceedingly complex defense mechanism against unwarranted social change, but one which functioned in very different ways depending upon the actor or group involved. It was not the only issue which brought ultimate victory to Lueger and his party by 1896, even if it did provide a useful initial principle of organization and cohesion in the early days of the movement.

Both religion and antisemitism operated in the context of a larger cluster of issues, namely, the desire on the part of all of the *Bürger* occupational groups involved to enhance their material and status security in Austrian society by manipulating a system of privileged political resources. Fin de siècle Viennese politics offered an excellent example of the use of hegemonic political rights for group identity and special interest particularism. At the same time, a more general value overlaid much of the interest fragmentation of the party, the ideal of the unitary Bürgertum which Lueger used so magnificently in appealing to the voters of all three curias in the heated campaigns of 1895 and 1896. The older German ideal of the Bürgertum as an *allgemeinen Stand* in positive, universalist terms was converted in Christian Social politics in Vienna to a more exclusive, defensive norm which stressed antiproletarian and anti-industrial virtues of the Viennese *Mittelstand*.[3]

Another important issue which the party's history raised was the role of Lueger himself in its development and the relationship between powerful personal leadership and neutral party structures. Karl Lueger and his movement were prime examples of two of the major structural features Max Weber characterized as typical of late-nineteenth-century party politics—the transformation from notable to mass party and the internal power struggle between charismatic leadership personalities and unwieldy, impersonal, rationalizing bureaucracies, whether party political or governmental in nature. Yet one value in studying the Christian Social movement lies precisely in the way in which it reveals the complexity and diffusion of such patterns of change. The Viennese experience shows that Weber was both correct and incorrect in his assumptions about mass politics in the late nineteenth century. Mass politics did arise, but rather than replacing the older politics of notability it simply incorporated notable politics into itself, so that the Christian Social movement by 1897 represented a curious blend of both kinds of political models. Indeed, the unique power and strength of the Christian Socials in their ability to attack the older Liberals and successfully defend themselves against the insurgent Social Democrats only made sense in terms of its twofold capacity for styling political change to social tradition and for adapting political tradition to the needs of social change.

Equally important, the collision between personal and rational rule, which Weber thought inevitable, took place in no other movement in Central Europe as prominently and as forcefully as it did in Vienna under Lueger's Christian Socials. Lueger was a classic leader, who dominated his movement in strongly emotional and personalistic terms. But men voted for the Christian Socials not only because they admired Lueger's courage and calculated extremism, but also because they sensed a deep strain of political accountability, integrity, and rationality in his own person. The history of the party cannot be limited to Lueger the person, for the success of the party depended upon Lueger's willingness to subordinate a charismatic politics of will to the larger rationality of the party as a whole. This process occurred slowly and informally before 1897, largely in the context of the tradition of club and rally politics so common to Viennese political history, which demanded of all leaders that some informal structure govern personal choice and ideals. After 1897 more ominous and fateful challenges to Lueger occurred, precisely in the fashion one might expect from an unraveling of the Weberian model: externally, the Christian Socials gained a ready-made bureaucratic framework by winning control of Vienna and Lower Austria, enabling them to create a modern political machine in the city, which obviated some of the strength of the older notable and charismatic politics; but they also began to develop an internal party bureaucracy as well, especially after 1907. They thus had available to them a new, two-track system of political control (city bureaucratic patronage and the inner party organization itself), which forced a revision in the operations of the party and, eventually, of the role of Lueger within the party. The prominent role of state-party which the Christian Socials were forced to play on the national level after 1905 simply added to the complexity of the party's internal authority structure and its external role in the Austrian political system.

The recent work of Carl Schorske has emphasized the transformational "new key" style of politics Lueger employed in creating or perhaps even conjuring forth the Christian Social movement.[4] This book will ask how "new" the new key actually was: Did Lueger employ novel organizational techniques to summon the party into existence? Was the party, as Schorske seems to suggest, from its very inception a mass party which broke sharply with the Liberal tradition, or is it necessary to define more closely what is actually meant by "mass" party and then measure the Christian Socials against this criterion? How different in method and technique, in social constituencies and electoral support were the Christian Socials from the Liberals? Was Lueger's politics of language a truly novel phenomenon, or was it an old political language thrust into a new, social interest and social class situation? Ultimately this book will suggest that both Schorske's and Adam Wandruszka's analytical hypotheses on the disjunctive, *Lager* nature of fin de siècle politics (in some ways Schorske's arguments depend on Wandruszka's triadic scheme of Viennese politics), while brilliant and ultimately acceptable, must be more carefully qualified in terms of the early history of the anti-Liberal movement. The idea of mass politics, while helpful (and valid), is also a Pandora's box of conceptual confusion unless the terms of the argument are carefully arranged and the evidence measured against them.

Central to the argument of this book is that Viennese politics between 1848 and 1914 were marked as much by continuity as they were by radical political change. Lueger's movement is to be understood much more in terms of its profound normative and social roots in the nineteenth century than in terms of its alleged paradigmatic role for twentieth-century politics on the radical Right. Austrian Christian Socialism was a movement of nineteenth-century social bourgeois protest, not a protofascist crusade or a total break with nineteenth-century Viennese political values and institutions. There was no absolute, precise boundary line between "rationalist" and "irrationalist" politics in nineteenth-century Vienna.

This interpretation of Viennese politics demands a careful review of Austrian Liberal history, as well as a detailed analysis of those who sought to modify and build upon that tradition. It is impossible to understand Christian Socialism without a prior consideration of Austrian Liberalism; hence the substantial attention accorded in this book to the Liberals and their political institutions and resources. For all of its cosmopolitanism and social change, the world of Bürger politics in the city of Vienna was a remarkably small and intimate one. The Christian Socials for many years were far closer to the Liberal world of small district and ward clubs, established upon traditions of informal social gatherings and small-group friendships, than they were to the mass, bureaucratized cadres of Austrian Social Democracy. After 1896, when the party began to move in the direction of systematization and bureaucratization, this change did not entirely displace the older informality and what I have called "petty notability" of Viennese Bürger politics. Down to its collapse in 1918 Lueger's *Bürgerpolitik* was a fascinating hybrid of modern mass political mobilization and Vormärz social traditions. This book is thus a study of the longevity of political traditionalism based upon broadly comparable social systems in Vienna in 1848 and 1895–96. Vienna's society changed drastically in the second half of the century in its lowest reaches (the industrial proletariat of the outer districts) and in the evolution of a very narrow capitalist elite on the top of the social pyramid, but the relative distribution and the social attitudes of the more traditional *middle* sectors of the Viennese Bürgertum did not change as drastically in the same time period. And, because of the peculiarities of the Viennese franchise system, it was the middle of Viennese society which held real political power.

Finally, this book will attempt to open discussion on the way in which Austrian political parties and their social constituents related to the Imperial government (and each other) in the period after 1890. The ultimate challenge both German and Austrian state systems faced after 1890—how to cope with the parliamentary influence and internal leadership resources of modern mass political parties against traditional ruling elites (such as the *state* bureaucracy or the army) and against the insurgent power of semi–public interest groups—found no better illustration than in the impact which the Christian Social movement had on the Hapsburg political system. Contemporary German historiography has developed a clear (almost *too* clear) set of assumptions and questions about the relationship of Wilhelmine political parties and interest groups to the state. For Hapsburg history during the same time period the slate is still embarrassingly blank. Not only are the "answers" missing, but in many cases historians have yet to formulate the right questions. The easy tags with which German history is now marked—social imperialism, Liberal nationalism, *Sammlungspolitik,* interest group pluralism—these are in large part inadequate for Austrian history. This results not only from the different role parties played in the Austrian system, but also from the different role the Austrian state bureaucracy played in managing "its" political universe. If this book and its projected companion volume (which will carry the history of the party to 1920) contribute to an understanding of the late Imperial political system as a functional whole, the role of the Christian Socials in that system will be more justly appreciated. Rather than emphasizing the themes of decline and disintegration in the monarchy's (and Vienna's) final decades, it may be just as appropriate to explore those features of the Imperial political system which contributed to its stability and functionality, however marginal. To adapt a phrase from Hans Mommsen, presented in the context of the history of the First Republic, the important fact about the monarchy before 1918 was not that it fell apart, but that it proved capable of surviving for so long.[5] Survival in this case was not predicated on individual rationality or irrationality, but on larger, structural features of the system as a whole, of which the Christian Social party became a significant part after 1897.

Acknowledgments

Among the many scholars in Austria who offered generous help during the writing of this book, I wish to thank especially Professors Grete Klingenstein, Erika Weinzierl-Fischer, Gerald Stourzh, and Adam Wandruszka. Above all, Professor Fritz Fellner offered advice and encouragement which contributed immeasurably to the completion of the book. Hofrat Dr. Willy Lorenz and Dr. Karl Schwarzenberg were of considerable help in locating and obtaining permission to use the Schindler and Vogelsang papers. Among the many archivists and librarians in Vienna whose kindness and attentiveness greatly eased the difficulties of primary research, I would especially like to thank Dr. Henriette Peters of the *Erzbischöfliches Diözesanarchiv*, Archivdirektor Dr. Felix Czeike of the *Archiv der Stadt- und des Landes Wien*, Hofrat Dr. Franz Stundner of the *Niederösterreichisches Landesarchiv*, and Dr. Andreas Weyringer of the *Katholisch-theologische Fakultät, Universität Wien*.

I owe a special debt to Professors Hans Mommsen and Wolfgang J. Mommsen in Germany, who offered advice and valuable criticism at crucial stages in the evolution of this work. To the extent that the book attempts a balance between the social history of ideas and the social-structural history of politics, it is owing to the influence of Hans Mommsen and Wolfgang Mommsen.

In America Professors Robert A. Kann and Klemens v Klemperer offered timely and welcome assistance throughout the course of my research. To Professor William J. McGrath I owe a profound debt for first introducing me to late-nineteenth-century Austrian culture in his 1969 seminar on fin de siècle political radicalism. Professors James J. Sheehan, William M. Johnston, and Richard S. Levy read various drafts of the manuscript and offered important suggestions for revision, many of which are reflected in the present book. In a more personal sense Jim Sheehan's conviction that Central Europe is more than a collection of random and isolated parts has been a sustaining principle behind the present work. At the University of Chicago Keith Baker, Jules Kirshner, Arcadius Kahan, Friedrich Katz, Peter Novick, and Arthur Mann have offered an ideal group of critics whose interests in urban political and social history challenged me throughout the long period of this book's writing. Karl Morri-

son and Barry Karl, as chairmen of the Deparment of History from 1970
until 1979, provided both financial and moral support which helped greatly
in bringing the book to a final conclusion. My research assistants Jonathan
Sperber, Tod Heath, and especially William Levine were also immensely
supportive of the project.

To Leonard Krieger, for his skillful blend of encouragement and criticism and for his deep interest in the impact of ideas on society, I am
extremely grateful. I am indebted to William McNeill both personally and
intellectually in ways I can only hope this book will begin to justify. To
Emile Karafiol, former teacher and colleague and present friend and *av-
ocat consultant* of Hapsburg history at Chicago, whose analytical percep-
tiveness is surpassed only by his profound kindness and generosity, I
offer my deepest gratitude.

To my colleagues in the Department of History at Chicago, for their
patience with the eccentricities of someone who teaches German but
writes Austrian history, I express the hope that neither culture has suffered unduly by being placed in a comparative, Central European context.

The major research for this book and its projected companion volume
(which will cover the years 1897–1920) was undertaken with grants from
the Social Science Research Council, the American Council of Learned
Societies, and the Spencer Foundation.

Finally, more than anyone else my wife Barbara, who has shown patience, sympathy, and good cheer toward the capricious demands and
foibles, as well as the pleasures of late Imperial Vienna for over a decade,
has made this book possible.

October 1979

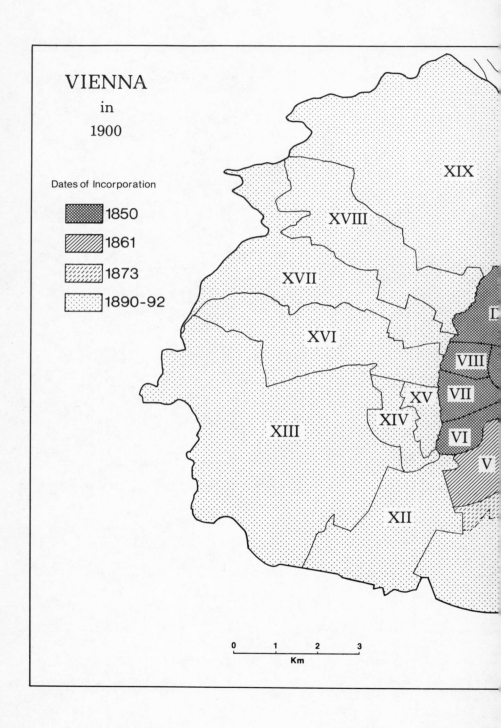

VIENNA
in
1900

Dates of Incorporation

1850
1861
1873
1890-92

XIX

XVIII

XVII

XVI

XV

XIV

XIII

XII

IX

VIII

VII

VI

V

0   1   2   3
Km

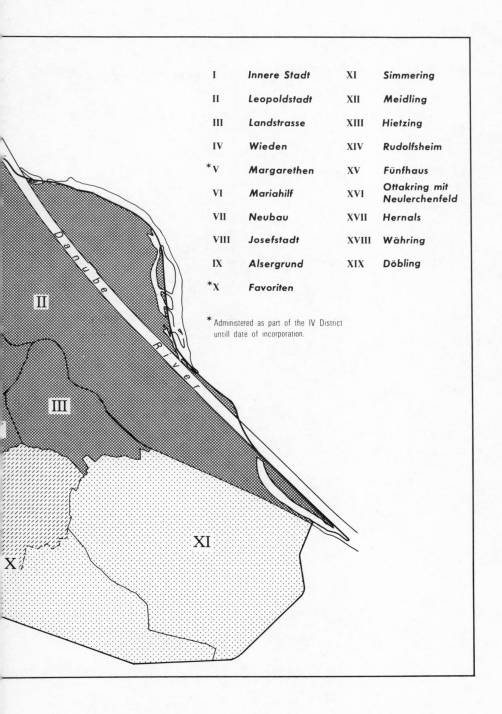

I	Innere Stadt	XI	Simmering
II	Leopoldstadt	XII	Meidling
III	Landstrasse	XIII	Hietzing
IV	Wieden	XIV	Rudolfsheim
*V	Margarethen	XV	Fünfhaus
VI	Mariahilf	XVI	Ottakring mit Neulerchenfeld
VII	Neubau	XVII	Hernals
VIII	Josefstadt	XVIII	Währing
IX	Alsergrund	XIX	Döbling
*X	Favoriten		

* Administered as part of the IV District untill date of incorporation.

I

Austrian Liberals and Liberal Politics, 1848–79

Bürger Privilege and the Fragmentation of Bourgeois Politics

Throughout Central Europe between 1880 and 1914 Liberal political parties found themselves on the defensive, both in terms of ideological consistency and the practical consideration of electoral success. The widespread popularity earlier Liberal parties found in the 1860s and 1870s quickly diminished with the impact of the economic depression of the later 1870s and with the rise of mass-based political movements, such as the Center and the Social Democrats, who appealed to more particularized kinds of electorates. The self-serving economic and social conserva-servatism which many Liberals espoused—the National Liberal Heidelberg program in 1884 is perhaps the best example—underscored the embattled state of Liberal politics on the national level in Germany. The very complexity of the German Liberal tradition, with its many nuances and particularities across the ideological (and geographical) spectrum, made it difficult for any single Protestant bourgeois party to claim for itself the role of principal spokesman for Liberal political theory or social philosophy. Opposition to the Liberals came not only from the big, mass-based parties of the Catholic Center and the Left, but also from Right-oriented conservative movements and from the splintered, factionalized German *Mittelstand*.

At the same time, German Liberals did have basic social and political resources to sustain them at some level of operational significance throughout the later nineteenth century. For all their weakness and disorganization several modes of Liberal politics did endure on the national and (especially) the local and regional levels of government in Germany. Paradoxically, the Liberals profited both from the experiential demands placed upon them by universal suffrage on the national level (from the very beginning of the Reich in 1871 they were forced to compete in a relatively open system of political resources with a diversity of electoral groups) and from the uniquely oligarchical franchise arrangements within various regional and local governmental bodies. The three-class voting system employed in many Prussian cities, for example, ensured Liberal dominance of major urban centers throughout the nineteenth century. The very same Liberals who profited on the municipal level from tight restrictionist legislation of voting rights were also capable of mounting respectable (if not always successful) competitions on the national level. The party organization of the Berlin Progressives, for example, maintained a stranglehold on the city itself before 1914 and did a reasonably effective job in saving at least some of the city's parliamentary seats (Berlin Wahlkreise I and II, the latter until 1893) from the Social Democrats. Where the party found itself in the minority, at least some semblance of respectable political organization and minority voter turnout was sustained. Crucial here, as in much of urban Germany, to such a pattern of survival was the lack of a third, bourgeois, yet secular anti-Liberal alternative to displace both the Liberals and the Social Democrats (or the Center and the Social Democrats).

In Austria and especially in Vienna such a third alternative (secular, non-Liberal bourgeois, yet anti-Marxist) did exist with enormous success: Karl Lueger's Christian Social party. The history of the Austrian Christian Socials necessitates, therefore, a prior review of the essential features of Austrian Liberal history, just as its later development requires a close inspection of the workings of Austrian Social Democracy. In Austria the German Liberal party was but one bourgeois interest group amid a conflicting network of national parties, all of whom depended upon the narrow Austrian curial system for their survival on the state level. The Liberal movement began in Austria in the 1860s with a much less arduous task before it than that faced by its German cousins both in terms of comfortable curial voting rights and in its effective detente with the Imperial administration. But unlike the Germans, the Austrian Liberals could not rely on the national issue or the issue of social imperialism as sources for their political universality after 1880. The nationalities issue itself proved far too attractive for Austro-Germans after 1900 to permit the survival of Austrian Liberalism even in German-speaking areas. To the extent that extreme German nationalism and the earlier national moderation of the Austrian Liberals were mutually exclusive—and most older Liberals felt they were—the former rather than the latter was bound to prosper.

If the Liberals in Austria were less impressive on the state level because of their passivity and laxity, and their inability to resolve or surmount the challenges of the nationalities problem, in Vienna itself they ultimately suffered because of the peculiar structure of the city's municipal franchise and the narrowness of their cultural and social programs. The situation in Vienna became almost the reverse of that in Berlin. In Berlin the Liberal party survived using a tightly oligarchical local franchise, while competing successfully in a universal franchise on the Reichstag level. In Vienna the Liberals relied far too much on the narrow single curia franchise for the Reichsrat, while creating in 1850 a municipal franchise with three broad occupational and tax curias which provided for a powerful, nonoligarchical bourgeois political presence in the city after 1885. The use which the Austrian Liberals made of both curial systems—national and local—was ultimately disastrous, since they ignored the social and economic needs of the lower levels of the *Bürgertum* (which many German Liberals did not do), while spending an excessive amount of their energies in quixotic attacks on the Church. It was not surprising that their principal opponents in Vienna by 1890, the forces of Karl Lueger, should unite a coalition involving pseudo-clericalism, lower-*Bürger* economic protest, and political antisemitism to begin a movement which would entirely destroy the local Liberal tradition.

The rise of a powerful anti-Liberal, bourgeois political movement like the Christian Socials in Vienna was dependent upon the special developmental characteristics of Austrian, especially Viennese, Liberalism as well as the role which religion and the state played in the formation of the Liberal movement in Austria. The view of Austrian society during the Vormärz and Liberal periods presented here reflects a comparative examination of recent trends in Prussian and southwest German historiography (Koselleck, Nipperdey, Gall, Walker, Krieger, Sheehan, Winkler, Böhme, Mommsen) with older and more recent research in Austrian history of the same period. Such a comparative view is helpful in showing how Austria differed from Prussia in the way each state developed between 1790 and 1848. It also illustrates how this difference created a special eastern brand of Central European Liberalism—the Austro-Viennese—which shared many common values with its German cousins, but which was singular in its essential properties and in the kind of political culture in which it was anchored. The peculiar middle-Bürger symbolism and rhetoric which Lueger employed in mobilizing political support in the Second and First Curias in Vienna after 1891, casting the Christian Socials as the party which would reunite the whole Bürgertum on the basis of shared cultural values and thus elevate the Christian Social movement above the desperate, artisan-based antisemitism which marked it before 1891, must be traced in a generic and genetic sense to the special properties of the Austrian Liberal experience in 1848 and in 1867–79 and to the collapse of the Viennese Democratic movement in the mid-1870s. Christian Socialism in Austria was significant for its technical political innovations and for its symbolic role as a movement of lower-Bürger protest, but its success lay far more in the traditional, retrospective quality of the party's coalition by 1895–96. To write the history of this party is not simply to write the social history of the Viennese Bürgertum, but much more to chart the gradual fragmentation and reunification of that Bürgertum between the Revolution of 1848 and the conquest of Vienna by

Lueger in 1896. The core strength of the movement lay as much in its traditionalism as in its mass social radicalism.

The Vormärz

Of crucial importance for understanding the conservatism and centrism of the early Austrian Liberals is the fact that unlike the Prussian, the Austrian state administration was not accorded a heavy interventionist role toward society before 1848. In Prussia, as R. Koselleck has recently shown, the *Verwaltung* was not only accorded powerful social responsibilities before 1848, but was encouraged to use and expand them to the point where the administration began to make forceful and at times almost vengeful probes into German civil society, recasting traditional institutions in its own image and likeness. The array of social innovations under Prussian bureaucratic hegemony extended from major reforms, such as the destruction of the nexus of rural dependency in the implementation of the Stein-Hardenberg reforms, to less obvious policy decisions, such as the systematization and modernization of the traditional Prussian *Heimatrecht* in the 1840s, itself reflecting the tremendous social and occupational mobility which characterized Prussian society in the later Vormärz.[1]

A distinction must be made between the theoretical power of the state and its actual value and impact in civil society. The Josephist bureaucracy in Austria was clearly as powerful in theoretical terms as its Prussian counterpart (if not more so), but because Franz I had a strong proprietary sense of society as a whole (society as an aspect of dynastic *Eigentum*, as Friedrich Walter has argued) and because he recast the role of the Austrian Verwaltung toward this patrimonial *Eigentum* to promote state stabilization and dynastic conservatism, the Imperial bureaucracy in Austria was caught in an almost schizoid state in which its original mandate, as conceived by Joseph II and Leopold II, was set at cross-purposes with its functional role after 1800.[2] Franz no longer thought of society as an object of social discipline which was to be forcibly and rationally pushed toward social rationalization and economic utility, as had Joseph, but simply as an object of social conformity in which the manifest occurrences of social change were to be limited to those natural to civil society itself and were not to encompass those induced by government intervention.[3] Precisely this tension between the role of the Austrian Verwaltung as a force for social rationalization and its use as a device for social immobility in policy terms led to its miserable public image and to the kinds of rancorous self-criticism common among mid-century Austrian bureaucrats (Ignaz Beidtel is a good example). In Prussia, in contrast, the

Verwaltung possessed the sense of actually exercising power in society in a productive fashion, leading eventually to the fateful self-conception of the Prussian bureaucracy as a state within a state (or a *Stand* which was the state). Although the Austrian bureaucracy had a sense of negative coercive force against society (the *Polizeihofstelle* with its censorship powers), a sense of itself as a positive *Stand* qua state was not legitimated by contemporary fact, but was simply the idealized heritage of vague "Josephist" principles. As in many future political dilemmas, when Austrians were uncertain how to justify their present expectations in terms of their present behavior, they simply summoned the mythical Joseph II, who became all things to all men. The Austrian Verwaltung did little in the Vormärz to merit its etatism in a dynamic power sense. The fragmented, haphazard way in which a few social policy areas were developed (such as occasional progressive decisions taken on industrial development) hardly matched the kind of collective self-esteem based on solid administrative accomplishment which gradually developed in the Prussian bureaucracy.

The upshot of this dualism was that although the Austrian Verwaltung was frequently despised and insulted, its relationship with Austrian civil society and especially urban society was ultimately less tense and less conflict-oriented than that of its Prussian counterpart. This was even more true after 1848. Austrians in the Vormärz did not see the growth of a new *ständisch* monster claiming to manage and coordinate social change. They simply coexisted with, and in terms of the role the Austrian Verwaltung played in facilitating bourgeois social mobility, occasionally profited from the more latitudinarian traditions of the Verwaltung's passive, regulatory role toward civil society.

The perennial chorus of complaints about censorship should not lead historians to exaggerate the impact of Austrian administrative service in the Vormärz. The haphazard and arbitrary pattern of censorship hardly suggested a state system with impressive and coordinated political resources. The upshot of domestic censorship before the revolution was that the Verwaltung became its own worst enemy. Censorship was largely directed against the small domestic intelligentsia, whereas educated Austrians could purchase with ease the works of foreign and especially north and west German authors. Most of these authors had a jaundiced view of Austria, and in both clerical and proto-Liberal circles in the Vormärz one often saw the curious phenomenon of native Austrians using foreign images of Austria as their own (e.g., Sebastian Brunner's dependence on the German Catholic view of Austria; the early Liberals' use of a wide range of north German and Saxon critiques of the Austrian "system").[4] This hapless situation was compounded by the tendency of the small, elite groups of *Gebildeten* in the monarchy to borrow foreign political and social theory in an indiscriminate fashion (the enthusiasm for the ideals of Guizot and pre-1848 French Liberalism in the *Juridisch-politischen Leseverein*),[5] the outcome being that both the Austrian Liberal and Clerical movements not only were weak from a lack of self-directed labor, but often tried to push off onto Austrian society ideal types which did not fit the special historical problems of that society. This long-term deficit in political theory was one which both the Liberals and the Catholics took nearly fifty years to make good. The pragmatic success of Karl Lueger cannot be appreciated except in the context of his insistence on retaining the older Austrian traditions of a conscious gap between theory and practice, amid the furious theorizing of the later 1880s and 1890s, whether Fabian, Catholic Romantic, or Social Democratic.

Such discrimination against the native Austrian intelligentsia and the university system, much of it owing to passivity and administrative immobility as much as to outright coercion, limited the quality of new applicants for the Verwaltung itself, so that a vicious circle of mediocrity producing more mediocrity ensued, which was not effectively broken until the reforms of Leo Thun in the 1850s. The very aggressiveness of the Prussian Verwaltung after 1820 owed at least something to the more vigorous intellectual and academic traditions of north German society, which if they did not lead to the dominance of a nonstatist Liberalism outside the state could at least find some room for hegemonic expansion within the state service.[6]

At the same time the fundamental role which the Austrian Verwaltung played in enhancing bourgeois mobility cannot be overestimated.[7] For it was precisely the essentially bourgeois character of the Austrian civil service which helped to reduce the possible ideological divisions between it and the Austrian Bürgertum both before and after 1848.[8] The secular, nonaristocratic ethos of the Austrian *Beamtenadel* in the nineteenth century, lacking as it did qualities of "feudalization" such as Left-oriented historians have postulated for the Prussian civil service, and the absence within the civil service of a Junker-caste mentality helped to counterbalance the deficit in trust and respect resulting from the Verwaltung's patrimonial coercive role before 1848. Many of the younger Liberals who fought the neo-absolutist state had won their spurs as government officials (many served as *Prokuratoren* in the financial service) before commencing careers as private lawyers.[9] Throughout the nineteenth century there remained this curious symbiosis between Liberal and state administrative values, culminating in the Fabianism of men like Eugen v Philippovich and Josef Redlich after 1890.

The Austrian administration has traditionally suffered from invidious comparisons with its German counterparts in the Vormärz (in part reflecting Austrian inferiority complexes generated from self-deprecating envy of Prussian economic success), but in fact the Austrian government had little sense before 1848 of using the Verwaltung to modernize anything. The administrative power of state existed to enhance social stabilization and state conservatism, not to manage social modernization. Not only did Austrian Josephism thus play a different role toward civil society before 1848 than its counterparts elsewhere in Central Europe, but the Liberal response to that model differed as well. Lothar Gall has suggested that it is precisely in the context of the tension between early state administrative modernization and the German Liberals' sense of themselves as an *allgemeinen Stand* (universal class) entitled to represent all of society and to make all of society like itself that the later history of German Liberalism must be seen.[10] In many areas of Germany, especially in the southern and western regions, Liberalism developed vigorous Left and Left-Center traditions before 1848, often in response to the kind of state interventionist schemes posed by the Prussian model (or by its emulation in other areas of Germany). Recent work on the history of German Liberalism has dealt extensively with this dynamic tension in the Vormärz between activist Verwaltung and a responsible, articulate proto-Liberalism.

In Austria, in contrast, the Bürgertum never developed as fully this sense of itself as a political *allgemeinen Stand* comprehending and representing all of society. This deficit resulted not only from the absence of real political opportunities and institutions in the Vormärz and from the more passive, timid nature of the Austrian bourgeoisie, but also from the lack of a state modernization program which might have stimulated or challenged the bourgeoisie to make such a response. Hence the Austrian Liberals never suffered the problems of conscience which the German Liberals' later betrayal of this ideal brought them between 1860 and 1880 (all recent historians of German Liberalism agree that this occurred, although there is some debate as to when). Austrian Liberals might later claim for themselves a "universal" responsibility toward society, but this was always more artificial in Austria than in Germany. "Universal" meant "unilateral" in Austria far more easily than in Germany; self-interest in support of bourgeois norms and privileges always took precedence over universal social interest.[11]

Since there were no effective urban politics in Austria before 1848, the Bürgertum remained a legal category and a cultural concept, but not a political agent. In Vienna to be a Bürger in the legal sense meant to possess a patent entitling one to a share in the city corporation's resources (charity, military service, etc.), but the term conveyed few meaningful political rights. Generally speaking, artisans, merchants, and property owners resident in the city for an extended period and paying a direct tax were eligible for membership in the *Bürgerschafts-Korporation* (subject to the payment of a special initiation fee). Master artisans who were not members of the regular guilds (such as the poorer artisans in the so-called *befugte* status) were not generally entitled to the *Bürgerrecht*.

The word also possessed, however, a broader social meaning, which included not only the legal Bürger but also the academically trained individuals and other bourgeois types in the city (for example, those who did not own a house).[12] Bürgertum in a more general, cultural sense included all who fitted into the nexus of social respectability and solidity which the ideal Bürger possessed. The more rigid distinction between Bürger and *Honoratioren* obtaining in Prussian cities was weakened in the eighteenth century by Joseph II's legal reforms which consolidated all nonnoble court jurisdictions into one central criminal court. There were social tensions between the two groups, but these were never as extreme and as pointed in Austria as in Germany. There was also less interest in Austria in viewing the Bürgertum as a model for all society—the boundaries between it and the lower orders of society were not only definite, but salutary.

In Austria it is also more difficult to isolate a pronounced Liberal tradition of any serious, systematic sort before 1848. This was not merely because of the more coercive sense of the "system," but also because of the different role of the Verwaltung toward society and, perhaps, the more stable nature of the Austrian Bürgertum during the Vormärz. Especially lacking was a serious Left Liberalism. This does not mean that there was no political or civic consciousness in Vienna before 1848, for the organization in the mid and later forties of a modest club system (the *Leseverein* was the most notable example, but there were numerous small coffee house circles and groups of friends on the local level) would suggest the opposite.[13] But such consciousness was more subtle, more diffuse, and less overtly politicized and far less polarized on the level of explicit social policy issues.[14] The political culture of the Vormärz abounded with the beginnings of ad hoc intellectual fashions (the fashionability of Hegelian political thought in some student circles in the 1840s), but few of them ever developed into systematic ideas or political action. The continued presence within the university system of a strong, conservative school of natural rights theory (unlike Prussia, Austria did not commit itself to German juristic historicism and common law studies until after 1851) provided a mixture of absolutized, state-oriented contractualism in which the theoretical powers of the state were elaborated, but in which the idea that society deserved the explicit attention of (and control over) such powers was much less prominent.[15] In 1848, Franz

Schuselka and a few other Left Liberals found their natural law training useful in developing a native brand of radical Democracy, but these were exceptions and not the rule, even after 1848.[16]

Also important for the political culture of Vienna and for later Austrian Liberalism was the decision of the state to retain and in Vienna to enhance eighteenth-century modes of managing urban affairs in the monarchy. Austria thus fell thirty years behind Prussia in the elaboration of municipal autonomy, but this ultimately worked in favor of a more aggressive local Liberalism (and anti-Liberalism) in the empire after 1861. The much praised Stein reforms not only gave the Prussian cities political autonomy (often against their wills) and the encouragement to develop antagonisms with the state; they also gave the Prussian Verwaltung the opportunity to interfere with and intervene in the cities by forcing new social policy responsibilities onto them. In Vienna the older Josephist *Magistrat* system (as modified in 1808) remained in force until 1848, and when it was replaced, the break was much more powerful and radical than in Prussia: the Austrian Liberals wanted everything Stein had accorded the Germans, and they wanted it in the context of a Verwaltung less accustomed to manage and exploit municipal autonomy for its own corporate purposes. Had municipal autonomy been instituted in Austria before 1848, the Austrian Liberals would have had to pay the same price in the reduction of autonomist privileges after 1848 (the 1853 Prussian *Städteordnung* in comparison to the original Stein charter) as their German cousins to the north.[17] Municipal autonomy was, however, a conceptual impossibility before 1848, not merely because of the conservative propensities of the "system," but much more because the Verwaltung saw no need to develop autonomy to manage political and administrative modernization. Form followed function throughout the Austrian Vormärz.

Later Austrian political traditions, rooted as all of them inevitably were in the subtle and recondite administrative politics of the later Vormärz, in which neocorporatism of a modest, reform aristocratic mentality played a complementary role (the younger Schmerling and Doblhoff, for example), tended to stress consensus rather than unbridgeable conflict in the settlement of public policy issues, to the extent that these did not explicitly involve the nationalities question (the one enormous genre of later political behavior which Vormärz culture had not prepared the Austrians to cope with). Austrian political administration always had a marked talent for never being too far behind or ahead of the given balance of forces within civil society. Josephist statism could give the constant impression of social neutrality because of the absence of a self-enhancing, petty gentry power elite and because the Verwaltung never defined itself before 1848 as the principal agent to shape endogenous social institutions and values in its own image and likeness. The social composition of the Verwaltung matched well the service's universalist claims to cultural neutrality in its behavior toward society. During the later Liberal period, when the Austrian *Beamtenbewegung* came alive in more vigorous terms than in Prussia, most of the social tensions within the Verwaltung were articulated along purely internal, organizational rank lines, utilizing achievement-oriented criteria rather than caste pretensions.[18] There was no Junker skeleton hiding in the public closet, as it were. Flexibility, as most party politicians in Austria learned, was at a premium in the Austrian system. Those few major political leaders, like Schönerer, who would not conform to Austrian traditions, were soon ground out of the system. As a Bonapartist intent on slaying the evil demon of semitic Republicanism, Schönerer might have made more sense in French politics, where language and consequent political behavior always had a far more literal and positive congruence than in Austria. In Austria, where political behavior was more disjoined from both theory and the rigidities of language, he was an isolated and eccentric figure.

The Vormärz gave to Liberal politics a sense of linguistic theatricality and expressiveness, from which most Viennese politicians in the 1870s and 1880s were not immune (whether this be older Liberals "killing" the monster of ultramontanism or antisemites "killing" the evils of Magyar-Jewish Liberalism). The informality and social integration of Vormärz society provided the strong sense of localism and the technical cohesiveness which marked Viennese politics throughout the later nineteenth century. The simulated sessions of the City Council staged in local cafes and *Gasthäuser* by the Christian Social political clubs as a form of political entertainment and political mobilization in the tense winter of 1895–96, with Lueger's confirmation struggle hanging in the balance, reaffirmed deeply Viennese notions of informal, localist politics qua *Vorstadt* theatricality and cafe friendships.[19]

The Revolution of 1848

Beyond the general euphoria in March 1848 of having dispensed with Metternich and his "system" (the vagueness of the term and the personalism of the target suggested the absence of a coherent political opposition, aside from demands for the end of censorship, which everyone wanted), the amateurs who conducted the revolution in Vienna during the first months of 1848 slowly evolved two patterns of political attitudes (they do not justify the term "theory") which were to prove of crucial importance for later Austrian Liberal politics.[20] The two were not wholly exclusive and certainly not always internally homogeneous, but in general they existed for both the participants in the revolution and its later historians:

1. Among the more conservative middle and upper bourgeois leaders, who now found themselves forced to create a formal system of politics, a rhetoric of Bürger unity and class defensiveness developed, based partially on pre-1848 traditions of Bürger privileges and cultural ambitions in reference to the central administration and especially in the context of the chicaneries and inefficiency of the Viennese *Magistrat* (the local arm of government in Vienna, before it became the city's own self-managed bureaucracy after 1850). This view postulated the existence of a uniform citizenry in the city for passive, civil liberties, but when the issue became one of explicit political rights it converted its Bürger mentality into a language exclusive of the lower orders of Austrian society. This was the conceptual world of the *Leseverein* and the supporters of the Pillersdorf Constitution and its restrictive franchise. Such a style of political rhetoric postulated a unitary Bürgertum for the city, including all wealth levels and professions, both *Besitz* and *Intelligenz,* from the highest bourgeois (most of whom were in fact proto or early industrial types—the number of *Seidenzeugfabrikanten* in the *Gewerbeverein* suggests something of its early industrial, Bürger mentality)[21] to the smaller artisans and shopkeepers of the *Vorstädte*. All of these strata were consciously delimited from the proletariat by status and caste mentalities, as well as wealth. This style of Bürger rhetoric was particularly prominent in the literature generated by the leadership of the National Guard, itself the symbol of the unitary Bürgertum, since its organizational charter of 10 April 1848 required that all taxpayers, property owners and officials in the city join, while intentionally excluding all day laborers, artisan journeymen, and factory workers from its ranks.[22] The debates in the *Gemeindeausschuss* of the city, elected in May 1848, were filled with language which glorified the united Bürgertum as an object of political progress and virtue on one hand and as a defense for social stability and status traditionalism on the other.[23] The intent was to recognize for the first time with explicit political rights what had always been a social fact in Vienna—that pre-1848 Vienna was a *bürgerlich* city of a comparatively uniform social consensus.[24] Pre-1848 intrabourgeois tensions, such as those between the artisans registered in the guilds and the so-called *befugte* artisans, who operated outside the guild structure, would now be eased by including both in a new political Bürgertum, just as both were now in the municipal defense forces. J. M. Häusle, the politically isolated Catholic leader, noted in 1849 that much of the bourgeoisie's political strategy in 1848–49 was deeply rooted in Vormärz cultural values.[25] These traditions were now transformed by placing them in the context of Liberal political rights, without

adjusting the traditions to meet the real intent of the rights. However, the working class of the city (the "masses" about whom the leaders of the *Gemeindeausschuss* were constantly worried) was granted recognition in a very tentative and uncertain fashion. The leadership of the National Guard constantly referred to the population as "Bürger, Garden und andere Bewohner," as if it could not invent a proper name or category for anyone who was not a Bürger or member of the Guard. Conceptually as well as politically the proletariat remained the *andere* of this style of rhetoric.

2. The second great political tradition which evolved was that of the small number of Left Liberal democrats, students, and ex-theater journalists who made up the Democratic movement.[26] Their protests were generational as well as ethnic and ideological in nature. Openly derivative from styles of Left Liberal rhetoric that had developed elsewhere in Europe, this language of political rights condemned the kinds of social and (based upon them) political distinctions of the Bürger category. It postulated instead a new Bürgertum in the sense of a fully enfranchised and socially free citizenry cutting across class and caste levels, the modern *citoyen* of the French Jacobin model. This approach was a categorical attack on the ideal of the Bürgertum as a privileged, corporate citadel of property, tax, and educational resources. Democratic newspapers like the *Constitution,* the *Freimüthige,* and *Gerad' aus* devoted much of their time during the months of April through September to criticizing the older idea of the Bürgertum as distinct from the masses of Viennese society.[27] At the center of this view were the radical forces in the Security Committee dominated by Goldmark, Violand, Fischhof, and colleagues. Not surprisingly, both the National Guard and the City Council found themselves constantly at odds with the Security Committee.[28] The leaders of both organizations rejoiced when the committee was disbanded after the worker disturbances of late August 1848. The view of a unitary citizenry on the *citoyen* model was also shared, at least in terms of manifest public behavior, by some members of the lower Bürgertum, especially some of the companies of the suburban National Guard (particularly those of Wieden and Mariahilf), a fact which proved of ominous significance for the later history of political rights in the city. To the extent that the revolutionary labor organizations in 1848 had any discrete political views beyond striving for an equitable level of material resources, this model served them as well.[29]

The difference in political views between Liberal Bürger representatives and the radical Democrats was, moreover, only the first installment in a long process of revolutionary conflict, for the ideal of the unitary Bürgertum was challenged as early as late April and May 1848 by a growing social disaggregation of sentiment within the putative Bürgertum it-self. Crucial here was the uncertain, vacillating quality of the lower Vien-nese Bürger, especially the small shopkeepers and poorer artisans of the *Vorstädte* who dominated many of the suburban National Guard com-panies. A major axis of intra-Bürger feuding was the constant series of complaints about the harassment of apartment house owners (*Haus-herren*) by their tenants and by the radical Democratic newspapers.[30] The first instance of collective behavior on the part of the lower artisan Bürgertum in Vienna occurred in mid-April when a crowd of craft masters assembled to demand that their *Hausherren*, who were fellow Bürger of a wealthier sort, reduce rent levels on business quarters and apartments.[31] The situation soon escalated to the point where radical Democratic news-papers were demanding that the *Hausherren* forego several months of rent as an act of charity toward the increasingly desperate artisans, while also insisting that many property owners were practicing rent gouging by secretly increasing the rate of monthly apartment rentals.[32] The remaining months of the revolution in Vienna witnessed numerous confrontations between lower-Bürger types and the *Hausherren*, who were the first and for many the most ominous representatives of "big wealth" in the city (the peculiar cult and culture of the Viennese *Hausherren* will be dealt with below in chap. 6).

The tendency of some of the companies of the suburban National Guard to sympathize with the Academic Legion and the workers in May and again in August 1848 also generated a latent suspicion against these arti-san petit bourgeois types on the part of the more middle and upper ranking Bürger.[33] The poorer masters may have had ambivalent feelings about helping the *Pöbel* achieve full political emancipation—certainly the be-havior of the German artisan groups who addressed petitions to the Frankfurt parliament indicated that there was a clear division between them and their journeyman workers in terms of social program and status esteem, a pattern of prejudice which was applicable to Vienna as well.[34] But the general euphoria of the early months of the revolution, and the commonality of interest on some social issues between workers and the lower Bürger (both had to deal with the local *Hausherr* in a tenancy relationship; both would profit from state financial support to subsidize their marginal craft shops in the economic depression of the revolutionary year) blurred the lines of class and caste slightly, toward the lower end of the Bürgertum. The worst sin committed by the lower Bürger, however, was not their occasional assistance of the workers, but their enthusiasm for schemes which seemed to undercut the sovereignty of property own-ership in the city. August Swoboda's famous proposal to establish a *Leihanstalt* in late April 1848, which would raise hundreds of thousands of gulden for interest-free loans to suffering master artisans by forcing wealthier Bürger types to submit contributions of 50–100 fl. and by requiring them to use their apartment buildings to guarantee their contributions, was hardly likely to create confidence in the minds of the property owners of the city.[35] Swoboda was finally able to launch a credit association (the *Privat-Darlehen-Verein*) in June 1848, with a plan to sell 200,000 investment shares at 20 fl. each to bourgeois contributors (with a 5 percent return on the investment). His distribution of undercapitalized share certificates as ersatz money to needy artisans in order to bolster their floundering businesses led to the *Actienkrawall* of 11–13 September 1848, when a crowd of angry artisans invaded the City Council chambers demanding a public guarantee on these investments.[36] Nothing served so well to show the degeneration of the alleged harmony within the Bürgertum in the early months of the revolution as the Swoboda scandal of September 1848.[37] Since forty-three of the one hundred delegates elected to the City Council were also *Hausherren,* their attitude toward the erratic and unpredictable poorer artisan masters became increasingly hostile.[38]

The history of the construction of a municipal franchise for the new *Gemeindeordnung* in 1848–49 illustrates this gradual retrenchment of the higher and middle Bürgertum against the poorer artisans. At no time in 1848 or 1849 was any serious thought given to enfranchising the lower orders of Viennese society on the *Gemeinde* level, so that the intense in-fighting which surrounded the August 1848 franchise (prepared as a temporary expedient) and the final version of 1849–50 dealt only with the Bürgertum itself and not with the ideal of uniform, equal political rights. When it came to Vienna itself, the city fathers repudiated the *citoyen* mentality.

When the City Council wrote a provisional franchise in August to elect its new membership in the autumn (before the final text of the full *Gemeindeordnung* itself was finished), many local leaders expected that the new franchise would be retained in the final statute. The Council which wrote this franchise had been elected in May under an extremely narrow, patricianlike franchise enforced (as a temporary expedient) by the Pillersdorf ministry, requiring at least 20 fl. annually in direct taxes in order to vote.[39] The Council delegates of 1848 were hardly political radicals. The franchise which they produced for the new *Gemeindeordnung* in late August (immediately after the repression of the worker disturbances in the Prater) idealized the Liberal hope of a unitary Bürgertum of rights and liberties. The franchise excluded all but taxpayers, and therefore remained a purely bourgeois instrument, but it avoided any curial structure and allowed all Bürger to vote, even the lowliest petit bourgeois craft masters.[40] That some of the Liberal delegates felt slightly uneasy about the liberality of the proposal was indicated by Leopold Neumann's suggestion that the *Intelligenz* section of the franchise be made as large as possible to combat the influence of the "Proletariat des Steuerminimums," an obvious reference to the group who became known in the 1880s as the five-gulden men.[41] But the majority of the Council, led by Moriz Stubenrauch, accepted the inclusion of the petite bourgeoisie in the unitary Bürgertum, hoping that the future behavior of these men would be marked by Bürger conservatism and not by proletaroid radicalism.[42] The earlier "comprehensive" view of the Bürgertum as argued in the National Guard literature was still sustained.

The other sections of the debate on the new statute in August showed that the Council was much more concerned with isolating the proletariat than it was with splitting the Bürgertum. Stubenrauch himself, one of the more progressive members of the Council, declared publicly that the *Bürgerrecht* and *Gemeindemitglieder* provisions of the new statute should be as restrictive as possible to prevent the flooding of the city with proletarian families looking for handouts from the public dole.[43]

Between April 1848 and March 1849, when the Council again took up the question of a new statute for the city (its deliberations had not been completed when the October days broke out), two events occurred which were of great moment for the future shape of the municipal franchise: the September artisan riots over the Swoboda credit fiasco and the October days. The behavior of the lower Bürgertum in September and the support given by the National Guard companies from Wieden and Mariahilf during the Latour riots in early October 1848 led many members of the council to rethink the advisability of giving these people political rights on par with those of the rest of the Bürgertum.[44] The involvement of some suburban National Guard companies in resisting Prince Windischgraetz was the last straw. As Johann Häusle noted caustically in June 1849, most of the conservative majority of the Council had fled the city by late October 1848 and were actually proud of having avoided the contamination of those revolutionary events.[45] When the Council reassembled in the spring of 1849 to continue its debates on the new statute (which Stadion and Bach expressly permitted it to do), a different attitude was apparent on the part of the majority of the assembly toward the lower artisans, reflecting the events of September and October 1848. The committee appointed to draft a comprehensive proposal for a new statute proposed to retain in large part the provisions of the August 1848 franchise, but in early June 1849 the majority of the Council went against Stubenrauch and, on the motion of Andreas Zelinka, voted to create a curial system for the municipality.[46] The curial system, which separated voters into three distinct categories based on an extremely complex evaluation of tax and educational criteria (see chap. 5), consigned all of the 5 fl. and 10 fl. artisans to the Third Curia, giving the *Intelligenz* and smaller property owners control of the Second Curia and the highest taxed in the city control of the First. Each of the three curias was entitled to elect the same number of delegates. Since the peculiarities of the Austrian real estate tax system gave the *Hausherren* of most apartment houses in the city the right to credit their tenants' rent taxes as their own personal tax (see chaps. 5 and 6), the First Curia was not simply the curia of a grand industrial bourgeoisie but, as *Die Presse* put it in defending the franchise, the curia of the wealthier part of the "grossen Mittelklasse der zunächts höher Besteuerten," namely, the Viennese *Hausherren*, who in many instances were simply wealthy artisans and merchants.[47] The curial system which the Council included in the final draft of the *Gemeindeordnung* approved in August 1849 was the imperative force behind the next sixty years of Viennese politics.

The final step in isolating the lower artisans occurred in the final edition of the statute, approved by Alexander Bach in February 1850. Whereas the council's draft of August 1849 had left in the franchise the artisans paying the lowest taxes and simply isolated them by setting them against the upper curias of *Intelligenz* and *Besitz,* Bach insisted that the minimum tax level for possessing the vote be raised to 10 fl. in direct taxes, thereby excluding the five-gulden men from Viennese politics for the next thirty-five years.[48] Lest one be tempted to see in this act the arbitrary behavior of a neo-absolutist bureaucrat, it must be noted that Bach's revisions of the August 1849 draft were undertaken in the winter of 1849–50 with the cooperation of a delegation of prominent members of the City Council, who met with him to discuss the changes which might be desirable in the final version. As *Die Presse* intimated in its commentary on the final version in March 1850, it was likely that the more conservative members of the Council actually approved of Bach's revisions.[49] The Liberals never complained about this exclusion. Given the behavior of the lowest Bürger types in October 1848, the Liberals deemed it a just revenge to punish them by excluding them at least temporarily. They could always be brought back in again if they proved themselves "reliable" in the future. Ironically they were brought back in at precisely that point— 1886—when they were even more unreliable than in 1849. The exclusion of the lowest Bürgertum from the Third Curia and the curia system itself became the albatross of the Liberal party in Vienna for the rest of the century.

The 1850 municipal franchise was of paramount importance for later Austrian Liberalism since this was the first time the Austrian Bürgertum had had free opportunity to determine a voting system after the collapse of the Revolution of 1848. Although the government forced some revisions, the final product was largely the work of the City Council itself, undertaken without serious government pressure or prodding. The later plans of Schmerling, Perthaler, and Lasser in 1860–61 for curial *Interessenvertretungen*, although they owed much to the ideas inherent in the 1849 Stadion constitution and Bach's proposals in the 1850s, employed the same kinds of ideological and social assumptions about the Bürgertum put forth by the 1849–50 city fathers (with the exception that until 1871 the minimum tax level to qualify for the Landtag franchise in Vienna was set at 20 fl. rather than 10 fl. as in the city ordinance).[50] The political Bürgertum on which the main Liberal party built its successes in the 1860s and 1870s was in large part the group of the *Mittelklasse* (with the addition of wealthier artisans and the *Intelligenz*) to which the *Presse* had referred: not a classic *Hochbürgertum*, such as provided the leadership for the curia of the Chambers of Commerce and Industry, but a solid middle- and upper-Bürger type of Mittelstand. Viennese Liberalism, even after 1850, was heavily pre- or protocapitalist in its electorate—most of its voters were *Hausherren, Beamten*, wealthy artisans, and prosperous shopkeepers. But by purposely excluding the lower Bürgertum from active political rights and by still insisting that the unitary Bürgertum as a whole was a creature of inherent virtue and goodness (against the proletariat), the early Liberals had created the anomalous situation in which the lower Bürgertum was left in limbo between 1850 and 1885.

Neo-Absolutism: State Modernization and the Concordat

Friedrich Walter argued in his last (posthumously published) volume in the *Zentralverwaltung* series that the Bach era was simply a return to the Vormärz, a "more of the same" mentality and practice.[51] This was clearly not the case. New research on the 1850s has stressed the powerful, transformational effects of the reformed Verwaltung on Austrian civil society after 1850.[52] With neo-absolutism one is dealing with a very different kind of state from the paralyzed, uncertain bureaucratism of the 1820s and 1830s. In part this new kind of bureaucratic absolutism was in response to the Prussian challenge: it is clear that Bruck's reform program for the economy and Leo Thun's parallel attempts to restructure the institutions of higher learning both owed much of their existence to the Prussian threat and to Prussian models developed in the Vormärz.[53] The powerful ministerial leaders of the Austrian regime now thought of their mandate in terms of making good the thirty-year gap between Austrian and Prussian institutional and economic development.

The novelty of the neo-absolutist experience was above all a technical one. Austria finally received a strongly centralized ministerial government with a clear mandate to proceed with a vigorous program of social management and economic development. The destruction of rural dependency under Bach in the 1850s, together with the elaboration of a new, powerful system of regional and local administration, signified the beginnings of an agrarian revolution which, although more gradual than the Prussian, was no less important in shaping the late-nineteenth-century Austrian party system in German and Czech electoral areas.

The historiographical debate about the formal nature of the ministerial system after 1852 is somewhat misleading. Schwarzenberg clearly intended to change both the form and the substance of Vormärz patriarchal absolutism into a system in which the ministers themselves would have far more leverage against the crown and the bureaucracy (as well as civil society).[54] After August 1851 Kübeck and Metternich did persuade the young emperor to abandon structural innovations in the ministerial system, but the other aspect of the Schwarzenberg and Bach program—the use of the Verwaltung for a more coordinated program of social and economic change—was not abandoned. The 1850s were a decade of enormous social-institutional readjustments, most of which were presided over by the Verwaltung. Conservatives fought a losing battle in their efforts to preserve the appearance of Vormärz bureaucratic passivity. The very quality of the ministers in the decade was geometrically higher than in the last years of the Vormärz. Franz Joseph, for all his inexperience and stubbornness, was not simply a young Franz I thirty years later.

In the introduction to the recent edition of the *Ministerrat* protocols from the mid-1850s, Waltraud Heindl has noted that the neo-absolutist regime also employed numerous quasi-Liberal bureaucrats in ministerial and subministerial positions.[55] The massive study of Harm-Hinrich Brandt on neo-absolutist state finances has confirmed the central role of what he calls the "staatliche Reformbürokratie" in provoking social and administrative modernization.[56] Inevitably this meant that the regime began to respond to 1848/49, if only in very autocratic and hierarchic modes. Traditional rubrics like "liberal" and "conservative" fail to convey the complexity of political behavior and policy options available to policymakers in the 1850s. Neo-absolutism envisaged a system in which state power would be employed to modernize the industrial and educational resources of the monarchy, not merely as compensatory devices to satisfy the expectations of the Bürgertum in nonpolitical modes, but to enhance the stability of the state in progressive terms. This mating of statist and Liberal-modernizing features was a peculiar trait of the neo-absolutist regime. The relative obscurity in which Bach left the institutions of local autonomy established by Stadion's law of 1849 (the government did not have the chance to revise Stadion's law before it fell from power in 1859–60) testified that this heritage of the revolution was still available to the Liberals of the 1860s.

Critical to the later relationship between the higher Verwaltung and the Austrian Liberals was the fact that the centralizing absolutism of the 1850s with its propensity for deep social interventionism and the remolding of traditional financial and economic institutions only lasted a short nine years. As Brandt has shown, neo-absolutism faced the enormous and problematic dilemma of balancing rapid state and social modernization against the destabilizing demands of excessive military expenditure and against an antiquated, inefficient tax system. From the very first, based as it was on an economy which lagged behind those of all other major European powers except Russia, neo-absolutism lived beyond its financial and political means. At the same time, however, it was precisely the regime's "financial misery," as Brandt called it, combined with its ambitious social modernization programs, that provoked the need by 1858–59 for the state to share its policy formation and control with wider sectors of the Austrian bourgeoisie.

Beginning in 1858–59 the whole system began to unwind, and by 1861–62 the early Liberal-bureaucratic forces under men like Schmerling, the elder Plener, Lasser, and colleagues were forced to integrate the new technical absolutism into a para-constitutional framework in which the crown, the army, and the Church would be subject to a moderate level of Liberal constitutional review. In Austria, one might argue, the Liberals were extremely fortunate to "catch up with" the new interventionist Verwaltung (itself staffed by policymakers who were not unsympathetic to a modest constitutional framework) before it had sufficient time to build up powerful defenses. This did not happen in Prussia, and it is precisely in the 1850s and 1860s that the Prussian Liberals struggled with much less success to win control of the Verwaltung, as well as of the army. The second crucial timing feature here was that the work of mediating between absolutism and moderate constitutionalism was done by a generation of Liberals who were sympathetic to a modified absolutist ethos, provided significant concessions were accorded to the German-speaking bourgeoisie in terms of consultative, representational, and neocorporate rights. Unlike the Prussian Liberals in their struggle over the Army Bill of the early 1860s, the Austrian Liberals ultimately won their constitutional battle. They won because they were opposing a very different culture of authoritarianism than in Prussia, one less sure of itself, less deeply rooted in Vormärz reformism and in antibourgeois social attitudes, and less immune to exogenous pressures (the indirect support which Deak and especially Andrassy gave to the Liberals in 1866–67). They also succeeded because they did not have to face a powerful conservative leader like Bismarck.

The Concordat

The Concordat of 1855 was a catastrophic mistake for the Austrian regime's internal policy in the 1850s.[57] The praise which the reforms for the modernization of the Austrian economy and society ought to have earned the regime was effectively undercut, in cultural terms, by the bad press of the Concordat. The Concordat was the Church's great negative gift to Austrian Liberalism. In spite of the disastrous financial and foreign policies of the middle and later fifties, without the Concordat to use as an ideological target, the Liberals would have had a much more difficult time in undermining the credibility of the administrative-authoritarian version of state modernization. Unlike the Prussian Liberals, the Austrians passed over the army as their immediate constitutional target, selecting the Church instead. Eduard Taaffe once noted this propensity among Liberal leaders to trade off the Church for the army.[58] The Church's claims to power in the 1850s ultimately helped the Liberals, although this was hardly the original intention of Cardinal Rauscher's attempt to satisfy the four interest groups behind the Concordat (the ideological conservatives in the government, the crown, the Vatican, and the episcopate itself).

The Concordat may be viewed in two rather different ways, depending upon which sections of the final text one wishes to stress.[59] Although the most frequently cited terms were those which gave school supervision and marriage law to the Church, much of the rest of the Concordat was remarkably "liberal" in a modern functionalist sense. Although the state sacrificed to the Church areas of public policy and law which it formerly claimed as its own—and in this sense its act was anti-Josephist in terms of power allocation—it also restored to the episcopate many of the areas of internal church administration (cults, ritual, seminaries, correspondence with Rome, etc.) which the later Liberal regimes in Austria never repudiated. The idea of removing from the state the prerogative of meddling in the internal affairs of the Church was remarkably "modern." One might view it as a conservative version of the Liberal financial reforms (the 1859 *Gewerbeordnung*) in which the state withdrew its antiquated restrictive legislation from areas of civil society in which "progressive" (in a technical, not a normative sense) social change could best be accomplished by state supervision *over* a more self-directed subsidiary social nexus. In the case of the Concordat the "progressiveness" was to be the greater cultural effectiveness of the Church in reducing social disharmonies in civil society (this was clearly Leo Thun's motive in fostering the Concordat, not ultramontanism for its own sake), accomplished by allowing the Church free reign to reassert conservative values on an increasingly secularized popular culture in Austria.

Later Liberals (on the ministerial level, at least) never desired to eliminate the influence of the Church in civil society. The 1868–69 and 1874 laws cannot be seen as depriving the Church of all of its newly won *internal* freedoms and returning it to Vormärz administrative subjection. Many early Liberals thought of the Church in a guarantist mode of anticlericalism. They were more interested in providing a guarantee for the state's sovereignty against the private intrusions of "alien" Catholic dogma and administrative fiat than they were in protecting society against the Church. Hans v Perthaler's theory of the Church as a semipublic, voluntaristic corporation which should be deprived of its autonomous power prerogatives but which should enjoy the privileges of self-enhancement and relative self-management was typical of many attempts to divide Joseph II in half. These attempts constitute a fundamental, as yet unwritten, aspect of the cultural history of this period.[60]

The Liberal Epoch

One of the essential difficulties in writing a history of Austrian Liberalism is the apparent homogeneity of the movement itself, from a social and administrative point of view.[61] With the exception of the great struggles between Schmerling and the Liberal delegation in the Reichsrat in the early 1860s, there are few "glorious" events in Austrian Liberalism providing distinctive attributes or analytical categories which the historian may use to describe the movement in its entirety (the term *Verwaltungsrathpartei* from the mid-1870s is hardly an appropriate analytical category). One obvious feature of Austrian Liberalism which immediately differentiated it from the Prussian variety was the absence within it of a comprehensive, long-range Left Liberal tradition, such as that generated in Prussia during the army crisis and continued under Eugen Richter through the Bismarckian period. The struggles of the 1860s in which the Austrian Liberals were entrapped were as much Liberal against Liberal as they were Liberal against Verwaltung and crown. Herbst's great antagonist in the early 1860s was not (in a formal sense) Franz Joseph, but, rather, Anton v Schmerling himself. And Schmerling was hardly an Austrian version of Bismarck. Hence the Austrian Liberal experiment in the 1860s was relatively less decisive and less catastrophic than the Prussian

Liberal experience. The Liberals felt disappointment and anger over the nonunitary implications of the *Ausgleich*, but nowhere does one find the kind of collective humiliation through which Bismarck put the Prussian Liberal party. By 1867 the Austrian Liberals had achieved (and, equally important, received) a Liberal state which largely fulfilled most of their political desires. The chronic lack of an impressive legislative program in the 1870s, often noted in the historical literature of the period, reflected this satiated quality of Austrian Liberalism in the 1860s.

Unlike their Prussian colleagues the Austrian Liberals obtained a significant level of direct policy control over the state between 1867 and 1879, although the emperor himself never accepted their presence or their cultural ideals. What was notably lacking in Austria was the aura of manipulation and demagogy which Bismarck brought to the German political scene in the 1860s and 1870s. The precise nature of Bismarck's authoritarianism has recently been the subject of vigorous debate (Bonapartism, social Caesarism, simple Prussian paternalism, or a mixture of all three?), but the commanding manipulative intentionality which stood behind most government policy in the period was clearly Bismarck's own.[62] The National Liberals may have felt themselves to be the party of power, but their illusions depended upon Bismarck's tolerance.

The Auersperg ministry, in contrast, was closer to Liberal direction and control. Both Auersperg and Lasser insisted that they would not depend upon the good graces of the Liberal parliamentary delegation in making policy, but such bravado could not obscure the deep social and ideological ties between the ministerial leaders of the 1870s and the conservative elements of the Liberal party. That Franz Joseph and Taaffe went to extremes during the 1878–79 crisis to keep the Liberals in power showed the difference between Bismarckian rule in Germany and the Austrian situation.[63] The party's doctrinaire behavior in early 1879 was principally responsible for the Liberals' abandonment of their ministerial positions, not the anti-Liberal machinations of conservative politicians. Many of his Liberal colleagues felt that Herbst's stubbornness in the 1878–79 occupation crisis should have given way to a more tolerant and flexible posture, even if his behavior was pleasing to the editorial board of the *Neue Freie Presse*.[64] The various feuds which erupted in the 1870s between the parliamentary Liberals and their colleagues in the *Ministerrat* characterized a party too complacent for its own good. At the same time, the popularity of Liberal rhetoric and Liberal ideals in Austria was closer to the French than the German model, although on more superficial terms—"everyone" in urban Austria became Liberal in the 1860s and 1870s. The fashionability of the mode made it irresistible for a culture in which theatricality and taste were intimately related. The very cultural and linguistic structure of Austrian political journalism during this early period illustrated the unique interdependence of aesthetic expressiveness and political choice.

It would be tempting to categorize the Liberals by generational differentiations, and, indeed, on the surface these seem to work. Schmerling and Lasser, Pratobevera and Perthaler, Doblhoff, Plener, and Kalchberg were all born before 1820, and many were imbued with a mixture of *ständisch* and Liberal ideals which they put in a broader Josephist administrative framework. Almost all of them had significant professional experience in the higher state service.[65] This was the first generation of Liberalism to get hold of the state and to ease the transformation between the hegemonic, uncontrolled neo-absolutism of the 1850s and the mesh of administrative power and Liberal constitutionalism operative by the 1870s. Their accomplishment was of the highest historical importance. They were truly the founding fathers of Austrian Liberalism not merely for what they did, but much more for what they avoided doing: because of their transitional labors, labors which Schmerling eventually felt bitter about,[66] a sharp break between the Liberals and the crown on one hand and the Liberals and the Verwaltung on the other was avoided in Austria.[67] They salvaged and confirmed the idea of consensus politics as a typically Austrian mode. They did this, however, in the spirit of Hans v Perthaler's theory of representational, consultative Liberalism, which was strongly influenced by the Liberal conservatism of Rudolf v Gneist.[68] Perthaler's theoretical writings, which Josef Redlich identified as one important source for the February Patent of 1861, affirmed a conservative, almost autocratic theory of the Liberal state in which the Bürgertum had more "duties" in implementing legislation on the local and regional levels than it had in policy determination and control on the national level. Freedom, for Perthaler, was essentially *Ordnung* in a well-organized, unitary state.[69] He spoke far more of the duties and responsibilities of the bourgeoisie to the crown than of its rights and inherent privileges in civil society. Although there was no exact congruence between Perthaler's thought and Schmerling's final political strategy (the latter was a flexible and shrewd politician when he wanted to be), this theory of a conservative, advisory Liberalism marked the collective ethos of the Schmerling ministry of the early 1860s.

Equally prominent was the next generation of Liberals—that of Herbst, Giskra, Stremayr, Glaser, Unger, Chlumecky, Sturm, etc., all of them born between 1820 and 1840, and for some of whom 1848 was a more radical experience than for the earlier group.[70] Giskra's role in the

Frankfurt Assembly might be compared with that of Schmerling, for example.[71] The ties to the tradition of the Verwaltung were still strong—many were lawyers or university teachers who had worked in the Austrian state service before 1848 as part of their *cursus honorum*, but their general political stance was one of a clearer, more French-style constitutionalism. The debates in the Reichsrat in the early 1860s illustrated their sense of constitutional power in terms of specific policy control by the bourgeoisie, to be exercised not only against the crown but against the Verwaltung as well. The state for them was more than a *Verwaltungsmaschine:* both the crown and the new post-1848 absolutism would have to concede some measure of political accountability to the unitary Bürgertum. Their cultural vision was no more flexible than that of Schmerling's generation. If anything, it was even narrower since they deemphasized the holistic aspect of the state (one still found in Perthaler's work the view of the state as encompassing all of society) and delimited areas of society which were to exert control on the state, rather than the reverse. This very act of delimitation gave their work a more explicitly oligarchical and interest-oriented cast than the more universal, normative approach of the early statist Liberals. Schmerling's *Interessenvertretungen* became more class-oriented in their hands. By denying the patriarchal quality of the state's role toward society (a heritage of Vormärz Josephist thought which survived in the work of men like Schmerling and Perthaler), the second generation of Liberals defined the state's beneficence in terms of a negative liberty possessed by those who needed the state the least—the middle and higher ranking Bürgertum, who had already demonstrated in Vienna in 1849 the self-serving way in which they could define the unitary Bürgertum to exclude both the "masses" and even the unreliable members of their own group.

Both of the Liberal ministries of the period between 1867 and 1879 had some of these men, and both are similar in their accomplishments, although the first-generation Liberals had a stronger representation in the Bürger ministry than they did in the Auersperg ministry. The Abgeordnetenhaus of the *Bürgerministerium* from 1867 to 1870 was the transition point between the two generations: of the forty-four most prominent politicians in this parliament (qualitatively determined by major plenary and committee assignments), thirty-one had served before 1867 but only eighteen would survive politically to enter the Reichsrat of 1873.[72] Of these eighteen, almost all were prominent Liberals of Herbst's generation—by 1872–73 most of the early administrative Liberals had largely disappeared from the active parliamentary scene.

The third generation of Austrian Liberalism, that born between 1840 and 1860, was, of course, the missing generation, for it never really had the opportunity to exist on broad, popular terms (that Ernst v Plener was born in 1841, three years before Karl Lueger, only confirms this point). Most of the top elite of the Christian Socials in Vienna belonged to this group, as did many of the prominent leaders of the Social Democrats and the German *völkisch* parties in the 1880s and 1890s. This generation was the one that managed the transformation of Austrian Liberal politics into new ideological and conceptual modes, not only violating the established canons of Liberal belief and taste, but also proving that political mobility and career development could be achieved outside traditional Liberal channels.

This triptych does not reflect all of the available biographical evidence, however, since within each generation were men who foreshadowed the behavior of the next generation and who, in rarer cases, were instrumental in bringing that new mode of behavior into being. Eugen Mühlfeld, although he belonged to Schmerling's generation, was among the most insistent critics of Schmerling's brand of authoritarian Liberalism and his overly delicate attempts to "deal" with the Church in less than categorically anticlerical terms. Similarly, Josef Kopp and Carl Rechbauer, the leaders of the so-called *Jungen* of the 1873 Reichsrat, were clearly part of the second generation of Austrian Liberalism, as were most (over 70 percent) of the Progressives of the 1870s.

The new franchise law of 1873, which provided for direct elections to the Reichsrat and in Vienna confirmed the decision of 1871 to include the ten-gulden artisans in the electoral Bürgertum, made possible the entry into the Reichsrat of a small band of Viennese Democrats, the group among the Liberals closest to having a Left Liberal mentality.[73] Ferdinand Kronawetter and Johann Umlauft were the most typical figures of this subculture, in which for a short time the ideal of the unitary Bürgertum was merged with the ideal of the *citoyen* polity. Umlauft's credentials as a radical Democrat in 1848 helped to legitimate this unusual mix of privilege and political egalitarianism in the 1870s. By and large, however, the Democrats remained isolated figures. When their local political bases in Vienna began to erode in the mid-1870s (largely as a result of a backlash of Bürger sentiment against the Democrats' use of *citoyen* rhetoric and their attempts to patronize the early labor movement, which was openly hostile to the artisan groups of the early 1870s), they were of little use to national Austrian Liberalism. Lueger had no difficulty in converting their sponsorship of the unitary Bürgertum into a more radical brand of second-generation Democracy, which he then used as a bridge to Christian Socialism.

The Progressive party organized by Josef Kopp and Max Menger in the early 1870s was more interested in strident nationalism than in non-Bürger political rights.[74] The career of Kopp illustrated this bias: by the early 1880s he returned to the mother Liberal party and abandoned the superficial *citoyen* rhetoric he had played with in the early 1870s, much of it in a rather dilettantish way. Menger's career was a similar exercise in political maturation along conservative lines, as Kronawetter noted in his attacks on the post-1885 Liberals.[75] The Progressives did represent a new sector's entrance into national politics, although this was not clearly a question of age alone. The recent historian of the party, Harrington-Müller, failed to explore the age/occupational structure of its members, but these data can be assembled from contemporary reports and almanacs. The mean age of the members of the Progressive Club in the Reichsrat in 1873 was forty-three; that of the *Klub der Linken* (the high Liberals) was forty-eight—hardly an impressive justification for using the terms "old" and "young" to distinguish the two groups.[76] The Progressives had more men from Eduard Herbst's generation than from Karl Lueger's. The difference in occupational distribution was more significant: twelve of the eighty-nine members of the *Klub der Linken* were either state officials or judges, whereas only one member of the Progressives was in this category. Both clubs had a full compliment of lawyers (seventeen for the Liberals, fifteen for the Progressives), but the Progressives had more bourgeois land-owners, local and regional officials (as opposed to *Staatsbeamten*), independently wealthy property holders, and middle-sized merchants than did the Liberal Club, whose ranks emphasized the higher commercial, industrial, and academic bourgeoisie (most of the delegates from the Chambers of Commerce curia ended up in the Liberal Club). The Progressives thus represented the more middle and private sectors of Austrian Bürger society. Their rise was coincident with the institution of direct voting in urban election districts in 1873. The indirect selection process through the Landtage before 1871 had a built-in oligarchical tendency which made the Liberals unrepresentative of their own voters, namely, the middle and upper Bürgertum. With the Progressives, the party's makeup was brought back to a closer harmony with the composition of Bürger society. The Progressives also had more "new" men among them who first entered parliament in 1873 than did the Liberals, who had more carry-overs.

The 1873 franchise was still harshly restrictive. In Vienna alone only 5 percent of the civil population could vote under the new *Ordnung*,[77] but the rise of the Progressives revealed a more subtle and complex national Liberalism, illustrating the larger social net which Austrian Liberalism began to cast just before the depression of the middle seventies. As a result the Progressives were both more irreverent toward the state and more defensive of it. Much of the controversy surrounding the 1874 confessional laws resulted from Progressive attempts to build into this legislation tougher protection against the Church. The Progressive's weakness lay, however, precisely in their tendency to mimic the mother Liberal party on anticlericalism and nationalism, offering more extreme variants of the Liberals' positions on both issues, but not attempting to go beyond the narrow range of these concerns to the *social* problems of Bürger society after 1873. They continued to use the traditional Liberal political techniques, showing themselves no more interested in popular mobilization than the Liberals. The Progressives were often suspicious of the Democrats, whose neoleftist rhetoric they found distasteful. Josef Kopp was an occasional ally of Ferdinand Kronawetter, not his political sibling. This party also shared the higher Liberals' ambiguity toward the unitary Bürgertum. The 1871 and 1873 programs of the Progressives demanded a *wahre Volksvertretung* and an end to "artificial" curialism, but this should not be taken to mean an overnight change to universal suffrage.[78] What they wanted was a unitary Bürgertum based on some tax qualifications, not a complete opening of political society to the "masses," as Kronawetter and Schönerer proposed, the latter for a very short time.

The depresssion of 1873 and the collapse of the Liberal ministry in 1879 played formidable roles in discrediting this slightly more flexible variant of Liberalism. Had the Austrian economy continued to prosper and had the Progressives (and the Democrats) learned to expand the range of their concerns about Bürger society, a legitimate Progressive version of Liberalism might have survived into the 1880s and obviated the need for (and the force of) anti-Liberal alternatives using Bürger social rhetoric. As it was, the fascination of the Progressives for anticlericalism and economic individualism blinded them to the economic needs of the Mittelstand they claimed to represent. When faced with strident calls for craft protectionism in the later 1870s, they were immobilized, in a classic case of collective indecision.[79] The rise of Taaffe and the simultaneous increase in the number of Slavs in the Reichsrat (the return of the Czech delegation after an absence of sixteen years) made it all to easy for the Progressives to use the national issue as a way of avoiding more fundamental problems in the areas of social and economic policy. By the later 1880s men like Kopp and Menger had returned to the Liberal party they had so harshly attacked ten years earlier. The likelihood of Austrian Liberalism's renewing itself without exogenous help was dead. When the next generation of German bourgeois politicians outside Vienna arose (in the Alpine areas and in the Bohemian lands), they understandably chose to define themselves first and foremost as nationalists, adding an assorted list of other kinds of issues to their credentials whenever this proved advantageous in dealing with the electorate. In a political community like Vienna, in contrast, where nationalism was an issue of little formal effectiveness, the absence of a respectable Left Liberal politics by the early 1880s made it possible for a talented politician like Lueger to create an ersatz Left Liberal alternative by adding new issues to the Liberal spectrum, first in the name of the lower Bürgertum and then, with great force, on behalf of the unitary Bürgertum itself. The tragedy of the Progressives was not merely their inability to support a comprehensive political citizenship for all, but their increasing suspicion of the lower Bürgertum, to whom they had directed their appeals in the early 1870s. They also failed to appreciate that political issues have discrete lifetimes, and that anticlericalism was not as meaningful to Bürger voters in the mid-1880s as it had been in the mid-1860s.

Three components of the Liberal platform of the 1860s and 1870s, however, were of crucial importance to Viennese politics: its anticlericalism, its devotion to the ideal of the local autonomy of Austrian cities, and its gradual political settlement with the neo-Josephist Verwaltung. The first proved the undoing of Austrian Liberalism, while the last two remained as its positive (and impressive) achievements.

Unlike their German cousins, for whom the *Kulturkampf* was above all a political issue which some Left Liberals acceded to only with shame and embarrassment, the Austrian Liberals viewed the Concordat of 1855 as violating long-standing traditions of Church-state relations in Austria. For many German Liberals the attack on the Church was a covert attack on the powerful Center party (as it was for Bismarck) and thus expressed their ambitions for political hegemony against a powerful, dissenting cultural minority within the new pseudoconstitutional German state.[80]

Austrian Liberals in contrast did not face a credible Catholic political opposition. Indeed, they denied that the Church had any constituency at all, with the possible exception of the misguided and uninformed, who did not yet recognize the beneficence of Liberal ideals. Catholic politics in Austria in the 1870s encompassed a diversity of feuding and ill-united interest groups, lacking any central direction other than a shared contempt for the Liberals. Perhaps the most formidable rivalry was that between the great Bohemian aristocrats (like Leo Thun and Heinrich Clam-Martinič) and Cardinal Rauscher in Vienna. The Bohemian Feudals were determined to make states-rights federalism an integral part of Catholic politics in the monarchy, whereas Rauscher was equally insistent upon differentiating between Catholic conservatism and provincial autonomism in the secular political realm.[81] The Thun-Rauscher rivalry also encompassed tactical positions on the response of the Catholics to the Liberal anti-Concordat legislation of the late 1860s and early 1870s: the pragmatist Rauscher, together with Bishop Johann Kutschker, argued for a "realistic" attempt to work with the state of affairs established by the new laws. Thun and Cardinal Schwarzenberg in Prague thought, in contrast, that a more vigorous program of resistance should have been launched, parallel to the intransigence of the Czechs in the 1870s in refusing to participate in the Reichsrat.[82]

To the extent that a public parliamentary presence was available to the Catholics in the 1870s, this was the so-called Party of the Right, which included Clerical Conservatives from the Alpine lands, Istria, Dalmatia, and Carniola, and a few isolated delegates from Bukowina and Lower Austria. This diverse assemblage was led by Count Hohenwart and generally affirmed the provincial rights program of the Bohemian Feudals.[83] Although the miserable performance of the Liberals during the later 1870s offered a few delegates of the Right, especially Georg Lienbacher, the opportunity to make a vigorous personal impact, the club as a whole was doomed to ineffective opposition. Until the secession of various Alpine Clericals in the early 1880s from the Hohenwart Club, no Catholic political group addressed itself to the interests and needs of the Viennese Catholic audience—that is, to an audience interested in German rights and governmental centralism, along with Catholic cultural values.[84]

Hence the Austrian Liberal confrontation with the Catholic Church was much more an explicitly constitutional and moral issue than a political and cultural one.[85] The German Liberals did not need the *Kulturkampf* to define themselves in constitutional terms. For that they had forty years of struggle with a powerful, interventionist government—whose army they both admired and intensely distrusted—and, more positively, a national crusade on behalf of a *kleindeutsch* German state. The Austrians had none of these antinomies or values, at least in quantities useful for meaningful action. After 1866 the value of the national issue for political self-enhancement was clearly limited to a defensive anti-Slavism. The army issue never played the role in Austrian Liberal politics that it did in Germany (the short-term outrage of 1879 notwithstanding). The Austrians avoided challenging the neo-absolutist state head-on. Instead they directed their confrontation not against the crown or the Verwaltung (the "state" before 1860), but against a secondary body which was hardly able to withstand the kind of popular force brought against it. The Church was used as a surrogate for the neo-absolutist state. In symbolic terms the Liberals found it far easier to undermine absolutism in the form of the Concordat than in the form of the army or the Verwaltung itself. Hence the kind of symbolic overkill which marked the long debates on the Church in parliament in the 1860s and 1870s. Their psycho-social theatricality dramatized the constitutional significance accorded to them.

Between 1861 and 1875 two general Liberal positions emerged on the question of Church-state relations, with a more extreme, third option occasionally vented but not taken seriously. Most of the high, ministerial Liberals adopted a position of state guarantism. Eduard Herbst summarized this position in a speech given in December 1873 in which he argued that the Liberals had no desire to destroy the Church or to undercut its religious effectiveness in civil society.[86] But the Liberals did see the need to deny the Church both the pretense and the use of political authority. A modern state of freedom and unity demanded that the Church forego the private use of public power. As a privileged public corporation the Church might enjoy the patronage and even the protection of the state, but the extent of such support should be determined by constitutional means and not by the private, discretionary authority of the Austrian episcopate.

The Progressives pushed this form of negative guarantism to the point where criticism of the Church itself as a religious institution was apparent. That is, they attacked not simply the Church's use of public power, as prescribed by the Concordat; they began to question as well the social value of the particular form of religious observance taught by the Church as it was presently constituted under the Austrian episcopate.[87] This was a more literal anticlericalism, consciously blurring the distinction between the Church as a public corporation and the Church as cultural force in society. This was not quite agnosticism or pure secularism, but it was closer to such a stance than the high Liberal one. The Progressive camp frequently assailed the Austrian bishops for using religion to their own professional ends. Such a position was shared by populist Progressives like Johann Fux, who was willing to provide more money for the "captive" lower clergy in order to reduce the power of the bishops in the Church, and by bitter, ideologically inspired critics like Friedrich Dittes and Theodor Haase (both German Protestants, working respectively in Vienna and Teschen), who wanted all of the Church's special privileges abolished and the influence of canon law eliminated from civil society.[88]

The most extreme position, that of a separation of Church and state, was advocated by a few radicals, perhaps the most notable of whom was Ferdinand Kronawetter. Kronawetter's stance testified to his consistent anti-Josephism, for it was clear in the 1848–49 Reichstag debates and again during the Liberal era that the Liberals and the Progressives had no intention of simply setting the Church free in civil society, without protective guarantees that the latent power of the Church might not be used against the Liberal state. Both the Liberals and the Progressives shared a Josephist sense of the subordinate role of ecclesiastical affairs in civil society (Josef Kopp openly admitted that he was using Joseph II as his model),[89] an assumption which the Clericals in parliament vigorously criticized, since it seemed to contradict the Liberals' pious claims about projecting liberty to all sectors of civil society.[90] The Conservatives in the Hohenwart Club argued that the Liberal state had no a priori right to grant liberty on a discretionary, sectoral basis.

The essential problem with the Liberal approach had to do not with the Conservatives' contention that the state was powerless (which was both naive and ahistorical in the Austrian context), but with the great complexity of the Josephist heritage itself. Herbst's position was at least theoretically consistent with the Josephist approach (subordinating the Church to the state, while implicitly retaining some patronage for it), but the bitter cultural anticlericalism of men like Dittes and Haase clearly superseded Joseph's careful attempt to integrate the Church into civil society under the subordinate direction of a statist episcopate. Their real intent was to isolate and if possible to eliminate Catholicism in society, which was not a Josephist position. The radical clerics of the 1880s, deeply imbued almost against their wills with the Josephist ideal of the lower clergy, realized the inherent dualism of the Liberals' anticlerical mystique. Since the conservative Liberals had the upper hand in the formation of legislation and since Franz Joseph would not tolerate more than a minimal tampering with the internal affairs of the Church (such as the *Religionsfondssteuer* of 1874, which made sense on utilitarian, fiscal grounds),[91] the actual impact of the May Laws of 1868 and the laws of 1874 was not categorically adverse to the Church's internal liberty. But in the popular culture of the day, especially the Viennese newspapers and public political language, the more anti-Catholic cultural slant could and often did raise its head.

Anticlericalism became the classic issue of Austrian Liberal politics. The Liberals pushed it successfully for all it was worth. But unlike in France, where the presence of a Catholic intelligentsia (both clerical and lay) gave anticlericalism a target, there was little point to the Liberals' crusade in Austria, especially after the wave of episcopal anarchism led by Bishop Rudigier of Linz was brought under control. There was no Catholic intelligentsia in Austria worthy of the name, either clerical or lay. The oppressive practices of the Austrian episcopate in the 1850s (Anton Günther) ensured that there could not be an intellectual revival among the clergy in the 1860s. Ironically, Liberal anticlericalism in Austria eventually suffered not because of the strength of the Catholic cause, but because of its essential weakness. Had religion found a more cohesive and socially popular group to defend it in the 1870s, one might have seen the development in the 1880s of a true political Catholicism, as occurred in Germany. Instead, anti-Liberalism in Vienna used (and misused) religion

through the secular mode of antisemitism, which was a far more dangerous enemy for the Liberals than clericalism or ultramontanism. The ultimate success of anticlericalism was to make everyone in urban Austria so
fearful of being called a "clerical" that the only way to create a non-Liberal political alternative was to use a new principle of legitimation, in this
case antisemitism, which did find a real social constituency. Dialectically
the Austrian Liberals summoned the means of their own destruction.

Moreover, the whole issue of Liberal anticlericalism was predicated on
a certain kind of internal Church authority system, the neo-Josephist-
episcopal. The bishops were the classic whipping boys of the Liberal fight
against the Concordat, far more than the lower clergy or the Catholic
congregations. Again, the Liberals had unwittingly selected what ultimately proved to be the most compliant and weakest sector of Catholic
resistance—Cardinal Rauscher's and Bishop Kutschker's response to the
Liberal legislation of the sixties and seventies was far more typical in
terms of future episcopal policy than was Rudigier's. What the Liberals
could not know, however, was that the Austrian lower clergy also had
conceptual and moral resources, apart from their bishops, which had been
developed over a long period of state sponsorship. When the lower clergy
broke with their bishops in the 1880s and developed their own ideas of
corporate self-help and professional renewal, the Liberals faced a movement which their older concepts of anticlericalism did not effectively
cover. Progressives like Fux had admitted that the "poor suffering lower
clergy" needed help against their bishops, even if these were tactical
ploys to embarrass and isolate the bishops. When the lower clergy took
the Liberals at their word and began to defend themselves with nonepiscopal resources, the whole universe of anticlerical rhetoric which
depended upon episcopal and ultramontanist referents was called into
question. The radical clerics could not easily be tagged as ultramontanist
or episcopal lackeys. Nor was Karl v Vogelsang's social theory particularly episcopal or Rome-oriented. Vogelsang's north German Lutheranism gave him the same sense of presbyterial independence that the
Austrian lower clergy possessed. The clergy thus came through the Liberal period ready to create a new brand of social clericalism against which
older Liberal models were often helpless.

The second (and more positive) achievement of the Liberals was their
insistence on retaining the ideals of *Gemeinde* autonomy first put forth by
the revolutionaries of 1848 and by Franz Stadion in place of the more
conservative, bureaucratized notions of Schmerling and Perthaler.[92]
Perthaler, who was influenced by Gneist on this point, saw the *Gemeinde*
in functional-economic terms (ensuring the *Produktivkraft* of society) and

as the locus of quasi-autonomous administrative authority in which the Bürgertum cooperated in fulfilling its "duties" toward the state by helping in the implementation and administration of local and regional policy. A narrow autocratic cooption defined urban freedom in what eventually became the typically late-nineteenth-century Prussian mode of urban administration.[93] The second generation of Liberals rejected this kind of insipid "autonomy" and demanded that the free *Gemeinde* actually receive a full measure of meaningful political and administrative rights, defined in terms of freedom from state interference and intervention. The resultant battles in the Reichsrat—well described by Redlich and Brockhausen—led to the *Reichsgemeindegesetz* of 1862, which was a victory for the younger Liberals' more expansive views. The free *Gemeinde* became the hallmark of Austrian Liberalism, one which later theorists like Lorenz v Stein and Josef Redlich celebrated in their discussions of the state political system, but one which also played a key role in the maturation of non-Liberal bourgeois political alternatives in the monarchy, like the Young Czechs in Bohemia and the Christian Socials in Lower Austria. Paradoxically, the very scope of political and administrative rights accorded to the *Gemeinde*, together with the curial franchise systems employed for voting purposes, made it possible for anti-Liberal political movements to turn the autonomous *Gemeinde* against the interests of the Liberal party after 1885.[94]

The free *Gemeinde* gave to Austrian Liberalism a variety in its social constituency and local political elites which it might otherwise have lacked. There was no model political bourgeoisie in Austria after 1848, and most Liberal voters in rural and city districts were hardly *Hochbürger* types. The free *Gemeinde* made it easier for middle-Bürger artisans and small merchants, as well as regional government officials, to find their way into Austrian public life in the 1860s and 1870s. Gradually there developed an intimate connection between local, regional, and national politics, especially in Vienna and Lower Austria. Although some Liberals entered national politics laterally from the top (e.g., Ernst v Plener), this often involved election through the privileged curia of the Chambers of Commerce and Industry. Many of the Liberal and Democratic politicians elected to the Reichsrat from urban districts in the 1870s and 1880s began their careers in the City Council, rising with personal patronage and experience to assume Landtag and Reichsrat responsibilities as time passed. The career of Josef Kopp was a classic example of this incremental political mobility. Perhaps the most famous case was that of Karl Lueger himself. Indeed, the intermixture of highly structured, local/district political interests and the relatively unstructured nature of the Liberal party on the national level gave rise to a style of qualified *Honoratioren*

politics in Vienna which was not simply "notable" in its avoidance of
society in a high bourgeois sense. Although this gap is often implied in
contemporary accounts of the style of Liberal politics, in Vienna at least it
is manifestly erroneous. Eduard Herbst once noted with considerable
frankness that the *Gemeindevertretungen,* filled with "Männer des
gewerbefleissigen, des thätigen Mittelstandes," were the bedrock of the
Liberal state and party of the 1860s.[95] The typical *Wahlcomité* structure
which both the Liberals and later the Christian Socials used to organize
their electoral campaigns in the city was dominated by the middle
Bürgertum, well before the rise of political antisemitism. Of the forty-nine
men on the Liberal electoral committee for the 1879 Reichsrat elections in
Vienna, fifteen were artisans or small factory owners and seven were
Hausherren, the rest being members of the City Council, many of whom
were themselves in similar occupational categories.[96] The Liberals who
arrived at the Abgeordnetenhaus from other provinces may have styled
themselves as high bourgeois notables, but the political world of the local
Liberals elected to the Reichsrat in Vienna itself was that of the local club
politics generic to Viennese society. Even before 1848 the coffee houses
and cafes provided more covert and informal opportunities for political
discussions. To believe that this generation of Liberals was divorced from
all political accountability to their constituents and had no social connections with them is to create fables in place of reasonable fact.

The third achievement of the Liberals was the most important, but the
least tangible, namely, the gradual detente they arrived at with the
Josephist Verwaltung. Josef Redlich argued that the Verwaltung would
have preferred Schmerling's kind of *Scheinkonstitutionalismus* to the
moderate, mixed constitutionalism which Austria achieved in 1867.
Doubtless this was the case, but the concessions wrung from the government in 1860–62 on the level of the *Gemeinde* and the *Land* (sustaining a
dual-track system of administration with potentially powerful local and
regional governmental structures) were supplemented in the period
1867–79 by a growing social and political accommodation between the
Verwaltung and the Liberal party, so that the original antinomy Redlich
proposed, which made sense in the later 1850s and early 1860s, was too
simplistic to represent Austrian politics in the later 1870s.[97] The very fact
that the Liberals controlled government policy during the period reduced
the dissonance between the higher Verwaltung and the party. This was a
very complicated sociological process, which has never been properly
analyzed, but it did result in a gradual meshing of sympathies and views
on the part of newer state officials who entered the civil service in the late

1850s and 1860s, to whom the Liberals gave patronage in the 1870s. Also, the Liberals gave the Verwaltung an extremely generous salary and benefits law in 1873–74, with the explicit demand that resistance to the Liberal state cease immediately.[98] The lack of a Junker-caste mentality in the Verwaltung made this possible, and the Liberals did respect the inherent rationality and internal organization of the administration. Their politicization of the service was a gentle and informal one—they expected state officials to vote Liberal and support the party. Administrative autocracy was still a useful tool for the Liberals themselves. If the crown could use it against the masses, so could the Liberals. The most generous treatment accorded the Socialists during the Liberal period occurred when Hohenwart, a Clerical Conservative who disliked both neo-absolutism and Liberalism, was in power (1871). Hohenwart felt, as Karl v Haller had before him, that neo-absolutism and Liberalism were ad hoc blood brothers.

The Conservatives frequently saw this symbiosis of Liberalism and administrative power as a nefarious tool for the enhancement of German centralism in the monarchy, which it was. The *Ausgleich* of 1867 and the Hohenwart episode may have shocked the higher civil service into seeing how closely its own political interests were allied to those of the Liberal party and how much it had to lose if the Federalists ever redesigned the system to reduce the central bureaucracy's role. Tension between the ministries and the parliament continued, but this now occurred in a routinized, professional sense of rival participants in the same, generally accepted political system. No political system has ever established perfect harmony between the state service, however liberal its sympathies, and the parliament. In dynamic terms such a congruence would be both impossible and undesirable. But by the later 1870s these tensions had been structured into a relatively predictable system of shared governmental power, in which the limits of probable behavior on both sides were at least being charted and institutionalized. Theoretical policy control of the system still rested in the hands of the emperor, but in terms of *functional* operations, power and policy were inevitably shared.

For the future of Austrian Liberalism, the relative universality and bourgeois character of the Verwaltung (in all but the highest regional and ministerial positions) made it easier for the later Social Liberals to ascribe to the Verwaltung an ethically charged and scientifically directed program of reforms. Unlike Weber's Prussian models, their Verwaltung was ostensibly universalist in its normative and social intentions, so that the Liberals felt they could afford to endow it with an ethically determined social science and law. The other component of the Verwaltung, the high aulic

and sub-aulic aristocracy, might be accommodated into this gradual dé-
tente. Erich Kielmansegg's behavior toward the Lower Austrian Liberals in the late 1880s and early 1890s illustrated this process. Many
second-generation Liberals before 1848 had put themselves through the
university by working as tutors for noble families.[99] This pattern of informal deference and patronage did not disappear entirely in later generations of Liberals and non-Liberals. The gap between the first and second
society did exist in Vienna, but there were bridges with which to cross it,
if only on a temporary basis. The antiaristocratic motif so common to
Liberal and Christian Social party rhetoric was directed more against the
secular aristocracy outside the Verwaltung, such as the Bohemian Feudals, and less against those socialized into the traditions of the Josephist
service mentality.[100] The one danger which this symbiosis of Liberalism
and statism implied, however, was that the Liberals could become overly
dependent upon it. What would happen if the Liberals lost power and
a new government arrived which promised to retain centralism and hierarchy of the system but which did not include the Liberals as a patronage
group? This was, of course, the fundamental dilemma the Liberal party
faced after 1880 and even more after 1890 on local and regional levels of
government. The Verwaltung had accepted the Liberal state, but could it
perhaps do without the Liberal party?

Conclusion: Viennese Politics and the Reconstruction of Bürger Society

The radical Democrats who engineered the Revolution of 1848 in Vienna
hoped that one result of their labors would be a homogeneous political
culture within the city itself. Goldmark, Violand, Fischhof—all were convinced that only a *Volk* possessing a moral and social, as well as a political
unity could resist the kind of deprivation and coercion which marked
Austrian civil society before 1848. The later willingness of the Austrian
Social Democrats to patronize their historical memory, even though the
Democrats were not socialistic, testified to the leftist thrust of their
utopianism. However, the student groups and democratic journalists who
formed the core of the movement found themselves faced with the un-
alterable fact not only that there was a Bürgertum and an *Arbeiterschaft*
by August 1848, but that even within the Bürgertum there were several
social and cultural factions which made political homogeneity impossible.
The course of Liberal politics in 1848 foreshadowed the gradual alienation
of the solid middle Bürgertum away from both the working classes and the
lower *Kleinbürger* types. A crucial social issue in the first months of the
revolution was the defense of real property rights. When artisan masters
finally managed to organize themselves, they demanded rent protection

against their *Hausherren*, not political liberty. The Democrats' attempts to cultivate these groups (Goldmark, Schuselka, and colleagues were responsible for the proposal in the Reichstag to allocate 2 million fl. of public funds to impoverished artisans in September 1848) met with some success, but the Democrats and artisans were on relatively distinct political wavelengths in their communications. With a tradition of relative so- cial conformity and nonviolent collective behavior (as opposed to the tradition of revolutionary protest sustained by the French petite bourgeoisie), the Viennese artisans made their peace with the neo-absolutist regime far more easily than did the small band of alienated, liberal Democrats. Because these groups of artisans were eliminated from the Austrian political system for the next thirty-five years, their opportunity for protest and collective self-definition was limited. When they did organize again in the later 1870s and 1880s, their behavior was as nonviolent in the realm of political action as it was violent in that of political language. The social violence of the artisans of 1848 was ahistorical and atypical of the Viennese. When political antisemitism provided a language of symbolic aggressiveness in the 1880s which obviated the need for violent social behavior, the lower-ranking artisans returned to the more traditional Austrian mode of political conflict. The Revolution of 1848 was not the logical turning point for Austria, if the methods and tactics of the year are seen as typical of a pattern of political behavior. Rather, it was a "turning point" which was judiciously avoided by all later Viennese-based political movements. Even the Social Democrats tended to celebrate March and not August of 1848.

The ideal of the unitary Bürgertum was the great Liberal heritage of 1848, one which the Liberals both sustained and consciously betrayed. The next generation of Austrian Liberalism redefined the nature of the *Volk* to exclude the proletariat in categorical terms and the lower artisan Bürgertum in relative terms. All Liberals shared the conviction that owning a "share of the corporation" should be the principal qualification for political rights. Maturity, property, social service—these were the attributes of political liberty which ultimately became the hallmarks of the Liberal patronage system as well. Politics existed not to reshape the contours of Austrian society, but to serve the privileged Bürgertum as it existed in cultural and economic terms. *Ständisch* and class-based social interests combined to define a new idea of political liberty which sanctioned social stability rather than mobility.

Between 1873 and 1895 the Liberal dream of political liberty based on the middle and upper reaches of the Bürgertum, in alliance with the small, yet powerful *Hochbürgertum* of industrial-capitalist dimensions which Austria gradually possessed after 1848, proved initially more persuasive than the dreams of a universal citizenship of the 1848 Democrats. The fledgling Democratic movement, which began in Vienna on an ad hoc basis in the early City Council elections of the 1860s and crystalized in the period 1868–73, floundered seriously even before the depression of the later 1870s because of its patronage of early labor groups after 1867. Hans Rosenberg's easy causal relationship between the depression and political "reaction" does not quite fit the Viennese context, since the essential social conservatism of most lower-Bürger in Vienna (the Democrats depended heavily upon the 10 fl. artisans who dominated the Third Curia until their lower ranking brethren were brought in in 1882–86) was openly manifest before the depression actually began. The career of Eduard Hügel, the editor of the *Konstitutionelle Vorstadt-Zeitung,* was typical of many of these Left Liberal Democrats.[101] After 1870 Hügel found himself cut off from the labor movement, which he had sought to patronize in the later 1860s. The profound isolation of Ferdinand Kronawetter after 1873, when most of his colleages in the *Demokratische Gesellschaft* repudiated the idea of a symbiosis between the unitary Bürgertum and the *citoyen,* illustrated the hardening of the lines of class conflict in Austrian society by the early 1870s.[102]

The new generation of Bürger politicians arriving by the later 1870s on the Viennese scene perceived the narrowness and inflexibility of the Liberal interpretation of the ideal of the unitary Bürgertum and realized the new social dimensions of politics. Politics no longer existed simply to recognize the social status quo, but to advance and assist the lower Bürgertum in regaining the kinds of political and economic "liberties" which it deserved. At the same time, new forms of linguistic and ideological discourse were needed if the dominance of Liberal anticlericalism was to be broken. As long as anticlericalism survived as a functional issue, the unitary Bürgertum would remain fractionalized and imbalanced. The lower artisan Bürger hardly possessed the resources necessary to protect himself against the social egalitarian demands of the early Austrian labor movement; only the classic ideal of the unitary Bürgertum, reestablished on new terms, could provide this historical service.

This double political revolution—the destruction of Liberal anticlericalism and the reincorporation of the lower Bürgertum into a realm of political privileges on the one hand, and the reconstruction of Bürger political society as a whole against Social Democracy on the other—was the work of Karl Lueger and the Christian Social party. When Lueger was elected mayor of Vienna in 1895–96, he not only depended upon the votes of the artisans in the Third Curia who had fought for and against the workers in 1848 and who had picked up the language of political antisemitism in the 1880s as an alternative to Liberal anticlericalism, but also added to his coalition a significant portion of the old Liberal Mittelstand in the First and Second Curias as well. The five-gulden men were Lueger's beginning point in mass politics, but hardly his destination. In September 1848 wealthier artisans and property owners (butchers, bakers, *Hausherren* of all varieties, *Fabrikanten, Beamten,* and other assorted Bürger groups) were fighting against their less fortunate bourgeois colleagues, but by September 1895 they were voting together in a joint attempt to establish a new variant of middle bourgeois politics in Vienna and Lower Austria.

This book is the story of this double revolution, the history of a dream and an illusion fulfilled—the final success of the unitary Bürgertum. Rather than designing his Bürgertum from the top down, as did the Liberals, Lueger reversed the process and built it from the bottom up, but the result was remarkably similar by 1900. The dream of universal homogeneity of the radical Democrats of 1848 was fulfilled, but on far more narrow, class-based terms than they would have wished. Society was politicized into antinomies and rejoined into social interest harmonies. Anticlericalism and antisemitism, the two principal modes of bourgeois politics in Vienna in the period 1848–1914, combined in the Christian Social party in a unique mix to Bürger liberty directed at collective self-enhancement and anti-Socialist defensiveness.

2

The Viennese Artisans and the Origins
of Political Antisemitism, 1880–90

Until the early 1880s the restrictive franchise of the 1850 *Gemeinde-ordnung* gave Viennese Liberalism a powerful hegemony in local politics. Most moderately well off artisans belonged to the Third Curia and adopted Liberal or Liberal-Democratic views. Although the Democrats might criticize the narrow electoral franchise in the city, they shared with the Liberals an uncompromising anticlericalism and at least a moderate economic Liberalism. The poorest artisans may have resented their loss of political rights, but they showed no disposition to attack the established order. Without spokesmen and without attractive economic issues to mobilize their energies, the lowest levels of the Bürgertum remained in a state of passivity.

In the wake of the Crash of 1873 and the ensuing depression, however, a protest movement among the lower artisans began which was to have enormous repercussions for the whole structure of Viennese Bürger politics. By 1880 those artisans (or their successors) who had lost their political rights in 1849 wanted to return to politics, but with a very different sense of themselves as economic men with uncompromising and desperate demands. There were also more of them: the relative percentage of 5 fl. artisan taxpayers in the city increased by 60 percent between 1848 and 1880, revealing the increasing poverty of many handwork shops. These men were simply one component of a diverse Bürgertum when the Liberals shunted them aside in 1849–50, but now they constituted a powerful and numerically impressive source for radical political discontent. Moreover, these men owed the Liberal tradition nothing. The Liberals made no effort between 1849 and 1880 to socialize these potential voters into a pattern of Liberal political behavior. Not surprisingly, they were prime material for a countermovement which affirmed their traditional status prerogatives but attacked the pieties of Austrian Liberalism.

Not all artisans in Vienna were 5 fl. men, and not all 5 fl. men were fire-eating Jew haters, before or after 1880. Such conventional stereotypes, which are often suggested in the historical literature, are absurd. Even after 1880 there were thousands of prosperous middle and upper ranking artisans, many of whom later came to occupy key positions in the mature Christian Social movement.

The importance of the lower artisans for the origins of the party cannot be ignored, however. They were the first social group to embrace political antisemitism. Without their massive repudiation of economic Liberalism and its advocates, the Christian Socials would never have established themselves as an alternative to Liberal conceptions of the privileged Bürgertum, while retaining the idea of the Bürgertum as an operational entity.

The artisans played a crucial role in the politics of the 1880s as a result of their enfranchisement on the national and local levels between 1882 and 1885. What the Liberals could not bring themselves to do—enlarge the active citizenry by including the lowest levels of the taxpaying Bürgertum in the franchise—Taaffe's clerical-Slavic Iron Ring did with a vengeance. The decline of political Liberalism on the national level as a result of its oppositional role after the crisis of 1879 inevitably led to readjustments in the whole Austrian political system as the 1880s wore on.[1] Not only did new policymakers gain political control, with new social and cultural goals, but also the kinds of issues which might shape and motivate public opinion altered as the decade progressed. The new isolation and defensiveness of the Liberal party drastically reduced its tolerance of political dissidence within its own ranks, as radical Democrats like Ferdinand Kronawetter and Karl Lueger soon learned. Anticlericalism ceased to have the magic, formulaic value as a central political issue that could ensure party unity by the early 1890s. Indeed, Austrian political culture seemed to explode around a multiplicity of new issues—nationalism, socialism, antisemitism—all of which had formerly existed, but none of which had ever enjoyed successful sponsorship by a broadly based, popularly legitimated political movement.

In Vienna, where nationalism hardly ranked as an issue in the first place and where socialism suffered in the early and mid-1880s as a result of the anarchist movement of 1881–84, antisemitism became the most dramatic new issue on the political horizon. Antisemitism functioned as a short-term panacea for discontented artisans searching for easy explanations of their economic woes and for bourgeois political activists looking for easy, unencumbered devices to capture their voters' imaginations. Inevitably, the Viennese Jewish community came to occupy the spotlight of public attention, in ways which Liberal Jews found both shocking and perplexing. Having worked for decades to achieve a satisfactory economic integration into Austrian society and having finally achieved full legal and political emancipation between 1848 and 1867, Viennese Jews found that the very success of their accommodation with and emulation of bourgeois society was now held up as unacceptable and even intolerable. By the end of the decade, with the increasing diversity and poverty of the city's

Jewish community, many younger Jews would begin searching re-examinations of their predecessors' assumptions about the workability of political parity within Gentile society.

Finally, the 1880s were the first decade in Austrian politics in which the new scope of political resources and the new latitude of political issues found an equally complex and fragmented social base upon which to operate. No longer did the Bürgertum exist as a monolithic entity, representing a consensus of political views. By the end of the 1880s it consisted, in social-psychological terms at least, of a number of anxious, self-serving interest groups, all of which sought to enrich their own cultural and material status within an economy which seemed to be faltering and within a state structure which seemed increasingly hostile to their particularistic needs. With the rise of the modern Austrian Social Democratic movement at the end of the decade, all of these groups found themselves facing an enemy which could force upon them an artificial political unity. Misery loves company, special interest ideologies notwithstanding. With the rise of the great ideological chasm in modern Austrian history—socialist versus bourgeois, with no credible, mediating Liberal forces in between—other ideologies became increasingly secondary and subsidiary as determinants of tactical political behavior in late Imperial Vienna.

The Decline of the Handwork Artisans, 1870–83

In 1880 in Vienna, 43,492 individuals were registered as operators of industrial businesses, while 22,670 persons identified themselves as active in retail and wholesale trade *(Handel)*.[2] In 1881 legally registered businesses sufficiently prosperous to be subject to the trade tax *(Erwerbsteuer)* numbered 28,474 for industry and 21,069 for trade.[3] Although Viennese industrial statistics for this period are unreliable and often provide a misleading view of the size of the businesses,[4] of those firms which paid the license tax in 1881, 20,214 paid the minimum tax of 5 fl. and another 17,084 paid the second lowest rate of 10 fl., indicating the modest size and annual profit levels of these firms.[5] From these two groups of taxpayers the Christian Socials derived their initial voting strength, dominating as they did the Third Curia in Vienna. Even as late as 1902, in Austria's first accurate industrial census, the significance of the small workshop or store (employing 1–5 persons, including the owner) in Vienna was still apparent. Of 105,525 businesses in that year, 90,281 had five or fewer employees.[6] Allowing for the fact that some of these "independent" businesses were not run by fully independent craftsmen, but by house-industrial sweatshop workers, the number of small firms was still exceedingly high.

In contrast to the new middle class of bureaucrats, clerks, and industrial or commercial employees, whose salary and social prestige might remain below desired levels but whose employment prospects were excellent in an industrializing economy, the small Viennese tradesman was involved by 1890 in a mortal struggle for survival in the face of newer, more efficient modes of production and distribution.[7] Because industrialization in Austria occurred at a far slower pace than in England or America and took place within delimited geographical areas, the Austrian (especially the Viennese) master handworkers were able to survive and to coalesce as a substantial political force in the mid-1880s. Political consciousness came before the final denouement inherent in their increasingly archaic situation and was infected with a particular urgency. The very forms which economic development assumed in Austria tended to lengthen the patient's sickness interminably, without either curing or killing him.

The economic modernization of Austria after 1848 and especially after 1859 presented the small craftsman with some severe challenges.[8] The most serious was increased mechanization and concentration in such industries as textiles; construction trades; metal, iron, and machine production; and furniture production. The Viennese textile industry, for example, was hard hit by foreign and regional (Bohemian) competition and by the technological obsolescence of small-scale manufacturing. In 1850 there were 452 silk manufacturers located in Vienna, employing 8,616 workers. By 1887 there were only 83 such firms left, with a total work force of 1,134 workers.[9] The old *Seidenzeugmacher,* with his solid middle-Bürger status, disappeared from the face of Viennese society between 1850 and 1880.[10] The cotton and wool weavers' guild suffered an even more catastrophic decline—from 1,281 master artisans in 1848 to 176 in 1887. To the extent that textile manufacuring survived in Lower Austria this occurred in a few larger, fully mechanized plants, many of which were located in rural areas to avoid the labor costs of Vienna. Similarly, large commercial firms in the Viennese clothing industry organized large-scale house-industrial systems *(Heimarbeit)* in the 1860s and 1870s to supply the export market and to cater to the desire of the local population for cheap new clothing (rather than used clothing).[11]

The new pace of mechanization and the changing market situation in Vienna, based on the steady influx of impoverished workers into the city, on the novelty and convenience of large retail establishments, on the growing availability of reliable freight transportation, and on the provisions of the 1859 trade laws, led to the encroachment by big producers and distributors on formerly secure artisan domains. Try as they would to preserve their independence, the small artisans were slowly caught up in impersonal economic processes beyond their understanding or control.

Gustav Schmoller, who was sympathetic to the artisans' plight, analyzed their dilemma accurately when he wrote in 1870 that "the crisis of handwork is not a matter unto itself; it is a consequence of general changes in our entire economic relationships."[12]

The 1873 crisis and ensuing depression, whose worst effects only gradually disappeared by the mid-1880s, hit hardest those artisans with the smallest capital bases, many of whom were already by 1873 practicing outmoded production techniques. After 1873 the larger and more powerful industrial units pursued an extensive policy of concentration and monopolization.[13] The decline in wages and, more significantly, the sustained drop in prices after 1873, together with the increased competition which Austrian exporters faced from abroad (notably from Germany, following the introduction of restrictive tariffs), meant more devastating competition within the domestic market.[14] No clearer example of this process could be found than the case of a Viennese shoe manufacturer, Alfred Fränkel, who established a highly mechanized shoe factory in a suburb of Vienna in the early 1880s hoping to enter the French and Balkan export markets. As a result of the uncompetitive prices of Austrian products against German, Swiss, and American shoes of similar quality, and because of the ill effects of the Austro-Rumanian trade war of 1886–87, Fränkel decided to shift the distribution of his shoes into the domestic market, concentrating on Vienna. In May 1887 he opened a series of ten retail outlets, threatening the livelihood of hundreds of small Viennese shoemakers. Not only did Fränkel undercut his competitors in price (for a similar pair of shoes Fränkel charged 10–20 percent less than did an artisan shoemaker), but he paid higher wages and provided his workers with company housing, attracting the most skilled journeymen to his own plant and away from local shoemakers.[15] Fränkel also enjoyed an advantage in terms of the antiquated Austrian commercial tax structure. Whereas the hundreds of master shoemakers whose livings he was destroying paid (as a group) over 6,000 fl. in trade taxes annually, Fränkel paid one flat rate of 210 fl.[16]

The depression which began in 1873 saw many such hostile confrontations between industry and handwork artisans. The Christian Socials were fortunate to gain political power in Vienna at precisely that moment (1896) when the city's economic situation took a sharp turn for the better, explaining perhaps the tendency of some commentators to look back on Lueger's tenure as mayor as an "era of good feelings."[17]

The Viennese artisan in 1880 was threatened by three developments: the mechanized factory, the house-industrial system, and a multitude of retail distributors, small and large, who interposed themselves as middlemen between producer and consumer, offering ready-made goods, often in attractive advertising displays, with whom the small master craftsman in his cramped, dirty workshop could not possibly compete. Not only middle-class consumers, but even many from the lower orders demanded more selection at lower prices—the specialty store and the dealer were in a position to destroy the artisan by appealing to these new consumer standards.[18]

The several hundred industrial trades in Vienna were not each threatened by the same enemy, though some trades, like carpentry and furniture making, confronted all three of these difficulties at once. In an investigation in 1894, Eugen Schwiedland differentiated between trades which were already surpassed by factory mechanization (textiles, watches, playing cards, pianos, machine parts and tools, candle and soap products, and beer) and those which, while seriously threatened, had managed to preserve some semblance of independence by drawing upon factory-made parts for final assembly in their own shops or by concentrating on repairs of factory products (hatmakers, glove makers, locksmiths, and carpenters).[19] Large artisan trades such as the carpenters and the turners survived, and the absolute number of master craftsmen even increased, but the inroads made by factory production were still apparent. The number of furniture factories between 1841 and 1890 in Lower Austria and Vienna grew from three to fifty, while the number of craftsmen merely doubled (from 2,188 to 4,573). In many trades the increase in artisan membership did not even keep pace with the growth rate of the population of greater Vienna. Also, much of the absolute growth of the artisan ranks must be explained not in relation to the prosperity of workshops serving individual customers—the classic handwork ideal—but rather, as in the case of the carpenters, in terms of the growth of retail furniture dealers. Many carpenters, using parts precut in a factory, served as dependent laborers for a local furniture dealer. With cheaper production costs, with a larger, regional market, with an effective division of labor, with raw materials in greater quantities purchased at a discount, the superiority of the factory made it only a matter of time until the small artisan was either forced out of business entirely or forced into repair service or sales of factory products, that is, compelled to join the already overcrowded ranks of the petty shopkeepers.

The second threat to the independence of these craftsmen was the *Verlag*, or house-industrial system, which was particularly widespread in the clothing trades. Here the formerly independent master became a "piece man" *(Stückmeister)* who worked in his own shop (usually a one- or two-room apartment in which he also lived with his family) with one or two apprentices or journeymen, producing one particular article of clothing or one type of shoe for a large clothing manufacturer *(Konfektionär)*.[20] The *Konfektion* system represented the power of a unique combination of commercial and industrial capital, since some manufacturers not only exported their goods *en gros,* but also established networks of retail outlets for the sale of ready-made goods and for orders of quality articles. In an investigation of the men's clothing industry in Vienna in 1895 Friedrich Leiter found that of 3,119 tailors in greater Vienna, approximately 1,900 worked as *Stückmeister* for large commercial manufacturers, the other 1,200 artisans being wealthier quality craftsmen working on order for individual customers *(Kundenschneider).*[21] In 1885 there were eighty-four large businesses involved in the manufacture of men's clothing in Vienna, employing a total of 4,574 workers, of whom 2,439 worked outside the place of manufacture. Almost all of these individuals worked for *Konfektion* enterprises.[22] In the manufacture of umbrellas, twenty large firms dominated the market, relying heavily on the smaller craft masters in a house-industrial status.[23] At least fifty percent of the 25,000 workers employed in shoe manufacture in Vienna, including many of the 4,400 master shoemakers in the city, worked for *Konfektion* firms.[24] The extent of house industry in the city can be gauged from the fact that over 50,000 rental units in the city (out of 400,000) functioned as both living and business quarters for a family. Only 25,000 units of rental space were used exclusively for business purposes.[25] Although the subject of considerable controversy, the *Konfektion* system was a response to critical market conditions in Austria and not simply the result of greed on the part of a few individuals to exploit the handwork masters.[26] As a transitional stage between the simple one-man craft shop and the fully mechanized and centralized factory, the house-industrial system served the Austrian market by providing cheap, average-quality clothing for growing urban markets.[27] House industry saved the manufacturer the cost of a large investment in a physical plant and enabled him to lower production costs and prices.[28] It also provided employment for those who could find work in no other industry.[29] Many wives of government *Beamten* and of other bourgeois functionaries, whose social position did not allow them to engage in work publicly, served as seamstresses for the Viennese clothing industry in the privacy of their homes.[30] The *Verlag* also brought with it, however, dysfunctional features, notably the low wages paid to the *Stückmeister* and their journeymen, the unregulated working day, and unsanitary working conditions. Many artisans hoped that by forcing the larger clothing manufacturers to designate their businesses as "factories" in the legal sense, thereby subjecting them to state labor regulations, the smaller and less viable firms could be driven out of business.[31] They were, as one critic remarked, interested not in "labor protection," but rather in "master protection."[32] The problem with this approach was that it exposed the handwork owners to the equally just demand that *their* shops be made subject to labor protection and rigorous sanitary inspection. The government's uncertainty about reforming the *Konfektion* system without injuring the already fragile state of Austrian exports and causing mass domestic unemployment made the abolition of this form of business before 1914 an impossibility.[33] The house-industrial system was so extensive, moreover, that even the wealthier masters employed subordinate artisans as house-industrial workers. The attitudes of the better placed master craftsmen toward the abolition of the system were, therefore, quite different from those of the less well situated artisans.[34]

The third and in some respects the most critical challenge faced by small industrial producers in Vienna was the expansion of the number of small- and medium-sized retail distributors after 1848. In 1852 Vienna had 2 retail shoe stores. By 1890 the same districts of the city had 79 shoe dealers. Instead of 5 retailers of men's and women's clothing in 1860, the city had 134 such establishments in 1890. In 1855 there were 17 furniture stores in the city, whereas by 1890 there were 134.[35] A more provocative form of retailing which threatened the artisan was the small general store dealing in an incredible assortment of foods and various articles of clothing, the *Gemischtwarenverschleisser*.[36] These stores competed with artisans accustomed to direct negotiations with their customers, while also generating hostility from other small merchants, such as the milk dealers and restaurant owners. The master shoemakers and many of the other large guilds hated the general store owners.[37] In 1890 there were approximately 3,600 of these small general stores in Vienna, many of which had done very well during the depression.[38] Independent storekeepers were not alone in dominating the retail market. Many artisans who found that their businesses could not be sustained on goods which they themselves made also went into retailing. At least one-fourth of the industrial shops classified as "hatmakers" in Vienna in 1890 were actually shops selling hats from domestic and foreign *Konfektion* firms.[39]

By the early 1890s, retail distributors had deprived the artisan of an essential part of his self-image—immediate control over his selling price by negotiation with the customer.[40] Most of the small and medium dealers in clothing, shoes, furniture, umbrellas, and watches also depended on the *Verlag* system for their supplies.[41] Furniture warehouses thus provided the major market for the products of hundreds of master carpenters, who were forced to sell at the dealer's price.[42] In 1886 the furniture dealers of Vienna were able to establish a price cartel to regulate the maximum prices paid to master carpenters.[43] Such arrangements worked to the disadvantage of the artisans, who had no effective interest organization to defend them. Retail establishments with a firm capital base and with newspaper advertising rarely lacked customers. But because the expansion of the number of dealers in the 1870s and 1880s also included many small, unstable elements, fierce competition soon ensued, often involving unscrupulous advertising and sales techniques.[44] The market itself, moreover, consisted increasingly of proletarian families who could afford only the cheapest goods, a fact which the handwork masters intentionally ignored in their polemics against alleged swindlelike tactics on the part of the dealers.[45] The result of retail competition might have been favorable for the artisan producers had their numbers stabilized by 1880 and had the dealers not had other sources of supply, such as the artisan centers in Bohemia and Moravia, whose products could reach Vienna with ease on the new rail system. Unfortunately, the ranks of the artisans in large Viennese trades like carpentry and shoemaking continued to grow even after the prohibitory trade amendments of 1883.[46] Because the small craftsman lacked credit and required immediate cash payment for the articles he delivered to the dealer, he was at a great disadvantage in price negotiations.[47]

Ironically, the rapid expansion of the retail sales trade in Vienna provoked cries for protectionism even among such mercantile groups as the *Verein der Specerei-, Material-, und Vermischtwarenhändler,* a group of older, more established food merchants than the small-scale general store owners. This group summoned a merchants' congress in Vienna in August 1884 to demand the same kind of protection against peddlers, cooperative societies, and small general stores as that which the craft artisans were insisting upon.[48] The government's lack of sympathy for their pleas reflected not merely the administration's unwillingness to interfere with commercial structures for fear of raising retail prices, but also the fact that these older, intermediate mercantile groups had no devoted political patrons. To the larger, Liberal-oriented *Konfektionäre* and wholesale merchants they were an anachronism;[49] to the smaller general store proprietors they were an undesirable competitor.[50] To the populace of Vienna, many of whom were confused by its innumerable legal and linguistic distinctions, the *Kleinhandel* movement was a stillborn affair which never reached a significant political level in the 1880s.[51] The craft artisans and not the mid-sized shopkeepers were the basis of the Christian Social party's initial electoral efforts before 1890. After 1890, when the party gradually arrived at a compromise with the small shopkeepers and the antisemites won control of their guild (1893), the older mid-scale merchants had no political home.

To examine each of the hundreds of craft trades in the city between 1870 and 1895 is certainly beyond the scope of this book, but certain trends are apparent. Although many trades lost relative and absolute numbers as early as 1862, the period 1873 to 1882/83 was probably the nadir for many of the larger artisan trades. Between 1873 and 1882 the ranks of the carpenters, the tailors, the shoemakers, the bakers, and other small artisans showed a decline. Between 1876 and 1882 the number of locksmiths dropped from 710 to 611, shoemakers from 2,692 to 2,651, carpenters from 1,750 to 1,531, turners from 750 to 732, tailors from 2,858 to 2,651, house painters from 286 to 267, bakers from 306 to 298, and jewelers from 595 to 546.[52] Available statistics list only artisans whose place of business was in one of the ten original districts of Vienna. Many of the poorer artisans gave up their trades in Vienna (thus explaining in part the numerical decline in their ranks) and simply moved out to the suburbs, where the cost of living was lower. This phenomenon was added proof of the dissatisfaction the decline in their social and economic status must have produced, since an artisan who was forced to give up his business in such citadels of Bürger respectability as the Josefstadt and the Landstrasse and to relocate in a suburb where much poorer consumers lived would be likely to harbor resentment over the disruptions in his life. Other groups such as that of the mechanics increased their numbers between 1876 and 1882, but available data provide no breakdown of tax payments by individual units. The rise in the number of machine shops may have reflected both the growth of larger, mechanized establishments and a modest (and for those concerned unprofitable) increase in the ranks of the smaller mechanics who served as subcontractors.[53]

Especially noteworthy was the fact that in most Viennese craft trades the low point in membership as well as the nadir in trade taxes occurred in 1880–81, precisely the years when political antisemitism began to infiltrate local artisan groups. The special committee of the *Wiener Gewerbegenossenschaftstag* which organized the First Austrian Craft Congress in November 1881 (the formal beginning of the artisan protest movement) consisted of the following individuals: a shoemaker, a tailor, a jeweler, a carpenter, a baker, a painter, and a chimney sweep—men who belonged to those trades suffering from declining membership.[54]

More convincing evidence of the commercial weakness and overpopulation of many trades was offered by the taxes paid by the smaller shops. Between 1852 and 1879 the number of businesses subject to the trade tax in Vienna increased from 33,943 to 48,861, but the total tax paid in 1879 was only 159,991 fl. greater than that in 1852. In 1852, 24.75 percent of all craft shops in Vienna were taxed at the lowest rate of 5 fl., whereas by 1879, the 5 fl. category included 42.5 percent of all producers. In 1852 the number of 10 fl. businesses amounted to 45.5 percent of all those subject to a tax, but by 1879 the number had fallen to 34 percent.[55]

After 1882 the downward trend in craft membership was arrested for some businesses. According to the reports of the Viennese Chamber of Commerce and Industry, 1881–82 was the first good business year since the mid-1870s.[56] In many sectors, however, the decade 1880–90 remained highly unpromising.[57] For some handwork trades, the rise in the total number of masters simply meant less profit per unit. Eugen Schwiedland calculated in 1894 that for twelve broad industrial classifications the total number of the larger-size plants paying 42 fl. or more in taxes between 1880 and 1890 had grown by 39 percent and had increased their tax performance by 59 percent. For firms under the 42 fl. borderline the growth rate was only 10 percent and their tax performance had actually decreased by 0.1 percent.[58]

The marginality of the poorer artisan was painfully clear. Unable to attract customers to his shop, he was forced to sell his wares to a dealer. He had little or no credit, and he could not buy his raw materials in bulk quantities at a discount as the *Verlag* could do.[59] His housing was often miserable, although it was probably superior to that of the typical journeyman, who was forced to rent a bed for the night in a filthy, lice-ridden room. His professional training was often surprisingly inadequate. Many master artisans were accustomed to making one specific part of one article or, at best, one kind of article, and never had the chance to enjoy an overview of the craft as a whole. One Viennese master shoemaker who was interviewed in 1902 had never learned the correct methods for constructing the upper part of a shoe.[60] In 1895 the government sponsored a "master course" at the Technological Trade Museum in Vienna for forty-nine shoemakers who already held the legal title of "master." A report on the previous training of these men when they entered the course noted that not one man could design and execute the pattern for a complete shoe. None of them knew anything about the anatomy of the human foot; all were ignorant of even the simplest method of basic book-keeping. One-third of the students could not even join the sole of a shoe to the upper portion in the proper manner.[61] This abysmal lack of training was not characteristic only of the shoe industry.

To survive as an independent producer and to maintain a respectable level of personal consumption, the master artisan exploited the labor of his journeymen and apprentices. Because he was in such close physical proximity to the proletariat, the craftsman's political encounters with the working class assumed a passionate, personal hostility which was often lacking in the more neutral (and more arrogant) behavior of the wealthier manufacturers.[62] The artisan master may have envied and resented *Grosskapital,* but even more did he fear the union movement as a force of social and economic egalitarianism. In this unenviable situation the traditional caricature of the Viennese artisan as the Babbitt-like *Spiessbürger* found great popularity.[63] For the Socialists Karl Lueger himself was the archetype of this aggregate of petit bourgeois vice and virtue: superficial, without serious convictions, humorous in a cynical, sardonic manner, lacking wholly in ethical principles.[64] Undoubtedly, behind the caricature there lay a certain degree of truth. It would be inaccurate, however, to conclude from this array of attributes that the artisans' behavior was "irrational," subject solely to affective motives. Although their gullibility for the slogans of the Christian Socials was extraordinarily high, the success of such propaganda lay in its promise of basic economic change. Where appeals to cultural hatred were involved, as in antisemitism, these often had a strongly rational core.[65] Some of the promises of the antisemites were absurd; but others involved rational, objective considerations such as better credit facilities, higher tax rates on big industry, the abolition of peddling, laws regulating competitive sales, and the like. The radical sounding language of the politicians, as in the case of Lueger, was intelligible only in terms of the special set of meanings given to such terminology in the popular dialect of the Viennese artisan bourgeoisie. The artisan Spiessbürger, although intolerant and chauvinistic, had, like most voters, a concrete sense of what he wanted and expected from the political elites who represented him. Berelson's comments on the American voter of the late 1940s may find some applicability to nineteenth-century Austria as well: "The voter does have some principles, he does have information and rationality, he does have interests—but he does not have them in the extreme, elaborate, comprehensive or detailed form in which they were uniformly recommended by political philosophers."[66] Although the Social Democrats often mocked the credulity and "stupidity" of the artisans, they did not underestimate them. The Socialists did not dare to ignore the possibility that they might persuade some handwork masters to vote for their candidates. Socialist propaganda on the issue of housing reform in Vienna (about which the Christian Socials would and could do nothing) usually included the artisan masters as well as the industrial proletariat as its targets.

One of the great tragedies of the Viennese labor situation involved the position of the apprentice (Lehrling).[67] The apprentice problem was almost solely a dilemma of the smaller artisans, since mechanized factories often did not accept apprentices and, when they did, apprentices were usually accorded more adequate educational opportunities and the better labor protection guarantees.[68] In no other sphere of Austrian society was the disjunction between law and reality greater than in the treatment of the apprentices.[69] Apprentices were a source of cheap, unskilled labor for artisans who did not want to spend the money to hire a journeyman. They were often used in menial capacities, as servants or delivery boys.[70] The level of training which apprentices received was usually minimal, and some masters used the unscrupulous technique of nachlernen (compulsory retraining periods) in order to get an additional year of work out of their apprentices before discharging them.[71] Numerous cases of physical abuse were reported.[72] Where masters attempted to provide vocational training, this often involved instruction in only a small part of the production process, since the master himself was caught up in a system with an extensive division of labor.[73] By learning only a minor part of the craft process, the apprentice compromised his prospects should his one skill, or "subskill," be rendered superfluous by advancing technology. A vicious cycle took hold in many trades, since the quality of vocational training for apprentices in the 1870s and 1880s was not impressive. In those schools which did exist, the drop-out and absentee rates were staggeringly high.[74] Apprentices were forced to attend their schools after work hours (usually after 8:00 P.M.) and on Sunday afternoons. The Austrian vocational schools had the lowest rate of successful annual completions of any school system in the monarchy. Many masters even refused to allow their apprentices to attend a school. In Lower Austria masters had been legally required to send their apprentices to school since 1868, but the fine for failing to do so was insignificant—some artisans simply wrote off such fines as a necessary business expense.[75] Ill-trained apprentices became ill-trained journeymen, and, in turn, journeymen of questionable competence managed to earn the title of "master" for themselves. The ill-equipped apprentices of 1875 were the desperate artisans of 1895.[76]

The fate of the artisan was the subject of considerable debate among late-nineteenth-century economists and sociologists. Many analysts, like Karl Bücher and Karl Kautsky, predicted a sharp decline of the various handwork crafts. Others, like Gustav Schmoller, were less convinced that artisans were faced with total ruin, although they admitted that their former scope of operations would be severely limited in the future.[77] A moderate assessment of the future of the craft trades was presented in 1899 by the Austrian economist Emanuel Adler. Adler distinguished between small industrial units which because of the technical and distributive superiority of the factory were completely uncompetitive, and craft trades which could sustain themselves providing a number of preconditions could be met, such as special market opportunities or customer desires for individualized products. Adler argued that the small shop *might* remain completely unaffected by large industry only in service trades like house painting or in those industries where transportation of the ware could not easily be effected.[78]

The *Handwerk* question also provided the Social Democrats with a major source of controversy in the Revisionist dispute of 1898–1904. In his book *Evolutionary Socialism*, Eduard Bernstein admitted that in Prussia the larger industrial units were increasing faster than the handwork trades, but pointed to the persistence of small economic units like bakeries which were able to sustain individualized markets. Bernstein suggested that three sets of conditions might enable the small shop to survive:

1. Some small trades were better adapted to produce articles, such as wood and leather products; other trades might survive by the assembly of parts of a product which were produced in a factory.
2. Where immediate consumer access to a product, especially fresh food products, was desirable, the small baker or butcher would survive; certain trades which could produce and service goods might also survive.
3. Large industry, by cheapening the costs of auxiliary materials and half-manufactured goods, might encourage small producers to take up the slack left by large manufacturers.[79]

Bernstein's conclusions were largely unexceptional—Adler came to similar conclusions. But where Bernstein saw hope, Adler saw only despair. The relevant question was not, however, whether these processes were operative, but whether they would permit a *large* number of the small workshops to survive. Could the artisan masters achieve financial self-sufficiency or simply a permanent seat on the edge of economic disaster?[80] Bernstein grouped the smaller- and medium-sized trades together against large industry, but he failed to mention that the economic interests of the medium-sized shops (six to twenty employees) might not be entirely congruent with those of the one- and two-man shops. In some Viennese trades a good deal of tension existed between wealthier artisans who employed fifteen or twenty journeymen and their impoverished colleagues with one or two apprentices. Both groups supported the Christian Socials, but their economic interests were not always identical.

A critique of Bernstein's theories as they applied to Austria would center on his failure to distinguish between the increase in numbers of the supposedly independent small workshops, on one hand, and the artisans' real economic function (were they really sweatshop workers going under a different name?) and the profit and tax base upon which these shops operated, on the other. Also, numerical growth would have to be qualified by data on the enormous turnover rate in the occupancy of the small businesses, the crucial factor being not numerical increases, but the length of time any individual owner managed to hang on before being replaced by some other hopeful.[81]

Alder's and Bernstein's approaches to the problem had one common omission: they did not consider the possibility that heavy governmental intervention might be brought to bear to "save" the master craftsmen, regardless of the consequences for other sectors or the economy as a whole. The question of what steps the government could take on behalf of the artisans—and not the question of whether such help would ultimately be of any avail (which would seem to have been the logical starting point)—occupied the imaginations of Austrian politicians, state bureaucrats, and the artisans themselves between 1880 and 1914. Although the hundreds of proposals and counterproposals which were aired after 1875 were often contradictory, even when presented by one political party, *two* basic policy orientations toward the fate of the artisans emerged in Austrian politics during the early 1880s. The first, which might be called the "positive" approach, was the official doctrine of the large commercial and industrial interests within the Chambers of Commerce and Industry and, implicitly, of the higher officials in the Ministries of Trade and Finance. According to this view, the master artisan could best be helped by measures providing him with remedies for his technological and educational shortcomings, encouraging the formation of associations such as cooperatives for the purchase of raw materials in bulk quantities, extending state aid for shops which wanted to mechanize their production, and promoting greater solidarity (occupational, not political) among the artisans themselves. This approach combined the Liberal tradition of cooperative self-help with a moderate dose of government encouragement. Help would be provided to the artisans, while the sanctity of the market would be recognized. The comment of the Lower Austrian Chamber of Commerce and Industry in 1874 on the artisan problem—"the artisans must realize that the improvement of their situation is only possible through self-help"—typified this attitude.[82]

The second approach, more "negative" because its intent was restrictive and regulative, involved a series of government-sponsored reforms to limit competition: a "proof of competency" *(Befähigungsnachweis)* for the title of master craftsman, the curtailment of the rights of the *Konfektion* to take orders for custom-fitted clothing, the establishment of obligatory guilds endowed with powers exercised ordinarily by the bureaucrats in the Ministry of Trade, and an increase in the tax rate on large manufacturers to limit their competitive advantage. Advocates of the second approach usually adopted many of the ideas of the "positive" school, placing emphasis on the extension of state credits to the artisans. Anti-Liberal reformers were less enthusiastic about vocational programs for artisans, since most masters had neither the time nor the willingness to participate and since support for such programs might be viewed as a confession that, technologically and structurally, the small craft shop was doomed to obsolescence unless serious reforms occurred among the masters themselves. While demanding government controls on their "enemies," the artisans and their political spokesmen rejected government controls on the crafts trades themselves. After 1885 this approach was usually described as the "antisemitic" one, but a restrictionist program was supported by many Liberal artisans as well.

The protest movement of the master craftsmen in the early 1880s took the 1859 industrial code *(Gewerbeordnung)* as its primary legislative scapegoat. In 1859 the government, bowing to pressure from large commercial and industrial entrepreneurs, abolished the old guild regulations of the monarchy and threw open trade and commerce to any individual or organization willing to venture the capital to establish a business. Much of the 1859 *Gewerbeordnung* simply sanctioned existing reality, for even before 1848 Liberal-minded bureaucrats and imaginative entrepreneurs circumvented the complicated, contradictory restrictions of Austrian trade legislation.[83] The 1859 law distinguished between "free" and "concessioned" trades, the former requiring merely a certificate of registration to open a new enterprise, the latter requiring permission from the Ministry of Trade. Most trades were declared "free," and few difficulties were placed in the way of those who wanted to secure approval for a concessioned trade.[84] Wide latitude was granted to the businessman in defining his particular craft. Artisans and manufacturers had the right to employ journeymen of other trades if they required additional presonnel. The old network of traditional guilds, a characteristic feature of the Austrian economy well into the twentieth century, was converted into a series of compulsory trade guilds *(Genossenschaften)*.[85] The rationale behind the older guilds was reversed, however. Rather than making membership in a trade dependent upon membership in a guild, the law specified that entry into a business constituted automatic membership in the local craft guild.[86] Although participation in the craft associations was compulsory, in fact neither the government nor the artisans themselves were seriously interested in developing the new corporate structures. Where such associations were founded (the government exerted no pressure to force establishment), as in Vienna, they languished from bureaucratic obfuscation, and from indolence and lack of interest on the part of the artisans. By the mid-1860s, 102 associations had been established in Vienna, but many were simply paper organizations. Those which did attempt to coordinate activities among their members usually restricted themselves to care of the poor and sickness insurance and did not, in the words of a report of a Chamber of Commerce, "encourage serious participation of their members in the vocational school system and an appropriate cooperation in all that which might further trade and industry."[87] The 1859 trade regulations (section 126) required that proposals for the common sale of craft products in a large hall or for the procurement of raw materials had to be approved unanimously by interested participants—compulsion was declared illegal.[88] This restriction was not, however, the real impediment to collective action. Most masters were too conservative and too suspicious of innovation to invest their savings in a cooperative venture. The haphazard and ineffective results of the craft guild system before 1883 owed much to this lack of a collective mentality on the part of the master artisans.[89] Those attempts toward self-help which were undertaken between 1867 and 1873 soon floundered after the Crash of 1873.[90]

The 1859 *Gewerbeordnung* helped to quicken the decomposition of small-shop craft production, but it was not the major, effective cause of the process.[91] The law was, however, notable in the context of antisemitic politics, since the patent opened industrial production and commerce to Jews.[92]

With the establishment of the Liberal regime in 1867, the leaders of Viennese artisan trades tried in March 1868 to assemble their guilds into an effective organ of interest representation, the *Wiener Gewerbegenossenschaftstag*. Consisting of the chairmen and other delegates of all recognized guilds in Vienna, the *Genossenschaftstag* met at irregular intervals. Its early history was most unimpressive.[93] The *Tag* participated in charitable and self-help ventures, collecting money in 1873 to establish the *Kaiser Franz Joseph-Stiftung* to assist needy artisans.[94] It also submitted a petition to Albert Schäffle in 1871 requesting moderate changes in the 1859 *Gewerbeordnung*, but its ethos was both nonprotectionist and nonpolitical. The *Tag* wanted tax reforms and the enfranchisement of the five-gulden men, but there was little talk of legislation to curtail competition. Between 1868 and 1871 the *Tag* summoned several assemblies of Viennese artisans for discussion of common issues, but the rallies often were broken up by groups of socialist journeymen who invaded the meetings, demanding the right to present their views.[95]

Artisan organization in Vienna in the early 1870s was, thus, insignificant when compared with the tumultuous history of the early union movement between 1868 and 1873. Indeed, the two movements soon came into bitter conflict, since many of the early unions were in the craft trades, like carpentry and shoemaking.[96] The principal hate-object of the masters until 1873 was not the 1859 *Gewerbeordnung*, but rather the 1867 Associations Law and 1870 Union Law, which legalized unions and strikes in the monarchy.[97] Whereas a few Viennese Democrats like Ferdinand Kronawetter continued to patronize the labor movement after 1870, many Democratic politicians became more circumspect in supporting journeymen who were striking against the membership of the Democratic base vote in Vienna, the artisan *Bürgertum*.[98]

On two occasions before 1880 the Lower Austrian Chamber of Commerce surveyed opinion within the Viennese craft guilds. In August 1868 a questionnaire was distributed to several dozen guilds in Vienna and Lower Austria; and in 1873–74 the Chamber of Commerce conducted a public *Enquête* with extensive testimony by artisan leaders on their crafts.[99] Respondents to the 1868 questionnaire favored hesitant restrictionism and self-help: limitations on entry into a specific trade by tests to measure the qualifications of journeymen; support for the obligatory guild system; affirmation of a collectivist ethos within the guilds. But the answers were still Liberal, if only in a negative fashion—many of the guilds apologetically stated that they believed in commercial freedom "in principle" and did not want a return to the old *Zunft* system, but desired more control than the 1859 *Ordnung* provided. Opinions expressed during the 1873–74 *Enquête* were often ambiguous or contradictory, if only because of the more ambitious scope of the proceedings.[100] Some of the larger guilds, especially those in the clothing industry, supported the proof of competency certificate—they held, in other words, restrictionist attitudes. Surprisingly, however, in contrast to those questioned in 1868, many of the participants in the 1873–74 *Enquête* were hostile to the compulsory guilds, viewing them as a burden to those artisans committed to the collective organization of the craft trades. Numerous masters suggested that the compulsory guilds be abolished and that artisans be permitted to establish voluntaristic guilds whose duty would be the running of cooperative sales, credit, and production societies.[101] The anti-Liberal motif of restrictionism was integrated with Liberal cooperative thought (Schulze-Delitzsch), which was strong in Austria in the early 1870s. To understand the anomaly of this union of protectionism and self-help, one must keep in mind the timing of the *Enquête* itself. Although it was held in late 1873, the long-term effects of the Crash of 1873 were not yet apparent. Most of the artisans who participated made no reference to May 1873. Their ideal of cooperative self-help obviously reflected pre-1873 attitudes, which had not yet been discredited. It would be misleading to suggest that the Viennese artisan trades never gave up their hope for legal protectionism before 1873.[102] Rather, older Vormärz notions of restrictionism were overlaid with a glib, uncertain enthusiasm for Liberal self-help notions fashionable in the later 1860s and early 1870s. Most artisans before 1873 were both restrictionist *and* Liberal in their view of the Viennese craft trades. Only in the light of this conjunction of protectionism and economic Liberalism was the later support for protectionist trade regulations by Liberal artisan leaders like Heinrich Matthies and Joseph Schlechter comprehensible.

A new set of social conditions in Vienna also gave the sponsors of more radical craft reform cause for confidence. The later 1870s saw the Viennese market being subjected to new external pressures. The importation of great quantities of low-quality, mass-produced personal goods from abroad and from other regions in the monarchy gave the Viennese artisans a new enemy to concern themselves with (the flooding of the Viennese market in the later 1870s with cheap Swiss and American watches and English shoes was a good example of this process).[103] Also, peddling provoked perennial complaints among local artisans, but the actual threat of the peddlers to the artisans became far more severe as the 1870s wore on and as thousands of impoverished Galician and Hungarian Jews and others journeyed to Vienna in search of quick employment. The number of legally registered peddlers in the city jumped from 927 in 1866 to over 1,600 in 1878–79.[104] Since much of the peddling was done illegally by men or women operating without a license, these data may reflect a larger and more threatening movement.

More important than the antagonisms engendered by peddlers and industrial imports (and the two were related, since it was the peddlers who distributed the cheap watches, umbrellas, gloves, and other personal goods imported from abroad) was the slight rise in retail food prices in the city in the years 1879–83. Following the Crash of 1873 food prices on most items had declined, a result of market response to mass poverty and to a temporary decline in personal consumption.[105] But beginning about 1879, as a result of disappointing harvests in Hungary and Galicia and a reduction in meat imports from Russia and Rumania, retail prices in the Viennese food market showed a slight inflationary curve in their behavior.[106] Beef, horse meat, light and dark bread, mutton, pork, and potatoes rose in price by as much as 5–10 percent between 1879 and 1881.[107] Each food item had a distinctive price pattern—meat prices stayed higher for a longer period than did bread prices, for example—but in all cases, the zenith of the price increases came in the years 1880–82, with a decline in retail prices after 1883 on most items.[108] Complaints about Vienna's first price inflation were evident in the popular and especially the antisemitic press after 1881.[109] Although the antisemites did not exploit the issue as effectively as they were to do ten years later when a more serious inflation occurred, the reduction in consumer purchasing power did affect the morale of the smaller, independent artisan masters. The first stages of political antisemitism in Vienna occurred precisely during the years of the inflation in retail food prices, intelligible in view of the fact that the typical artisan master expected to be able to eat (and drink) at a slightly higher level than that of his journeyman workers. The artisans were not starving—starvation riots among the lower Mittelstand were a thing of the past—but they were being pushed into consumer positions not very different from those of their workers.

Indications of a more hostile attitude on the part of Austrian artisans to their occupational distress came in September 1879 when a congress held in Prague by the Society for the Encouragement of the Morale of the Craft Trades passed resolutions demanding the retention of the compulsory guilds and the introduction of the test of competency.[110] The Viennese *Gewerbegenossenschaftstag* followed suit in October 1879, issuing a statement repudiating the moderate proposals it had put forth during the 1873–74 *Enquête* and replacing them with a stronger statement on the desirability of governmental protectionism.[111]

The Liberal regime which controlled the government until 1879 intended to submit a bill for the revision of the 1859 *Gewerbeordnung,* but legislative work which the Liberals considered more important always took priority. That the Liberals were dragging their feet on the issue was obvious. When Eduard Taaffe assumed control after the elections of October 1879, the Ministry of Trade submitted to parliament a series of weak amendments to the 1859 *Ordnung,* most of which dealt with worker-employer relations (section VI of the *Gewerbeordnung*) and none of which appeased the growing protectionist mentality among the artisans. These drafts, the work of Liberal officials in the Trade Ministry, were based on previous drafts formulated in the mid-1870s.[112] Taaffe himself did not favor a strong artisan legislative program. To the extent that he reversed his opinion and supported the restrictionist law of 1882, this was a concession to the Clerical Conservatives in the Iron Ring and not an act of conscience.

The draft bill of late November 1879 provoked a storm of protest from artisan groups throughout the monarchy. If any single event was the starting point of the modern, anti-Liberal artisan movement in Austria, it would be the public reaction in craft trades circles to the November draft. Ferdinand Kronawetter noted in January 1880 that many simple artisans in Vienna, who heretofore had scarcely concerned themselves with the puzzling issues of craft reform, were now heatedly discussing the sins and omissions of the government's draft in their local cafes.[113] An assembly of artisans in Brünn led the way in November 1879 with a tough memorandum demanding a more comprehensive reform than that which the Trade Ministry envisaged. In early February 1880 Franz Löblich submitted a resolution to the lower house of parliament urging the government to withdraw the November draft and introduce legislation which would curb the "unscrupulous trade freedom" afflicting the artisans.[114] After speeches of support from Georg v Schönerer and several others, Löblich's motion passed by a large majority. Many Liberals voted for it.

Löblich's intervention in the Reichsrat on behalf of an extremist program was paradigmatic of the confused political situation on the issue. Löblich was an old ward politician from Alsergrund with staunch Democratic credentials. In the early 1870s he became active in the artisan movement, and eventually was elected to the chairmanship of the *Wiener Gewerbegenossenschaftstag*. Under his direction the *Tag* adopted a more protectionist stance. For Löblich the craft trades issue was one which transcended conventional politics. He insisted that political Liberalism was entirely consistent with protectionism. His mating of Viennese Democracy and the "reactionary" artisan program illustrated the powerful pressure which economic issues were beginning to exercise within local politics.

The government stalled on the artisan issue for almost a year, but eventually gave in to public opinion and withdrew the November draft in December 1880. An important change then occurred in the makeup of the *Gewerbe* committee of the lower house, which would determine the structure of any reform proposal brought before parliament. Originally the *Gewerbe* committee had been constituted to deal with one minor issue, the peddling question. By early 1881 it was apparent that such a modest rule would not suffice to appease the artisans. Until 1881 the committee was chaired by Ferdinand Weigel, a Liberal from Galicia. Its first spokesman was Heinrich Reschauer, a well-known Democratic-Progressive journalist who wrote for Moriz Szeps's *Neues Wiener Tagblatt* in the 1870s when Szeps still claimed to support the Progressive movement. Reschauer advocated collectivist self-help and tax concessions for the artisans and was often heard in lectures and newspaper articles to condemn the "unprincipled freedom" of the 1859 *Ordnung*.[115] In fact, Reschauer had little sympathy for the protectionist ideas of Löblich and Schönerer and the later antisemites. He supported collective organization of the craft trades and was even willing to allocate state credits, but he was adamantly opposed to such restrictionist measures as the proof of competency. He was also militantly anticlerical.

In November 1881 the Clerical Conservatives insisted that the leadership of the committee have a closer relationship with the balance of forces within parliament as a whole.[116] The Iron Ring used its decisive voting majority over the Liberals on the committee and elected Franz Zallinger, a clerical delegate from Tyrol, as the new chairman. Count Egbert Belcredi, a protégé of Karl v Vogelsang and other Austrian Catholic social leaders, replaced Reschauer as *Referent*.

The takeover of the *Gewerbe* committee by Austrian rural Catholics from the Bohemian and Alpine lands had a decisive effect on the program of social legislation which passed the Reichsrat in the 1880s. Unlike the situation in Germany, where the Center party led by Ludwig Windthorst and Georg v Hertling refused to support the extremist artisan demands of neo-Romantic theorists like Franz Hitze in the early 1880s, in Austria prominent rural conservatives (Belcredi, Alois Liechtenstein, Lienbacher, Zallinger, etc.) who concerned themselves with the artisan issue favored a rigorous program of protectionism.[117] They were closer in many respects to the Prussian Conservatives than to the leadership of the German Center. Belcredi's confidant and adviser in drafting the craft amendments of 1882–83 was Rudolf Meyer, a former editor of the *Berliner Revue* and a journalist and social theorist of conservative propensities.[118] Belcredi was also influenced by Hermann Wagener, the social mentor of the activist wing of the Prussian Conservative party.[119] A few other aristocrats became interested in neocorporatist social reform during the 1870s.[120] In 1877 Alois Liechtenstein published a pamphlet ("The Idea of Representation of the Interest Groups") in which he argued that the corporate principle of diverse occupational *Stände,* possessing considerable public power, would curb the excesses of political and economic Liberalism.[121] Liechtenstein was also in contact with Rudolf Meyer, reporting to Vogelsang on Meyer's great fund of knowledge about contemporary social problems.[122]

Not all of the Bohemian and Alpine aristocracy in parliament shared Liechtenstein's anticapitalism, but their resistance to a program of Mittelstand social reform was half-hearted. Only when Liechtenstein and Belcredi began to consider labor legislation for the proletariat which would have been too "expensive" for Austrian industry did the more liberal members of the Catholic aristocracy raise questions.[123] Their firm opposition to radical anticapitalist measures, such as a stock exchange tax or usury prohibitions, prevented the more utopian schemes of their fellow aristocrats from turning into reality. As a short-term method of accentuating anti-Liberal politics, moreover, the artisan question was irresistible, especially when it was coupled with Taaffe's reform of the national franchise lowering the minimum tax requirement to 5 fl. Unlike Germany, where the major political parties had to concern themselves with a more diverse electorate in national elections, in Austria the antiquated curial voting system encouraged conservatives to subsidize special interest groups on a piecemeal basis. In view of the fact that the Iron Ring under the conservative fiscal leadership of Julian v Dunajewski passed higher tax rates on key consumer goods like petroleum and raised import tolls on goods like coffee and tea in the spring of 1882, the artisan *Novelle* in the fall of the same year was a useful way for the Clericals and the agrarians to win the urban artisans' sympathies while blocking embarrassing Liberal accusations about the antiurbanism of the government.[124]

In Vienna artisan protest occurred within the context of larger ideological issues and with the sponsorship of established political groups anxious to accommodate themselves to artisan discontent. It was apparent by mid-1880 that many wealthier artisans, and not simply the proverbial five-gulden men, were interested in legislation to curb competition with the craft trades. The negative view of the Chamber of Commerce on *Gewerbe* reform did not always reflect the sentiments of the wealthier Mittelstand. In September 1880 the City Council, in response to growing hostility against the peddlers, arranged for public hearings to be held.[125] The hearings were the first opportunity for artisan leaders in Vienna to speak out since the 1873–74 *Enquête*.[126] Virtually all of the guilds represented at the inquiry proposed a complete prohibition of peddling. One of those who spoke was Josef Buschenhagen, a poor watchmaker who felt that his trade was being destroyed by the foreign watches sold on street corners and in local taverns by Jewish peddlers.[127] Buschenhagen decided, for motives which remain obscure, to hold a protest meeting of artisans from the Landstrasse two days after the city hearings ended in order to reaffirm the consensus of his colleagues that peddling had to be stopped.[128] This rally was held 11 October 1880. The success of the assembly and the public sympathy which it engendered (several of the Democratic associations in the city supported the artisans on the issue, and a delegation from the meeting was ceremoniously received by Mayor Newald) encouraged Buschenhagen to call a second rally with longer-range goals. As yet there was little explicit antisemitism, although everyone knew the ethnic background of the peddlers.[129]

On 25 October 1880 Buschenhagen held a second mass rally for Landstrasse artisans at which a number of local Liberal and Democratic politicians showed up, including Karl Lueger. Devoted to a review of artisan complaints, the meeting went beyond the peddling issue and urged the organization of a political society to lobby for artisan demands. Lueger suggested that the meeting appoint, for organizational purposes, a steering committee of fifteen individuals, among them his friend Ignaz Mandl and himself.[130] Lueger's initial interest in the artisan question showed his desire before 1883 to keep the artisan movement within the traditional framework of Viennese Democratic politics.

The leadership of the Viennese artisan movement did not devolve, however, upon Buschenhagen's new Society for the Protection of Handwork (which was established in the spring of 1881, but accomplished nothing). Rather, it was Franz Löblich and the older *Wiener Gewerbegenossenschaftstag* who assumed control of the burgeoning *Gewerbe* movement by calling a national craft congress in Vienna for the autumn of 1881. An ad hoc committee from the *Tag,* including Löblich and a newcomer to Viennese craft politics, the mechanic Ernst Schneider, organized the congress, which met 13–15 November 1881. It was attended by approximately 1,500 men in an atmosphere which was a far cry from the placid deliberations of the Chamber of Commerce.[131]

The resolutions of the congress, written by Löblich, included the following: (1) The compulsory *Genossenschaften* of 1859 were to be reorganized and strengthened. (2) In the future, anyone wishing to practice a handwork trade would have to qualify for a *Befähigungsnachweis,* based on several years of practical experience in a trade. Also, in the establishment of new trades, the local *Gemeinde* was to have the right to determine if such businesses were needed, or whether they would lead to overcompetition. (3) Regulation of apprentices was to be left wholly to the artisans. (4) Peddling was to be completely abolished. (5) Special chambers of commerce and industry for the petite bourgeoisie were to be established apart from the existing Chambers of Commerce, in which the artisans had had little weight or authority. (6) All adult males practicing a handwork trade as a master and paying a direct tax were to have the right to vote.[132]

The overt purpose of the congress was to pressure parliament to pass as restrictionist a *Gewerbenovelle* as possible. That the congress had implications for the future of artisan antisemitism only became obvious later. In 1881 the leadership of the artisan movement was still in the hands of Liberal Democrats like Löblich and Johann Steudel, wealthy artisans who were known in Vienna for the harsh attitudes they had toward the workers in their own businesses.[133]

When the Imperial government withdrew its November draft in December 1880, it substituted for it a more comprehensive reform bill which retained the obligatory craft guilds and allocated to them more management of intracraft affairs, conceding one long-sought point to the artisans. But the draft had some serious defects, or so the artisans thought.[134] Not only did the new draft deny the masters their cherished test of competency, but it gave the journeymen membership in the guild with full voting rights. The latter idea was totally abhorrent to both Liberal and antisemitic artisan leaders.

After a first reading in parliament the proposal was sent to the Clerical-dominated *Gewerbe* committee. Here Belcredi and Zallinger made significant revisions. After prolonged negotiations with the officials of the Ministry of Trade, Belcredi presented to the full committee in February 1882 a revised version of the government draft.[135] To expedite passage of those sections of the craft reform which pertained directly to the artisans, other parts of the proposal relating to labor protection for workers were dropped from view for over two years.[136]

The autumn of 1882 saw two more significant steps in the politicization of the artisans. In October 1882 the emperor sanctioned legislation opening the franchise on the national level to all males over twenty-four who paid at least 5 fl. per year in direct taxes. In Vienna this meant the enfranchisement of the thousands of artisans who had never enjoyed the national franchise.[137] For Taaffe and the conservative majority in parliament, who pushed the legislation through over the objections of the Liberals, the five-gulden men were instruments to disrupt the bastions of Liberal power in Vienna and other urban areas. By 1890 Taaffe came to regret his haughty attitude toward artisan radicalism, but in 1882 the minister president was too fascinated with the punitive reduction of Liberal power to consider long-range repercussions. In view of the new suffrage law, the Second Craft Congress (also organized by Löblich and Schneider), which convened in Vienna 12–14 November 1882, assumed a larger significance.[138]

During the debates in parliament on Belcredi's draft in December 1882, interesting repercussions were to be noted among Democrats like Löblich and Reschauer who were veterans of the radical and moderate wings of the artisan campaign. Löblich assured the house that the proposed legislation was not an attack on large industry. He admitted that many craft trades had been surpassed irrevocably by large industry and that no amount of legislation could turn back the clock.[139] Reschauer went further. He rejected the proof of competency for entrance into the craft trades, arguing that a stronger guild system, with increased credits and better education, was the only appropriate means to solve the artisan problem.[140] He condemned the intervention of Alois Liechtenstein and the other Clerical Conservatives in the artisan problem as sheer opportunism.[141] Disillusioned by its anti-industrial and antisemitic aspects, Reschauer abandoned the artisan movement after 1883 and joined the Liberal party.[142] His inability to endorse full protectionism was typical of many Progressive Liberals and accounts for the decline in Progressive and older Democratic popularity among artisan voters. Löblich, in contrast, was a protectionist, but one with serious conscience problems. He gradually realized that protectionism, even if it was consonant with political Liberalism, could be easily exploited by non-Liberal ideologies. As long as restrictionism was only a demand of the Viennese artisans themselves, it was acceptable. But once Clericals and antisemites began to exploit the issue, Löblich found himself in a highly compromised position.

Belcredi's bill was approved by parliament in December 1882 and became known as the *Gewerbeordnung* of March 1883.[143] Because the law regulated Austrian craft policy (with some amendments) until 1907, its provisions are noteworthy. The three principal achievements of the 1883 law were the creation of a trialistic structure of free, concessioned, and handwork trades, the establishment of a proof of competency, and the revision of previous statutes concerning the obligatory craft guilds. All independent businesses were henceforth classified as either free, that is, not requiring a special legal title for their pursuit, or as concessioned or handwork trades. All factories, retail and wholesale commercial establishments, and house-industrial systems were designated free trades, effective immediately, and hence not subject to the restrictions applied to crafts. Whether a given trade was to be considered a handwork craft was not regulated by the law, but left to the discretion of the minister of trade, who would specify the crafts by administrative decree. Factory establishments producing goods which were also manufactured by artisans were excluded from any of the legal controls applicable to the latter.[144]

Entry into a craft as a master artisan now required a proof of competency. Such competency was not by examination, but simply by time served as an apprentice and journeyman ("for several years"), although the trade minister could grant exemptions from these restrictions on appeal. Two key provisions of the law, later the sources of much controversy, were sections 37 and 38, by which owners of commercial establishments (Handelsgewerbe) could produce handwork articles only if the owner or one of the managers possessed competency for that particular craft.[145] Craft masters and factory owners were permitted to employ dependent workers to produce other handwork articles, if such articles were vital to the final product. The law retained the 1859 system of compulsory associations, excluding, however, factory owners and their employees from membership. Belcredi's draft rejected the idea of voting equality for the journeymen in the craft guild. Workers were not members of the association, but were simply "attached" to the guilds with a separate assembly of their own (Gehilfenversammlung).

The proof of competency, in the words of the committee's report, would be a defense for "honest labor and the existing craft trades against competition and cut-rate production, a defense against inexperience, insufficient ability and capital, as well as rashness in entering a craft, and a defense for the consumer, the buyers of 'unsolid' wares."[146] The committee denied that the intention of the proof of competency was to limit entry into a trade, but the real reason behind the test was the hope that the growth of the trades would be stopped and existing tradesmen given a respite agianst intratrade competition. Reschauer's accusation that the 1883 Gewerbeordnung was an anti-industrial step was only partially justified in terms of the text of the law, but in terms of the hopes to which the document gave rise and did not fulfill, Reschauer was correct by 1890.

With the exception of section 38, which placed formal (but easily avoided) restrictions on wholesale and retail shops in handwork production, the 1883 law exempted most of the competitors of the artisans from its scope. It did give the artisans an advantage in that the separation it created between factory and handwork permitted the government to apply more comprehensive categories of labor protection to the factories after 1885. The *Gewerbeordnung* of 1883 must be viewed as an imperfect attempt by the artisans to secure some relief from the pressure of economic modernization. In 1882 both Schneider and Belcredi were satisfied with the new law.[147] By 1890 it was clear that the law was having little effect and that the proof of competency was of no value. From a present-day perspective, it is clear that the 1883 legislation was likely to fail, especially since it came at a time when the urban working masses were deprived of the franchise and, thus, had no opportunity to express their antagonism to laws providing expensive support for the masters. A contemporary Austrian economist and former leader of the *Volkspartei*, Stefan Koren, has noted that the only result of such legislation in the long run was to allow the artisans to avoid facing economic reality and to facilitate their resistance to economic modernization.[148]

The 1883 law put Austria far in advance of Prussia in artisan protectionism. Not until 1897 did the Reichstag adopt some restrictions (involving compulsory guilds) similar to the 1883 Austrian bill. The Center's role in the 1897 legislation, although crucial, was also appropriately moderate and pragmatic, avoiding the kind of extremist protectionism common among the Christian Socials. This difference in governmental and Catholic political accommodation to the artisan movement in each state was important. In Germany the *Kleinbürger* protectionist movements remained fragmented and localized, wallowing in their own internal acrimony and disorganization. In Austria all artisan groups could look to the 1883 bill as a precedent and proof of governmental approval. If the 1883 law proved inadequate, the answer was more and not less legislation to "fill the gaps." Together with the more stratified, petty-elitist national franchise structure in Austria and the extraordinary patronage given the artisans by the clericals, the very existence of the 1883 law gave Austrian Mittelstand movements a respectability and effectivity which their German counterparts frequently lacked. This was "their" law, one which became a psychological center point of three decades of political attention. That Austrian Social Democracy and its union movement reestablished itself at the same time as its German counterpart (1890–95) was of little help in matching the artisans' political head start. The German Social Democrats never found themselves faced with the inflated respectability which the Austrian artisans contributed to parties like the Christian Socials. For the thousands of masters who saw the 1883 law as a panacea, bitterness was not long in coming. An initially fragmented group was gradually transformed into a hostile subculture in search of further legal remedies. Precisely this mood of social disenchantment and economic anxiety after 1883 provided a climate conducive to the rapid spread of political antisemitism.

Political Antisemitism and Artisan Resistance, 1880–86

Social Orientations and Antisemitism

The principal cultural ideal of the artisan was a belief in social traditionalism with a sense of social hierarchy—he valued the honored status position which his predecessor (ideal or real) had once occupied and hoped to secure such a niche for himself. During the parliamentary *Enquête* on the craft problem in 1893, the chairman of the *Wiener Genossenschaftstag,* Johann Jedlička (who proudly insisted that he represented more than 25,000 taxpayers), claimed that before the free trade legislation of the 1850s artisans were respected and honored: "As long as we had this (protection), we were honored, we were *somebody* in the state. Today, because of free trade, we have sunk so low that we are only seen as obstacles to resolving the social question." To Jedlička the solution was "to clean up our trades, so that, like our forefathers, we can appear as respected citizens."[149]

Contemporary artisan propaganda from the 1870s and 1880s was filled with complaints that, without paternalism, it was impossible for masters to control their journeymen. Artisan spokesmen responded by trying to differentiate their *Stand* from other strata, particularly the Austrian working classes. The *Oesterreichischer Volksfreund* complained in 1882 in an article entitled "Sins of Bourgeois Society" that "the unholy doctrine of equality of all individuals has taken control of the heads of many people, leading them blindly into corruption. According to this doctrine, no one is interested any more in *Stände;* whoever is loyal to his *Stand* is laughed at as mentally limited."[150] Tension between the artisans and their workers was ultimately a far more pervasive force in artisan politics than the programmatic anticapitalism which the masters so fiercely espoused. With the increasing separation of work place and home in the nineteenth century, and with the rise of new associational forms for social and political organization, which provided journeymen with cultural alternatives to the former socializing patriarchy of the artisan workshop, the masters increasingly found the paternalistic, conformity-oriented atmosphere of the shop to be a thing of the past. Conflict rather than coerced conformity became the typical mode of social interaction between worker and master. Georg Simmel long ago remarked that social conflict in the form of an external threat may function as a unifying force, legitimizing strong inner organizational discipline.[151] The anxiety produced by the formation of a powerful Social Democratic leadership cadre at Hainfeld in early 1889 was a factor equal in importance to Lueger's personality in producing the Christian Social coalition.[152]

The actual cleavage between the masters and their journeymen is difficult to estimate accurately. Poorer masters doubtless led lives only slightly more comfortable than better paid laborers, and within the artisan group as a whole broad differentiations existed. Many craftsmen worked for wages by the piece and failed to keep accurate financial records. Of the two sets of statistics from this period which might be used to provide some tentative comparisons, the general income tax in Austria after 1896 provided a far more accurate index of actual income than the mere fact that an individual was registered to pay a trade tax. For 1898 the annual number of taxpayers in the category *Industrie und Gewerbe* in Vienna was 91,471, of whom 43,240 were workers, 36,195 were independent businessmen, and 12,036 were white collar employees. For the category *Handel und Verkehr* there were 24,575 businessmen, 19,046 employees, and 14,119 workers. The lowest possible income on which a tax could be paid was 600 fl. per year. The great majority of both small businessmen and workers in commerce and industry fell within the 600–1,200 fl. range.[153] For the combined categories of *Industrie* and *Handel* nearly as many workers (57,359) were paying an income tax as were independent businessmen (60,770). However, using only those businessmen and workers who paid an income tax reflecting the lowest income level (600–1,200 fl.), if one correlates the number of businessmen paying a tax to the total number of businessmen in Vienna and then compares the ratio with a similar correlation for the working class, the chance that a small businessman would pay an income tax is almost 2.2 times greater than the odds for a typical skilled or semiskilled worker:

Number of independent businessmen according to the 1900 census in industry, commerce, and transportation	140,655	(58,313)
Number of independents paying an income tax in 1898 (based on salary of 600–1,200 fl.)	37,682	
Number of full-time workers in Vienna in 1900	430,865	(108,336)
Number of workers paying an income tax in 1898	52,385	

(Values for females are given in parentheses.) Even these statistics are probably too pessimistic about the situation of the *male* small businessman (the only one who could vote), since the percentage of females listed in the 1900 census as independent businesswomen is greater than the percentage of females listed as workers (41.5 percent against 25.1 percent), although women in both categories earned less than their male counterparts. The likelihood that a male artisan or shopkeeper would earn at least 600 fl. was greater, therefore, than the above data would indicate.[154] There was, in other words, no "ideal" type of artisan voter, financially speaking. The city never ceased to have a rich culture of prosperous artisans, some of whom were property owners. That the' antisemitic movement did not begin with *these* people was obvious; but by 1896–97 it was well on its way toward incorporating them into its ranks, not because they had become impoverished, but because the social foundations of political anti-Liberalism were becoming more broadly Bürger in their appeal.[155]

Another set of data which necessitate some qualification in categorizing *all* artisans as impoverished are the statistics on investments in savings associations *(Sparkassen)*. After 1873 *Sparkassen* investments became the most popular form of financial investment in Austria, aside from real estate, because of the psychological advantage of fixed interest rates.[156] The distribution of savings books in relation to the size of individual investments provokes some suggestive, if only tentative hypotheses. In 1898 there were 562,633 savings books registered at the six Viennese *Sparkassen*. The number of books with deposits of over 100 fl. was 324,177, 128,744 of which had deposits of 500 fl. or more. Who were these depositors?[157] Five hundred gulden was a considerable sum of money in Vienna in 1898. It was more than many male workers earned all year long. The number of individuals or households in Vienna in 1898 paying taxes on income of more than 1,200 fl. per year was 78,810.[158] Is it possible, therefore, that some of the individuals in 1898 having savings accounts of over 100 or 500 fl. were individuals whose annual income fell between 600 and 1,200 fl., specifically, the antisemitic master artisans and white collar employees?[159] These speculations are meaningful only when viewed in conjunction with Lueger's word of caution to Vogelsang in 1889, when the latter expressed a dislike for interest bearing paper, that many artisan voters had small investments in stocks and government securities. After the stock exchange panic in November 1895, Albert Gessmann remarked that many of the "smaller" people of Vienna (specifically, his voters) had been hurt during the panic.[160]

These facts also suggest the ambiguity and tentativeness of artisan "anticapitalism" in Vienna. Many artisans used such rhetoric not only to express their frustration and bitterness, but also to show their desire to share in the resources of the Austrian capitalist network. Hence the frequent demands by artisan groups that the large commercial banks devote some of their funds to small-business loans. In attacking the "Jewish-Liberal *Börse*," many artisans felt the problem was with the adjective rather than the institution itself.

The first and most prominent issue used by the artisan movement in the early 1880s to respond to its economic problems and status concerns was political antisemitism. Artisan movements elsewhere in Central Europe also used the resources of antisemitic propaganda, but nowhere else did artisan antisemitism become the basis for a major successful upheaval in municipal politics. Antisemitism in Vienna was notable not for what it was, but for what it eventually made possible—the destruction of Liberal rule in the city. The specific function which Jew hatred played in the party depended upon the organizational location and spatial consciousness of the individual political actor, a fact which has often been lost sight of in much of the literature on antisemitism.

Most political parties, especially a party as polyglot and diverse as the Christian Social coalition, have various elite levels. Before 1895, when the party's social culture was diversified and yet more simple because it did not yet have the financial and administrative resources of the city of Vienna to bolster its efforts, there were at least *three* levels of elite behavior within the antisemitic coalition. These elites cut across the various sectors of the party electorate which will be surveyed in this book. Central control and management of the coalitions's affairs on regional and national levels depended on Karl Lueger and a group of centrally located political associates, including Albert Gessmann, Robert Pattai, Prince Alois Liechtenstein, and Franz M. Schindler. This top elite, which was recruited out of the coalition's Reichsrat delegation with the addition of Schindler, who had connections to the *Reichspost* (the party's principal newspaper after 1897) and the Church, was underpinned by two distinct, yet interconnected sets of sub-elite personalities. On the municipal level the members of the antisemitic City Council delegation, the affiliated party journalists of local and city-wide newspapers, the *Vorsteher* of districts where the antisemites had control of the *Bezirksausschuss,* the chairmen of the larger craft guilds and other professional interest groups (some of whom sat in the City Council delegation), influential clerics like Joseph Scheicher and Roman Himmelbauer who were involved in radical clerical political agitation—these elements constituted a second, subsidiary elite which had important and distinctive rights of its own, given the federalized nature of the antisemitic coalition. Members of this secondary elite often challenged Lueger's or Gessmann's tactics for party strategy. Beyond this secondary elite of leaders and journalists with some city-wide or even regional exposure, the antisemites, like the Liberals, had a large cadre of ward activities and supporters constituting a tertiary, ground-level elite: clerical leaders of Catholic voluntary organizations, prominent members of local *Hausherrenvereine*, antisemitic members of the local *Bezirksausschüsse*, antisemitic parish priests, proprietors of local *Gasthäuser* which served as meeting places for antisemitic political clubs, and simple Bürger types with a craving for election-eve cronyism and agitation (a type one sees in any large urban political machine, whether in Europe or America). These men had no national or even regional political significance. Their importance lay in a derivative, organizational sense, but without their readiness to demonstrate and to contribute money the antisemites would have been hard pressed to match the Liberals' electoral efforts.

This elite structure was highly fluid in nature. The distribution of power and roles presented here in "horizontal" terms should not disguise the fact that much of the political culture of Vienna was both local and "vertical"—political feuds were fought out and settled within the local worlds of district (club) politics and the victories then transplanted onto municipal and regional levels of government. Similarly, for the purposes of candidate selection in City Council elections, the top two elites tended to merge—Lueger did not simply dictate who would run and where. After 1895 this tripartite structure was immensely complicated by the assumption by the Christian Socials of public administrative power. For the history of antisemitism before 1895, however, the multi-elite structure is crucial. American political theorists have shown that in many cases the most ideologically hostile and combative actors in a political organization are the subleaders or sub-elites involved in the secondary policy levels of the party. In a recent study of the political structure of Hallein, a small city in western Austria, G. Bingham Powell found that the second level political activists in both major parties, especially journalists and those in the lower echelons of political mobilization, were likely to be far more polarized than the population as a whole.[161] Local and municipal sub-elites not only shape opinion by their frequent, intimate contact with the party's voters, serving as channels of vertical communication to the top elite, but also exert the greatest pressure on that elite to maximize ideological distinctions, prevent compromise negotiations, and incite the voters to greater party loyalty.[162] On the other hand, relations between the elite and the sub-elites usually, as Robert Dahl has noted, assume rational and pragmatic features. Party loyalists may act in public out of conviction, but they also insist on rewards, usually in the form of patron-age or jobs, which are the easiest for the elite to manipulate.[163] In situa-tions where plural sub-elites are in conflict, each attempting to impose its views on the movement, the party elite is forced to aggregate such ten-sions into a workable model of compromise without destroying the party itself. Such inter- and intra-elite conflicts were everyday occurrences in the Christian Social movement between 1889 and 1914.

These comments are relevant to understanding the place of anti-semitism in the Christian Social party for several reasons. The growth of the party represented an interesting model of political evolution in that much of the party's infrastructure of sub-elites and secondary organiza-tions was in place *before* any centralized leadership existed. The major leaders of the Christian Socials in the later 1890s—men like Lueger, Gessmann, Liechtenstein, Weiskirchner, Schindler, Strobach, and Funder—were only informally or marginally associated with the anti-semitic movement before 1887. After Lueger and his colleagues achieved party unity and won the elections of 1895–96, very few of the earlier antisemitic politicians or journalists, with the exception of Robert Pattai, remained within the upper elite of the party. Men like Ludwig Psenner (founder of the Christian Social Association in 1887), Ernst Schneider, Cornelius Vetter, Ernst Vergani, and Josef Gregorig found themselves isolated from the central leadership of the party, even if in their own realms they retained great prestige. With the exception of Franz Schindler, the same was true of most of the radical clergy: they were used by the party as talented, versatile agents and rewarded with church funds and seats on the school board, but the party leadership never became pre-dominantly "clerical." This meant that the racial antisemitism of men like Ernst Schneider, Ernst Vergani, and Joseph Scheicher did not infect the central party leadership.

The hypothesis that the sub-elites of a party tend to be the most aggres-sive and militantly ideological probably fits the situation in Vienna in the 1880s and 1890s. Among the dozens of poorly paid journalists and aggres-sive ward politicians, political antisemitism was clearly a forceful motive in their behavior. But there was less systematic evidence as to how these ideas worked themselves out in the voting public at large. Did every member of the *Wiener Genossenschaftstag* share the full range of Ernst Schneider's opinions about the Jews? Did a vote for the United Christians or the purchase of a copy of the *Deutsches Volksblatt* indicate that the voter shared the logical consequences of Vergani's racial antisemitism, that is, that the Jews should be legally restricted *even if* economic pros-perity returned? Or might such behavior have indicated that, although sharing some kind of antisemitism, the voter had other issues in mind as well—in the case of a teacher, a salary raise; in the case of an artisan, a government contract—the satisfactory resolution of which might obviate the appeal of antisemitism? Admittedly, such data as the enthusiastic sales of Pater Deckert's racial antisemitic *Sendboten* and the words which were used in singing the "Lueger March" in place of the original text ("Lueger will live, and the Jews will croak") could be used to show a diffuse atmosphere of seething, violence-prone hatred.[164] Similarly, the frequent fistfights and brawls associated with Viennese elections in the 1880s and 1890s might indicate an active propensity to violence on the part of the Christian Socials (although it should be noted that both Socialists and Liberals were as adept at starting election-eve brawls as were the antisemites, and reports of such violence must be carefully scrutinized in this regard). Against this kind of evidence, one encounters the autobiographical testimony of Ernst Waldinger, a Viennese Jew who grew up in Neulerchenfeld (near its border with the Josefstadt) in the late nineteenth century. Waldinger reported that in his neighborhood social and business relations between Jewish and Gentile shopkeepers and artisans were both normal and peaceful: "The small-business people, however, Jew and Christian, lived in relative peace with each other, and in the evening, in the few hours remaining to them after a long business day, sat in the *Gasthaus*."[165] Paul Molisch, a German Nationalist historian, once noted that in the 1890s most Gentiles were not supporters of exclusionist actions against the Jews: "A great part of the Aryan population resisted, consciously or unconsciously, such attempts to work in this direction."[166] Considering that the Jewish community in prewar Vienna was qualitatively different from that after 1915–16 in its social makeup and in the strength of its small group structures, such an attitude would not be surprising.

The prewar Gentile might approach the Jewish community and the Jewish family with hostility, but also with a grudging respect for their energy, industry, and general stability. Currents of external and formalized political hostility were counterposed to inevitable social interaction at home and at work. Nearly 60 percent of the Jewish population in Vienna in 1900 lived outside the ghetto areas of the Leopoldstadt and Brigittenau.[167] There is no substantial evidence to show that these Jews voluntarily segregated themselves from Gentiles by selecting apartment buildings in which only Jews lived, as may have happened in Prague.[168] The scarcity of decent housing for upwardly mobile bourgeois and petit bourgeois types was so extreme that selective segregation would have been difficult in many areas of the city. One took what was available in terms of housing, without asking detailed questions about the ethnic mix or the tenants of the building. Since Jewish ownership of real property was not common outside the Leopoldstadt and the Innere Stadt, many Jews lived in buildings owned by Gentile landlords. Jews who were financially and psychologically able to move out of the poorer ghetto areas were not necessarily seeking complete assimilation with Viennese Gentile society. What they were affirming was their functionality as members of a viable economy. Although many antisemites decried this functional intermixture of Gentile and Jewish economic life, their hate-rhetoric could not abolish it. Social interaction and economic integration (rather than assimilation per se) tied the two groups together in a thousand informal ways.

Even for poorer Jews who remained in the ghetto areas, common interests resulting from shared occupational and class concerns tied them to their Gentile rivals. Otherwise the extraordinary occurrence of a meeting of Jewish tavern owners in 1892 in which a local Jewish leader publicly thanked Rudolf Polzhofer, a nationalist antisemite, for assisting their organization in negotiating with the government on trade and licensing matters made no sense. Polzhofer's presence at the meeting and his magnanimous reply were embarrassing neither to him nor to his hosts.[169] Similarly, Jewish butchers had no difficulty in voting for the antisemitic chairman of their craft guild in his race for a Council seat, since they were confident that his antisemitism had little to do with his ability to represent the internal affairs of the guild. If anything, it might even enhance his leverage with the city.[170]

The complexity of Viennese society, its diversity, multiethnicity, and subtle intrabourgeois status patterns, offered numerous opportunities for social interaction between Gentile and Jew on an individual, personal basis. If these occurred less frequently in a formal associational structure than they did in Prague, this was owing to the informal, small-social-group mentality of Viennese society. Personal identity was not defined simply by family and associational connections; it also depended heavily upon one's circle of friends in the cafe or *Gasthaus*. Close personal proximity did not prevent the Gentile from harboring antisemitic feelings or using antisemitic concepts in a collective way to explain individual distress. But it did make such impersonal hostility more ambiguous and less harsh.

For most Viennese artisans economics and politics were related but distinguishable entities. Politics might ease economic unrest, but it should not stand in the way of mutual economic advancement. The fierce tone of antisemitic rhetoric should not disguise the fact that much social consciousness remained outside the conventional scope of politics, whether of the old or new key. The traditional Liberal dichotomy between politics and economics was taken up and continued by the Christian Socials. From the party's viewpoint this was a safety device to diminish their responsibility for solving economic problems by political means, but it also left vast areas of Viennese society free from political enmity. In other words, consideration should be paid to the multiplicity of issues which faced a voter in the late 1880s and 1890s, and the extent to which anti-semitism registered the same kind of affirmation and the same degree of significance in the individual voter as it did in the party's sub-elite of journalists, priests, and ward politicians. Wise and successful elite politicians in fin de siècle Austria were rarely "one issue" men. In view of the fascination the Viennese petite bourgeoisie had with law and order, an issue instigating violence would have been most unsuccessful.

Economic rivalries within the antisemitic camp also helped to defuse the impact of antisemitism. This was especially apparent at the 1893 *Gewerbe* hearings. One section of the 1883 craft law which outraged the artisans in the clothing industries was the regulation that distributors could take measurements for clothing or shoes and then have them prepared for custom sales *(massnehmen)*.[171] The antisemitic chairmen of the guilds of tailors and shoemakers demanded that this practice be brought to an end. Since most of the shoe and clothing dealers in the city were Jews, anti-semitism was an easy way of dramatizing their grievances. However, clothing dealers were not the only ones who profited from this practice. Most Jewish retailers and wholesalers had white collar clerks in their firms, many of them Gentiles who voted regularly for the Christian Socials after 1897. They were led in the early 1890s by Julius Axmann, later a Christian Social parliamentarian. The thousands of small general store retailers, most of whom were Gentiles, also profited from *massnehmen*. Their guild elected an antisemitic leadership in 1893 after years of conflict. Consequently, both Axmann and a representative of the small-store owners, W. Zimmermann, rejected the demands of the tailors and the shoemakers that the government prohibit *massnehmen* and voted with the delegates representing the dealers.[172] This internal conflict affected, in turn, the antisemitic issue. As long as *massnehmen* was practiced only by Jewish businessmen, antisemitism was an effective device to elicit public sympathy. But once Gentile businessmen or employees had a stake in such practices, the utility of antisemitism was reduced. Getting rid of the Jewish dealers would not suffice: the artisans would have to force the Gentile store owners and Christian Social clerks out of business as well. This did not mean that the artisans ceased to dislike the Jews, nor did it mean that small shopkeepers ceased to feel envy against their Jewish competitors. But for the party as a whole more attention had to be paid to the fundamental structures of economic development than to the occupants of particular roles within those forms.

Popular antisemitism in Austria was hardly the creature of the 1880s. Clerical, aristocratic, and Bürger antisemitism had a long history in Austrian society.[173] Before the integration of Jews into civil society in 1848–61, their acceptance was generally a measure of self-enhancing utility. The Austrian aristocracy's defense of the Jews against Maria Theresa was a classic example of informal tolerance based on mutual need. Joseph II's reforms universalized this corporate utilitarianism and expanded its operational area—Jews were to be made into functional, productive citizens because the good of society and the state dictated that this should be done. The traditional reverence felt for "good Emperor Joseph" by Austrian Jews was an expression of gratitude more for Joseph's results than for his motives.

When Franz Joseph offhandedly remarked to Philipp zu Eulenburg in 1895 that the "eastern Jews" controlled the Austrian press, he was speaking as a member of an aristocracy who might dislike the "Jewish" control of the *Neue Freie Presse* but who saw the utility and functionality of the paper for the Austrian business community.[174] Austrian Jews shared with the high Austrian aristocracy a critical value and a common circumstance—both groups were utterly loyal to the dynastic Hapsburg state, and the culture of both groups depended on the flexible, multinational character of the empire as a whole. As long as the empire remained a balanced, multinational amalgam in which the high aristocracy played some leading administrative and judicial roles, the Austrian Jews had no need to fear radical antisemitism. Although he felt ambivalence about the quality of the Jewish-owned press, Franz Joseph never doubted its dynastic loyalty.[175]

During the classic period of Jewish liberation in the 1860s the functional utility of integrating Jews in civil society was augmented by tributes to the natural rights of man. Liberalism introduced into the competitive political sphere a sense of universal right and responsibility, although, as has been previously noted, many of these "rights" were quickly qualified in strict proprietary terms in regard to their actual social consequences. The Jewish bourgeois community in Vienna found this combination of universal right and class patriarchy compatible with its own secular, quasi-assimilated attitudes. The organizational statute of the *Israelitische Kultusgemeinde* read like a miniature version of the 1850 *Gemeindeordnung*. The ability of modern bourgeois Jews to affirm corporate/class privileges against the Jewish lower classes and against the more orthodox factions within the Jewish rabbinate should not be surprising in the light of a similar mixture of corporate, class, and anticlerical elements in the Liberal movement.

It would be extremely naive, moreover, to believe that most educated or even semieducated Gentiles in Vienna in the 1860s and 1870s accepted the integration of Jews into Bürger society simply out of respect for an idealized set of eighteenth-century rights. The "silence" about the Jewish issue in the 1860s and 1870s, the allegedly idyllic period when many wealthier Jews claimed they even stopped thinking of themselves as Jews, is misleading. If there was a silence, it was deliberately cultivated on both sides. Jews were accepted, but only because their economic and social integration seemed both useful and decent.[176] Decency did not replace utility—it simply postulated a mutual advantage. The Austrian Liberal party, in its majority Gentile sense, showed itself just as capable of a utilitarian "silence" on the Jewish question in the 1890s, when many Viennese Jews desperately wanted it to speak out in defense of their rights and liberties.[177]

There was a definite continuity, therefore, between early and modern antisemitism in Austria: on one hand, the real standard for popular tolerance of the Jews was utility and not idealized human rights; on the other, public reaction against the Jews was carefully modulated and controlled by the deep respect for public order inherent in the Viennese Bürger culture (foreign visitors might call this laziness), and by a careful respect for the role of law in society, but not for Liberal economic philosophy.

Popular antisemitism during the early 1880s was a mixture of economic protest and racial hatred, rationalist opportunism and irrationalist anxiety. An early example of the kind of pamphlets distributed in Vienna giving expression to economic antisemitism was one in 1880 by "Austriacus," *Oesterreich ein Juwel in jüdischer Fassung*. "Austriacus" feared both Jewry and Social Democracy at a time when accusations about "Jewish" Socialists were irrelevant (itself significant in demonstrating that the most dangerous enemy for the artisans was not the Jewish Socialists, but *any* kind of Socialists.) He defended the landed nobility with its "solid wealth" against the "money aristocracy" of finance capital. The Jews refused to engage in manual labor, since "their exclusive purpose in life [was] to get wealth, without work and without sweat."[178]

The Austriacus pamphlet had most of the early stereotypes used in economic antisemitism. The key to his argument was the alleged laziness of the Jews and their propensity toward fraud. That the other stereotype of the crafty, overly eager Jew was difficult to relate to this one did not bother Austriacus. He was not concerned with logic. The author might have summarized his arguments by stating that the Jews no longer offered the public the kind of functional utility necessary to justify their tolerance. His arguments were not racial in a formal sense, but were radical economic-utilitarian in nature.

In his 1892 pamphlet, "The Situation of the Jews in Vienna," Ernst Vergani used the same stereotypes, but went beyond Austriacus in introducing a motif of racial hatred.[179] Vergani distinguished between economic and religious antisemitism on one hand, and racial antisemitism on the other. Even if the Jews might assimilate on economic or religious terms, their racial characteristics made their exclusion both inevitable and desirable. Vergani's racialism was the fundament on which his newspaper, the *Deutsches Volksblatt,* was built, but the business operations of his paper revealed much about the utilitarianism of racial antisemitism.

His newspaper survived and prospered as a result of the advertising fees paid to it by large commercial, industrial, and banking concerns anxious to buy the paper's goodwill and (often) its silence.[180] That many of these firms were owned or managed by Jews (wealthy "capitalistic" Jews) did not bother Vergani in the least. By 1903 he had even come to see the virtues of the *Börse,* defending it against plans to implement a more severe *Börsesteuer* as the goose that laid the golden eggs.[181] His newspaper was unusual in that after 1907 its subscription revenues declined but its gross profits increased—Vergani was not about to kill the growing goose.[182]

Racialism as the most extreme form of antisemitism was rarely to be found in Vienna in an unalloyed state. Usually it was intermixed with more traditional economic, religious, and cultural arguments. Virtually all of the major leaders of the Christian Social party by 1891 had explicitly repudiated racialism and the exclusionist legalism which accompanied it.[183] Nevertheless, a subculture of crackpot journalists and district political leaders, largely on the fringes of the power structure of the party, adhered to racial antisemitism both before and after 1896. Although the rhetoric of the racialists was ferocious, this form of antisemitism was an ineffective means to intimidate the Jewish community and most antisemitic leaders knew it. Racialism made no sense in a city with a Jewish community of such extraordinary proportions, especially when so many members of the community were involved in businesses which were linked with middle-class Gentile concerns and where so much of the private philanthropy devoted to Gentiles was funded by Jewish wealth. The hypocritical letters between antisemite and Jew which the Liberal press loved to publish in exposé format (such as that sent by the "arch-antisemite of the Landstrasse" Cornelius Vetter to the Jewish communal leader Salo Cohn, obsequiously telling Cohn that he had been a better friend to him than most of the antisemites in Vienna) were neither surprising nor avoidable.[184] Jewish economic and social *integration* (not as-similation) had proceeded too far by the later 1880s for categorical racialism to make any sense. As a public policy, pure racialism was absurd in the context of late-nineteenth-century Viennese Bürger culture. As a weapon to terrify the Jewish community, it had little effect. An examination of the debates of the *Oesterreichische Union*, the Jewish political club organized in 1886, would show that between 1890 and 1896 most bourgeois Jews who were interested in politics feared antisemitism's economic and clerical implications far more than they did its racial rhetoric.[185] Liechtenstein's *Kauft nur bei Christen* campaign caused far more anxiety than did Vergani's pronunciamentos. Most Jews were con-fident that the government would protect their civil liberties; it was the Gentile reaction in the economic marketplace that worried them.

Viennese Jews and Liberal Politics

The Jewish population in Vienna grew rapidly between 1857 and 1880 as a result of the availability of cheap, rapid transportation and because of the abolition of residence prohibitions in Austrian cities. The Jewish commu-nity in Vienna in 1854 numbered less than 16,000.[186] By 1869 there were 40,230 Jews (6.6 percent of the total city population); by 1880 this figure had increased eighty percent to 74,523 (10 percent of the total popula-tion).[187] Most of this growth resulted from immigration from Galicia, Hungary, Bohemia, Moravia, and other more rural areas of the monar-chy.[188] The community which resulted was both younger and had rela-tively more males than did Viennese Gentile society.[189] The discrepancy in the ratio of males to females (for the city as a whole 1,000:1,061; for the Jews 1,000:951) was significant in terms of the challenges presented by the Jews in the employment market.

The magnetism of the learning and employment opportunities offered by Vienna drew rich and poor, learned and illiterate to the city to stay and find a niche in the new urban society. The Jewish community soon be-came diversified and complex, with newer migrants in the 1870s and 1880s bringing different cultural and social views to challenge the older, established elites. The bitter conflicts between Orthodox and Reformed Jews in the *Kultusgemeinde* in the early 1870s were merely the first stage in a long process of intracultural competition.[190] The response of the established elites within the *Gemeinde* was to insist that voting rights within the community remain a privilege of those paying the annual com-munity tax.[191] By 1893, the majority of Jewish households in Vienna were so poor that they were exempt from the minimum tax of 10 fl. (of the 26,000 families only 11,000 were taxed at all, and 90 percent of these were charged the minimum contribution of 10 fl.).[192] The Viennese Jewish community may have been rather different from those in German cities like Berlin or Frankfurt with its poverty and its exploding level of eastern Jewish immigration.[193] In Vienna the majority of the community consisted of poorer immigrants from Galicia, Bukovina, and Hungary, who constituted the second society of Viennese Jewry.

Economic antisemitism predicated the Jew as an agent of commerce rather than "productive" industry. Indeed, the majority of Viennese Jews did earn their livelihood in trade or in one of the free professions. In the monarchy as a whole, the census of 31 December 1900 revealed that over 35 percent of all employed Jews were engaged in commerce or transportation.[194] Six times as many Jews per thousand were employed in credit institutions as were Gentiles (13:2).[195] Jewish concentration in commerce and finance resulted from pre-1848 restrictions which forbade Jews the right to practice a handwork industry.[196] The post-1848 processes of industrial concentration and centralized commercial distribution were not the immediate work of the Jews. Many of the first clothing and shoe Konfektionäre were Gentile tailors who accumulated sufficient capital to expand their plants.[197] The first retail and wholesale furniture dealers were also Gentiles.[198] After 1867, however, Jews gained a majority position in both of these industries. Many of the merchants in the personal goods industries for which Vienna was famous, such as buttons and combs, which employed hundreds of master artisans on a commission basis, were Jewish. The interposition of dealers between the producer and the consumer has led everywhere in modern times to tensions with the small artisan. In Vienna antisemitism was an easy means to exploit such economic dependence for political purposes. In a bad year, the dealer's market demand might drop and with it, his prices for wholesale goods, leading to lower wages for the artisans whom he employed. Who was responsible? It was far easier to grumble against "the Jew" than to attempt to comprehend the impersonal forces at work.[199] Artisan antisemitism in Vienna thus reflected the extensive interdependence between Gentile artisans and their Jewish employers.

The most serious complaint lodged against Jewish businessmen was the use of fraudulent business practices. Statistics for the monarchy on crime rates for felonies and misdemeanors indicate that Jews generally suffered a higher rate of convictions for misdemeanors in financial affairs, while Gentiles generally had higher rates for crimes of violence.[200] Considering their relative share in the commercial sector, such statistics were neither surprising nor shocking. Such data fail to reveal, however, the social realities of Vienna in the 1880s. The sudden entrance of the city into the industrial age after 1848 (if only in terms of light and medium industry), with its burgeoning population levels, gave rise to new business procedures, some honest, many dishonest. Jewish merchants, anxious to make a decent living for their families, often disregarded customary Viennese business practices such as long midday lunches, early closings, and an easy, unrushed labor schedule. This competitive quickening of the business culture shocked many Gentile artisans and shopkeepers, forcing them to keep pace or lose out. The new business attitudes were hardly fraudulent in legal terms, but they were jarring in cultural terms.[201]

Examples of real business fraud, moreover, could easily be found among the antisemites as well as among Jewish merchants and credit managers.[202] Of value on this point were the comments of Josef Leb, a local Catholic notable in late-nineteenth-century Vienna, about his father's experiences with the business ethics of the 1870s and 1880s. Leb reported that his father was a respected Viennese merchant but that in the 1880s "other business principles," introduced (Leb charged) by Jewish retailers, had disrupted his father's business. The elder Leb refused to "write false accounts" and therefore lost many of his former customers. However, the younger Leb then made a very interesting comment. He was sufficiently fair to note that Jewish businessmen were not the only ones using such techniques: "Even the clerical buyers from the great monasteries demanded false statements."[203] Obviously, the problem of business fraud as Leb saw it was not confined to one particular ethnic or confessional group. Since Jews played a decisive role in the service sector, they were particularly exposed to such accusations, even if Catholic abbots and monks used identical business practices.

The formidable Jewish presence in literature and the arts has been discussed sufficiently elsewhere to eliminate the need for a discussion here.[204] Before 1870 many Jews who attended a university chose medicine, because the skills obtained were easily transferable and because there were no quota restrictions on doctors as there were for lawyers under the antiquated *Advokatenordnungen* of the Vormärz. After 1872, when the standards for medical study at Austrian universities were made more rigorous, the absolute number of Jewish medical students declined until 1880, and again from 1892 to 1910. The relative percentage of Jews studying medicine before the Liberal era (approximately 23 percent for the years 1851–69) was not significantly lower than that after Jewish liberation in 1867. Jews who might have been inclined to study medicine after 1885 chose to attend technical colleges instead.[205] The majority of Jewish medical students in Austria before 1885 were extremely poor. They often represented first-generational attempts at significant social mobility, eliciting contempt from their Gentile counterparts and professors for their eagerness to find success.[206]

After 1868 legal careers were freed from the restrictions of the Vormärz. The volume of civil, criminal, and commercial litigation grew as the city's economy expanded and its culture became less stable. The need for lawyers was met by a sudden rush by university students to Austrian law faculties, many of them Jews.[207] The University of Vienna outdistanced national percentages. Whereas in Austrian law faculties as a whole in 1880 only 15.4 percent of the students were Jews, in Vienna 22.3 percent were Jews.[208] A far greater percentage of Jewish law students entered private practice than did their Gentile counterparts, because of continued informal restrictions on Jews entering public service. Most Jewish lawyers in Vienna before 1890 came from lower or middle bourgeois families, unlike their Gentile counterparts, who often came from well-to-do situations (another reason why Jews did not enter the civil service—their families could not have afforded to subsidize their training as unpaid or poorly paid *Praktikanten* while waiting for a tenured position). In law, therefore, the equation of resentment from the commercial world was reversed: Jews in this case were hated not by poor Gentiles because of their wealth and success, but by wealthier Gentiles because of their attempts at an occupational mobility.[209] The influx of young Jewish students into medical and legal careers was paralleled by a similar process in the philosophical faculties. In 1860 the Jewish students constituted merely 6 percent of the Vienna philosophy faculty; by 1880 their share had jumped to nearly 16 percent, not as impressive as the Jewish presence in law and medicine, but more important because of the problem of employment for university-trained Jews in the humanities. Although the number of Jews teaching in gymnasial-level schools increased slowly, this was not a realistic employment option. Not surprisingly, many turned to journalism as a career.

The influx of educated, anticlerical Jews into Austrian journalism coincided with the establishment of the Liberal political press in the 1860s and 1870s. This conjunction gave Austrian Jews the opportunity to make a decisive intellectual contribution to the letters and the arts, but it also tempted such writers to exhibit the unseemly sides of Austrian Liberalism, most notably in its behavior toward those whom Liberal politicians felt to be their social inferiors. One of the first issues of the *Oesterreichischer Volksfreund* in 1881 criticized the arrogance of the *Neue Freie Presse* in making derogatory comments about the handwork artisans and using the word "we" as a sign of intellectual superiority.[210] Although there was anti-intellectualism and cultural philistinism among the antisemitic voters and their local leaders, one need only read the memoirs of Sigmund Mayer, a wealthy Jewish merchant in Vienna, to understand something of the cause of the artisans' resentment.[211] His condescending attitude toward the artisans did not disguise the fact that he considered them to be stupid oafs on whom political rights had been wasted. Intellectual excellence was often confused with and distorted by the arrogance of an upwardly mobile, quasi-assimilated bourgeoisie. That Jewish journalists created this posture of social contempt was not true; that some Jews shared such attitudes with Gentiles who styled themselves as political Liberals was.

Study at the university required completion of an academic *Mittelschule*. Jewish enrollments in Lower Austrian gymnasien and realgymnasien rose rapidly between 1851 and 1880 (6.1 percent in 1851, 10.4 percent in 1865, 25.6 percent in 1880). The social history of Austrian intermediate education remains to be written, but it is likely that some Jewish students were sent to the city to study while their families remained elsewhere in the monarchy and that many more were sons of first-generation immigrants to the city struggling to make a go of it—hardly a grande bourgeoisie. Even so, the relative rise in enrollments indicated an expansion in the size of the bourgeois elite of the Jewish community in Vienna by 1880, although for both Gentiles and Jews the absolute numbers of students remained pitifully small in comparison with the general population. What is most interesting, however, is that the relative Jewish enrollment in Viennese *Mittelschulen* after 1880 never rose above 28 percent for the rest of the Imperial period, declining from 28.8 percent in 1885 to 27.6 percent in 1912. Jewish participation in classical gymnasien remained relatively stable (in 1885, 30.9 percent; in 1900, 32 percent; in 1910, 27.6 percent), while Gentile enrollments in the rapidly expanding *Realschulen* (which prepared students for graduate training in engineering and technology) mushroomed. *Realschule* enrollments on the whole increased by 82 percent between 1895 and 1912, whereas those of the gymnasien grew by only 34 percent. These data suggest that the Jewish share in higher bourgeois secondary educational resources never surpassed the level of 1875–85 and in fact even began to decline slightly. Assuming that a *Mittelschule* education for a son was an important criterion of bourgeois familial status, the relative size of the Jewish elite which participated in these educational institutions did not increase in Vienna after 1880.[212] Antisemitic propaganda about the Jews "taking over" the elite positions of the city was absurd. After 1880 their share was stable at best.

Of all occupational groups, Jewish doctors were subjected to the most vulgar accusations, owing to the possibility of sexual allusions in discussing their relations with patients (most Christian Social leaders never employed this kind of vulgarity, but a few, notably Ernst Schneider, did so with regularity).[213] Such language may have appealed to latent irrationalism involving aggression or sexual anxiety among the voters, but among the party leaders themselves it was often nothing more than cheap opportunism. Many antisemitic notables continued to seek medical assistance from Jewish physicians and surgeons in Vienna during the 1890s and 1900s.[214] Public attitudes toward Jewish doctors were probably more conservative than Schneider's speeches might lead the historian to expect. Where hostility did exist, it may have been owing to such mundane irritants as the high treatment fees charged by both Gentile and Jewish physicians (against which both the Social Democrats and the Christian Socials constantly complained).

Of greater social importance for political antisemitism was the entrance of Jews into white collar jobs in public and private bureaucracies. The Austrian civil service was closed to Jews before 1867, and even after 1867 relatively few Jews gained access to jobs in state, regional, or local government.[215] Those who did were usually converts to Christianity.[216] Of the 817 higher level officials in the Austrian judicial bureaucracy in 1894, only 16 were Jews.[217] Similarly, the Liberal party in Vienna had a poor record of employing Jews—with a few exceptions they were excluded from the higher ranks of the *Magistrat*.[218] The Liberal ministries of the 1860s and 1870s conscientiously excluded Jews from state service to avoid antagonizing their voters in the larger cities of the monarchy. Not until Taaffe's ministry did a few Jews find places in public life.[219]

It was therefore to private industry, banking, and commerce that Jews looked in search of jobs carrying the status of "employee." The business bureaucracies of Vienna absorbed thousands of Jews who otherwise might have entered retail commerce.[220] Since Jews did not occupy all such jobs, antisemitism found enormous support among thousands of Gentile employees, who competed with their Jewish colleagues for appointments, promotions, salary raises, and positions in institutions like the *Handelsakademie*.[221] Jewish policy control of the business community was more a myth than a reality. Most of the boards of directors of large banks and corporations contained a majority of Gentiles. Some refused to seat Jews at all.[222] That the higher administrative management of banks and industrial concerns was strongly Jewish was true, but Gentile elites within the city did not find it difficult to integrate themselves in subtle and not so subtle ways with their Jewish peers. Hence the invention by the antisemites of phrases like "Jew-Liberal" or "Friend of the Jews," popular political language revealing the integration of Gentile and Jew.

Especially noteworthy, however, was the fact that Viennese Jews did not make an effort to gain a dominant position in city property ownership. Official statistics of the *Magistrat,* assembled on the basis of the 1880 census, showed that approximately 8 percent of the house owners in the city were Jews.[223] Given that the Jewish community in Vienna constituted approximately 10 percent of the permanent population, its share in house ownership was not greatly disproportionate. In the decades after 1880 the share of Jewish property ownership did not increase substantially. More important, the issue of Jewish *Hausherren* never became an effective or widely used antisemitic device. The property owners were the one voting group affiliated with the Christian Socials who were not immediately interested in antisemitism. By and large, the majority of the Viennese *Hausherren* before and after 1890 were Gentiles. The unwillingness of Jews to invest heavily in real estate reflected the burdensome rates of house and rental taxation in Austria, as opposed to Germany. In Berlin, a tenement house would be taxed at the rate of 13 percent of its annual rentals (including state and local taxation), whereas in Vienna the same house would be taxed at a rate of over 40 percent (including the *Zins-kreuzer*). Although property owners tried to adjust their rent levels to cover this taxation (giving Vienna the reputation of being one of the most expensive cities in Europe for housing costs), such discriminatory taxation did not make most urban real estate an attractive investment (per capita rent taxes were almost three times higher in Vienna than in Berlin). Jews who sought security might buy a house, but those who wanted to invest their money in opportunities with higher appreciation looked elsewhere. Given the cultural propensity of Viennese bourgeois Gentiles to seek security and "roots," their urge to buy real estate was quite intelligible. Mortgage money was usually available at rates and under terms which made it possible for even a prosperous artisan to invest in a house. But for Jews, especially those not entirely confident of the success of their assimilation, property holding as a cultural statement of "security" was not justifiable in terms of the lost profits incurred.

This fact had several implications for the roles the Jews and Gentiles played in municipal politics. Because the First Curia and (to a lesser extent) the Second Curia were dominated by the *Hausherren,* and because wealthy Viennese Jews generally invested their money elsewhere (and not in districts like Landstrasse, Josefstadt, or Neubau), the Jewish vote was never a hegemonic factor in the higher reaches of local Liberalism. Sigmund Mayer, a member of the City Council from 1880 to 1890, estimated that the number of Jews serving in that body never rose above 6 percent at any given point, and was frequently below it.[224] Jews rarely served on the local district councils or on the school board. Although the Liberal base vote for the Innere Stadt and for the Leopoldstadt depended partly on Jewish votes, the political elite which ran the city generally came from outside these two districts.[225] All of the Viennese mayors from Felder to Lueger had their home constituencies in old Bürger districts like the Landstrasse or the Josefstadt. The same was true for most of the assistant mayors *(Bürgermeister-Stellvertreter)*. Jewish money played a major role in financing Liberal campaigns in a few of the city's districts, but urban politics in Vienna in its ethnic makeup stressed social continuity rather than radical change between 1848 and 1896.

This lack of control over local political institutions was a prime reason for the feelings of defenselessness often verbalized by Viennese Jews after 1890. As Peter Pulzer has shown, Jews in Wilhelminian Germany occupied major positions of power in municipal institutions. The last mayor of Imperial Berlin, Adolf Wermuth, estimated that 25 percent of the Berlin City Council was Jewish.[226] In Vienna, with its poorer Jewish community and with a different curial franchise structure, Jewish voters were less numerous and tended to be thrust into the Third Curia, even though they might pay more taxes than the Gentile state officials and teachers who were given a privileged voting position in the Second Curia. Until 1891 wealthier Jewish *Privatbeamten,* for example, voted in the Third Curia, where their votes were overwhelmed by the masses of Gentile artisans.[227] The political deficit of the local Jews within the all important Second Curia during the Liberal era made it all the easier for the Christian Socials to take power during the 1890s.

Economic antisemitism faced a profound challenge after 1848, when Jews in increasing numbers entered industries closed to them in the Vormärz. This movement perplexed the antisemitic sloganeers in their attempts to retain consistency in their propaganda. The statistical significance of this shift was clearly revealed in that in 1900, out of a total of 1,224,711 Jews employed (male and female, full-time jobs), 351,212 persons were active in industry, while 535,247 were employed in the traditionally "Jewish" commerce.[228] Employment in commerce still predominated but was now challenged by a Jewish presence in the industrial sector as well.

In 1840 Josef Wertheimer, one of the leaders of mid-nineteenth-century Viennese Jewry, established the *Verein zur Beförderung der Handwerke unter den inländischen Israeliten.* Its purpose was to sponsor vocational training for poor Jewish youths in order to undermine the legend of the Jew as *Handelsmann* who disliked physical labor.[229] By 1875 the *Verein* supported 258 apprentices in craft industries which were Gentile preserves, such as machine production, carpentry, lock making, and turning.[230] The *Verein* was the most successful apprentice organization of its time, placing its charges with Gentile artisans without difficulty, largely because it assumed the financial burden of supporting its apprentices during their instruction period (usually three to four years).[231] In the early 1880s Baron Hirsch provided the *Verein* with an annual subsidy of 14,000 fl. a year, enabling the association to expand its activities. By 1890 the association had 479 corporate and individual contributors and was sponsoring annually over 1,300 Jewish apprentices in Viennese craft trades.[232] Among the trades frequently selected were carpentry and shoemaking, the crafts in which competition was the fiercest and antisemitism the strongest.[233] Since the training period lasted three to four years, a substantial number of well-trained Jewish craftsmen were entering the labor market in Vienna each year, perhaps 100–200 persons.[234] The *Verein* also made available grants and loans which would help the young Jews trained under its auspices to establish independent shops. Gentile artisans found themselves training Jewish competitors in their own trades, if not in their own districts.

This was a perfect issue for the antisemitic newspapers to exploit. That the funding for the *Verein* came from large industrial and commercial interests in the city made the issue doubly heated—not only antisemitism but also anticapitalism was involved.[235] The *Oesterreichischer Volksfreund* attacked the *Verein* as "very significant" for the future of the Christian trades. The newspaper charged that "it has been known for a long time how harmful an effect on handwork the semites have had, destroying and spoiling everything." Not only had untrained Jews previously attempted to "sneak" into the industrial trades, but now, Jews equipped with superior training, qualified for a proof of competency, were entering the market. Nowhere was the hypocrisy of arguments for the test of competency more clearly evident. A Jew with training was still as unacceptable as an unskilled Jew. More important, the antisemites now realized that the 1883 trade law would not prevent Jewish entrance into the craft trades. The *Volksfreund* urged Gentile masters to hide their trade secrets from Jewish apprentices and to make certain that the guilds were controlled by Gentiles[236] (many guilds had, by 1890, Jewish minorities, owing to the success of programs like that of the *Verein* and to Jewish immigration to Vienna from elsewhere in the monarchy in the 1870s and 1880s).[237]

Whether the readers of the newspapers felt as strongly as the journalists may be doubtful, since most Gentiles continued to accept Jewish apprentices. Popular anxiety was not motivated by racial feelings, as in the case of the journalists, but by fears of competition. Jews entering craft trades offered competition. Since they had been well cared for, the average Jewish apprentice was more capable than most apprentices at the conclusion of his training—the *Verein* even paid to send its apprentices to additional schools.[238]

However, the *Verein* did far more than simply train apprentices; it also broke down the old stereotype of the Jew as a greedy moneylender or old-clothes dealer. Jewish craftsmen now began to function in occupational modes indistinguishable from those of the Gentile population.

Jewish writers like Joseph Bloch and businessmen like Sigmund Mayer applauded this diversification, seeing it as a source of pride for the Jewish community.[239] But for the antisemitic journalists this expansion caused grave conceptual anxieties. The old categories of hatred by which one had judged a Jew—usury, laziness, moneylending—were becoming inoperative. Even the social distance which encouraged hatred and suspicion of the Jewish "foreigner" in the large, impersonal city now seemed shaken, for how could the artisan master hate the Jewish youngster whom he had personally trained for four years, imputing to him subhuman behavioral traits? If the Jewish apprentice was lazy and incompetent, was this not just as likely to reflect badly on the Gentile master who trained him as on inherent ethnic traits? The *Volksfreund* tried to revise its conceptual categories by arguing that the Jews would now destroy the craft trades just as they had poisoned commerce, but the paper was unable to invent so easily new shibboleths in place of the Jew as *Handelsmann*. The author of the article had to fall back upon the *Handelsmann* stereotype by insisting that the Jews were always speculators: "He [the Jew] always tries to become rich, not by means of honest labor, but by effortless speculation using all means and especially in commerce."[240] The myth remained, but its social referent was changing.

Racialism as a serious political policy was inappropriate for the diffuse, personalist culture of Bürger Vienna. This was not because of the success of Jewish assimilation, which was never even marginally successful in an ideal sense, but because of the functional integration of the large Jewish community into the Viennese commercial, educational, and industrial worlds. In spite of the antisemitic rhetoric, Jews did serve necessary and valuable economic roles. Antisemitic carpenters might hate their local Jewish furniture dealer, but, in order to survive, they had to work with him and not merely for him. Hatred and pragmatic tolerance were at a crucial balancing point; politics in Lueger's style served to defuse the more dangerous racialism of Schönerer by converting racial antisemitism into the more traditional, utilitarian mode. Lueger promised his constituents that under an antisemitic municipal regime, the Gentile artisans' role in society would be enhanced, obviating the need for extreme forms of antisemitism. This was a far cry from idealized rights—beer hall politics hardly recognized such ideals—but it was not racialism either.

Artisan Political Antisemitism, 1880–86

Viennese antisemitism in the early 1880s had contemporary European models and domestic antecedents. In 1878 Adolf Stöcker organized his Christian Social movement in Berlin and soon took advantage of the antisemitic issue. In March 1881 Bernhard Förster and Max Liebermann v

Sonnenburg founded the *Deutschen Volksverein,* popularizing a mixture of racial antisemitism and handwork protectionism.[241] Pogroms in Russia, initiated under the auspices of the new czar, Alexander III, began in the spring of 1881, encouraging thousands of Jewish refugees to stream across the borders of Austria-Hungary in the late summer and fall of 1881 (some of them made their way to Vienna, where they worked, some legally, most illegally, as peddlers in 1882–83).[242] In 1880 the first Hungarian antisemitic association was set up in Pressburg, fifty miles from Vienna. September 1882 saw riots in Pressburg over the Tísza-Eszlár ritual murder trial.

Along with such developments came a flood of pseudoscholarly tracts wholly or partially directed against the Jews, typified in the work of Wilhelm Marr, Eugen Dühring, Paul de LaGarde, and Augustus Rohling.[243] A priest and since 1879 a professor of Hebrew at the Catholic Theological Faculty at Prague, Rohling had published *Der Talmudjude* in 1871. This book was a clever rewriting of lies and superstitions originally published in 1711 by Anton Eisenmenger in his *Entdecktes Judenthum.* After Rohling's appointment at an Austrian university his writings became more widely known. By 1882 the alleged admonitions to Jews in the Talmud that they should mistreat and cheat Gentiles were widely discussed in Vienna, largely as a result of Rohling's book.[244] The feud between Rohling and Joseph Bloch, the hot-tempered Viennese journalist, led to a libel trial between 1883 and 1885 which ultimately revealed Rohling to be the charlatan that he was and forced his resignation from the University of Prague in 1885.

In Vienna the first stirrings of modern antisemitism in the 1870s came in the nationalist circles in the universities. In 1875 the famous Viennese surgeon, Theodor Billroth, called attention to the influx of poor and (in his mind) ill-prepared Jewish students from Hungary and Galicia into the University of Vienna medical school. Insisting that Jews were a distinct ethnic and national group, he argued that their attempts to achieve assimilation with the Germans were destined to fail. The precise nature of Billroth's antisemitism was never clarified,[245] but his less than flattering comments on the educational background and financial status of eastern Jewish students led the *Leseverein der deutschen Studenten,* a German National student group, to congratulate the surgeon for his remarks.

Student antisemitism at universities like Vienna and Graz was largely racialist. Various *Burschenschaften* in Vienna began to exclude Jews from membership in 1878.[246] By 1889 all of the leading Viennese student societies had forced out their Jewish members, even those who were baptized.[247] One result of university antisemitism was that younger faculty members in some secondary schools were influenced by antisemitism in their teaching and administrative policies.[248] Complaints were heard in Jewish circles in the 1890s about antisemitic remarks against Jewish students made by gymnasial teachers,[249] a result of the recruitment of new instructors from the university system. In some gymnasien, antisemitic articles in student newspapers were even published.[250] When the government decided to harass the leadership of the German National movement in Vienna in 1887–88, it had only to restrict the right of gymnasial professors to draw salaries while sitting in the Reichsrat—many of the early supporters or sympathizers of Schönerer in Vienna, such as Josef Fiegl and Otto Steinwender, taught in municipal realgymnasien.[251]

Schönerer maintained close ties with nationalist student groups in Vienna in the late 1870s. Their antisemitism, together with the German and Russian paradigms, was influential in persuading him to incorporate Jew hatred into his organization in 1882.[252]

The first stirrings of popular antisemitism in Vienna were narrowly journalistic. In February 1881, Karl v Zerboni, a bankrupt army officer whose antisemitism dated from the late 1860s, founded a small, biweekly newspaper, the *Oesterreichischer Volksfreund.*[253] The material for his paper came almost exclusively from foreign sources. The first year of the paper saw long selections from the speeches of the Hungarian antisemite Victor v Istoczy and several German antisemitic leaders, all of whom Zerboni knew personally. Aside from selections from Rohling's *Talmudjude,* however, Zerboni made little progress toward an Austrian variant of antisemitism. The paper found a moderately large audience of free professionals and artisans as subscribers, but it was never able to survive without extensive secret subsidies.[254]

Zerboni used the paper to campaign for an antisemitic political party. In February 1882 he saw his dreams fulfilled. On 11 February 1882 a small group of artisans (most of them affluent) and smaller factory owners, together with a few lawyers and schoolteachers, established the *Oesterreichischen Reformverein,* the first association in Vienna devoted exclusively to an antisemitic program.[255] Most of the founders of the *Reformverein* were political unknowns who retained that status in the future, but in Robert Pattai the club found a leader with promise.

Pattai was a young German National lawyer from Graz who studied at the University of Graz in the 1870s. At first Pattai involved himself in Liberal politics in the Neubau,[256] but he had also met Schönerer and took part in the preliminary deliberations leading up to the Linz program. In 1882 he decided to strike out on his own by organizing what he hoped would be a movement appropriate for his inflated ambitions. Antisemitism was for Pattai, as it became for other "new men" in the 1880s, an easy way to break into politics without having to spend long deferential years gaining the confidence of the Liberal party in Vienna. The *Reformverein* offered to Pattai (who became its president in May 1882) a perfect forum for his long-winded speeches on the need to rejuvenate Austrian society by radical economic reforms.

Pattai's self-interest not only won him a lucrative legal practice, but eventually gave him a reputation for backsliding on issues that purist racialists like Schönerer thought sacred. He became known as a "salon-antisemite," whose rhetoric never reached the vulgarity of Schneider's or Gregorig's. His ability to sustain social contacts with ministerial officials was always a source of suspicion to the more orthodox German Nationalists.[257] Under Pattai the *Verein* cultivated the artisan issue as its major political capital, although it also organized histrionic ventures, such as the protest assembly in April 1884 against the *Nordbahn* franchise.[258]

Many of the novel forms taken by early antisemitism in the years 1882–83 arose under the auspices of the *Reformverein*. Historians have all too frequently mistaken, however, the tone of early Viennese antisemitism for its substance, for by 1885–86 not only the *Reformverein,* but much of the early antisemitic movement as a whole was floundering in internal discord and factional bickering, discredited as much in its own eyes as among the Viennese voting public. How this nadir was reached revealed much about the possibilities of using new forms of political behavior and voter mobilization within a political culture with strong traditionalist biases.

The organization of the *Reformverein* in February 1882 was immediately followed in March and April 1882 by several controversial artisan assemblies. The Viennese watchmaker Buschenhagen organized an assembly of 400 artisans on 20 March 1882, ostensibly to support Clerical proposals before parliament to grant the five-gulden men the franchise. The rally soon degenerated into a crowd of screaming men, incited by a minor journalist, Franz Holubek.[259] Schönerer was also present, and gave a long speech condemning the Austrian press and the influence of Jews in public life. The assembly was a curious mixture of old public issues (the Democrats in Vienna had been arguing for 5 fl. suffrage for nearly twenty years), *Kleinbürger* enthusiasm, and antisemitic crudities. It would be erroneous to mark the assembly and those which followed it as wholly novel in terms of Viennese politics. The rowdiness and histrionics of the assembly were quite in the style of similar Democratic assemblies of the 1870s, although it was larger in size.[260] What was different was that radical, Left Liberal rhetoric was being forcefully pushed to the side by antisemitic jargon, which could be exploited for a certain amount of notoriety, but which would hardly provide the substance of an organized political movement. Schönerer's petitions to parliament in May 1882 against the immigration of Russian Jews were an excellent example of the limitations of this kind of random antisemitism with little occupational focus.[261] Such issues (the *Nordbahn* railroad franchise in 1884 was another) were useful for momentary publicity, but they had little effect in developing and orchestrating a systematic anti-Liberal alternative. The outrage (in the Liberal press) which the March 1882 assembly provoked led Holubek and Buschenhagen to arrange for a second rally, held in the Wieden on 4 April 1882.[262] Here Holubek concentrated on the Jewish question by presenting a ten-point program for ridding Austria of the Jews. Holubek's program—which he never had the chance to offer because the police representative intervened to stop the rally—included limitations of residence, the reinstitution of a head tax, prohibition against owning land, rigid employment limitations, and elimination from all public service jobs.[263] Holubek justified this program with long quotations supposedly from the Talmud, most of which he had plagiarized from Rohling's book. With Schönerer in the chair the meeting took a predictably unsettled course.[264]

The Holubek-Buschenhagen-Schönerer meetings of March and April 1882 have become part of the lore of early antisemitism, but in fact they were of minor significance. Holubek soon left the movement and returned to the political obscurity he so richly deserved.[265] Buschenhagen became a minor pan-German, completely isolated from the mainstream of Viennese artisan antisemitism by 1885.[266] Holubek's outrageous program was a standard variant of early racist antisemitism, intelligible by its context but little else. There were numerous programs circulating in German antisemitic circles in the early 1880s; what marked Holubek's efforts were their wholly derivative, plagiarized character. Neither Buschenhagen nor Holubek had any political roots in Viennese politics—their assemblies were spectacles for the curious, for the eager, for those who thought they disliked the Jews and wanted some excuse to say so.

Perhaps the most significant development in Viennese antisemitism in 1882 was the increasingly dominant role played by Schönerer. Schönerer faithfully joined the *Reformverein*, although he had doubts about its lack of a strong nationalist component. During its first year Schönerer was a featured speaker at each monthly meeting, along with Pattai and other, minor notables.[267] But Schönerer had other, loftier plans for his movement than simply dealing with artisan complaints. After months of preparation, he founded his *Deutschnationalen Verein* in Vienna in June 1882.[268] It was in the context of this association, filled with a few hundred journalists, school teachers, gymnasial professors, and wealthier small businessmen that Schönerer intended to develop his new creed. Unlike the *Reformverein*, which was both local (in a municipal sense) and implicitly political-agitorial, the new pan-German association aimed at a national constituency. It soon turned into a small group of hateful, racist sub-elite leaders whose tastelessness in their antisemitism shocked many conventional Bürger in Vienna.[269] Owing to a few small groups of Schönerian agitators in Vienna and Lower Austria, gruesome, "drive the Jew out" types of propaganda began to filter into Vienna and the smaller towns of Lower Austria, some of it imported from Hungary and Germany, the rest locally produced.[270] The impact of this material was not great, since the government was careful to confiscate it as soon as it was located and identified, but coming as it did in the years 1882–83 when anti-Jewish riots were breaking out in Russia and in Hungary, it was hardly likely to calm public emotions.[271]

Schönerer's rhetoric and his followers' unsavory devices generated short-term interest, but the leaders of the *Reformverein,* especially Pattai and Schneider, were anxious to convert the *Verein* into a functional political movement. Up to 1884 the *Verein* held monthly assemblies, each in a different district of the city or suburbs, like a traveling circus with paid performers and occasional guest stars, but this was hardly the stuff out of which a major political party could be made. The *Verein* had no roots, it developed no local elite support, it was an outsider seeking admission at traditional political doors. It claimed a membership of over 1,000 men, but these were spread throughout the city. In spite of its bravado, the *Verein* was a head without a body.[272] For Schönerer political integration and accommodation were a moot question, since he had already begun by mid-1883 to reveal those propensities toward ideological and organizational dogmatism which characterized the Austrian pan-German movement for the next thirty years. The core of Schönerer's movement in Vienna was never more than an ill-integrated group of quasi-sectarian professionals. Periodic purges and loyalty tests protected the inscrutable facade of the master. Schönerer enjoyed an enormous personal popularity, but structurally the formal pan-German movement (as opposed to a more diffuse nationalism) was stillborn in Vienna from the early 1880s on. Many of the talented upper Mittelstand politicians recruited to its ranks, such as Fiegl, deserted Schönerer after 1889–90.

The *Reformverein* had three options for its strategy. For the small band of Schönerians the *Verein* was a useful tool for propaganda without bothering with the compromise-ridden culture of Viennese local politics. Schönerer preferred a small, innocuous *Verein* with a wholly German constituency to one which depended upon the assimilated Czech master artisans in Vienna for voting support. Ernst Schneider sensed this peculiar sectarianism when he wrote to Vogelsang in March 1883 that

Schönerer's interest in craft reform was gradually evaporating: "What Schönerer is doing with regard to social-political affairs is, in my opinion, not to be taken seriously."[273]

At the other extreme stood Ernst Schneider. As ambitious as Pattai to gain notoriety, Schneider ran for parliament in a by-election in Hernals in April 1882 without using antisemitic rhetoric. He styled himself as an honest, self-made businessman with a medium-scale machine shop, whose *Fabrik* employed over fifty workers.[274] Schneider's self-effacing Democracy failed miserably (he came in a poor third in the race), and he decided to give his artisan program a sharper, more antisemitic focus. Schneider's relations with Schönerer quickly degenerated into extreme personal acrimony. Schneider told Schönerer in April 1882 that he would have no part in "Prussophilic" schemes within the *Reformverein,* proposing that the association restrict itself to a program of artisan reforms.[275] Schönerer never trusted Schneider, considering him a tool of the Clericals and a spy for the police.[276]

Although he admitted to Vogelsang that Schönerer did deserve credit for "bringing the antisemitic movement into motion," Schneider decided by mid-1883 that he would no longer tolerate Schönerer's pan-German machinations.[277] He began plotting to become the "new Schönerer" of Viennese craft politics, hoping to "paralyze" the latter's influence in the city by developing a rival program of antisemitic crudities which would emulate Schönerer's tone without affiliating the association with nationalism.[278] Schneider assumed the worst in human motivation and the least in voter intelligence. Voters existed to be manipulated by radical rhetoric and secret plots.[279] This made him an excellent conspirator and special interest organizer; it also made him a poor district politician in a political culture where friendship and personal loyalty counted for much. Appropriately Schneider finally found a political home for himself within the more oligarchical structure of the guild system rather than within Viennese ward politics. His endless conspiracies could proceed among a small group of guild chairmen without having to depend upon the development of a broad nexus of friendships in local *Gasthaus* political clubs. In his own way Schneider was as much a sectarian as was Schönerer, with one difference—Schönerer's isolation was ideological and programmatic, Schneider's was personal and emotional.

Schneider thought that the *Reformverein* had the responsibility to combat pan-Germanism among the Viennese artisans. After his election to the vice-presidency of the *Reformverein* in late 1882 Schneider expanded the association's social base by recruiting smaller, less wealthy artisans to join.[280] Many of these men were first- or second-generation Bohemians or Moravians who had become assimilated into Viennese culture and were far more interested in implementing the craft programs of the 1881 and 1882 craft congresses than they were in promoting Schönerer's pan-Germanism. These "Czechs," especially those from the larger craft guilds like the shoemakers, gave the *Reformverein* a more diversified character. Schneider also made sure that the *Reformverein* developed close ties to the *Gewerbegenossenschaftstag*—the club sponsored special social events for the delegates to the Second Craft Congress (November 1882).[281]

Robert Pattai represented a third alternative for the *Verein*. He respected Schönerer's power and the loyalty this man generated among his coterie of supporters. Schönerer had financial resources at his command, and these were not to be ignored in a city in which an election race might cost as much as 5,000 fl. On the other hand, Pattai realized that Schneider's option of restricting the *Reformverein·* to a craft context and of bringing in as many of the poorer artisans as possible, even if some of these people were assimilated Viennese Czechs, was the only realistic one if he hoped to win elections in Vienna. The stark fact of Viennese politics in 1884 was that most of Schönerer's relatively small number of urban supporters already had the vote, since they had generally been recruited out of the middle and upper levels of the Viennese Bürgertum (especially the white collar, professional classes). Schneider, in contrast, was attempting to politicize the new 5 fl. voters who would exercise their franchise for the first time in 1885 and who had little interest in nationalist strife. Pattai was caught in the middle.

The first rupture in the *Reformverein* occurred in the spring of 1884. In mid-March 1884, Schneider urged the leaders of the *Reformverein* to support the reelection of Karl Lueger to the City Council in the Landstrasse.[282] Lueger faced a difficult election, and he welcomed support from all quarters. Although several of Pattai's loyalists (Cornelius Vetter, an antisemitic book dealer in the Landstrasse and Pattai's brother-in-law; and Leopold Hollomay, a friend of Vetter and a poor lithographic printer) had doubts about Lueger's acceptability, they joined Schneider in urging the *Verein* to support him as a "friend" of the movement. Following this decision Schönerer announced that he and his faction were resigning from the *Reformverein* because of its increasingly diluted principles.[283]

Schönerer's precipitous reaction embarrassed Pattai.[284] As president of the *Verein,* he could hardly repudiate Schneider's negotiations with Lueger and Gessmann. Schneider's tactics were one way of bringing the *Verein* into local politics—not by running its own candidates, but by supporting other groups' candidates with the assumption that the reelected politicians would gradually be coopted into the antisemitic movement.

At the same time, Pattai was clearly unwilling to break with Schönerer. He wrote to Schneider urging him to continue his work in the *Verein*, but pleading for a more conciliatory stance toward Schönerer (who, Pattai claimed, was gradually moving toward the *Reformverein*'s position on artisan politics in the city).[285] The Schönerian newspaper, *Unverfälschte Deutsche Worte*, claimed Pattai as a member of "our party" in June 1884. In fact Pattai was looking out for his own interests.[286]

In May 1884 Pattai decided to try his own hand at politics by running in a by-election for the Reichsrat seat in Mariahilf which had been vacated by Josef Kopp. To do so, he needed financial support and made a deal with Schönerer and the executive committee of the *Deutschnationalen Verein*. Pattai agreed to run his campaign on the basis of the Linz program (including the separation of Galicia and Dalmatia from the Cisleithanian half of the monarchy) and to join a pan-German club in parliament, should Schönerer organize one. He also agreed not to accept Schneider's help in raising money (meaning money from the *Reformverein* or from Schneider's aristocratic friends).[287] In return Schönerer underwrote his election expenses (nearly 4,000 fl.). Luckily for Pattai, he lost the election by a narrow, but respectable margin. His promise to Schönerer was moot, although it returned to haunt him in late 1885.[288]

Two developments in 1885 helped to clarify Pattai's situation. In late 1884 Schönerian loyalists led by Fiegl in Mariahilf, the district where Pattai had run unsuccessfully for parliament six months previously, organized a local district association, the *Politischen Bezirksverein Mariahilf-Neubau*. For the history of Viennese antisemitism this was a crucial development, since it was the first *effective* antisemitic association in one of the traditional *Vorstadt* districts.[289] Pattai and his followers in Mariahilf immediately joined the club, and within a few months they took control of it. Conflict soon broke out over the issue of section 19 of the Linz program, which called for a tariff union with Germany. For the artisans and *Fabrikanten* in Mariahilf, who were the majority of antisemitic voters, this clause was wholly unacceptable. A tariff union with Germany would have made their precarious economic existence impossible. Pattai and his friends agreed to abandon section 19, but Fiegl and the more rigid pan-Germans refused to compromise.[290] In mid-April 1885 the Schönerian dissidents seceded and formed a rival organization, the *Deutschen Bezirksverein Mariahilf*, but it was the original *Politischer Verein*, dominated by Pattai, which achieved a workable constituency within the district and eventually won control of the *Bezirksausschuss*. Pattai now had an organizational base of his own, apart from the *Reformverein*.

The City Council elections in March 1885 led to the second crisis in the *Reformverein*. In the Landstrasse the *Verein* voted to abandon the precedent of the previous year—supporting Democratic candidates against the Liberals—and to run its own slate. Cornelius Vetter and Leopold Hollomay were slated to run against the two Democrats, Ignaz Mandl and Franz Schallaböck. Although the *Reformverein* voted to support Vetter and Hollomay, Schneider lobbied for Mandl and Schallaböck, reasoning that it was better to coopt the Democrats into antisemitism than to run isolated antisemitic candidates against them. Mandl and Schallaböck both won their races. More important, Schneider did nothing to support the campaign of Anton Schnarf for the Second Curia in Mariahilf. Schnarf was a nationalist gymnasial professor whose views on topics aside from antisemitism were unacceptable to Schneider. He lost his election. For Pattai this was unbearable. In late March 1885 Pattai sent an angry letter to the executive committee of the *Reformverein* demanding an end to the "pro-Czech" machinations within the *Verein*. Unlike Schönerer Pattai was not anti-Slavic, just anti-Schneider. Disgusted with the constant feuding caused by Schneider, Pattai resigned the presidency of the *Reformverein* on 10 April 1885.[291] A week later, in an election marked by voting irregularities, Schneider had himself elected president. As a result of these internecine quarrels active membership in the association began to slip badly.

Pattai's rejection of Schneider (but not of Schneider's pro-artisan tactics) helped to conciliate pan-German opinion in his favor, and, when he ran for the Reichsrat in June 1885 from Mariahilf, he was successful in assembling a coalition of newer 5 fl. voters and older pan-German voters still loyal to Schönerer. This time, however, he did not depend on Schönerer for his finances; it was the new *Politischer Verein* which supported Pattai's campaign.[292] Pattai's election was a milestone in the history of early Viennese antisemitism, for it showed how antisemitism might be used effectively within one district by a traditional independent club organization. With this precedent in mind, the utility of the more loosely organized *Reformverein* diminished rapidly.

The final denouement of the *Reformverein* occurred in April 1886 when most of the Pattai faction left the association after a stormy meeting in which Hollomay accused Schneider of fraud and other assorted sins. With this secession the *Verein* was dead—it vegetated for a few months but had no further effect on local politics.[293] Schneider's defense of himself was accurate when he stated that personality conflicts and not strategic issues led to the break.[294] In the Council elections of March 1886 Pattai and his *Politischer Verein* supported Vincenz Wessely, an artisan master of

Czech origin, against an orthodox German Nationalist in Mariahilf, Josef Himmelbauer.[295] Pattai was no less "pro-Czech" than Schneider, but he wanted Schneider to stop encroaching on his political territory.

The idea of an antisemitic district association was so appealing that Vetter and Hollomay organized a parallel *Politischen Verein* in the Landstrasse in October 1886.[296] Here, however, they ran up against a well-organized Democratic club organization dominated by Lueger. As the events of 1890–91 revealed, when Lueger destroyed both Vetter's and Hollomay's political careers, it was difficult to steal districts away from accomplished Democratic politicians, provided that the Democrats would accommodate themselves to antisemitism. Both Pattai and Schneider were shown to be partially correct in their strategies—Pattai because he realized that effective organization meant district-level organization and not the nebulous *Reformverein;* Schneider because within each district compromises were still to be made with existing Democratic elements.

Only after antisemites like Pattai and Vetter realized that antisemitism had to begin on the ward level and work up to the municipal level and that it had to accommodate itself to existing Democratic leadership cadres did the movement as a whole become a serious, effective threat to traditional Liberal political groups. Schneider, too, by abandoning the *Reformverein* after 1886 and concentrating on the craft guild movement, realized the importance of an effective infrastructure in spreading the new faith. Once antisemitism did develop local affiliations and roots, a process of compromise and integration with existing Democratic elements was inevitable.

From the point of view of early 1886, however, political antisemitism had reached an abysmal nadir with its feuds, acrimony, and petty quarrels. Viennese Liberals looking at the movement in 1886 were properly contemptuous of its future. But the Reichsrat elections of 1885 and the City Council elections of 1886 showed the remarkable response awaiting candidates who could combine Democratic traditionalism, district localism, popular cultural appeals, and a respectable (that is, nonviolent) brand of economic antisemitism. As a political issue, especially among voters in the Third Curia, antisemitism was an immensely rich vein to mine, but it required the proper organization and discipline.

The years 1885–88 saw two processes at work which improved these aspects of Viennese antisemitism. On the one hand, owing to the influence of Ludwig Psenner, Karl v Vogelsang, and the cadres of lower-order Catholic priests, a subtle yet effective pseudoreligious facade was brought to the antisemitic movement which provided it with more ideological and cultural respectability and further internal resources. On the other hand, these years saw the gradual personal transformation of Karl Lueger and

Albert Gessmann, the two Democrats most responsible for the leadership of a revived Christian Social antisemitism after 1889.

The Radicalization of the Artisan Movement, 1886–92

The years following the *Gewerbeordnung* of 1883 made it apparent that the law offered the artisans no panacea. In 1885 Ernst Schneider complained to Vogelsang: "In early 1883 we got the craft law and ask yourself, what has happened, what can happen? . . . Are not the Jews and their friends everywhere? Do they not attempt to undercut the law in every possible way?"[297] In 1890 the annual report of the Viennese Chamber of Commerce indicated that "the economic situation of the handworkers is very precarious."[298] Since no fundamental changes occurred after 1883 in the haphazard system of apprentice training, the proof of competency did not provide the labor market with new artisans of higher quality. Nor did it reduce competition in the trades. Many crafts in 1883 had too many legally registered apprentices and journeymen to begin with. After the passage of the law there was no substantial decline in the annual rate at which new master craftsmen entered the Viennese market.[299] Most of these men had all of the experience necessary to obtain a master's certificate. Since the 1883 law did not require an examination but merely stipulated years of work experience as a journeyman, there was no method by which the quality of training could be evaluated. Richard Weiskirchner, later a Christian Social minister and party dignitary, admitted in 1895 that the proof of competency certificate, when applied to such crafts as Viennese hat making, was of no significant value.[300]

The 1883 law also contained loopholes by which the certificate could be avoided. The government was authorized to grant exemptions from the requirement, and the first level of authority responsible for making such exemptions in large cities like Vienna was the *Magistrat*. Until 1896 this authority was under Liberal political control.[301] Naturally, the Liberal municipal bureaucrats were not miserly in promising exemptions. Also, any citizen of the monarchy who obtained recognition as a master in one province of the state could, upon moving to another area, simply have his proof of competency registered in the new area. He did not have to repeat the process of obtaining official certification. This had two consequences: the 1883 law did not stop entry into the Viennese labor market of émigrés from Bohemia or Galicia; and, if all else failed, by means of bribery or some other illegal device a competency certificate could be obtained elsewhere and then simply transferred to Vienna. Finally, section 38 of the 1883 legislation, which required that owners of new commercial establishments such as *Konfektion* houses have a certificate, could be avoided by hiring a "straw man" as codirector or supervisor of the firm or by restricting the house's orders to artisan subcontractors who did have a master's certificate (as opposed to independent journeymen). In any event, since this provision was not retroactive, the many large establishments which competed with the artisans in the various clothing trades were not affected.

Conflict soon ensued over whether shoe and clothing dealers and shop owners might take individual orders by measurement and handle repair work, rather than ordering or producing large quantities of goods in standard sizes. The antisemites claimed that section 38 of the craft law did not permit *massnehmen*, but the *Verwaltungsgerichtshof* decided in a controversial case in February 1888 that this interpretation was erroneous.[302] The decision of the court led to massive protests on the part of the craft guilds in Vienna and elsewhere, with the leaders of the *Genossenschaftstag* organizing a mass petition with 100,000 signatures.

The 1883 law also gave rise to excessive intercraft bickering over the range of articles which any given trade could manufacture. After 1883 hundreds of cases involving contested articles and procedures were submitted by the government to the Chamber of Commerce for its evaluation and recommendations.[303] Ironically the chamber, which was controlled by the large manufacturers and industrialists, was called upon to mediate complaints from quarreling guilds whose members were in large part antisemitic. The disputes between artisans over their boundaries exemplified the serious divergences of opinion among leading economic groups which supported the Christian Social coalition. The guild of general store owners was as anxious as organizations of wealthier businessmen like the *Wiener Kaufmannschaft* to prevent restrictions on Sunday opening and closing hours, although Sunday closings were demanded both by the Social Democrats and by many artisans in the industrial crafts.[304]

The second major provision of the *Gewerbeordnung*, the strengthening of the craft guilds, proved more successful, but not in economic terms. By 1890, 120 associations had been organized or reorganized in Vienna in accord with the 1883 law. The goal of the Clerical politicians in designing the craft guild system had been to develop among the individual masters a consciousness of membership in a larger corporate entity, using these associations to create other institutions such as cooperative sales halls, cooperative materials procurement centers, and sickness insurance systems.

Reality proved, however, less attractive. The post-1883 guilds suffered from several weaknesses. Artisans who defended their integrity against large commercial and industrial enterprises often viewed the collective goals of the guilds either as impossible or as a threat to their own independence. The attendance rates at most meetings of the various craft associations were low. In 1894 the total number of general membership meetings held by the 125 craft and commercial guilds in Vienna was 227—less than 2 per year.[305] Fifty-three associations held only 1 annual meeting, while 45 held merely 2.[306] Election meetings held to determine the executive leadership of the guilds were also marked by low attendance—it was unusual if more than 30–35 percent of the legal membership of the major craft guilds participated in these elections.[307] Such statistics explained the observation commonly made in industrial circles on the lack of corporate spirit in many trades.[308] Given the long work schedules of most masters, their self-reliance, and their suspicions of one another, guild leaders were probably satisfied at achieving 1 or 2 successful meetings each year. The process of creating a collectivist economic ethos among the artisans proved long and difficult, much more so than among more stable and educated segments of the Christian Social party like the clerics, the *Beamten*, and the property owners.

The network of cooperative associations which Belcredi and Schneider hoped the guilds would generate proved impractical. Section 115 of the 1883 *Gewerbeordnung* prohibited compulsory cooperative associations established by the guilds—only voluntary organizations were permissible. More important, most master craftsmen were either unwilling or unable to put out the necessary capital to join a cooperative. The guild of the turners (one of the largest in the city) reported that, although its members realized the value of cooperatives, the majority of the membership was so poor that they were unable to come up with a contribution.[309] When cooperative institutions were established, they usually favored the wealthier artisans, who needed assistance the least. When the guild of the master carpenters arranged for a common sales hall, only 75 out of 2,580 craftsmen were willing to join.[310]

The cooperative principle was, however, one of the more auspicious aspects of the 1883 *Gewerbeordnung*. Although it was a failure in the late 1880s, after 1896 the Christian Socials were able to channel government credits and city contracts to the craft guilds to encourage such undertakings.[311] Only after 1896 did many of the guilds come to play a vital role in enhancing the economic prosperity of some members. That this occurred under the aegis of external political power and that it was often limited to the personal friends and acquaintances of the guild chairmen eventually had dysfunctional consequences for the internal stability of the guilds.

The other institution which the craft guilds were to sponsor was sickness insurance for artisan employees. The law of 30 March 1888, which created a system of compulsory occupational sickness insurance in Austria, directed that workers in the craft trades join their own guild's insurance society *(Krankenkassen)* rather than one of the district or independent institutes.[312] Since the societies were established for the sake of the journeymen (for whom the employer had to pay at least one-third of the cost) and not for the benefit of the masters themselves, and since the committees of workers which ran the insurance societies frequently had a Socialist majority, they were extremely unpopular with the master artisans.[313]

If the craft guilds were unsuccessful by 1890 in improving the quality of their members' lives or the stability of their businesses, they did serve another, more latent purpose admirably. Real power in the Viennese craft guilds rested in the executive leadership (*Vorstehung*). The executive committees of the Viennese guilds varied in size from four to thirty-eight persons, and the major offices of the associations often included a salary and a loosely controlled expense account. In fact, of the total income the 120 Viennese craft guilds received in 1890 from such sources as membership fees, entrance fees, and investments, nearly 50 percent (201,453 fl.) went for internal administrative expenses rather than for vocational schools, charitable activities, or sickness insurance costs.[314] Johann Jedlička, the chairman of the carpenters' guild, who was an intimate colleague of Ernst Schneider and a supporter of Lueger, earned 1,000 fl. per year for his official duties.[315] This meant that many of the guilds, especially the larger ones, possessed well-paid agitators and lobbyists and special budgets for their propaganda and political expenses. The larger guilds often owned their own houses, which served not only as administrative headquarters, but as convenient centers for political coordination.[316] The major orientation of the executive boards was more political and legislative than economic—the Chamber of Commerce noted that the only activity considered worthwhile by many chairmen was "trade politics and administration" as opposed to economic or cultural interests.[317]

The guild boards used their organizations by the early 1890s to mobilize electoral support for various antisemitic candidates.[318] Within the antisemitic movement as a whole, the executive boards became what Gabriel Almond has called "distinct sets of communications subsystems," providing both horizontal and vertical channels of communication for the antisemitic elite, ensuring a reciprocal performance on the part of the political elite in favor of artisan economic demands.[319] Not surprisingly, election to the chairmanship or another leadership post of a large craft guild after 1890 frequently meant a seat in the City Council on the antisemitic ticket as well.[320] The post-1883 guild thus provided the recruiting grounds for a number of the local notables who served in the lower elites of the Christian Social political organization after 1891 (few were ever elected to the Landtag or Reichsrat). In this the antisemites were no different from the Liberals—guild chairmen like Heinrich Matthies and Joseph Schlechter had long enjoyed Liberal patronage for election to the

City Council on the Liberal slate, but the Christian Social practice depended on the ability of the individual guilds to provide their leaders with independent means of support to be able to take up public office. Moreover, the presence of so many guild officials from the Third Curia in the Council inevitably led to conflicts within the antisemitic coalition when Leopold Kunschak tried to organize a Christian Social labor movement.

One significant result of the 1885 Reichsrat elections, aside from the election of Lueger and Pattai to office, was the defeat of Franz Löblich for reelection in Alsergrund by a Liberal candidate, Karl Wrabetz. Löblich's pro-artisan parliamentary efforts between 1880 and 1883 caught him in a Liberal trap. The Liberals suggested that Löblich's cooperation in the craft movement with antisemites like Ernst Schneider had assisted the rise of political antisemitism in the city. They were able to swing a sufficient number of voters in the district to Wrabetz, returning Alsergrund to the Liberal fold after twelve years in the hands of the Democrats. Löblich's defeat was symbolic of the collapse of a credible non-antisemitic movement among the handwork artisans. He was hated and distrusted by both the Liberals and the antisemites.[321]

More significant than the technical reorganization of the guild system itself and the election to parliament of politicians sympathetic to the artisans was the political transformation of the cover organization which had the potential to coordinate the guild system for antisemitic political endeavors. Until 1884 the *Wiener Gewerbegenossenschaftstag* was a neutral political body. There were latent pressures within the craft movement to entice the artisans en masse into political antisemitism, but until 1884 antisemites like Ernst Schneider sought to work from the outside in, that is, to use clubs like the *Reformverein* to politicize the artisans in an external, nonprofessional context. The requirement of the new *Gewerbeordnung* that all existing guilds be reconstituted and their executive boards reelected or reorganized offered new opportunities for the insinuation of antisemitism into the internal politics of the guilds themselves. This is precisely what happened after 1885. As early as August 1884 Schneider wrote to Vogelsang, arguing that Löblich was dispensable and that his removal from the craft movement would help solidify antisemitic support in the various guilds.[322] At the 1884 craft congress which Löblich called, acrimonious confrontations took place between antisemitic speakers like Buschenhagen and Liberal leaders like Matthies.[323] The Liberals still controlled the board of the *Genossenschaftstag,* but these disturbances were a portent for the future.

Until 1885–86 Schneider was busy with the affairs of the *Reformverein* and did not devote his full attention to the guild movement. With the collapse of the *Reformverein* and his efforts to style himself as a new, pro-Austrian Schönerer, Schneider withdrew from district-level politics in Vienna (he was never elected to the City Council) and concentrated on the political potential of the reformed guild structure itself.[324] At the urging of Vogelsang and Lueger (each for different reasons), Schneider created a kind of power base for antisemitic politics different from the more traditional, district-club nexus which Robert Pattai had chosen in Mariahilf and Landstrasse. If the executive committee of the *Genossenschaftstag* could be integrated into the antisemitic movement, the artisans would obtain a powerful, city-wide representation. Instead of representing individual artisans, the *Tag* represented guilds as institutional entities. For this reason, and because the guilds were both obligatory and given to oligarchical domination by small political elites, it would be a far more stable and effective force to intervene in Third Curia politics than a mere club of individual artisan voters.[325] Representing guilds with considerable financial resources, the *Tag* had money for political organization, even though its ostensible function was that of a nonpolitical pressure group. As Schneider never tired of telling Vogelsang, to fight the Liberals in Vienna one needed considerable sums of money; the *Tag* was one way to provide such funds.[326]

Beginning in 1885 the antisemitic representatives within the executive board of the *Tag* made life unbearable for the older Liberal delegates, with the result that Löblich and Matthies resigned their positions in the summer of 1886.[327] By October 1887 many of the older Liberal guild chairmen had resigned their positions in the *Tag*.[328] Schneider engineered the election of Ferdinand Mayer, an ex-Democrat from Mariahilf and the chairman of the ornamental feather-makers' guild as the new chairman of the *Tag*. Schneider retained the position of executive secretary, which he was to use (with a short break in 1891–92) for the next twenty years to dominate the affairs of the organization, running it with a close circle of cronies among the chairmen of other large craft guilds.

More important, Schneider and his lieutenants began to organize conspiracies in many of the larger guilds, winning control of the positions of chairman and vice-chairman.[329] This process required ten years; not until well after 1896 had the antisemites gained control of the majority of the guilds, but as early as 1890–91 Schneider's allies had won control of the three largest craft guilds in the city—the shoemakers, the tailors, and the carpenters.[330] These were precisely the trades whose artisans were deeply involved in the consumer goods industries dominated by Jewish dealers and *Konfektionäre*. The process was not uniformly successful. Many of the smaller crafts, and especially those which represented more stable occupations and wealthier constituencies, such as the bakers, the printers, and the restaurant owners, remained in the Liberal fold for some years to come. But by the early 1890s the decisive momentum favored

Schneider and the antisemites. In 1894 Georg Hütter won control of the wealthy butchers' guild for the antisemites. In the same year the general store dealers went antisemitic.[331] Even in the case of the nominally Liberal guilds, their own interest in protectionism and their hostility to a common range of targets (Jewish peddlers, cooperative societies, accident insurance for journeymen) made it easier to cooperate with the antisemitic-dominated *Genossenschaftstag*.[332] In some cases after 1895 guild leadership was divided between the two parties, as occurred in the restaurant owners' guild.[333]

Much of the feuding between "Liberal" and "antisemitic" factions in an individual guild related as much to personal rivalries among local notables as it did to differences in political ideology. Guilds like the shoemakers had a long history of intraorganizational conspiracies against the existing leadership.[334] Now the antisemitic-Liberal antinomy overlaid these endogenous conflicts.

The Liberal party, assisted by wealthy Jewish merchants, organized a countermovement among the artisans by establishing the *Deutschen Gewerbegenossenschaftsverband* in Vienna in 1887, but this met with little response. Liberal trade newspapers like the *Deutsche Gewerbe-Zeitung* tried to invoke the nationality question as a way to undercut Schneider, accusing him of helping "Czech" factions in the guilds.[335] This too had little substantive effect on artisan opinion in the voting place. Many of the new chairmen had Czech names, but most had become assimilated into Viennese bourgeois culture. A more objective appraisal in the *Allgemeine Handwerker Zeitung* in 1888 admitted that there were often as many Czech-Viennese artisans supporting the Liberal candidates for chairman as there were the antisemitic candidates.[336] The nationality issue was not an effective ploy to counter artisan antisemitism in Vienna in the 1880s. As long as the antisemites avoided insulting the national background of the émigré artisans, the issue was stillborn. Just as bourgeois Jews had no place to go other than the Liberal party, the assimilated Czechs had few realistic options other than the antisemites, at least before 1900.

The success of this twofold drive—capturing control of the individual guilds themselves and capturing control of the cover organization, the *Genossenschaftstag*, which represented their interest to wider society— gave Schneider a powerful weapon to use in articulating the demands of the movement. Schneider and the antisemites had a far more activist and interest-oriented role in mind for the *Tag* than had the older Liberal-Democratic leaders of the 1860s and 1870s.

One opportunity for the *Tag* to stir up trouble came in June 1888, when a minor scandal erupted over Alfred Fränkel's shoe factory in Mödling. Fränkel's decision in 1887 to distribute his shoes primarily in the domestic market outraged the leaders of the shoemakers' guild. In February 1888 the artisans organized a committee to monitor the quality of shoes produced in the Mödling factory (in hope of showing Fränkel's wares to be inferior), and also sent angry protests to the Ministry of Trade and the City Council. In late May and early June 1888 the Council acted on a resolution brought by the antisemitic delegation which condemned Fränkel's business practices and urged the government to intervene. The stormy debates on the resolution had the unenviable distinction of being the first occasion of antisemitic rhetoric in the City Council's history.[337] The histrionics surrounding the Fränkel episode were of little help to the shoemakers, but they were enormously useful to Schneider and the *Gewerbegenossenschaftstag.*[338] Schneider even manufactured false evidence against Fränkel. Henceforth, "Fränkel's shoe factory" became a battle cry for the artisans' political organizers. It was worth literally thousands of votes.

The culmination of Schneider's agitation came in 1890–91 when the now antisemitic *Genossenschaftstag* proclaimed its new, maximal anticapitalist program. In September 1890 Schneider organized the Fourth Austrian Craft Congress.[339] Over 4,000 delegates representing 446 guilds gathered to hear Schneider present a new set of demands for future revision of the *Gewerbeordnung.*[340] The Liberal press claimed that the congress did not represent the majority of Austrian artisans, but such grumbling merely revealed Liberal bitterness. Schneider's program contained amendments to thirty-seven sections of the 1883 *Gewerbeordnung.*[341] He lengthened the list of trades designated as "handwork" and wanted this designation fixed by law, rather than left to the whims of the minister of trade. He also proposed rigid criteria for defining a factory. Independent cooperative associations which challenged the masters were to be abolished. Large businesses in the construction industry incorporating several trades were to be split up. Schneider answered complaints that the proof of competency had been ineffective by lengthening the time a worker had to serve in a training capacity before applying for the certificate of competency from six to eight years. He also wanted an actual test created and suggested that the craft guilds be given sole responsibility for administering and evaluating such tests. The house-industrial system was forbidden to produce handwork products of any kind, and the program of independent journeymen working in the *Verlag* system was to be abolished immediately. Distributors in retail or wholesale goods were forbidden the right of *massnehmen,* and all retail trade in handwork goods was henceforth restricted solely to the artisans. No retailer or wholesaler, whatever his area of production, could possess more than one store within the city limits.

Schneider's program, had it ever been enacted, would have wrought chaos in the Austrian economy.[342] The proposals were designed to return the city to a preindustrial age in which all light and most medium industry would be centered in small handwork shops. In an attempt to add some respectability to the 1890 program Alois Liechtenstein gave Schneider's ideas a rhetorical dressing-up in parliament in June 1891. Liechtenstein insisted that the proposals could be implemented gradually and would not have the character of expropriations, and that economic chaos need not result.[343] Liechtenstein wanted the Chambers of Trade and Commerce split into two sections, one of which would be consigned to the artisan guilds. Large-scale commerce, such as the *Konfektion* system, would be abolished, but since "acquired rights must be respected in a state of law," existing factories and plants would not be immediately affected. Only new establishments would be prohibited by law. Existing factories which dealt with goods claimed by the handwork artisans as their own could not be sold or bequeathed, but would be taken over by the craft guilds. At the same time, the guild system would be "built up and expanded." The guild in each craft area would buy up factories by using "continuous bank credits." The circle of factory owners and large retailers would disappear "gradually," thus avoiding any disturbances in the state's production system. The managerial talents of the manufacturers would be superfluous, since the new guilds would rule their members with iron discipline and would control the production of the various masters. Rather than attacking the technological existence of the factory and the large store, as Schneider had done, Liechtenstein accepted both, but simply replaced private ownership and its managerial elite with craft guilds run by artisans.[344] Where Schneider sought to turn the economy backward, Liechtenstein wanted to turn it upside down.

Liechtenstein went far beyond Schneider by introducing a neocorporation which would supersede privately owned manufacturing and distribution. Schneider stopped short of this, and with good reason, since Liechtenstein would have destroyed the very independence of the individual artisan which Schneider and his colleagues hoped to preserve. Under Liechtenstein's plan the individual master artisan would become simply a skilled laborer in a large guild-supervised production process, losing the independent status which he coveted. Ostensibly, Liechtenstein wanted to reduce government intervention. But his proposals would have given rise to a governmental bureaucracy so complex that any vestige of guild independence would have become mere myth.

The absurdity of Liechtenstein's plan was obvious. Lueger, Gessmann, Weiskirchner, and other Christian Social leaders never endorsed his ideas. He never went beyond the vague generalizations of the 1891 speech to explain in detail how the craft guilds would assume responsibility for the production and distribution of large quantities of goods and services or what he actually considered to be a "handwork" good.[345]

The question remained after all of the rhetoric: Did Schneider and Liechtenstein believe in the efficacy of their proposals in 1890–91? The question is important, since upon it hinges an understanding of the anti-capitalist impulse of the early antisemitic movement. Schneider was un-doubtedly in earnest about his program, although in 1906–7, when the Christian Socials succeeded in pushing through parliament the long sought reform of the 1883 *Gewerbeordnung,* they settled for considerably less than the 1890 scheme.[346] In Liechtenstein's case he admitted that he was projecting a utopia, the practical aim of the speech being a device for political mobilization and little more.

Liechtenstein often misjudged the potency of his verbal radicalism. In 1889 he gave a harsh anticapitalist speech to the Second Catholic Con-gress, urging corporate organizations to regulate large industry in Austria. Given the trend toward cartelization and industrial concentration after 1885, this demand was not outrageous. What made it unacceptable was the apparent regulatory role which Liechtenstein accorded to government agencies in supervising these cartels and the implication that worker wage levels would not depend on market mechanisms, but would be coordi-nated by external political authority. Liechtenstein's comments generated considerable opposition among the Bohemian nobility, many of whom had large industrial investments in sugar and mining. When Liechtenstein learned of this reaction, he wrote a shocked letter to Vogelsang explaining his innocence and his basic sympathy with Austrian capital develop-ment.[347] He then asked Vogelsang to publish an essay in *Vaterland* to "clarify" any misunderstandings which had arisen as a result of his speech. He insisted that his corporate theories, far from injuring Austrian industrial development, would assist it. Liechtenstein's "anticapitalism" thus fell between the explicit reactionary planning of Ernst Schneider and the illusory monetary utopianism advanced by Joseph Schlesinger, a Christian Social parliamentary delegate and a professor at the Imperial agricultural college. Schlesinger was a self-appointed, self-taught economist who spent years in a simpleminded effort to advance his idea of a "people's money" to replace the Austrian currency. His notions made for good antisemitic propaganda, but few serious Christian Social leaders, even those who represented the artisans, paid any attention after 1896 either to him or to his *idée fixe.*[348] In Schneider's case and in the case of artisan anticapitalism it might be argued that the tone of their rhetoric was fiercer than the intended consequences of their proposals, although the proposals were both real and potentially damaging to Austrian commercial development. Emil Lederer once noted that "the Austrian petite bourgeoisie, most prominently in its Viennese form, appears to be radical...but this radicalism lies more in its tone than in concrete postulates."[349] In the case of Liechtenstein, however, behind the radical posturing stood not only a man who lacked the courage of his convictions, but whose convictions themselves were largely the stuff from which crass political opportunism was made. His prudential concern for the feelings of his fellow aristocratic sugar and mining industrialists in 1889 found many parallels in the years to come.

Eugen Schwiedland pointed out in 1897 that Liechtenstein's plan to replace private industry with an empire of guild ownership would have profited only a few of the wealthier, elite craftsmen who had the capital, technical expertise, and administrative ability to rise to the top of such guild organizations. Private capitalist oligarchy would be replaced by guild capitalist oligarchy.[350] Liechtenstein's admission that legal compulsion and government supervision would have to force all artisans to participate in the new associations misread the real psychological needs of the individuals whom he genuinely wanted to assist.

The most important factor in evaluating the anticapitalism in the 1890–91 proposals was that it came at a period when Social Democracy and the union movement were only beginning to make themselves felt as powerful political forces in Vienna. In the 1870s when the Viennese labor force began its first successful efforts to organize, the artisans were fearful of pushing their own internal development too far in the face of socialist reprisals. The period during which antisemitic artisan protest first seized public attention was precisely the period during which the Austrian labor movement was most fragmented and persecuted. The government was far more concerned in the early 1880s about the political activity of the radical and moderate factions of early Social Democracy than it was about protest meetings of antisemitic master artisans.[351]

Liechtenstein's anticapitalism could therefore occupy center stage in the public view at a very low cost in logic or responsible economic theory. Because there was no effective, massive Socialist presence, he could afford the luxury of "saving" the masters, not only at the cost of the industrialists, but also at the expense of the proletariat. In 1890 he did not have to choose between the two. Sigmund Mayer pointed out in 1893 that Liechtenstein's ideas might very well backfire in that he was willing to confiscate the private property of the big capitalists in order to enrich the small capitalists. Why, Mayer asked, could not the proletariat force the process one step further and simply confiscate *all* private property? Why replace capitalist stock corporations with guild stock corporations? If masters could replace managers, could not journeymen replace masters?[352] Heinrich Reschauer, the erstwhile Progressive who abandoned the movement once the Clericals began to exploit it, had warned the artisan leaders in 1882 that a crusade against big business was, for the artisan's own interests, dangerous since the real enemy lay on the Left.[353] Liechtenstein himself sensed that his plans for the Austrian economy would run aground if the workers were given a voice in approving or rejecting such reforms. Although fulsome in his sympathy for the "poor" workers, he rejected the idea of universal suffrage for them.[354]

Formal tensions between labor and the artisan masters had existed since the 1860s, but the late 1880s saw heightened conflict between the two subcultures. The points of conflict were manifold, ranging from strikes and wage demands to the movement in labor circles to establish cooperative societies. Socialist groups captured control of the journeyman assemblies in many guilds, as well as the committees administering sickness insurance.[355] In many guilds the leaders among the journeymen were more active in political agitation than their employers.[356] Most journeymen were indifferent or hostile to religion, and the pseudo-clericalism which artisan leaders preached to their underlings met with open resentment. The union movement, having made significant organizational progress in the early 1890s, was the gravest threat faced by the artisans, so much so that the editor of a prominent Catholic craft newspaper, Joseph Blaschek, urged the government in 1891 to prohibit all Socialist unions.[357] That Socialist labor leaders in key craft industries like carpentry, shoemaking, turning, food products, and metal and machine production held national congresses in the summer and autumn of 1890, simultaneous with the Schneider craft congress, was symbolic of the growing gap between the artisan masters and their journeymen.[358]

The level of conflict between masters and workers by the later 1880s simply reflected a long-range decline of preindustrial work norms, especially those which implied a union of workshop and home as the moral and physical nexus for employer-employee social interaction.[359] Increasingly by the later decades of the century journeymen lived apart from their masters, often as *Sitzgesellen,* and even when they did reside with them they did so in the status of cash-paying *Bettgeher,* not as integral members of an extended, patriarchal community.[360] With the establishment of a new network of *Gehilfen* assemblies and union organizations in the later 1880s, as well as the cultural organizations of the Socialist party itself, activist journeymen finally obtained legally and culturally sanctioned agencies for collective action against their employers. At the same time, precisely because labor activism centered on institutions such as the

Gehilfenversammlung which were legally a part of the artisan-dominated guild structure, the level of hostility between artisan and worker assumed dramatic proportions, if only because of the institutional and social proximity in the context of which labor conflicts evolved.

Rather than personal loyalty to his master, the journeyman frequently felt far more allegiance to his colleagues in the *Gehilfen* assembly or other, Socialist-inspired organization. Gradually the cultural loyalties of journeymen shifted to external sociabilities and associations carrying enormous potential in the political marketplace. As Michael Mitterauer has noted, this process of cultural alienation between master and journeyman had commenced in Austria long before 1848 on individual terms, but only after 1870 did it assume institutionally significant political proportions. By 1890 it was possible, if only tentatively, to attribute class-oriented behavior and a sense of "class-belonging" to many artisan-employed workers, who now found acceptable political and ideological alternatives to the culture of paternalistic obedience and subordination which their masters so fondly remembered (or, more accurately, claimed to remember).[361]

With the establishment of a central union organization in Vienna in December 1893, and with the growth of regional and national craft unions between 1890 and 1895, workers gained collective mechanisms to challenge the artisan-dominated guilds. That Liberal-dominated guilds, like the bakers, suffered as much from Socialist antagonism as did the large Christian Social craft guilds eased the way for the two bourgeois parties to collaborate on local and regional levels against the union movement.[362]

Particular points of conflict between the labor movement and the artisans were the gaps in social legislation passed between 1885 and 1888. The law of 8 March 1885, which established guidelines for worker protection, granted concessions to the artisans. Artisans could employ children from the age of twelve on, whereas factories could not hire children less than fourteen years of age. Most important, although no maximum work day was set for handwork industries, factories were limited to eleven hours per day.[363] In 1887 another law, establishing accident insurance for laborers, completely excluded all employees in artisan shops from its competence.[364] In January 1895 a law regulating Sunday rest allowed the minister of trade and the provincial *Statthalter* to authorize exemptions from the general rule that shops were to be closed on Sunday. For some retail businesses as much as six hours of Sunday work might be allowed. In April 1895 the *Statthalter* of Lower Austria, Erich Kielmansegg, granted exemptions to a series of industrial crafts and retail trades. The *Arbeiter-Zeitung* called this practice a "parody" of the law's intent. Many artisans and small retailers vehemently protested any Sunday rest and continued their custom of working on Sundays. By September 1895 3,600 complaints had been filed against 100 master bakers for repeated violations of the legislation.[365]

All three laws gave rise to demands in worker circles that the artisans be made subject to the same restrictions which their larger industrial counterparts faced. When the government attempted to secure legislation in December 1895 introducing a maximum work week for artisan trades (seventy-seven hours) and placing the shops under accident insurance, a series of antisemitic protest assemblies were held, bitterly rejecting such ideas.[366] By 1896 it was apparent, therefore, that artisan anticapitalists would have to adjust their rhetoric from criticism of the industrial Right to meet a massive challenge from the political Left.

Johann Jedlička may have come to this conclusion in July 1896. During a strike of several hundred carpentry journeymen, he tried to organize a lockout among 600 of his artisan colleagues against the workers. To support this endeavor, he sought cooperation from an ad hoc committee of 25 industrialists in the wood and furniture business.[367] Without the support of the *Fabrikanten,* the lockout would have failed. In his momentary desperation Jedlička sensed that even the staunchest of antisemites could not burn the economic candle at both ends and win. Cooperating with industrial capitalists was certainly more palatable than sacrificing one's status dignities and economic security by conceding nine-hour working days to "Red" workers. Later in the month, when a delegation of leading Viennese industrialists visited Count Badeni to protest the ongoing wave of Socialist strike activity in Vienna, they coopted into their group artisan leader Johann Köhler to present the artisans' side of the story.[368] These informal occasions of antisocialist cooperation between industry and the artisans did not mean that the anti-industrial propensities of the craft movement were evaporating—they remained a viable force until the end of the empire. But it did mean that the political system in which this kind of protest was out of proportion to the natural balance of political forces in late Imperial bourgeois society was clearly dying.

The renewed antisocialism of the artisan masters after 1891 found an effective voice in the *Gewerbegenossenschaftstag.* The success of the *Tag* in mobilizing artisans to vote antisemitic in the 1891 Reichsrat and City Council elections led the Imperial government to suppress it in June 1891, ostensibly for violating its professional, nonpolitical charter. The prohibition, much celebrated in the Liberal press, could not be sustained. In 1892 the government relented and allowed the chairmen of the larger craft guilds to reestablish the *Tag,* again with Ernst Schneider as executive secretary.[369] By 1895 the *Tag* had become an effective voice for a protectionist program with newer antilabor tenets complementing older, anti-industrial demands. When Lueger, in his new capacity as *Bürger-meister*, attended a festive banquet of the *Tag* in July 1897, a precedent of cooperation between the city and the guilds was set which was to endure for the next twenty years.[370] The *Gewerbegenossenschaftstag* had now become "respectable," its leaders received individually or collectively by the emperor, its designated spokesmen pushing with eventual success for a more radical reform of the existing craft laws (the Novelle of 1907).

The political success of artisan protectionism in Austria did not result, however, from the politicization of the craft guilds per se, but rather from the inclusion of the new guild structure in a broader, more powerful anti-Liberal party. Had political antisemitism in Vienna stopped short in 1886 with Schneider's conspiracies in the *Genossenschaftstag* and Pattai's limited efforts in the Mariahilf, the Viennese Liberals would have retained control of the city until 1918, just as their German cousins to the north and west did in their cities. Schneider's efforts in the *Tag* resolved the deficit in collective consciousness and behavior among the Viennese artisans, but they did not give the artisans a workable, secular framework in which to use their new institutional resources. By themselves, with only their limited resources to depend upon, the Viennese artisans would have been crushed by the Austrian Liberal party.

Religion and Artisan Antisemitism

In order to enhance the ideological effectiveness and organization of the antisemitic movement in the mid-1880s and to provide a focal point for non-Schönerian antisemitism, a few antisemitic leaders urged introduction of a strong religious motif. In the early 1880s Schönerer and Pattai had used the phrase "practical Christianity" to describe a normative ethos in contrast to that of "Jewish culture," but they had no serious thought of committing the movement to a religious direction.[371] One character in the later 1880s who wanted to join the two subthemes was Ludwig Psenner. Psenner was an antisemitic journalist from Bozen who took control of the *Oesterreichischer Volksfreund* from Zerboni in mid-1884. By 1885 he had introduced into the paper a bizarre mixture of social Darwinism and vague Christian theology, although he refused to call himself a clerical.[372] Psenner soon met Vogelsang and, by his own admission, became a protégé of the elder journalist (Psenner also received a secret subsidy from Egbert Belcredi for his paper). Gradually, he became more orthodox in his religious views, although antisemitism was uppermost in his value system. Psenner felt that antisemitism alone would not provide the necessary unity for a successful political crusade. Something more positive was required.[373] He devoted his newspaper to furthering the union of antisemitism and Christian religion, arguing that Christian institutions, religious ideals, and cultic practices were being threatened by Austrian Jewry. By using religion, the antisemitic artisans would obtain greater diversity of ideological support and new weaponry to defend their much abused economic status. Simple economic competition from Jewish merchants or artisans could be transformed, using Christian theology, into earth-shattering confrontations possessing a transcendent significance and involving the very existence of Christianity.

In Psenner's essays the Jews symbolized the ultimate principle of evil. Jewish "world domination" was evident in commerce, industry, banking, credit, and insurance. "Asiatic foreigners" now dwelled in villages and towns where a socially homogeneous population had once existed. Psenner seemed to object not so much to large corporations and capital structures in themselves as to the fact that they appeared in the guise of semitic *Grosskapital*. The ideal society was an organic one, dominated by Mittelstand occupational groups. Psenner recalled the balmy days of a past where there were no Jewish professors, when there was strict censorship of the press by the "Christian conservative state," when the youth were protected from "false doctrines," when state permission to marry was obligatory, and when the government protected artisans from "dirty competition."[374]

In March 1887 Psenner, together with a Viennese Catholic priest Adam Latschka, established the Christian Social Association in Alsergrund. Its first public meeting was held in April 1887. The association replaced the defunct *Reformverein* and rested on a gamble that antisemitic voters would tolerate Catholic priests as subleaders and agitators. The association soon established sections in each district in Vienna and by 1890 had recruited 1,300 members.[375] It resolved the structural problem of the old *Reformverein* by providing itself with a local anchorage in each district of the city. Prime emphasis was placed on encouraging artisans and shopkeepers to attend the meetings.

During the second meeting of the association (May 1887) Psenner gave a speech advocating confessional schools as a precondition for effective social reform. An uproar occurred when socialist workers who had found their way into the meeting replied to Psenner with cries of "those we don't need!" A master carpenter in the audience responded by regretting that the "familiar relations" of the patriarchal environment of pre-1848 Austria had disappeared. "Dirty competition" was undermining "honest labor." Following these comments, the leader of the workers asked Psenner for permission to speak. When Psenner refused to relinquish the podium, a near riot ensued between the masters and the socialist laborers.[376] The meeting was, in perspective, a microcosmic expression of the

hostile relationship between the anti-Liberal movement and Austrian Social Democracy. Less than two months after its establishment, the Christian Social Association had become a vehicle of class conflict.

The Christian Social Association served two purposes: it advanced the
idea and the practice of a coalition of clerical and antisemitic sentiment in
an anti-Schönerian mode; and it provided a useful city-wide organization
to replace the defunct *Reformverein* and to provide a political complement to the more oligarchical power represented by Schneider's *Gewerbegenossenschaftstag*. Psenner's efforts to interest artisans in religion were
moderately successful, at least in political externalities. Clerical agitators
such as the Jesuit Heinrich Abel soon began working in Vienna, supporting the quasi-missionary activity of the association.

Two questions must be asked about this clerical revival: Why would
religion appeal to the antisemitic leaders as an effective political tool to
win voter support? Also, what were the nature and the extent of this
popular religious response, assuming that there actually was some kind of
religious motivation aside from mere Jew hatred beneath the rubric
"Christian?" In the early 1880s most of the members of the *Reformverein*
were anticlerical. Pattai, for example, told Schneider in 1884 that he
feared that Psenner was diluting the antisemitism of the artisan movement
by introducing religion into its affairs.[377] Priests were associated with
"the Establishment" and, ironically, with economic Liberalism as well.
The passivity of the clergy in the 1870s exposed them to the charge, often
seen in the letters of Schneider to Vogelsang, that Catholic priests befriended influential Jews and other Liberals while refusing to involve
themselves in artisan economic problems.[378] The image of the Concordat
Church bore heavily on the clergy's professional reputation. Although the
antisemitic leaders detested "Jewish domination," they did not want to
replace it with a return to clerical omnipotence in public affairs. Great
efforts were made in the meetings of the Christian Social Association to
persuade the artisans of the sympathy for and interest in their cause on the
part of the clergy, subject to a prior declaration by the clerics involved
that they were in fact loyal antisemites.

This general fear of "clericalism" was gradually reduced by the Christian Socials in the 1890s and 1900s, by demonstrating that the traditional
cultural principles for which the Catholic Church stood were in harmony
with the mentality of the artisans, especially at a time when the Socialists
were enunciating their radical egalitarianism. This appeal depended on the
party's ability to use the Catholic clergy in a series of nondominant
agitatorial roles and on its distortion of the religious values of the Church
to serve the political purposes of the party machine. In the early 1880s,
however, the possibility that the clergy would willingly acquiesce in such

political dependence seemed unimaginable. The general cry of "clerical-ism" was sufficient to make strong men tremble, even if they were anti-semites. No greater tribute could have been paid to the vigor of Liberal sec-ularization than the fact that the principal enemies of the Liberal party feared a demonstrably Liberal image of "clericalism" in associating with the common clergy, their real political allies, for many years before 1914.

Religion thus served several functions in the antisemitic movement. One primary use was as a source of social solidarity and cultural com-panionship. Anticlericalism among the lower and middle strata of the Viennese Bürgertum predated the coming of the Liberal era in Austria. Before 1848 this anticlericalism was informal and unarticulated, reflecting the absence in Josephist ritual of appeals to emotion and spirit. The cul-tural world of Vormärz Vienna was not openly anticlerical, but it was secular and moral in a traditionalist way. Viennese Bürger society was rich in secular cultural attractions—the immensely popular *Vorstadt* theaters with their humorous and moralistic farces, for example—which compensated for the decline in spectacle and congregational cohesion wrought by the Josephist revolution in matters spiritual. To this traditionalist secular culture of the Vormärz, unreflective and almost anti-intellectual in ethos, the Liberal era brought a formidable barrage of openly anticlerical symbols, not the least of which was the new school system. Whether or not the schools performed their promised pedagogical accomplishments was irrelevant; as cultural symbols of a new order of life they were immensely powerful. The popular press of the 1860s and 1870s which cultivated Bürger readers, like the *Vorstadt-Zeitung* and the *Morgenpost,* was openly anticlerical, a posture reinforced by the new pseudo-Liberal humor magazines like *Kikeriki.* The Viennese popular novel after 1860 in the hands of men like Moritz Bermann and Heinrich Blechner assumed a similar anticlerical stance. Not only did popular liter-ature begin to censure the Church in more open and daring ways, but the secular morality of the older theater culture of the Vormärz eventually declined. This curious combination of more anticlericalism and less popular morality in the 1870s led to a reaction against the moral super-ficiality of Liberal literature in the later 1880s and early 1890s which found expression in new aesthetic modes stressing everything from social utopianism to Wagnerian social regeneration.

With the breakdown of the Liberal-Democratic political consensus in the later 1870s, moreover, the possibility of overturning popular anti-clericalism seemed to beckon. To the extent that the clergy could per-suade the artisans that their occupational decline was the result of not merely economic but also of cultural lawlessness, some sympathy might be stimulated for the Church. A questioning of Liberal economic norms might encourage a rejection of secular cultural norms as well. The Church could also exploit the popular theism which survived in spite of anti-clericalism in Viennese Bürger strata during the Liberal period. This theism, often expressed in a belief among middle-class Viennese in the *Herrgott,* had little to do with institutional Catholicism. It was a last vestige of popular religious culture transplanted to the middle and lower urban Bürgertum. The popular agitator Hermann Bielohlawek, a classic Christian Social self-made man who rose from a lowly *Handlungsgehilfen* status to political power and wealth, proudly proclaimed his belief in the providence of the divine Saviour, while insisting that the Roman Catholic Church in its organized, clerical sense had absolutely no control over his personal or professional life.[379] Karl Lueger was also a Bürger theist of this sort, believing in the providential protection afforded by the *Herrgott* to his city and his nation, but clearly distinguishing the actions of providence from those of Rome. Popular Bürger theism, often with vague Christological overtones, was equivalent to high Liberal beliefs in the providential power of Progress.

Although Vienna was in the midst of a demographic explosion throughout the century, the decades after 1861 were particularly unsettling for the lower and middle bourgeoisie. Statistics fail to convey the relative decline in social stability, specifically among lower-Bürger families (as opposed to the general population, which would include the Viennese working classes). Frequent loss of or change in residence was a crucial problem which afflicted lower artisan families, who were forced to stay one step ahead of the previous *Hausherr* to whom they owed rents.[380] There is little evidence to show a radical breakdown in formal family structure among the lower artisans. Most illegitimate children born in the city throughout the period came from the ranks of the proletariat, not the independent craftsmen of the lower Bürgertum. But cultural isolation in a large city with a tumultous and increasingly heterogeneous ethnic culture may have been all the greater for those who did affirm the values of a stable family. The classic ideal of the artisan was economic independence, but many felt that some kind of social hierarchy was both necessary and desirable if such economic independence was to be preserved. Hence the singular situation of artisans who refused to join cooperative societies for business purposes (which seemed to violate their independent status), but who were willing to join political clubs and attend meetings which emphasized paternalistic, hierarchical authority systems. What the workplace could no longer offer—cultural authority as well as social stability—new, external contexts would have to provide.

To the extent that the antisemitic coalition was able to entice the votes of higher strata within the Bürgertum, a different set of cultural and social preconditions applied, as they did with the voters of the First Curia. In these higher levels support for popular religion and histrionic antisemitism were less fervent and less necessary. The more rooted and stable the target group with which the Christian Socials had to deal, the more emphatically their propaganda concentrated on purely economic and technical-professional issues. *Hausherren* or *Bürgerschullehrer* of the First or Second Curia did not need symbols of patriarchal community or ways to reinforce their social integration as badly as did poorer artisan voters of the Third Curia.

The guild system was one effort to correct this troubled situation—to re-create the sense of social community with which the medieval guild had imbued its members while defending their economic individualism. Antisemitism, in contrast, was an essentially negative weapon. It was a cudgel against Jewish penetration of the city's economy, but could it offer social certitude and normative roots? Georg v Schönerer apparently thought not, since the pan-Germans used antisemitism after 1890 only in conjunction with the promise of a new Germanic culture and national state. Schönerer's ludicrous attempts to provide the months of the year with new, Germanic cultic names was, from a sociological viewpoint, a part of his campaign to demonstrate the fraternal elements of his new world view. Similarly, the corpus of Germanic myth brought forth during the *Los von Rom* crusade in Vienna was not simply anticlerical. Teutonic myth was to anchor the loyal pan-Germanist in a new normative and social system.

Religion was not the only alternative, but it was one possible answer. Many master craftsmen and most anti-Liberal white collar voters never seriously adopted an active interest in Christian religious beliefs or cultic practices even after 1889, relying instead on the vague theistic moralism which the Christian Social party sponsored in its propaganda and on the efficacy of secular occupational organizations, which also offered a way of belonging to a larger, corporate entity. For many antisemitic artisans the typical district political club with its histrionic speeches and good fellowship provided a form of cultic spectacle which lessened the personal isolation many felt in their individual lives.[381] The devotional social clubs dedicated to Lueger's personality, like the *Luegerbund* in 1894–95, served as secular counterparts to more explicitly religious institutions. Politics itself was the theater of the lesser and middle Bürgertum. The major manifestation of this new cultic politics came only after 1895 and did not thus contribute fundamentally to the initial successes of the party, but it served to foretell a major cultural development within the party after 1896.

For those who did assent to religious belief, however, a feeling of social unity was readily obtained. Franz Eichert, an antisemitic journalist and sometime railroad clerk who turned Catholic in the late 1880s, described the spirit of social cohesion which existed in meetings of Catholic voluntary associations in Vienna in the late 1880s, as if the joy of common struggle and the sense of unity was as important as the final goal of the organizations: "Almost every Catholic meeting which I attended at that time so energetically was a fiery furnace for the souls, from which a torrent of sparks and flames of holy enthusiasm was generated; a powerful forge, in which the armaments were hardened for a battle for the Cross, now threatened from all sides."[382]

One of the claims of the religiously oriented antisemites was that the union of religion and antisemitism filled the Catholic churches, encouraging attendance at Catholic rites by people who had never before interested themselves in Catholic cult and ritual.[383] This was undoubtedly true, since even the bishops noted in 1901 that in recent years church attendance had climbed dramatically.[384] It should be noted, however, that the motivations which led individuals back to the churches may not have always been religious in nature; many of the sermons given in Catholic services were so overtly political in their content that the line between cultic worship and political mobilization was frequently difficult to draw. Also, the phrase "filled the Catholic churches" is misleading, if taken literally and not metaphorically, since with the exception of the First District, Catholic churches were so few in number that only a small percentage of the adult population could possibly have been accommodated at any given time.

One of the most influential forms of religious celebration was the popular missions and pilgrimages organized by Heinrich Abel in the early 1890s combining frenzied revivalism and political demagogy.[385] Before 1867 the Imperial government's tight supervision of Catholic cult and the ritualistic conservatism of the Austrian episcopate prevented the Church from exploiting the popular mission as an instrument of mass clericalization. Not until well into the 1880s did isolated Catholic clerics (usually regular clerics) revive the practice of holding missions.

Abel's rallying cry was that used earlier by Schönerer ("Back to practical Christianity"). His sermons were litanies of traditionalist values— paternal authority, family prayer, obedience and submissiveness of children and wives, and the stability of the family.[386] One of the participants in Abel's crusades, Josef Leb, reported on the mood and motives of the men in Abel's audiences. The very language Leb used—Abel as the "father" of his "group of children"—revealed the need many of these men had for joining a hierarchical social group. Leb admitted that religion was not the only motive which led his companions to listen to Abel: "It is above all the spirit of a peaceful Christian family. There in Maria-Zell the unlimited admiration of the men for their fatherly leader revealed itself. Everyone wanted to greet him, to shake hands.'' The high point of the service was a night parade with each man carrying a candle, at the head of which was Abel, the father figure, the man one could trust.[387] That many of the lower clerics who propagated this kind of conservative familial hierarchism among the artisan masses were themselves highly dissatisfied with the paternal authority culture their bishops used against them was one of the contradictions which afflicted the Christian Social movement, giving it the half-modern, half-reactionary ethos it so successfully exploited.

The very catalog of sins against which Abel thundered—everything from marital infidelity to alcoholism—reflected a deeper quest for social order at a time when the secular promises of the nineteenth century seemed for many artisans to be socially barren and emotionally unacceptable. That Abel's crusades overlaid an enormous amount of ordinary human hypocrisy in his followers was inevitable.

Another social group which the purveyors of artisan political clericalization in Vienna tried to reach was that of the lower bourgeois female. Beginning in the early 1890s a series of Christian Family associations were organized in the various districts and parishes of the city.[388] The radical clergy were especially active in patronizing these clubs. Lueger hoped to use these clubs for pseudopolitical purposes, since he was convinced that artisans often listened to their wives before formulating their personal voting decisions.[389] Some leaders in the anti-Liberal movement sought to use Christian Social women's organizations in the *Kauft nur bei Christen* campaign against Jewish merchants. But for the women themselves social companionship and symbols stressing family solidarity and normative conservatism against the unseemly social doctrines of the Socialists were the crucial attractions. The history of the Christian Social women's movement properly belongs in the second volume of this study (which will deal with the period 1897–1920), since its major impact came after Lueger's political victories in 1895–96; but its origins lay in the formative years of the antisemitic movement.

Religion also opened organizational resources to the antisemitic leaders which they would have otherwise missed. The small parish associations devoted to a variety of pietistic purposes now became centers of agitation. More important, larger, city-wide Catholic associations, some with their own buildings, staff, and newspapers, such as the Catholic School Association, offered the antisemites more diverse opportunities to establish lines of communication with thousands of potential voters, as well as to recruit future party activists. All Catholic organizations, whether the small parish group, the local charitable association, the local women's society, or the suburban monastery, were targets for possible campaign contributions.

Throughout the religious history of the Christian Social movement there was also a strong note of bourgeois class opportunism which had, at best, a pseudoreligious facade. For example, artisan masters thought their apprentices should receive more religious instruction because it would encourage their discipline and keep them from the "Reds." It was Alois Liechtenstein's view that more religious instruction would increase the level of obedience in the population by means of "a tightening of loosened discipline."[390] The *Oesterreichischer Volksfreund* informed the farmers in the 1890 Landtag elections that religion was a useful tool in their role as budget-conscious employers:

> Peasants, remember one more thing: the men who accord no respect to Christianity are not the proper [workers]. When you have a laborer who is a good genuine Christian, he does his work orderly and conscientiously, energetically, loyally, and honestly, even if you are not standing behind him. On the other hand, if you have a worker who has abandoned his religion, as a rule he is the one who is not conscientious and not satisfied, and you cannot pay him enough. And even when you stand behind him, he does not perform what a genuine Christian does.[391]

With such efficacious results it was not surprising that many artisans and farmers, even if they were personally indifferent to religion, welcomed the addition of Christian theology and Catholic voluntary associations to their political party. Hierarchical paternalism, if no longer justified and sustained by natural social forces, might be artificially induced by legal and political means.

3

Catholic Politics in Vienna
The Radical Clergy and the Restoration of Mittelstand Society

The Viennese clergy were the first professional group to join the anti-semitic movement after 1886. Although artisan leaders like Schneider tried to convert the craft guilds into a base for antisemitism, the guilds alone would not suffice to provide the sub-elite leadership and associations necessary to revive Viennese antisemitism and make it a viable opponent of the Liberal party. The Liberal party had formidable resources at its command. Not only did it possess the practical things to win elections in Vienna—money, voluntary organizations, rally speakers with experience in facing crowds, local and municipal propaganda vehicles—but also it conveyed the image of a reliable, responsible party. As much as voters might repudiate specific Liberal policies, they did feel that the Liberals could manage city government in an orderly fashion. This sense of administrative responsibility was precisely what the antisemites lacked in 1886. They possessed a viable principle of political legitimacy (anti-semitism), but they lacked an ethos of stability to make their views acceptable to the more tradition-oriented voters in the electorate.

The lower clergy were useful to the antisemites in terms of technical resources and ideological conservatism. Not only were they to prove themselves adept at local, ward-level agitation, using the resources of their Catholic voluntary organizations and parishes to support the work of the secular political clubs and district committees of the Christian Social movement, but also they brought to antisemitism a much needed corrective to the nationalist radicalism of men like Schönerer. Though individual clerics might behave "radically," the very fact that they represented a large, conservative social institution—the Church—gave the movement a solidity it desperately needed. Behind the surface fears of "clericalism" in pan-German propaganda against the clergy was Schönerer's very real expectation that this group would help to moderate Viennese anti-semitism. Ironically, to prove their worthiness, individual clerics had to act in quite the opposite fashion, as the most aggressive and acerbic agitators in the antisemitic fold. But there was a distinction to be drawn between individual behavior and the broader impact of the clergy as a group. Joseph Scheicher, as a priest, was among the most radical of all antisemitic politicians, but in the long run his presence inevitably helped to turn the antisemitic movement into more conservative, *Hapsburg-treu* channels. The clerics were not the only conservative force of this kind (Lueger's Democratic movement and the property owners were ultimately of greater importance for the Christian Socials in this regard), but they were the first such group (1887) to assent clearly and openly to political antisemitism.

The clergy found strong support in their attempt to join radical politics in the persuasive journalism of Karl v Vogelsang. This pragmatic neo-Romantic made his most important contribution to the Catholic wing of the Christian Social movement by defending and legitimating the presence of the clergy as a social interest group within the party's elite and cadre structures.

Unlike the political Catholicism in Prussia, where the *Kulturkampf* and the more aggressive behavior of the German bishops gave the Church a tradition of independence and energy, modern political clericalism in Austria was effected in large part against the Austrian bishops. Antiepiscopalism was a central component of the Catholic side of the Christian Social movement. One priest, Joseph Scheicher, made a virtue of such antihierarchical rhetoric, using it to show that the clergy were "democratic" in an antiauthoritarian sense and thus not "clerical" as often defined. The difference between Germany and Austria can be explained in part by differing traditions of canon law, episcopal appointments, and internal organizational practice. Its origins are also deeply rooted within the special traditions of Austrian Josephist Catholicism as they defined the status and role behavior of the common cleric.

Ideals and Realities of the Clergy, 1780–1848

The modern history of the lower clergy in Austria begins in the 1750s and 1760s when reformers in Vienna demanded both an upgrading of clerical education and discipline and a more effective utility for the common clergy.[1] Education was the sector in which the state's new role for the clergy was most obvious. The reform of the Viennese Theological Faculty in 1774, the establishment of general seminaries in 1783, the limitation of the supervisory powers of the episcopate over seminarians and priests, and the willingness of the crown to tolerate Jansenistic, Febronian, and Protestant-reformist literature in lower clerical circles all characterized the state's patronage of the clergy as a distinctive subculture within the Church.[2] The state encouraged the development of a new curriculum of priestly education.[3] Antischolastic pastoralism; statist canon law; secular natural law; Church history in a critical, Protestant mode; historical dogmatics rather than formal dogmatic theology—these became the key elements of the new *cursus* of priestly training.

The educational ideals developed by Rautenstrauch and other Catholic reformers in the 1760s and 1770s, were, moreover, the harbinger of a new concept of the priest as a *pastor bonus* with powerful eudaemonistic, civic, and antihierarchical implications. The state allocated to the Catholic pastor and his assisting priests a series of secular responsibilities which would integrate the clergy into the nexus of civil society.[4] The state also guaranteed the legal rights of the clergy in case of disciplinary confrontations with their bishops. Just as the bishop was now liberated from the Curia, so too were the lower clergy brought under the protection of civil law.[5] The ambiguous position of the Josephist episcopate was evident in their being held accountable by the state for the effectiveness of their clergy, without having full control of the education or the secular behavior of the priests. As often happened, enlightened absolutism used the protective, liberating force of law to intervene in traditional, closed authority networks only to establish alternate systems of control and accountability in their place. The new "liberty" of the clergy was, in fact, a dual system of control by governmental and episcopal authority; since social opportunities often occurred in the 1780s in which the clergy could play the one side off against the other, this regime was not entirely unacceptable to many clerics.

After 1780 Joseph II completed the portrait of the reformed clergy by allocating to them important responsibilites in sponsoring his program of radical religious and cultural reforms, as well as serving the state in administrative and social welfare functions. In return the state established a system of income guarantees for the common clergy—the *Congrua* system—with which Joseph expected to eliminate the discrepancies in the lower clergy's livings.[6] For an elite few, cooperation went beyond pastoralism and offered opportunities for professional advancement. For all, the model of the *josefinischen Pfarrer* stressed the qualities which would have been admirable in any religious group. Self-discipline, asceticism, social service—it was to inculcate such ideals that the general seminaries were organized. The emperor thought of these institutions much less in terms of restricting the powers of the bishops (which they did) than in terms of his well-known demand for symmetry and system in the administration of the state's business. For Joseph II professional education was to be both a liberating and a disciplining experience. He wanted priests who, like his ideal bureaucrats, would not only know and respect the ideals of the state, but pursue these ideals without heavy governmental or episcopal direction.[7]

Joseph's dicta met with a mixed response from the clergy. Rarely did a lower cleric become wholly "Jansenist" or "Jesuit" in his behavior, as opposed to his opinions—the authority culture of the period was too subtle and too personalized to permit rigid public factions among the clergy. But there was evidence that large numbers of lower clerics in Vienna and elsewhere in the monarchy affirmed the ideal of *pastor bonus*.[8] Clerics became more interested in social ethics and civic morality than in devotions, rituals, or mysticism. For a half-century this anti-devotional, antiritualistic component remained a part of the clergy's mentality.[9]

In Vienna and in other dioceses significant numbers of young clerics cooperated with the emperor, even if in many cases they were more interested in the religious-ethical aspects of the reforms, as opposed to their purely political utility.[10] Cardinal Migazzi's effort to crush Ferdinand Stöger and other Catholic *Aufklärer* who tried to reconcile statist and reform Catholicism reflected his fear of losing control of his prerogatives over the clergy.[11] When Leopold II solicited the opinion of the Austrian episcopate in 1790–91, both Migazzi and Bishop Kerens complained about the arrogance and disrespect of younger clerics in their dioceses.[12]

Also present in the 1780s, if not before, was a movement of synodal thought. The bishops' complaints about the lack of discipline in the clergy were supplemented by their outrage at the popularity among certain clerics of the works of Edmund Richer and other French Jansenists advocating synodalism in the Church.[13] During the Josephist period this synodalism was covert (with the exception of the experimental synod held in Pistoia in 1786 under the patronage of Leopold of Tuscany).[14] The latent synodalism of the late eighteenth century was to play, however, a vigorous and enduring role in the later self-conceptions of Austrian clerics in the nineteenth century.[15]

The Josephist ideal of the priest as a self-sustaining agent of civil and moral administration created a revolutionary tradition in Austrian ecclesiastical history. It provided the lower clergy with a visible identity and a powerful rationale. The prime concerns of the cleric were social morality and rationality, and divine observance. Each was supportive of the other. The symbiosis between the state Church and the internal Catholic reform movement was sufficiently attractive in the 1780s and the 1790s to make clerics accept the burden of the state in order to enhance their personal and professional interests, including a relatively free intellectual development. The combination of state support and professional reform became a classic feature of the Josephist compromise with the eighteenth-century lower clergy.[16] The new ideal of the *pastor bonus* in Austria was approved not by a revolutionary but by a conservative-absolutist tradition. As long as the basic terms of the compromise could be sustained, as long as the clergy derived some satisfaction from their association with the state, there was little reason to reject the integration supported by the state.

After the death of Joseph in 1790 and the interlude of his brother Leopold (1790–92), the situation of the clergy changed along subtle, yet decisive lines.[17] Even under Joseph the ideal of the civically interested cleric was ambiguous. The ideal prescribed the role of social and civil educator as a predominant one, but it is clear that the emperor conceived of the role in terms of the narrow conception of "rights" with which he approached Austrian civil society. The state would educate its citizens in all of the rights conducive to tolerant, rational, and productive behavior, but it would do nothing more. In this mode of passive, directed liberty, the clergy came very close to being assigned positions which were almost disciplinary and certainly regulatory toward Austrian society. The model was such that the clergy's supervisory and pedagogical powers could be misused for conservative goals without the potential force of the model itself being obviated. The state, in other words, might shift its own priorities from encouraging civic autonomy and social rationality to social regulation and repression of the citizenry and expect that the lower clergy would follow it.

The Franciscan regime did not abandon the ideal of the Josephist priest, but converted it into a more conservative instrument of state policy.[18] Especially after 1800 the state adopted what Eduard Winter has called an "Austrian restaurationist" mentality, involving a series of changes designed to preserve the statism of the Josephist Church but insisting upon a more conservative ideological orientation.[19] Given that this process enhanced the local jurisdictional powers of the bishops, it was not surprising that the state curtailed the support it had accorded the lower clergy before 1790. The state now committed the lower clergy to a negative, repressive role toward Austrian society and placed the clergy in an ambivalent situation not only toward state power, but toward itself as a professional group. In the eighteenth century state power was used to consecrate and legitimize the clergy *in* lay society; now it was aligning the clergy with its own power *against* lay society.

The state still viewed the clergy as agents for *Staatspolizei,* but now the concept received a narrower, more exclusively coercive meaning. Priests were expected to supervise public discipline and religious morality, without demonstrating the eudaemonistic, libertarian individualism which was a part of the original image of the *pastor bonus.* The state's regulation of

Church affairs remained unimpeded throughout the Vormärz. In the hands of Josephist administrators like Martin Lorenz and Joseph Jüstel (both of whom were clerics) state policy toward the Church gradually accepted conservative ideological claims without sacrificing state power to the Curia in Rome. The advocates of a more ultramontane restoration in Austrian Catholicism were never satisfied with this arrangement, but most of the episcopate loyally supported it.[20] As Eduard Winter has noted, the episcopate's treatment of Michael Fesl after his condemnation in 1820–24 was far more harsh than that meted out by the state.[21] After 1792 the state retained control of cult and ritual, but it did eliminate the blatant sources of tension between the traditionalists and the clerics. By 1800–10 in most areas of the monarchy the religious situation had stabilized.[22] The government discouraged attempts to develop Catholic associations, but Joseph's extreme iconoclasm was rescinded.[23] The Vormärz thus initiated a new version of the Josephist compromise. The original promise of the 1780s—that of the *pastor bonus* leading his flock to a better world of civic morality, tolerance, and Christian virtue—was more limited in the Vormärz. The state replaced the original Josephist vision of the rational integration of the clergy into society with a more limited assignment emphasizing social conformity and discipline.

The reaction of most clerics was to accept the new status quo.[24] Rather than dynamism and self-initiative, humility was the quality expected of the Vormärz cleric in the performance of *Dienst*. For most clerics the conditions of life in the Vormärz, while not ideal, were tolerable. The Church was protected by the state, and its seminaries were filled with Josephist-minded professors, many of whom had learned the ideal of Josephist *Pfarrer* in the period 1780–1800.

In urban areas especially, the secularization of culture continued and increased as the century wore on.[25] Traditional clerical historians have blamed the de-religiosity of the Austrian Bürgertum in the Vormärz on the prevalence of dull and banal Josephist religious practices which alienated some and bored others. Doubtless such criticism had some truth, although secularization was not simply the result of the old Josephist prayer books.[26] The Church itself in an institutional and hierarchical sense became an easily accessible symbol of the rigid, seemingly stagnating state.

Against the loss of active support for the clergy in urban areas were two important trends which continued to make the symbiotic relation of the clergy with the state rewarding. Contemporary reports show that, for rural areas, the clergy retained public respect and influence down to 1848.[27] This was not merely owing to the traditionalism of the Austrian peasant; the Austrian peasant community, unlike the Prussian, was not set in a process of revolutionary agrarian upheaval after 1815. Since many rural communities remained stable (if impoverished) in the Vormärz, it was not surprising that the local priest still enjoyed his prerogatives in the village. More important, the state ensured that the clergy did enjoy a minimal level of public respect, even if that respect was one which simply masked indifference.[28] There was no public politics in Austria before 1848, but by enhancing the clergy's right to supervise the school system (the 1804 Schools Edict) and by confirming its involvement in charitable administration, the state shared its formal administrative "politics" with the Church.

The apparent lassitude of the lower clergy began to change after 1820. Clemens Maria Hofbauer, a Redemptorist priest with an emotional style of neo-Baroque preaching, introduced a nonrationalist approach to Christian piety and religion.[29] Hofbauer's contribution to Austrian ecclesiastical history was more exemplary than substantive. Although he offered Viennese society a Romantic alternative to the aesthetics of the Austrian Catholic Enlightenment, the actual impact of his pietism was limited. Hofbauer's stress on the spoken word to educate the masses was a continuation of a Josephist tradition, although the sermon itself might change radically. More important was his personal influence on a number of talented men who came to view Catholicism as a religious vocation, including Joseph v Rauscher, Anton Günther, and Johann Emanuel Veith. Hofbauer's order never received the cooperation from the secular clergy it would have needed to pursue its mass catechetical work effectively.[30] This in itself testified to the strength of Josephist piety in the Vormärz clergy.

After Hofbauer's death in 1820 three circles of lower clerics pursued the tradition of lower clerical activism established during the Enlightenment, but with radically different implications. Those around Bernard Bolzano in northern Bohemia and Anton Günther in Vienna became the center points of influential theological movements in Central European Catholicism. The third, best represented by Joseph v Rauscher, was a more diverse tradition closer to Hofbauer's original values which became the seedbed for the reconciliation between the Josephist episcopate and curial authority. This third tradition served as the basis for the Concordat of 1855.

The most notable continuation of the rationalist eudaemonism of the Josephist clergy was represented by the Bolzano circle in Bohemia.[31] Bolzano was a religious philosopher at the University of Prague with deep roots in eighteenth-century rationalism. His unique integration of Leibnizian monism and Platonic realism as the basis for a eudaemonistic view of religion led to his persecution by ultramontane and conservative statist forces in 1819–20 and to his dismissal from his university post in 1820. The Church, for Bolzano, was a brotherly community devoted primarily to social ethics. Bolzano deemphasized both the institutional and the sacramental aspects of Catholicism, concentrating on man as a part of a cosmos of ideal ethical behavior.[32] Ethics were not merely a part of religion; to a great extent they were the essence of religion. Bolzano's political views made the collectivist implications of his ethical theory explicit. Influenced by Rousseau and Saint-Simon, Bolzano developed a utopian system for the "best state" which combined social egalitarianism (redistribution of property by the state to achieve social harmony) with a regulating and directing state administrative power.[33] Bolzano refused to publish the work setting forth this system, fearing that it would be misused by the Democrats and Liberals of 1848, whom he distrusted. In their politics the Bolzanoists reaffirmed the rationality of an enlightened, bureaucratic state with quasi-absolutist powers, if only because they were unable to distinguish between politics and ethics, on the one hand, and the individual and the state, on the other, as separate spheres of action and of rights. As William Johnston has observed, this system was so intent on the ideal good of all it was inevitably led into a quietistic acceptance of each of the parts of the existing society.[34] In its social ideals Bolzano's *Vom besten Staate* would not have been entirely unacceptable to Joseph II.

As a teacher in Bohemia Bolzano had a valuable, if limited, effect on the history of the Bohemian clergy. Bolzano showed that it was not necessary to consign the Josephist vision of the priest to the rubbish heap of history. Bolzano's most notable disciple, Michael Fesl, a professor of biblical studies in Leitmeritz until 1820, tried to implement some of Bolzano's notions in ways that did not observe the caution of his master.[35] In 1816 Fesl organized a *Christenbund* among his seminary students, a relatively harmless secret society aimed at enhancing the effectiveness and morale of younger clerics in his diocese.[36] For this "revolutionary" activity with a Josephist ideological bent (Fesl's sermons on the ideal cleric were sharply reminiscent of the neo-Jansenism of the 1780s), he was placed under arrest in 1820, deprived of his teaching position, and forced to repudiate his affiliations with Bolzano in 1824.[37]

Fesl's imprisonment, the resignation of Bishop Hurdálek of Leitmeritz for his reformist sympathies, and the firing of Bolzano and others from university posts did not end, however, Bolzano's influence among the Bohemian clergy. Several of his own students or students of Fesl later managed to achieve important ecclesiastical positions. More important, members of the Imperial bureaucracy and the Bohemian nobility, for very different motives, offered some Bolzanoists positions of minor pedagogical influence throughout the Vormärz.[38]

A second group of clerics who reaffirmed the ideal of an independent nexus of lower clerical rights and responsibilities was the small circle around Anton Günther in Vienna.[39] Günther was both a former student of Bolzano and a man initially attracted to the piety of Hofbauer.[40] His originality of mind led him to create another option for the Austrian Church, one which remained Romantic in its personalism, subjectivism, and organicism, but which also posited a rational philosophical framework for Christian belief and action. Günther was a dualist who sought to overcome the dominance of idealist pantheism in early-nineteenth-century philosophy by postulating the existence of two realms of being in which man stood simultaneously.[41] Man was a creature of nature and spirit, of freedom and necessity, of self-conscious thought and nature-oriented, logical abstraction. For Günther salvation began not with God but, in epistemological terms, with man. Revelation could only assist the individual once he had realized his own spiritual, anthropological being. Man was thus an imperfect organic unity of nature and spirit who looked to Christ as the model as well as the initiator of his perfection. Man was a being of perfect freedom and imperfect necessity. The semirational anthropocentrism in Günther's thought was not identical with the man-oriented Christology of the Enlightenment, but both traditions placed a high valuation on man's rational integrity in society.[42]

The Church for Günther expressed the historical process of salvation. In contrast to Bolzano, Günther's Church had powerful sacramental components oriented toward knowledge of God and ethical service for man.[43] Man enjoyed a double sovereignty: his integrity as a creature of spirit and nature and his freedom as a part of the perfect spirit standing beyond material necessity. Man was both a free individual with rights in this world and a free spiritual being with dignity beyond this world.

This dualism implied, not surprisingly, a different kind of relationship between citizen and state on one hand, and Church and state on the other. Günther and most of his disciples rejected the absolute bureaucratic state and favored a moderate constitutional monarchy in which individual freedom and some degree of active individual political participation would be allowed.[44] More important, because Günther's conception distinguished between the Church as the union of all individual spirits with Christ and civil society, he was less inclined to accept state control over the Church than was Bolzano.[45] Günther proposed a political system in which the Church would work as a free agent, not subject to the state's political goals or motives. He did not want to diminish the influence of the Church; but the relationship between a state set free of political repression and a church seeking to maximize its own advantage without the power of law needed greater clarification.

Günther's dualism also led him to reject Bolzano's utopian communist proposals. Communism denied the inherent inequality in man's nature. Thus, the Güntherian position was one which, theoretically, was not uncongenial to a Liberal bourgeois movement.

Günther's work in Vienna in the 1830s and 1840s attracted numerous friends, some of whom met in small discussion circles to exchange ideas. Among the most important was Johann Emanuel Veith, a former protégé of Hofbauer who had left the Redemptorists. Veith favored abandoning the mass catechetical approach of Hofbauer and concentrating on spreading Catholic doctrine among the elite sectors of society.[46] In this intellectualism he found a firm supporter in Günther, who decried the low level of education among both the clergy and the Austrian Bürgertum. Veith took from Hofbauer, however, a commitment which all of the Güntherian priests shared, that of the responsibility of the clergy for public moral instruction.[47] Most of the Güntherian priests were excellent preachers, a fact that became obvious in 1848. Veith was the most famous preacher of his day. If the Bolzanoists sustained the Enlightenment ideal of the priest as activist in ethical-social service, the Güntherians reaffirmed the ideal of the lower cleric as a public educator through the spoken word. The Güntherians' formulation of this responsibility in a more elite, philsophical sense reflected the new speculative environment of early-nineteenth-century German culture. They abridged the universal duty of the ideal cleric by defining his audience in more exclusive terms. In contrast, the lower clerics of the late nineteenth century limited the ideal of Josephist universalism in an opposite sense by adapting it to the needs of social-class politics.

One disciple of Günther, Sebastian Brunner, demonstrated that it was possible to combine features of the Austrian ultramontane-restaurationist mentality with elements of Günther's theological system. Brunner was a crude, but effective propagandist with strong Romantic aesthetic interests. As a young priest in the later 1830s and early 1840s he was greatly influenced by the work of Joseph Görres in Munich and by the vigor of the Rhenish Catholic Church in the Cologne mixed marriage affair.[48] His world was as much that of Jarcke and Metternich as it was that of Günther and Veith—although Brunner became a deadly foe of the Josephist domination of the Church, he did not want to set the Church free in a competitive, secular environment. Rather, with some allowance for clerical synodalism, his political program was not greatly different from that of Joseph Rauscher, namely, the maintenance of the monarchy which would voluntarily permit the dominance of the Church over the state (using state power to enforce monistic cultural norms). Both Günther and Brunner found a protégé later in the nineteenth century in Joseph Scheicher, the most influential of the radical antisemitic clerics.

By 1848 there were three distinct ways for the Austrian clergy to view themselves as a social and cultural group. In the vision of Bolzano, they would accept state control of the Church, while hoping for an internal democratization of the Church and a more enlightened policy of social service for the Church in society. In the Güntherian option, the Church would reduce (but not end) its ties to the state and compete with other cultural forces in a moderate constitutional polity. Finally, in the view of Rauscher, Madlener, and Brunner, the state would relinquish to the Church its authoritarian powers, allowing greater internal freedom for the Church, but not necessarily for civil society.

Each of these options was little more than a cluster of small-group attitudes. Especially for the Güntherians there was little that could be called coherent political philosophy before 1848. In view of the particularized, fragmented nature of Vormärz culture, it was inevitable that the behavior of these clerics was highly sectarian and exclusivist. Günther and Veith's fascination with the trappings of order life did not end once they became diocesan clerics.[49] Their introverted and intellectualist exclusivity, which often denigrated the educational background of their fellow priests, stood in stark contrast to the more collectivist attitudes of the radical clerics at the end of the century.

When the Revolution of 1848 broke out, both the Güntherians and the Bolzanoists reacted to the challenges it presented with programs which revived Josephist claims about the responsibilities and rights of the lower-order clergy.[50] Both groups of priests formulated programs for the reform of the Church's internal structure along the more synodal, presbyterial lines, which not only recalled the clerical ideals of the late eighteenth century, but went far beyond them.

In Vienna the revolution brought forth a wave of crude anticlerical protest. After Archbishop Milde fled Vienna during the first week of April, the lower clergy were left to their own devices. Before departing Milde had ordered his clergy to refrain from politics and to confine themselves to pastoral activities.[51] One of Günther's disciples, Johann Michael Häusle, a lower cleric who worked as a *Hofkaplan*, wrote a pseudoanonymous pamphlet attacking Milde's conservatism and demanding that the archbishop recognize that his priests were citizens as well as clerics.[52] Milde's intransigence was more extreme than that of some other members of the Austrian episcopate, such as Friedrich Schwarzenberg in Salzburg, but it did reflect the uncertainty of all the bishops in the face of radical political change.[53] Until the autumn of the year, when the Austrian episcopate tried to prevent a loss of privileges for the Church in the Reichstag, the record of the Austrian bishops was uninspiring.[54] They never made a coordinated response similar to that of the German episcopate.[55]

In mid-April several priests from the Günther circle began to organize their colleagues in a program of self-help. Sebastian Brunner published the first issue of his *Wiener Kirchen-Zeitung,* which became an influential local Catholic newspaper during the revolutionary year. But the major step toward clerical defense was taken by another student of Günther, Wilhelm Gärtner, the preacher of the University Church.[56] Gärtner summoned a meeting of the clergy on 17 April. The seventy priests who appeared at the meeting authorized a delegation including Häusle, Brunner, and Gärtner to submit a petition to the archbishop urging that the clergy be permitted to defend themselves and to seek greater independence from the new revolutionary regime.[57] This led to an unpleasant confrontation between the clerics and Milde on 18 April. Milde refused to respond to the priest's petition, and when the clerics tried to summon another meeting of their group the archbishop prohibited any further gatherings. An attempt in May by over a hundred priests to obtain Milde's permission to organize reading and discussion circles also met with a flat refusal.[58] Beyond issuing one petition to the provisional government and another to the citizens of the city requesting freedom and protection for the Church, the attempt of the clergy to create a semi-independent nexus of authority was a total failure. A few priests ventured into politics— Häusle served on the Viennese City Council—and a few others became involved in minor journalistic endeavors, but Milde had effectively curbed the clerical dissent by the summer of 1848.[59]

There was little consensus among the priests involved in the events of April and May about the aims of their movement other than to defend themselves against street corner anticlericalism and to enhance their pastoral effectiveness in the chaos of the revolution. Disagreements soon occurred over the prudence of challenging the archbishop in the manner Häusle and Gärtner had done.[60] Even so, Milde's inflexibility and the absence of organizational opportunities led to a verbal backlash. Sebastian Brunner published a series of articles in the *Kirchen-Zeitung* proposing diocesan synods in which the lower clergy would have rights of expression and deliberation in running the affairs of the diocese. Priests from St. Pölten, the neighboring diocese in Lower Austria, organized similar lists of claims and desiderata.[61] Other members of the Güntherian circle suggested that the clergy deserved greater jurisdictional prerogatives, including pastoral conferences, elections for ecclesiastical appointments, synodal opportunities, and greater disciplinary protection against the episcopate. These complaints were the result of frustration, but they also had two other sources. The clergy began to internalize the political rhetoric of 1848 and to transform it into ecclesiastical terms. Given the confused nature of secular democratic rhetoric in 1848, it was not surprising that the clergy's proposals for Church power became more diffuse as the year went on. More important, the Güntherians' desire for a more democratic Church made sense only in terms of their perception of their own continuity with older Josephist traditions. It was not accidental that Wilhelm Gärtner, a principal organizer of the 17 April assembly, was not only a friend of Günther, but a protégé of Bolzano and Fesl as well.[62] Both Bolzano and Fesl warmly supported the work of the Viennese clergy, seeing it as an expression of the dignity of lower-order clerics in the neo-Josephist tradition. Moreover, the plans of the Güntherians were closely related to their view of the cleric as a public educator of civil morality. Häusle, Gärtner, Veith, Günther, and the other clerics who committed themselves to the revolutionary cause were all imbued with this ideal.

The lower clergy also sought to organize themselves in Prague.[63] Franz Náhlovský, the rector of the Wendish seminary in Prague and a former student of Bolzano, summoned a meeting of common clerics on 18 May to discuss their situation. Náhlovský was far more extreme in his presbyterial and synodal arguments than anyone in Vienna. He not only demanded synodal rights for the clergy, but attacked the hierarchical power of the papacy, insisting that the revolutionary year would end with the victory of conciliar thought against curial ultramontanism in Rome. He also called for drastic liturgical reforms, for an end to celibacy, and for a redistribution of clerical income between wealthy episcopal sees and impoverished local parishes. The social egalitarian component in Náhlovský's thought was a feature which more socially conservative Güntherians in Vienna found difficult to accept.

For all of their dissimilarities, however, the clerics of Vienna and Prague had a common heritage in struggling to create more democratic authority structures for the Church. Both were operating in a tradition of *pastor bonus* which had survived for sixty years in the work of men like Bolzano and Günther. That their movement failed reflected continued dominance of the episcopate over the clergy—a testimony to the effective legitimacy of the Austrian Josephist episcopate until after *its* catastrophe in 1867–70. Also, the radicals were unable to persuade many lower clerics to join them. Even in Vienna many lower clerics remained neutral or became indifferent as the year passed.[64] The events of 1848 occurred too rapidly for many priests, and the chaos which ensued was hardly a proper atmosphere for a program of self-help. To act against the episcopate was to act against the state, and until the coming of the Liberal era, the state was the traditional patron of the clergy. The symbiosis of person and state which played such a central role in the Enlightenment and Vormärz versions of the clerical ideal did not magically disappear overnight.

The problem of an audience for Christianity beyond the state led several Güntherian priests in Vienna to attempt what one historian has called Vienna's "first political Catholic movement." Because the Güntherians could differentiate between individual and polity more effectively than the Bolzanoists, they tried to convert their uncertain rejection of the absolute state into a source of popular support. In May 1848 a group of clerics and laymen, several of whom were converts from Judaism, met to organize the *Katholikenverein für Glaube, Freiheit, und Gesittung.*[65] The principal leader of the Catholic Association was Veith, who saw the association and its journal, *Aufwärts*, as a way to restore the prestige of the Church in Vienna. The association was not a political party—Veith explicitly rejected such an idea. Rather, it was an educational vehicle for Catholic values which, Veith believed, were compatible with the more moderate, Liberal ideals of the revolution. Günther refused to involve himself in the organizational affairs of the association, but contributed essays to its journal. In spite of its initial enthusiasm, however, the *Verein* made a poor showing in the city at large. By October 1848 the *Verein* claimed to have 2,000 members, but this figure was doubtless as exaggerated as were most of the statistics for political clubs in Vienna in 1848. Beyond its small social gatherings it had little impact. Four Güntherians, out of 120 men, were elected to the City Council in the October 1848 elections, hardly an impressive showing. Veith became embittered over the lack of support shown by other leaders of the *Verein*, such as Häusle, who thought that Veith's *Aufwärts* was too intellectualist to appeal to the simple Bürger types on whom the *Verein* would necessarily depend for its support. Veith, in turn, spoke deprecatingly of these "low-brow" readers, preferring to concentrate the *Verein*'s attention on the higher sectors of Viennese society.[66]

The real shortcoming of the *Verein* lay in its inability to appeal to a wide spectrum of social opinion in the Bürgertum on explicitly social terms. It had, for all practical purposes, no political program other than recruiting support for the Church. Its leadership structure was so ill organized that it accomplished little. Günther, always the academic critic, refused to involve himself in the trivial and boring work of associational planning. The central action of the *Verein* was essentially negative: the leaders of the association, especially the clerics, spent most of their time in the later months of the revolution conducting a vigorous propaganda campaign against the German Catholic movement in Vienna.[67]

The *Katholikenverein* survived the occupation of the city, but its days were numbered once Archbishop Milde returned. Milde was completely opposed to the idea of an independent Catholic associational system. He allowed the *Verein* to continue, but under a revised statute which emphasized devotion and piety as its aims. In 1852 its name was changed to the *Severinus Verein* and it became one of the small, nondescript devotional groups which marked Viennese Catholicism before 1887.[68] During the course of 1850–51 most of the original Güntherian adherents of the association, like Veith and Ludwig Croy, resigned from the *Verein* and from its newspaper. Veith was so embittered by the hostile treatment accorded him by the archdiocese that he left the city for Prague.[69] Güntherian clerics met with outright enmity from Milde and (after 1852) from Milde's successor, Rauscher.[70] Sebastian Brunner, always the opportunist, eventually ended his pleas for synods. In Bohemia, with the death of Bolzano in 1848 and the dispersion of many of his disciples and with the onset of neoscholasticism as a powerful rival in training the clergy, the formal coherence of the Bolzanoist group was destroyed.

With the ascendancy of Joseph v Rauscher the Church inaugurated a new strategy in church-state relations. As archbishop of Vienna, Rauscher ruthlessly isolated the remaining Güntherians in the city. By 1853 he moved to secure Günther's condemnation in Rome for theological and Church-political reasons. Not only was Günther's philosophy adamantly antischolastic, but Rauscher's fear of the "agitation for a constitutional church government" made it doubly necessary to obtain Rome's repression of Günther in 1857.[71]

Under neo-absolutism there was no place for Güntherian or Bolzanoist lower clerical independence. Perhaps even more than for the Liberals and Democrats of 1848, the revolutionary year ended on a note of degradation and despair for the clergy. The next two generations of lower clerics would use the ideals of the reformers of 1848, but within a radically different social context and with a very different perception of the nature of the Catholic priesthood.

Neo-Absolutism and the Liberal Challenge

The crushing of the lower clerics in 1848 and the victory of the episcopate's Concordat mentality represented a crucial turning point in the history of the Austrian clergy. The defense of progressive ideals which might have restored to the clergy their original universalist role of the *pastor bonus* had failed miserably. The signing of the Concordat, and its subsequent collapse under the pressure of Liberal constitutionalism, was a threshold from which there was no turning back. The episcopate gambled with the fortunes of the Church as an institution and the clergy as a professional group. The result was humiliation and failure.

After 1867 the lower clergy faced a secular political regime which no longer pretended to affirm the older eighteenth-century or newer Vormärz versions of the Josephist compromise. It offered no *political* guarantee of the service mentality of the clergy; it even allowed its press to denigrate the very terms of that mentality. The Liberals saw no value in the compulsory, artificial integration of the clergy into society. The more radical Liberals would have preferred that the clergy remain socially isolated. For clerics who did resist the new state's authority there was only humiliation and disgrace. The example of Bishop Rudigier in Linz was at most bittersweet—Rudigier became a hero, but his opposition to the regime was ineffective and degrading.

Liberal culture in Vienna and in the smaller towns and markets of Lower Austria devastated the tolerance and respect the clergy had formerly enjoyed. In Vienna the Liberal newspapers deflated clerical prestige. Austrian Liberalism was closer to its French than its German cousins in that the Austrian Liberals had utterly no rivals for respectability. Everyone in urban Austria suddenly became "Liberal" after forty years of nonpolitical behavior. The more isolated status of German Catholics in a nation whose majority was Protestant found no parallel in Austria. In a country where everyone was nominally Catholic, Catholicism became a subject of personal indifference. The religious sentiment among the urban Bürgertum which endured the Vormärz and the neo-absolutist periods had, by the 1860s, leveled off into a diffuse, vulgar theism which applauded the *Herrgott* while denigrating the clergy. Bürger theism in Vienna after 1860 set popular religion against the Church in a way which minimized the utility of the clergy as a professional group. The Liberal press took special pains to hold up to public ridicule the *Pfaffen* who tried to run other people's lives while being unable to control their own.

The secularism of the 1860s had an immediate effect on the recruitment of the clergy. The new network of secular *Mittelschulen* established in the 1850s and 1860s reduced the numbers of young men entering Catholic seminaries. Beginning in the 1860s enrollment in most seminaries in Austria suffered a steady decline.[72] By 1875 there were only 179 students in the first academic year of the eighteen diocesan seminaries of Cisleithanian Austria. Anton Erdinger, the director of the seminary in St. Pölten, noted in 1876 that Bürger families in his diocese, formerly the source of most candidates for the priesthood, now considered "the clerical garb to be a disgrace, which is now thought of as a symbol of personal stupidity and a plot to encourage public ignorance."[73] The new normal schools for public school teachers also drained off many young men of lower or middle bourgeois status. The intense hostility between teachers and clerics in Austria after 1867 must be understood in the context of the *similarity* of their social backgrounds.

The renewal of the free *Gemeinde* structure gave the Liberal movement the opportunity to establish a rival system of local elites who were jealous of the clergy. The *Gemeinde* became the agent for enforcing Liberal anti-clericalism, more so than Liberal legal activities on the national level.[74] For the local notables who affirmed the urban corporatism of Austrian Liberalism, ultramontanism was not merely attacking Josephist absolutism. It was also creating a rival system of corporate power, much more dangerous than neo-absolutism, since it competed within the city rather than dominating it from above. Local Liberals fought the Church not only because of its distinctiveness from Liberal thought, but also because of its similarities with it.

The challenge which the clergy faced after 1867, therefore, was to move beyond the boundaries of the ideal of the universal *pastor bonus* and to apply a new, radicalized self-concept to a new path of social integration, one of an essentially antistatist, party-political mode. Yet, only in the context of the collective memory of the Josephist ideal could the late-nineteenth-century clerics proceed. They were men about to re-create their history by escaping from it.

The Occupational Revival of the 1880s

The 1870s were not without some clerical responses to the problem of Liberal hegemony. In 1869 a group of clerics organized an association of priests in Vienna, the *Associatio perseverantiae sacerdotalis,* emulating an idea of pietistic associationalism which began in France in the 1860s.[75] By 1880 the organization had over 500 members, but it was controlled by higher officials of the archdiocese associated with Cardinal Rauscher. Its liturgical functions had little impact on the clergy. The Viennese clergy never overcame the deficit in popular organization caused by Rauscher's insistence on purely pietistic and devotional associations in the 1850s. Johann Veith's description of Rauscher's *Severinus Verein* in 1858 as the center point of "an arrogant pietism draped with ignorance" was only too true.[76]

In the diocese of St. Pölten a small Catholic political revival occurred in the mid-1870s, largely because of the single-handed leadership of a young Catholic cleric, Joseph Scheicher, who started a meager associational movement (a few casinos, a constitutional *Verein,* etc.).[77] Even here the results were very discouraging. Scheicher met with opposition from his bishop, from many of his clerical colleagues, and from apathetic peasants disinterested in politics. By 1879 most of the seats in the Lower Austrian Reichsrat delegation and all the seats from the smaller towns and markets were still held by the Liberal party.

In Bohemia, especially in the diocese of Leitmeritz, where the tradition of clerical activism went back deep into the Vormärz, isolated clerics like Ambros Opitz with his *Nordböhmisches Volksblatt* waged a vigorous, if very lonely, war against Liberal politics and culture.[78] The Bohemian Church, closer as it was to Germany and more directly confronted by rapid social and ethnic change than other areas of the monarchy, was extremely sensitive to Bismarck's attack on Prussian Catholicism. Opitz became a ferocious opponent of the Old Catholic movement in Bohemia, anticipating the conservatism combined with actional vitalism which marked late-nineteenth-century Austrian clerical culture.

But such stirrings of clerical protest were ultimately as fruitless as those of the Güntherian circle in Vienna in 1848. The clergy had as yet no sense of itself as a modern, collective occupational group, and it had not yet discovered a bourgeois *social* role by which it could reestablish its cultural influence. Güntherian intellectual exclusivity was being replaced by anti-Liberal religious protest. Each was ultimately unworkable. What was needed was a broader social constituency in a new group *élan* to mobilize the clergy into acting on its own behalf.

In the early 1880s the passivity of the Austrian clergy was challenged by a group of energetic clerics in Vienna who organized the *Correspondenzblatt für den katholischen Clerus Österreichs*. The *Correspondenzblatt* was the first significant newspaper devoted exclusively to the interests of the Austrian clergy. The paper was a *novum* in Catholic journalism since it was financed by subscriptions and advertising income, without the subsidies from aristocratic sources on which other Catholic journals depended. By 1888 the paper had collected nearly 7,000 subscriptions, a remarkable success in a decade when most Catholic newspapers barely survived.[79] The *Correspondenzblatt* was the first "self-help" model for dissenting Catholic journalism, one which was emulated a decade later by the Christian Social *Reichspost*.

Priests of all age levels supported the *Correspondenzblatt*, but the paper's major audience was the priests trained in the 1860s and 1870s and the seminarians of the 1880s. The paper recruited most of its writers from these generational groups, priests for whom the philosophical disputes of the Vormärz were either unknown or an impersonal myth. The paper reflected the anxieties of younger clerics who lived through the failure of the Concordat or who were trained in the 1870s and who felt disgust with the collapse of the Church.

The men who formed the cadres of radical priests after 1885 were also the products of post-Concordat seminaries, where for the first time in a century alternative views of Church-state relations were openly discussed and where the new facade of neoscholasticism discouraged the kind of vigorous, hothouse philosophizing of the 1820s and 1830s.[80] These clerics were forced to come to terms with the condemnation of Günther and the eclipse of Bolzano. Perhaps, in retrospect, they were better for it, since the sectarian exclusivity which hindered the effectiveness of the Güntherians and Bolzanoists was not a problem for the radical clerics of the later nineteenth century. As in France, after the second great wave of anticlerical legislation in 1900–1905 the Austrian Catholic Church was now thrown back on its own resources with less public power at its disposal, but with more discretion in ordering its internal affairs.

At the same time these clerics profited from the social dynamism and organizational flexibility which the Liberal age brought to Austrian society. By its vigorous press, by its reduction of state censorship, by its political sponsorship of the middle levels of the Austrian Bürgertum, the Liberal movement offered younger clerics a vision of society which was less authoritarian, less hierarchical, and less static than that of the Vormärz. The Liberals may not have been conscious of their role as political models, but the clerics soon learned that the only way to surpass the Liberals was to imitate them. Competition rather than prescription became the key to the new clerical mentality. Just as the Liberals were to qualify the classic idea of individual freedom' with political corporatism—the ideal of the Gemeinde—so too were the clerics to realize that individual rhetoric after 1867 needed backing in social action.

The Correspondenzblatt was founded and edited by two Viennese Augustinians from Klosterneuburg, Berthold Egger and Roman Himmelbauer. The Augustinians contributed other important activists to the paper, like Rudolf Eichhorn and Gustav Piffl. The presence of these canons on the newspaper's local editorial staff gave the Correspondenzblatt some independence from the archdiocesan authorities in Vienna. It was also an ironic reposte to the antimonastic traditions of Austrian Josephist Catholicism.[81] Most of the paper's contributors, correspondents, and readers, however, came from the diocesan clergy of Vienna, St. Pölten, and Linz. The paper also found a responsive audience in Bohemia and Moravia and became a model for the more nationalistic Czech and German-speaking clergy of Bohemia in their own attempts at clerical self-renewal in the later 1890s and 1900s.[82]

The single most influential figure behind the paper was Joseph Scheicher.[83] Scheicher was a Lower Austrian priest of poor peasant origins whose career was among the most colorful and provocative in modern Austrian ecclesiastical history. After his ordination in 1869 he was assigned a rural parish in southwestern Lower Austria, where, as noted, he proceeded to organize a small Catholic political movement. He was later sent by Bishop Fessler to the Frintaneum in Vienna for his doctorate and eventually in 1878 was appointed a professor of theology at the local seminary. In cultural terms he was among the most radical members of the Christian Social party—an outraged Liberal once labeled him the violet revolutionary.[84]

Like many of the top Christian Social leaders (Lueger, Schindler, Weiskirchner, Bielohlawek, and others) Scheicher was a self-made man. He admitted frankly that he became a priest because, as the son of a peasant, he could afford no other kind of advanced education, a motive which, he insisted, many of his colleagues shared.[85] More than any other quality in his personality, his pride in personal mobility and his resentment against those who would denigrate the terms of such hard-won achievement were always apparent. As the provincial seminary professor with one foot in the door of "intellectual" respectability, at the same time intensely proud of and apologetic about his background and education, he was an archetypal leader of Austrian Christian Socialism. Scheicher was not a "have-not"; he simply wanted more prestige and recognition for what he did possess.

Scheicher had two important links to the Güntherian tradition of priestly independence. One of Günther's most notable disciples, Karl Werner, was Scheicher's teacher in St. Pölten.[86] From Scheicher's memoirs it was apparent that he sympathized with Günther and had no loyalty toward Rauscher's ultramontanism, even if he did accept neo-scholasticism as the basis of his thought.[87] More important, Scheicher was a personal friend and protégé of the elder Sebastian Brunner. Scheicher admired Brunner's fight against Josephism and his tough political journalism.[88] Much of Schleicher's later synodal and presbyterial thought (such as his call for a "reformation in head and body" at the Clerustag in 1902) derived from the programs of the Güntherian priests and Brunner during 1848.[89] In contrast to some of the more libertarian Güntherians, Scheicher shared Brunner's insistence on the absolute hegemony of Catholic culture—his antisemitism was an obvious reflection of this nonpluralist view of society.

There were important differences between the two men, however. Unlike Brunner Scheicher disliked both aristocratic culture and Austrian Romanticism. The conniving side of Brunner, so apparent in the 1850s, was foreign to the more aggressive and intransigent Scheicher. Scheicher's aesthetic tastes were closer to those of the eighteenth-century Jansenists and the Bolzanoists than to Brunner or Hofbauer. He disliked mysticism, devotional pieties, and elaborate ritual. Anything reminiscent of the baroque he termed "Byzantine" and dismissed. His support for Heinrich Abel's mission movement in the 1890s was on political rather than aesthetic grounds. Scheicher was willing to contemplate reform of the celibacy question and other radical cultural reforms within the Church, which put him closer to the Bolzanoists than the Güntherians. Scheicher also shared the Bolzanoists commitment to social involvement for the clergy, but for very different purposes. Like Bolzano he reduced the ritualistic component of the Church, preferring that clerics use their time to study social affairs and involve themselves in practical politics. As a Güntherian he recognized the sacramental force of the Church, but accorded it a reduced significance. In contrast to the Bolzanoists, however, he launched a crusade of priests against the state, not in support of the state. In his personal combination of the Jansenism and eudaemonism of the Josephist/Bolzanoist tradition and the antistatism and synodalism of the Güntherian tradition, Joseph Scheicher summarized a century of Austrian clerical history.

In spite of Scheicher's prominence, however, the circle around the *Correspondenzblatt* comprehended a collective and often anonymous effort. Scheicher was the most articulate and vocal of these priests, but the paper and its circle did not depend on him alone. One profound difference between Scheicher and Brunner lay in the fact that Scheicher guided a mass, *collective* movement of priests, not simply a quixotic, individualist effort like that of Brunner in the 1850s.[90]

That lower clerical radicalism first occurred in the Imperial capital and Lower Austria and not in the more isolated Alpine areas was hardly surprising. In Vienna and St. Pölten men holding the office of bishop during the Liberal era were both conciliatory to the Liberal regime and acceptable to the Viennese press.[91] Matthäus Binder in St. Pölten (1872–93) and Johann Kutschker (1875–81) and Cölestin Ganglbauer (1881–90) in Vienna, bishops with neo-Josephist sympathies, avoided quarrels with the government while maintaining a traditional authority system over their clergy. All were uninspiring leaders. Lower clerics in Vienna and Lower Austria had to look elsewhere for their political leadership.[92] In Rome none of these bishops generated much enthusiasm. In Ganglbauer especially the Vatican saw a man with secret Liberal proclivities who refused to follow a hard-line opposition to the Liberal regime.[93]

Beyond the problem of poor episcopal leadership, the pressure of the Liberal press on the Lower Austrian clergy was greater than that on clerics in dioceses where social change moved at a slower pace or where the nationality question intervened to defuse a direct clerical-anticlerical confrontation. That Catholic politics in Lower Austria were practically nonexistent by 1880 also meant that the lower clergy had no episcopal-aristocratic rivals when they did come to take an interest in politics. Unlike Tyrol, where a bitter feud continued well beyond 1900 between Catholic conservative and Christian Social factions, conservative politics in Lower Austria were so weak that the lower clergy began with a blank slate.[94] In many rural districts in Lower Austria there were no Catholic political associations. Where they did exist, as in St. Pölten, they existed at the tolerance of Bishop Binder, not because of his support. In Vienna serious Catholic politics simply did not exist until the late 1880s, when they immediately became an appendage of Christian Social antisemitism.

The Congrua

The first and most persistent issue treated by the new priestly authors in the 1880s was their demand for increased salaries and retirement benefits, the so-called Congrua question. The Congrua problem was noteworthy since it was the first, dramatic issue in the 1880s to shake the priests out of the apathy and silence which had afflicted them since 1849.

The Congrua was the legal minimum salary guaranteed the Austrian clergy by the government.[95] The Congrua levels of the clergy in 1880 were still those which Joseph II had fixed when he established the Religious Fund (Religionsfond) between 1782 and 1786.[96] Under Joseph II the Religious Fund was made responsible for providing salaries in Vienna of 600 fl. to each pastor and 250 fl. to each assisting priest in parishes where the local endowment was insufficient to meet such levels.[97]

For decades the question of clerical incomes had perplexed the episcopate. Requests from individual bishops during the Vormärz that clerical salaries be augmented met with indifference from the Hofkanzlei. The neo-absolutist regime, although it accommodated the Church on legal and political matters, did nothing for the clergy's material welfare. Similarly, when the Liberals came to power after 1867 they pushed through a generous revision of public employees' salaries, without any improvement for the clergy. The Liberals announced in 1871 that they would consider such a law, but the second stage of anticlerical legislation in 1873–75 occupied most of their attention. In 1872 the parliament did pass emergency legislation creating a fund of 500,000 fl. to assist needy clerics, but the episcopate were hostile to this patronage, fearing that it was an attempt to exclude them from the right to negotiate on behalf of their own clerics.[98] In fact, the grants were a rather unsubtle attempt by Stremayr, the minister of education, to lessen clerical discontent with the legal revolution wrought against the Church by ad hoc salary supplements.[99] That the Liberals financed these grants by a new tax on wealthier clerical incomes in favor of poorer benefices only embittered the Austrian clerical hierarchy. In many dioceses the Austrian bishops forbade their clerics from applying for such assistance. Even if they abstained from the extreme statism of their predecessors, the bishops placed a high symbolic value on the legalism of the Church-state problem.

In 1876 the Auersperg ministry finally initiated serious negotiations with the Austrian bishops and sent a proposal to the Reichsrat which would have raised the Congrua. Negotiations over the bill stalled in 1877, however, and the bill languished until the parliamentary session ended in 1879.[100]

In the 1870s the lower clerics waited for improvements in their salaries which would do for them what the Liberals had done for the state officials. They had no way of publicizing their distress—the Reichsrat received no mass petitions from the clergy, as it was to do in the 1880s after the priests began to behave more aggressively. Many clerics were embittered by the stalemate between the government and the bishops, not only because of the Liberals' superciliousness, but also because of the episcopate's apparent lack of concern for the priests. The legalism of the bishops might be satisfying for those with comfortable incomes, but for the common cleric such legalism did not buy new clothes or new books. The problem of clerical salaries was intensified by the inflation in consumer prices in Vienna in the years 1878–82, precisely the period when antisemitic artisan agitation began.

The *Correspondenzblatt* group was the center point during the early 1880s for lower clerical agitation for salary increases. Indeed, the paper's support of this issue first justified its existence in the minds of priests throughout Austria. In 1884 the editors of the *Correspondenzblatt* organized a petition to the Reichsrat which argued that many clerics lived under the old Congrua levels in "necessity and deprivation."[101] The petition noted that the Congrua itself was so confusing that many priests were uncertain what income they actually deserved. In view of the quietude of the clergy in the 1870s, the petition was an astounding success—in a few months 6,000 priests signed the document.[102] The newspaper also opened a line of argument by challenging priests to view themselves as political men, as active citizens who should awake and use their political rights.[103] An acceptable Congrua was not a concession from the government; it was among the "rights" of the clergy.[104]

The activism of the priests reflected situations of true social distress. In 1879 the minimum yearly income necessary for a single adult male to survive in a large urban area was between 350 and 400 fl. and for a rural area at least 250 fl.[105] Measured against this minimal standard, the pre-1885 rates for Vienna and for Lower Austria were clearly inadequate.

Under pressure from the bishops and their clerical coalition partners, Taaffe's ministry reintroduced Congrua legislation in parliament in 1880, and after a series of technical delays the Reichsrat finally enacted a law (19 April 1885) providing a comprehensive reform of the salary system of the Austrian clergy.[106]

The law eliminated the distinction between "old" and "new" parishes and set up a graduated system for measuring the Congrua, depending upon geographical location, by which men residing in or near large urban centers, where the cost of living was appreciably higher, were alloted more money. For Vienna, pastors received 1,800 fl. For the rest of Lower Austria, pastors received between 800 and 1,200 fl. Younger priests who served as assistants *(Cooperatoren* or *Kapläne)* received 500 fl. in Vienna and between 350 fl. and 400 fl. elsewhere in Lower Austria.[107] The government also permitted clerics to retain up to 30 fl. of the fees *(Stola)* paid for Church rituals.

The reforms of 1885 went a long way toward improving the situation of the clergy. Information on wages in Austria before 1900 is notoriously unreliable, but a source of comparison may be found in wage statistics from strike disputes assembled by the Statistical Office of the city of Vienna beginning in 1894. According to the 1894 data, the weekly wage for skilled male laborers in the metal, woodworking, and turning industries in Vienna averaged between 8 and 13 fl., or approximately 400– 600 fl. per year.[108] The income of a newly ordained cleric, including his salary of 500 fl., funds from the *Stola,* and his wages as a catechist (usually between 200 and 250 fl.), surpassed the wages of a skilled factory laborer and those of many artisan masters as well. Clerical salaries now compared well (in purchasing power) with those of Rank X of the Imperial *Rangclassen* system, the entry rank of most academically trained state officials.[109]

That the anger of the clergy over their salary situation grew even more abrasive after 1885 illustrated the relation between the clergy's resistance to perceived injustice and their rising expectations for satisfaction.[110] Between 1885 and 1897 a long series of articles argued that the financial situation of the common clerics was still serious.[111] In 1894 the *Correspondenzblatt* circulated a petition demanding further changes in the Congrua legislation, this time collecting over 8,000 signatures.[112] In 1896 the clergy of St. Pölten submitted to the Reichsrat a long petition demanding twenty-nine different revisions in the 1885 legislation. In the same year, 150 priests, representing nearly all of the dioceses in Austria, met on their own initiative in Vienna and formed a Delegates' Conference of priests. Organized by Rudolf Eichhorn from the *Correspondenzblatt,* the meeting drafted yet another memorandum on the Congrua question.[113]

Following the protests of the main body of the clergy which led to the legislation of 1885, a movement for higher wages began among the young priests serving as part-time catechists. An article appeared in 1886 in the *Linzer Volksblatt,* the newspaper controlled by the bishops of Linz, accusing the *Correspondenzblatt* of stirring up discontent among the younger clerics and threatening the authority of the bishops. Berthold

Egger settled the matter quietly by meeting with some of the bishops in Vienna and explaining the idealism behind the agitation. In his newspaper, however, Egger insisted that the clergy were independent and would defend their own rights. If the bishops do not act vigorously, "we must use our own intelligence in order to do away with injustices."[114] The negotiations of the episcopate with the government and public pressure by the priests themselves produced tangible results in the Imperial law of 17 June 1888.[115] Even this legislation did not satisfy the priests, however, since they resented the gratis hours they had to teach and the slowness authorities took in making salary payments.[116]

The most interesting aspect of the lower clergy's aggressive stance on the Congrua question after 1885 was the social implications of the language they used.[117] Were the clergy still so desperately poor as the rhetoric of the *Correspondenzblatt* might lead the reader to believe?

Many of the assertions of the priests about their financial situation *after* 1885 were exaggerated. From various random accounts in the *Correspondenzblatt,* which discussed the living arrangements of both pastors and assistants, such relative luxuries as domestic servants, three decent, warm meals a day, and clean, comfortable housing conditions were definitely the rule, especially in Vienna and in the small towns of Lower Austria, where over 80 percent of the common clergy in the province lived.[118] Further, clerics did not have marital and parental responsibilities, although they were quick to point out that their roles demanded that they give money to charity.[119] In most cases the cleric lived at his parish house at minimal expense, thus lowering food and housing costs.[120] That the newspaper ran a regular column for its readers, "Der kleine Kapitalist," on the structure of the Austrian investment system was proof that the clerics maintained essentially bourgeois life-styles and self-conceptions. In rural areas the peasants usually envied the situation of the local priest.[121]

But social superiority was an elusive concept, precisely because the priests measured their income in ways which obscured their superiority over the lower classes. It was large enough to separate them from the working class, but not always substantial enough to provide them with personal consumption on a par with the Austrian *Bildungsbürgertum.* Objective facts collided with subjective standards.

The clerics' disaffection was, in fact, a problem of relative deprivation in which the uncertainty of social status played a major role. Two related themes appeared in the petitions and essays written to dramatize the clergy's needs: the use of bourgeois reference groups for comparison with the clergy, and the need of the clergy to achieve not only a minimally acceptable salary but recompense compatible with their dignity *(Würde)* and social position (a *standesgemäss* income).[122] One petition argued that the priests had been "pushed down" to where their salary was similar to that of governmental servants, a "lower" *Stand*.[123] Another article in 1892 emphasized that the *Würde* of the cleric depended on his "material position" and that a lowly Congrua would endanger his "dignity and independence."[124] Low Congrua levels would hinder the cultivation of *anständig* (socially respectable) habits.[125] The statements of the St. Pölten priests and the Delegates Conference of 1896 admitted openly that the young clergy could never accept salaries merely equal to those of a worker or a governmental attendant, since this would be a "humiliation" *(Demüthigung)* for the priest. Workers had a very "cheap" *(wohlfeil)* education, and the priests demanded compensation commensurate with their more extensive education.[126]

For men who believed that their cultural heritage and education qualified them for high status positions, the lack of a suitable Congrua was evidence of social marginality. The Delegates' Conference implied this when it argued that a low Congrua showed the state's "disdain" *(Geringschätzung)* for the clergy, discouraging new recruits from joining the priesthood.[127] The "humiliation" of the priests in being compared with wage laborers is significant in view of the chronic inability of the Austrian clergy to win even a modest following among the working class.[128]

Although the radical clerics occasionally used cultural justifications for their salary demands, their most frequent argument was the more functional assertion that they were an "educated class" *(gebildeter Stand)* who deserved treatment consistent with their training.[129] The 1894 Congrua petition had noted, in a distinction based on personal achievement, that the cleric's education amounted to twelve years of training (eight years gymnasium, four years seminary), whereas the school teacher found employment after only eight years of advanced schooling (without the financial burden of attending a gymnasium), and concluded that an assistant priest deserved more money than his counterpart in public education.[130] This self-serving distinction with its overcompensatory rhetoric showed the clergy's similarity to late-nineteenth-century white collar protest movements among Austrian *Staatsbeamten* and school teachers in learning to articulate their discontent about status and income. The second great wave of clerical petitions on the Congrua (1894–96) occurred after a parallel movement among Austrian state officials in the years 1888–93 had led many of them to political antisemitism. By selecting the bureaucrats and teachers as their referents, the priests demonstrated their desire to be included as a part of the new Mittelstand culture of special interest demands.[131]

The clergy's claim to a valid level of *Bildung* also showed a craving for bourgeois respectability in a society in which older corporate values were being forced to compete with achievement criteria of education and work performance. The clergy now recognized the criterion of achievement for the allocation of prestige and work rewards, but they wished to mix this new attitude with older corporate claims. The clerics affirmed their conservatism in static religious-cultural terms, but by emphasizing their education as a basis for their salary claims, they also placed themselves on a level with the more stable sectors of the antisemitic coalition. The clerics thus were a prime example of nonmobile and dynamic conceptions of social status within the same occupational group.[132]

The proud, yet defensive assertions by the *Correspondenzblatt* group that their *Bildung* was as good as any other inevitably led them to realize that it was not as good as they (or their predecessors in 1848) wanted it to be. In 1848 Veith and Günther had stressed the need for a truly educated Catholic clergy, but for the good of society more than for the clergy's own good. The priests of the 1880s adopted a more complex attitude. To the outside world their training was as modern as anything available. But among themselves they admitted that clerical education needed improvements, not so much for society's good as for their own self-justification to the world. They reaffirmed the older Josephist value of education as a source of moral improvement, but they added to it the idea of education as the criterion for competition as a modern occupational group. Competitive self-interest replaced pure social service as the reason for *Bildung*.

The politics of clerical incomes, reflecting traditional prerogatives which had been forgotten or ignored and new claims which were not yet recognized, played a decisive role in motivating younger clerics to search for political solutions for their disaffection. By discovering the collective dimensions of their social devolution, the clerics took the first step to prepare themselves for entry into the Christian Social coalition. By breaking with the state over salaries, the clerics ended the umbilical dependence which had held them to the state for nearly a century.

With their traditional cultural values, the clergy were suitable allies for groups equally dependent upon past-oriented conceptions of their now threatened social status, the artisans and shopkeepers in the Third Curia. At the same time, because the clerics had a basic social rationality, their claims to respectability equal to that of state officials or older school teachers were not absurd and did reflect an inflation in personal values of all middle bourgeois groups in late-nineteenth-century Vienna. The clergy were thus compatible allies, in pure class terms, for more established and educated segments of the Christian Social coalition: the property owners, the thousands of *Staatsbeamten,* and the middle and upper ranks of many private bureaucracies. Culturally the priests might affiliate with the artisans, but socially their guidance points were the more elite sectors of the Christian Social movement. This placed priests at a crucial equilibrium point: they were able to exploit the resources of both sectors, which they did to a remarkable degree in the years 1895–1918.

The Schools

Even if the culture of the pre-Liberal era was dismissed by the *Correspondenzblatt* as "Josephist," the absence in that society of rivals to the Church permitted the clergy to view it as an age in which the image of the priest was suitably lofty. The paper constantly referred to the priest as the bearer of the "holy fire"[133] and as the "teacher of the people."[134] Joseph Scheicher recalled with a mixture of nostalgia and bitterness a past age, fast disappearing even in rural areas, in which the priest and the local church formed the center point of the community, where the youths admired the *Cooperator* and wanted to emulate him.[135]

The clergy viewed the place their religious values occupied in Austrian society in a holistic sense, going well beyond the boundaries of approved Josephist ideals. Not only should the state be infused with Catholic values in a way which would destroy the uneasy harmony between church and state existing since 1780, but no compromise could be made with rationalistic nonbelief.[136]

In rejecting liberal culture, the clerics demanded a return to the values of the past. Scheicher voiced a common refrain when he urged the Church to reclaim its *alten Besitzstand,* its past cultural influence. What Scheicher did not make clear was what past he wanted the lower clergy to return to. The great burden of these clerics was their ambivalent historicism. These were men whose apparent past was one which was of merely ambiguous legitimacy—the "past" of the Austrian Church was as much the property of Josephists like Jüstel and Heinke as it was of ultramontanes like Hofbauer and Brunner. Their radicalism was uniquely ahistorical in a dual sense. The clerics drew upon a long tradition of Josephist sponsorship for the Church, measuring their present predicament against the fruits which this past *should* have provided for them. At the same time, for tactical reasons, they were forced to repudiate the very legitimacy of their statist past, since the traditional symbiosis of clergy and state in Austria seemed to be at the root of all their problems. The clerics thus had to invent a past and then destroy it, using it as a mythic guarantee for their present demands, but in fact not wanting to make myth into contemporary history. The Austrian ecclesiastical past was being used against itself by men who felt cheated by their own history.

The alienation of the clerics from Liberal society found its most poig-
nant expression in the confessional schools controversy.[137] The school
supervision law of May 1868 and the Imperial school law *(Reichsvolksschulgesetz)* of May 1869 had removed from the bishops and the common
clergy the extensive supervisory and administrative power they had enjoyed. Catholic priests, at least in Vienna and Lower Austria, were not
made permanent members of the local school councils, but were allowed,
along with representatives of other religious groups, to attend sessions in
which religious matters were discussed. The clerics, like other religious
groups, received only one seat on the Vienna School Board. Provincial
and district school inspectors assumed powers formerly exercised by the
Church.

The clergy never accepted this state of affairs. Until 1879, when Taaffe
assumed control, little could be done. In 1880 Alois Liechtenstein and
Georg Lienbacher introduced proposals in the Reichsrat which would
have reestablished a confessional school system. Although the government and the Reichsrat were not prepared to go so far, Taaffe eventually
forced through the law of 2 May 1883, which conceded an optional six-
year instruction period for rural areas.[138] The bill also required school
principals (the law did not apply to state secondary schools) to obtain a
proof of competency *(Lehramtszeugnis)* in the teaching of the religion of
the majority of the students in the schools. The law was a minor victory
for the bishops and Clerical politicians, but little more. Even before 1883
Taaffe's ministry had often allowed local communities to decide teaching
appointments on the basis of religious affiliation, although this was illegal.[139]

In the spring of 1890 the Austrian bishops made one last effort to push
for national legislation on the schools, but soon withdrew their demands
after receiving assurances from the government that the Church's interests would be met through sympathetic administrative decrees.[140] The
episcopate's strategy after 1890 resumed a more traditional, conciliatory
direction, preferring private negotiations with the Verwaltung in the belief
that fragmentary concessions were better than nothing.[141] The new
quietism of the episcopate on the school question was also tied to the rise
of lower clerical agitation—the bishops urgently desired after 1890 to
maintain control over the Church's stance on educational policy.

The episcopal campaign to confessionalize the schools met with enthusiasm on the part of the lower clergy. The motives of the clerics,
however, were different from those of their ecclesiastical superiors. The
lower clergy viewed their roles as catechists and teachers in the schools as
a last opportunity, short of nonecclesiastical functions, to revitalize their
profession. For the parish priest, who often devoted twenty hours a week

to religious instruction, the problem of youth socialization was crucial. If the irreligiosity of the Liberal era were not reversed in the children of the next generation, the cause of the Church and of their own profession would be doomed. The clerics had only to look at Republican France to see the power of long-term anticlerical attitudes among the lower and lower middle classes. On no other issue did the fortunes of religion as a system of belief and the subjective occupational interests of the clergy coincide so imperatively as they did on the schools issue. Professional self-enhancement depended upon the revival of a broad current of popular belief. The clerics' animosity and extremism on this question reflected its dual function for their lives: more religion in the schools would re-legitimate the ideological foundation of their belief system, as well as strengthen the subjective roles which they played in that system. For the lower clergy it was a question not simply of the desirability of law, but of the logic of social reality.

More important, public education was one of the few areas which seemed to offer to the priest public influence beyond his ritualistic duties. After 1869 the clerics were forced to compete for honor and esteem with the Liberal-trained public school teachers. For all their contempt of the new school system, most priests (especially those in Vienna) were im-pressed with its technical and financial resources. Their hostility resulted from envy at being excluded from what they saw as a system improved in technical terms, but increasingly godless in moral terms. Education was the great commodity which the Liberal party offered nineteenth-century society. It was seen as one of the few areas in which the state might justifiably intervene in society and recast social opportunities and re-sources. The clerics simply imitated the Liberals in making a political fetish of public education. As *Gebildeten* conscious of their credentials they felt that they had a rightful leadership role to play in the new system beyond that of catechetical instruction. Hence the outrage of clerics when Liberals insisted that they were acting in the "true" spirit of "the Great Emperor Joseph II" in isolating the Church from public education. It was precisely the Josephist tradition which allowed the clerics a significant role in social modernization. The Liberals seemed to be inventing a new portrait of Joseph II.[142] The clerics felt doubly cheated and deceived. Not only were their prerogatives curtailed, but they were put in the ironic position of having to defend "rights" which were the result of Joseph's sense of the secular utility of religion for civil society.

The Catholic campaign for the school system inevitably preoccupied the group around the *Correspondenzblatt*. The Viennese priest who wrote regularly for the paper on education, Bernhard Otter, insisted that the new school system should not simply provide religious instruction as a "certain mass of religious knowledge," but that it must be able to shape the total life of the student, forcing a religious disposition *(Gesinnung)* into all of the powers of the soul.[143]

Questions of social status also found their way into this discussion. The priests, who served as the local school inspectors before 1868, were angered at their loss of such prerogatives and by their lack of permanent membership on the school councils.[144] Catechists resented their subjection to the administrative supervision of the head teacher *(Oberlehrer)* and to the district school inspectors, in addition to their immediate supervision by episcopal authorities. Bernhard Otter remarked indignantly that the Vienna School Board treated teachers of religion "just like the other instructors, in that it includes them among all those teachers under the supervision of the school principal, and in that the principal is supposed to report on fulfillment of their responsibilities."[145]

The public school teacher, whether Gentile or Jew (and the vast majority were Gentiles), posed the greatest menace for the priests. In the decades following the 1869 school law two generations of teachers received their education in the spirit of the new interconfessional system. As in France, these teachers not only dominated the system pedagogically, but frequently displaced the cleric as the local notable to whom families or individuals would turn for advice on personal affairs.[146] Most teachers tolerated the clergy's catechetical efforts, but they refused to function as the clergy's religious surrogates.[147] Nor were they willing to recognize the clerics as their equals for policy or administrative purposes. Relations between the clergy and the teachers were always tense, but they worsened in the mid-1880s under the pressure of the Catholic drive to regain control of the schools.[148] In rural areas the social superiority which the *Pfarrer* played over the village *Schulmeister* before 1867 also changed radically. As the teachers became more conscious of their professionalism and refused to function as unpaid servants for the local parish, social relations often degenerated into outright hostility.

In 1888 the latent feud between the two groups erupted when the editors of two Liberal educational journals in Vienna, the *Freie pädagogische Blätter* and *Schule und Haus,* published a series of controversial articles combining anticlerical rhetoric with harsh personal attacks against individual clerics.[149] The Viennese clerics responded by forming an "Observation Corps" to protect themselves against insults and to investigate the contents of school libraries.[150] Liberal teachers' associations in turn charged that the group was nothing more than an "espionage system" to dominate the schools.[151] The corps, consisting of seventy-eight Viennese priests, demanded that the government remove the offensive issues of *Schule und Haus* from school libraries. After some delay, the ministry of education complied with the clerics' wishes. The *Correspondenzblatt* saw the victory as an example of what the priests could achieve if they united under their own leadership. Scheicher admitted, however, that bishops were extremely suspicious of the Observation Corps, fearing a breakdown in organizational discipline.[152]

Between 1888 and 1890 the clerics saw another way of enhancing their educational roles, which drew upon their new group self-awareness but put it in a wider political context. At a time when the bishops ended their confrontations with the government and negotiated privately for concessions, the Viennese clergy opted for political antisemitism as a way of legitimating their demands through electoral politics. Not surprisingly, most members of the Observation Corps ended up as militant sub-elite agitators in their parishes after 1889. Rudolf Eichhorn was one of the first clerics to suggest this strategy when he argued in 1887 that clerical support for the artisan antisemites would "reawaken trust in the priest and thus offer to the Church supervision of the school system, which she deserves."[153] Clerics like Eichhorn found the bishops' strategy of slow, gradual negotiations tiresome and sterile. The schools issue thus became a primary motive for the clerics to join the antisemitic crusade in 1887–89. Rather than the state, they chose bourgeois society as their ally, hoping to use mass social pressure to turn the schools in a more Catholic direction.

Ironically, opting for political confrontations never gained the clergy the hegemony for religion which they wanted. Between 1890 and 1895 the anti-Liberals gradually penetrated the ranks of the public-school teachers in Vienna, not so much because of Jew hatred, but as a practical alternative in voting behavior reflecting many teachers' dissatisfaction with the local Liberal party.[154] Most of the tenured teachers who became Christian Social supporters after 1895 did so for frankly opportunistic reasons, not from a love of Catholic cultural values. Anticlericalism among white collar professional and paraprofessional voters was always a factor in the Christian Social party before 1914.

The schools were one area of policy where the clerics were forced to back down on their absolutist demands for hegemony. Rather, they received what the party was willing to give them: seats on the school board, some control over teachers' appointments, guarantees against direct hostility by local teachers' associations, and other practical concessions. The grandiose expectations of the young clerics during the late 1880s proved exaggerated, but at the same time militant anticlericalism among the older, tenured teachers also diminished considerably as time passed.

The rise of the Social Democrats in Vienna was probably most significant in persuading many bourgeois anticlericals to take a second, more favorable look at the "usefulness" of a religious revival. This was especially true when a group of younger teachers *(Unterlehrer)* led by Karl Seitz brought enormous pressure to bear on the Christian Socials in 1897–98, a movement which older teachers found difficult to accept. Better a "Christian" nationalism under Lueger than social egalitarianism under Karl Seitz and Victor Adler.[155]

Clerical Status and the Role-Set of a Lower-Order Priest

Issues like Congrua reform and the schools spurred many clerics writing for the *Correspondenzblatt* to inquire more generally into the reasons behind their decline in public respect. Scheicher described the typical experience of a young Lower Austrian *Cooperator,* full of enthusiasm from the seminary: "Above all he finds in the first and perhaps also in the second and third place of his work absolutely nothing. No one is waiting for him, except a few beggars and some children. The profession of a priest appears, at least to some people, as the lowest, as something which one would take up who either is mentally ill or doesn't have the material means in order to choose another occupation."[156] Matthäus Bauchinger estimated that 95 percent of the male population of Vienna was, for all practical purposes, non-Catholic.[157] In rural areas the situation was no better. Not only had Liberal values infected the urban electorate, but the peasants had seen their lives radically transformed by the agrarian reforms of 1848–49. For those peasants who prospered, Liberal politics and the independent communal institutions obviated their cultural dependence on the local priest. For those who suffered from the reforms, the Church was simply part of an establishment with no sympathy for them. The clergy were hated or ignored.

Encouraged by the newspaper, an informal public debate was organized in the years 1885–90 to discuss why the clerics found themselves so isolated. Two kinds of explanations emerged, one having to do with the new social and political context within which the clergy had to work, the other relating to the internal organization of the Church itself.

Many priests now believed that the long association of the Church with the Imperial government was responsible for their decline. The clergy were viewed by many as a civil arm of the government at best and as a branch of the *Gendarmerie* at worst. Scheicher quoted Ernst Vergani's famous vulgarism that he would rather sit down at table with ten Jews than with one priest. For Scheicher this mentality arose from the fact that "the Church in Vienna has lost its popular sense. It became in the course of time a state Church, a court Church, or a government institution."[158]

Although Scheicher would have denied it furiously, the Austrian clergy could not afford to simply write off the state. Unlike the Prussian clergy, for whom the state was at best an object of tolerance and at worst an object of fear, the state was for the Austrian clergy a realm of opportunity as well as hostility. The clerics ignored the contradiction in their logic when, at the same time, they demanded freedom from the state and control of such institutions as the educational system. Their demand for a "Christian state" revealed that their distinction between state and society was a tenuous and arbitrary one. It also showed that most radical clerics were uncertain just how far they wanted to carry their antistatism. As a political tactic it was useful, but as an ultimate goal it raised troublesome questions about ending Catholicism's privileged relationship with the state.

In attacking the *Hofkirche*, the clerics came close to a confrontation with the dynasty and self-incrimination on the basis of their own Josephist past. It was thus convenient for them to transpose their critique of the state itself into a critique of the Liberal state by means of antisemitic rhetoric. Again, as in their convoluted notions of history, the clerics distorted and manipulated the past in a way which maximized their political maneuverability. When Rudolf Eichhorn insisted that a small group of capitalist plutocrats ran the government and that "capitalism" was somehow responsible for the miserable state of the Church, he was combining descriptive and analytical accounts of the Liberal state in an effort to excuse the generic antistatism of the *Correspondenzblatt*.[159] Logic demanded that the clerics condemn the Concordat Church as much as the Church created by the confessional laws of 1868–69 and 1874–75. Political prudence and self-interest dictated, however, that the latter rather than the former bear the brunt of the enmity. The clerics found themselves in a curious dilemma: they had to account for the perversity of the Liberal state toward the Church, without impugning the fact that the Church had privileges to begin with. Clerics like Scheicher and Eichhorn were clearly willing to see a restoration of the Church's privileges, but they sought to justify this by insisting that a new kind of Church and a new kind of state and society would be the parties to the arrangement. Rather than all forms of statism or even Josephism being "bad," it was the Liberals' perversion of Josephism and the episcopate's passive authoritarianism which merited contempt. As if to square a circle, the clerics insisted that they would now "earn" their privileges by secular action—by democratizing the Church and making it "popular," a new Church would be created which would deserve the privileges enjoyed before 1860. At the same time, by eliminating certain "corrupting" influences from the state and society, both would be purified and readily assent to a return to Catholic hegemony. Clerics like Scheicher rejected both Bolzano's statism and Günther's division of church and state into separate realms. They did not want a Catholicism regenerated by a new absolutism. Rather, they sought to use Bürger society as the agent of this religious renewal, against both the traditional state and the traditional episcopate.

One easy explanation of the clergy's predicament was antisemitism.[160] Of the various groups in the antisemitic movement, the clergy alone could not project economic competition from the Jews as the basis for their antisemitism. Jews ran the Liberal newspapers which degraded the clergy's image, however, creating a form of cultural rivalry the clergy found as ominous as economic competition. Poorer Jews served clerics as objects of invidious self-esteem; to enhance their own social status, clerics attacked a nondominant minority group.[161] For a few clerics (probably not the majority) racialist hatred even reflected themes of violence—Heinrich Abel recalled with delight how his father had once beaten up a Jew with a club.[162]

Perhaps the most singular use to which the clerics put antisemitism, however, was to explain the devolution of the Austrian state after 1867. Of all the priests associated with the *Correspondenzblatt,* Joseph Deckert was probably the most vulgar antisemite, but it was precisely in Deckert's numerous pamphlets and articles that the Jew was repeatedly used to explain the perversion of government and society in the Liberal era. Deckert insisted that the Jews were responsible for the disappearance of a state in which Christian culture reigned supreme.[163] "Jewish domination" changed the essential nature of the Austrian state, forcing it to deny its Christian origins and ethics. Society had now become a "sick organism."[164] The tough exclusionist legislation prescribed by Deckert would in an indirect way eliminate the interconfessional laws of the Liberal period. If the bishops could not achieve this in the name of Catholicism, perhaps it could be done in the name of "Christian antisemitism."[165] Deckert thus explained away the problem of state power by suggesting that once "Jewish" influence on such power had been eliminated, its use by the clergy would again be permissible. Equally important, once the Jews had been isolated from Austrian society, society would again recognize voluntarily the privileges of the Church.[166] Deckert also showed his fellow clerics how profitable antisemitism could be in a personal sense, even if this meant exploiting half-demented *Lumpen* (e.g., Paulus Meyer of the famous Meyer-Bloch libel trial in 1894) to achieve his ends.[167]

The Church's dependence on state power led the clerics to current problems of internal organization and conflicts within the set of roles traditionally prescribed for a priest. Precisely because the Church was a *Staatskirche,* living out its existence under a state dominated by "Jewish" rationalism, its weaknesses soon became apparent. The

Correspondenzblatt priests were unanimous in accusing their colleagues of a dangerous level of passivity and even laziness. Many thought that the clergy had concentrated on mere sacramental-ritualistic duties for too long.[168] Bauchinger hit upon this issue when he insisted that before 1885 the clergy had "trusted our prestige and the deep faith of the folk and did not notice that both became weaker with each day; we thought that we could retain the Christian folk on the right road with the sermon and the confessional. In a word: we did not understand our time." Scheicher later put it thus: "Today to go before the masses with apologetics or defensive rhetoric is anachronistic. Today I must take the rights of the mass of the people into account."[169]

Equally problematic was the narrow range of education for younger clerics. Not only did the Liberal state deprive the Church of financial resources to upgrade its training facilities, while channeling funds with great generosity into the secular universities where the clergy's "enemies" were trained, but theology itself had become sterile. It lacked a connection to the "sociological area." This generation of clerics was no longer interested in arid philosophical disputes, Scheicher proudly announced. It wanted "scientific" training in social theory as it applied to moral theology, not simply Church dogma.[170] Scheicher may have been exaggerating, but the group of clerics who led the Viennese clergy into antisemitism were marked by the prominence they gave to a socially oriented moral theology. Franz Martin Schindler and Joseph Scheicher, for all their differences in personality and political style, shared this commitment. Both defended Albert Ehrhard in Vienna in 1901 against accusations of modernism precisely because they saw in Ehrhard a new standard of quality education which the Austrian clergy desperately needed if they were to compete successfully with secular rivals.[171]

Demands by the lower clergy for the modernization of seminary education were not restricted to Austria in this period. Such hopes played a role in leading many Italian clerics to join Murri's Christian Democratic movement after 1898, much to the Vatican's unease. During the 1880s such demands seemed innocuous enough, but with the rise in the later 1890s of reform Catholicism and theological modernism, these demands became very sensitive.

Beyond problems of education, the roles prescribed for the lower clergy by tradition also seemed increasingly unproductive. For the Vormärz bureaucrat, clerics served as agents of social control. Their prime loyalties were to go to the state rather than to society. For the hierarchically minded bishops, whether Josephist or ultramontane, the cleric was an ecclesiastical agent whose ultimate roles were almost identical with those postulated by the government. Service to the state was not questioned;

the sacral responsibilities of the clerics were simply stressed as a complement to their service duties. For the pre-1848 Hofbauerites the clerics' role in society was not wider, but deeper, more mystical, and more pietistic in nature. More emphasis was placed on individual sacramentalism in the priest's contact with the public, but the Hofbauerites never relinquished the service mentality entirely. In Cardinal Rauscher the two modes met and meshed so intricately that it was difficult to tell where the Josephist left off and the ultramontane began.

Both traditions promised to the cleric that the dutiful fulfillment of his roles—pastoral care, charity, school teaching, civil administration—would ensure public respect.[172] With the coming of the Liberal era, both traditions proved worthless. The state itself drastically abridged the roles involving charity and school teaching. The clergy were left with simple pastoralism and the onerous tasks of civil administration, at a time when urban population rates were soaring and a shortage of priests made such work intolerable. The priest not only was expected to perform the tasks of Church administration in his parish, but was also responsible for the *Matrikeln* (the conduct and reportage of all significant civil statistics relating to birth, death, marriage, legitimation, and care of the poor) plus the preparation of testimonies of moral character for individuals requiring such documents for employment or educational purposes. Many priests felt that the last role made them petty civil bureaucrats.[173] At least twelve parishes in the city of Vienna had over 40,000 people each. In the parish of Meidling, which had over 50,000 inhabitants in 1890, the assistant priests each spent between twenty-six and thirty hours weekly giving religious instruction, and the pastor reported that he could "scarcely manage the bureaucratic part."[174] During the Vormärz, when most clerics placed few intellectual and no political demands upon themselves, such bureaucratism was tolerable. But the clerics of the 1880s saw the priest as a public man of greater dignity and political responsibility who needed the leisure of free time to read, study, and act upon the issues of the day. As with other Austrian middle bourgeois groups of the period, dignity was defined in terms of personal freedom from formal bureaucratic control.

A Return to Society through Politics

The priests of the *Correspondenzblatt* offered their colleagues two solutions to the decline in clerical effectiveness: a more aggressive and, in a narrow sense, a more democratic tone with which the clerics should respond to the issues affecting the Church; and, more important, a commitment by the clergy to interest themselves in the social and economic demands of certain occupational strata, a stance which after 1887 committed the clergy to enter competitive party politics. The solution to the role problems of the priest was to be the addition of a new role to his traditional set—that of a political activist in support of special interest groups. Also, the new spirit of aggressive behavior (Scheicher borrowed Schönerer's phrase, *die schärfere Tonart*) would revitalize the other roles. A new, sharper "key" in the everyday lives of the clerics would demonstrate to the nominally Catholic population of Vienna and Lower Austria that the clergy were seriously concerned in its social as well as moral well-being.

Political action might generate an image of the clergy as a group genuinely sympathetic to the needs of their constituency, and thus remove the stigma from priests who both resented their roles as bureaucrats and yet wanted control over such public institutions as the educational system. The clergy should join the antisemitic movement in Vienna and Lower Austria because, as the *Correspondenzblatt* proclaimed, antisemitism would serve as a "bridge" to "true Christianity": "Through it [antisemitism] the respect for the clergy, so undermined by the Liberal newspapers, will again be somewhat improved."[175]

During the early and mid-1880s the clergy's interest in politics was confined to speculation about the social question. The *Correspondenzblatt* ran a regular column, "The Clergy and the Social Question," in which priests ventured suggestions on the ways and means to approach social reform issues. Joseph Scheicher in his small book *Der Clerus und die soziale Frage* (1884) portrayed the economic misery of the master handworkers, the small farmers, and the urban workers, and attributed the unrest in all three groups to a godless capitalism. He insisted that the social question arose from economic misery, not moral failings. But most of the book was an apology for handwork protectionism and special favors for property-owning peasants. The only real way to solve the worker question, argued Scheicher, was to emphasize the "striving for the eternal goal," which could best be achieved by "unity between state and Church, the subordination of the material to the spiritual."[176]

Other clerics such as Rudolf Eichorn and Matthäus Bauchinger were sympathetic to the urban working class, but their approach was equally unsystematic and uncertain, mixing antisemitism and antiplutocratic appeals with calls for morality and for the supervision of workers by priests. Bauchinger presented a good analysis of the attractiveness of Social Democratic ideas, but could only suggest as a response that conferences for priests be organized. Eichhorn was active in a number of worker causes, ranging from alleviation of the plight of the Viennese tramway workers to organization of guilds of small handwork journeyman groups. He even tried to establish a Catholic labor newspaper. By 1890, however, realizing that his efforts had resulted in almost total failure, he turned to the Lower Austrian peasantry as a more sympathetic "target group" for social activism.[177]

The record of the clerics was neither better nor worse than that of other groups in the Christian Social coalition, as far as the *Arbeiterfrage* was concerned. On the secular side of the Christian Social movement, the attempt of Leopold Kunschak to establish a subsidiary Christian Social Workers' party was a long-standing source of anger, suspicion, and contempt. The "poor" workers were a useful foil against the political and economic power of the higher bourgeoisie in Vienna. Once labor interests began to demand parity with the groups who dominated the Christian Social movement, sympathy for them declined sharply. The clerics' emotional inability to deal with these problems may excuse their confusion and hesitation. Their caution also reflected the chronic disorder of the Viennese labor movement itself in the mid-1880s. When order did come, in the person of Victor Adler, it was not to the clergy's liking.

In beginning to explore "society," with all of their self-centered and class-limited biases, the clerics stumbled onto a great opportunity to circumvent their isolation from Austrian public life. If they could not change the preconditions of their religious heritage, perhaps the other side of the equation—the society to which they directed their cultural efforts—might be viewed in a different light.

The clerics found a more congenial relationship with anti-Liberal artisan, merchant, and white collar groups in Vienna and the small and middle peasantry in Lower Austria, even if the bond which united them to these groups was a class-based secularism (in the ad hoc form of antisemitism) rather than shared religious experiences, as might have occurred in Germany. After 1885 many of the Viennese clerics came under the intellectual influence of Karl v Vogelsang. Their natural inclinations to support the Bürgertum and *Kleinbürgertum* in social conflicts were intensified by Vogelsang's arguments.

The key turning point was the year 1887. Several priests from the *Correspondenzblatt* were active in establishing the Christian Social Association, first in Alsergrund and then throughout the city. More important, Joseph Scheicher was instrumental in obtaining Catholic support in Lower Austria for Joseph Ursin, a nationalist supporter of Schönerer running for a seat in the Lower Austrian Landtag in November 1887. The idea of the "United Christians" was born, a coalition of clerical, nationalist, and antisemitic protest against Viennese Liberalism. Scheicher now recognized that his earlier efforts at a purely Catholic politics were doomed to failure and that the clergy had to ally themselves with other anti-Liberal groups.[178]

Scheicher and Eichhorn were among the first to identify themselves openly as antisemites, but by 1888 dozens of other clerics were moving in the same direction. Priests began to show up at secular political rallies; gradually they were permitted to share the speaker's platform with other petty notables. The Catholic School Association was infiltrated by anti-semitic clerics, as was the whole network of small Catholic voluntary organizations. In 1890 two antisemitic priests were elected to the City Council, and one, Josef Schnabl, won a runoff election for the Landtag. Although Scheicher's personal example and his urgings in the *Correspondenzblatt* doubtless played a decisive role, the actual movement of clerics into ward politics and electioneering was truly a collective and often an anonymous phenomenon.

In the 1870s Scheicher's attempt to found a small conservative movement was ignored by most of his fellow clerics. Now, fifteen years later, their enthusiasm was overwhelming. The clergy had changed. Not only did they possess a new level of professional self-awareness, but they discovered a secular protest movement which seemed sufficiently powerful to make their gamble worthwhile.

In 1888 the *Correspondenzblatt* began to register a new tone in the comments of clerics who found that their prestige had increased dramatically. Having joined the "United Christians," clerics found that "now the way stood open to all associations, and meetings; we were accepted with joy, our words found approval, even our newspapers found estimation."[179] Running under Lueger's sponsorship, Schnabl was elected to the Lower Austrian Landtag in 1890 because "the people again trusts its clergy."[180] One priest commented, "We priests are again getting the opportunity to speak with the people, to encourage the power of truth in those who up to this point might have viewed it as an insult to talk with a priest."[181] In October 1894, 200 Viennese priests signed a statement of appreciation and presented it to Lueger, expressing their confidence in the efficacy of political action: "In association with their political friends, they [the priests] attempted to make firm the loosened bonds, to join the bonds torn apart, so that the mass of the people looks again with trust to its priest, seeing in him its friend and adviser, hears his word, and does not allow its trust to be affected by one or another unworthy occupant of the priestly office." The statement then listed the results of this new revival: clerics now had a defense against criticism, politics helped to raise church attendance in Vienna, and the clergy had been awarded "influential political rights."[182]

Of the various professional groups which joined the antisemitic coalition, the priests were numerically the smallest. Even at the zenith of their electoral work, in the elections of 1895–96, not more than 200 to 300 clerics, as compared with thousands of *Beamten* and *Hausherren* voters, were actually involved. But it must be remembered, lest these figures be taken to detract from their importance, that not only were the priests the first to join (clerical agitation clearly predates serious, organized *Beamten* unrest by at least two years), but their movement to self-awareness as a bourgeois interest group was path breaking for the similar processes which occurred later among the other groups in the coalition. More important, they brought key assets to the antisemitic coalition which their rivals for bourgeois status did not. Whereas most of the antisemitic agitators and leaders who were property owners and state officials tended to remain at first within the organizational context of their home movements, the priests found it easier to play a multifunctional role in party agitation. Police reports from 1895–96 indicate, for example, that the clergy were often behind a variety of different kinds of rallies, political events, and money solicitations.[183] Whereas Christian Social leaders like Strobach, a property owner, were specialists at representing their own interest group, the clergy tended to become "all-purpose" agitators to whom Gessmann and Lueger could assign a variety of mundane organizational tasks. In part this reflected the clergy's role in society—they had time and opportunities for day-to-day social contact which other persons often did not enjoy; it also reflected their tendency to overcompensatory behavior. Strobach had no need to apologize for owning property. But the clerics were suspect by many within their own coalition. They had to work harder at being accepted.

The clergy were important, thus, not simply as a voting group, but much more as a source of local, sub-elite organizers. The clergy constituted a subsidiary group of organizers who gradually integrated themselves into the other, larger sub-elite structure of the party which was based on the secular political clubs, the guilds, and the district electoral committees. The two groups were not identical (and there were tensions between the two), but to the extent that Catholic associations gradually were converted to antisemitic rallying points (the work of Josef Dittrich in the Leopoldstadt was an excellent example of this process—his Catholic *Verein* became a leading element in the local Christian Social organization in this ward), the lower clergy made a meaningful contribution to the successes of 1895–96.

The priests did not restrict themselves to political agitation. As the system of rural credit societies began to grow in Lower Austria, clerics took a serious interest in these organizations, often joining the boards of the local chapters and serving as financial advisers for the local peasants. What had been impossible in the 1870s because of the absence of a neutral and workable institutional framework within which peasants and clergy could meet on equal and yet mutually dependent terms was now possible by the later 1880s and early 1890s.

Some clerics must have felt uneasy, however, about their new careers as antisemitic agitators. This was suggested by Gustav Piffl, a young Viennese priest in the 1890s and later Cardinal of Vienna during the inter-war period, who wrote in his private diary: "When one has been so involved in political action as I have up to now, one becomes fearfully 'tolerant,' one allies oneself with anyone who seems minimally com-patible. Are there any alternatives, if one wants to succeed?"[184]

The uncertainty expressed by Piffl over clerical politics was also shared, ironically, by many secular politicians and ward heelers in the antisemitic movement in Vienna. To prove their worthiness, clerics were forced to surpass the aggressiveness of even the staunchest ward politi-cian in local electoral rallies. Psenner's *Oesterreichischer Volksfreund* warned Catholic priests in 1890 that "we want no clerical domination and we will vote for a priest only then, when he has actually shown that he is concerned selflessly and fearlessly with law and justice, with the public welfare."[185]

The most important strategic effect of the clergy's antisemitism was that it set the antisemitic movement on a collision course with the Aus-trian bishops and the emperor himself. Franz Joseph had no fondness for Bürger antisemitism, but his greatest mistrust was directed against lower clerics playing non-Establishment politics. As a good Josephist he found this intolerable.

Isolated examples of the involvement of priests in public affairs were not unusual in the 1860s and 1870s, especially in the Alpine provinces and Galicia. Joseph Greuter from Tyrol was such a man. The Viennese move-ment in the late 1880s was quite different from these earlier episodes, however. Not only was it collective in its dimensions, but it was totally divorced from the Austrian episcopate's political judgment. Politics in itself were not anathema to the bishops, as long as such politics were restricted to confessional issues. The conservative *Linzer Quartalschrift* even published an article in 1876 encouraging priests to take an interest in politics, but stressed that this was to be on an individual basis and in a purely nonpartisan format. The priest should be a conciliator between political parties, rising above narrow political interests.

Antisemitism was not the root issue which divided the priests from their bishops, since Greuter was certainly as antisemitic as Scheicher, and the bishops had no fondness for "atheistic freemasonry" and the like. Doubtless the bishops felt some unease over the popular agitation of the clerics and the oft touted claims of the Christian Socials that they were about to launch a new "Christian democracy" in secular society, but the most immediate and probably the most important tension between the episcopate and their clerics involved intra-Church authority.[186] This was apparent in the bitter feelings many bishops bore against Joseph Scheicher after 1887. Beginning in the late 1880s Scheicher published a number of essays defending the right of clerics to pursue their own politics and calling into question the hierarchical authority structure of the Church.[187] Scheicher's revival of Josephist synodal ideas was of critical importance to the clergy's participation in antisemitism. For the clergy had to prove to their allies that religion could be differentiated from at least one form of "clericalism," namely, episcopal domination of public policy. His derogatory comments on the "failure" of the Church in Austria, over its seeming loss of nerve, must have seemed to the bishops to be a direct affront to their work. That a faction of the Roman Curia and the papal nuncio in Vienna, Antonio Agliardi, agreed with the lower clergy in their low estimation of the episcopate only intensified the bishops' anxiety. In Germany the Center party's and the German episcopate's hostility to Bismarck created tensions for them with Rome. In Austria the reverse was the case—Rome wanted a more aggressive posture from the Austrian episcopate, a desire which was never fulfilled.

The initial reaction of the Austrian episcopate to the clergy's radicalism was hesitant. In 1890 the bishops announced that clerics running for public office would have to obtain the consent of their bishops before taking the oath of office.[188] The episcopate also issued a joint pastoral letter on the eve of the 1891 Reichsrat elections condemning nationality agitation and making some coldly unsympathetic references to the Christian Social movement, but stopped short of an outright condemnation.[189] Between 1891 and 1895 a few bishops became more concerned with the growing power of the party, but their response was still uncoordinated, having neither the power of the government nor that of Rome behind it.[190] Cardinal Gruscha warned his clerics that protests of priests against governmental policies had to be approved by the Consistory Office of the archdiocese. He also forbade the distribution of literature other than devotional materials in churches, a clear, if ineffective reprimand against the political use of church buildings by the lower clergy.[191] Gruscha was over seventy when he was appointed to Vienna in 1890. Not only did he fail to inspire his clergy as a professional leader, but his passivity and administrative pettiness made him a caricature of a strong leader like Rauscher. Although petulance prevented Joseph Scheicher from speaking before Catholic voluntary associations, there were many other antisemitic clerics who soon dominated these groups.[192] Gruscha found it impossible to control or discipline all of them.[193]

Both Cardinal Schönborn of Prague (the senior Austrian cardinal and the representative of the episcopate to the government) and Gruscha hesitated to issue a direct condemnation of the Christian Social movement until late 1894.[194] When Schönborn and the Austrian Foreign Ministry undertook jointly to appeal to Rome in February 1895, the effort came too late and was handled too ineptly to have any hope for success.

There were few, if any, examples of individual priests disobeying their bishops. The uncertainty of the episcopate about how to deal with Christian Socialism worked to the clerics' advantage. Not until Schönerer's *Los von Rom* campaign after 1898 did the Austrian clergy find it necessary to resume the Güntherian and Bolzanoist drive for a synodal Church organization. In the 1890s the Christian Social movement itself was the clergy's synod, offering them protection and encouragement in their efforts to end their political isolation.[195]

The movement for renewal among the lower clergy in Austria soon found parallels in France, Germany, and Italy. The decade of the 1890s not only marked the rise of Christian Socialism in Austria, but also saw the beginnings of the French clergy's congress movement (Reims, 1896; Bourges, 1900), the German clergy's intense involvement in the *Volksverein* and in Christian labor unions in the Rhineland and Westphalia, and, most important, the organization of Romolo Murri's Christian Democratic movement in Italy (1898).[196] The clerical revival in Austria was native and autonomous, however, in its first stages. The clerics in the *Correspondenzblatt* were concerned with the fate of other European clerical groups, but their organizational responses derived more from their own traditions than from foreign models, most of which were not available until after 1890.

In contrast to the experience of Murri in Italy, where lower-order clerics actually did involve themselves in a liberal, democratic movement for the benefit of Italian society, in Austria the clergy consciously associated themselves with a thoroughly bourgeois social movement which became a major anti-Marxist power in Austrian politics and whose economic policy was not merely conservative, but increasingly capitalistic as well. Clerics in Austria protected themselves from the heretic-emotionalism of the later years of the reign of Leo XIII and the first years of Pius X because of the respectability of their mother party. Once Rome had approved of Lueger's movement in 1895, the clergy could rest easy about their politics in the secular world. There were, however, limits to the level of *internal* independence which Rome and the Austrian episcopate would tolerate, and these limits were firmly established after the catastrophic attempt of Scheicher and the other priests of the *Correspondenzblatt* circle to establish a clerical congress movement in the Hapsburg Empire in 1900–1902: Scheicher's *Clerustag* was repressed by the episcopate in 1902 without difficulty, as was the *Jednota* movement of Czech priests in 1907.[197] Rome was interested in a politically active clergy; it was not interested in setting the clergy free of their disciplinary responsibilities to the episcopate.

The rise of political clericalism was also shocking for the government.[198] The clergy were a premodern social group whose behavior, like that of the *Staatsbeamten,* had always been closely supervised by the state. After 1861 Liberalism destroyed the control which the Josephist tradition had exercised over both social groups. The *Staatsbeamten* picked up impressive support from the Liberal party, which tried to politicize them to accept its own modest party-political values. But for several decades this politicization was only gradually effective, and, in any event, it simply reimposed on the *Staatsbeamten* a new control device, political rather than legal, but effective nonetheless. When the clergy gained their civil liberty, there was no ongoing political movement to welcome them into the age of Liberal freedom. Like the officials, they looked to politics to define their group self-interest, but their politics was more radical and less predictable—Christian Socialism. Whereas the higher Verwaltung always retained disciplinary authority over the *Staatsbeamten,* even after they had become Liberal voters, the analogous source of controls and sanctions over the lower clergy, the episcopate, showed itself by 1895 to be inadequate to supervise its subordinates.

The radicalism of the lower clerics also showed the government the dangers resulting from Taaffe's attempt to play off economic unrest in the lower Bürgertum against the Liberal party. By tolerating collectivist rhetoric among the clergy, the government was subsidizing explosive models which could be converted into national as well as social terms. Viennese priests with social issues were an annoyance; when Czech priests in Bohemia used their Viennese brethren as models and recast antisemitic issues into national ones in the later 1890s, the government realized the gravity of its error. The emperor himself noted this danger before it was recognized by many of his advisers. On several occasions in the early 1890s Franz Joseph expressed grave concern over the radicalization of the lower clergy in Vienna and its implication for the nationalities problem.[199] By the mid-1890s the ability to exercise tight disciplinary control over the diocesan clergy became a new criterion used by the government to judge candidates for the Austrian episcopate.[200] The Austrian government suddenly wanted "strong" men for its bishops.

Catholic Social Theory in Vienna: Karl von Vogelsang

The collective and anonymous decision of hundreds of lower-order priests to join the antisemitic coalition between 1887 and 1890 proved important in providing Viennese antisemitism with a cultural legitimation apart from pan-German nationalism. But the priests drew upon one other source of Catholic support in Vienna, the journalistic politics of Karl v Vogelsang. Most of the young clerics who rose to the upper leadership levels of the Catholic wing of the Christian Social coalition after 1890, most notably Joseph Scheicher and Franz Martin Schindler, depended heavily upon the patronage and the encouragement of Vogelsang.[201] Indeed, it was precisely Vogelsang's unique combination of neo-Romantic theorizing and shrewd journalistic maneuvering in his newspaper *Vaterland* that gave the clerics the leverage they needed to secure respect within the party as a whole. In previous histories of the Christian Social party Vogelsang has usually been placed on a par with Lueger as a "cofounder" of the early Christian Social movement, with the clergy relegated to obscurity. The situation was actually quite different. The clergy were the major force for integrating Catholic culture and politics into the Christian Social coalition, both before and after 1890. Vogelsang, in turn, provided a much needed, but more diffuse, legitimation and support for "his" clerics, who often felt more loyal to him than they did to their nominal superiors Cardinals Ganglbauer and Gruscha. Not only did Vogelsang inspire and defend clerics in their anti-Establishment behavior, but he provided secular anti-semitic leaders with a neutral referee and sounding board for conflicting opinions and tactics. He listened to all of them, dispensing advice, and, more important, coverage in his newspaper. By his very presence in the crucial years 1885–90 he forced other anti-Liberals to recognize themselves as part of a common endeavor which had goals and moral justification aside from that of mere Jew hatred and personal gain. Even if his new political associates differed profoundly in evaluating his theory or sharing the literalness of his Catholicism, he provided the movement with an earnestness and moral ballast which helped to stabilize it in its newly won Third Curia successes. In this sense his leadership was more indirect and derivative than was Lueger's. Like the clerics, Vogelsang was part of the second stage of Viennese Christian Socialism. He was among those who profited from the initial unrest among the artisans by bringing to bear on this inchoate radicalism a definite view of its usefulness and future. Vogelsang, like Lueger, did not create the antisemitic movement, but he did have the shrewdness to jump on the bandwagon when it was just beginning to roll.

Karl v Vogelsang was born in Prussian Silesia in September 1818, the son of a retired Prussian army officer.[202] His family was of Lutheran, lower noble stock, with its principal seat in Mecklenburg. Vogelsang's early childhood environment was that of a rural, north German *Rittergut* with all of the feudal, patriarchal associations and values accompanying the life-style of the provincial aristocracy in pre-1848 Germany.[203] Following the conclusion of his university training in law, he entered the Prussian judicial service as a young *Referendar*. He experienced the revolution in 1848 while stationed in Berlin, which proved of decisive significance for his future. Depressed by the weak performance of Frederick William IV, Vogelsang resigned from the Prussian civil service and returned to Mecklenburg to assume the duties of a provincial landowner. When revolutionary trends manifested themselves in Mecklenburg and the local archduke was about to concede a constituent chamber in place of the traditional Estates, Vogelsang joined his fellow nobles in opposing this reduction in their political privileges.[204] The revolution made him doubt, moreover, the reliability of existing cultural and (especially) religious institutions in Mecklenburg to provide social stability. He later recalled that ''the revolutionary confusion of the last years, which also struck Mecklenburg...led my thinking to the final reasons for this sickness of human society.''[205] Vogelsang had always been deeply interested in religion and during his stay in Berlin had met the young Wilhelm v Ketteler with whom he had discussed the possibility of converting to Catholicism.[206] His Lutheranism seemed to be increasingly inadequate as a cultural barrier against distressing social and political change. Following the suggestion of Ketteler, Vogelsang went first to Munich, where he joined a circle of men in the Görres House, and then to Innsbruck to receive catechetical instruction from the Jesuits. On Easter 1850 he converted to Catholicism.[207]

When he returned to Mecklenburg in late 1850, Vogelsang encountered the hostility of his fellow Lutheran landowners, for whom Protestantism was a political as well as a social attribute. Rather than face the humiliation of living as an outcast, Vogelsang rented his estate and left Mecklenburg in 1854, beginning a twenty-year odyssey in search of economic security and professional satisfaction. Finally, in the early 1860s he purchased a small estate on an isolated hilltop outside of Vienna (the Bisamberg). He eventually settled there with his family (1865). For several years Vogelsang struggled to survive by managing a small cement factory (he eventually leased it to another company, which, in turn, went bankrupt after 1873 and left Vogelsang with huge debts), but he abandoned his tenuous status as an émigré lower noble proprietor in a society in which the status levels for the ranks of the landowning aristocracy were very different from those of Mecklenburg.

After several years of itinerant journalistic work in Hungary, Vogelsang returned to Vienna in 1875, having been appointed editor of the Catholic newspaper *Vaterland*. The newspaper had been established in 1860 by a consortium of Bohemian, Viennese, and Moravian aristocrats, with the Bohemians led by Count Leo Thun having decisive control. *Vaterland* represented the Catholic, federalist-oriented nobility in the struggle against both administrative centralization and political Liberalism. By the middle 1870s the paper was floundering, with declining subscription levels and a bland, uninspired style of journalism which, if nothing else, reflected the morbidity of the Viennese Catholic political situation.

Vogelsang later described the weak position of the Austrian Catholics as he first observed it in 1875: "When I came to Austria, educated circles viewed the so-called Clericals as a group of feebleminded people; the so-called Feudals, however, as a group of egoistic and power-seeking people. The former were ridiculed, the latter hated."[208] One issue which Vogelsang thought might unify the warring Catholic factions (Thun and the Feudals against Rauscher's centralist supporters) was the social question. During his sojourn in Hungary Vogelsang had devoted considerable attention to Catholic social theory, particularly the ideas of his friend Wilhelm Ketteler and to the social and political writings of early-nineteenth-century Catholic Romantics like Adam Müller. Of the two, Müller was to prove far more influential for Vogelsang's own contributions, although Vogelsang's view of the state was much less a summation of the whole of society (as it was for Müller) than it was a subsidiary mechanism he was forced to accept.

Vogelsang's decision to redirect his newspaper's editorial interests toward the social question, although it reflected his own personal interest in social theory and the social turbulence of the 1870s, also had the marked utilitarian function of bridging intra-Catholic political feuds.[209] But his insistence on introducing the social question in *Vaterland* collided with the tastes of his chief sponsor, Leo Thun. The once progressive and enlightened Thun had become by the 1880s a suspicious, autocratic, and sickly old man, with a propensity to use Vogelsang as a lightning rod for his frustrations over modern Austrian society and politics. Vogelsang's stubbornness and defensiveness did nothing to help the situation.

His life in Vienna was fundamentally influenced by the world of Mecklenburg which he had relinquished for his religion. This was important, since it provoked the isolation which Vogelsang initially felt in Viennese society. Not only was Vogelsang not the equal of the great nobles who funded his paper and for whom he often felt a scarcely concealed contempt because of their easy, unintensive life-style, but he did not fully comprehend Bürger traditions of Viennese society. His world was almost as foreign to that of Karl Lueger as it was to that of Leo Thun. He remained the struggling, intense *Rittergutsbesitzer,* having neither the latitudinarian qualities of the great Austrian aristocracy nor the full sense of competitive politics which imbued the Viennese Democratic movement. It said much about the poverty of early clerical politics in Vienna that the clergy had to rely on an outsider twice-over for their intellectual and emotional support. That Vogelsang finally chose Lueger over Thun reflected the dynamism and openness of the Christian Social movement, qualities which Vogelsang found refreshing and appealing.

Moreover, Vogelsang never overcame the chronic financial insecurity of his early life. The crash of 1873 was not simply a historical construct for Vogelsang. He felt it and was injured by it every time he looked at his bank balances. His biographers have tried to avoid associating his bitter anticapitalism with his personal misfortunes (such as the debacle of his cement factory), but there was clearly a connection. Vogelsang was not a petty man, but he was not above taking vengeance on a system which had caused him so much personal grief.

However bitter he felt toward the Lutherans in north Germany, culturally he was clearly one of them.[210] Vogelsang's ease in granting to the state a wide range of temporary social and economic powers may have been due, in part, to his Lutheran background. More important, Vogelsang brought to Austrian Catholic politics a very different self-conception and aesthetic tone from that which local aristocratic leaders affected. He was never comfortable with the ritual and aesthetics which some Catholics of the Concordat generation had seized upon to revive Catholic morals. In spite of his friendship with the Görres circle in Munich, Vogelsang's Romanticism was an ideational and abstract conception of the public social good, not simply a subjective personalism cast in larger institutional terms. He was far more insistent in his moralism than Austrian Catholic political commentators were prone to be. Vogelsang's reputation for analytic radicalism reflected his bent toward north German, Lutheran piety and morality, which was difficult to transplant into the more latitudinarian traditions of Austrian Catholicism, especially the Catholicism of the Bohemian nobility and the Alpine peasants, as opposed to that of the inhabitants of cities and small towns or of the Josephist clergy themselves.

Vogelsang's tenacity reflected his self-image as an active, ministerial Christian. His social theory was a part of a system of publicly preached social morality coming from a former Protestant who still felt the calling of a lay Christian to social ministerial duties. The ex-Lutheran was in fact closer to the Austrian Josephist tradition with its statism and eudaemonistic social welfare activities than he was to Vormärz Romanticism, although doubtless he would have denied this irony. Vogelsang shared with the Viennese lower clerics like Scheicher and Schindler a belief in self-reliance and individual responsibility, as well as a contempt for the laxity and passivity of Catholic aristocratic culture. Vogelsang loyally supported the bishops on policy questions, but he never indulged in the kind of unctuous, paternalistic rhetoric which characterized the other Catholic journals of the day. Vogelsang's Protestant background immunized him against this heritage of Vormärz paternalism and made him an ideal spokesman for a brand of social politics which respected the bishops without idolizing them. The clergy for Vogelsang existed for the good of society, as well as of the Church.

After 1875 Vogelsang cultivated a small group of Austrian nobles and clerics in Vienna, who provided lasting contacts for his years in the city. In 1875 he met Count Gustav Blome, also a convert from north Germany, who was associated with the Geneva Union, an ultramontane association organized in 1870 to defend papal interests, which also held discussions on the social question.[211] In the later 1870s Vogelsang met Egbert Belcredi, Alois Liechtenstein, Anton Pergen, and Franz Kuefstein, representatives of a small faction of the higher nobility whose political interests surpassed a narrow concern for federalist constitutionalism.[212] Vogelsang's connections with these aristocrats enabled him to launch in January 1879 the first Austrian learned journal devoted to social reform, the *Österreichische Monatsschrift für christliche Sozialreform.*[213]

During the 1880s two decisive changes occurred in Vogelsang's life and work. The artisan protest movement organized by Löblich and Schneider quickly proved to be a subject of irresistible fascination for him. Not only did the substance of artisan protectionism fit in well with Vogelsang's corporate theory, but the relevance of the problem as a local Viennese phenomenon offered the journalist an easy, legitimate way to center more attention on Vienna itself. Until the early 1880s *Vaterland* had not really addressed itself to a Viennese audience. Now Vogelsang suddenly discovered a ready-made constituency, eager and willing to use the space he made available in his paper for their cause. Given the propensity of the Liberal papers to ignore or minimize artisan protest, Vogelsang had a rich field of exploitation before him. He soon shifted the paper to a much greater coverage of the artisan movement.

Equally important, Vogelsang was able to use the process of legislation which led to the 1883 *Gewerbeordnung* as an example of the harmonious cooperation between the conservative aristocracy and the secular state. Much of his early social theory hinged on the expectation that the Catholic aristocracy working with the Church would show itself to be a natural, aggressive leader of the new Christian *Volk.*[214]

Had Vogelsang simply directed his newspaper toward the handwork issue per se in the early 1880s, however, this stage of his career would not have differed markedly from what went before. His own essays in the first years of his Viennese sojourn dealt primarily with agricultural problems and proposals for agrarian reform. The fundamental shift which occurred in his work in the later 1880s—away from an exclusively agrarian perspective and away from a dependence upon the aristocracy to regenerate society—took place largely because Vogelsang began to associate with a variety of local Viennese political figures. The earlier circle of aristocratic friends remained, but to them was added a second, more diverse line of radical clerics and ex-Democratic politicians, all eager to make the acquaintance of someone who controlled a large daily newspaper. As early as 1880–81 Vogelsang met Joseph Scheicher and Rudolf Eichhorn, initiating friendships which developed in intensity over the decade.[215]

Equally significant, Vogelsang met Ernst Schneider in 1882. Vogelsang exploited Schneider as a source of information, listening to his complaints, gossip, and sarcasm with patient interest. It said much about the isolation of Viennese Catholics in the early 1880s that Vogelsang had to rely on a man of Schneider's character to gain knowledge of the artisan movement.[216] As a contact man and judge of local personalities Schneider was invaluable to Vogelsang. Through Schneider Vogelsang met Albert Gessmann in 1883. Gessmann in turn eventually introduced Vogelsang to Lueger. Vogelsang also became acquainted with other antisemitic leaders, including Robert Pattai and Ludwig Psenner. He engaged in a regular correspondence with all of them, to broaden his contacts with artisan political circles and to encourage unity among the various antisemitic factions.[217]

This range of new personal contacts and new issues exploded Vogelsang's earlier satisfaction with Austrian clerical conservatism and the Austrian aristocracy. During the early 1880s Vogelsang hoped that Taaffe and the Iron Ring would sponsor a comprehensive program of social reform legislation. When by the later years of the decade it was apparent that this expectation was false and that many aristocrats thought of social reform as merely a convenient ploy to embarrass the Liberals, Vogelsang became disgusted with the tameness and passivity of the high aristocracy.[218] At the same time he was forced by the vagaries of "Christianity" in Vienna to recognize that his own personal literalness and scrupulosity as a convert to Catholicism was not characteristic of Gentile voters in the city. Gradually he became more flexible in his perception of what it meant to be a Catholic, hoping to gain for the Church at least some share of the power and achievements of political antisemitism.[219]

Vogelsang's personal transformation thus paralleled that of the lower clergy. Just as they abandoned the illusions of the late 1870s and early 1880s in favor of a more radical, self-help approach to Catholic politics, so did Vogelsang after 1887 abandon his former aristocratic sponsors in search of a new Catholic politics in the city. In both cases the tradition of synodal and lay Christian activity provided ex-Josephist clerics like

Scheicher and a former Protestant like Vogelsang with a common heritage of individual and small-group action.

Vogelsang's growing contact with the antisemitic movement inevitably produced tensions with Leo Thun. When Liechtenstein praised Vogelsang in 1888 as an "organizer of the first rank, who knows how to adapt the needs and desires of the middle classes in Vienna toward a welcome change of opinion," he was not speaking for the majority of the aristocrats.[220] After 1887 few leaders in the Hohenwart Club had serious interest in additional social reform legislation. Indeed, Vogelsang met with sullen tolerance or scarcely disguised hostility from aristocrats and higher clerics, who felt that *Vaterland* should avoid the artisans and concentrate on less volatile issues.[221] Ernst Schneider probably expressed the feelings of his constituents against this attitude of the aristocrats when, with his customary crudeness, he wrote to Vogelsang that "if one excluded a few highly respectable [individuals], one could easily throw the aristocrats together with the Polish Jews in a pot."[222]

Upon Leo Thun's death in late 1888 a new sponsoring committee for the newspaper was established which allowed Vogelsang more editorial flexibility. These were the golden years of Vogelsang's journalism. Never before had he enjoyed such freedom to shape the paper as he desired. The prominent support he gave the radical clergy, encouraging them to intensify their political agitation, was an important example of the new role of the paper.[223]

Vogelsang's early efforts at proselytizing on behalf of a conservative, anticapitalist approach to the social question were disillusioning. In 1882 he helped to organize the *Vereinigung katholischer Sozialpolitiker,* a joint Austro-German committee to study social reform topics and make regular reports to the annual German Catholic congresses.[224] By 1885 many of the lower clerics of the *Correspondenzblatt* group, including Scheicher, Eichhorn, and eventually Schindler, joined the *Vereinigung* on Vogelsang's sponsorship. The results of the first two conferences at Haid (Bohemia) and Salzburg in 1883 offered conservative, totalist interpretations of the social question, rejecting the justice of the wage contract and demanding instead a corporatist reorganization of large industry and the elaboration of a "social contractual relationship" *(Gesellschaftsvertrag)* between industrial workers and capitalist employers.[225]

The reaction of the German Center party to Vogelsang's efforts was openly hostile.[226] Ludwig Windthorst had no desire to involve his party in what he thought were arcane and irrelevant theoretical disputes between Liberal Catholics, who recognized the morality of modern capitalism (who were in the majority in the Center party leadership), and Catholics, like Vogelsang, who did not.[227] The *Vereinigung* never recovered from the negative response of the Center's leadership. As a sounding board for German social Catholicism the association had a limited significance after 1885, but for Austrian Catholics its importance was minimal. After the bitterness of 1884–85 Vogelsang felt isolated from German Catholicism and was more inclined to reinvest his energies in Viennese politics, where he might at least enjoy a modicum of respect. The Germans, in turn, resented the attempt of the "Lutheran convert" who had left Germany for Austria to dictate to them on the shape of their social theory.

Not surprisingly, when Vogelsang became involved in a second discussion circle in 1889–90, the terms of the arrangement were quite different from those of the *Vereinigung*. The *Entenabende* was a Viennese discussion group organized in 1888 by Schindler and Vogelsang to prepare for the social section of the Second Catholic Congress in April 1889. After the congress ended, the group continued to meet, drawing a far more diversified audience than the *Vereinigung* and serving as an agitatorial planning group for early Christian Social elite and sub-elite leaders. Lueger dominated the meetings, having made it clear to Schindler that he wanted "hints" and suggestions on pragmatic policy options, not abstruse metaphysics or neo-Romanticism.[228] The *Abende*'s lack of ideological coherence was compensated for by the political relevance of its agenda and the impact of its propaganda.[229] As in his journalism after 1886, Vogelsang sacrificed the virtue of theoretical consistency for the vice of political success. What the arid sectarianism of the *Vereinigung* could not do (force Vogelsang to conform to Viennese political reality) Lueger did with a few abrupt sentences. Now, like the clergy, Vogelsang had a political world of his own, one which far surpassed the isolation of his earlier career.

The traditional historiographical approach to Vogelsang has centered on the distinction between social reform and social politics, with Vogelsang cast as a neofeudal fanatic and Lueger as the moderate pragmatist who had little connection with Vogelsang's work. This interpretation has been guided in two directions, depending upon the politics of the individual author. Some militant adherents to Vogelsang's thought in the Austrian First Republic, like Wiard v Klopp, Anton Orel, and Karl Lugmayer, the so-called Social Romanticists, characterized the development of the Christian Social party after 1890 as a "betrayal" of Vogelsang's ideas in the sense that the Christian Socials gradually became a more conservative, procapitalist party.[230] Others, like Franz Sommeregger, representing the main body of the Christian Social party after 1911 and anxious to counter the accusation of Orel and others, dismissed Vogelsang's ideas as those of a mere journalist and a "noble-minded pessimist," which could best be forgotten as an embarrassment.[231] A recent American interpretation by Alfred Diamant has sustained the distinction between the idealist Vogelsang and the pragmatists Lueger and Schindler, emphasizing the statist aspects of Vogelsang's thought.[232]

The extent to which the party abandoned Vogelsang's ideals depends upon the relative importance the historian chooses to place on means as opposed to ends. If one emphasizes the technical means of Vogelsang's proposals (usury, social contracts, the *Stände* system itself in a completely literal sense), then one might well assume that Lueger, Gessmann, and Friedrich Funder (the editor of the *Reichspost*) led the party in repudiation of Vogelsang. If, in contrast, one sees these structural ideas as defining broader policy goals in a general system of conservative morality (the preservation of the artisan Mittelstand, the economic welfare of the peasant proprietor), then in one sense the Christian Social party never abandoned Vogelsang's moral heritage.

To argue that Vogelsang represented a brand of social theory which was wholly abandoned in political action after 1890 is both unrealistic and untenable. Such a view ignores the common assumptions shared by all anti-Liberal activists in the later 1880s, the period in the evolution of the Christian Social party when the major enemy of the artisan Bürgertum seemed to be the fledgling industrial capitalist establishment in Vienna.[233] Virtually all anti-Liberal radicals shared this view, even if for Lueger "anticapitalism" was political rhetoric with which to attack the local Liberal party (itself heavily protoindustrial in its voter makeup) and not a policy unto itself. Precisely in the years 1891–97 the party discovered that it needed other sources of support beyond the artisan-dominated Third Curia to protect its electoral constituency against the powerful assault of the Austrian Social Democrats. Increasingly after 1891 the Socialists, rather than the Liberals, loomed as the major enemy of the movement, a perception which Vogelsang had not encountered in his lifetime. Party leaders now came to the rude perception that the "poor" were a far greater threat for the Mittelstand than finance capitalism. Since the *bürgerlicher* Mittelstand in Vienna comprised voter groups more wealthy and stable than the artisans, the party was forced to tailor its rhetoric and policy to accommodate a broader cross section of bourgeois interests, many of whom were less interested in "anticapitalism" than were the 5 fl. artisans. Inevitably party policy became more moderate, not in a direct attempt to repudiate Vogelsang, but in an effort to provide the artisans and peasants with a broader contextual defense, based on all three electoral curias, against the Social Democrats.

Vogelsang's thought must be viewed within the context of the period in which he wrote, a period dominated by the agrarian depression of the later

1870s and by the credit difficulties of small and middle proprietors, with falling wholesale grain prices and rising interest rates. It was not surprising that Vogelsang's first essay against usury in the *Monatsschrift* in 1879 took as its subject the usurious exploitation of the peasantry.[234] The symbolic world which defined his views of usury was the immediate post-1873 chaos.[235] That his work distorted an extremely complex agrarian development is undeniable, but it perceived and expressed with accuracy the great human costs of such a transformation.

Vogelsang's thought was markedly historicist in nature.[236] Like many other nineteenth-century conservatives Vogelsang naturalized history, making arbitrary, idealized reconstructions of the past the "natural" basis and focus for contemporary social institutions.[237] Historical continuity, the valued heritage of the past, had to be preserved at all costs.[238] His economic thought was more reactive than analytical, representing more his disenchantment with economic Liberalism than a positive logical view of how the economy should function. The capitalism issue was Vogelsang's key to rejecting large-scale commercial and industrial development, even though he admitted that the moral perversity of "loan capital" *(Leihkapital)* had infected earlier civilizations as well. The domination of interest-bearing capital on the large industrial level deprived other forms of wealth of their "social character and social power."[239]

The most controversial aspect of Vogelsang's thought involved the usury question, a question which also had a profound influence on Joseph Scheicher and Rudolf Eichhorn, making the clerical wing of the party after 1890 somewhat more radical on the question than the main party elite. Vogelsang's preoccupation with usury was not unusual for conservatives of his generation, but he proved more imaginative than others in providing historical explanations.[240] He believed that the medieval legislation of the Church against usury and the notion of money as "dead" or "unfruitful" were still viable, operational concepts in the nineteenth century.[241] He rejected late scholastic devices for circumscribing prohibitions against interest (such as the title of *lucrum cessans,* by which an investor might accept a moderate rate of interest for a loan or an investment if, by so extending his own resources, he missed another, more profitable investment possibility).

John Noonan has commented on Vogelsang's work and on the later Viennese Romantics: "They are unfaithful to the scholastic tradition in its developed form and they do not accurately or fully present even the medieval theory."[242] Noonan's evaluation is a fair one, but it does not comprehend Vogelsang's psychological and emotional dependence on the usury problem. In political practice Vogelsang deferred to Lueger and suspended judgment on the problem as an operational issue,[243] but in his theory usury remained a cardinal explanation of his own generation's economic misfortunes. His position was one of interpretive excess, and it was precisely because Vogelsang realized that absolute prohibition of interest was impossible in the nineteenth century that he felt free to belabor the point in his moral polemics. The anti-interest position was far more a statement of political morality than of economic policy. Lueger, for his part, could live with extreme moralisms in a way that he could not tolerate extremist policy. Vogelsang himself admitted that he was proposing ideal moral situations which could not hope to have any effect in the foreseeable future.[244]

The linchpin of Vogelsang's system of social theory was corporatism, not usury condemnations. The importance of corporatism in his thought can be appreciated only when the double function of the ideal is recognized: not only would the corporations restructure Austrian society, but they would create a new system of economy and labor value as well. In one blow all of the problems raised by Liberalism, by usury, and by a pathetic and weak aristocracy would be resolved. The *Stände* were the uniform panacea for all of modernity's ills. Vogelsang's ideal society was one in which horizontal class divisions would be replaced by vertical, hierarchical divisions of various broad economic sectors, the three most important being large industry, the small craft trades and shops, and agriculture.[245] Vogelsang arbitrarily insisted that small and large industry be separated into distinct corporations, while refusing to recognize that the proletariat constituted a separate socioeconomic group apart from the other three *Stände*.

The ideal agents for this process of corporate cultural renewal should have been the Austrian aristocracy. And, indeed, for some years Vogelsang bent over backward to cast the nobility in a favorable, progressive light. The extent to which he misread the potency of aristocratic conservatism was obvious in the rude and indifferent reception which his mentor, Leo Thun, received after 1848 in articulating ideas he had acquired in the later Vormärz about a reformed *Stände* system.[246] The Austrian aristocracy was no more prepared to resist the Liberal state than it had been to look beyond a narrow program of economic self-interest in the 1830s and 1840s.

Perhaps because he finally recognized that the Austrian aristocracy was neither a creature of the state (as was the Prussian) nor its determined opponent (as was the French), Vogelsang was forced to admit that the constitutional state itself was a necessary factor in bringing the corporate idea into operation: the legislative machinery of the state had to be used "for speeding up the process." Those Catholics (including the bishops) who rejected temporary state intervention were guilty of the "error of social materialism."[247] Vogelsang's statism was, however, a two-edged sword. Greater state power would not mean in Austria, as it might have in Prussia, an enhanced influence in civil society for the aristocracy. Thus, although Vogelsang was willing to use the bourgeois state to introduce the corporate motif, he would not have wanted Austrian society to remain in permanent bondage to that state.[248] With their own ambiguity about the state, radical clerics like Scheicher and Franz Schindler found Vogelsang's mixture of statism and corporatism supremely attractive. Neither the clergy nor Vogelsang wished to dispense with or abolish the state, given its ultimate utility as an agency for hegemonic Christian ethics. But the present state, the state of Liberal values, needed an extensive inner transformation. In view of the Liberal state's seeming permanency, however, the Christian Social party offered to the clerics and Vogelsang a satisfactory antistatist substitute. The party was sufficiently antisemitic to provide a legitimate cultural alternative to the Liberals, while sufficiently conservative to ensure that public policy control, if achieved by the party, would serve Catholic social interests and remain subject to bourgeois society. It was hardly surprising that Schindler, the most "Liberal" of Vogelsang's protégés among the radical clergy, retained Vogelsang's combination of corporatism and statism, while rejecting the master's prohibition of usury and his labor theory of value. Schindler's later attempt to view the city of Vienna as a Catholic corporation, having both statist-interventionist and private-autonomous powers against the national state, was a classic manifestation of Vogelsang's admixture of state power and corporate right, which also harmonized well with the latent Josephist-Bolzanoist strain in the Austrian lower clerical tradition itself.[249]

In some instances the result of Vogelsang's corporatism was not altogether different from the pragmatic goals of the secular politicians in the party, such as the exclusion from his new, corporate-based state franchise of most workers and servants. In contrast to Vogelsang, however, the theoretical basis for the franchise manipulations of the Christian Socials was the political Bürgertum itself in all of its diversity, and not a social *Stände* system per se. Lueger was willing to manipulate franchise legislation to make sure that guild chairmen stood an excellent chance of election, but he was far too imbued with the sovereignty of the political party itself as an institution to relinquish *its* power prerogatives to corporate social groups. Social corporatism as a reconstruction of Bürger society was foreign to most of the nonclerical elements in the party. Whereas Lueger sought to reintegrate the lower Bürgertum into a general reconstruction of bourgeois society, Vogelsang and the clergy stopped short and converted the artisan craft trades into a hegemonic political structure without attempting to make their demands congruent with those of the rest of Viennese Bürger society.

Vogelsang also shared the propensity of most Catholic social theorists to deny to the proletariat an independent political or social role. Lueger, however, did not want to achieve a social consolidation of the working class with the Viennese Bürgertum. For all of their Liberal Democratic rhetoric about the unitary *Volk,* most party leaders were more interested in achieving a defensive strategy to provide for the political homogeneity of the Bürgertum against the working classes than in sponsoring a symbiosis between the two groups. On an empirical level, most Christian Social voters, especially those in the First and Second Curias, had little sympathy with schemes which seemed to deemphasize the social distance between themselves and the working classes. The psycho-social world of the typical *Hausherr* or antisemitic state official hinged on a deeply rooted horizontal separation of classes and caste levels. Thus, Catholic corporate social rhetoric of vertical, supraclass unity may have been a misreading of Bürger society, a society Vogelsang failed to understand in all of its complexity.

Vogelsang was more than a social instrumentalist. He disliked his society and sought to replace it, not simply to reform its more unsightly features. To deny this utopian aspect of his work would be both unfair and pointless. But his literalness in theory was counterbalanced both by flexibility in practice and by a willingness to allow others to draw upon his political morality in general terms without having to subscribe to all of his theories. This was perhaps the most important feature of his Viennese career. What had begun as an exercise in conservative dogmatism ended as a moral crusade for utilitarian benefits for the Mittelstand.

Vogelsang's most dogmatic theoretical statements were usually circumscribed by an abundance of qualifying clauses (he consistently referred to his own work as that of a *Vorstufe,* with real social reconstruction coming generations later).[250] He was thus able to avoid the charge of writing fantasies by suggesting that it was as a moralist and a prophet as well as a social architect that he had formulated his theories. And as a product of a moralist, Vogelsang's writings make sense in a way which obviates the charge of technical utopianism. Hence, what he had begun by 1890 could never really be accomplished. In Vogelsang's case the moralism was mediate to social reality but never made congruent with it.

His historical accomplishments within the Christian Social movement were of tactical and strategic importance. His role as editor of *Vaterland* between 1885 and 1890 cannot be overemphasized. Until the founding of the *Deutsches Volksblatt* and the *Reichspost* the antisemites and especially the clerics were enormously dependent upon his editorial patronage. Even if the circulation figures of the paper were not impressive (4,200 in 1890), its influence in a city with such a strongly politicized newspaper culture as Vienna was significant. Unlike the press in Berlin, the major

Viennese newspapers were extremely sensitive to local political developments. A party without a daily newspaper *of record* in Vienna simply did not exist. The symbolic presence of the paper was far more important than its circulation figures.

More important, Vogelsang's social theory gave to the clerics in their initial ventures a public credibility they desperately needed. This was both a significant and a necessary accomplishment, since Vogelsang's theories, however unworkable or antiquated they may have been in an applied sense, did elevate the antisemitic movement to a level of discourse where oppositional leaders like Victor Adler had to react on intellectual terms.[251] This was one of the marked points of difference between contemporary German antisemitic movements, like Stöcker's Berlin movement, and Lueger's efforts in Vienna. The joining of Catholicism to antisemitism with the mediation of Catholic social theory and lower clerical politics helped to justify the movement in terms other than the impoverished eclecticism of *Kleinbürger* Jew hatred. Even if Lueger was unwilling to accept any single part of Vogelsang's theory, he accepted the *whole* of the theory as a principle of justification to which he could point to define the party's mission. Vogelsang's theory became a classic case of the whole as more than the sum of its parts, not simply in a quantitative but also in a qualitative sense.

Long after Vogelsang's death in 1890 the legitimacy which he provided the clerical wing of the Christian Social party contributed to the variety and complexity of Viennese political antisemitism. By themselves the clerics might have found it difficult to attain a full partnership in the movement in the early years of the struggle. But with Vogelsang's help and guidance the clergy effectively confronted the "clericalism" issue by pointing to this Catholic social theorist who owed both "Rome" and the local episcopate nothing, but who challenged both to tolerate "Christian" antisemitic politics in Vienna after 1887.

Josephism: Upended or Fulfilled?

In discovering Mittelstand society the clerics found that it was possible to reactivate and modernize the service mentality with which their late-eighteenth-century predecessors had been so carefully imbued. Antisemitic Bürger politics offered both to the clerics and to Vogelsang an obvious invitation to apply traditions of nonepiscopal social action on behalf of social groups formerly alienated from traditional Austrian Catholicism. This time, however, it was civil society, as opposed to the Lutheran *or* Josephist state, which would profit exclusively from their energies and resources.

The renewal of the clerics' professional mentality in the 1880s on the basis of Congrua agitation and school activity played a crucial preliminary role. The passive legitimacy of the eighteenth-century *pastor bonus* was now exploded, since the clerics gradually perceived their own role in reference to other bourgeois groups. By becoming more conscious of themselves in social terms and by articulating this new ideal in a brash collective framework, the Austrian clergy expanded the basis for the meaning of *Dienst* beyond Josephist service. No longer was *Dienst* valuable because the state said so; it was valuable because a just appraisal of the framework of bourgeois status esteem in late-nineteenth-century society seemed to dictate that the clergy be accorded privileges similar to those granted to similar public service groups.

By joining radical politics, the clerics undid their isolation from the *bürgerlichen Gesellschaft* of mid-nineteenth-century Austria. Not by means of a Concordat, nor by means of isolated journalistic feuds in the manner of Sebastian Brunner, but by a mass movement of priests into electioneering and propagandizing, into agrarian societies and credit institutions, was this goal accomplished. Joseph II's goal of integrating the Church into civil society was finally completed, but in a way which would have shocked the emperor. For the clerics accomplished this integration not in the universal pietistic style of the Josephist tradition, but by the competitive, secular, antiproletarian strategy demanded by the interest groups of the Viennese Mittelstand. The more the priests became politicians, the less they could sustain their pretense of service to all society. A similar process occurred within the secular sectors of non-Liberal politics. Both politicians and priests found themselves using old language and old cultural expectations in dynamic political situations which often found it difficult to sustain them. The clerics were acting against their language, as it were. Lueger's "new" political language was really quite traditional in terms of popular rhetoric and religion. But the use of this popular language in a new class situation was revolutionary. Karl Kraus was wrong for the right reasons—men were despoiling their language in Vienna, but its misuse was intelligible and predictable.

In Germany the Center party served as both an alternative and an antidote to political antisemitism; the Catholic clergy in Prussia, thus, had no need to endorse antisemitism. In Austria in contrast the clergy sacrificed religion for a mildly nationalist and secular antisemitism; they expected that other middle bourgeois social groups, like the tenured school teachers, would sacrifice their anticlericalism in return. In Germany the clergy could rely on religion as an integrative force for political and social cooperation with the Catholic Bürgertum. The Austrian clergy had to find other, more secular modes of cooperation. Rather than seeing political antisemitism as a threat, as the German clergy did, they welcomed it as a last chance to prove their social usefulness and political effectiveness.[252] In Vienna the bourgeois groups involved were playing with stylized political issues which masked deep interest group self-aggrandizement. Cultural conflict over the "clericalism" issue within the antisemitic coalition never ended; indeed, it created a rich theme of inter-party tensions before 1914. But when the issue became one of the maintenance or loss of class prerogatives, the ranks could be closed.

Unlike the fate of the lower clergy in France and Italy, the Austrian clergy's social conservatism and their good fortune in discovering an anti-Marxist political movement combined to provide the Viennese clerics with a safe and comfortable secular home. By discovering the Austrian Mittelstand, the clergy could conveniently forget about the proletariat to a degree which was unparalleled in German or Italian political Catholicism.

This informal decision to abandon the Austrian working class in favor of an anti-Marxist Mittelstand movement was taken well before Leo XIII's *Rerum Novarum*. When the encyclical came out in May 1891, the clergy had no trouble interpreting it in a way which justified their bourgeois secularism. For the lower clerics of Abbé Lemire's Democratic movement in France or of Murri's Christian Democracy in Italy, *Rerum Novarum* was the beginning of a movement out of the enforced political ghetto of their respective churches. In Austria it was simply the final touch to a movement which created a more dynamic and more powerful party-political ghetto for the Church.[253]

More important, by joining a coalition of social protest which was based in the lower and middle ranks of the Bürgertum, the clergy resolved the problem which Veith and the Catholic reformers in 1848 had encountered in defining their social audience. The priests did not abandon the "middle classes" for the "lower middle classes," as one historian has argued, for many members of the Veith circle were also interested in the Bürgertum as a whole, and not just in the university-educated strata of society. The Christian Socials in turn were not simply a party of the *Kleinbürgertum;* they soon moved to encompass in their rhetoric the whole of the Bürgertum in a new sense of status unity. Now the clergy had a political movement in which to situate themselves, whereas in 1848 they tried to create their own constituency without outside assistance.

The upshot of this campaign for occupational renewal was that the lower clergy in Austria came full circle within one hundred years. In the 1780s a group of reformist priests, who for the sake of internal reforms tolerated and even supported the state control of Josephist Catholicism, was opposed by the episcopate, led by Cardinal Migazzi, who was both antireformist and antistatist. By the 1890s in contrast the Lower Austrian clergy were fiercely anti-Josephist in a state-church sense (although they retained an interest in internal reform), while the Austrian episcopate had turned to a complacent Josephism in hope that the state would protect the Church's prerogatives and privileges. The radical clerics mingled the best and the worst of the Josephist tradition. They combined a remarkable commitment to intellectual pluralism within the Church (Scheicher's espousal of a variety of semimodernistic views after 1900) with a profoundly antipluralistic view of civil society. That they were forced to coexist with rival social and ideological forces does not mean that they accepted such coexistence as a permanent feature of the general political system. The clergy's intolerance for ideological "oppositionalism" was no greater than that which their anticlerical opponents manifested toward them, but their historical defensiveness and the latent hostility the priests often encountered from many "Christians" within their own party made their monism even more embattled.

The end of the internecine bourgeois conflict in Vienna in 1896–97 and the beginning of a more fundamental conflict with Social Democracy brought the clergy, by trial and error, to the great watershed in Austrian political history. In dealing with culturally alienated bourgeois groups, the clergy might at least have recourse to social interest compatibility. Hence the kind of forced interchange of concessions which went on within the Viennese school system after 1898. But in Austrian Social Democracy the clergy (and the other bourgeois groups of the Christian Social coalition) confronted a culturally *and* socially alien group. The Social Democrats were both anticlerical and antibourgeois. This union of cultural and class hostility on both sides of the Austrian *Lager* system tore Vienna's civic culture apart for the next forty years.

4

Karl Lueger and the Radicalization of Viennese Democracy, 1875–90

The commitment of Catholic resources to the discontent initiated by the artisans helped to stabilize the early antisemitic movement, but neither the priests nor Vogelsang was able to provide the personal leadership to lift antisemitism out of the morass into which it had fallen by the mid-1880s. Only with the accession to leadership of Karl Lueger and the integration of older traditions of Viennese Democracy into artisan anti-semitism in the later 1880s did the movement stand a chance of long-term survival. Without Lueger and his Democratic tradition, antisemitism, even with a religious aura, would never have survived competition with the Liberal party. If the first six years of the movement showed anything, it was how desperately top leaders were needed to direct the inchoate forces of artisan discontent. The clerics could provide the manpower to assist in sub-elite electoral work, but they were unsuited to lead the movement. Vogelsang, though articulate on the level of propaganda, was always an outsider to the city's political culture. If "Christian" antisemitism was to succeed in a city with a deeply conservative social culture, it would have to adapt itself to older political norms and methods of the Liberal tradi-tion. Radical language and acerbic journalism was not enough to win elections. Social radicalism in bourgeois Vienna could succeed only by being tempered with a good dose of political traditionalism. The artisans needed leaders schooled in the patterns of deference and notability of the Liberal tradition, trained in electoral management and agitation, with a flair for styling political change in terms of the historic virtue of the Vien-nese Bürgertum.

In the history of the Christian Social movement Karl Lueger played several key roles, so much so that many writers, then and now, have simply identified Christian Socialism with him.[1] The inadequacy of this notion in view of the complexity of the movement ought to be apparent. Unquestionably Lueger was dominant in shaping and leading the hetero-geneous party. The relationship between this complex and often mis-understood personality and a movement prospering amid a variety of internal tensions now requires consideration.

Perhaps the most significant question which must be confronted is whether Lueger, by the force of his personality, created the Christian Social movement and, if so, how this was accomplished. Was the party the result of some charisma which only Lueger possessed? Or were other, more structural factors at work which led to party unity in the 1890s? Is it true that the Christian Socials lost the 1911 elections because they no longer had Lueger to lead them? Or may the historian look to such factors as consumer price levels, unemployment figures, and conflicts within the party elite to account for the decline in party fortunes? Was Lueger, even during the high point of his power, an autocrat who controlled each aspect of municipal and party politics?

It has often been accepted that Lueger's humor led thousands to vote for the antisemites and to "fill the churches" as a bonus. It may be more correct to believe, however, that Lueger and the rest of the party elite found themselves involved in a rational relationship of reciprocity among themselves and the subsystems of the party's membership. There were limits and standards of accountability beyond which no party leader dared to go, and a carefully circumscribed series of economic interests to which all leaders were required to demonstrate loyalty. If such sensitivity was lacking, as was often the case after 1907, all the charm and wit in the world could not maintain party unity.

Karl Lueger was born in Vienna in October 1844, the son of a retired soldier who worked as a servant at the Theresianum and later as a laboratory assistant at the Polytechnical Institute. His family was petit bourgeois and committed to the values and social orientations of the Hapsburg dynasty. Lueger's father idolized Marshal Radetzky; his mother was a model of devout piety. His family may have served, to use Harold Lasswell's phrase, as a "hothouse of ambition," since Lueger's parents took an extraordinary interest in his academic and professional training, possibly to compensate for their own modest situation.[2] Lueger attended local schools and then entered the famous Theresianum for his gymnasial studies. He was among the small number of students permitted to attend on a nonboarding basis. Lueger worked with furious energy and graduated with high honors. Very early in his life, therefore, Lueger was placed in competition with the progeny of the wealthy and powerful and learned to associate with them on terms which forced his competitors to accord him respect. He learned how to make the power system work for him and how to compensate for material disadvantages by aggressiveness and initiative. The traditional values of Bürger society were by no means alien to the young Lueger. He simply added his own version of the work ethic. His later inability to sympathize with the Socialists' schemes for an egalitarian society may have reflected his early track record in dealing successfully with an inegalitarian society by means of sheer personal talent and energy.[3] During his stay at the Theresianum he so disliked the teaching and the excessive piety of one of his religion teachers, a cleric by the name of Anton Gruscha, that he lost whatever interest in religion he may have carried away from his familial environment.[4]

Lueger entered the University of Vienna to study law in 1862. He avoided close ties with German National student groups, preferring to concentrate on his academic work.[5] His talent for leadership soon manifested itself, however, when he was elected to the executive committee of the *Deutschakademischen Leseverein* in 1863. His driving political ambitions were already evident in his university days: he announced to his fellow students that some day he would become mayor of Vienna.[6]

Of the little that is known about Lueger in this period, several traits stand out which were decisive for his career. Lueger took great pride in the efforts of his father, a man with little schooling, to obtain an education by attending the lectures of the professors whom he served as a laborer.[7] Lueger loved to refer to himself as a "child of the people," and this, together with his admiration of men of dynamism and power *(Kraftmenschen)* who could rise above their status disabilities, suggested that his relentless pursuit of political influence functioned as a compensation for the deprivation of his early family circumstances.[8] This motive explained his frequent efforts to gain recognition in aristocratic and high bourgeois circles. Success itself was not sufficient. It must come at high levels and under conspicuous circumstances. Lueger's passionate commitment to the Hapsburg dynasty and to a Bürger-patrician social structure never clouded his perception of the shortcomings of the aristocracy. Erich Kielmansegg later remarked that Lueger considered himself more Hapsburg than the man sitting in the *Hofburg,* vying for public honor and practicing a not too subtle form of one-upmanship on occasions when the Kaiser or his senior officials were present.[9]

An unflagging patriotism and a marked cultural conservatism reduced the ambiguities Lueger perceived in his social reform stance. The state represented a higher unity and an ultimate value for the good of which consistency in political action might easily be sacrificed. Lueger was a model of a more general type among the Christian Socials: the *Streber* who adored and yet surpassed the values of his father's humble environment to seek a reconciliation with and a co-option into higher social strata, doing so on terms reflecting social achievement and not merely ascribed status. Lueger believed in the virtue of both Bürger and aristocratic privilege in nineteenth-century Austria, but he insisted that such status positions be made available to a wider range of the citizenry. His political machine in Vienna after 1896 became a vehicle for just such a redistribution of status privileges to members of the achieving middle and lower bourgeoisie. Through his unmitigated search for power, Lueger hoped to make the political culture of the Austrian bourgeoisie more flexible and resilient, not to destroy it.

Lueger's noted egotism and pride of place were therefore intimately related to the realities of power for a man of his background in late-nineteenth-century Vienna. He was the kind of leader needed for a bourgeois democratic protest movement. What separated Lueger from so many of his contemporaries in similar straits was his fierce personal integrity and his sense of the professionalism of politics. No other qualities of the man impressed the voters more than his absolute honesty in personal affairs and his total dedication to public political norms. Wealth had no attraction for him. His only goal was the professional exercise of political power.[10]

Lueger began his career as a young assistant to several prominent Liberal lawyers in 1870. Establishing an independent practice in 1874,[11] he might have pursued a successful legal career, but instead became involved in the convolutions of local Viennese politics. Lueger's political beliefs at the time were in a state of flux, but generally fell within the accepted confines of the Liberal-Democratic creed on social and economic questions. In the theses which he defended for his law degree in 1870, he argued for universal suffrage for all fully literate males and for a rudimentary system of labor protection. Such statements were not in fact very radical (the literacy qualifications would have denied the franchise to tens of thousands in Vienna alone), but they might have signaled the beginning of a more socially conscious, third generation of Austrian Liberalism. That this did not happen, that Lueger was soon forced out of the traditional Liberal camp, was one of the decisive events in the political history of Vienna.

The Viennese Political System and Karl Lueger's Early Career

With the return of parliamentary control on the national level in 1861 the city of Vienna regained its autonomous rights as established by the *Gemeindeordnung* of 1850.[12] Free elections in all three curias were held, and a new mayor, Andreas Zelinka, took office. The slumbering political atmosphere of the 1850s found itself replaced by the vigorous, aggressive political culture of the 1860s. Mayor Zelinka was a good-humored, well-meaning lawyer from the Innere Stadt who despised neo-absolutist bureaucratism, but who proved ineffective in controlling the often uproarious behavior of the new City Council. When he died in 1868, he was succeeded by Cajetan Felder, a tough, hard-nosed lawyer from the Josefstadt who represented the largest bloc of votes in the Council, the conservative Liberal *Mittelpartei*. Felder believed adamantly in both administrative politics and urban development. Under his regime Vienna celebrated its first great age of municipal reconstruction since the eighteenth century.

During the 1861 election campaign for the Council, informal political factions emerged which later adopted more institutionalized forms as political clubs. The most significant early party in municipal politics was the *Mittelpartei*, a collection of 60 and eventually nearly 80 councilmen (out of a possible 120) who united behind Zelinka and Felder to establish a conservative, Right-Center bloc in the Council.[13] Most of the Liberal party derived from the First and Second (electoral) Curias. The club was formally constituted in 1862 and endured (under various names) for over four decades as the bastion of Center conservative power. It was not a party of *Grosskapital* in a literal sense, but many of its members did enjoy positions of wealth and education representative of the traditional elites of the mid-century bourgeoisie.[14] The *Mittelpartei* defended the existing curial system, which excluded the lowest levels of the Bürgertum from political rights and isolated the more prosperous artisans from the rest of bourgeois society. The club thus sustained and idealized the conservative bourgeois solution to the problems posed by the events of 1848–49.

In contrast to the *Mittelpartei* and its political allies (such as the so-called *Reformpartei*, which was established in 1872) a tradition of Liberal-Democratic politics also asserted itself, in part reflecting a rehabilitation of ideals and values first articulated in 1848–49. In 1861 Left-oriented factions also appeared in the council; adopting the rubrics *Linke* and *Äusserste Linke* by 1865, these factions reflected the moderate progressive and radical democratic views of their respective supporters.[15] The *Äusserste Linke*, the true bastion of Viennese Democracy, was led by prosperous artisans like Johann Steudel and Franz Löblich. Its support was largely from the Third Curia, mostly from the *Vorstadt* districts like Wieden and Josefstadt (occasionally the Democrats did make inroads into the Second Curia), and most of its delegates were artisans, self-employed businessmen, or white collar professionals.[16] With the passage of the Associations Law in 1867 both the Left and the Right in the Council began to establish district political associations to underpin their electoral recruitment and organization on the local, ward level. Between 1868 and 1873 each district (with the exception of the Innere Stadt) received one or more Democratic *Vereine*, and under Felder's guidance the *Mittelpartei* also set up in 1871–73 a network of *Bürgervereine* to match the Left's efforts.[17]

Before 1885 each district in Vienna organized a series of officially sponsored voter rallies on the eve of each City Council election (conducted in March or April of each year), at which candidates of various persuasions might present themselves and during which test votes *(Probewahlen)* were taken to see who enjoyed the greatest popularity. The semiofficial status of these rallies did not obviate, however, the functionality of the rival political clubs, since each prospective candidate depended upon the support of "his" club to gain public legitimacy before the voters. Indeed, rival clubs frequently contested this form of candidate selection, and since the test votes were not legally binding, the political system slowly moved toward a more competitive structure in which rival candidates fought for voter support for the same seat on election day.

In spite of their early successes in monopolizing the Third Curia, the Democrats never came close to winning more than 30 percent of the seats in the Council. Inevitably they endured the fate of many factions permanently consigned to a minority, oppositional role, raising the same issues year after year, always subject to internal feuding and external humiliation by the dominant Liberals. Democracy also suffered from a chronic lack of municipal-level organization. Each district club cherished its autonomy vis à vis its neighboring associations. Most important, the Democrats never achieved a programmatic unity of purpose toward their own Mittelstand voters or toward the growing working-class movement which emerged in the later 1860s. In theory the Democrats claimed to be the heirs of the Left of 1848, and in their fundamental anticlericalism and long-standing opposition to the curial franchise system this linkage was doubtless justified.[18] Many of the Democratic voters and some of the local party leadership had been National Guard members in 1848–49. The problem for Democracy came in its adherence, often unenthusiastic and half-hearted, to a fuller version of the Left's ideal of 1848—the true *citoyen* state. Some Democrats, like Ferdinand Kronawetter, went beyond the Democratic view of the unitary Bürgertum (including all bourgeois strata, even the lowest artisan master, in a noncurial franchise system, but excluding the proletariat) and advocated equal political rights for all. Democratic journalists like Eduard Hügel took an active interest in the incipient working-class movement of the later 1860s, trying to convert workers to the Democratic cause by sponsoring Liberal cooperative ideas. As noted in chapter 2, however, these years were a most inauspicious time to preach social and political cooperation between the bourgeoisie and the working class under any terms, especially those of 1848. The journeyman strikes of 1870–73 and the political evolution of early Social Democracy effectively killed any hopes for a united, social-Liberal, progressive-labor coalition, such as might have been aspired to by the extreme Democrats of 1848.[19]

Equally problematic was Democracy's view of the artisan problem. Although most of the party depended upon the 10 fl. artisans of the Third Curia for their election to the Council, most Democratic politicians adopted moderate, nonprotectionist attitudes about the artisans in the early 1870s. It was an open question whether the party could abandon what soon proved to be politically anachronistic views in time to retain the loyalty of its voters by the late 1870s and early 1880s.[20]

In 1873 the Democrats tried to redress their organizational inadequacies by creating a central Democratic association, the *Demokratische Gesellschaft*.[21] The party did well in the fall 1873 Reichsrat elections, winning five seats in Vienna. But unfortunately for the Democrats, their attempts at organizational renewal came too late and proved too little. As Felder noted in his autobiography, by late 1874 much of the Democratic party was on the decline.[22] In part this reflected the demoralization attendant upon the Democrats' permanent minority role. They began to feud with one another as much as they attacked the Liberals. Those Democratic politicians who won election to parliament in 1873, like Steudel and Johann Schrank, neglected their local constituencies in favor of their new parliamentary roles. Perhaps most important, the mid-1870s saw a short-term decline in voter interest as a result of the incipient depression. Voter participation rates, high for the period 1861–68, sank progressively after 1869 until the rise of Lueger's second-generation Democracy in 1877–78. As many older Democrats now recognized, Third Curia voters had become suspicious of the human rights rhetoric of radical Democrats like Kronawetter and Umlauft. Ignaz Krawani, the leader of the Democratic Association in the Landstrasse, confessed bluntly in 1875 that the Democrats should abandon their self-image as a party of all society and worry more about the master artisans, who were increasingly antilabor in their political views.[23] The *Demokratische Gesellschaft*'s membership sank from 1,400 in 1873 to little more than 200 men by 1876.[24] The depression led many voters into a state of apathy and political introversion. The exercise of older Democratic propaganda from the 1860s became increasingly ineffective. The Liberals under Felder did their share to discredit the Democrats, robbing them of many of their issues (such as control of the schools).

By the mid-1870s, thus, Viennese municipal politics had entered a new stage, marked by apparent stagnation and high bourgeois hegemony. The gap left by the older Democrats invited the rise of new, aggressive political personalities. Democracy continued to find a home in the city's Third

Curia, but it was clear by 1875 that unless some new political group arose to challenge Felder's *Mittelpartei,* the outlook for Democracy would be bleak.

When Karl Lueger entered Viennese politics in 1872, he joined the *Deutsch-Demokratischen Verein* in the Landstrasse. This Democratic club was run tyranically by Krawani, an old 1848 Democrat. Among the first persons Lueger met in the club was a young Jewish physician interested in civic reform and muckraking, Ignaz Mandl. Both Lueger and Mandl detested Krawani's tyrannical behavior and left the *Verein* within months of joining it. Mandl, together with eight other men, all of whom were wealthy artisans or mid-level merchants, organized a rival Democratic club, the *Eintracht,* in June 1872. By January 1873 Mandl had recruited 300 men for his club, many of whom found their way into the sub-elite structure of the Christian Social party twenty years later.[25] Although some Lueger apologists have cast Mandl as a "spoiler" who rode along on Lueger's coattails, Mandl expanded Lueger's intellectual and ideological horizons, not vice versa.[26] Mandl's Democratic movement was important since the *Eintracht* represented the beginning of a second generation of Democratic Liberalism in Vienna, one which ultimately enriched the long-term history of Austrian politics.

Ironically, Lueger was not among those who cast their lot with Mandl's revisionist Democracy. After resigning from Krawani's club, Lueger joined the Liberal *Bürgerklub* in the Landstrasse, earning the patronage and support of Franz v Khunn, a confidant of Felder. Lueger's rationale for making this choice was made clear in a speech he gave in April 1875 in which he referred to the older Democrats as "men of little consequence, unsuited to political leadership."[27] Lueger obviously hoped to use Felder's support to make a career for himself, enabling him to shorten the conventional waiting period for novices in municipal politics.

Mandl also made a temporary truce with the Liberals in 1874, although he was less inclined to insinuate himself into Liberal social elites. Mandl had tried to run for the Reichsrat and the Landtag in 1873 with local Democratic support, but in both cases the *Demokratischer Verein* supported other candidates.[28] Not surprisingly, when Mandl ran successfully for the Council in 1874, he did so against Krawani's candidate and with the Liberal *Bürgerklub*'s unofficial support. Personal ambition, coupled with intense intra-Democratic feuding, thus led to Mandl's revolt. Nominally he joined the *Mittelpartei,* as did Lueger when he followed Mandl to the Council in 1875.[29]

Lueger's accommodation with Felder did not last very long. Lueger's ambition and turbulent energy, which led him to denigrate the inactivity of older Democrats like Steudel, soon turned against the autocratic Felder.

Lueger resented the mayor's iron discipline and high-handed parliamentary practices in the City Council. More important, Felder's emphasis on age and experience as prerequisites for responsibility (ideas which are manifest throughout his autobiography) seemed to leave the young lawyer no room to develop his own political profile.

From the very outset of his career, Lueger conceived of the role of a politician as something more than a part-time, unpaid public servant whose deliberations took place apart from society. Politics needed discussion; it grew rich on controversy and debate; it needed a healthy input of diverse social representation to make its administrative actions effective and responsible. A system with no controversy was a contradiction in terms and irresponsible as well. Thus, more than simple generational ambition was responsible for Lueger's adopting an overtly antagonistic stance.

The new style of politics suited to Lueger's needs was provided by Ignaz Mandl in the autumn of 1875. In the municipal elections of March 1874 the district committee (Bezirksausschuss) of the Landstrasse received a Democratic majority dominated by Mandl's club. In October 1875 the Landstrasse committee sent a petition to the City Council, protesting abuses and administrative irregularities which, it claimed, were damaging city services in its district: municipal services were paid for but never performed; contracts were let but never fulfilled; street cleaning services were abysmal; corruption in the poor care system was rampant.[30] The immediate target of the report was the Magistrat, the city's executive bureaucracy under whose purview services and expenditures fell, but Mandl was obviously trying to embarrass Mayor Felder as well. Given that Felder had asked the Council for an increase in local taxes in 1873 to cover the growing deficit in the city budget, Mandl's exposé on the abuse of public funds was especially telling.[31] In 1876 Mandl found an even more attractive issue in the mismanagement of the Central Cemetery by the Magistrat—payroll padding, false accounting, and poor management gave Mandl more ammunition to use in his attack on Felder's competence.[32]

Felder's reaction to the report was to bury it in the Council and to ignore Mandl. Felder saw the petition as an attempt by the new Mandl Democrats to stir up a "revolt" against the municipal bureaucracy by the local district committees, who were traditionally jealous of their petty rights and who claimed to be independent legislative bodies not subject to the direction of the Magistrat. By mid-December 1875 the Mittelpartei, to which Mandl still technically belonged, was up in arms because of his "insults" to Felder.[33]

Until late 1875 Lueger watched the tumult provoked by Mandl from the sidelines, cautiously evaluating his options. During the debates on the

1876 budget Lueger joined Mandl in criticizing the secrecy and inconsistencies which surrounded the budget.[34] His comments were milder than Mandl's, but it was apparent that Lueger had joined Mandl in repudiating Felder. Felder tried to persuade the Liberal Club in the Landstrasse to throw Lueger off the 1876 ticket for reelection (Lueger's first term had been a one-year replacement position), but Lueger still had sufficient credibility to prevent this.[35] Following his reelection in April 1876 his attacks on Felder became more open. The climax came in early September when Lueger submitted a motion to the Council asking Felder to behave in a more nonpartisan fashion and questioning Felder's political autocracy.[36]

Lueger's motives in challenging Felder were in part generational—he undoubtedly considered his own political base secure and thought he had nothing to lose and much to gain by the notoriety which the role of a young gadfly brought with it. But Lueger also disliked Felder's pronounced bureaucratism in managing the city's political system. The central theme which ran through Lueger's rhetoric in this early period was the importance of the Council as the ruling body of the city to which the executive (the office of the mayor and the *Magistrat*) must remain responsible. Lueger was much more concerned with this procedural and jurisdictional problem than with the substantive issues Mandl was raising.

In October 1876 Felder had the Council dismiss the Landstrasse committee for not performing its administrative duties properly. Felder's act was punitive, and everyone in the city knew it. New elections for the committee were called, setting up a test case for Mandl's and Lueger's renegade version of Democracy. Not only did the Liberals sweep the First and Second Curias by wide margins, but they even defeated Mandl in the Third Curia. Lueger took the election results as a repudiation of his actions by the voters and resigned from the Council.[37]

Lueger's defeat was a shocking experience for the young, arrogant politician, but it was also an important learning experience. Much of the anti-Felder rhetoric in 1875–76 generated by Mandl and Lueger sounded both petty and ad hominem. Despite his autocratic behavior Felder enjoyed considerable esteem among the Bürgertum of all three electoral curias. His strong-handed paternalism and his ability to defend the city's autonomy won him widespread support. It would take much more local-level agitatorial work (rallies, club gatherings, local contacts) to undermine public confidence in him and his party. Moreover, neither Mandl nor Lueger had concentrated on a program of positive alternatives to the Liberal style of urban administration. It was not enough to deliver public insults to Felder; a clear set of policy alternatives had to be formulated and sold to the voters.

Lueger and Mandl spent the next two years creating such a program. Using the *Eintracht* as an organizational base, they retained control of the Third Curia City Council seats in the Landstrasse in the 1877 elections. They called their new alliance the "Economic party." A year later, in March 1878, Lueger reentered political life by running for the Council from the Third Curia. He won convincingly with 531 out of 958 votes, in an election in which 13 anti-Felder Democrats won seats in the Council.[38]

As important as practical political work was in 1877–78, these years also saw the evolution of a new rationale for Lueger's and Mandl's programs, providing them with force and coherence. Mandl became acquainted in the later 1870s with a Viennese economist, Wilhelm Neurath, and was much influenced by Neurath's social collectivism.[39] Influenced by the work of Adolf Wagner and Wilhelm Roscher, Neurath preached a doctrine of Liberal organicism in which economic progress and a healthy economy depended upon socially eudaemonistic attitudes on the part of the wealthy in society and upon the social sponsorship of the poor by the state.[40] Mandl was particularly intrigued by Neurath's stress on a collectivist ethics for society to be encouraged by governmental bodies. To serve as a model for social morality, however, government had to operate under more honest and responsible norms. Mandl derived from Neurath's theory a doctrine of public social responsibility which would not only improve urban administration in Vienna, but would create a new set of political virtues in Viennese society as well. Ethics had always played an important role in most variants of Liberalism in Central Europe; it was not different for Lueger's and Mandl's new Landstrasse Democracy. Now, however, the ethics became a social ethics in an urban mode, serving as the instrument of administrative reform.

Neither Mandl nor Lueger blindly adopted all of Neurath's discursive and often inconsistent ideas. And much of what Mandl proudly touted as an ethical revolution was merely his own voice stirring up trouble where none had existed before. Like most radical Liberals, Mandl had a vision of himself as a savior, as a servant of the people as a whole. The line between ethical renewal and simple demagogy in Mandl's behavior was always fluid.

Lueger had less trouble with ethical dogmatism, since his life centered around his ambition to gain and exercise political power. He differed from Mandl in that his use of Left Liberal rhetoric always depended upon its marketability with the electorate. Lueger shared with Mandl the Left Liberal collectivism of the late 1870s, but he merged this with traditional Viennese pragmatism, the end goal of which was to lead him to power in the city. Lueger carried with him Liberal universalist rhetoric—he spoke constantly of the *Volk* as the object of his dedication—but this universalism was modified by his Bürger roots. He valued the traditions and privileges of that society and culture as much as he did the reformist Liberalism of Mandl. When called upon to defend Julius v Newald during the Ring Theater scandal, the highest tribute Lueger could pay to him was that he was a traditional "Bürger durch und durch."[41] Older Democrats often accused Ferdinand Kronawetter of harboring socialist ideas, but this was hardly possible in Lueger's case. His Democracy was fundamentally utilitarian, with a strong bias toward antiproletarian privilege. The *Volk* for Lueger was the Bürgertum in the newer, more generalized mode in which he used the word to include the *Kleinbürgertum* as well. He thus suffered none of the inflexibility of Mandl on issues like anticlericalism and antisemitism. Bürger society in Vienna had long been both anticlerical and antisemitic; Joseph Schöffel was as willing to use the word *Saujud* as he was *Pfaffe* in the world of Democratic politics in the 1870s.[42] Lueger's achievement was to build a new political movement which played these traditional cultural reflexes off against each other. The inflexible idealism of a Left Liberal model never worked well in Vienna. It fitted neither the pragmatic political traditions of the Viennese nor their lateness in political maturation. Lueger realized that the model had to be scaled down and made to serve the privileges and prejudices of Viennese Bürger society.

Lueger took from this tradition the idea of universal service to the "people," but defined the people in question in nonproletarian terms. He thus sustained the antinomy in Viennese Liberalism which had emerged in 1848, namely, the ambivalent self-interest pursued by the Bürgertum in defining itself both as a privileged order and as the whole of society.

The result of Mandl's and Lueger's interest in civic ethics and municipal reform was what might be called a civic-service Democracy. Their initial program was modest in its actual content, confining itself to city finance and administration. The idea of municipalization of city utilities which gradually became a key point in Mandl's arguments was based on Neurath's social collectivism. Not only was the administration to be responsible to the Council, not only was urban government to be moral and honest, but the city itself, by assuming the ownership of privately managed utilities, was to serve the people in a general way. Initially absent in Mandl's municipalization schemes was the expectation that the city would profit financially from such businesses.[43] The idealist Mandl was much more interested in the social service and morality such programs would offer than in the revenues they might generate.

Mandl took up the idea of municipalization earlier than Lueger.[44] As late as 1881 Lueger denied that he wanted to municipalize the tramway.[45] What he did want was tight regulatory controls on the private companies, just as he wanted more effective controls on the *Magistrat*. For Lueger both entities (private capital and public administration) had to be subject to political control. His motives in supporting municipalization after 1882 were far more pragmatic than Mandl's. Lueger became more interested in the revenue and the political power which city-owned industries would provide than he was in their contribution to civic morality.

What Mandl and Lueger accomplished with their contentiousness in these years was to present a view of the city as something more than the defender of political or cultural autonomy in the fashion of the older Democracy of Steudel or Krawani. Now the city had to provide a model of public services in the most efficient and economic manner possible. In theory this view had always been a part of the Liberal creed, but in practice the Liberals under Mayors Zelinka and Felder concentrated their energies on large-scale building programs (the *Rathaus*, the water supply system, the sewage system, school construction, etc.), financed through major loans. Protecting the city's autonomy against the Imperial state was a cardinal Liberal virtue—the expansive, historicist aesthetics of the *Rathaus* were shaped by the need for a symbolic home equal in stature to that of the *Hofburg* or the Imperial ministries. The Liberals were not disinterested in public service, but they saw as their role the establishment of the institutional matrix of a large metropolitan area. One should worry about efficient water and sewage systems, decent school buildings, and an effective *Magistrat* before worrying about better service on the tramway. Felder was less opposed to municipal socialism on philosophical grounds than from the priorities of practical policy, especially after the Crash of 1873. Getting immediate cash subsidies and rental revenues from private companies to bolster the city's overburdened budget was of greater concern to him than was experimenting with novel municipalization schemes.[46] Not all of his fellow Liberals agreed with him (there was sentiment in the Liberal party in favor of Mandl's ideas), but Felder had his way. The civic-service Democracy of Mandl and Lueger depended logically and administratively on earlier Liberal successes. Lueger could not have preached the new mentality without depending upon the impressive progress which the Liberals had made in the city's institutional development.

The clash between Felder and Lueger also resulted from conflicting views of urban administration. Throughout his autobiography Felder stressed the "nonpolitical," purely administrative nature of local politics.[47] He took great pride in his modernization of the *Magistrat*, but ironically his success proved to be his undoing. Before 1868 the City Council exercised considerable influence over the city bureaucracy, creating chaos by meddling in its activities. Felder tried to eliminate political influence from the *Magistrat*, but carried the practice too far.

What angered even his Liberal supporters were not Mandl's accusations, but Felder's inability to discipline members of the *Magistrat* who were guilty of poor judgment, laziness, or possibly worse.

Especially after Felder's reelection to second and third terms as mayor (1871–77) the *Magistrat* ran the city with increased independence. An attitude of sovereign disregard was displayed by officials in the bureaucracy. A notable instance came during a libel trial in the late 1870s when a city finance official admitted under oath that he never gave a thought to what the members of the Council felt. Such arrogance ran against deep-seated traditions in local Liberal politics.[48] What Felder seemed to be doing smacked of Vormärz bureaucratism in an updated framework.

Felder disliked competitive politics. He could bring himself to do no more than call Lueger perverse and Mandl mentally disturbed. That many of his fellow Liberals also enjoyed political intrigue was a sign of their lack of dignity. At heart Felder was an administrator called to live his life in politics. With Lueger it was the reverse; he was a politician summoned to live a life of administrative rationality. Lueger never lost the love of competitive politics and the belief in the political control of administration which was first nurtured by his revolt against Felder. After the Christian Socials assumed power in 1896–97 he was forced to work out a new relationship between administration and politics which preserved the normative and operational effectiveness of the first while maintaining the legitimacy of power of the second. In Lueger's regime one found a fascinating example of the rationalization of politics by administrative force merged with the manipulation and control of administration by political power.

The United Left and the Revision of Democratic Politics, 1878–82

Cajetan Felder insisted that the *Zentralfriedhof* scandal and other irregularities cited by Mandl and Lueger were groundless and based on spite, but the commission of the City Council which investigated the cemetery affair reported in mid-March 1878 that widespread minor corruption had occurred.[49] Other areas in the city suffered from mismanagement and abuses (one serious problem was that many officials held outside jobs, some of which involved conflict of interest questions). Felder's reorganization of the *Magistrat* neglected to provide for its close supervision by elected officials. In retrospect, the total elimination of corruption may have been impossible—cases of such minor corruption occurred in each mayoral regime in Vienna in the nineteenth century, regardless of party affiliation. Felder's real political sin was not that he allowed corruption to occur, but that he responded to the charges in a clumsy way. Instead of using Lueger's later practice of delay, evasion, and outrage (denounce corruption in general, isolate the cases involved by token disciplinary actions, delay any serious investigation for an inordinately long time, and then quietly bury the matter once the initial journalistic outrage had subsided), Felder handled the Council's investigative reports ineptly. He refused to initiate even token disciplinary proceedings against the officials involved and tried to still the controversy by ignoring it. By the spring of 1878 even the Liberal press began to be uneasy over Felder's behavior.[50] Articles appeared in Liberal journals urging a revitalization of the Liberals' leadership. Had Felder been more artful and flexible, he might have deprived Lueger and Mandl of their ammunition. As it was, the results of the 1878 Council elections revealed that traditional political loyalties were becoming more diffuse. By the late spring of 1878, Felder could count on no more than sixty-five to seventy votes in the Council. Weakened by a long illness and profoundly tired of the turmoil in which he was caught, Felder resigned his office in June 1878.[51]

Felder's successor was Julius v Newald, a local politician from Alsergrund who had served as the chairman of the *Mittelpartei* during Felder's regime and a former protégé of Mayor Zelinka.[52] Like most of the mayors of the Liberal and Christian Social periods, Newald's career was the product of extensive local- and district-level experience and ward-level friendships. He knew his enemies and friends at first hand, having dealt with them on a daily basis since 1864. Newald's education was in law, but he spent much of his mature life working as a commercial and military agent and had connections in the business world. He was a conciliatory, well-meaning person, with none of the abrasiveness of Felder. His administration assumed a very different style from that of Felder.

Newald's election offered the *Mittelpartei* no cause for confidence. For the next few years the party was mired in acrimonious in-fighting between rival claimants to Felder's position. Newald was seen as a stopgap candidate who satisfied no one, but whom everyone thought they could live with. Most of the opposition, including Lueger and Mandl, also voted for his election as mayor.

The next four years of Viennese politics were shaped by two new trends. In August 1878 the first anti-Liberal Democratic coalition, the United Left, was formed by the merger of three Democratic clubs, Lueger's Economic party, the older Extreme Left of Steudel, and the centrist Left Club. Lueger represented his club in the coalition negotiations and wrote the program of the new bloc, which was published in August 1878.[53] The program attacked the curial franchise system and urged a common electorate of all Bürger taxpayers. Interestingly, it avoided any mention of municipal socialist schemes.[54]

From the outset the United Left was a most heterogeneous creature. Combined within it were younger Democrats and Liberals with inflated ambitions like Lueger and Johann Prix (Lueger's political nemesis after 1890), and older *Vorstadt* Democratic types like Steudel and Löblich whose real political interests were not always served by Lueger and Mandl. The coalition functioned well on traditional issues (like the school system), but on economic and social issues the United Left was as divided as the Liberal party frequently was.[55] Löblich was far more protectionist on the artisan issue than Mandl, but far less progressive on the question of municipalizing the gas works.[56] The older Democrats felt uneasy about attacking the *Magistrat*. They had no scruples about criticizing state-level administrative actions, but the *Magistrat* was part of the city, for better or worse. Having won their spurs in the 1860s when any kind of municipal autonomy—political or administrative—was preferable to a return to neo-absolutism, they were less enthusiastic about undercutting the municipal bureaucracy.[57]

More important, serious generation rivalries soon arose, pitting the young "upstart" Lueger against the older Steudel and Löblich.[58] Mandl proceeded to alienate Löblich by accusing him of corruption in soliciting contracts for his private business interests.[59]

The organization of an alternative to the Liberals in the Council gave Mayor Newald the opportunity to initiate a second important development, namely, his personal shift toward the Left in 1880. Newald differed from Felder in believing that a mayor must assemble support from a variety of political groups. But because the *Mittelpartei* retained a majority in the Council, Newald's attempt to work with the United Left while retaining nominal leadership of the Liberals often meant that he was governing the city with minority support. When Newald was up for reelection in 1881, a group of younger Liberals led by Raimund Grübl and Guido Sommaruga (both from Lueger's home district of the Landstrasse and both rivals of Lueger) sought to oust Newald and replace him with a more orthodox candidate.[60] Although they failed, it was clear that Newald could not count on the Liberal party after mid-1881 to extricate him from serious political embarrassments.

These were years of considerable social upheaval in Vienna, but none of the clubs found ways of responding to the incipient artisan protest movement effectively.[61] When antisemitism entered local politics in 1882, it did so outside traditional Liberal or Democratic structures. The signs of disunity which became apparent in the United Left by late December 1880 weakened the base on which Newald could rely in the Council. Eleven older Democrats, led by Steudel and Löblich, announced their resignation from the coalition.[62] A more serious blow came in December 1881 with the Ring Theater fire. The fire, which took the lives of nearly 400 members of the audience, provided the *Mittelpartei* with the long-awaited chance to rid itself of Newald and to undercut Lueger's political career.

The Ring Theater fire provoked a controversy of long-range importance.[63] The issue on which all of the accusations centered was the responsibility for the inadequate fire defense at the theater on the night of the disaster. Immediately after the fire the United Left passed a resolution absolving Mayor Newald of any culpability and suggesting that the police had been laggard in their responsibilities.[64] This brought the Lower Austrian *Statthalter* into the fracas, since the police were an Imperial agency. *Statthalter* von Possinger insisted that fire defense was a responsibility of the city itself as an autonomous entity, and not part of the administrative duties that still belonged to the state. Von Possinger accused Newald and the city authorities of intentionally refusing to issue and to enforce the "Regulations on Theater Safety" for which the city was accountable by agreement with the Imperial government.[65]

For several weeks an uneasy peace reigned, but on 22 December Guido Sommaruga brought an interpellation before the Council, demanding that Newald answer the charge that he had failed to discharge his responsibilities in providing for fire protection at the theater.[66] Von Possinger followed this attack by publishing a series of letters between city officials and his office which suggested that Newald and the *Magistrat* had consciously refused to issue the theater regulations out of reasons of petty administrative politics (by denying that the city itself was responsible for establishing legal regulations governing fire defense). Newald's actions may have been intelligible in light of the long-standing feud between the city and the state over responsibilities for public services in Vienna. The administrative duties the *Magistrat* had to perform for the state (e.g., tax collection, craft trades supervision, voter registration) cost the city great sums of money each year for which Vienna received little or no financial recompense from the state (although each year insistent demands were made for such compensation). This was part of the classic deal from which the autonomous *Gemeinde* in Austria had emerged—the cities were given substantial political freedom in return for assuming the burdens of delegated, state-level administrative duties. Von Possinger insisted that fire protection defense was not even part of the delegated authority of the state exercised by the city, but rather a part of the city's natural area of competency *(natürlichen Wirkungskreis)*. Newald, anxious to prevent the imposition of yet another difficult burden on the city without any hope of financial recompense, denied von Possinger's assumption that fire defense was a responsibility of the city as an autonomous entity. Rather, in terms of policy planning (and accountability) it was the concern of the Imperial government exclusively. In other circumstances Newald might have been applauded for his defense of the city's integrity; as it was, his luck ran out and he was caught politically short.

Von Possinger was a tough, skilled bureaucrat with an instinct for survival. He sent a representative to the City Council on 17 January 1882 to read what amounted to a personal indictment of Newald for incompetence.[67] This event was not merely political, but symbolic as well. Newald had brought the government into the city's autonomous sphere. Never before had a Viennese mayor been publicly humiliated by an Imperial official before the City Council. Shame was the cross on which the Liberals could now crucify Newald. He was visited by a delegation of Liberals (including Grübl and Sommaruga) who urged him to resign for the sake of the city's reputation.

In a desperate, last-minute move, Lueger attempted to enlist Eduard Taaffe to mediate between Newald and von Possinger. Taaffe saw, however, the political dimensions of the power struggle and could only suggest to Lueger that Newald try to make his peace with the *Statthalter* and accept the inevitable humiliation which would result. Lueger in turn advised Newald to refuse a compromise which would have been tantamount to an admission of guilt. On 22 January Newald resigned his office, a broken, hapless man.

Lueger's role in the scandal was extensive, and for his later career, problematic. In late December 1881 the second vice-mayor of Vienna, Johann Schrank, had died. The election to fill Schrank's post was held 12 January. The United Left nominated Lueger, and to all appearances he would win. A week before the election, however, his voting support began to fade. Key members of the coalition, especially the remaining older Democrats, refused to support him. When the election took place, many Democrats threw their support to Johann Prix, who was elected by a fifty-nine to forty-seven vote. Prix ran as the candidate of the *Mittelpartei;* his victory was an important sign that the Newald affair had weakened Lueger's credibility in the Council. Lueger's career, so promising less than a year before, now fell apart. By 1 February a rash of resignations from the United Left began, with former adherents scurrying to dissociate themselves from Newald and Lueger.[68] Lueger's secret visit to Taaffe had injured his esteem in traditional Democratic circles—local Liberal clubs summoned rallies to gloat about the "clerical" and "pro-Slavic" Lueger, who seemed to be on such intimate terms with the anti-Liberal minister-president.

If Lueger decided to forsake the label of a Liberal Democrat after 1882, the vindictive treatment which the Liberal press accorded him on his visit to Taaffe was the beginning of the process. That a man of Lueger's ego did not take such biased criticism lightly should be remembered in considering the personal motives behind Lueger's antisemitism. Lueger was a cautious politician, but the Liberal press regularly called out the vengeance motif in his behavior.[69]

From a high point as the leader of a city coalition who had personal contacts with the ruling mayor, Lueger now found himself deserted. He was now a free agent in Viennese politics. Some Democrats returned to their old factional affiliations; others joined the Liberals. District particularism, personal vendettas, and a lack of organizational and ideological coherence doomed the alliance. No one, even Lueger, was certain what it meant to be "anti-Liberal." The United Left's major weakness lay in the fact that its necessity was not acknowledged by the enfranchised citizens. Unlike the 5 fl. artisan voters of the mid-1880s, the voters who dominated the upper curias of the city's electoral system were not yet convinced that a new political alternative was necessary, especially one which demanded that they abandon long-cherished ideological tenets in favor of interest group politics. Given the more conservative behavior of typical Second and First Curia voters before 1890, it was doubtful whether the kind of anti-Liberal alliance envisioned by Mandl and Lueger could have succeeded by relying on those curias for support. Many Third Curia voters before passage of the 1882 suffrage amendments were equally uncertain about the need for radical politics. Once the 5 fl. men provided the material for the "takeoff" period of an anti-Liberal coalition in 1885–86, other bourgeois social groups could be attracted by the movement's momentum. Groups like the state officials and schoolteachers were poor material with which to build a fundamentally different political alternative. Once the alternative had been launched (antisemitism), and once middle bourgeois groups like the *Beamten* and the clergy had become sufficiently dissatisfied with their standard of living, they could be coopted into the new pattern of non-Liberal, bourgeois politics.

The experience of leading a large coalition was valuable for Lueger. Now nearly forty years old, he had established himself as a skillful political leader with experience in managing a city-wide coalition. He came to know the strengths and the weaknesses of such an organization. When he had the opportunity to lead a second coalition after 1888, he did not make the same mistakes twice. The pressure for party discipline which he brought to bear within the Christian Socials reflected his earlier disillusionment with voluntaristic politics.

Lueger also gained an appreciation of the utility of a strong party base for a successful mayoral candidate. Newald's fiasco in governing against the majority of the Council showed Lueger that this was an impossibility in the local, faction-ridden world of Viennese politics. He also recognized the need for a strong mayor. As much as he had profited from Newald's patronage, he now saw the merits of Felder's administrative autocracy. After 1897 he tried to merge the two models—he retained Newald's emphasis on cooperation with the Council, insisting that a mayor must work with and not simply against or over the parties and the electorate, but he did so in a fashion which often differed little from the autocracy of Felder. In contrast to early Liberal administrative autocracy, Lueger developed a machinelike party autocracy to accomplish his ends.

Lueger's Accommodation with Political Antisemitism

The period from February 1882 until the end of 1887 was the most significant in Lueger's oppositional career. Only in defeat and humiliation did he begin to expound to the voters (and to himself) the need for a drastic reconstruction of popular politics in Vienna.

Lueger reacted to the destruction of the United Left with bitterness. Two days before the dissolution of the coalition, he gave a speech in the Landstrasse before the *Eintracht*.[70] After insisting that he was not a supporter of Taaffe, Lueger revealed that substantial bribes had been offered him in the fall of 1881 in conjunction with the construction of the new urban railway for Vienna, the *Stadtbahn*.

The *Stadtbahn* was a vital element in the modernization of the city's transportation network. Even Lueger admitted that there was substantial economic justification for building the railroad. Kielmansegg reported in his memoirs that Lueger confessed in 1881 that he would oppose the *Stadtbahn* because influential landlords and property owners in the Landstrasse opposed the project.[71] The railway would have devalued the real estate along its tracks (because of the noise, soot, and vibrations in the buildings), as well as leaving the city with an ugly system of aboveground trestles and viaducts on which the tracks would run. Lueger, like many Viennese, was critical of the aesthetic failings of the project, but his covert motives before 1882 were essentially political—real estate owners were voters. The "foreign capitalism" issue, so prominent in Mandl's concerns, did not play a role in Lueger's initial evaluation of the railroad.

The consortium which hoped to build the *Stadtbahn* was led by two Englishmen, Joseph Fogerty and James Bunten.[72] Lueger was appointed chairman of the committee of the Council which was to examine the Fogerty proposal. He immediately began to raise objections.[73] In his February 1882 speech Lueger charged that on several occasions in the first week of November 1881 he had been approached by intermediaries representing the English concern and offered bribes to secure his cooperation. Lueger also mentioned two other councilmen, Theodor v Goldschmidt and Rudolf v Gunesch, who allegedly had accepted promises of administrative posts with the new railway should the Council pass the measure.[74] The two men sued Lueger for libel, and Vienna found itself in the spring of 1882 in the midst of a sensational libel trial.

Lueger portrayed himself as the innocent victim of the evil forces of finance capitalism. He may not have been aware of the effectiveness of the "capitalism" issue before the *Stadtbahn* controversy (he rarely used it), but he now organized his public defense around it. His accusations about the bribes were undoubtedly accurate, but his revelations were dictated wholly by pragmatic considerations, since he had waited three months to make his charges public. In November 1881 he still led the United Left, and such accusations might have compromised members of his own coalition, as well as his friend Julius Newald. Lueger was not the innocent victim of moral turpitude. Only after the coalition's collapse, when Lueger was looking for revenge, did he summon the outrage necessary to act against the bribery conspiracy. At the trial itself Lueger's assertions were not given sufficient attention (the word "cover-up" might be too strong) and Lueger was fined 100 fl. for remarks to the City Council based on hearsay evidence, but he was cleared of the libel charge.[75]

The trial brought Lueger to the attention of the antisemites. Zerboni, the editor of the *Volksfreund,* sent Lueger a letter congratulating him on his newfound anticapitalism.[76] In early March 1882 Lueger presented his first rally speech in his role as a political outcast. The speech was the plebiscitary type which he loved to give—a recital of the evils of his opponents and of his own political virtue, and a call for public approval in which he "thrust" his fate into the hands of his voters ("My political life lies before you open and clear"). The international money cliques and big capitalists were poisoning Austrian public life. What was worse, they recognized no fatherland.[77] Coming two weeks before the famous antisemitic rally staged by Holubek and Buschenhagen, Lueger's performance showed his new perception of the utility of anticapitalism as a symbolic device for voter interest. In November 1880, as chairman of the council committee investigating peddling, Lueger had adopted a guarded, judicious position. He had refused to support a total abolition of the peddlers, preferring that existing regulations be more adequately enforced.[78] Now in the spring of 1882 he suddenly turned against the *überwuchernden Hausierhandel* which was destroying the artisan Mittelstand.[79]

Although he later expanded the range of his attacks on capitalism to include the Jews, the Liberals, and the Socialists, his real discomfort with investment capitalism was largely a question of its international nature. Lueger's anticapitalism was closer to that found in the *Hausbesitzer* associations in the 1890s than anything else. Most Viennese property owners did not want to "do away with" the stock exchange. The typical *Hausherr* of moderate to wealthy social background resented the tax advantages accorded to capital investment and speculation, but he himself, by virtue of his one or two mortgages, had a direct interest in preserving the stability and growth of the city's economy. In direct terms the *Hausherr* did not feel himself dependent upon the stock exchange—he might even grumble about the attempts of the Liberal newspapers to persuade potential house owners of the attractions of speculative capital investment as opposed to land and house ownership, but he would never condone attacks on any form of private property. He did not seek to destroy the *Börse;* what he wanted was more attention paid to his own tax burdens and his desire to amortize and appreciate his house investment as quickly as possible. In spite of their awesome rhetoric, Lueger and his colleagues (most of whom were also *Hausherren*) never considered themselves state socialists in the classic sense of opposing "international capital" with a broad program of national socialization.[80] Rather, the preferred Christian Social alternative was a concentration of Austrian private capital in Austria (especially German Austria), under a benevolent regulation by the government.

Lueger's talk in March was his first effort to style himself as an anti-plutocratic underdog, as a "child of the people." Because his public rhetoric was so controversial, it must be examined more closely. Karl Renner once described Lueger's speeches as being vacuous and lacking in any original ideas, as collections of clichés to which a few radical phrases were added for voter appeal.[81] A careful reading of hundreds of Lueger speeches in a multiplicity of situations between 1880 and 1910 would confirm this assertion.[82] When he spoke in parliament on political issues, Lueger revealed an excellent memory for administrative and legal detail and a sound knowledge of the internal workings of the Austrian bureaucracy. On economic and cultural matters, however, his lack of training and his Bürger philistinism showed up immediately. To comprehend his speeches, one must realize that Lueger differentiated sharply between the worlds of public and private communication and between words as symbols to effect political mobilization and words for managing governmental affairs. In May 1887 in a speech before parliament Lueger made one of those occasional comments unusual for their candor. He tried to excuse the radical language used by Ferdinand Kronawetter by arguing that a politician's words must not be taken in their literal sense: "If he used some hard expressions, these are not to be taken literally in the way in which the representatives of the government took them. When he speaks about 'fraud,' for example, he really doesn't mean to say that officials are cheating for their own personal advantage. Rather, he is using the word in the way that it is popularly used in Vienna. Dr. Kronawetter speaks in dialect, and the phrases used by him are to be understood in the popular Viennese dialect.''[83]

Lueger's commentary revealed more about his own language than that of Kronawetter. Very often there was a marked discrepancy between what he said and what he meant. Joseph Bloch touched upon this quality when he argued that Lueger was not a great radical, but that he was a great actor.[84] Lueger was conscious of the difference between public and private channels of communication, as were most Christian Social leaders (Ernst Schneider was an exception).[85] Much of the irrational behavior which has been imputed to these men on the basis of their wild rhetoric was actually a commonly understood and accepted system of public discourse current among the particular strata to which the Christian Socials appealed. Such language was the expected verbal response to situations of tension and conflict. Lueger implied that not only did the speaker understand his linguistic manipulations, but that his audiences understood them as well.

The banality of many of his speeches reflected Lueger's own social background and that of his audience, but also the danger which dogmatic or innovative statements could create for a political coalition embracing so many mutually suspicious interest groups. The makeup of the Christian Social party did not afford its elite the luxury of the dogmatics which the Socialists trundled out at will.

Lueger was not the first politician in Vienna to exploit the Viennese dialect. In his autobiography Cajetan Felder noted several early Democrats from the 1850s and 1860s who preceded Lueger in exploiting language. Lueger's linguistic power resulted from his combination of dialect with older organizational forms and newer social issues. His linguistic resources were effective only because they were integrated into an electoral system with its own traditional rationale (the district-political nexus of Viennese politics) and because Lueger had available a new set of public policy issues with which to excite the public imagination.

Between 1882 and 1885 Lueger's ambitions suffered from the uncertainties of the municipal political situation. The Liberals finally buried the factional differences which had split them in the later 1870s and organized a single political club, uniting the old *Mittelpartei,* Prix's *Wiener Club,* and Steudel's *Äusserste Linke.*[86] In the 1882 Council elections they exploited the problematic image which Vienna had attained under the last months of Newald's and Lueger's rule, implying that the United Left had been unfit to govern the city.[87] Johann Steudel admitted that the same accusations had been leveled against him and other older Democrats in the early 1870s, but the present accusations were effective nonetheless.[88] Lueger soon gained a profound respect for language stressing "solidity" and "respectability" in the city's affairs. In stressing Liberal inadequacies, he distinguished between the Liberals and the city itself as a political community. No Viennese, whatever level of the Bürgertum he might occupy, would tolerate a lack of sanctimonious reverence toward the city. This was more than affectation or nativist pride—it was a vulgarized and popularized version of early Liberal *Gemeinde* rhetoric from the 1850s.[89]

The Council elections of 1883 were even more depressing for Lueger. Six Democratic candidates in the Third Curia were denied election or reelection in mid-March.[90] Lueger found himself totally isolated with the exception of Mandl and a newcomer to the Council from Neubau, Albert Gessmann. A young librarian in the university library elected to the Second Curia in 1883, Gessmann was one of the few bright spots in Lueger's future. He quickly became Lueger's lieutenant and principal adviser. His great talent was not only his famous organizational ability, but his flair for manipulating new political issues. If Lueger brought to Vienna the idea of political professionalism, Gessmann contributed the discrete sense of political time. Always one issue ahead of his opponents in plotting new public interest demands, he had a superb sense of timing. One of his remarkable innovations was that his party and its bourgeois rivals came to see the Austrian political process as possessing an inherent dynamic of its own. The responsibilities of a party did not consist of reacting to popular needs, but rather lay in stimulating and guiding such needs in the electorate's consciousness. If a party could control and shape issues rather than merely reacting to them, its primacy as an instrument of public policy would be guaranteed.

Gessmann also helped bring to the antisemites a level of organizational cohesiveness after 1897 which far surpassed the informal procedures of the earlier Liberals. The Liberal idea of a political party also required, like the Christian Social, that it be free of interest domination, but the Liberals' view of their party on the national and regional levels as a collection of sovereign individuals led to fragmentation rather than strength. The Christian Socials gradually came to possess a more collectivist sense of the nature of a modern political party, one which demanded subordination not to a single leader *or* to a fragmented series of interest groups, but to the party as an institutional and functional whole. The achievement of this kind of operational cohesion occurred only after the party conquered the *Rathaus* in 1896, but Gessmann was its principal architect.

Gessmann soon established contacts with leading antisemitic agitators like Schneider and Psenner, while Lueger concentrated on district-level campaigning in the Landstrasse and Margarethen. The issue of obtaining voting rights for the 5 fl. artisans on the municipal and regional levels of government was at the forefront of Lueger's attention. Anticapitalist rhetoric would be wasted on these men if they could vote only in national elections.[91]

In the City Council itself after 1882, the lines between the Liberal and anti-Liberal clubs were fluid.[92] When the Council voted in April 1884 on Lueger's motion to nationalize the *Nordbahn*, the motion was defeated by a vote of fifty to forty-one (with a public roll call). Many Liberal councilmen deserted their party to support Lueger on the issue.[93] The most prominent difference dividing the two sides was the question of the city budget and the possibility of municipalization of key utilities. When the Liberals considered measures to alleviate Vienna's financial problems, they thought in terms of long-term loans and modest increases in direct taxes (such as the *Schulkreuzer*). In this mode of thought they were usually following policy proposals prepared by the administrators in the *Magistrat*, whose conservatism in dealing with municipalization was more finance-technical than ideological.[94] Although some Liberal councilmen may have been influenced by personal favors from the private utility companies, Liberal caution on this issue during the debates of October 1885 and April 1887 reflected other factors. The city authorities were uncertain about the outcome of judicial appeals then being litigated against the private utility companies to clarify disputed clauses in the original contracts. For the city to withdraw its monopoly contract from the Imperial Gas Company in 1886 and build a new municipal gas works by 1889 without first being certain that it could legally prohibit the company from continuing to pump gas through its mains until 1899 (when the city had the contractual right to take possession of the physical plant) would have been suicidal in terms of reaching an acceptable profit level.[95] Similar considerations were raised by the Liberal Club during the tramway disputes in April 1887.[96] Liberal policy in 1894–95, when Mayor Grübl made a serious effort to plan for the municipalizaiton of the gas works, suggested that the "procapitalist" stigma Lueger sought to impose on the Liberals was an exaggeration and simplification of a complex issue.[97] Most Liberals realized, if only from the models offered by Germany, that municipalization was coming. The question was how and when, rather than what. Vienna in the 1880s was burdened with continuous deficits and an outdated system of taxation. Most of the city's revenue was generated by indirect taxes and surtaxes on state taxes levied in the city. Capital improvements undertaken before 1873 were financed by loans, all of which proved to be financial disasters. When Lueger was demanding that the city again resort to loans to build large public utilities in the mid-1880s, the last of the earlier loans was being retired. Many officials opposed burdening the city's deficit-ridden budget with more loans. Lueger promised (and rightly) that such utilities would be so successful that they would repay the initial capital investment many times over. The unimaginative Liberals thought more in terms of current needs than future resources.

Lueger's search for a new political affiliation before 1885 led him to join Adolf Fischhof in June 1882 in organizing the abortive *Deutsche Volkspartei*. Fischhof sought to organize a nonnational party based in Vienna which would mediate between German and Slavic interests in the monarchy.[98] The base of the party was to be the former United Left—Kronawetter, Newald, Lueger, Mandl; these were the Viennese leaders who responded to Fischhof's call for a centrist party which would oppose the Liberals.[99] Not only was the party a dismal failure (it was quickly abandoned by its proponents after receiving no popular support), but the *Volkspartei* idea illustrated the problems inherent in maintaining the status of a "Democrat" in the 1880s.[100] What gave the Democracy of Steudel and Löblich in the 1870s security and justification was that it created a more flexible mode of local Liberal politics without sacrificing anticlerical or national ideals. Democracy did not endanger the German bourgeoisie and thus was not a threat to the cultural substance of Liberalism. After 1879, however, to be anti-Liberal in municipal affairs also meant to be accused of being anti-Liberal on the national level. Since the Liberals were now in the opposition, and since Taaffe's ministry rested upon a series of compromises with the Czechs and Clericals, Democracy could be viewed as a treason against the German nation. Ferdinand Kronawetter was viciously attacked in the Liberal press in the early 1880s for being a secret "friend of the Slavs" and a "crypto-Clerical" simply because he dared oppose the Liberals on economic issues.[101]

With the radicalization of voter opinion among the newly enfranchised lower-Bürger voters, Democracy found itself undercut from below on economic and cultural issues. Fischhof sought to give Democracy a new lease on life by making a virtue out of a commonplace fact, the indifference of most Viennese artisans to the national question. But he was unable to respond effectively to the other challenge, that of artisan protectionism. Most lower-Bürger voters were not "pro-Czech" or "pro-clerical," but they were increasingly interested in special interest policies which would enhance their economic security. The Liberal counterattack on Fischhof and the Democrats was effective in the short, but not the long run. Among older voters enfranchised in the 1860s national rhetoric still had some years of legitimacy left, but for most of the Third Curia voters enfranchised in the 1880s nationalism and anticlericalism were rapidly becoming secondary issues. The most ominous threat to Democracy came from the other direction, from those who ignored national and anticlerical rhetoric and preached pure artisan protectionism. Hence, neither Fischhof's *Volkspartei* not Schönerer's *Linz* program was the pace-setting idea behind contemporary Viennese politics.

How serious Lueger was in joining Fischhof was difficult to determine. Doubtless he saw the *Volkspartei* as one option among many. Gessmann's parallel exploitation of contacts with the antisemites might indicate that Lueger was hedging his bets in 1882–83. When Kronawetter asked Lueger what he made of antisemitism's potential, he replied that "on that one has to wait and see where and how the whole movement develops." Fischhof, for one, soon came to distrust Lueger's sincerity. When someone suggested to Joseph Bloch that Lueger serve as his lawyer in the Rohling libel trial, Fischhof warned Bloch: "Beware of Karl Lueger! He may support you now, but I am not at all certain that he will not abandon you in the end, perhaps even put you in danger before the jury."[102]

Lueger's priorities led him to avoid anticlerical propaganda after 1882. Not only did he see the fallacy of helping his local political enemies by supporting their principal cultural issue, but he saw no reason to alienate the Church. That this was due to a secret "clericalism" on Lueger's part was absurd. Lueger measured political events with a steadfast and unshakable realism—there was no political or cultural "clericalism" in Vienna worthy of the name. To attack it in defense of Liberal honor seemed pointless. His position led to a temporary break with Ignaz Mandl in May 1883, when Mandl proposed at a meeting of the *Eintracht* that a resolution be passed approving of the Liberals' opposition to the clerical school amendments of 1883. Lueger opposed the motion, noting that he was willing to affirm the ideals of the 1869 school law but that he would not support the Liberal party's propaganda rage.[103] Mandl resigned from the *Eintracht* and published a series of bitter newspaper articles accusing Lueger of clericalism and federalism.[104] The seeming pettiness of the dispute was misleading. Lueger had begun to pull away from his former Democratic comrade on the all-important issue of anticlericalism. Having repudiated that part of the Liberal heritage, Lueger did not find it difficult to go one step further and find something to replace it. As Lueger was soon to learn, he could not afford clericalism without antisemitism, and he could not accept antisemitism without clericalism.

Lueger's chief tactical need in the mid-1880s was to reinforce his credibility as a prominent municipal politician with the new 5 fl. voters who would appear on the scene in 1885. Issues like the *Nordbahn* were attractive because of their simplicity and symbolic character, but they also invited competition from the rival anti-Liberal clubs. An issue which was shared by all belonged to none of them. Lueger devoted a good deal of effort to the *Nordbahn* question, not so much on the merits of the case itself, but because not to have done so would have meant being overshadowed by Schönerer and the *Reformverein* antisemites.[105]

By the spring of 1884 Lueger's credentials with the antisemites were strong enough to win him the backing of Schneider and Pattai in his reelection race for the Council. The *Volksfreund* recommended that antisemitic voters support Lueger because of his anticorruptionist stance, although it regretted that Lueger was not an antisemite.[106] Lueger won the election, but by a surprisingly small margin (845 to 728), indicating that antisemitic support may have proved crucial. His narrow victory margin led Lueger to redouble his preparations for the upcoming Reichsrat elections in 1885, where he would have a voting constituency greatly enlarged by the 5 fl. men. In the city as a whole voter registration almost doubled, primarily because of their enfranchisement: from 24,264 in 1879 to 46,226 in 1885.[107] The new voters presented Democracy with a serious challenge by breaking up the predictability of traditional political loyalties. The very ardor with which campaigns in Vienna now came to be waged indicated that no politician could be certain that his followers were not in fact inclined to follow someone else. Candidate nominations and electoral campaigns were still within the matrix of the district clubs, but now there was a potentially large swing vote which all non-Liberal politicians had to deal with.

Lueger prepared for the 1885 election by holding a series of campaign rallies at which he concentrated on issues attractive to the artisan masters. He also managed a reconciliation with Mandl, healing the rift in the Democratic Club structure in the Landstrasse. This touched off a minor revolt among radical antisemites in the *Reformverein,* but Lueger steadfastly insisted that he was not an antisemite and that he would not tolerate outside interference with his decisions on Landstrasse politics.[108] The antisemites eventually backed down (after some grumbling), and the rift was repaired. The Democrats and the antisemites refrained from running rival candidates in the same electoral districts in June 1885.[109] This cooperation was merely tactical, since both Pattai and Vogelsang distrusted Democrats like Kronawetter and Mandl. Pattai wrote to Vogelsang in 1885 that Lueger could be depended upon to support artisan protectionism, but Democrats like Kronawetter were unreliable and hence dangerous.[110]

On 27 April 1885, at the largest rally of his campaign, Lueger presented his program.[111] This was a noteworthy document, since in his later years Lueger scrupulously avoided programmatic statements of any kind. Lueger announced that he represented a "new" Democratic movement, one which would not involve a class party, but which would base itself on the "broad and sure fundament of the whole people, without difference of nation or confession, rank or status." He rejected Schönerer's suggestion that Galicia and Dalmatia be separated or given autonomy from the monarchy. He also rejected a tariff union with Germany, suggesting protective legislation to save "domestic industry" from German domination. Against antisemitism Lueger took a mildly negative stand, defending all confessions as equal before the law but never mentioning the Jews. His silence on the Church and "clericalism" indicated the Lueger wanted no trouble from the clergy. In any event, "equality of confession" and the "free evolution of the school system" could be interpreted in various ways, as Lueger was later to prove.

To compensate for hedging on the antisemitic issue, he hit hard at "large capitalism." He reminded his voters of the past glory of the Fogerty episode: "I have fought corruption everywhere, and I have opposed large capital at every moment, when it wanted to enrich itself at the cost of the public." After promising high tariffs and laws to restrict competition, he urged the "gradual" nationalization of insurance and credit systems, but avoided any mention of industry or the stock exchange in this context.

Lueger made two points on the labor question which were incongruent with the rest of the speech. He suggested universal suffrage and the abolition of curial voting, and advocated laws to protect the workers against "big industry." He also went on record against Taaffe's anti-Socialist law. These views must be placed in the context in which they were given. Lueger did not advocate a general series of labor laws, only laws which would cripple the artisans' chief competitors. At a time when the working class was politically disorganized Lueger could easily afford prolabor rhetoric. His espousal of universal suffrage was an extreme measure, which he later repudiated. Lueger may have been using the suffrage issue to strengthen his credentials as a social reformer in working-class circles, since he succeeded in obtaining the services of some workers in his campaign organization.[112] He was careful, however, to append to the word *Arbeiterschaft* the phrase "in the widest sense of the word," meaning all nonsocialist white collar employees. After 1886 Lueger made no mention of universal suffrage. If he was actually willing to support such a law (which was doubtful), he was willing to do so only on the national level, not on the local or provincial level, where real administrative power lay.[113]

The speech was an extraordinary performance. Lueger rejected pan-Germanism and distanced himself from extremist antisemitism, yet reaffirmed his loyalty to the recipients of the antisemitic message, the master artisans. He also made enough "good government" promises to engage the interest of other middle class voting groups. Even so, the June election was a difficult one and the results were uncomfortably close. Lueger ran against Steudel, now a regular Liberal but still with some popularity among the 5 fl. voters. Lueger won the race with 1,403 votes to Steudel's 1,346, not an impressive victory considering the effort expended.

The 1885 elections were a milestone in Viennese political history, since voter turnout amounted to almost 70 percent of those eligible to vote.[114] In previous state and regional elections in Lower Austria the turnout rate rarely went above 55–60 percent. The new trend resulted from two factors: the excitement generated by the more elaborate and costly campaigns arranged by the candidates, and the impact of the 5 fl. men, who were eager to exercise their new right to vote.

In the municipal Council elections after 1885 the same pattern was to be seen (the Taaffe ministry finally put sufficient pressure on the Lower Austrian Liberals to force the Landtag to give the city and Landtag vote to the 5 fl. artisans, beginning in 1886), although the staggered nature of municipal elections in Vienna until 1891 made it difficult to estimate the exact dimensions of the increase. In 1883, 8,502 voters participated in elections out of a total of 27,869 eligible voters, but the fact that in some districts no seats were up for reelection and in others one-year replacement elections were being held (these usually generated little interest) made the 30 percent participation rate a statistic of limited value. In 1887, 19,084 men voted out of a total eligibility pool of 47,757 (40 percent), so that a relative increase in voter interest did occur after 1885.[115] In city elections, however, much depended both before and after 1885 on the candidates and issues in each specific district. A lively contest between rival candidates in the Third or Second Curia during the Newald period usually generated a remarkably high voter turnout.[116]

One change in 1885 which did alter the shape of local politics had to do with the city-sponsored *Wählerversammlungen,* which had been a customary part of Viennese politics since the 1860s. The original idea behind these nonpartisan rallies, held in the spring of each year, was that they would provide a neutral forum at which various candidates could appear and appeal for popular support from the voters of a given district. Also, because in many districts the Liberals made informal deals with the local Democratic clubs that the Democrats could run their candidates in the Third Curia unopposed, in return for a similar privilege for their candidates in the Second and First Curias, the nonpartisan assemblies functioned as neutral meeting grounds for candidates of opposing parties who were *not* competing with each other (since their curial assignment was already agreed upon). After 1878 the Democrats in various districts constantly violated these "arrangements" and ran candidates in the Second Curia as well, turning the city *Versammlungen* into modern political rallies.[117] It was increasingly apparent, in other words, that the allegedly nonpartisan nature of Viennese *Rathaus* politics was a charade and that the partisan, club basis of municipal politics was winning the upper hand. This occurred long before the establishment of the antisemitic United Christians in 1888. In March 1885, on a motion from Lueger, the City Council abolished these rallies and threw open the electoral process to the market.[118] Henceforth voters of Democratic or antisemitic persuasion went to their rallies, and the Liberal voters did likewise. An increasing polarization of the voters of all clubs and parties ensued, since there were no social opportunities for candidates of different viewpoints to debate the issues before a common audience. Lueger found this development beneficial; the Liberals were equally confident that they would profit from it.

The modest victory Lueger had eked out in 1885 gave him a seat in the lower house of the parliament, but little else. Three Democrats, Kronawetter, Anton Kreuzig, and Lueger, took their seats in the Reichsrat in late 1885, but they hardly constituted a political party. When Lueger claimed pompously in 1886 that he belonged to a new party, he was mocked by other politicians with shouts of "Where is it?" and "What kind of party is that!"[119] His isolation must have been embarrassing. Even if his prestige as a local leader in Vienna made him a force to reckon with in the City Council, he counted for nothing in the parliament without a strong delegation behind him.

Lueger's behavior between 1885 and 1887 may be compared with Kronawetter's, who should have been his closest colleague. Kronawetter enjoyed the isolated position of a gadfly. By temperament choleric and by conviction a strong civil libertarian, he increasingly took to the floor of parliament to criticize government proposals. In contrast, Lueger's interest in cultivating the artisans and his tacit detente with Taaffe and the Church were soon apparent.[120] Lueger sponsored a plea from the antisemitic *Gewerbegenossenschaftstag* that artisans be allotted, through the craft guilds, access to the credit resources of the Austro-Hungarian Bank.[121] He insisted that the Clericals were not traitors to the Germanic cause and suggested that attacks on the Church had no place in a discussion of the labor question.[122] He also defended the legislation on accident insurance proposed by Alois Liechtenstein, but refused to support its extension to workers in the craft industries or on the farms.[123] Kronawetter, on the other hand, wanted to expand the law to cover *all* workers, whatever their occupational locus.[124] More significantly, Kronawetter played an active role in fighting the 1886 anti-Socialist Law, giving speeches and attending a rally with Victor Adler and Engelbert Pernerstorfer.[125] Lueger studiously avoided the rally and did not utter a word during the acrimonious debates on the legislation.

The one novel political tactic Lueger introduced in these years remained an effective ploy with him well beyond the turn of the century. His opposition to pan-Germanism never wavered, but he substituted for the nationalism issue hatred of the Magyars. In rejecting the government's renewal of the *Ausgleich* in October 1886, Lueger complained that the Germans living in Hungary were forced into a near slave status *(nationale Knechtschaft)*. The Slavs happened to be another group oppressed by the Magyars, a shocking situation in that the Slavs were equal to the Germans in cultural development. It was deplorable that "two highly developed nations, like the Germans and the Slavs, are held in slavery by the Magyars, who surpass them neither in culture nor in numbers."[126] Later in the speech he repeated this ploy—the Germans and Czechs were "Cisleithanians," "without difference of nation," whom the Hungarians held in subjection and persecution. Lueger's talk was a clear feint against Schönerer, as well as a clever attempt to diffuse the nationality question in Lower Austria by setting up an alternative target for political mudslinging. The Hungarian threat was a rich subject for the Christian Socials, and one which made increasing sense as Budapest came to rival Vienna for the economic leadership of the empire. It also possessed considerable flexibility—after Lueger joined the antisemites he expanded Magyar into "Judeo-Magyar" as the epitome of social evil.

In 1884 and 1885 the antisemites and the local Democrats had cooperated informally to support each other's candidates, but Lueger could not be certain how long this kind of tenuous relationship would last.[127] To prevent internecine warfare, he proposed a temporary antisemitic-Democratic coalition for the 1886 Council elections. Rather than merely voting for each other's candidates, various Democratic and antisemitic district associations agreed in February 1886 to run a common slate of candidates.[128] The goal of this strategy was to prevent confusion in the minds of the newly enfranchised 5 fl. voters, who were participating for the first time in municipal elections.

Lueger denied that he had officially joined the "Schneider party." But the ad hoc coalition was significant enough to move Ferdinand Kronawetter to write a sharply worded protest against antisemitism in a local Liberal newspaper. For Kronawetter tactical cooperation with the antisemites was the same as adopting their program; he would have none of it.[129] The electoral cooperation worked effectively, however, with the result that eighteen Democratic anti-Liberals (of whom twelve were closely associated with Lueger and one was officially an antisemite) occupied seats in the new Council.[130] Many of these Lueger Democrats were men of his own generation, recruited in the mid-1880s, with no direct ties to the Democracy of the 1860s. Lueger's Reichsrat victory in 1885 was crucial in restoring his prestige in some of the more enterprising Democratic circles.[131] Many of these men would follow Lueger into antisemitism after 1888.

In April 1886 the antisemites and the Democrats in the Council joined a new club, the "Democratic Left," thereby institutionalizing the temporary coalition. The Democratic Left of 1886 was the first germ of the Christian Social party. Lueger again had a small, but devoted band of followers.[132]

Antisemitism itself was becoming harder to resist. The movement was so fragmented in 1886 that Lueger might have pushed himself forward as a compromise leader. However, to move too quickly might create more jealousy and further fragment the anti-Liberals. The crucial factor in Lueger's calculations was Schönerer. A direct challenge of Schönerer for the position of senior leader of the antisemites was neither feasible nor desirable. Lueger avoided antagonizing Schönerer and his loyalists; when the pan-Germans in parliament asked Lueger to sign a petition in favor of legislation to cut off the immigration of foreign Jews into the empire in May 1887, he complied. The Liberal press immediately denounced Lueger as an antisemite, but in fact Lueger was simply buying time for his own uncertainty.

A month later Lueger delivered an important speech in Margarethen which came close to confirming Liberal fears. If any single talk may be designated as Lueger's "first antisemitic address," it is this talk and not the September 1887 speech usually cited by historians.[133] Lueger launched a diatribe against the Hungarians, accusing the Magyars of using "foreign capitalism" to undermine the Cisleithanian side of the monarchy. The same charge could not be leveled against the Slavs, since they too were oppressed by the Magyar capitalists. Rather than stopping with this now familiar juxtaposition of the poor Czechs and Germans against the evil Magyars (the Magyar problem was not a "national" issue for Lueger, but a problem of state power and sovereignty), he then threw in a gratuitous insult against the Jews: Liberal politics were a "masterpiece of cunning which are fit for the Talmud."[134] This remark drew "strong and extensive applause" from the audience. The antisemitic reference was clear to anyone even vaguely familiar with Rohling's *Talmudjude*. Lueger was drawing closer to political antisemitism.

Early in September 1887 Lueger had traveled to Linz to participate in the Upper Austrian Craft Congress.[135] His famous speech of 23 September 1887, often referred to as his first antisemitic address, was originally intended to have little to do with antisemitism. Lueger spoke before a plenary meeting of the Christian Social Association to report on his impressions as an observer at the Linz congress.[136] He was to speak in a pro-artisan capacity, not as an antisemite. The speech must be read in this context. Since the first speaker of the evening, a rabid Hungarian anti-semite by the name of Komlossy, delivered a harsh attack on the Jews, Lueger, who spoke second, was forced to deal with the antisemitic issue.[137]

Lueger began by trying to obliterate the distinction between antisemites and Democrats: "Whether Democrats or antisemites, the matter comes to the same thing," since the Democrats confronted the Jews in their anti-corruptionist struggles. Despite this bow to the antisemites, Lueger knew that the terms were not equivalent. He even offered a qualification to the Jewish community by adding that there were as many evil Christians as there were dishonest Jews. He then turned to the "Christian religion" (a term which carefully avoided any reference to Catholicism) and defended the right of lower clerics to engage in radical political agitation if they so desired. For himself he promised that he would never betray "my religion" to the Jews. If there were orthodox Catholics in the audience, they would have had some difficulty in identifying their religion amid the tortuous circumlocutions and postures which Lueger was offering.

Lueger's speech was an unequivocal commitment neither to anti-semitism nor to political clericalism, but it was evidence that he was now willing to bargain with each group in the hope of achieving some higher political unity. The rest of the talk (the principal part) dealt exclusively with artisan complaints.[138] The major opponent threatening everyone was capitalism, "which is international, having no fatherland and no religion." This role for religion, which made it little more than a substitute for patriotic chauvinism, was characteristic of the speech as a whole.[139]

Lueger's sympathy for the antisemites and the lower clergy showed that he was beginning to consider a new model for Viennese politics, typified by the social structure of the Christian Social Association itself. Antisemitism could be balanced by a vague appeal to Christianity and religion, making Jew hatred seem more respectable and distinctly less pan-German. Clericalism, on the other hand, while opening up the organizational resources of the Church (and its money), could be made inoffensive by mixing it with a good dose of secular antisemitism. As a force for cultural traditionalism religion might prove exceedingly helpful. Religion also offered a useful insurance policy for a non-Establishment politician who wanted to make certain that the government took note of his loyalties to the empire.

The September 1887 address began the final rupture of the Democratic ranks in Vienna. Lueger spoke at a Democratic rally in early November to defend his reputation as a Democrat, but the charade was beginning to wear thin. Vogelsang touched upon the dilemma of Democrats like Kronawetter, when he wrote that their belief in absolute political equality prevented their perception of the justification of antisemitism. Lueger may not have been infatuated by antisemitism, but he never demonstrated any profound commitment to absolute political rights. He was now contemptuous of those "1789 Democrats" who dared spread such "foreign" notions in Bürger Vienna.[140]

Talk of a potential anti-Liberal coalition soon filled Vienna's political clubs and salons in the autumn of 1887. Such a coalition would extend the informal alliance of Democrats and antisemites organized for the 1886 Council campaign, but it might also involve a more permanent alliance with other groups as well. Lueger first mentioned the idea of an "Anti-Liberal League" in October 1887 at a rally in Landstrasse.[141] The idea proved attractive to other groups, especially the Viennese clerics and Vogelsang, although some antisemitic leaders, like Robert Pattai, were suspicious of a grand coalition, fearing a loss of local autonomy. In late November 1887 Pattai denied that there was any such thing as a league.[142]

Pattai's denial did not conform to political reality. In July 1887 Dr. Johann Ofner, an old, main-line Liberal who ran the St. Pölten Liberal party, died. Ofner sat in both the Reichsrat and the Landtag, and his death necessitated the holding of special by-elections in the fall of 1887. When the election for the Reichsrat was held on 13 October 1887, three candidates were on the ballot: Leopold Wimmer, a Catholic factory owner and a protégé of Joseph Scheicher; Joseph Ursin, a follower of Schönerer and the mayor of Tulln; and Georg Granitsch, a wealthy Liberal lawyer from Vienna. In the first round of voting no candidate received an absolute majority, necessitating a runoff between Ursin and Granitsch. Scheicher persuaded the local Catholic *Pressverein* in St. Pölten to back Ursin in order to deprive the Liberals of the parliamentary seat. On 15 October Ursin narrowly defeated Granitsch and became the first non-Liberal elected to the Reichsrat from an urban constituency in Lower Austria since 1870.[143]

Six weeks later, in the Landtag election on 24 November 1887, the Schönerians and the Catholics repeated the same maneuver, this time running Ursin alone against his Liberal opponent, Karl Heitzler. Again, Ursin won, to the astonishment of Scheicher and the Catholics, who had been trying for years (with no success) to break down Liberal power in provincial Lower Austria. Vogelsang devoted several long editorials to the cooperation engineered between the German Nationals and the Catholics, urging them to continue the process as an ongoing venture.[144] Scheicher and Vogelsang immediately proclaimed the existence of a new tactical alliance of all antisemitic groups in Lower Austria, the "United Christians."[145]

The degree of Lueger and Gessmann's involvement in the St. Pölten affair was uncertain (probably very small), but five days after the Landtag election Lueger acknowledged that the victory of Ursin was the first example of the "quiet alliance of antisemites, Democrats, and conservatives" which he had advocated earlier in the year.[146] In Vienna the concept of the United Christians had less immediate relevance, since the formal Schönerian contingent there was rather weak, especially in the all-important Third Curia. But the pan-German contingents in districts like the Landstrasse and the Josefstadt might provide the crucial margin of victory in Second Curia elections. For Lueger the United Christian alliance in Vienna was therefore a dual investment. On the level of artisan voters the coalition of antisemitic, nationalist, and clerical sentiment would help to solidify the anti-Liberal front without making any explicit commitments to support a narrow Schönerian ideological program. Among Second Curia voters, where nationalist sentiment was slightly more emphatic, the United Christians would guarantee pan-German electoral cooperation without handing the curia over to Schönerer.

From the very first, the enthusiasm for coalition politics was not shared by Schönerer. Schönerer carefully limited his response to the United Christians to self-interested utility. As long as such talk helped his candidates (like Ursin), the former Viennese Democrats and the clericals could call their alliance with him whatever they pleased.[147] But Schönerer was far too rigidly ideologized to encourage dreams of a permanent anti-Liberal alliance.

The increasing dissatisfaction of some older Democrats with Lueger's association with antisemitism confronted Lueger with a critical choice.[148] By November 1887 it was not only clear that antisemites of various persuasions could unite to support coalition slates, but it was also apparent that Democrats like Kronawetter and Kreuzig would vehemently reject such compromises.[149] Lueger decided in January 1888 that his personal future lay in cooperating with the antisemites: he announced that he would join the new anti-Liberal *Bürgerclub* in the City Council, which replaced the Democratic Left. The new club, which explicitly played upon older Viennese ideals about the unitary Bürgertum, explicitly avoided the term "Democratic" in its title.[150]

The ultimate direction in which this decision would lead him was by no means clear. Lueger would eventually have to find a new label to consecrate his envisioned amalgam of Mittelstand politics and Bürger virtue. His situation in late 1887 introduced the fourth stage of his political career.

The United Christians, 1888–90

The United Christian coalition was not a political party. There was no central leadership; there was no program; each of the groups in the alliance cooperated on an ad hoc basis while exploiting the coalition for their own particularistic ends. Because it was able to draw upon the pan-Germans and the Clericals, as well as the Democrats and antisemites, it did signify a decisive change, however. At this stage in anti-Liberal politics the name itself was its most notable aspect, since the very fact that all groups would accede to a linguistic expression of their unity could be viewed by Lueger as progress of a sort.

The presence of Schönerer, although many thought him a mixed blessing, was decisive for the later history of the Christian Socials. Once Schönerer had eliminated himself from Lower Austrian politics, leaving his own party in chaos, many Nationalist subleaders and voters felt free to transfer their allegiance to a new group—whether this be the Christian Social party or the more vaguely defined *Bürgerclub* in the Council. In the broadest sense the United Christians (minus the extreme Schönerians) did not cease to exist until 1896, and only the precedent of the alliance of 1887 made the later Christian Social experiment in political cooperation possible.

Lueger soon had an opportunity to assert a profile distinct from that of Schönerer. The Christian Social Association organized a public banquet in February 1888 to celebrate the fiftieth anniversary of the priesthood of Leo XIII. Dignitaries from both Church and government were invited; even old Cardinal Ganglbauer made an appearance. The banquet was not, however, a confessional event, but rather a propaganda spectacle for the antisemites. Pattai and Schneider showed up, along with the chairmen of several craft guilds. Lueger and Gessmann, as well as a contingent of Viennese lower clerical types, also attended. Later in 1888 Vogelsang referred to the February banquet as the day on which the United Christians "came to exist as a united party." In fact, the banquet involved everyone *but* the pan-Germans, an open sign to Schönerer that political exclusivity might work in more than one direction. When Lueger spoke about the categories of membership in the United Christians, he used sweeping criteria—anyone willing to call himself a Christian was welcome. But the context of the speech was a clear indication that Lueger saw "Christianity" in a potentially anti-Schönerian sense.[151]

Lueger's lack of enthusiasm for the anticlerical campaign against the second Liechtenstein *Schulnovelle* in January 1888 and his appearance at a Clerical-antisemitic banquet in honor of the pope led a number of Democratic politicians to cross over to the Liberal party.[152] Whether they were frightened by clericalism or antisemitism was unclear; that they would not tolerate a combination of the two was obvious. During the Council elections in March 1888 a few anticlerical Democrats like Wilhelm Rasp and Ludwig Dotzauer threw their support to the Liberals.[153] Ultimately, however, a majority of ward-level leaders among the Democrats followed Lueger into Christian Socialism, to the extent that they chose to remain in politics after 1888. The Democrats of the *Eintracht* in the Landstrasse, for example, simply switched the association's nominal allegiance from Democracy to Christian Socialism.[154] The subleaders and voters who crossed over from Democracy constituted an important secular core for the early Christian Socials, helping to balance the party against the special interest pressures from the radical clergy and the craft guild leaders. Former Democratic leaders and voters helped to diversify and strengthen the anti-Liberal crusade by adding to it a sense of political experience and traditionalism neither the clergy nor the guild leaders possessed.

Tactical cooperation between renegade Democrats, craft guild anti-semites, and political Catholics was encouraging, but neither Lueger nor Vogelsang had any idea of how to cope with the enigmatic Schönerer. Fate soon resolved their riddle, however. In one of the great blunders in the history of Austrian politics, Schönerer and a band of drunken followers broke into the editorial offices of the *Neues Wiener Tagblatt* late in the evening of 8 March 1888 and violently threatened the terrified editorial staff with bodily injury. Early editions of the paper had carried contradictory stories about the alleged death of the German emperor, Wilhelm I. Schönerer had become infuriated and lost control of himself.[155]

Within hours the events at the *Tagblatt* were known all over Vienna. The intruders were arrested, but since Schönerer enjoyed parliamentary immunity, the government could not act against him without the public spectacle of a debate in the Reichsrat. The opportunity to settle accounts with Schönerer, who had now become something more than the embarrassing annoyance to the Liberals which Taaffe had originally intended, outweighed the publicity Schönerer would gain. After heated debate in the lower house, Schönerer's immunity was revoked and the trial began in May 1888. He was found guilty, was sentenced to four months in prison, and had his patent of nobility revoked. The government also withdrew his political rights for five years; he would be unable to vote or hold public office until late 1893.

Schönerer's chief defenders, aside from Karl Türk, were Lueger and Pattai. The parliamentary debate offered Lueger an opportunity to portray himself as a model anti-Liberal, sacrificing personal squabbles to defend a colleague. He could marshal few arguments to prove Schönerer's innocence, but managed to attack the Liberal press for its "insatiable desire for revenge." Lueger seemed to argue that Schönerer was legally guilty (he admitted that the latter's conduct was a "great act of stupidity'' and the behavior of a "choleric man"), but morally justified in view of the crass opportunism and biased reporting of the Viennese Liberal press.[156]

Lueger was not so certain in 1888 that Liberalism was as "dead" as his speeches might have indicated. The superficial bravado of his rhetoric masked a real fear that a political reconciliation between Taaffe and the Liberals might lead to the Liberals' reentering the ministry. When Taaffe fell from power in late 1893, such a compromise did occur, and the presence of the Liberals in the government in early 1895 helped to generate official intervention in Rome against the Christian Socials.[157] A successful prosecution of Schönerer for a criminal act might encourage the Ministry of Justice to use the vast "administrative" pressure at its command to harass the rest of the antisemitic clubs. Lueger could not be certain. Since he had only recently joined Schönerer in the United Christians, Lueger was defending not only Schönerer but, far more, his own actions in the past twelve months.

Lueger's real motives were elucidated by a confidential letter which Pattai sent to Vogelsang in late March 1888.[158] Pattai admitted that a court conviction would end Schönerer's career in parliament, but he argued that this would not profit the Austrian antisemities, since there were other Nationalist leaders who were ready and willing to replace Schönerer. Schönerer had been useful against the Liberals and an indirect source of strength for the Clerical Conservatives. But, Pattai predicted, should Schönerer be convicted and driven from public life, he would become dangerous. Four months' imprisonment would not do him any physical harm, but it would turn him against the Austrian political system in a way which would give his movement a "highly subversive character." Precisely the possibility of pushing Schönerer to extremes worried Pattai.

Pattai's amoral calculations—he had no regard for the fact that Schönerer and not the Austrian government had taken the first extreme step—illustrated his and Lueger's self-serving considerations. If Schönerer radicalized his movement, the whole antisemitic effort might be brought under governmental persecution. Pattai's prognostications about Schönerer's future behavior were remarkably accurate.

Schönerer's jail sentence at hard labor ran from August through December 1888. If Schönerer's imprisonment taught Lueger anything, it was that he must immediately concentrate his energies on unifying the non-Schönerer elements in the United Christians. Schönerer's hard-core followers, especially those in a leadership role, retained their loyalty to the imprisoned idol. For the short term their behavior was unpredictable. Lueger realized, probably under the pressure of Gessmann, that his own political security would depend on establishing a more moderate antisemitic profile. The most obvious counterweight against the racial anti-semitism and political irrationalism of the Schönerians was the Church. Not surprisingly, in the year following Schönerer's political collapse Lueger's relations with Vogelsang and other Clericals in Vienna became much more prominent.[159]

According to Franz Schindler, Vogelsang first organized a series of meetings for anti-Liberal politicians and Catholic journalists in a villa in Hietzing in late 1887. Gessmann persuaded Lueger to attend. In a letter to Anton Pergen in November 1887 Vogelsang commented favorably on a talk which Lueger had given in which he had used the phrase "social reform on a Christian basis." To him "Christian" meant something far different from what it meant to Vogelsang, however.[160] Marie v Vogelsang, the journalist's daughter who also served as his personal secretary, later recalled that when Lueger first appeared at this gathering in late 1887, he announced belligerently to Vogelsang that "a whole world view separates us."[161] Peter Abel noticed a similar disposition in Albert Gessmann—when he first met Gessmann, the latter was "indifferent to religion."[162] Not until after the Schönerer affair was Lueger interested in a closer partnership with the Viennese Clericals.

During 1888 his situation changed rapidly. Vogelsang was on the podium at the February banquet in honor of Leo XIII, at which Lueger gave a stirring defense of the United Christians. The following day's issue of *Vaterland* praised Lueger fulsomely. During the summer of 1888 Lueger began to correspond with Vogelsang regularly, discussing practical politics. Lueger was especially concerned with rumors about the delay in organizing the second Catholic congress, asking Vogelsang if there was a move afoot to repudiate the antisemitic movement. He warned Vogelsang that "a work will be destroyed that could never again be duplicated," meaning a broad Democratic-Clerical alliance. Lueger was open in his personal admiration for Vogelsang, "the old man of our movement."[163] As he later put it, "You, Herr Baron, are one of the few people whom I respect and love." Vogelsang was "a man of principle, the old man from the mountain."[164] Lueger admired Vogelsang precisely for those qualities which he himself found so inconvenient—exact principles and a high sense of theoretical integrity based on such principles.

Lueger's alliance with the Catholics was openly utilitarian in nature. Vogelsang greatly admired Lueger's "magnificent sacrificial activity in the interests of the Christian people," but he was under no illusions about the extent of Lueger's personal Catholicism.[165] Neither were clerics like young Gustav Piffl, who observed Lueger close up.[166] Lueger was burdened not at all with scruples about Catholic social theory. Ernst Karl Winter's suggestion that "what Lueger later implemented goes back to the intellectual impulse of Vogelsang" in the Christian Socials' municipalization policies is not historically correct.[167] Lueger was convinced of the merits of urban municipalization long before he encountered Vogelsang or Catholic social theory. Similarly, Lueger's later expansion of his movement into the higher reaches of the city's electorate—the *Mittelbürger* who dominated the Second and, to a certain extent, the First Curia—found no ready analytical justification in Vogelsang's social theory. Property owners and state officials were less malleable in terms of utopian social theory; they had their own, self-serving visions of a renewed order of corporate value claims, which they had developed under the Liberal regime in Vienna. Social theory had to deal with these groups more gingerly and more carefully; sweeping statements about recasting society meant little to them. Because they were not categorical "losers" in the industrialization process, they did not fit into neo-Romantic schemes as easily as did Vogelsang's idealized artisans and peasants. Lueger did see two important contributions which religion might bring to a new anti-Liberal political alternative, however. In a cultural sense religion, in the vague theistic form which Lueger found acceptable, might serve as an effective antidote to the ideological attractions of the Social Democrats.[168] More important, Catholic social theory could play a major supportive role in providing additional moral justifications for embarking on programs of artisan protectionism and urban municipalization so rapidly and with such intensity. Lueger clearly did not learn from the Catholics *what* should be done to bourgeois society; but he was certainly willing to accept Catholic public relations and ideological assistance in justifying *why* such policies ought to be implemented with a minimum of delay.

During the months following Schönerer's conviction Lueger came to respect Vogelsang's journalistic and ideological leadership. In September 1888 he attended a private birthday celebration for Vogelsang in the latter's home. Heinrich Abel was present and later recalled that Viennese politics occupied everyone's attention. Lueger gave a brief, but impassioned, talk. Although Lueger reiterated his disinterest in religion, Vogelsang was said to have exclaimed, "Now we have found the leader for the United Christians." If this comment was not apocryphal, Vogelsang was making a two-edged assertion: that Schönerer's imprisonment necessitated a new central leadership for the United Christians and that a single set of leaders from all factions was important in place of a loose association of rival politicians.

Vogelsang then called for a change in the title of the coalition: "The word Christian will remain, but we will replace the word 'united' with the word 'Social.'" Instead of the "United Christians" one would have the

"Christian Socials." Vogelsang's adjustment would have consolidated Viennese anti-Liberalism against Schönerer (for whom the term "Christian Social" was intolerably "clerical") at a time when Schönerer had just been excluded from public life for five years. Less than six months after Lueger led a sympathy march to protest Schönerer's conviction, he was being invited to stage a stunning political coup. According to Abel, Lueger reacted to the change in rubrics with "ardent zeal," as well he might.[169]

The September meeting may have planted in Lueger's mind the idea of a "Christian Social party," "Christian" in its dual meaning of Jew hatred and quasi clericalism, "Social" in its sense of reviving the Viennese Bürgertum. Lueger already had one example of an institution operating successfully in Vienna under a similar linguistic maneuver, Psenner's Christian Social Association. But neither Lueger nor Gessmann took any immediate steps to implement this idea. Extant police reports on the 1888 and 1889 elections indicate that the rubric "Christian Social" was not used in either campaign. Lueger wanted to avoid any action which might prevent pan-German leaders on the ward level from supporting a common slate of candidates in the 1889 municipal elections. He wanted to convert Nationalist voters and exploit them for his own ends, not to compromise with the top-level Schönerians. But he was willing to allow Schönerer to make the first move, and given Schönerer's bitterness over his imprisonment, Lueger did not have to wait very long.

Lueger's speeches immediately after the Schönerer incident concentrated on relatively innocuous topics like the artisans and "big business."[170] But by November 1888 he had dropped his usual custom of referring to himself as a Democrat—the Christian Social Association was now "our" rather than "your" club.[171] Having decided to move nearer to the clerical camp, Lueger became much more sensitive to intra-Catholic feuding. He began to talk publicly about the value and importance of a reformed Catholic aristocracy, an idea completely foreign to his own political past. The closer he drew to Vogelsang, the more likely it was that he would be embarrassed if the Catholic conservatives openly condemned the antisemitism of Vogelsang and the Viennese clergy.[172]

One threat to both Vogelsang and Lueger in late 1888 was the establishment by Ernst Vergani of a daily German National newspaper in Vienna, the *Deutsches Volksblatt*. Vergani began his career as the mayor of a small town in rural Lower Austria. He was elected to the Reichsrat and Landtag as a pan-German in 1886–87 and for a short time seemed to be a rising star in the Schönerian ranks, until his ego and venality got the best of him. A shrewd, autocratic, and cunning businessman, he ran his newspaper in the tradition of the Austrian Liberal press, accepting bribes, arranging special contracts, exploiting the city's vice structure, building expensive houses for himself, and abusing mercilessly an army of under-paid and overworked editors and writers.[173] Much more than the *Reichs-post,* which was controlled by Albert Gessmann, the *Deutsches Volks-blatt* became the voice of the most antilabor elements in the Christian Social coalition. Leopold Kunschak often wondered if Ernst Vergani was not a greater threat to the fledgling Christian Social labor movement than all of the Social Democrats in Vienna put together. Vergani offered no one free publicity. Even groups with whom he was politically sympathetic, like the *Genossenschaftstag* and the antisemitic guilds, had to keep Ver-gani happy by means of gifts or subsidies. It was sometimes said in fin de siècle Vienna that the prestige of a journalist could be measured by the size of the bribe it required to control him. If this was the case, Vergani could certainly take pride in the price of his support.[174]

Much of Vergani's success was due to his catering to Gentile white collar voters whose antisemitism was tinged with a certain degree of anticlericalism. Vergani announced that his paper would be neither *ver-judet* nor *verpfafft.* His anticlericalism, which became more extreme after the *Reichspost* was founded in 1893 and after the *Deutsche Zeitung* took a moderate German National–Christian Social stance in 1895, was a con-sistent point in his program. Here an inevitable hostility with Vogelsang arose. Vergani's nationalism and his glorification of Bismarck intensified the quarrel. Vogelsang (like Lueger) found himself in a cross fire between Vergani and the Catholic conservatives, who now had concrete evidence that much of the new anti-Liberal movement, about which Vogelsang wrote with such enthusiasm, was a religious fraud and a patriotic menace.

By the end of 1888 Karl Lueger was nearing the final turn in his checkered political career. As if to dramatize the end of one age and the beginning of another, Lueger broke publicly in February 1889 with Ignaz Mandl, the man from whom he had learned so much of his political rhetoric. Yet the Mandl affair also showed the complexity of Lueger's motives and his hesitation to abandon totally the Democratic past which had long nurtured him. Mandl, who was a Jew, was offered informal support from the local Liberal club in the Landstrasse in his reelection race for the Council in March 1889. For the Liberals this was an excellent way of embarrassing Lueger. Mandl was inclined to cooperate with the Liberals, since he was certain that his ethnic background would lose him many of the traditional Democratic votes on which he had counted in previous elections. He refused to repudiate Liberal support.

Mandl had long been hated by the more "vigilant" antisemites like Cornelius Vetter and Leopold Hollomay, as much from envy of his successful political career as from his religious background. Conflict over Mandl had almost destroyed the antisemites' Council campaign in the Landstrasse in 1888, but Lueger was able to intervene and smooth things over.[175] As the Council elections of 1889 approached, pressure increased on Lueger to jettison Mandl. At first Lueger ignored Mandl's negotiations with the Liberals, telling Gessmann that Mandl would overcome antisemitic opposition and that it would be foolish to oppose his reelection.[176] Lueger told Vogelsang confidently in early February that Mandl would run unopposed for reelection.[177]

Lueger had not counted, however, on the violent emotions stirred up against Mandl by Hollomay and Vetter in local Landstrasse voters. When he attended a huge political rally in the Landstrasse on 19 February, he encountered a barrage of demands that he repudiate Mandl and support a regular antisemitic candidate for the Council seat. Slowly but inevitably Lueger backed down, announcing that since Mandl had refused to relinquish Liberal help, he no longer considered him a political ally.[178] But Lueger refused to give the extremists the pound of flesh they wanted, and when Hollomay claimed that Mandl had used secret Liberal funds to finance past elections, Lueger angrily rebuked him.

Lueger's ambivalence toward Mandl, his oldest and most influential friend, was dramatized by a letter which Schneider sent to Vogelsang in late January. Schneider made it clear that Lueger was aware of Mandl's machinations, but that loyalty to his friend and his desire to preserve the fiction of an "independent" stance within antisemitism led him to refuse to take any decisive action. Schneider was shocked by Lueger's indifference on the Mandl problem, since it was endangering the possibility of coopting former Schönerian Nationalists into the antisemitic crusade. With Schönerer out of the way, his former supporters might be captured by the more Austrian elements of the United Christians, but not if Mandl remained on the anti-Liberal ticket. Schneider also raised the troublesome question of Lueger's apparent "lack of character." Lueger seemed to have no principles: "First Liberal, then Democratic, then antisemitic, then Clerical, and now through Mandl Liberal again!"[179]

A month later Lueger jettisoned Mandl, trying to make it seem a free decision on his part rather than the result of public pressure. In fact the Mandl affair showed the parameters of action which limited Lueger. Schneider, with his racism and vulgarity, had touched upon a salient point: Lueger could not afford to ignore the emotions and prejudices of his constituency, especially if he hoped to enlarge that constituency by stealing votes from the Nationalists. Lueger never forgave Vetter for the insults directed at Mandl (in 1891 Lueger made sure that Vetter was denied a place on the antisemitic slate for the new metropolitan Council elections, destroying his career), but personal friendship had to make way for party unity.

During February and March 1889 the various antisemitic clubs made preparations for the spring elections.[180] The antisemites ended up with 21 seats in the Third Curia (a gain of 9) and 4 seats in the Second Curia. Of the total votes cast the antisemites won a clear majority—15,036 against the Liberals' 14,027.[181] In the council the *Bürgerclub* now had 25 members, becoming for the first time a significant voting force on the floor of that body.

When the Second Catholic Congress convened in late April, it was only natural that Lueger should attend. As if to confirm the fears of the high clerics and conservatives who had wanted to postpone the congress again, Lueger seized the limelight by offering a "welcoming address" to the delegates (most of whom were lower clerics) which completely overshadowed those of the clerical dignitaries. In contrast to his usual dramatic flair, Lueger was curiously subdued, emphasizing his respectability and cultural conservatism rather than the novelty of his politics.[182] Such conservative posturing had a pragmatic purpose. On 10 April 1889 Karl Türk, the pan-German who tried to fill the void in parliament left by Schönerer, made some controversial comments about the Austrian army. Speaking during the debates on the Defense Law, Türk cautioned "God protect Germany if it ever needs help from Austria. It would receive very lukewarm help, if any at all."[183] His comments raised a storm of criticism. In some quarters there were accusations of outright treason. Lueger's appearance at the Catholic congress a few weeks later had the manifest intention of differentiating *his* politics from the dangerous rhetoric of the Schönerians. The Church was a useful tool to undercut Liberal assertions about the undifferentiated, homogeneous nature of antisemitic radicalism.

One aristocrat at the congress who was impressed with Lueger's arguments was Alois Liechtenstein. Following the victory of the Young Czechs over the more conservative Old Czechs in the Bohemian Landtag elections of July 1889, Liechtenstein withdrew from the chairmanship of the German-Conservative *Centrumsklub* and resigned his seat in parliament in the fall of 1889.[184] Liechtenstein had no intention of abandoning political life, however. He was in contact with various Christian Social leaders by early 1890 to pave the way for his reentry into parliament on a Christian Social election slate in June 1891.[185] Most Conservatives never comprehended Liechtenstein's behavior, but he realized ten years earlier than his aristocratic hunting partners that the best defense against the egalitarianism of the Socialists lay in the political anti-Liberalism of the Viennese antisemites.

Lueger's alliance with Clericals like Vogelsang and Liechtenstein exacerbated the latent feud within the original United Christians between

the Schönerians and the rest of the antisemites. Schönerer's imprisonment, together with the loss of his cherished patent of nobility, made him
paranoid and overtly hostile to real or perceived rivals. His celebrated
ill-temper and his penchant for jealousy and self-pity totally undermined
his public effectiveness. The famous feud which he conducted with his
former protégé Vergani must be seen in the light of his psychological
imbalance during this period. In the months following his release from
prison, Schönerer adopted the habits of a hermit, refusing to take command of his weakened party organization. He renounced any interest in
Viennese politics, returning to his estate in Lower Austria to sulk. When
he did consent to speak out, he used harsh, distinctively anti-Austrian
themes which reflected the personal bitterness he felt. In a speech delivered in late May 1889 Schönerer praised Bismarck as "our leader" in
national affairs, making flattering comments about the Hohenzollern
dynasty.[186]

The absence of effective leadership and the new anti-Austrianism
alienated thousands of voters. Schönerer's weekly newspaper admitted
that a "fading of the German National idea" was taking place.[187] A police
report from Vienna in 1890 noted that the new Christian Social party had
won over to its ranks many peasants and artisans who had formerly supported Schönerer.[188] When Erich Kielmansegg toured the northwest
areas of rural Lower Austria (the districts of Waidhofen an der Thaya,
Horn, and Zwettl) where Schönerer enjoyed his greatest support, he
found that interest in pan-Germanism had declined markedly in the small
towns and villages which made up the city electoral districts.[189] Kielmansegg's observations were confirmed in the Landtag elections of October
1890 when the pan-Germans lost all but one of the urban contests they
entered.[190] Kielmansegg found that many peasants felt strong personal
loyalties to Schönerer, not because of Schönerer's nationalism, but because of his generosity as a local landowner and his pro-peasant record in
parliament. By 1893, however, police reports indicated that even in rural
areas the Christian Socials were capturing large numbers of peasant voters from the Schönerians.[191]

Schönerer's intent to commit political suicide did not make anxious
ministers and government officials rest any easier. Erich Kielmansegg
wrote to Taaffe, calling Schönerer's new political style nothing less than
"high treason."[192] Following Türk's speech against the army the government began to crack down on pan-German political associations. The
Verband der Deutschnationalen, the parliamentary club of the pan-
Germans, voluntarily dissolved itself in October 1889. In July 1889 the
Schulverein für Deutsche was abolished by government decree; in mid-
September the *Deutschnationaler Verein* met the same fate.[193] Kielman-
segg instructed lower echelon officials in Lower Austria to "devote full

attention to a possible reappearance of Schönerer, to watch carefully the meetings organized by Schönerer, and to combat disorderly or illegal gatherings."[194]

Eduard Taaffe found the new radicalism of the pan-Germans a personal embarrassment as well as a political danger.[195] Personally indifferent to antisemitism, Taaffe used it in the early and mid-1880s as a weapon to weaken the resistance of the Liberals to his coalition, making them more amenable to "cooperation" with the ministry.[196] Taaffe once remarked cynically to Eduard Sturm that only the Liberal party and not he, Taaffe, had to fear "twenty Schönerians."[197] Taaffe never expected that nationalism and antisemitism would have such an attractive and, for the government itself, such a devastating impact on the loyalties of thousands of Austrian white collar employees and professionals, especially those employed in the state bureaucracy. The pressure of the Czechs for more government appointments and the increasing dissatisfaction of lower and middle officials with current salary levels combined to produce a highly combustible political situation. Plener noted on several occasions in his autobiography the first signs of a radicalization of German-speaking *Beamten* in Vienna in the late 1880s.[198]

Not only did Schönerian nationalism exceed acceptable political limits by mid-1889, but it coincided with an equally grave threat from the Young Czechs to the north. Like many high officials and politicians, Taaffe was taken by surprise by the magnitude of the Young Czech victories in the Bohemian Landtag elections in 1889. The emperor was extremely disturbed by the upsurge of the Young Czechs (who in some respects were a Slavic version of a secular Mittelstand protest movement, with wider compass and more ambitious ideological intentions), and the long-term fate of Taaffe's carefully constructed ministerial coalition was now cast into doubt.[199] Liechtenstein's resignation from parliament was the most explicit indication of conservative German unrest over a resurgent Slavic nationalism. Other Clerical politicians felt as Liechtenstein did, although few had his option of avoiding the nationality conflict altogether by switching to Viennese politics.[200]

Taaffe was faced with a three-headed monster: pan-German treachery, the infiltration of the traditionally austere, Liberal-Josephist bureaucracy by the antisemites, and the destruction of his Conservative-Slavic coalition by the Young Czechs.[201] In February 1890 Schneider reported to Vogelsang a conversation which Liechtenstein had had with Taaffe: Taaffe's former benevolent tolerance of the antisemites seemed over, and they might expect a more hostile relationship in the future. Taaffe warned Liechtenstein that antisemites who dared to encourage "public provocations" would find themselves crushed.[202] When Ernst Vergani tried to organize an antisemitic congress in November 1890 with speakers from Germany, France, and Hungary, Taaffe wrote to Kielmansegg urging him to have the police prohibit the assembly.[203]

When riots broke out in Ottakring and Neulerchenfeld in April 1890, with crowds of youths chanting antisemitic slogans (amid their other vulgarities), the Christian Socials had serious cause for concern.[204] They issued heated denials that their voters had anything to do with the commotions. Socialist-led factory workers were not involved in the actual disturbances, although the weeks preceding the riots had seen four thousand construction workers involved in a bitter strike in the two districts. Rather, crowds of apprentices, day laborers, and unemployed journeymen, as well as school youths and university students (with a good number of itinerant *Lumpen* thrown in), formed the center point of the disturbances. The riots were triggered by collective, imitative behavior. Early in the evening of 8 April 1890 large groups of striking Socialist-led workers gathered at key points in Neulerchenfeld and Ottakring to cast insults at the scabs being employed by the construction companies during the strike. Minor incidents occurred when the police intervened to break up fistfights. Crowds of onlookers and rowdies drawn by these incidents quickly surpassed the controlled protests of the striking workers. In several places the crowds got out of control; rock throwing and minor plundering began, and the police who were summoned to the scene met with verbal abuse.

When the union leaders realized what was happening, they lost no time in bringing their workers under control (most bourgeois newspapers grudgingly admitted that the workers had maintained a *ruhige Haltung*). The youthful mobs then took control, many of whom were by this time drunk, spending the rest of the evening smashing windows and brawling. Bourgeois papers insisted that tens of thousands of rioters were on the streets, but such a number would be absurd—two or three thousand would be more reasonable. The antisemitic vulgarities shouted by some of the crowds against Jewish-owned *Branntweinladen* were, however, an ominous demonstration to the government of the informal effect of ten years of political antisemitism.

Although a few industrial workers were arrested, the great majority of the fifty men detained by the police were either artisan apprentices and journeymen or unemployed day laborers. No individual was arrested who might be conceived of as a Christian Social voter. The Ottakring riots were the work of young men, men of no property whose status levels were so low as to make them almost social nonentities. They were also men who belonged to no cohesive, disciplined political organization. The riots showed both Socialist and antisemitic leaders the difficulties in dealing with younger, unskilled workers in a formal political context. The Socialists responded with a renewed and successful effort in the 1890s to create disciplined union organizations for craft journeymen and apprentices. Among bourgeois circles in the city, however, whether Liberal or Christian Social, the riots left a deep and abiding fear. The occurrence of these riots less than a month before the Social Democrats organized their first May Day celebration (1890) provides an insight into the genesis of bourgeois fears about this date. Would 1 May become an Ottakring and Neulerchenfeld written on a larger and more destructive scale? That the government saw a connection between the two events was indicated by edicts issued by Kielmansegg in mid-April 1890 instructing the district offices of the province (the *Bezirkshauptmannschaften*) to take appropriate measures to control worker excesses.[205]

Coming as they did on the heels of Schönerian radicalism and the government's repressive response, the disturbances might have been used by the authorities as an excuse to crack down on the Viennese anti-Liberals for alleged ''social revolutionary'' tendencies. Did not some of the rioters use antisemitic language? Taaffe's displeasure over Schönerian antisemitism has been clearly charted. It was also well known in high governmental circles that the emperor thought very little of antisemitic rhetoric. In such instances such as the Neulerchenfeld riots where a few hotheads took such rhetoric seriously Franz Joseph responded with demands for repression. He had already faced one urban revolution in his lifetime and had no intention of repeating the experience.[206]

In spite of such preconditions for intervention, the government took no action against Lueger and the non-Schönerian antisemites. Why was this the case? In part this reflected the ministry's preoccupation after April 1890 with the Socialists. In fact, both bourgeois and aristocratic circles in the city were far more inclined to view the Ottakring events as worker events than they were as antisemitic events. The class dimension was the preeminent one, not the cultural thrust of the riots. The government in Vienna was increasingly disturbed by worker organization as 1890 passed, and the antisemites profited from this distraction of official interest. Compared with Victor Adler, Lueger seemed almost tolerable, and it was precisely this ''almost'' status which kept the antisemites in the good graces of the government throughout the early 1890s. The costs of repressing them were too great in the short run to justify the effort involved, especially when limited police resources had to be committed to careful supervision of the burgeoning Socialist movement. Also, Lueger's clever use of the Church as a mantle of cultural respectability may have made any drastic action against the antisemites seem inopportune. Finally, the antisemites themselves made a concerted effort to establish before key government pesonalities their credentials as respectable bourgeois politicians. The language of the rally halls was quickly dispensed with in an effort to show the government through an informal pattern of personal contacts that the anti-Liberals were acceptable elements of the traditional political system. An excellent example of this informal bargaining came in September 1890 when Lueger sent a confidential letter to Kielmansegg insisting upon his party's respectability. Lueger had delivered a tough, hard-hitting attack on the Liberals' plan for the unification of the suburban areas and Vienna in the City Council. Since Kielmansegg was responsible for drafting the bill with the Liberals' cooperation, the speech might have been construed as an insult against the government and the emperor's personal representative in the unification negotiations. Lueger assured the *Statthalter* that he held him in great personal regard. His speech was not a diatribe against the government, although the Liberal newspapers tried to construe it as such. From his previous encounters with Kielmansegg he had learned to "value and respect" him. Lueger claimed he was outraged by Liberal self-indulgence in their version of the unification laws, but even more by the Liberal claim that the provincial government was intrinsically hostile to the *Bürgerclub* and an ally of the Liberal party. The latter assertion seemed to Lueger to be extremely dangerous, since it would have undercut any possibility of an equitable, two-party system in the province.[207]

Lueger's obsequious (and ego-smoothing) behavior toward Kielmansegg paid off. When Kielmansegg was called upon in 1895 to evaluate Lueger's qualifications for the office of mayor, he was forced to admit that Lueger was a moderate, bourgeois politician who would not dishonor the office to which he had been elected. Kielmansegg's personal loyalties were with the Liberals, but the careful sense of the limits of permissible behavior which leading Christian Socials always manifested made it impossible to tag them as "revolutionaries" and consign them to the same pariah group as the pan-Germans. Lueger forced the government, clearly against its will, to observe a functional neutrality toward a competitive, two-party bourgeois political system. As the antisemitic movement picked up support and momentum, the Imperial government no longer had any choice—what might have been repressed in 1887 or 1888 was there to stay by 1895. The demands that the new coalition regime "crush" the Christian Socials which were occasionally heard in the hysterical Liberal press in 1895 were pure utopianism.[208] Unless the regime was prepared to resort to illegalities of its own and perhaps even political repression, such talk was nonsense and responsible government officials knew it. Was Lueger worth a local *Staatsstreich* in 1895? The absurdity of the question was even more apparent in view of the government's failure to take any action against the nonnationalist antisemites since their unification in 1887.

Most Christian Social voters were as frightened by disturbances like those in Ottakring as a Ringstrasse banker was apt to be, perhaps more so. In the suburban districts, where most *Hausherren* were voting antisemitic by the mid-1890s, *their* property was being stoned and *their* windows broken. Unlike the Social Democrats, the Christian Socials were unwilling to use the streets as a principal forum for political agitation. They were closer to the Liberal political style, preferring closed, self-contained rallies with controls over entry and exit. The artisans of 1890 differed from their predecessors of 1848 in their habituation to social order and nonviolent protest. Much more typical of the Bürger attitudes toward collective street activities was the behavior of the *Hausherr* (a wealthy shoemaker) whom Karl Renner knew in Vienna in the 1890s. On 1 May he locked up his strongbox (which was well supplied with money from his several large tenement buildings) and took his family to the country for the day, fearing public violence.[209] That Christian Social election meetings took place in beer halls (as did the Liberal rallies), with occasional fistfights and gate crashings by opposing groups of voters, did not indicate that the antisemites were plotting social revolution. Most of the big voting blocs from which the Christian Socials drew their support were composed of men who saw a difference between an isolated beer hall dispute and a riot. Jail was hardly the place for an artisan master who hoped to open his shop the next morning. As for the white collar elements in the party, they observed a very cautious line of behavior—no public or private bureaucracy in Vienna gave job promotions or salary raises to anyone guilty of unseemly public behavior.

Schönerer's verbal violence made inevitable an open break between him and the other United Christians. Vergani, for one, seeking to exploit Schönerer's hysteria, set himself up as a general press lord of Viennese antisemitism. When Schönerer threw him out of the party, this was a great boon to his fortunes—he could still claim to be a racial nationalist, but without the millstone of Schönerer around his neck. Vergani quickly selected Vogelsang and Pattai as targets of his arrogant posturing, Vogelsang because of his "clericalism," Pattai for his betrayal of "true nationalism." By late 1889 the original United Christians seemed mired in intracoalition feuds dangerously similar to those which had destroyed the *Reformverein* in 1886.

Pattai responded to Schönerer and Vergani with a declaration of independence. He had always styled himself as an "independent" Nationalist. Now he simply chose to take the rubric literally. In a controversial speech in October 1889 Pattai assailed Türk's army speech and uttered some unflattering remarks about Schönerer himself. He tried to balance his performance by criticizing the "clericalism" of the Catholics, but the pan-German press took the talk for what it was, a personal repudiation of Schönerer.[210]

Pattai's strategy of outmaneuvering the pan-Germans was successful, but only because there now existed a reasonably viable coalition of antisemitic groups who had a real stake in maintaining party unity. This was the message Lueger continually hammered home: tolerate Vergani and if necessary even Schönerer for the sake of party unity. Lueger intervened with Pattai, urging that personal vanities and private interests be repressed in favor of public unity.[211] Pattai refused, but Lueger's efforts at conciliation suggested much about the source of his political esteem. He was one of the few major anti-Liberal politicians who were not hated by any of the other rivals in personal terms. Schönerer might envy Lueger, but he was forced to respect him as a professional for whom politics possessed its own impersonal rationale. Whereas Pattai and Schönerer fought duels in defense of their "honor," Lueger categorically rejected such subjective, individualistic behavior as unacceptable for a modern political movement. Lueger came out of the period 1887–90 as the man who stood above personality disputes and rivalries, as a professional politician who could reconcile and lead the faction-ridden cadres of Viennese antisemitism. Even if Lueger later indulged in a personality cult, he did this with the conscious knowledge that this was as much a tool for voter mobilization as it was a gratification for his own ego.

Fortunately for Lueger, Schönerer took the decisive step. In late October 1889 Schönerer announced that he was repudiating any past and present support for both Lueger and Pattai, accusing them of having sold their souls to Catholicism and of refusing to rise above artisan economics to the pure heights of German nationalism.[212] Lueger was still talking about the formation of a "great German-Christian" party in early October,[213] but he was now free to dispense with artificial attempts to conciliate the Schönerians. Schönerer was responsible for the break, not Lueger—Lueger's patience had finally paid off. By late November Lueger conceded the inevitable and announced that he was now leading the new Christian Social party.[214] In February 1890, in his first speech before parliament in six months, Lueger formalized his new allegiance, asserting that a new party now existed to which he had the honor to belong.[215] This time, unlike his experience with political rubrics in 1886, there were no catcalls from the floor of the house. Lueger was beginning to make his mark in an impressive way.

Lueger's odyssey had finally ended. The relentless tempo of Schönerer's radicalism, the threat of the nascent Social Democracy, and his own carefully modulated ambition to return to a city-wide leadership role overcame any residual doubts about committing himself to an explicit blend of antisemitism, Democracy, *and* political Clericalism. For most of

1888 and 1889 Lueger was the cautious observer of the mistakes of others, rather than the initiator of centripetal processes. Once it was apparent that the United Christians in their original form could no longer survive and that Schönerer's pan-Germanism was endangering the whole enterprise, Lueger felt free to search for a new framework, one which would replace his former affiliation with Democracy and create an effective political organization for Vienna and the rural areas of Lower Austria.

Lueger had long desired to force the Schönerian elite into a subsidiary leadership position in Lower Austria. His caution and circumspection throughout 1889, however, together with his role as the loyalist who did nothing to insult Schönerer personally, made his position even stronger. Because Lueger refused to condemn categorically the idea of some kind of nationalist defense against the Slavs (all the while insisting that it was not a vital necessity), he was able to prevent an antisemitic civil war in Vienna.[216]

The old spirit of cooperation among the various anti-Liberal factions which was first enunciated in 1887 was perpetuated in Vienna after 1890. With Schönerer's voluntary isolation and his hermitlike behavior, his supporters had no indication of a feasible pan-German alternative. Many of the district political organizations which operated before 1890 under a German National aegis continued to exist. Some, like the *Politischer Bezirksverein Währing,* led by Anton Baumann, all the while insisting that they were loyal to Schönerer personally, in fact shifted to a moderate, independent-nationalist stance which enabled them by 1895–96 to become de facto members of the Christian Socials.[217] Other clubs, like the *Politischer Favoritner Bürgerverein,* led by W. Ph. Hauck, remained pan-German, but still cooperated with the Christian Socials and ordered their representatives to sit with the antisemitic *Bürgerclub* in the City Council. The *Bürgerclub* itself remained an amalgam of various factions, but by 1896 the Christian Socials were in the great majority. Still other pan-German associations collapsed entirely or became outright Christian Social *Vereine.*[218] Many of the newer clubs established after 1890–91, especially in the newly incorporated suburban districts, adopted neutral names (like *Bürgerverein*), but were in fact dominated by Christian Social leaders.

A similar pattern of diffusion and reorientation occurred among nationalist politicians, who now found themselves in the quandary of affirming loyalty to Schönerer while quietly disassociating themselves from his movement. As late as March 1896 over one-third of the Christian Social City Council delegation publicly insisted that they were "nationalists" of one sort or another, and still more wanted it to be known that they harbored nationalist sympathies.[219] In fact a shift away from pure pan-Germanism to a more vague, nationalist reformism on social

Bürger principles was in progress, as the party neared the realities of political power in 1896. Pure nationalism was not an effective issue in Viennese politics, even after Schönerer provoked the *Los von Rom* controversy. The shift of political loyalties was only possible because of the shared Bürger cultural values common to most potential antisemitic voters and sub-elite leaders. The social force of these values was far stronger for political unity than the nominal differentiations of the various sects would suggest. Dr. August Kupka, a lawyer from the Josefstadt, exemplified such a movement. Originally a Liberal Nationalist, then a Lueger Democrat, he became a Christian Social and after 1896 a powerful member of the Christian Social *Stadtrat*. Similar patterns occurred in the political careers of prominent Christian Socials like Leopold Tomola and Leopold Steiner. Other antisemites, like Rudolf Polzhofer and Robert Pattai, considered themselves German National and Christian Social simultaneously, as did Theodor Wähner, the influential editor of the *Deutsche Zeitung*.

Nor should the willingness of Lueger and Gessmann to work with moderate nationalist politicians—as opposed to simply stealing their voters—be construed as an act of political magnanimity. They had no alternative. In many districts of the city, especially those with a strong sense of local, particularistic loyalties, local antisemitic politicians were more than men bearing a party label. They often were popular local business and municipal leaders who were respected by a variety of voters. In Währing, where Anton Baumann held sway, it would have been political suicide for Lueger to try to destroy the indigenous leadership cadres.

Lueger's great talent amid all of this terminological particularism was not a magic charismatic presence, but rather his hard-nosed bullying of and shrewd mediation between the disparate elements of the anti-Liberals, encouraging a gradual process of assimilation into the Christian Social ranks. He was far more an instructor in political tactics and a conscience who could remind all anti-Liberals what was at stake and what the prizes of victory might be, than he was a spiritual high priest. Men reacted positively to him because he persuaded them that it was in their own interest to do so. To make compromises and achieve political unity were cardinal necessities, a point Lueger never tired of reiterating. Lueger was a modern political educator, drawing on nearly thirty years of active experience.

Early Party Structure

What was the Christian Social party at this stage? For several years it would remain little more than a linguistic designation of the status quo in which Lueger and Gessmann found themselves: an association of ex-Democrats, ex-nationalists of various colors, and radical Catholics, united in a search for municipal hegemony. Lueger's role was not and was never to become that of an absolute dictator with arbitrary discretion over everyone and everything within his purview, although he did not hesitate to crush the attempt by a few pan-Germans led by Paul v Pacher in 1896 to revive an independent Nationalist movement in Viennese politics.

Before 1896 each district in the city had one or more antisemitic political clubs which managed local political mobilization during election periods. Each club had a base constituency of loyalists, usually working out of a regular cafe or *Gasthaus*. The petty leadership cadres of these clubs were based as much on personal friendship and mutual business interests as they were on ideological commitments. Clubs might have diverse ideological attachments—most of the party's clubs were either formally Catholic (such as the Christian Social Association's branches or the *Katholisch-politischer Verein* in the Leopoldstadt) or more secular and Democratic (such as the *Eintracht* in the Landstrasse or the Christian Social *Bürgervereine* in Hernals and Hietzing). The natural rivalry between the clubs of a given district (most districts had several) rarely produced serious disruptive consequences for the party. The duties of constituency politics were also shared by the craft guilds and Catholic voluntary organizations. These groups played diverse roles, sometimes working on a municipal level in support of a common list of candidates, sometimes putting their money and energy behind a select group of party candidates who were especially sympathetic to their own interests (such as the support given by the guilds to Lorenz Müller, a master baker in the Leopoldstadt, when he ran for a Council seat in 1895). The clergy played important roles in the Catholic associational network, but also worked extensively in the district clubs. After 1890 the formal development of professional organizations like the local *Hausherrenvereine* in each district and the *Beamten* clubs enhanced the organizational matrix in which the Christian Socials could work. Men came to see themselves in a more complicated series of external social roles, each one demanding a distinct organizational affiliation. The party did not always demand or expect explicit political loyalty from these professional organizations. In many cases it was far more useful to have them maintain a surface neutrality (as many of the property owners' associations did), since this expanded the recruitment possibilities for undecided voters who might find a partisan political atmosphere unpleasant or unacceptable. Political life in Vienna under the Christian Socials was, as it had been under the Liberals, localized and mediated by a large number of small, voluntaristic social and professional organizations.[220]

Until well after 1897 Lueger and Gessmann made no attempt to create a permanent central party bureaucracy on any level. Organizational prowess was not one of the virtues of the early party. Election planning above the club and association level was generally handled by a committee of *Wahlmänner* in the district, which usually included the antisemitic city councilmen, the members of the District Committee *(Bezirksausschuss)*, leaders of the key clubs in the district, guild chairmen (if they resided in the district), influential priests, and other local notables.[221] The *Wahlmänner* coordinated on an ad hoc basis many of their tasks with the leaders of the clubs (to the extent that the latter were not represented on the district *Wahlcomité*) in arranging political rallies and printed propaganda. Where the Christian Socials controlled the District Committee and elected the district *Vorsteher* (increasingly the case after 1896), they had at their command the resources of municipal government in arranging their rallies and electoral agitation. Rallies might be of a general, district-wide variety to listen to candidates' speeches and give a final voice-vote approval of the party slate (previously arranged by the committee and cleared with the central leadership), or they might be restricted to one club's base constituency. Usually each campaign saw a mixture of several forms of such assemblies. The party usually restricted rallies to the district level, or at most to neighboring districts. It also made a practice of calling rallies on a regular basis in between scheduled elections to provide for social interaction and to retain the interest of the voters. On some occasions campaign rallies might be the scene of oppositional movements within the local party groups, usually provoked by irate sub-elite leaders who had been denied a place on the slate.

Beyond the local level a higher directorate, the *Zentralwahlcomité*, was organized for each election, usually bearing a neutral political rubric under which all of the interests and factions in the party could unite. The typical name before 1896 was the United Christians, although *Bürgerclub* was used on some occasions. This central committee system was a standard feature of much of the local and regional bourgeois politics in Central Europe. It provided flexibility and maneuverability; and it could be disbanded after each election, in conformity with Lueger's preference for avoiding the image of a rigid party bureaucracy.[222] The most prominent members of the party, with Lueger as chairman, occupied positions on the central committee. These were the high-profile politicians who were the party's leading vote-getters and who could be relied on to bring out a respectable audience at club or rally assemblies in any of the city's districts. The numerical size of rallies was crucial—both loyalist and opposition newspapers paid careful attention to the size of the previous evening's rallies, as did the police. Small assemblies were a chronic embarrassment and also an open invitation for rival clubs or factions to "invade" the meeting by sending a cadre of their supporters to the meeting to disrupt the proceedings. This was a standard practice among the Liberals, Christian Socials, and Socialists in the city, although the last two parties were larger and their disruptions gained more publicity. The best, indeed, the only protection against disruptions was to fill the hall rapidly with one's own supporters. Without a "name" speaker such as Lueger, Liechtenstein, or Pattai a rally might flounder for lack of interest.

Candidate designation was one of the most sensitive and least systematized processes in the city's political system. Lueger denied that he had sole control of the overall nomination process for candidates, and there is no reason to doubt him. Leopold Kunschak discovered that the artisan masters and property owners were loath to accept Christian Social laborite candidates on the party ticket in any election. Lueger, whether he wanted to do so or not, was forced to comply with their wishes. Nor was it uncommon for local candidates to generate support for themselves in their districts and then present the central committee with a fait accompli. Lueger and his elite colleagues exercised the right of final approval over all candidates and did arrange for the nomination of some individuals through direct intervention with the district committees, but there were a variety of structures and processes at work simultaneously. Lueger's problems with Anton Baumann on candidate selection matters illustrated the accommodation and compromise necessary for survival in Viennese politics. In 1891 Baumann tried to resist the imposition of Alois Liechtenstein on his district as its candidate for the Reichsrat election. He resented Liechtenstein as a *fremdartigen Candidaten* who had no connection with Während, did not live there, and was not a man of the *Gewerbestand*. He also distrusted Liechtenstein's billowy, nonracial antisemitism and his obvious clericalism.[223] Lueger was unable to dissuade Baumann from running an independent candidate, Franz Frassl, against both Liechtenstein and the Democrat Kronawetter, but Liechtenstein easily crushed Frassl in the first round of voting and went on to beat Kronawetter in the runoff election.[224] Baumann was not always so unsuccessful in manipulating the local party slate. In the summer of 1895, for example, he decided to dump Johann Jedlička, the chairman of the carpenters' guild, from the Council election slate in Während. Jedlička was a Lueger loyalist and a crony of Schneider, but his financial incompetence and his friendship with several prominent Jewish innkeepers, as well as his Czech background, made him an easy target for Baumann, who wanted to replace him with his own man.[225] After Baumann's *Politischer Bezirksverein* threw Jedlička off the ticket for the September elections, Lueger was forced to accept the situation, even though the incident created embarrassing problems with groups of guildsmen who saw the anti-Jedlička movement in Während as an attempt to curtail the rights of the craft guilds in the party.[226]

Crucial to Baumann's leverage was the fact of district localism as a prerequisite for any kind of Viennese bourgeois politics. Not until the stormy campaign of September 1895 did Lueger seriously contemplate moving beyond the exigencies and restrictions of the localized, district mode of politics. Even then he did not fully emulate the Social Democrats in their municipal consciousness and regular party bureaucracy. Before 1895 it is difficult to call the Christian Socials a "mass" party, for reasons which will be discussed in chapter 6. Even in 1895 the heritage of district patronage and power remained strong. When the antisemites wished to maintain public interest during the lag which occurred between the November 1895 confrontation with the government and the February 1896 Council elections, one effective technique they exploited was to engage in political drama in the local *Gasthäuser* and club headquarters of the districts. Local notables staged simulated City Council sessions in local taverns and rally points, with some of the antisemitic sub-elite playing "Liberal" and some "antisemitic" roles to entertain and edify the local clientele.[227] Although this particular technique was novel, it was also deeply Viennese in its use of political theatricality on a local, district-level base. Lueger always felt uncomfortable with a mass, street and parade style of politics—he disliked crowds outside traditional rally halls. He differed fundamentally from Victor Adler in this regard. Lueger preferred to modernize traditional Liberal techniques and to improve upon them, rather than abandoning them completely.

By 1895 the Christian Socials were beginning to evolve cadres of ward organizers in each of the nineteen districts, attempting to make one political worker responsible for as few as ten to fifteen voters (making certain of their loyalty, making sure they got to the polling place and cast their vote in the proper fashion, and then leading them off to a local drinking spot). This kind of precinct-level efficiency was not a total break with previous Liberal practice. The Liberals were also capable of mounting such a concerted effort (including the use of a fleet of election wagons to carry Liberal voters to and from the polling place), but they rarely did so with such panache and enthusiasm.[228] What the antisemites improved was not the political structure itself, but the efficiency and rapidity of technique. The party emulated the Liberal rally style, for example, but held more and larger rallies per district in each campaign, using more ferocious propaganda.

In terms of campaign funding the Christian Socials did not break fundamentally with Liberal practices, largely because they were dealing with the same kinds of voters. Each of the opposing central committees assembled a *Zentralwahlfond* from which to pay the expenses incurred in printing propaganda, renting rally halls, paying for refreshments, and engaging in an occasional bit of "honest graft." Each district *Wahlcomité* had a reserve fund of its own, solicited through voluntary contributions from local businessmen and party loyalists, as well as grants from outside organizations. Neither party was a "membership" party in a strict sense, so that neither could rely on membership fees or contributions from a predictable and stable constituency, as could the Socialists through their unions and party cards. The *Zentralwahlfond* was a larger collection of revenue, which supplemented local resources; the cost of a typical rally might run as high as 200–300 fl., an expense beyond the resources of many local clubs. The central party treasury also depended upon contributions, as well as grants from "secret" outside sources such as banks or monasteries. Each party also profited from informal concessions and donations from "nonpolitical" sources—the Catholic School Association was a well-endowed group capable of mounting its own rallies. By allowing the antisemites to use these occasions for their party propaganda, the association was in fact subsidizing the party's *Zentralwahlfond* by allowing its funds to be used elsewhere. Sympathetic business interests played a crucial role in funding for both parties. The typical Liberal contributor might be larger and more "capitalist," whereas the antisemites (at least before 1896) had to put together more diverse and smaller business contributions. The Liberals were undoubtedly the wealthier party, but Lueger never lost an election for want of money—the Christian Socials never had as much as they wanted, but they did have enough to win control of the city in 1896. By 1907 the Christian Socials were receiving large-scale business subsidies from industrial and banking interests who wanted insurance against a Socialist victory in the 1907 elections.[229]

District localism was thus a component of antisemitic as well as Liberal politics. Inevitably it influenced the workings of the broader municipal political system. Lueger was on a first name basis with many of the Liberals from the Landstrasse with whom he fought for political control of the city. He knew Raimund Grübl for thirty years; Ludwig Vogler was once employed in Lueger's law office.[230] Many of the local political leaders in both parties were members of the same district *Hausherrenverein,* where they often associated with each other both socially and professionally outside the world of competitive politics. The elites and sub-elites of the Christian Socials and the Liberals shared a profound sense of rootedness and social permanence in terms of local *Bezirk* life, a quality which made each of them distinct from the mass organizational ethos of the Social Democrats. Precisely this shared social and cultural *Sesshaftigkeit* made the transition from Liberal to Christian Social rule in Vienna smooth and uninterrupted, compared with the violent dislocations which occurred between the Christian Socials and the Social Democrats in 1918–19.

Lueger had to respect not only the personalities of his colleagues, but also the powerful social interests they often represented. Schneider could afford to play the role of the drunken bad boy of the party for this reason: his influence with the craft guilds afforded him protection. Within the party elite Lueger was the indisputable first leader, but he exercised his power in a collegial fashion, rarely taking important actions without consulting his colleagues. Albert Gessmann, who controlled the distribution of party funds, was a powerful figure in his own right. Ernst Schneider demonstrated the flexibility demanded of Lueger when he wrote to Vogelsang warning him that he would allow no one to "push him around."[231] Joseph Scheicher was a similar character, who fiercely resented being treated as anything but an equal. Yet Scheicher emphasized in his memoirs that Lueger treated his colleagues in a "democratic" way. Scheicher's reports on the way in which the Christian Social parliamentary club meetings were managed indicated that Lueger often had to rely on rational persuasion and argumentation rather than an endless series of dictatorial commands.[232]

The elite structure of the Christian Social coalition in 1890–91 is best described by the idea of petty notable politics, not based on a rationalized, hierarchic local-regional-national control system such as the Social Democrats were soon to develop. Rather than Liberal *Honoratioren* dominating local and regional politics, a new group of bourgeois notables, most of whom were slightly below typical Liberal wealth levels, moved into prominence in Viennese politics. But the organizational forms of politics remained much the same as before 1890, even though Lueger contributed to them a new dynamic of political language.

A survey of the occupational and social backgrounds of the sixty-eight men who were elected to the City Council on antisemitic/anti-Liberal election slates between 1886 and 1891 in the Third and Second Curias reveals the integrated, socially stable nature of the Christian Social municipal elite. In terms of professional status, twenty-six were artisans of the *Kleingewerbe,* twenty-two owned businesses or stores of a larger, *Mittelgewerbe* size (*Stadtbaumeister,* owners of firms listed in the trade register, medium-sized factory owners, etc.), four were lawyers, nine were teachers (most of them senior teachers with a considerable amount of tenure), one was a medical doctor, and the rest were public or private employees.[233] Thirty-nine of these candidates were property owners, some owning lucrative apartment houses. Ten were officials in one of the craft guilds, while many of the others had involved themselves in district-level charitable or educational councils or accepted professional responsibilities before their election to the Council. In general, they fell into one of two categories: either they were highly politicized, local sub-elite leaders who ran political clubs in the districts in which they were elected, or (and this was the majority) they were comfortably situated and (in some cases) wealthy Bürger types on whom the antisemitic coalition could depend to run for office as a form of civic duty and honor. Few of them were men with no organizational or political backgrounds before election to the Council. Almost none of them were from the class of 5 fl. artisans. Most were fairly prosperous members of the Bürgertum for whom the paradigm of the "poor artisan" was a symbolic construct, not an element of their present experience. The mean age of the candidates (upon their election to office) was forty-five; two-thirds (forty-six out of sixty-eight) had been born before the Revolution of 1848. If this was slightly younger than the mean age of Liberal candidates in the mid-1880s, it was still a far cry from the youthfulness of the local leaders of the Social Democrats.[234] Less than 55 percent of them (thirty-six of the sixty-eight) were natives of Vienna or Lower Austria—many had, therefore, an acute sense of personal mobility and achieved success in their newfound *Heimat*.[235] At the same time, they overcompensated for their newness by redoubling their efforts to style themselves as traditional, reliable members of the Viennese Bürgertum. Like converts to a new religion, these men were anxious to demonstrate and even to flaunt their new social stability. There was some irony in the fact, however, that they were no more a part of the generational traditions of Viennese society than were the newly immigrated Jews they claimed to dislike. Politics became for them a way of enhancing their integration into Bürger values and mores.

These were not high Liberal *Honoratioren*. They were not men of regional or even municipal prominence, but rather of local, district-level notability. Extreme wealth was not (and has never been) an essential value in Viennese society, but solid Bürger security and respectability were. In the aftermath of each municipal election the Austrian police examined the personal records of each new candidate to establish whether such Bürger-level solidity and lawfulness did in fact exist. Between 1886 and 1891 not one antisemitic politician was rejected as unfit for public office.[236] The argument of Reinhold Knoll, reversing the logical order of Max Weber's terminology, that the Christian Social party was a "mass" party in the 1890s and only later became a party of notables (*Honoratiorenpartei*) fails to consider the subtle, differentiated system of stratification within Viennese Bürger culture before 1890 and is thus very debatable. Few men could afford to hold public office in Vienna in the 1890s without an independent means of support, since officeholding on the municipal level did not carry with it a salary. More important, these notables were men who were well integrated into local cultural circles and associations, who had a clear conception of themselves as putting the Liberal system aright, not overturning it in a structural sense. After 1896 a more elaborate and more hierarchical system of nobility gradually did evolve, but it was a system which built upon and expanded the formative system of petty notability rather than replacing it. If anything, both periods exhibited some qualitative features of mass and notable politics, mixed in a confusing, but highly successful matrix. The party's loyalty to property, social respectability, and cultural philistinism, and its distrust of full electoral democracy and egalitarianism, were as strong in 1895 as in 1911.[237]

The conjunction of *Beamten* (with and without comprehensive university training) and schoolteachers with the handwork masters and shopkeepers in the party after 1890 also gave rise to more integrated patterns which helped to create a stronger bourgeois sense in the party's direction and goals. Hansjoachim Henning has recently explored the process of attitude change toward their social situation on the part of late-nineteenth-century German *Beamten* in terms of an increasing emphasis on *Bildung* as an attribute of social prestige.[238] A similar process took place among the Austrian *Beamten*. Even though *Bildung* may be considered a more competitive, progressive justification for bourgeois prestige than attributive *ständisch* justifications, such as those used by the artisans, the two sets of value justifications were not, in terms of day-to-day political operations, mutually exclusive.[239] Both sets of claimants realized that each depended upon the other and could offer something vital to the other, namely, the absolute control of a Viennese electoral curia.[240] The presence in the party of *Hausherren* and wealthier artisans helped to bridge the psychological gap between the two groups. It was not uncommon for *Beamten* to run as candidates in the Third Curia and industrial or commercial Bürger to run in the Second Curia. The older double meaning of the word Bürger—as a description of nonacademic, bourgeois types involved in business or property holding in the narrower sense, and as a description for the whole of the middle bourgeoisie, including the *Intelligenz,* as opposed to the very poor and very wealthy in society—which dated from the Vormärz, was still a viable dual usage in Vienna in the 1890s. The Catholic clergy, although they might have relied on attributive cultural justifications for their interests, usually emphasized achieved-class distinctions, so that they were appropriate class partners for the *Beamten*.

Even among the lowest levels of the *Besitzbürgertum* in Vienna there was considerable admiration for the prestige and life-style of the academically educated *Beamten*. To the extent that a master artisan did not want his son or sons to carry on his business, he would have preferred for them some kind of *Beamten* status. That this attitude was not reciprocated by *Beamten* voters explained the superiority and importance of being able to vote in the Second as opposed to the Third Curia (artisans who ran in the

Second Curia as candidates had to have solid financial credentials to prove that they belonged there and were not intruders from below). Many artisan voters in the party had the opportunity to mimic the status of the *Beamten*, if only on a part-time basis. The municipal government of Vienna depended upon hundreds of part-time *Armenräte* and *Ortsschulräte*, not to mention the more prestigious positions of the District Committee itself. Even during the Liberal era most of these positions were filled by voters with little formal education, but who did have aspirations to bourgeois status. [241] The job of an *Armenrat* (each district had eighty to ninety such individuals) carried with it a title, an office of sorts, and the possibility of an order or certificate of merit of some sort, if only the city's *Bürgerrecht* title.

The later history of the party was to show that tensions between the two groups were in some respects inevitable, but these became operatively significant only after 1906. As early as 1894–95, therefore, there were a number of occupational strata in the party who claimed "notable" status, or at least hoped to emulate those who had achieved such success.

Only with the Landtag elections of October 1890 and the Reichsrat elections of March 1891 did a slightly clearer focus of the uncertain identity of the new party become apparent. The Council elections in the spring of 1890 proved that Viennese anti-Liberalism had met the challenge of pan-German separatism successfully. Ten new candidates were elected to the Third and Second Curias. [242] In Franz Schindler's mind the campaign for the Landtag in the fall of 1890 was the real operational starting point of the Christian Social party. [243] With the unification of the suburban districts and Vienna in 1890 the party would have an impressive opportunity—the possibility of ruling a metropolitan area of nearly 2 million people.

5

The Transformation of Viennese Politics
Metropolitan Vienna, White Collar
Radicalism, and the Elections of 1891

In late 1890 a series of revisions in the political and administrative structure of the city of Vienna took place which changed the course of urban politics in Vienna before the First World War. Not only were the social resources of the city considerably enlarged by the unification with Vienna of the suburbs surrounding the city in December 1890, but the unification itself necessitated revisions in and rethinking of the strategies of all competing political groups. The creation of a new statute, designed by the ruling Liberal party to ensure its future dominance of the city, offered Liberals and anti-Liberals alike new opportunities to prosper or flounder in future municipal conflicts.

Nor did these changes fail to influence the rising tide of antisemitic politics which had slowly swept over the city since the mid-1880s. Antisemitic politics in Vienna before 1890 had been fitted, if only in a haphazard fashion, to the given administrative and constitutional structures of the city. They were no more and no less ambitious than the given electoral structures allowed. Before 1890 anti-Liberal strategy had concentrated largely on the Third Curia, and within that curia on the large antisemitic base vote of the 5–10 fl. men. Between 1886 and 1890 the various factions in the antisemitic coalition had run twice as many candidates in the Third Curia as in the other two curias. Whereas the antisemites in the Third (and poorest) Curia soon ran up an impressive record of success, seats in the Second Curia were far more difficult to obtain, and when they did fall to the anti-Liberals, they usually did so by uncomfortably small margins. Once the political structure of the city had been radically reformed by the changes of December 1890, both the possible scope and the potential rewards of expanded political activity became a spur to creative political imagination. Only after 1890 did the antisemites seriously begin to consider how they could put together a winning majority within the city's three electoral curias. When they began to address this question, they were forced to make a much greater emotional commitment to winning the votes of more prosperous and more status conscious citizens in the Second and First Curias, whose interests and needs were not always identical with those of the five-gulden men.

Following the municipal elections of 1889, the German ambassador, Prince Reuss, had written to Berlin commenting that the antisemites were winning not only the votes of disgruntled Jew haters, but far more those of the "genuine Viennese Bürger," who, in his judgment, was voting not because of racial, antisemitic hysteria, but from a disenchantment with the ineffectiveness of Liberal administration of the city's affairs.[1] Only after 1890, however, did the Christian Socials try to convert this Bürger disenchantment into privileged Second and First Curia votes.

Finally, the period after 1890 in Vienna saw the evolution of several major mid- and upper-Bürger occupational movements such as those of the government employees and the property owners, all of which affected the later balance of power in the city. Because of the peculiar structure of the 1890 Gemeindeordnung, many of these groups proved effective bargainers in advocating their narrowly conceived interests. In asserting their power and in installing themselves as permanent features of the Viennese political system, such interest groups inevitably modified the political movements which sought their support. The beginning of a more considered and a more moderate policy basis for the Christian Social party—all radical-sounding rhetoric aside—is rooted in the period 1891–95 when the anti-Liberal forces began a slow, but clearly discernible movement into the middle sectors of the Viennese Bürgertum.

Metropolitan Vienna: Genesis and Political Consequences

The formal unification of the city and the suburban communities completed a process of vast urban growth and consolidation in Lower Austria dating from the 1840s. Before 1840 the numerous small villages which surrounded the central Innere Stadt and its satellite districts (after 1850 the Second to Ninth Districts) were relatively isolated and had little direct economic significance for the city's growth. As the population of the city expanded, however, and as the city's industry and commerce became more diversified and complex, the suburbs became the natural areas of residence for tens of thousands of industrial workers, handwork journeymen, small retail merchants, poorer artisan masters, and others of modest means. During the negotiations in 1849–50 between the Imperial government and the representatives of the city which resulted in the 1850 Gemeindeordnung, the negotiators for the city rejected the proposal put forward by Franz Stadion that the Ordnung unite the small suburbs with the city, forming a Greater Vienna.[2] Fearing a proletarianization of the city and the probability of escalating poor care costs, the Committee of Twelve which represented Vienna recommended that the city include only the present-day First to Ninth Districts, those lying within the old consumption tax lines (Verzehrungssteuerlinie) of 1704.[3]

Between 1848 and 1890 the population of the suburban communities rose from less than 200,000 to 536,000.[4] Many of the tens of thousands of immigrants who came to Vienna between 1850 and 1890 in search of work settled in the suburbs because of their cheaper cost of living and their proximity to new industrial plants on the fringes of the city. A lower percentage of the adult population of the suburbs incorporated in 1890 were *heimatberechtigt* in their current place of residence than the population of the city itself.[5] The initial semirural character of many of the suburbs (for example, Hietzing, Simmering, and Döbling) meant that work was available for agricultural laborers in the truck garden and wine-producing industries. After 1880 agricultural industries in the suburbs declined rapidly, but the population density of these communities was still lower than that of the city itself.[6]

The suburbs served as an escape route from areas in the city which became overcrowded or overpriced (in the 1870s and 1880s). Between 1857 and 1890 a revolution in residential housing patterns occurred in Vienna.[7] Large numbers of Vormärz-*Biedermeier* houses of two or three stories were torn down and replaced with (or remodeled into) the four-, five-, and six-story tenements which came to dominate the city by 1914. Between 1840 and 1914, 75 percent of all pre-1840 houses in the city were either replaced or radically remodeled.[8] With the rapid commercial development of key business streets in the First to Ninth Districts after 1857 and with the demolition of the bastions which separated the Innere Stadt from the *Vorstädte,* land values in most inner districts rose precipitously.[9] Rising land values, a steady decline in interest rates for mortgages, tax concessions by the government to the owners of new or remodeled buildings, the availability of capital in the 1860s and 1870s for investment in housing construction, the new 1859 building code of Vienna which permitted higher and larger housing units, and changing patterns of taste on the part of the middle- and upper-Bürgertum who wanted larger and more functional apartments—all of these factors encouraged rent increases.[10] Between 1869 and 1890 per capita rent expenditures in the First to Ninth Districts rose from 53 to 80 fl.[11] That the housing market in Vienna continued to expand and prosper in the face of such rising rent levels testified to the increasing wealth diversity of the city's Bürgertum, or at least to the willingness of many Bürger families to devote a larger share of their income to maintaining their achieved or claimed social status by residence in new or remodeled apartments.

For others the rising rents made continued residence in the older areas of the city impossible. In addition to rising housing costs in the First to Ninth Districts, another problem faced those with limited budgets. Because of the *Verzehrungssteuer* (the tax on consumption of a number of specified goods), the cost of living in Vienna was appreciably higher than in the suburbs. The *Verzehrungssteuer* was an indirect Imperial tax instituted in 1829 throughout the monarchy. In Vienna it replaced the older *Thorsteuer* from 1704, which had been a municipal tax. After the change in status of the tax in 1829, the Imperial government collected and retained the bulk of the tax revenue, but allowed the city to affix surtaxes *(Zuschläge)*. By 1890 the city depended heavily on these surtaxes for a substantial portion of its budget.[12]

The *Verzehrungssteuer* was doubly discriminating against Vienna and its populace. Not only were merchants, wholesalers, and even common citizens of the city subject to inordinate delays and often embarrassing searches when transporting goods through the tax lines (the tax was collected at the lines by a small army of officials), but the government set much higher revenue levels and employed a more complicated tariff schedule for the tax in Vienna than it did for small villages and rural areas.[13] In 1889 the city paid a consumption tax on over two hundred different articles, arranged in fifty-one different tariff posts. Many of these articles were basic consumer goods like cereals, bread, soap, eggs, cheese, meats, wine, and beer. In rural areas, where the tax was collected not by tax inspectors but through an indirect system of *Abfindung,* only a few articles were subject to taxation. In many villages, because of the technical inadequacies of the Austrian tax administration, even this lower level of taxation was haphazardly collected.[14] More important, the relative rates at which the tariff levels in rural areas were set were significantly lower than those imposed on Vienna.

The desirability of uniting the suburbs with the city was recognized by the municipality after its political autonomy was restored in the 1860s. From the mid-1870s various councilmen and some local political clubs submitted proposals to the City Council with the intent of planning for the administrative incorporation of the suburbs.[15] Only a few of the suburbs, such as Währing, reacted with any enthusiasm to these proposals. The differences separating the city and suburbs were immense, including legitimate fears by suburban businessmen about the competition they would encounter if their districts were united to Vienna.[16] The major issue preventing unification, however, was a financial one. As long as Vienna was subject to a different kind of *Verzehrungssteuer,* and as long as the tax lines disrupted the free flow of goods and population between the suburbs and the city, unification was a technical impossibility.

The complaints of the city about the inequities and burdens of the tax system eventually led to legislative reform proposals. In the process the problem of the political and administrative unification of the city was shunted aside, only to become the subject of serious consideration after the tax question had been settled in March 1890.

In 1886 the lower house, on the motion of the Liberal party, appointed a special subcommittee of its standing Consumption Tax Committee, to be chaired by Max Menger, to discuss various tax reform proposals and to draw up a compromise formula.[17] Menger's subcommittee attempted to draft a law which would have completely revised the national system of the consumption tax by abolishing the tax advantages which rural areas in the empire held over the cities.[18] Menger's strategy immediately encountered the hostility of the Cabinet, representing as it did a powerful agrarian-Slavic majority. Without the approval and support of Julian v Dunajewski, the Imperial minister of finance, any piece of legislation involving municipal tax reform stood no chance of success. Dunajewski, who represented an ardent anti-German clique in the Cabinet, combined allegiance to fiscal conservatism (in matters which did not pertain to the many tax privileges Austrian Poland enjoyed) with a disinterest bordering on hostility toward the plight of the inhabitants of the *Reichshauptstadt*.[19]

In October 1888, however, the emperor intervened. In a speech given at the opening of the Türkenschanz Park in Währing he stressed his personal interest in seeing the consumption tax walls abolished, which would necessitate a reform of the tax itself.[20] Franz Joseph made the speech at the suggestion of Eduard Taaffe, who was undoubtedly aware of its implications.[21] Taaffe's motives were complex, and the speech did not necessarily mean that he would push for unification. But Taaffe was interested in gaining leverage against Dunajewski within the cabinet on the problem of German/Slavic relations. By activating the Viennese tax issue, he won for himself an additional reward that he could dangle in front of the German Liberals.

Following the emperor's speech, the Ministry of Finance (at the request of Taaffe) organized hearings on the *Verzehrungssteuer* at which representatives of Vienna and the suburbs participated. Then, during 1889, the government formulated a counterproposal to that offered by Menger's subcommittee. After the first stage of the negotiations on the German-Czech *Ausgleich* had been completed and an agreement had been initialed in late January 1890, Taaffe ordered the government's bill placed before the *Abgeordnetenhaus*. Taaffe hoped to make a symbolic, placatory gesture to the Liberals at a key moment in the *Ausgleich* negotiations.

In October 1889 the tax reform received another boost when Erich Kielmansegg was appointed the new *Statthalter* of Lower Austria. Kielmansegg helped the prospects of the bill enormously, although he had to exercise care in his relations with the Lower Austrian Liberals to avoid creating resentment about a government-based initiative to reform the city's political structure.[22]

The submission of the government's tax reform proposal to parliament on 2 February 1890 took the Liberals completely by surprise. The bill extended the collection lines for the tax to include thirty-four of the largest and most populated suburban communities. The old tax walls were to be torn down and the land on which they sat consigned to an expansion of the metropolitan transportation system (the *Stadtbahn*). The bill favored Vienna in that it eliminated thirty of the fifty-one posts of the 1829 consumption tax, releasing over 130 articles from all indirect taxation. Henceforth, inhabitants of the city could purchase cereals, eggs, dairy products, and numerous other items free of the octroi. To balance these reductions, the bill brought the suburbs, together with Vienna, under a revised system of tariffs which would tax meat, wine, beer, and poultry, articles which either had never been effectively taxed in the suburbs or, if taxed, had been so at merely nominal rates.[23]

The suburbs reacted to the bill with bitterness. Petitions were submitted to parliament from suburban business groups, property owners' associations, craft guilds, and local political clubs of all ideological persuasions to stop the legislation.[24] All disputants, including the Liberals, admitted that the suburban poor would suffer some increased tax load.[25] The petitions of the suburban Mittelstand groups demonstrated, however, that the groups who would feel most disadvantaged by the new taxes were lower- and middle-Bürger families who were accustomed to consume meats and poultry, wine and beer more frequently and at higher levels of quality than were working-class poor. Friedrich Suess and Ferdinand Kronawetter repeatedly stressed the antagonism these new taxes would produce among the thousands of lower ranking state officials, private employees, and artisans who lived in the suburbs.

The Liberals, led by Herbst and Menger, were not unsympathetic to the suburbs. With the exception of Wilhelm Exner, Friedrich Suess, and the Democrat Kronawetter, however, they voted for the government's plan. Their dilemma was not a pleasant one: either to reduce the indirect taxation on the city and thus try to curb the social unrest within the Viennese Bürgertum which the antisemites were exploiting, or to extend the tax to the suburbs and earn the permanent enmity of suburban voters.

The most interesting behavior during the tax debates was that displayed in March 1890 by Karl Lueger, Robert Pattai, and the few other antisemites in parliament. With the exception of Vergani, who rose once to defend the interests of the Lower Austrian vintners, the antisemites maintained complete silence throughout the proceedings. Lueger's atypical quietude was the first step in a cautious political strategy which netted the Christian Socials a good deal of electoral support in the newly incorporated suburbs after 1891. As representatives of Bürger electoral districts in Vienna (Margarethen and Mariahilf), which stood to benefit from the reform, Lueger and Pattai neither could nor would speak out against the *Verzehrungssteuer*. Nor could they try to thrust the blame for Vienna's financial isolation on the system of agrarian privilege which the

Taaffe ministry sustained, as the old Democrat Kronawetter was wont to do. The Lower Austrian Landtag elections were scheduled for September/October 1890, and the antisemites hoped to win support among peasant voters. By accepting tacitly the consumption tax reform, however, both Lueger and Pattai accepted the probability of the unification of the city and the suburbs. Both men actually favored the general concept of unification. Lueger was on record several times in the early 1880s advocating unification. In late 1890 Lueger opposed unification for two tactical reasons: not only did he object to specific provisions in the new statute, but the Liberals had the votes to pass the unification bill in the Landtag even if the antisemites opposed the measure. Opposition to unification was a "safe" issue in that it endangered nothing while offering Lueger the opportunity to pose as a defender of suburban rights and traditions against the bill's alleged discrimination against the suburbs. Had Lueger and the other antisemites really been interested in defending suburban interests, they would have opposed the consumption tax reform, not unification itself. They chose instead to allow the Liberals to alienate the suburban electorate through the consumption tax reform, and then to present themselves in late 1890 as defenders of suburban autonomy and localism.

Once the tax reform had been passed and approved by the emperor in May 1890, many Liberals and Imperial officials felt that no further changes involving Vienna were desirable in the immediate future. Only Erich Kielmansegg thought that tax reform both necessitated and eased the way for Vienna to incorporate the suburbs. The various officials and politicians to whom Kielmansegg presented his ideas showed no interest.[26] Neither Taaffe nor Dunajewski thought the idea worth supporting. Taaffe also doubted the practicality of the project and did not want his ministry embarrassed by an attempt at unification which the Lower Austrian Liberals would not accept.

In December 1889 a new Liberal mayor of Vienna, Johann Prix, took office. Like Cajetan Felder before him and Karl Lueger after him, Prix was a strong, domineering mayor during his short term in office (1889–94). He led the largest faction among the local Liberals, the *Mittelpartei,* which was dissatisfied with the indecisiveness and political ineptness of Mayor Eduard Uhl during the later 1880s.[27] In the light of the successes which the antisemites had enjoyed after 1887, Kielmansegg might have expected that Prix would listen with some interest to a unification scheme. If successful, such a plan might have brought the Liberal party badly needed prestige.

When Kielmansegg approached Prix in early April 1890, however, the mayor was very uncertain about the advisability of such a plan.[28] To incorporate the suburbs into Vienna would bring in thousands of hostile suburban voters, men alienated by the tax reform passed the preceding month. More important, Prix was unsure about the nature of the new *Gemeindeordnung* for an enlarged Vienna. Although a conservative Liberal, Prix was, like Lueger, a staunch defender of the city's autonomy against the Imperial bureaucracy. Would the government try to use the occasion of a new statute to reduce Vienna's political independence?[29] Would a government which was unsympathetic to the Liberal party give the Liberals the kind of privileged election franchise they needed to ensure their dominance of the city?

By the late summer of 1890 the government was willing to consider the possibility that cooperation with the Liberals, rather than continued feuding between the Iron Ring and the city's political elite, might be in the best interests of both parties. The successful collaboration of the Viennese Liberals with Kielmansegg (and through Kielmansegg with Taaffe and his political advisers) after August 1890 meant that Kielmansegg had effected a subtle change of attitude in the leadership of the Cabinet and among influential Viennese Liberals.

Kielmansegg gained his most important ally in his effort to push both groups to consider the advantages of a *Gross Wien* in the emperor himself. Franz Joseph was gravely concerned about the tide of political and national radicalism which seemed to be rising in 1889–90. He felt that Taaffe was not doing enough to stem such developments.[30] Following the Ottakring riots in April 1890 the emperor ordered Kielmansegg to draft proposals for reorganizing the Viennese police *Rayon* to establish more effective controls over future disturbances. Kielmansegg used the occasion to broach his unification scheme. He told the emperor that a more effective system of police control depended upon more centralized administrative control over the city and its suburbs. Administrative unity was a prior condition for curbing social violence. Franz Joseph was impressed with the logic of Kielmansegg's proposals and gave them his immediate unqualified support.[31]

The issue which finally brought the question into sharper focus, however, was the disposition of future tax revenue to follow the tax reform. Having brought the suburbs into the *Verzehrungssteuer* net, the government was responsible for securing a compromise formula for the apportionment of the surtax revenue between Vienna and the suburbs which could be presented to the Landtag immediately. This task fell to Kielmansegg.

Following Taaffe's instructions, Kielmansegg organized a conference in late June 1890 involving representatives of Vienna and the suburbs to settle the surtax problem. Before the conference Kielmansegg let it be known in ministerial circles (specifically to Dunajewski) that if a compromise formula for the sharing of the revenue was impossible, he would press for the unification of the suburbs and the city.[32] That Kielmansegg deliberately planned to have the conference fail was unlikely. But the negotiations lived up to his expectations. As early as April Kielmansegg had instructed his staff to prepare drafts for a new *Gemeindeordnung* for Vienna in the event unification could be achieved. After two fruitless meetings in late June all of the participants realized that the conference was deadlocked. The five representatives of Vienna (four Liberals and one antisemite) demanded that the city should receive at least 75 percent of the annual surtax. The officials of the suburban municipalities, in turn, held fast to a demand for not less than 50 percent of the revenue.[33] Kielmansegg did nothing to facilitate a compromise.

By the third session of the conference Kielmansegg decided that an opportune moment had been reached to push the negotiations into a discussion of unification.[34] Beginning with the fourth session on 7 July, he transformed the hearings into a planning conference on the expansion of the city.[35] He appointed a subcommittee of prominent Liberals to formulate draft proposals for the consideration of the plenum, using the drafts for a new *Gemeindeordnung* which his staff had already prepared as the basis of subsequent negotiations. The ease and rapidity with which this move was accomplished suggested that Kielmansegg had carefully coordinated his tactics with the leaders of the Liberal party, especially Johann Prix and Josef Kopp. Moreover, the Liberals survived their first test of strength with Kielmansegg when they forced him to repudiate a suggestion he offhandedly made during the meeting involving the mode under which the mayor of the new *Gross Wien* would be selected. Kielmansegg admired the Prussian tradition by which the German emperor was able to confirm the appointments of trained administrative officials (and not local politicians) to key mayoral positions in the larger cities. Kielmansegg proposed to surpass even the Prussians and simply have the Viennese *Bürgermeister* named by the emperor.[36] Both the Liberals and the antisemites reacted with genuine outrage, and Kielmansegg was forced to issue a denial that this was anything more than a "suggestion."

Doubtless, when Kielmansegg first raised his proposal for unification in April 1890, he thought that an appointed mayor was the safest way to assure that level of "control" which he had promised Franz Joseph. Now he was faced with a continuation of the older mode of autonomous municipal government, while having to support the kind of *Gemeindeordnung* the Liberals would find acceptable. Indeed, the two were intrinsically related—once Kielmansegg had conceded to the Liberals the position of elective mayor, he was forced to provide them with a franchise and an administrative structure which would be unassailable by radical political groups.

The results of the conference, in the form of a preliminary draft, were

ready by late August 1890.[37] Kielmansegg then circulated a summary of
the conference's recommendations in the form of another questionnaire to
the offices of the suburbs and to the Viennese City Council for comments
and approval (he did not circulate the actual text of the draft, since his
office had not yet finished the final editorial work on the document). The
questionnaire met with stiff resistance in many of the suburbs.[38] In
Vienna the Suburbs Commission of the Council met late in August 1890
to consider the proposal. Although Lueger and the other antisemites were
respresented on the commission, the Liberals dominated the body and
gave the summary proposals a favorable recommendation.[39] The full
Council debated the questionnaire for over a month (9 September to 10
October), during which time the antisemitic forces bitterly opposed the
bill (Lueger had not opposed it during the debates of the Suburbs Commission).[40] Before the debates on unification could be completed, however, the antisemites and the Liberals vied for seats in the Lower Austrian
Landtag in the elections of 25 September (for rural areas) and 2 October
(for city districts). Of crucial importance for the future of Viennese Liberalism was the fact that the Council debates and ministerial negotiations
on the new *Gemeindeordnung* had not yet considered those sections of
the reform proposals which dealt with white collar voting rights before the
Landtag elections occurred.

The Lower Austrian Landtag Elections of 1890

The Landtag elections of 1890 were important for the future style of
Viennese politics. The antisemitic coalition which Lueger had held together since Schönerer's imprisonment entered the struggle with a slate of
candidates whose suspicion of each other was often offset only by the
ferocity of their rhetoric against the Jews.[41] Ruthlessness with words and
money, pressure on various white collar and artisan groups, and unscrupulous campaign practices marked the behavior of all political
groups, including many of the local Liberal clubs. The levels of rhetorical
venom spewed during the campaign set models for the future behavior of
the various factions in the Landtag itself between 1891 and 1896.

Nor was the style of these years exclusively a Lower Austrian
phenomenon. Much of the aggressiveness of public politics in Vienna after
1890 was modeled on the uproarious behavior of the Czech Nationalist
parties in Bohemia, with whom the Christian Socials soon developed social
and agitatorial connections.[42] In the case of the antisemites the need
for public gratification and audience response, the frustration engendered
by Liberal contempt, and the opportunistic calculations of experienced
politicians like Lueger, Gessmann, and Pattai contributed to the maelstrom

of verbal conflict. Local Viennese Liberals were hardly more conciliatory or moderate.

The Landtag elections of 1890 effectively eliminated the Schönerian pan-Germans from Lower Austrian politics. They also revealed a marked decline of Liberal support in rural and in some urban areas. In many electoral districts the Schönerian loyalists had difficulty in persuading anyone to stand for election, since this meant opposing not only the Liberals, but also the antisemitic coalition.[43] Only three of the nine candidates fielded by the Schönerians were successful. Of the twenty-eight successful non-Liberal candidates, only three were willing to associate their names with Schönerer.

For the Liberals the election was devastating. From the position of hegemony in the Landtag which they had enjoyed before 1890 (over fifty-five of a possible seventy-two seats), the Liberals salvaged forty-one seats. This number was misleading, moreover, since nineteen of the forty-one came from the privileged curias of the Chambers of Commerce and Industry and the *Verfassungstreu* noble landowners. In Vienna itself the Liberals lost half of the city's eighteen districts. Their residual strength in the twelve urban districts of rural Lower Austria owed less to their attractiveness and efficiency than to the absence (as of yet) of effective antisemitic political organizations in these towns. In the twenty rural districts of the province, the Liberals retained only four seats, and those by very narrow margins. The rural losses of the Liberal party were the beginning of the political transformation of the more prosperous elements of the Lower Austrian peasantry from reliable Liberal electors, controlled by a privileged system of indirect voting, into collectively organized agrarian interest voters open to the appeals of the clerical wing of the antisemitic coalition. This transformation hinged upon the later development of peasant protest organizations (especially the Lower Austrian *Bauernbund*) and the introduction of direct voting in rural districts in 1896, but the process was rooted in the events of October 1890.

Most distressing and shocking about the results was the loss to the antisemites of key bourgeois districts in Vienna, like the Landstrasse and the Josefstadt. Antisemitic successes in these districts were owing in part to the presence on the Landtag registration rolls for the first time of the five-gulden artisans (who had received the provincial franchise in 1886, but who only now had the chance to vote), but in districts like the Josefstadt, where artisans were generally more prosperous than elsewhere in the city, the five-gulden men were not alone responsible for the Liberals' losses.[44] The Josefstadt in October 1890 had 3,907 registered voters, yet fewer than 2,000 of the resident small businessmen in industry and commerce paid a trade tax of 5 *or* 10 fl.[45] Although an important factor in

Landtag elections, these voters were neither sufficiently numerous nor sufficiently united to play the hegemonic role in election competition. This was especially the case in the Josefstadt, where many artisan voters had long supported Democratic candidates. Not all of these voters would immediately desert their traditions to vote for the antisemites. Rather, the election results of October 1890 demonstrated the attractiveness which political antisemitism had for the hundreds of private employees, school and gymnasium teachers, lower and middle ranking state officials, and other white collar types who lived in these districts, especially the younger members of these groups.[46] Of the nearly 53,000 registered voters in Vienna for parliamentary and Landtag elections in 1890, approximately 13,000 were men employed in the state, provincial, or municipal bureaucracies.[47] The incidence of political antisemitism among these voters was to be crucial in the modernization of Viennese party systems, as well as in the evolution of a modern social *Beamten* movement in Austria. That political antisemitism spread to the Viennese officials at precisely the time when the Liberal party was about to enlarge the city's boundaries and rewrite the city's franchise (1890–91) was a momentous factor in the development of modern, interest-group politics.

The Viennese *Beamten* and Radical Politics, 1886–90

In 1890 the idea of collective *Beamten* protest in Austria was still a novel one. Beginning in the mid-1860s a number of *Beamten* welfare and insurance organizations had established themselves in Vienna, the most notable being the *Erster allgemeiner Beamten-Verein,* which developed a wide-ranging program of welfare and credit facilities.[48] In March 1872 a general congress of state officials met in Vienna and formulated requests for salary raises to present to the Liberal ministry. Opinion within the Liberal party was divided on the propriety of such quasi-political activity by the state officials. A delegation of the congress visiting Franz v Hopfen and Carlos Auersperg, the Liberal presidents of the lower and upper houses of the Reichsrat, was received with sympathy and encouragement. When the delegates met with the Liberal minister-president, Adolf Auersperg, however, he coldly informed them that he did not consider them to be the legal representatives of the state officials and expressed suspicion over their failure to express their grievances through traditional hierarchical channels.[49]

Once the Liberals had regulated the salaries of the officials in a relatively generous fashion in March 1873, *Beamten* political discontent subsided, and with it, any motivation to develop an independent political organization.[50] The *Beamten* salary improvements in 1873 came at a propitious time for the middle and lower level officials, since the later 1870s saw a decline in food prices from which all employees and workers with regular salary or wage positions profited.[51] Not only did the state officials have steady sources of employment, but as a group, they entered the depression of the seventies with enhanced purchasing power.

For almost a decade the *Beamten-Verein* served as the representative of the Austrian state officials, having no rivals to challenge its organizational supremacy. By the early 1880s, however, the decline in the prices of basic consumption articles was temporarily arrested (it resumed at a much slower rate between 1885 and 1890; then a significant price inflation occurred again). This reduction in the real value of salaries, together with growing housing costs, led to sporadic social discontent in the ranks of the intermediate and lower officials. In response to these economic pressures, at first incidental and not yet forming a clear trend, two *Beamten* organizations were organized in Vienna which reflected the dissatisfaction of some officials with the *Beamten-Verein*.

In March 1884 the *Verein der k. k. Staatsbeamten zur Wahrung der Standes-Interessen* was organized by a small group of middle ranking officials in the Imperial Post Office and Finance Ministry to serve as a more effective representative of the views of the non-elite members of the bureaucracy. Its newspaper, the *Sprechsaal des Beamtentages*, began a heated press war against the *Beamten-Verein*, accusing the latter of being little more than a glorified insurance agency and credit union from which only the wealthiest officials profited.[52] Despite the ambitions of its leadership, however, the new *Verein* made little headway, due to the indifference (or cautiousness) of most Viennese officials—between 1886 and 1889 it accomplished little, aside from issuing an occasional propaganda blast at its rival. The *Verein* never created a large organizational apparatus; nor were the times sufficiently desperate to make the officials realize that they needed a professional group to sponsor their interests in competitive fashion. The older notion of the *Beamtentum* as a *Stand* apart from the rest of civil society made it difficult for many *Beamten* to realize that in a modern system political privileges, sustained by law, could result only from vigorous interest group representation. That the *Verein* reserved its "tough" language for its rival, the *Beamten-Verein*, and not for the government, was a deficiency its more aggressive successor in the 1890s, the *Verein der Staatsbeamten Österreichs*, was to correct.

The leadership of the *Verein* like that of the *Beamten-Verein* was staunchly Liberal, although of a Democratic variety. Liberal partisanship at a time when political antisemitism was becoming a major power on the local scene made the *Verein*, in its politics, an anachronism. It lacked the courage to challenge the Liberals and had too many convictions simply to associate itself with the antisemites, who at this stage (1884–85) were not yet interested in using the officials for their purposes.[53]

In April 1885 a second association of officials was organized in Vienna, the *Verband der Wiener Beamten*. This group was dominated by the municipal officials of the city, but many state officials also joined. Implicitly it was a "political" association, using as its model the organizations through which the schoolteachers in the late 1870s and early 1880s had so successfully made their occupational grievances known to the municipal government of Vienna.

In the 1885 parliamentary elections the *Verband* supported the complete slate of Liberal candidates, opposing Lueger, Pattai, and the other antisemites. Indeed, much of the *Verband*'s early leadership consisted of younger men employed in the higher levels of the city *Magistrat*. As long as the officials voted Liberal, the Liberal party in the city administration was willing to tolerate the fledgling organization.[54]

Within two years, however, the *Verband* was languishing in the same dilemma from which the new *Verein* was suffering. Both associations were Liberal-Democratic in their politics. It was questionable whether any such association could achieve practical results for its membership when it denied itself the one lever which any such group might possess, the option of voting for the oppositional party. Also, both of these groups were to a large extent the figments of their creators' imaginations—neither was a true membership association, and neither had any momentum. In the spring of 1887 Albert Gessmann and several minor antisemitic and antisemitic-Democratic politicians (the terms in the public mind were still confused and interchangeable) made a concerted effort to take over the *Verband der Wiener Beamten*. In the weeks immediately preceding the City Council elections the *Verband*'s executive committee issued the endorsements of the association: included were the names not only of Democratic candidates, but of several antisemitic candidates as well. The reaction of the Liberal administration and press was not long in coming. In April 1887 over fifty of the original founding members of the *Verband* resigned, all of whom were *Conceptsbeamten* in the municipal bureaucracy. The Liberal party would not tolerate oppositional organizations whose members owed their employment to the beneficence of this party.[55]

In 1888 a group of commercial clerks and other white collar employees gained control of the *Verband,* almost by default, and guided it into antisemitic politics. Felix Hraba, an antisemitic official with the *Erste österreichische Sparkasse* and later *Stadtrat* under Lueger in Vienna, was elected chairman. The effectiveness and influence of the *Verband* was still marginal, however, since its leadership structure was too loose to provide effective control over prospective members. A report on the association in early 1891 indicated that its membership levels were low and that it had few, if any, financial resources.[56] The major role of the *Verband* became that of an elite action cadre, dominated by a small group of antisemites, to mobilize opinion, spread propaganda, and organize protest assemblies. The *Verband* made no effort to influence the 1888 municipal elections, and in 1889 it was only slightly more effective in making its presence felt.[57] Like many fledgling political clubs in Vienna the *Verband* suffered from a lack of popular credibility, compounded by the hostility of the city and the Imperial administration to radicalism among teachers or officials, even if such behavior fell within the rights of the individual under the constitution. Austrian authorities were not as repressive or manipulative of middle and lower level public officials as their Prussian counterparts, but there were clear limits to what they would tolerate.

Precisely this hostility of the government, however, toward individual radicalism on the part of teachers and state officials necessitated their collective organization on interest group lines. Well into the 1890s the Imperial authorities harassed individual teachers and officials who engaged in radical political activity in too ostentatious a fashion (although this was done very inconsistently; Liberal teachers enjoyed much more freedom in political propagandizing than antisemitic teachers, for example).[58] Under such circumstances professional associations offered a measure of security in numbers.[59] Associations also offered a much more efficient mechanism for transforming group interest into political power. The upshot of the hostility of the government toward individual political activity was that the officials came to equate public action with their own group self-interest, clogging the political system with particularistic demands.

The existence of the *Verband,* and the salary and other work-related dissatisfactions to which it appealed, was clearly analogous to earlier trends of social disaffection in the Catholic lower clergy. What the Liberals now faced was not a unity of antisemitic protest among bourgeois service groups with identical grievances, but a coalition of varying social disenchantments running parallel to the antisemitic coalition of artisans established in the mid-1880s.

Of crucial importance to the history of antisemitism was the fact that the disaffection of white collar service groups occurred ten years after the rise of radicalism among the artisans. Because the artisans were exposed, as small, self-employed businessmen, to the effects of the price deflation and unemployment of the 1870s far earlier than the state officials, their protest movement predated a modern *Beamtenbewegung* by over ten years.[60] The first ten years of the anti-Liberal movement were spent in establishing for the antisemitic coalition a firm and unassailable base in the artisan Third Curia. Once the anti-Liberals had created this firm base, they could exploit social groups of greater prestige and political resources. Lueger's vision of the fruitfulness of coalition-type politics on the Democratic model mitigated the need for doctrinaire policy consistency and provided the flexibility needed to accommodate diverse groups. At the same time Lueger's staunch personal commitment to the primacy of party politics over the interest demands of any single group meant that no one group would be permitted to dictate party policy unilaterally. The success of the Christian Social movement in Vienna lay in the opportunity which the movement's time-history gave it: the party had ten years to organize itself and mobilize artisan discontent; it then had the opportunity to do the same for the white collar contingent of the city's Bürgertum. That it could perform these tasks synchronically and consecutively in two distinct time periods maximized the party's efficiency.

Relative to the artisans, however, the officials moved at a slow and deliberate pace in their radicalism. Occupationally and socially such men had more to lose. It took years of social frustration and political education before the officials as a group learned to deal more aggressively with the Imperial government as an employer. In learning this new behavior, they were assisted after 1890 by the network of social-oriented parties which competed for their allegiance.[61] The nationality question also played a crucial role in politicizing the Austrian state officials earlier and more effectively than their Prussian counterparts, since each national group and its affiliated party assumed the sponsorship of the officials of its nationality.

As long as the officials could attack the government through the mediating agencies of the parties, their isolation from political reality could be ended in a way which did not infringe upon their idealization of themselves as a privileged cultural stratum with corporate claims to honor. Indeed, the possession of political rights within the framework of franchise privileges now became a crucial symbol of social exclusiveness and cultural worthiness, while also offering a more practical way of getting their demands transformed into legislative reality. Privileged voting rights offered the best of both worlds—a sign that the older notions were now of practical value in obtaining modern interest group rewards. Not surprisingly, when the antisemitic *Verband der Wiener Beamten* scored its first and most stunning success (after five years of humiliating struggle), in October 1890, it did so not in advocating welfare rights for white collar employees, but in defending the privileged political rights of the teachers and state officials in the new statute the Liberals and Kielmansegg were writing for the city.

Beginning with the City Council elections of March 1889, in which the Liberals lost several Second Curia seats to the antisemites by narrow margins, both the Liberal party and the Imperial government became concerned about a certain slippage in *Beamten* voting support for the Liberal party in the Second Curia, where most state officials had the privilege of voting.[62] As the party holding unchallenged municipal and provincial power in Lower Austria before 1890, the Liberals were cautious in making the kinds of expansive promises which the antisemites could conjure up with the ease that administrative nonaccountability brought. Because of the leisurely, more universalistic style of politics the high Liberals had been wont to practice, both the need for and the respectability of narrow interest group promises seemed questionable. By the spring of 1890 the Liberals could not avoid facing the fact, however, that some segments of the Viennese state officials were becoming sensitive to the benefits of competitive politics.[63]

The Liberal party had two options in dealing with the consequences of the social unrest which the antisemites were beginning to exploit: it could preemptorily thrust the officials and similar groups out of the privileged Second Curia and into the artisan Third Curia for municipal elections, thus obviating the need for any serious confrontation with the *social* bases of white collar unrest; or it could try the more dangerous strategy of winning back the loyalty of the alienated officials through a combination of hierarchical pressure and social welfare guarantees.

Precedents for professional pressure on the part of the government to influence the political behavior of state officials were not unusual in late-nineteenth-century Austria. During the municipal elections of 1890 the Imperial government issued a confidential *Erlass* to the directors of many offices in the state bureaucracy in Vienna ordering them to enforce the abstention of bureaucrats from active election agitation. Indeed, some of the more conservative supervisory officials in the higher levels of the bureaucracy found it unfitting that lower and middle ranking officials should have the vote at all.[64] The government also decided in 1889 to institute a new uniform code *(Uniformzwang)* for the officials: new, quasi-military uniforms would serve to differentiate officials from the civilian population and encourage professional discipline.[65] By 1890, however, it was apparent that hierarchical pressure and new uniforms were not sufficient to control lower ranking state officials, whether the question was campaign agitation before elections or choice of candidates at the polling place. The crucial dilemma was now more categorical: either the state officials and related groups like the municipal employees would be persuaded that the Liberal party was interested in their welfare and that it would accomplish something on their behalf, or these groups would have to be neutralized in an absolute fashion by reducing their voting rights. External pressure and internalized norms were no longer enough.

The dilemma the Liberal party faced on the *Beamten* issue in late 1890 was made more acute because the party would soon have to make some very explicit decisions on the shape of the new franchise which had to be written to accompany the new Viennese *Gemeindeordnung*. Repression of the officials by depriving them of their political rights was a dangerous step, but the alternative seemed just as formidable—the Liberals would have to abandon their former universalistic, principled style of politics directed at the middle and higher bourgeoisie in general and begin to formulate strategies directed at specific social interest groups.

What made the situation difficult for the Liberals was that the voting groups involved were former clients who had never challenged Liberalism in such a frank, utilitarian fashion. That the Liberals were blindly re-affirming their support for municipal autonomy was a fateful conjunction in the history of Viennese politics.

Liberal fortunes in the Landtag elections took a decisive turn for the worse when it appeared suddenly in mid-September 1890 that the party had decided to use the option of repression in dealing with the *Beamten* problem. On 11 September 1890 an antisemitic member of the City Council, Rudolf Polzhofer, announced that he had obtained possession of a secret text of a Liberal proposal for the new city franchise which had been secretly developed in the offices of the Lower Austrian *Statthalterei* during August 1890. The next day, 12 September, Karl Lueger revealed that the draft provided that many categories of lower and mid-level officials (those in salary ranks XI–IX) would be dropped to the Third Curia and that all schoolteachers, although remaining in the Second Curia, would henceforth be prohibited from running for political office.[66] Polzhofer refused to disclose from whom he had obtained the document, but its authenticity was beyond doubt. Furious over the security leak in his office, Kielmansegg immediately issued a statement to the press denying that the Polzhofer text was the current position of the government.[67] He insisted that he had ordered the draft prepared after the conclusion of the surtax *Enquête* in mid-July 1890 and rejected the notion that the Liberal party had known anything about the plan. He also affirmed that the government had long since given up the idea of tampering with white collar voting rights.[68] That Kielmansegg had not given up his scheme for reducing the rights of the teachers was indicated by a communication to him from Baron Gautsch on 3 October, however, in which Gautsch informed him that, because they were state, not local, employees, schoolteachers could not be deprived of the passive franchise.[69] As late as early October, therefore, Kielmansegg was still dreaming of curbing the political rights of white collar voters.

Kielmansegg's denials were solemnly confirmed by Liberal spokesmen. Mayor Prix told his voters in an election rally on 22 September that he knew nothing about Kielmansegg's proposal and that he would not support a curtailment of the political rights of public officials. Prix's disclaimer was probably untrue, since Kielmansegg had kept Prix informed of the government's work. Moreover, other prominent Liberals in the Lower Austrian provincial government must have known about it and approved of it.

Because of the Polzhofer-Lueger revelations, it seemed to many officials on the eve of the Landtag elections that the Liberals had decided to eliminate hostile voters by electoral geometry. Since Landtag elections in Vienna were not conducted by curias, the voters who would have suffered the loss of their electoral privileges under the Kielmansegg plan had the opportunity to express their outrage by deserting the Liberals en masse. The now antisemitic *Verband der Wiener Beamten* made skillful use of Kielmansegg's blunder. On 24 September 1890 it organized a protest meeting against the proposed franchise changes which was attended by over 2,000 disgruntled governmental employees.[70] A similar assembly of hundreds of worried Viennese schoolteachers was held on 27 September.[71] In both instances the antisemitic speakers charged the Liberals with being secretly behind the Kielmansegg plan. The Liberals realized the extent of the outrage the antisemites had stirred up and summoned a meeting of the Liberal Club of the City Council to disavow the idea of depriving officials of their franchise. But with the election less than a week away, it was too late to repair the damage. On Polzhofer's document, the *Neue Freie Presse* gloomily suggested that "the last word has not yet been spoken about this unfortunate piece of paper."[72]

Liberal propaganda denials aside, the antisemites' accusation that Prix and other ranking Liberal leaders had known about Kielmansegg's plan did have convincing circumstantial support. In March 1890 the antisemites elected Josef Sturm, a municipal gymnasial professor, to the Council in a bitterly contested election, but the Liberals, arguing that secondary-school teachers were municipal employees and thus ineligible for local office, since they were covered by the city's *Dienstpragmatik,* refused to seat Sturm. Robert Pattai took Sturm's case to the Imperial Court and won an easy reversal of the decision on the grounds that the 1850 city statute accorded full political rights (active and passive franchise), to higher ranking Viennese teachers, in contrast to other municipal officials, who could vote in elections but not hold elective office.[73] The court ruled in Sturm's favor in mid-July 1890. Less than a month later, Kielmansegg and the Liberals secretly attempted to circumvent the court's decision by writing an express prohibition against the teachers into the new statute.

If the timing of the Sturm case and Kielmansegg's draft was purely coincidental, then it was a coincidence for which the Liberals paid dearly. Prominent Liberals like Raimund Grübl in the Landstrasse and Eduard Uhl in the Josefstadt went down in defeat.[74] Grübl's loss in the Landstrasse to an antisemitic priest, Josef Schnabl, was an important indication that anticlericalism was a useless and even dysfunctional tool when it was not combined with a program of positive social benefits and privileges for the white collar electorate.[75] Schnabl's success did not prove that antisemitism was stronger than anticlericalism in the consciences of the voters who had elected him. The Liberal attempt to abridge *Beamten* political privileges was the necessary first proof which gave credibility to all of the other antisemitic claims and accusations.

The support which younger and lower ranking state officials gave to the antisemites in October 1890 was impressive. One of the leading professional newspapers of the officials, the *Sprechsaal des Beamtentages,* estimated that over 80 percent of the officials in the XI *Rangclasse,* over 50 percent of those in the X *Rangclasse,* and over 13 percent of those in the IX *Rangclasse* had voted antisemitic.[76] The three lowest salary ranks in the Austrian state bureaucracy were staffed by men with a bewildering variety of educational qualifications and social backgrounds. In general, however, three categories of officials existed in Austria, each with its own set of educational qualifications: those with some level of university training who served as *Praktikanten* and were then appointed to judicial or administrative and, eventually, to higher policy posts (the *Concepts-beamten*); those with some *Mittelschule* training (who may or may not have completed a full course of instruction in a gymnasium or *Realschule*) who occupied intermediate positions (for instance, the *Rechnungs-beamten* or *Cassenbeamten*); and finally those who usually had served twelve years as a noncommissioned officer in the army and who eventually won posts as subaltern officials in *Kanzlei* work (the *Zertifikatisten*).[77] Rarely did a member of the first group of officials ever find himself appointed to the XI *Rangclasse,* which was filled with men from the last two groups. The X *Rangclasse,* however, contained a number of younger university-trained jurists and administrative officials, as well as intermediate employees.[78] The IX *Rangclasse* was the traditional home of a great number of university-trained officials in the age group thirty to forty-five, as well as many older men from the intermediate group who had won hard-earned promotions over the course of their careers. Few *Kanzleibeamten* were to be found beyond the X *Rangclasse.*

The estimates published by the *Sprechsaal des Beamtentages* are of interest in that large numbers of younger *Mittelschule*-trained officials, who had a higher level of education but who were included in the same rank (XI) as the former army noncoms, chose to vote antisemitic along with those lowest ranked officials, even though many of them fiercely resented being placed in the same salary category as the *Kanzlisten*.[79] Such resentment was one of the clearest motifs in the various officials' newspapers of the period. The *Mittelschule* graduates complained that the government expected of them an appropriate *Bildung*, but refused to promote them higher than the IX *Rangclasse*. The *Kanzlisten*, in turn, felt themselves despised by the *Mittelschule* types in the Verwaltung.[80] Also noteworthy was the infrequency with which the *Beamten* newspapers (which were controlled largely by men from this intermediate category and which supported the radicalization of the *Beamten* movement in the mid-1890s) referred to these men as "subaltern," the category to which they would have been summarily dismissed in Prussian bureaucratic rhetoric. They did not think of themselves in such terms, and their language about themselves was correct in avoiding the term. The resentment of these men over a loss of privileged voting rights was intense, since they felt that their earned educational and rank achievements entitled them to these rights. Their voting behavior was characteristic of those half-mobile Bürger groups in Viennese society which, like the public-school teachers, had one foot in the door of bourgeois respectability and who were loath to lose any of their privileges.[81]

This group of officials with some education (even if it was in fact a caricature of true *Bildung*) was of crucial importance for the history of Austrian Bürger politics. Its membership constituted almost 40 percent of the total tenured civil servants in Vienna in 1892. Most of the leadership for the more aggressive officials' organizations after 1890 came from this group. These were men who were not academically educated *Gebildeten*, but for whom Hansjoachim Henning's term "nonacademic educated" is also misleading, for they, together with the public-school teachers, increasingly thought of themselves as members of the *Bildungsbürgertum*. They thus fell between two extremes: the ex-military *Kanzlisten*, on one hand, who would have been completely unable to sponsor an independent political movement, and the university-educated *Juristen*, on the other, whose career patterns made discontent probable only at the younger age levels. Once a *Jurist* in the court system or the administration had passed rank VIII or VII, his personal interest in occupational aggressiveness diminished tremendously. This explains the rather strange phenomenon that the Christian Socials tended to pick up the votes of older intermediate officials and younger *Juristen*.[82]

The voting behavior of the X and IX *Rangclassen* indicated, moreover, that some men of higher educational achievement or higher relative rank may also have cast their votes for Lueger's party. To the extent that university graduates were members of these salary ranks, they would have been younger men who had recently finished their training period as *Praktikanten* and who were beginning their careers as *Conceptsbeamten*. Doubtless, generational tensions, membership in nationalist student clubs, and salary inadequacies played a formidable role, but the immediate grievance of these men in 1890 was the prospect of the loss of their political privileges at the beginning of their professional careers.

The *Sprechsaal des Beamtentages* insisted that few of these voters were antisemites by ideological conviction. Rather, they had voted for Lueger's party in reaction to Liberal arrogance and indifference to their socio-occupational needs and their political rights. Even so, the results of the 1890 Landtag elections seemed to bode ill for the future of Liberalism in Vienna, if not for the monarchy as a whole. Prince Reuss described the election results to Berlin in the most pessimistic terms, blaming the losses on Liberal indifference and overconfidence, on the laziness of Liberal voters who did not bother to vote, and on the estrangement from the Liberals of important Bürger groups who found that the propaganda of the antisemites answered and indeed defined their social needs far better than did that of the Liberal party.[83]

Reuss's despair was understandable, and from the vantage point of 1896 it might be accepted as evidence for a momentum on the part of the Christian Socials that was all but unstoppable. In fact, however, there was nothing "inevitable" about the victories scored by the Lueger movement in 1895–96. Christian Social success in 1895 hinged upon four years of intense and fateful policy decisions by the Liberal party after 1891, the most significant of which was the catastrophic involvement of the Liberal party in the coalition of 1893–95, and not upon the resources which the antisemites mustered to win the elections of October 1890. Rather than causing the Liberals to despair, the election losses of 1890 spurred them to complete their work on the new *Gemeindeordnung* as quickly as possible and to attach to the new statute a revised franchise which would correct the strategic deficiences that had cost them the Landtag elections.

The *Gemeindeordnung* of 1890

While the Liberals in the Council completed their deliberations on the last sections of city statute and the new municipal franchise (in early October, in the week after the Landtag election), the legislation for the reform as a whole was also debated in the *Ministerrat*, where Taaffe personally supervised some final revisions in the bill.[84] At the opening session of the newly elected Landtag on 14 October 1890, Erich Kielmansegg presented the revised, Liberal-approved bill. By mid-December 1890 after stormy debates provoked by the antisemites, the narrow Liberal majority pushed the law through without substantial alterations.[85]

The key structural reform of the 1890 *Gemeindeordnung* was the creation of an Executive Council *(Stadtrat)* within the City Council which would replace the ten committees *(Sektionen)* of the Council as the agency responsible for all preparatory legislative work. In the decades after 1861 the inability of the various committees to handle efficiently the growing volume of administrative and legislative business given over to their supervision was apparent.[86] Legislation frequently languished in these committees for months, especially when jurisdictional disputes arose between committees. But the committees did give opposition members in the Council, whatever political title they bore, opportunities to control the majority, if only by creating interminable delays in processing legislation. Lueger, for example, even in the days of his most bitter opposition after 1885, was a member of several of these standing committees and often functioned as the influential *Referent* for the Judicial Committee. The committees made effective political opposition possible within the municipal government, especially after the resignation of Cajetan Felder. Their very existence demonstrated that the homogeneity 'and policy uniformity which has often been ascribed to Liberalism in Vienna before the rise of antisemitism simply did not exist. Through the committees the political clubs in the plenum were able to ensure that the *Magistrat* did not become informally what the Prussian institution of the same name did become through law—an independent policymaking body with little accountability to the Council as a whole.[87] Austrian municipal systems, whether Liberal or Christian Social dominated, usually maintained a staunch commitment to popular-curial and mayoral control over professional administrative elites.[88]

The new Executive Council would consist of twenty-two members, each elected for a term of six years, plus the mayor and the two vice-mayors. The mayor would sit as permanent chairman. As the only executive committee within the Council, the body would have enormous powers. Unlike the full Council, its sessions would be closed to the public, with its debates published only in summary form. Because its members were to be elected for six years and because they would be powerful ward politicians in their own right, the Liberals were in fact creating an institutionalized political oligarchy for Vienna, such as the city had not experienced since 1848. Until the Executive Council drafted and released legislation, the full Council was powerless to act on any significant bill.

The powers of the Executive Council were, moreover, much greater than those of a preliminary legislative commission. The new statute also gave to the Executive Council control over all appointments and promotions within the municipal bureaucracy, formerly a responsibility of the full Council, without establishing any principle of accountability by the Executive Council to the plenum. The mayor retained the authority to discipline members of the *Magistrat,* but the powers of patronage for all jobs within the city bureaucracy became fragmented among the various politicians on the Executive Council.

The loss of the committees and the establishment of one powerful central committee naturally led to shifts in power elsewhere in the municipal system. A strong, yet pliable Executive Council would enhance the powers of the mayor. No longer would the mayor have to deal with ten different committees to develop the kind of legislation and administrative policy he desired. If the mayor proved strong enough to dominate the Executive Council (which was a separate and crucial question) and if his political bases were secure within the City Council, he might run the city with machinelike efficiency, or so the Liberals and Kielmansegg hoped. Before 1890 the mayor could effectively supervise only the *Magistrat;* now he had the clear opportunity to dominate a second power center as well.

The *Magistrat,* represented by the older and higher ranked career officials, also gained from the abolition of the committees. No longer would the senior *Räthe* have to deal with a large number of politicians gathered in rival committees to explain their policy proposals. All contacts between the administrative and legislative sectors of municipal government would flow through the mediating Executive Council. In terms of power, however, the Liberals left the mayor and the Executive Council in tight control of the *Magistrat,* a decision consonant with the traditions of Austrian, as opposed to Prussian, urban administration after 1848. Not only was the mayor given the right to intervene in the administrative processes of the *Magistrat* (such as the power to withdraw certain policy areas to his own office if he so chose), but the members of the Executive Council themselves bore little resemblance to the nonprofessional members of the Prussian *Magistrat* on whom Rudolf Gneist had centered so many of his hopes for a nonpolitical self-rule in Prussian urban administration. All members of the Executive Council were paid a generous salary. Their presence on the Executive Council meant a politicization of administration, not a neutralization of party politics.[89]

To balance the centralist, oligarchist tendencies of the new statute, the Liberals established a modest federalism on the ward level. Before 1890 each district in the city had elected a District Council *(Bezirksausschuss)* together with a district chairman *(Bezirksvorsteher).* The power of these local councils, was, however, limited in that they exercised only an advisory function toward the chairman. The new statute enhanced the councils by granting them the power to make district budgetary requests and the right to give instructions to the chairman in his capacity as district representative to the central administration. The council also retained some administrative control over the local school boards and the systems for relief of the poor in their districts.[90]

For the Liberals these structural changes were administratively useful and politically vital. The reduction of the power of the City Council was a strategic defense against the disruptive behavior of the antisemitic opposition.[91] The administrative reforms gave the Liberals a more efficient management of a city with a burgeoning population of a million and a half. Municipal centralism and political oligarchy would, so the Liberals hoped, ensure their political survival. By making the municipal administration more effective and less subject to anti-Liberal machinations, the reform would also offer the city the most realistic defense against power encroachments by the Imperial bureaucracy. A city with an incompetent and divided administration invited the intervention of the Lower Austrian *Statthalter*. Even after 1891 Erich Kielmansegg threatened on several occasions to send an official representative of the government to "observe" the often tumultous proceedings of the Council.[92]

The conflicting themes of centralism and oligarchy within the city and autonomy and liberty from powers beyond its boundaries demonstrated the Liberal party's ambiguous relationship to the heritage of an authoritarian and enlightened Josephist state, a state whose systems and ethos were twice revised after 1861 by the accession to power of the Liberal party in the 1860s and by the intensified growth of the nationality conflict in the 1880s. As Germans, Liberals in Vienna could applaud the necessity of a centralized bureaucratic regime on the national level. German administrative centralism was the most powerful device to ensure the control of the non-German social and ethnic majorities within the monarchy. At the same time Viennese Liberals, as Liberals, needed to stake out their own claim for municipal autonomy as evidence that the post-Josephist state had been brought under Liberal control. They affirmed one version of a Josephist model—German administrative hegemony—while emphasizing the value of urban autonomy as a way of limiting that hegemony. In trying to keep an important sector of Austrian society, the city of Vienna, free from total bureaucratic absolutism, they were using models of the relationship between state and society with which German political theorists had been experimenting since the beginning of the Stein era in Prussia.[93] The Liberal dilemma was a problematic one: could one isolate in a power sense subordinate areas of political society by freeing them from the direct executive control of the state, in the hope that in doing so the state as a whole would be strengthened?[94] Their dilemma was all the more imposing since the Austrian Liberals worked with two very extreme models of state-society interaction: eighteenth-century Josephist absolutism and the 1849 Stadion *Gemeinde* law. On one hand, Austrian political traditions offered them the option of a centralized, anticlerical (although not anti-Christian) German state with few theoretical limits to the state's sovereignty. On the other, because Austrian municipality law assumed a far more "Liberal" form and ethos after 1848 than had Prussian urban law and because municipal freedom survived during the neo-absolutism of the 1850s, the ideal of municipal freedom had a special pride of place among Austrian Liberals. Unlike Prussia, municipal autonomy in Austria did not precede parliamentary constitutionalism, but occurred within the same revolutionary situation. One of the most impressive accomplishments of the Austrian Liberals with their less richly endowed heritage of Liberal thought and action was the renewal of local autonomy in 1862.[95]

Ironically, the Liberals' reconstruction of the city's political system in 1890 was an attempt to emulate, in explicit political terms, the kind of centralized control they desired to retain on the national level. The new *Gemeindeordnung* did not deny the fact that Vienna had become since the 1870s a competitive political system and not simply an economic-administrative system, although more conservative Liberals in their despair over the "outrages" of antisemitism often expressed admiration for the businesslike, nonparty atmosphere in which most Prussian cities operated.[96] But the statute did place rigid parameters on the free operation of the system—parties could compete for power, but the rewards would never be fairly and equally distributed. This half political, half oligarchical-authoritarian ethos of the 1890 *Gemeindeordnung* was a first step of the Liberal party toward the more extreme act of despair which many Liberals took after 1900, namely, a repudiation of municipal autonomy and of municipal politics, because of the infiltration of radical social and national parties into local government in the monarchy.

The Christian Social coalition in the City Council saw the new statute in a very different light. To Karl Lueger the new statute granted the Liberals an enormous political advantage. Because they lost any possibility of effective opposition in the committees after 1891, the antisemites escalated their political rhetoric in the Council in the period 1891–96. Wild rhetoric compensated for effective political participation, as well as providing a useful source of propaganda and a way of keeping the public's attention on their movement. Ultimately, the Christian Socials profited from the Liberals' designs. Liberal political blunders between 1892 and 1895 handed to the antisemites a ready-made system of institutionalized oligarchy, anchored within a broader system of municipal autonomy. The real victors of 1890 did not claim their prize until 1896. It was precisely because of the reforms of 1890 that the prize won by Lueger in the victories of 1895–96 was so attractive.

The Franchise of 1890 and White Collar Politics

More central to the hopes of the Liberals for survival was the new municipal franchise. The Liberals fashioned an electoral structure which, in theory, provided them with a strong advantage. The weaknesses which they later demonstrated in 1895 were owing not to a faulty design in the 1890 statute, but to their failure to play the political game in 1895 according to the new rules they themselves had written.

The franchise provided for a City Council of 138 seats, divided, as in the 1850 franchise, into three electoral curias. Each member of the Council would be elected for a six-year term, as opposed to the three-year term previously in force. A major change was made in the way in which the curia members would be reelected. The 1850 franchise had prescribed that one-third of the members of each curia would stand for reelection each year, so that no year went by in Vienna without a municipal election. According to the new regulation, elections would be held on a staggered basis every two years, and at a given election the seats of a whole curia would be subject to reelection. To start the system, a general election for all three curias was called for March/April 1891. The next election would then be held in 1893, at which time the seats of the wealthiest curia, the First, would be vacated and reelected. Elections for the Second and Third Curias would follow in 1895 and 1897. The cycle would begin again in 1899.

The cyclical-curial arrangement gave the Liberals several advantages. The antisemites had always profited from yearly elections before 1891. Each March brought more agitation and more violent rhetoric. Annual elections offered antisemitism the opportunity to build psychological momentum through the electoral process itself. Also, voter participation rates in these elections tended to work to the advantage of the anti-Liberals. Higher percentages of voters in the Third Curia participated in the elections than in the Second and First Curias. This meant that the antisemites might be able to pick off Second Curia seats one at a time, while retaining unchallenged control in the Third Curia. After 1891, however, the possibility of sustaining momentum through annual agitation was cut off.[97]

Because a whole curia would vote at one time, the Liberals thought that they would be able to bring more pressure to bear on traditional nonvoters (whether Liberal or undecided) to participate in the Second Curia elections. Also, because the Third Curia always voted first, allowing the anti-semites to assemble impressive victory margins at the beginning of each annual election, the Liberals feared that the voters in the upper two curias might eventually find the antisemitic "bandwagon" effect irresistible. Now the antisemites would no longer enjoy a political advantage. Since the First Curia would be the first to be reelected, the Liberals thought they would have at least four and perhaps six more years of relative peace before they had to face the rebellious Third Curia in 1897.

As an added measure of security, the Liberals did not distribute the 138 seats of the Council on a strict per capita basis among the nineteen districts of the city. The First through Tenth Districts, which had profited from the consumption tax reform and whose voters were more enthusiastic about unification, received 93 of the 138 seats. The suburbs received only 45 seats, below the number they should have received on a proportional basis.[98] The First through Tenth Districts also contained more wealthy and white collar voters than did the suburbs, as well as a majority of the Jewish vote.[99]

Lueger was aware of the implications of the new cyclical system. He offered amendments to the bill in the Landtag to reduce the electoral term to three years and to give the suburbs more seats.[100] But his efforts failed miserably. The upshot of this new cyclical system was that it helped to foster the same kind of rhetoric and disruptive tactics by the antisemites as had the creation of the Executive Council and the reduction of the powers of the plenum. Because Lueger could no longer count on using annual spring campaigns as a method of exposure for his party, he decided to take the language and the behavior of the rally halls into the plenum of the Council and the Landtag. Once there, the formal powerlessness of the antisemites encouraged a redoubling of their efforts at disruption. Mayor Prix antagonized the antisemites further by pushing through the Council a new *Geschäftsordnung* with tough exclusionary powers to deal with the disruptors.[101] The style of political language used between 1891 and 1895 was not the result of antisemitic irrationalism. Lueger knew exactly what he was doing in encouraging his colleagues to escalate their political rhetoric.

The most significant technical innovation which the Liberals made in the franchise, however, was a redefinition of the tax and educational requirements for the various curias. Their goal was to expand the size of the Second Curia in each district, increasing the base vote on which they might count. To do this, they engineered a complex transfer of selected groups of voters from other curias into the Second Curia.

The 1850 franchise for Vienna had divided the electorate into three distinct groups.[102] The First Curia contained the highest taxed property owners in the city, as well as individuals paying a trade and income tax or special income tax of 100 fl. or more. The Second Curia contained all house owners paying a rent tax of less than 500 fl. per year; selected groups of higher state, provincial, and municipal officials; pastors and rabbis; all those holding an academic doctorate; and the higher ranks of the city schoolteachers. The Third Curia contained all men paying a trade and income tax or a special income tax of less than 100 but more than 10 fl. per year. The lowest curia contained, thus, not only small tradesmen but also owners of or employees in medium-sized commercial and industrial establishments.

A curious aspect of this franchise was that it excluded large numbers of officials and teachers whose salaries did not enable them to pay at least 10 fl. in income tax (to do so, they would have had to earn at least 1,000 fl. per year in taxable income).[103] In 1850 the lower ranks of the bureaucracy who had no university training and most schoolteachers in Austria were not considered to be full, integral members of the *gebildeten Stände*. Those men who entered the civil service with university training but who because of the workings of the seniority system had to wait years for promotion to supervisory positions were also not considered worthy of full electoral privileges. Since the Second Curia was designed to function in part as the "curia of the intelligentsia," all such groups—those without academic training or those with it but in lower ranking positions—had no inherent right to membership in the curia, unless they could rise in their occupations to more senior ranks. The rank achievements of older schoolteachers who were without university training but who had achieved the position of school principal, for example, were considered the political equivalent of university training or *Mittelschule* training and later job promotions. The 1850 law did not place the nonacademic intelligentsia (journalists or artists) or middle level employees of private commercial establishments in the Second Curia, largely because the question was not relevant—the numerical growth of these categories did not occur until after 1860. And after 1860 many of them would be educated or semieducated Jews.

Interestingly, the original draft of the *Gemeindeordnung* prepared by the Council in August 1849 had excluded all lower ranking teachers from the vote, but it did include most of the officials in the franchise.[104] But when Alexander Bach revised the Council's August 1849 draft in the winter of 1849–50, he not only excluded the five-gulden men from the Third Curia, but also eliminated all officials earning less than 1,000 fl. per year from the Second Curia. Bach's motives were complex—he doubtless wanted to keep the officials out of the process of political bargaining for disciplinary purposes, and he may have feared that they would support more radical democratic types in their choice of candidates—but the Council itself was not without ambiguous motives on this point.[105] The Council put the officials in the franchise as a testimony to the ideal of the unitary Bürgertum which would stand against the proletariat to defend the city's Bürger nature. Even in the August 1849 version, however, the middle- and higher-Bürgertum would have dominated the city because of the curial structure passed in June 1849.[106] The Council's draft was marked, therefore, by an explicit conservatism in which the 5 fl. artisans would be isolated in the Third Curia and by the hope that the officials would conform to new Liberal political standards and not cause trouble for the party in the Second Curia.

Even within the Council, moreover, there was a latent, ill-disguised distrust of the younger and lower ranking state officials. They were given the franchise in 1848–49 in order to balance the 5 fl. men,[107] but once Bach had eliminated the artisans, the need to keep the lower officials quickly disappeared. The Council was close in its political views to the more conservative sectors of the National Guard in Vienna. From contemporary literature on the Guard, it is clear that Viennese Bürger circles regarded the lower and younger officials as potentially unreliable, since they might be pressured into voting whichever way the government wanted.[108] They had no sense of themselves as mature Bürger types, and therefore did not deserve the vote until they had achieved higher rank and status levels.

The franchise of 1850 also put some of the property owners into the Second Curia, a move which integrated the older Besitzbürgertum, many of whom were wealthier small businessmen with little formal education, with the academic and white collar elites of the city. The patrician authors of the 1850 franchise had no trouble justifying this intermingling of intelligentsia and Hausbesitz, since both groups, by virtue of their stability and conservatism, had earned the right to vote for the Liberal party. Viennese Liberalism from the very inception of its dominance was not simply a party of academic and high industrial or commercial elites. Its success was rooted in the votes of thousands of property owners in the First and Second Curias, most of whom did not desert the Liberal party even after the financial and economic disasters of the mid-1870s.

The 1850s franchise's combination of Bildung and Besitz into one privileged political classification indicated that earlier political distinctions in central Europe between the Stadtbürger and the Intelligenz were now eliminated in Vienna, since both groups now shared the same electoral category.[109] After 1850 franchise privileges became a new criterion for status unity in a way which tended to ameliorate the gaps

existing between occupational classes before 1848. When the newspaper
of the early Austrian *Beamten* movement announced in 1884 that the ideal
candidate for public office was a man who was a "Jurist und Bürger in
einer Person," it was idealizing the amalgamation of *Bildung* and *Besitz* in
a typological sense to legitimate the sharing of political resources and
power between both groups.[110] Although tensions between the *Juristen*
and the Bürger in municipal politics never ceased entirely (witness the
1861 elections for *Bürgermeister,* in which a faction led by Leopold Mayer
tried to elect a true "Bürger" as opposed to a *Juristen* as mayor), these
strains never hindered either the Liberals or the later Christian Socials
from drawing upon both groups for their elite leadership. With Karl
Lueger one sees a *Juristen* who went out of his way to style himself as a
pre-1848 Bürger, much to the advantage of anti-Liberal politics.[111]

Several significant changes occurred in the 1850 franchise between 1850
and 1890, the most important coming in December 1885.[112] When the
five-gulden men were admitted to the municipal franchise in 1885 by
being integrated into the Third Curia, the reform legislation also made
significant adjustments in the political status of white collar professional
and quasi-professional groups that had been excluded from the franchise
in 1850. After 1885 all schoolteachers and lower ranking state, provincial,
and municipal officials could vote in the privileged Second Curia. The size
of the Curia increased by over 3,000 voters between 1885 and 1886.[113]

The decision of the Liberal party to expand the Second Curia in 1885
was one expression of a change in attitude which occurred between 1850
and 1885 within the professional groups in the monarchy. In establishing
its political and social predominance in the 1860s, Austrian Liberalism
styled itself as the patron of the state officials and the Viennese schoolteachers. This occurred in large part within a rhetoric of the principles of
humanity and anticlerical liberty; that is, the Liberals did not present their
support of the German-speaking bureaucracy in an explicit, quid pro quo
electoral sense.[114] But the Liberals did make certain that state officials
were aware that the substantial salary improvements obtained for them in
March 1873 and the perfection of the ministerial system in the 1860s and
1870s were the work of their party.[115] The Liberals were also strong
supporters of the upgrading and relative independence of the *Mittelschule*
and of the university system and the expansion of the ranks of the medical, legal, and philosophical faculties after 1860, even though much of this
work was begun in the 1850s under Leo Thun.[116] Even more significant
was the cultural ethos of Liberal politics and administrative hegemony.
The Liberals expected that members of the bureaucracy of all ranks and
backgrounds would share their ideological principles and social assumptions.[117]

The introduction of constitutional government in Austria in 1861–66 met at first with some hostility on the part of many of the older officials, who were accustomed to think in terms of administrative absolutism. On numerous occasions members of the first Liberal ministries in the 1860s vented their anger at the negative behavior of some state officials. Carl Giskra was notably outspoken in this regard.[118] During the debates on the salary legislation for officials in 1872–73, one Liberal, Johann Fux of Moravia, made it clear that the officials should not expect assistance from the Liberals unless they changed their attitudes and became supporters of the new constitutional regime. Fux meant by "constitutionalism" nothing less than loyal support for the German Liberal party.[119] Few of Fux's colleagues were as explicit as he in stating such expectations, but most agreed with him. After 1873 Fux's demand was largely, if involuntarily, fulfilled. During the 1870s and early 1880s most state officials in Vienna and Lower Austria became reliable, habitual supporters of the ruling Liberal regime.[120] In doing so they involved themselves in an implicit patron-client relationship with the Liberals which, most of them probably hoped, would work to their mutual benefit.

With such patronage, even if it was meant in a utilitarian sense, and with the rising numbers of university-trained young men entering the various state and local bureaucracies after 1850, a slow, but certain wave of rising status expectations manifested itself among the lower and middle orders of the *Staatsbeamten*.[112] The tremendous rise in university and *Mittelschule* enrollments in Austria between 1851 and 1881 (the relevant time frame for the generations employed in the government in 1891) far outdistanced general population growth. In 1851, 1,034 students were enrolled at the University of Vienna in the law faculty; by 1881, this number had jumped to 2,200. In 1851, there were 76 successful completions of the three juristic state examinations at the university; by 1881, there were 919. The university granted 14 doctorates in law in 1851; by 1881, it was granting over 100 annually.[122] By 1890, nearly 39 percent of the 33,850 full-time tenured officials in the service of the state had on their records some kind of training at universities or other institutions of higher education. Another 38 percent had attended a gymnasium or other kind of *Mittelschule*. This latter group of officials, who were so important for the leadership of the Austrian *Beamten* movement, represented a tranformation in intermediate education which had occurred in Austria after 1850. In 1854, the province of Lower Austria had two *Realschulen* (enrollment 1,102) and no realgymnasium. By 1881, Lower Austria had eight real-gymnasien and seventeen *Realschulen*, nineteen of them with seven- or eight-year programs. Their enrollment totalled 5,445. Between 1851 and 1881 the enrollment at Lower Austrian classical gymnasien more than doubled: from 2,194 in 1851 to 5,089 in 1881. The general population growth of the province (including Vienna) during this period was 49 percent.[123] More significant, however, was the fact that the educational system through which the students had passed was that which had been substantially reformed and upgraded after 1850. The extreme emphasis which the Liberals placed on the value of higher learning and on free research was internalized by those who went through the new system in the expectation that their personal investments of time and money would be valued more highly than had been the case in Vormärz society.

The merits of achieved status through better-quality education and through adherence to "correct" and fashionable Liberal principles and the merits of inherited corporate claims to status based on the prestige of the traditional Josephist bureaucracy merged into a politically sponsored group self-importance. State employees began to think of themselves as members of a profession having social rights, as well as members of a traditional service group having rigid responsibilities. This process occurred first among German-speaking state officials, but the mobilization of social sentiment among non-German groups in the bureaucracy also began, with important results for the evolution of a more powerful bourgeoisie among the Slavic-speaking peoples of the empire.[124] Within the bureaucracy lower ranking and younger officials began to consider the kinds of rewards which ought to flow to them as members of a modern professional group, rewards in terms of the values of a class society based on political privilege (curial voting rights) and in terms of economic and social resources. Adherence to Liberal principle soon invited expectations that the personal satisfaction which such principles brought was no longer sufficient in itself to fulfill, especially after the traumatic economic crises of the 1870s and 1880s.[125]

The Liberal party spent thirty years telling state officials that they were important in ways which they or their predecessors had never heard before—through party-political mechanisms, through a libertarian political language, and through the powerful Liberal press. This campaign served Liberalism as much as it did the state employees, since it constituted one axis of a dual attack on absolutist sovereignty. Austrian Liberalism relied on the parliament and the cities as one angle of opposition to the throne, but it also attempted to take the ideal of an *Obrigkeitsstaat*, modified by an independent civil law, and instill within members of the bureaucracy new Liberal mentalities. In doing so the Liberals thought their party would provide a new party-political bond to hold the formerly independent administration together. Officials in all areas and ranks of the administration and the judicial system would have one important shared value: they would consider their political allegiance to lie with the Austro-German Liberals. Equally important, this revolution in social and political self-esteem was not confined to university-trained or *Mittel-schule*-trained officials. By the late 1880s and early 1890s even groups like the *Kanzlisten* had begun to mimic their betters' behavior.[126]

Of vital importance, however, was the fact that the Liberal party lost control of the Imperial government in 1879. The rise of a powerful clerical-Slavic national coalition meant that the Liberals were no longer in a position to respond to the grievances and hopes of the Imperial bureaucracy. Count Taaffe and his finance minister Dunajewski were unwilling to provide the Liberals with gratuitous support by helping the German-speaking officials in the ways in which the Liberals might have tried to do. The more conservative Iron Ring refused to implement the program for the officials which the Liberals had originally proclaimed in the early 1870s. All prospects for the passage of a national *Dienstpragmatik*, for example, ended after 1879. Pension reforms, the demand for which was frequently voiced in *Beamten* newspapers, languished under Dunajewski's tight fiscalism.[127] In those semiautonomous or federal areas of the state—such as the city of Vienna or the province of Lower Austria—where the Liberals retained control of the public purse strings, some financial and organizational improvements for local and provincial officials were implemented. It became a standard and frequently recited complaint in petitions and newspapers in the 1890s that the municipal officials of Vienna were far better off than their unfortunate colleagues in the national bureaucracy.[128]

The end of Liberal dominance was both the occasion for and the result of the growth of powerful national movements, the most significant of which, the Czech, was especially interested in obtaining a greater share of the appointments to the local and state offices in Bohemia and Moravia. Although this "Slavicization" of the state bureaucracy has not been studied intensively and seems to have been confined to Bohemia and Moravia until the 1890s, it is likely that the input of Czech-speaking candidates for jobs and promotions reduced the availability of public employment opportunities for German-speaking candidates on all levels.[129] The virulent student nationalism in the universities in the 1870s found its major impact in the 1880s, when the graduates of the 1870s had completed their training periods as *Praktikanten* (which often lasted five or six years) and were placed in responsible positions. A growing sensitivity to nationalism was undoubtedly to be found among the other two classes of German-speaking state officials, although the strength of such sentiment was clearly stronger in Bohemia and Moravia than in Vienna itself.

These developments were matched by fundamental changes in the social living standards of white collar employees. The organization of a broad network of *Beamten* credit and savings societies in the 1870s and

1880s under the direction and control of the *Erster allgemeiner Beamten-Verein* meant that state employees now had available to them credit resources which were often more dangerous than helpful.[130] The seven credit societies of the *Beamten-Verein* in Vienna had outstanding loans to their members of over 1 million gulden by 1890.[131] The problem of personal credit for public employees, credit often available only at extremely high interest rates, became a major subject for public discussion in the 1890s and 1900s.[132] Such heavy personal indebtedness resulted in part from the long-term rise in the cost of living in Austria after 1860, especially the cost of housing, which increased astronomically in many cities between 1860 and 1890. But it also derived from higher and more tempting standards of consumption—the social expectations of a white collar family in 1890 were different from those forty years previously.[133] By 1890 each official expected to carry a life insurance policy for the protection of his family. Family prestige and hopes for some level of social mobility also entered into the drive for better and more expensive forms of schooling for male children. Bürger families in Germany during this period spent between 2.5 percent and 3.5 percent of their total income on educational expenses; the situation was probably not very different in German Austria.[134] The advertising and consumer revolution of the later nineteenth century did not fail to affect the mentalities of public employees and their wives.[135] The Liberal party had the difficult task in the early 1890s of persuading these men, as consumers and as increasingly frustrated nationalists, that it was both willing and able to respond to their needs.

A similar pattern of status upgrading in the 1870s and 1880s occurred in the Viennese and Lower Austrian teaching corps. The Liberals made the improvement and the training programs and living conditions of the public-school teachers one of the cardinal points of their program after 1867. Because anticlericalism constituted the most powerful impulse in Austrian Liberalism, the teachers became one of the front-line units in the battle against the "clerical menace." In Lower Austria the battle against the Church gave the Liberal teachers some decided advantages. It was not accidental that Friedrich Dittes, the man responsible in the 1870s for the organization of the *Wiener Pädagogium* (a modern center for the continuing education of teachers in Vienna) and a staunch defender of the teachers' salary and occupational rights, was one of the most vehement anticlerical spokesmen in the Lower Austrian Liberal party.[136] Because of men like Dittes, schoolteachers came to have a higher ideological and political opinion of themselves.[137] If teachers, having been trained in the new Liberal teacher institutes, were to serve as the force of Liberal light in the clerical darkness, could the higher bourgeoisie continue to deny to the teachers some of the attributes of the *Gebildeten?* Attendance at the postgraduate, continuing education courses of the *Wiener Pädagogium* raised the self-esteem of schoolteachers, who began to conceive of their training in terms of professional competence established by "scientific principles."[138] In an absolute sense traditional prejudices against the strivings of men of the lower-Bürgertum to gain social recognition and economic security by entering the ranks of the schoolteachers certainly persisted. But compromises and adjustments were inevitable. The contempt and derision with which schoolteachers had to contend in the 1840s had definitely been reduced by the 1880s. The Imperial school law of 1869, one of the most sacred accomplishments of Austro-German Liberalism, made this readjustment of prestige allocation within the Bürgertum inevitable.[139] In 1889 even the Imperial government recognized the achievements of the teachers when it accorded the one-year reservist right *(Einjährig-freiwilligen-Recht)* to students who had completed four years in a teacher training institute.

By the early 1880s schoolteachers in Vienna had developed aggressive professional organizations to express their wishes.[140] The fact that appointments to many school positions in Vienna, especially those of the city's *Bürgerschulen* (which were more coveted jobs), were arranged through the political patronage and sponsorship of the more powerful members of the Council who sat on the Vienna School Board gave to the teachers a sensitivity toward the city's political system from the very beginning of their careers.[141] Both schoolteachers and municipal employees were psychologically and socially closer to a competitive political system than were the state officials, for whom party politics for some years possessed a more doubtful legitimacy.[142] Party politics could be accepted more easily by these local officials, since the administrative system controlling their careers was more open to direct party manipulation. It was not accidental that the first instance of white collar group public "interviews" of and accountability sessions with candidates for public office came in the early 1880s when the senior Viennese schoolteachers began such a practice in the Council elections. The *Verband der Wiener Beamten* in 1885–86 was indebted to the older schoolteachers for this model of aggressive political behavior. The municipal officials who created the *Verband* provided state officials in turn with a model for mobilizing their profession and integrating it into the party system in 1890–91.[143]

This modeling experience revealed one way in which the city of Vienna influenced national politics. The city was not merely the receptacle for national policy decisions; as a competitive political unit in its own right, the city could start trends in organization and method within its political culture that would later spread to the national context. Mass social interest politics had a richly endowed political system within which to experiment before "going" national. Not only was Vienna the seedbed of political ideologies and movements, but, more important, it gave these movements the temporal, legal, and social framework within which the all-important connection between interest and power might be articulated. In Vienna the antisemites could actually win control of a city government and force the Imperial government to recognize their existence by recognizing their right to administrative power.

Similarly, because the "payoff" potential in Viennese politics was somewhat higher than in other local political systems, the network of white collar interest organizations could tie itself into the more visible party system and use this system to encourage its own organizational prowess. Not only did the 1,200 schoolteachers and 850 municipal officials employed by the city in 1889–90 constitute an important bloc of white collar voters in the Second Curia, but they were ideologically and politically the closest members of the officialdom to the Liberal party. Little likelihood remained that, if the Liberals ever lost the loyalty of these groups, they would hold on to the votes of the state officials.

The decision of the Viennese Liberals in 1884–85 to bring the mass of lower and middle public officialdom and the schoolteachers into the "curia of the intelligentsia" was, thus, not surprising.[144] If the five-gulden artisans were to receive the franchise, the public employees could hardly be denied it. In their own minds these officials and teachers possessed the four criteria which the *Sprechsaal des Beamtentages* formulated in 1885 as preconditions for the privilege of voting in the Second Curia: education, social service, corporate honor, and public respectability.[145] The newspaper's combination of two criteria of individual achievement and two of corporate honor was typical of the transitional state of Mittelstand politics in Vienna. By giving these groups a privileged franchise, the Liberals accorded them a symbolic recognition of their advancing status claims. More practically, putting them into the Second Curia would also keep them away from the more radical tendencies of the new artisan electorate.

Unfortunately, as often happened with the Liberals, their well-intentioned actions came too late. The Liberals were shocked to learn in the later 1880s that some of the newly enfranchised officials and teachers could disassociate without difficulty their hopes for solid bourgeois respectability and their intention to vote for Liberal candidates. Many state employees began to question what Liberal rhetoric about the importance of well-educated state officials was worth without its translation into financial reality. For some, the *idée fixe* of the 1870s, that the concepts of Bürger and Liberal were synonymous, now became unacceptable. By 1890 social unrest had slowly begun to affect all levels and ranks within the bureaucracy, although in different forms. The greatest overt hostility to the Liberals was manifested among the younger jurists who had joined the state service in the mid-1880s. Liberal parliamentarians anxiously complained about their nationalist and antisemitic sympathies.[146] Nor were the ministerial officials in the central administration immune to the idea of voting against the Liberals: Count Kálnoky told Eulenburg in 1895 that most of the younger, university-trained *Conceptsbeamten* in his ministry openly admitted that they had voted antisemitic in the City Council elections that year, while the older men on the level of councillor were preserving a sympathetic "neutrality" toward Lueger and the antisemites.[147]

Each level of officials might have its own particular reasons for finding antisemitism attractive. Although few Jews were allowed into the judiciary, the majority of trial lawyers in Vienna in the 1890s were Jews, and this meant that hostile, conflict-oriented interaction occurred in court cases with Gentiles on one side and Jews on the other. Frustration over slowness of promotion and the threat of competition by Slavic-speaking candidates (or even other German-speaking candidates) were easily converted into scapegoatism against Jews in the legal profession and on the university law faculty, but some real referents to Gentile-Jewish hostility also existed. In the case of the thousands of *Mittelschule*-trained officials who occupied the middle ranks of the bureaucracy, antisemitic propaganda about the overrepresentation of Jews in the universities had a powerful reverberation. Many of these men had attended or even finished a gymnasium or other *Mittelschule* and had the talent to go on to higher levels of academic achievement. Because of a lack of financial resources, however, they opted to join the state bureaucracy early in their careers (often at the age of nineteen or twenty) and were thus channeled into rank levels which were never comparable in prestige or salary to those of their university-trained colleagues.[148] When Lueger and the other antisemites thundered against "wealthy Jews" who had taken over the universities, they were manipulating real feelings of inadequacy and envy on the part of these intermediate officials, many of whom wanted a university education but could not afford it. Antisemitism became the externalization of feelings of personal inadequacy and self-hate.[149]

At the root of the officials' political unrest, however, were issues which were far more powerful than mere antisemitic rhetoric. The *Sprechsaal des Beamtentages* insisted that most of the officials in 1890 were not "antisemites by conviction," an evaluation confirmed in separate analyses by Prince Reuss and Joseph Baernreither.[150] Rather, salary discontents, the lack of a fair and clear *Dienstpragmatik*, the absence of vacation time, the miserable pension system, nepotism and political favoritism in appointments and promotions, fears of nationalist competition, resentment against the long, low-salary probationary periods which younger officials had to endure—these were the important issues which provoked the state employees to begin to question their allegiance to the Liberal party.[151]

Liberal uncertainty over whether to push these men into the Third Curia in 1890 had cost them the Landtag election. In the final version of the 1890 franchise Kielmansegg and the Liberals decided to leave all of the white collar voters in the Second Curia. But they did make some important changes in the composition of the "curia of the intelligentsia," which collectively became known as "Prix's electoral geometry." The new franchise transferred all home- and landowners paying less than 200 fl. annually in taxes from the Second to the Third Curia. This group of voters was not large, since most *Hausherren* in Vienna paid far more than this.[152] The vast majority of the property and apartment house owners in Vienna were left in the First and Second Curias. Indeed, the First Curia was still dominated by these voters. Also, more categories of professionals and semiprofessionals not in the government were elevated from the Third to the Second Curia. Pharmacists, notaries, military officials, men holding a certificate or degree from an institute of higher learning other than a doctoral degree, and other groups which had not enjoyed the privileged Second Curia franchise in 1850 received it now. More important, the law transferred to the middle curia a large number of the new class of private employees working for banks, industrial and commercial bureaucracies, and newspapers. Many of these individuals were Jews whose votes had formerly been useless to the Liberals since they had to vote in the Third Curia. Finally, by adjusting the tax requirements of the franchise, the Liberals shifted a number of owners, managers, or partners in commercial or industrial businesses of moderate size out of the Third and into the Second Curia. This was especially true for owners of firms listed in the official trade register and for segments of the artisan elite of the city. Both Jewish and Gentile businessmen profited from this change.

The Third Curia was generally left untouched, although its numerical size was reduced by the transfers into the Second Curia. The result of these manipulations was apparent in the movement of registered voters from one curia to another between 1890 and 1891. Between 1886 and 1890 the annual growth in the Second Curia was rarely more than 4 percent. Between 1890 and 1891 the curia increased by over 3,000 voters, or 9 percent per district.[153]

By combining in the new Second Curia the broadest possible representation of the educated elites of the city (including journalists and writers) with middle level industrial, commercial, and property-owning sectors of the city's economy, the Liberals fashioned a curia with a dual bourgeois nature. Membership in the new curia, so the Liberals hoped, would function as a recognition that the concept of Bürger had both traditional corporate and achieved-class status justifications. Older representatives of the political bourgeoisie (as constituted between 1850 and 1885) such as property owners and university-trained academics were united with occupational groups which, like the schoolteachers, had only recently claimed recognition as respectable Bürger types or which, like the employees of large private commercial bureaucracies, had not even existed on mass terms before 1850. The franchise demonstrated the Liberal hope that by delineating as sharply as possible the Second and Third Curias all Bürger types would be carried along in a spirit of status loyalty to support the Liberal party.[154]

Crucial to the Liberals' electoral strategy in the 1890s was, therefore, the assumption that they could manipulate the First and Second Curias to compensate for the losses to the antisemites in the Third. That the Liberals left the officials in the Second Curia did not mean that they fully trusted these men.[155] The new recruits from the commercial bureaucracies, the newspapers, and the mid-sized industrial firms would provide a welcome ballast against a white collar revolt. But the Liberals did hope in 1890 that the political behavior of the officials and teachers might be stabilized by a careful admixture of enticement and repression.

One disgruntled Liberal voter thought little of the franchise strategy. He wrote anonymously to Kielmansegg in October 1890, warning that the new franchise was suicidal for Liberalism and that the antisemites would surely conquer the Second Curia in the elections of April 1891. For the "Wiener Patriot" there was an inevitable tension between the higher and lower ranks in the bureaucracy which no rhetoric of status harmony could mitigate: if the higher-ups voted Liberal, then the underlings (whatever their educational or family background) would automatically vote antisemitic. The Patriot urged Kielmansegg to revise the franchise so that the two lowest Rangclassen (X and XI) would vote in the Third Curia.[156]

The pessimism of the Patriot's letter was unfounded, for the Liberals proved in 1891 and the antisemites in 1895–96 that voting patterns in the bureaucracy often had very little to do with rank alone. Political grievances among members of the state bureaucracy involved social issues which cut across rank and educational barriers.

For Lueger and the Christian Socials the 1890 franchise was a mixed blessing. From a tactical standpoint Lueger was appalled at the electoral advantages which the government would award the Liberals by its sanction of the Ordnung. During the Landtag debates he proposed amendments which might have lessened the Liberals' self-gratification, but they were defeated. His critique of the franchise centered on the need to reform the curial system. To the Liberal arguments that the Christian Socials would use a noncurial system to infringe upon property rights in the city, Lueger pointed out that most Third Curia voters usually elected men to the Council who possessed voting rights in one of the higher, privileged curias and who thus represented some measure of wealth.[157] To confirm his real stance on democratization of voting rights, however, Lueger soon moved from a demand for noncurial suffrage to a series of detailed amendments which would have enlarged the Second Curia even more by adding to it a larger number of private employees, especially those men who did not earn enough to justify their inclusion in the new reformed Second Curia (the Liberals set the income boundary line for the officials at 1,407 fl., upon which the tax would have been 30 fl.). Lueger implicitly acknowledged his general sympathy with the idea of a curial system when he noted that it was entirely appropriate that men of some academic training be grouped together in one voting curia.[158]

The antisemites were also disturbed by the six-year terms of office and by the distribution of seats to the various districts. They were less concerned about the transfer of voters from one curia to another, perhaps because of an overconfidence encouraged by Liberal disasters in the Landtag elections. The antisemites were certain that, even if the Liberals juggled the Second Curia, they would win a significant number of Second Curia seats, and pick up a few in the First Curia as well.[159] With this assumption went a related one that the kinds of propaganda the anti-Liberal coalition had used up to 1890 were entirely appropriate for the political conquest of Vienna. The leaders of the antisemitic movement were in for a rather rude shock, however, since Viennese Liberalism was not as "dead" in 1891 as the editors of the *Deutsches Volksblatt* wanted to believe.

The Elections of 1891

The two elections held in the spring of 1891 tested the effectiveness of the Liberal franchise strategy of 1890. On 5 March 1891 the national elections for six-year terms to the Reichsrat took place. They were followed in late March and early April by the City Council elections. Both elections occurred well before the new consumption tax rates were scheduled to go into effect.

The antisemites mounted an effective campaign for the Reichsrat elections and came away with some encouraging victories. Of the fourteen seats in Vienna and the suburbs the antisemites captured seven (Wieden, Margarethen, Mariahilf, Neubau, Josefstadt, Sechshaus, and Hernals).[160] Although the franchise requirements for Landtag and Reichsrat elections were almost identical, there was a substantial relative increase in voter turnout for the national elections, an increase of nearly 10 percent over that of October 1890. The results indicated that the increase in new voters worked to the benefit of the antisemites in Mariahilf, Neubau, Margarethen, and the Josefstadt. In the Landstrasse, Wieden, and Alsergrund the Liberals held their own or actually profited from the entry of new voters.[161]

The greater voter turnout was undoubtedly attributable to voter fascination with the kinds of issues raised by the antisemites and by the style in which those issues were discussed. Reichsrat elections offered the antisemites the opportunity to deal with each district as a whole, running their single most attractive and publicly respected candidate.[162] Such elections focused on the candidates' personalities and on national issues in addition to specific occupational grievances. In such elections the Liberals had less opportunity to control the behavior of such voters as the state officials because there was no way to hold them accountable as a curial group. There was also no way to ensure that specific kinds of propaganda would necessarily find their way to intended social groups.

Even so, the antisemitic victories in the Neubau and the Josefstadt indicated that the hostility many white collar voters had vented against the Liberal party in October 1890 was a persistent phenomenon. On the other hand, the Liberals stabilized the antisemitic challenge in the Fourth District (Wieden) and reversed the pro-antisemitic trends in the Third (Landstrasse) and Ninth (Alsergrund) Districts which were manifest in October 1890.[163] The crushing victory of the Liberal candidate, Guido Sommaruga, in the Landstrasse proved that solidly Bürger districts could still return a Liberal if presented with the right candidate and with effective preparation.[164]

The real test of Liberal survival came three weeks after the Reichsrat elections. The Liberals used the interim to bring massive pressure to bear on public employees of various categories to vote the "correct" way in the municipal election. Indeed, the party seemed to come alive in the final days of the Council campaign in a way it had not for the national elections.[165] Even the *Deutsches Volksblatt* was amazed at the vigor and tenacity with which the Liberals organized their campaign.[166] Although one-half of the Reichsrat delegation was now lost to the antisemites, Mayor Prix was determined to keep the city government out of their hands.

The antisemites and the Liberals prepared for the Council elections with considerable care, selecting candidates whose occupational backgrounds made them appropriate to the curia in which they were to run.[167] Of the forty-five candidates slated for the Third Curia by the antisemitic coalition, twenty were clearly identifiable as owners of artisan businesses or small shops, sixteen were owners or managers of businesses of a slightly more prominent nature which might be called *Mittelgewerbe* (*Stadtbaumeister,* factory owners, merchants owning firms which were enrolled in the trade register, etc.), three were lawyers, three were property owners *(Rentier),* two were journalists, and one was a Catholic cleric. Of the forty-five candidates, twenty-one were *Hausherren.* The anti-semitic artisan candidates were usually older men of some prominence in their respective trades—many bore the designation of *beeideten Schätz-meister* and had been elected previously to the local District Councils. Seven of the antisemitic candidates were chairmen of craft guilds in the city.[168]

None of the forty-five Liberal candidates for the Third Curia in 1891 represented large-scale wealth (except for Victor Silberer and Constantine Noske, who ran in the First District). Seventeen of the Liberal candidates were simple artisan types; another twenty-two were *Mittelgewerbe* individuals, many with retail or wholesale firms enrolled in the trade register. Some of the Liberals were businessmen with special professional distinctions—several served on the board of the Viennese Chamber of Commerce. The Liberals also ran one medical doctor, one public-school teacher, one private employee, and one journalist. No lawyers were slated by the Liberals for the Third Curia. Nineteen of the Liberals were *Hausherren.*

Liberal candidates in the Third Curia were thus not greatly different from their antisemitic counterparts in occupation, but they did occupy ranks within shared occupations of higher prominence and wealth.[169] The typical Liberal candidate in the Third Curia was a man of proved business success within his small or mid-industrial or mid-commercial occupation. The Liberal nominees were at that point of economic security and professional prosperity where the antisemitic candidates and their voters wanted to be. There does not seem to have been, however, a significantly higher level of formal educational achievement on the part of the Liberal, as opposed to the antisemitic, candidates.[170]

For the Second Curia a similar imbalance between the two opposing slates existed. Of the forty-six candidates put up by the antisemites, only six could be classified as artisans. Thirteen antisemites were *Mittel-gewerbe* types, most of them owning or managing a registered firm. Four lawyers and three physicians found themselves listed, together with seven schoolteachers, six *Kleingewerbe* artisans, and one dentist. All of the teachers were men who had achieved a relatively high status position within their profession—the director of a *Bürgerschule,* a supervisory teacher *(Oberlehrer)* at a large *Volksschule,* etc. The rest of the antisemitic slate consisted of middle level state officials, real estate administrators, independently wealthy *Hausherren,* and one journalist.

The Liberals slated candidates of similar occupational designations (twelve *Mittelgewerbe* types, seven artisan types, seven middle or high level state or private officials, four physicians, eight lawyers, four teachers, and several journalists and technicians), but like the Liberal Third Curia slate, their candidates occupied more prominent economic ranks within their occupations than did the antisemites. The typical anti-semitic *Mittelgewerbe* candidate owned a wholesale food business or a small perfume factory; the Liberals in contrast owned a brick factory or an architectural firm. Antisemitic white collar candidates were generally in the lower middle or middle range of their occupational hierarchies (a librarian in the university library, a senior bookkeeper in a commercial firm, a retired chief inspector of a state railroad); Liberal white collar candidates in contrast often represented middle to upper ranks in their bureaucracies (an official in the Imperial Mint, an accountant with the Lower Austrian provincial government, an accountant in the Finance Ministry). Liberal lawyers were generally men of greater income than their antisemitic colleagues, not because of greater talent, but because of their wealthier clientele. Among the schoolteachers and school officials nominated by both parties there was no significant difference in rank. The antisemitic candidates had thirteen *Hausherren* among them, the Liberals sixteen.

In sum, the antisemitic coalition had no trouble finding candidates for the vitally important Second Curia whose occupations matched those of the Liberals' slate. They did, however, find it difficult to obtain candidates who could match the opposition's social rank achievements within shared occupations. In perspective, this ultimately worked in their favor, once the voters of the Second Curia had become sufficiently alienated from the Liberal party by 1895 because of the latter's inability to fulfill the promises it had made in 1891. In turning to an alternative party, Second Curia voters would never venture too far afield in terms of status, rank, and value privileges. Their candidates had to be superior to the Third Curia candidates, or the curious mixture of old *ständisch* value claims and new class and rank privleges which all Second Curia voters found comforting would be destroyed. The Christian Socials soon realized this fact. On the other hand, it did not hurt the antisemitic coalition's chances to put up for election men of slightly lower success levels, since this might help to secure a kind of negative solidarity and identity which would attract the Second Curia voter in his own disenchantment.

The Third Curia elections on 2 April 1891 went as the antisemites had expected and hoped.[171] Issues about Jewish "treachery," economic decline, and the antisemitic ability to straighten out the "mess" in city government, standard fare for any Third Curia election, were brought out again by the antisemites. The results were predictable: the anti-Liberal coalition won all of the districts except the Inner City, Leopoldstadt, and Fünfhaus, capturing thirty-three seats to the Liberals' thirteen. With a bravado generated by such success, the antisemites expected that the Second Curia elections on 8 April would produce similar results. They were greatly mistaken. By the evening of 8 April the Liberals had earned for themselves an additional five years of hegemony in Vienna. The Liberal party captured thirty-eight of the curia's forty-six seats. The antisemites won two seats in Ottakring, two in Währing, two in Favoriten, and two in Hernals. The rest of the city went solidly to the Liberals.

Not only did the Liberals win in districts like the Josefstadt and Neubau which had caused them so much anxiety in recent years, but they won with overwhelming margins. In the Landstrasse Baron Sommaruga's cadres performed their work with efficiency: the Liberals averaged 1,124 votes per candidate, while the antisemites obtained only 759. In the Josefstadt the ratio was 572:460; in Margarethen, 405:269. In contrast to these margins, the antisemitic candidates barely won in Ottakring and Währing. In the latter district, with a total pool of 1,562 voters, of whom 1,129 voted, the antisemitic victory ratio was only 589:527. This was especially notable in that over 1,000 voters in the Second Curia in Währing were lower ranking officials of the X and XI *Rangclassen*.[172] Obviously, the Liberals had somehow managed to neutralize the threat of a revolt on the part of many of these potential antisemitic voters.

Liberal success resulted from several factors. During the Reichsrat elections earlier in the month there were indications that many of the white collar voters whom the Liberals had alienated in October 1890 might be willing to return to the fold if given sufficient reason to do so. As the *Sprechsaal des Beamtentages* insisted, these were men who were looking for convincing reasons to vote Liberal, not to desert the party.[173]

In the weeks immediately preceding the Second Curia election, the Liberals, led by Johann Prix, took this advice to heart and committed themselves to an important revision in their political campaigning. The Liberals organized voter assemblies in many districts devoted exclusively to the material welfare demands of the *Beamten* and the schoolteachers.[174] The most successful venture of this kind was organized by Guido Sommaruga, even though he insisted that he deplored the new kind of interest-oriented politics into which the Viennese campaign had moved, lacking any discussion of general Liberal principles.[175] Sommaruga called a special *Beamten* congress for the white collar voters of the Landstrasse at which he presented his "program" for improving the welfare of state and municipal officials in his district. He offered an explicit, point-by-point commitment to work for a *Dienstpragmatik*, for salary raises and pension benefits, for a reduction of the time in grade required for promotion, and for similar issues. Following Sommaruga's speech Raimund Grübl, Prix's close ally (and in 1894 his successor), repeated the party's devotion to the material welfare of all *Beamten*, whether they were employed by the state or the municipality.[176] Given the enormous margin by which the Liberals carried the Landstrasse, Sommaruga's ability to overcome his scruples and lobby for interest-oriented votes was probably decisive in ensuring the Liberals' success in the district.

More important, however, was the behavior during the campaign of Mayor Prix and Ernst v Plener, the leader of the Liberal Club in the Reichsrat. Prix organized several election assemblies at which he promised the municipal officials and teachers a new era of material improvements and security, if only his party were allowed to continue its control of the city. At an assembly on 31 March in the hall of the Chamber of Commerce he shared the podium with Plener. Prix spoke first and argued not only that the Liberals intended to take up the problem of salary reforms for municipal employees as soon as the new Council met, but that the party would push ahead with the decentralization of the municipal bureaucracy through a new system of district offices (*Bezirksämter*) and would institute a new system of rank classifications for the Viennese officials. Plener then gave a major address in which he recalled the long tradition of support and interest which the Liberal party had shown the state officials and their municipal colleagues. Plener found it inconceivable that any state or local official could think of voting against the Liberal party.[177] By the following day the Liberals had printed 10,000 copies of Prix's speech and distributed them all over the city, a remarkable reflection of their new aggressiveness.

Prix's preelection promises were in fact little more than an opportune restatement of a commitment he had given on the question of the structural reorganization of the Viennese bureaucracy when he first assumed the duties of mayor in December 1889.[178] In February 1890 the *Magistrat* had submitted to him a series of reform proposals involving new rank classifications and salary adjustments, but Prix had refused to act on them. Now, immediately before the election, Prix announced that he was ready to proceed with the reforms.[179]

Prix's and Plener's assurances were important in persuading uncommitted or uncertain voters in the Second Curia to give the Liberal party one more chance. In March 1891 the Liberals had no power to do anything for the officials on the national level, but the absolute control which they held in Vienna itself served in a multifunctional sense. To the local officials and teachers employed by the municipality the Liberals promised real and immediate improvements. At the same time, these improvements were intended to represent to the white collar voters in the city what the party would do for *them* if it ever regained power in the Imperial Cabinet.[180] Not only could Prix's behavior after April 1891 be held to a strict standard of accountability by these voters, but Ernst v Plener put himself and the national Liberal Club in the same situation. When Plener finally engineered the Liberals' return to power in the coalition of 1893, the Second Curia voters of the city expected that the promises of March and April 1891 would be made good. That Plener either refused or was unwilling to do so in good part secured Karl Lueger's victory in 1895–96.

The ability of the Liberal politicians to survive in suburban districts like Rudolfsheim and Fünfhaus and to come very close to winning in Währing and Ottakring was in no small measure owing to a definite change in the political responses of many subaltern and middle level *Beamten* voters.[181] The party was also assisted in all of the city's districts in 1891 by the neutrality of the fledgling *Hausherrenvereine,* which had only begun to be organized in 1891.[182] From the election results of the First and Second Curias it was clear that most property owners had continued to vote Liberal, just as they had faithfully done in the past. Unless the Liberal party gave these voters some definite provocation not to continue to vote Liberal, it seemed likely that their support would remain a proprietary possession of the party.

The massive Liberal majorities in the older districts, however, also hinged in part upon the results of the "electoral geometry" of October 1890. The *Deutsches Volksblatt* bemoaned the fact that Prix's calculated voter transfers had stolen the election from the antisemites' grasp.[183] Indeed, in the Second, Third, Fourth, Sixth, Seventh, Eighth, and Ninth Districts the average victory margin assembled by the Liberal slate of candidates was smaller than the number of new voters transferred into the Second Curia by the 1890 reforms. These results indicated that in some cases the extra cushion for a Liberal victory had probably come from the transferred voters. However, it was likely that some of the newly eligible did not vote and that the Liberals had been able to secure the votes of men who might have turned to the antisemites in 1890. In the Fifth District (Margarethen), for example, the Liberal victory margin was 137 votes, even though the Second Curia in this district had been enlarged by only 48 voters under the 1890 reforms. Here the Liberals relied successfully on older Second Curia voters who chose to remain loyal or officials who were persuaded to return to the Liberal fold. The Liberal *Neues Wiener Tag-blatt* was so grateful for the loyalty of the officials that it commented on the day after the voting: "Yesterday was a day of honor for the teachers and officials. The Liberal party must now try to obtain for these voters the promises which Mayor Prix gave them in his speech in the Chamber of Commerce."[184]

Having successfully resisted the antisemitic challenge in the Second Curia, the Liberals had no problem in winning forty-four of the forty-six seats in the First Curia. They entered the new City Council of metropolitan Vienna with a delegation of ninety-three, almost as strong, on paper at least, as they were before 1890. Their election victories were at the same time reality and illusion. They had bent every effort to keep control of the crucial Second Curia, and they had succeeded. Their victories were not the result, however, of long-term strategy and permanent organizational strength. The Liberal party realized the importance of the white collar social issues only in 1891, exploiting its powerful communications resources to persuade a large enough group of voters that it would be able to secure meaningful changes in their lives. The Liberals thus put themselves on record with a specific sense of political accountability to several district *Beamten* subcultures. When the next Second Curia election came in 1895, the voters would be able to compare promise with performance and judge accordingly. The Liberals had learned the rewards of converting their party into a middle class social interest movement; their problem now was whether they could deal with the responsibilities which accompanied that role.

Before 1885 Liberalism always tried to style itself as the party of the people in a universalistic, nonpolitical sense, even though its politicians did in fact represent very distinctive attitudes toward the shape of Austrian society.[185] Before 1885 its universalism was challenged by the Democratic politicians and voter associations, but because these groups continued to insist that they too were "Liberal," the problem of the *party-political* expression of social fragmentation was never a major one. Although the antisemites were in many respects the organic heirs of the older Democrats, their insistence on being a new and alternative political network which repudiated all that Liberalism stood for left the Liberals in a puzzling dilemma. Universalism was no longer possible—the Viennese political system ceased after 1887 to be one movement divided into several factions and became two parties sharing between themselves the same unitary social interest groups. Had Liberalism and antisemitism completely distinct constituencies, the new party system would have been easy to comprehend. But both parties claimed to be acting in the name of the Bürgertum, not just the old artisan class, but the middle sectors of

Viennese political society as well.[186] For the Second Curia in Vienna represented a fundamental sociopolitical fact: in it the extremes of "capitalism" on one hand and "anticapitalism" on the other merged into linguistic and normative confusion. A handwork artisan might be "anti-capitalist," a banker might be "capitalist," but where should a school principal or a construction company owner be placed?[187]

Both parties had "home" territories marked out by 1890: the Liberals in the property owners of the First Curia, the antisemites in the artisans and tradesmen of the Third Curia. These groups constituted one-half of the relative base votes of the respective parties (with some overlapping and exchange). But both parties also conceived of themselves as being rooted in the Bürgertum, not in the struggling *Heimarbeit* artisan or the industrial plutocrat, but in the middle-sized merchant, the factory owner listed in the trade register, the gymnasial teacher, the wealthier artisan elites. This meant that socially and ideologically the two movements overlapped, however much the propaganda organs of the parties denied any similarity between the two.

The sharing of voter groups by the two oppositional parties illustrated the fact that the categories of *Kleinbürgertum* and *Grossbürgertum* were simply inadequate to describe the complexity of social and occupational stratification in the city. Members of the First or Second Curia in Vienna, to the extent that they were wealthy artisans who owned a profitable apartment house, were certainly not members of a *Grossbürgertum* of bankers, university professors, and industrialists, but they were certainly not to be ranked as *Kleinbürger* either. Culturally they might share many of the values and cultural symbols of their colleagues lower down the ladder of success and income, but they considered themselves to be proud, independent Bürger of a middle level of society in terms of economic and political achievement.

In this first competition for the Second Curia the Liberals won. Their success hinged upon the inherent conservatism of many Second Curia voters, which was not quite the same as giving the Liberals the "benefit of the doubt," but which had the same result. In 1891 many governmental employees and property owners, when faced with a barrage of promises from both Liberals and antisemites, were inclined to give the Liberals the first opportunity to sponsor bourgeois social reform. The very idea of such a program was so novel that both parties were still developing their positions toward it. The Liberals' alleged administrative ineptness in running municipal affairs as portrayed by the antisemites seemed to be disproved by the relatively successful transition of the city to its new metropolitan status. The voters of the higher curia had a greater sense of the city as their proprietary responsibility. Many voters, even those who within five years would desert the Liberals for Lueger, were probably unwilling to entrust the immediate fulfillment of unification to a new, fledgling party without significant administrative experience. To vote for antisemites for the Reichsrat was one thing, especially since the actual power of the parliament was always rather ambiguous and uncertain. Even to vote for isolated antisemitic candidates for the Council was an acceptable way of expressing frustration against the social status quo. But to hand over to the antisemites the city of Vienna in one blow was more than most Second Curia voters were willing to do in 1891. Only after the Liberals had made policy decisions in the early 1890s which unfavorably affected the lives of property owners, teachers, and municipal officials in the city did many voters finally conclude that the administrative experience was not necessarily a prerequisite for good or responsible government.

The antisemitic issue proved to be of only limited value to the antisemites in undoing confidence in the Liberals. No better proof was offered than by an election analysis which appeared in Vergani's *Deutsches Volksblatt* the day after the Second Curia voted. The writer, who remained anomymous, was clearly dissatisfied with the front-page argument attributing the antisemites' failure to Prix's electoral geometry. Rather, the antisemites themselves had failed to present their issue in a form which the "educated" voters of the Second Curia could appreciate and find meaningful.[188] The writer's prescription was for a sharper emphasis on nationalism and antisemitism, but one which would not insult the intelligence of the Second and First Curia voters. This article was important, since it revealed a problem which both parties now faced: how to differentiate between the social subcultures of their voters in a way which did not fragment their parties, but which at the same time allowed for flexibility in assembling a variety of tactical options. Ironically, the article confirmed the assertion made by the *Sprechsaal des Beamtentages* that most officials and teachers voted against the Liberals out of occupational dissatisfactions and not out of hard, ideological conviction. The same was to prove true for the *Hausbesitzer* as well. In this sense Second and First Curia voters in Vienna in the 1890s constituted the most dangerous of all constituencies which a party could face—these were independent voters who could swing one way or the other depending upon their own personal judgments. Neither the Liberals nor the Christian Socials were accustomed to dealing with such voters, the Liberals because they had been able to take such voters for granted in the past, the antisemites because they wanted to take them for granted in the future.

The defeat in April 1891 embittered and disillusioned many of the local antisemitic leaders. Far from having won Vienna, they found themselves controlling less than a third of the Council (45 seats out of a possible 138). If the Liberals' confidence in the new cyclical election procedure proved correct, perhaps they would never win Vienna. The bitterness of April 1891 found its way into the public rhetoric of Lueger and his colleagues for the next several years. Lueger was accustomed to losing elections, but his inexperienced colleagues were not. Their emotional intensity was a weapon which henceforth Lueger made no effort to control; he was forty-six years old and did not intend to spend the rest of his career leading powerless oppositions in attacking windmills. The vituperous and often furious political rhetoric of 1892–95 cannot be understood except in the light of his intermixture of frustrated political enthusiasm by novices and of cold, caluclated despair by a political professional.

Beyond setting the tone and style of antisemitic politics in Vienna, the election results made a fundamental contribution to the future direction in which Viennese antisemitism would head. Before 1890 political anti-semitism in Vienna had been largely an affair of the Third Curia. The leaders of the movement were often men of some educational attainment, but the kinds of issues raised and the kinds of organizational methods utilized were most appropriate for artisan voters. To win Vienna, how-ever, it was not enough to seize control of the Third Curia. The election of 1891 made the antisemites painfully aware that, like the Liberals, they had to make some fundamental readjustments in the way in which they would view competitive politics in the city. Issues which worked within the Third Curia might prove useless in the First or Second. The style of election agitation and the aesthetics of political rallies differed funda-mentally, for example, between the Third and Second Curias. After 1891 the antisemites were forced to orient their coalition toward a far more diversified range of issues. They had to prove that they were in fact what they claimed to be—a Bürger party. Given the importance of white collar employees and *Hausbesitzer* for the future success of the party in the two privileged curias, it was not surprising that after 1891 representatives of the property owners (Joseph Strobach), the nationalist-oriented senior schoolteachers (Leopold Tomola), as well as the university-educated city employees (Richard Weiskirchner) gradually gained more prominent roles in the coalition's elite.

Political Resources and White Collar Politics: Vienna versus Berlin

The significance of municipal franchise resources for the structure of urban politics is clearly revealed by a comparison of Vienna with Berlin and Cologne, the principal representatives of the two variants of *Städte-ordnung* in Prussia.[189] In Vienna, because the curial tax scale for munici-pal elections was more flexible and less plutocratic than in Berlin, with more exceptional interminglings of different kinds of Bürger groups, political rights did become a real and valued index of social mobility and prestige. This may explain why, even in the 1870s and 1880s, typical Viennese voter participation in municipal elections was usually somewhat higher than that found in Prussian municipal elections. Political rights and privileges in Vienna, because they were city-wide and predictable, offered to Viennese voters a useful and reliable criterion for defining subtle status distinctions between various kinds of nonproletarian social strata.[190] Also important was the fact that in Vienna, unlike Berlin, voting was by written ballot, making the exercise of political choices less subject to external pressures (or threats) to conform to the status quo. In Berlin, where municipal elections were conducted by oral, public voting, this kind of interest group solidarity against the ruling political establishment was not always possible.

Moreover, in Prussian cities, where most of those men who voted in the Second Curia in Vienna would probably have been consigned to Third Class because they did not fall into the second "third" of the total tax revenue for their specific districts, the kind of political culture resulting was markedly different. Contemporary reports on local agitation in Berlin's Third Class suggested that the Social Democrats faced a resilient core of Liberal voters who were small- and mid-scale artisans and state officials.[191] In 1891, for example, in Vienna 6.8 percent of the total electorate voted in the First Curia, 28.0 percent voted in the Second Curia, and 65.1 percent voted in the Third Curia. In Berlin, in contrast, which did not use a fixed index for income or educational achievement but which relied on a three-way distribution of voters according to total tax performance, the respective proportions in 1893–95 were 1.6 percent, 11.0 percent, and 87.4 percent.[192] In 1892, Cologne (with a total enfranchisement of 25,278) had a voter distribution similar to Berlin's: 1.5 percent, 10.2 percent, and 88.3 percent. As late as 1905–15 Cologne averaged only 1.2 percent, 12.7 percent, and 86.1 percent for taxpayers possessing franchise rights.[193] In Berlin or Cologne, where no provision was made to compensate the lower and middle levels of the *Intelligenz* by placing them in the privileged Second Class on the basis of their educational or occupational achievements alone, the kind of intermixture of smaller *Bildung* and *Besitz* voters on a nonoligarchical level which was obtained in Vienna could not occur. The special character of the Viennese Second Curia was a classic political formulation of a nonproletarianized Mittelstand in search of status.

Of equal comparative importance in Vienna's electoral system was the special nature of its First Curia. In Berlin the top class of voters were often members of a *grande bourgeoisie* on a Western European model. Even commercial corporations, banks, and other legal entities had the right to exercise a vote in Prussian city elections. In Vienna, however, the First Curia was dominated by middle and upper level *Hausbesitzer* who obtained the right to vote because the rent tax which their tenants paid to the state (and city), the *Hauszinssteuer,* was credited to them in a personal sense and not to their tenants. Thus an apartment house owner in Vienna whose building produced 3,000 fl. in rentals might pay as much as 42 percent of the adjusted gross income annually in taxes on behalf of his tenants in the building. According to the Viennese franchise the state's tax share (26.6 percent) enabled him to vote in the First Curia. The upshot was that the First Curia in Vienna was not really a curia of the *Grossbürgertum* in a modern, capitalistic sense. Wealthy artisans in Neubau or Landstrasse, for example, might save enough money to purchase an apartment building and win a position in the First Curia, simply because the *Hauszinssteuer* of the building was credited to them. One did not have to live on the Ringstrasse in Vienna in order to vote in the First Curia.

The Bürger character of the First Curia in Vienna was of critical importance to Karl Lueger and the Christian Socials. Lueger's victories in September 1895 and March 1896 were in part owing to the willingness of many *Hausbesitzer* in the First Curia to switch their support to the antisemites. Joseph Strobach, the replacement for Lueger as mayor in 1896–97, was vice-chairman of the Viennese *Hausherren* association when he won an elite position in the Christian Social party. Strobach brought with him impressive voting support from other sectors of the *Hausherren* as well.

These factors, together with the less industrialized nature of the Viennese economy, made it possible for the Viennese to create both sociologically and psycho-linguistically a *Mittelbürgertum* which in political terms occupied the middle and higher reaches of the Mittelstand. The structural-legal difference in franchise regulations between Vienna and Berlin also explained why the Progressive-Liberal party was able to retain control of the Berlin municipality until 1918, while the Liberals in Vienna suffered such ignominious defeats. The Second Curia in Vienna was far more mixed in income and status claims and more varied in social values than was the floating Second Class in Berlin. A more vigorous kind of party politics evolved in Vienna precisely because the civic culture required more management and direction owing to the less homogeneous structural basis for political privileges. In absolute terms the municipal political system of Berlin was more ''democratic'' since more citizens had the vote. But in Berlin a rather complacent ruling party could rely on two extremely narrow curias between 1860 and 1914. In Berlin political opposition had to come from the Social Democrats, since the structure of the municipal franchise dictated this option as the only feasible one. In

Vienna, where the Second Curia was a large, stable, and representative cross section of the Mittelstand (in Austrian terms), a non-Liberal bourgeois political movement, such as the Christian Socials, could succeed. Function followed form in Vienna's politics.

A final point of comparison between urban politics in Vienna and those practiced in Prussia lay in the significance of Vienna's *Bürgermeister* system. As noted earlier, both political parties placed great emphasis on retaining the tradition of an elective *Bürgermeister*.[194] In a strict sense this practice was not different from that of Berlin or Cologne, where the city assemblies also elected the mayor, subject to ultimate confirmation by the Imperial German government. A crucial difference between the Prussian and Austrian systems lay, however, in the fact that the position of *Bürgermeister* in Vienna was a local party office, that is, the mayor was a local notable politician, usually a lawyer or wealthy businessman who had no experience in the state administration. In Germany the position of *Oberbürgermeister* was one which usually demanded a long *cursus honorum* of proper state administrative experience. In Vienna the local Liberals and anti-Liberals took pride in the fact that their mayor was not connected with the state administration and was, thus, only accountable for his behavior to his political club. The maneuvers of the Liberals against the hapless Julius Newald and the uncreative Eduard Uhl demonstrated something of the kind of informal political accountability and independence from state bureaucracy which made the position of *Bürgermeister* so attractive in Vienna. When Lueger assumed the office of mayor, he became an executive of the *Reichshaupt- und Residenzstadt* who had an independent party-political base and who stressed that he was neither culturally nor politically affiliated with the Austrian *Beamten* ethos.

The Price Inflation of 1891–92

After the elections of 1891 the Liberal party prepared to integrate the suburbs into the city's administrative system. Before they were able to proceed with their long promised reorganization of the communal bureaucracy, events occurred in the economic sector which seized public attention. Beginning in the late spring and summer of 1891 the metropolitan economy suffered a mild commercial and provisioning crisis which grew worse as the winter approached. Cereal, bread, and fuel prices rose sharply from their 1889–90 levels. Retail prices during the last six months of 1891 for beef, pork, bread, mutton, and horse meat reached their zenith for the period 1886–94.[195] Investment in and the execution of public and private construction fell off in 1890–91, while the new transportation network for Vienna which promised to offer employment to thousands of semiskilled and skilled laborers was still only in the planning stages. The Lower Austrian Chamber of Commerce reported that export opportunities for Viennese goods did not improve immediately from the ending of the Rumanian tariff dispute, while the newly concluded trade treaties with Germany, Switzerland, and Italy were not approved until January 1892 and thus offered no immediate improvement over the trade situation of 1890.[196] For the thousands of artisan shops and plants in the city neither 1890 nor 1891 offered anything but the specter of a "vielfach traurigen Lage."[197] Unemployment during the harsh winter of 1891–92 proved exceptionally high (winter unemployment was a chronic feature of many seasonal Viennese industries even in good years).[198] In February 1892, 3,000 unemployed workers, including many women, met at Mandl's *Gasthaus* in Hernals and threatened to march on the *Rathaus* in protest over their misery.[199] Throughout the winter of 1891–92 the *Wärmestuben* were supplying an average of 8,000–9,000 people daily with free meals.[200] The food situation became most critical, however, in late February 1892 when for eight days the city authorities established distribution points where the thousands of unemployed might obtain free bread.[201]

The rise in food and fuel prices also produced reactions on the part of white collar employees, both in government service and in the private bureaucracies. In November 1891 a deputation of officials summoned courage to visit Ritter v Taussig of the *Österreichische Boden-Credit-Anstalt* to request emergency salary increases to cover the extraordinary rises in food and housing costs.[202] In some cases the inflation provoked or strengthened the organization of more aggressive professional associations. On 10 December 1891 over 600 officials of the city met to establish the *Verein der Beamten der Stadt Wien* which surpassed the older and smaller *Club der Conceptsbeamten* as a vigorous representative of municipal employees of all ranks and educational backgrounds.[203] Although the leaders of the *Verein* were jurists employed in the higher ranks of the *Magistrat*, they concluded that any organization which did not fight to improve the life situations of all the officials, whether they were of a *Concepts* status or not, would prove politically ineffective. The prime goal of the *Verein* was to provide the employees with greater collective leverage in bringing pressure to bear on Mayor Prix to fulfill his campaign promises of earlier in the year, but the force behind the *Verein* was the inflation in food prices.[204]

The unsettling conjunction of rising prices and aggravated unemployment of later 1891 became known in the public mind as the *Theuerung*. Numerous public organizations and legislative bodies drafted memorandums urging the government to take action against the price inflation.[205] A series of district consumer protest associations was established in Vienna in December 1891, the *Verein zur Verbilligung der Lebensmittel.*[206] The idea of a student *mensa* at the University of Vienna dated from the winter inflation of 1891–92.

Public pressure resulting from the inflation led to acrimonious recriminations in parliament in December 1891 between agrarian and urban political interests, the former blaming the Liberal city of Vienna and "Jewish" meat shippers for the rise in food prices, the latter demanding that the government end its protectionist tariff policies.[207] Erich Kielmansegg felt the situation serious enough to warrant a major statement to explain the inflation. Kielmansegg argued that the consumption tax reform had nothing to do with rising consumer prices.[208] Food prices had begun to climb as early as June 1891, and the new consumption tax rates, which might increase the relative burden of some foodstuffs in the suburban districts of the city, were not scheduled to go into effect until December 1891—a difference of six months. Kielmansegg's analysis was correct. Tariff disputes with the Balkan countries, temporary restrictions on meat imports from Galicia out of health considerations, a temporary drop in meat imports from Hungary to Lower Austria in 1891, the long-term decline in Alpine meat production—these factors contributed to the rise in retail meat prices in 1891.[209] Similarly, the dramatic upsurge in retail cereal and bread prices was caused by the rise in wholesale prices resulting from the harvest disasters of Russia in 1891 and from the poor showing of the Hungarian and Rumanian harvests of 1890–91.[210] Wine prices were inevitably affected by shortages brought about by the damage done by the phylloxera and peronospora.[211]

In the short run, Kielmansegg and the Liberals had little to worry about politically. The municipal and national elections in 1891 had been held early enough to allow voter opinion to be uninfluenced by the consumer hysteria of later 1891. Had the economy gone through the disruptions of 1891 and simply recovered, the political profit made by the antisemites with their accusations that the Liberals were to blame for the price rises would have been minimal. But other factors were soon brought to bear.

On 21 December 1891 the new tariff rates on the revised consumption tax were activated. These rates had a dual effect on the city's populace, depending on where one lived in Vienna. Because the new tax eliminated indirect taxation of bread, soap, eggs, and numerous other items in the older districts of the city, prices on these items gradually declined in the period 1892–93.[212] Thus, relatively speaking, the cost of living in these districts (First through Tenth) became slightly lower after 1892, although the cost of housing continued to surge. In the suburbs, however, a very different pattern of events occurred. After December 1891 consumers in the Eleventh through Nineteenth Districts were subjected to additional price increases to account for new consumption taxes on various kinds of meat and fowl, as well as beer, wine, and spirits. In many instances, moreover, local retailers raised their prices far beyond what they needed to cover the expenses of the new consumption taxes on goods which they brought into the city in bulk quantities. And some retailers even raised the prices of goods like dairy products which were not affected by the new taxes. The butchers' guild perpetrated a number of price abuses, leading Kielmansegg to consider executive sanctions against the organization's members. Even in the inner districts of the city, many butchers simply absorbed the savings provided to them by the new tax rates on meat and poultry as additional profit, instead of passing them on to their customers.[213] Housing costs, formerly more stable than those of the city, also began to soar as land values rose and as the kinds of new housing being constructed demanded more capital investment.

Because of the new *Verzehrungssteuer* and the way many merchants in the city reacted to the tax, the inflation of 1891 became for those living in the suburbs a quinquennial inflation. While the residents of the inner districts found some relief with the return of more modest wholesale prices in 1892 and with the discounts caused by the lower tax rates, residents in the former suburbs found themselves hit by a new, relative inflation in 1892 and again in 1893. The 1891 inflation and its aftermath in the outer districts set up a vocabulary of anxiety and deprivation which conditioned voter behavior in Vienna throughout the mid-1890s. The word *Theuerung* became a part of the daily individual and collective rhetoric of Viennese white collar groups on fixed incomes. Statistically, food prices fluctuated and, after 1893, even declined in some areas of the city, but in psychological terms the period 1891–95 was one of uninterrupted price inflation.[214]

To a certain extent the massive crescendo of complaints concerning this issue in the years 1891–95 reflected true social distress. Many individuals among the lower and middle suburban state officials, who had not enjoyed a salary raise since 1873 and whose financial worries were connected with their family responsibilities, felt that the inflation made already tenuous levels of financial security unbearable. In the course of the nineteenth century the Austrian officials had faced many economic crises to which the government failed to respond—those between 1800 and 1815 and between 1850 and 1859 were only the most extreme examples of a steady pattern of ill-treatment by the state of its officials. However, the inflation of 1891–92 was different from previous price inflations in the response to it by the petty and middle officialdom. For now the officials had a weapon which they could use against those who became the targets for blame: the privileged municipal and national vote. The decision of the German-speaking officials to desert the Liberal party between 1892 and 1896 was not simply owing to antisemitism. It involved a challenge to the Austrian state itself. Given the propensity of all Bürger groups in Vienna after 1890 to define their own interests as "progress" for society, while rejecting the egalitarianism of the Socialists, it was not surprising that *Beamten* groups should come to believe that Karl Lueger and his political movement could combine progress and privilege simultaneously. The idea of progress did not die with the Liberal party; it was simply (and brutally) diluted to fit the social-psychological interests of a wider section of the Austrian Bürgertum.

The Heritage of *Beamten* Unrest: Social Interest Politics after 1891

In May 1891, two months after the Reichsrat elections, the Liberal *Erster allgemeiner Beamten-Verein* pressured the Taaffe ministry into taking action on the complaints of the state officials. Although the association was dominated by the more senior members of the state bureaucracy, the *Verein* decided that the state of the economy necessitated a more active stance. Members of the group requested and obtained a personal audience with the emperor to present on behalf of the lower and middle ranks a petition containing most of the programmatic issues (salary raises, a *Dienstpragmatik,* pension benefits, etc.) around which much of the political wrangling of white collar politics in the 1890s centered.[215] Once the petition campaign had been initiated, there was no end to it. Within the next two years four separate "monster" petitions signed by thousands of state officials, plus dozens of petitions from local *Beamten* groups, were forwarded to parliament.[216] The Liberals ceased to be the principal advocates of the state employees in the parliament. Both the antisemites, especially Albert Gessmann, and the Young Czechs assumed a much more aggressive stance, sensing that a political gold mine lay before them. By 1892–93 Gessmann began to organize regular protest meetings for state and communal officials, urging them to take a more independent stance against the Liberals and condemning "capitalist plutocracy" for debasing their *geistige Arbeit.*

The government's response to the petition campaign was predictable and, for the Liberals, disastrous. After some delay a government bill was brought into parliament in early 1892 which proposed a one-time-only salary supplement for officials in the three lowest ranks, the total cost of which was set at 500,000 fl. Even this legislation was not sanctioned by the Emperor until late 1892. The antisemites quickly exploited its modest dimensions by summoning a rally of 2,000 state and communal officials to ridicule the bill.

On the municipal level the founding of the *Verein der Beamten der Stadt Wien* was a direct challenge to the Liberal regime in the city.[217] By late 1892 membership in the *Verein* had reached almost 700. That Mayor Prix distrusted the *Verein* was a sure sign that it was not simply a house associational organ of the Liberal party. Prix managed further to antagonize the city officials in 1892 with his decisions on the new *Rangclassen* system which had been promised during the 1891 elections. In June 1892 the City Council passed legislation providing for generous salary increases in the context of a new rank system which was similar to that used by the state bureaucracy.[218] But the hopes of the municipal employees were soon deflated, since the actual effect of the new salary legislation could not be measured until a second bill was passed, which reassigned the municipal officials in the new rank/salary system. The Liberals dragged their feet on this second and far more critical piece of legislation, and when Prix finally released it from the *Stadtrat* in November 1892, the bill was extremely unfavorable to the lower and middle ranks of the municipal bureaucracy.

In the same way, the period 1891–96 also constituted for the state employees in Vienna a decisive stage in their political experience. In late 1894 the state officials took an important step toward political power when the *Verein der Staatsbeamten Österreichs* was organized in Vienna.[219] This association was different in ethos from the older *Beamten-Verein*. In 1907 Victor Schidl, later a leader in the Austrian *Beamten* movement, noted that after 1894 the state employees stopped forwarding "hopes" or "pleas" to the government and began to draw up "demands." The change in language was significant.[220]

The *Verein* was organized and led by a different class of officials than that which ran the *Beamten-Verein*. Of the nine top leaders of the *Verein* in 1896, all came from the intermediate ranks of the state bureaucracy (five treasury officials, three post office officials, and one man connected with the state lottery). The *Verein* was far more aggressive in its language and behavior than the older group. Its newspaper, *Der Staatsbeamte,* avoided the kind of sweet, half-unctuous rhetoric of respectful loyalty so common in *Beamten* statements in the 1870s and 1880s. The power base of the *Verein* centered in the *Mittelschule*-educated employees and then spread up and down the ranks. These were men who were conscious of their superiority to the mere *Kanzlisten*. They valued their job security, but were also able to articulate their right to better treatment and higher salaries. They also had sufficient organizational sense to be able to express their discontent. By late 1896 the *Verein* claimed over 13,000 members and demonstrated its prowess in the autumn of 1896 by summoning dozens of local and regional *Beamten* congresses all over the monarchy.[221]

The inflation and disruption of the city's economy in 1891 were also a powerful stimulus of political unrest among salaried employee *(Angestellten)* groups who were not in the public service sector, but who were as fearful of proletarianization and status decline as were the state and communal officials. In April 1892 the antisemitic *Verband der Wiener Beamten* presented to parliament (through Albert Gessmann) a petition which paralleled the Liberal-organized petitions, but which differed in one important respect. The *Verband* petition dealt with the plight of the thousands of men employed in the state and private railways in Austria, concentrating on the needs of the officials of the railroads. The Liberal party was willing to support white collar officials in public service whose wages and benefits were paid from public tax resources. But in the case of the railway employees the issue was raised whether the Liberals would abandon the profit motive to assist Bürger voters in the employ of private businesses or corporations. The franchise in Vienna rested on the assumption that the Liberal party only needed to rely on the votes of a specific range of older Bürger occupations (such as the *Hausbesitzer* or the state officials), the support of which cost the Viennese business community nothing. With the development of large private commercial bureaucracies and with the massive growth of the railways, new occupations were created which did not easily fit into this traditional scheme. The Liberals were not anxious to move beyond their narrow definition of what constituted a politically respectable Bürger occupation. The Liberals thus left most of the railway employees to the Christian Socials and the Social Democrats, both of whom quickly moved into the ranks of the railway bureaucracies to recruit supporters for the time when universal suffrage might become a reality. The Christian Socials restricted their propaganda to the higher and middle ranks of the railway workers, while the Social Democrats cut across class and rank boundaries.[222] When the Social Democrats emerged victorious in the struggle for the railways by 1907, the basis for the unionization of white collar and other quasi-professional workers was clearly apparent, creating a precedent for a more radical structure of *Angestellten* politics.[223]

More central to the immediate fate of Liberal politics in Vienna was the radicalization of private commercial employees in the city after the inflation of 1891. Larger mercantile and commercial firms listed in the trade register belonged to the Liberal-oriented *Gremium der Wiener Kaufmannschaft,* a professional merchants' association with a long and distinguished tradition. In 1890–91 the *Gremium* had approximately 4,000 member firms, of which perhaps 300 were active in the association's politics.[224] The other major commercial association, aside from the suburban merchants' associations of Sechshaus and Hernals, was the

Genossenschaft der Gemischtwarenhändler und Verschleisser, whose members owned shops of a more modest size than those belonging to the *Gremium.* After 1893 the antisemites won control of this association, putting the resentment of the general stores against the Jewish peddlers in the city to good use.[225] That some of the storekeepers were former *Handlungsgehilfen* (salesmen or retail clerks) who began their careers working for the larger firms belonging to the *Gremium* but who were forced by economic necessity to strike out on their own with insufficient capital did not lead to high mutual regard between the two groups.[226]

Within this network of competing commercial associations, several classifications of private employees existed, whose common interest was their fear of proletarianization and their obsession with personal security. Higher ranking (and older) white collar employees with a set of specific commerical skills, such as accountants and senior clerks who were employed by the firms of the *Gremium,* usually joined the *Wiener kaufmännischen Verein,* a social and welfare organization founded in 1870. In 1890 the *Verein* had approximately 2,500 members and enjoyed close ties with the *Gremium.*[227] Many of the larger firms belonging to the *Gremium* also belonged to the *Verein* in a patron status; the purpose of the *Verein* was to encourage a patriarchal, nonadversary relationship between the higher commercial employees and their employers.

The principal interest of these higher ranking employees in the early 1890s was their social welfare rights, especially an adequate pension system. Neither the petitions of the *Privatangestellten* to the Reichsrat nor their journal, the *Kaufmännische Zeitschrift,* indicated any interest in salary or promotion reforms. The traditions of private commerce dictated that all arrangements for salary level and promotion within the commercial and industrial bureaucracies be left to market forces and to individual negotiations between the *Chef* and his employees. Because market determination of salaries worked relatively well (salaries in these occupations seem to have been slightly ahead of similar ranks in the state bureaucracy)[228] in the period before 1890, the kind of collective dissatisfaction and radicalization of opinion which occurred among the officials was not yet present here. Also, the age structure within these ranks made them more comparable to the higher ranks of the state bureaucracy, where radicalism was less prominent. Younger men entering a higher commercial occupation would often serve for a number of years as *Handlungsgehilfen,* as *Praktikanten,* or in some other modest jobs before winning promotion to a level where they would be interested in joining the *Verein.* The unsuccessful visit paid to Ritter v Taussig in 1891, however, by a delegation of his bank employees hoping for salary raises indicated that the inflation of 1891 had not left the *Privatangestellten* untouched.

And the insistent demand of the private officials for pension reforms in the early 1890s foreshadowed a more articulate and confident movement among the private employees after 1900 to secure privileged social rights.[229] Until after 1900 private officials lagged behind their counterparts in government because of their timidity and occupational conservatism; but the lag was not a permanent feature of Austrian white collar politics.

The other major employee organization in Vienna was the association of *Handlungsgehilfen* (or *Commis*), which was legally a part of the *Gremium* of the Viennese merchants. The occupation of *Handlungsgehilfen* was traditionally one in which a young man, usually of humble social origin, decided to apprentice himself to a merchant and then work as a shop salesman or junior office clerk in order to learn the business and eventually be able to control the business or, at least, to occupy a higher and more respected position within it.[230] The life of the *Commis* was always a problematic one with low pay and long working hours, but the prospect of future security and the fact that being a *Commis* was a relatively honored and respected role within the traditional merchant's hierarchy and that the position offered exposure to tasks of increasing responsibility made the position a tolerable and even desirable one. To be a *Commis*, whether this involved serving as a junior clerk or a salesman or some combination of both, was definitely not to be a worker. Precisely this status differentiation between *Handlungsgehilfen* and the workers (or, in commercial terms, the *Handlungsdiener*) made the job attractive.

The commercial revolution of the second half of the nineteenth century in Vienna saw, however, a consistent devaluation of the honor and the security attached to the occupation of the *Handlungsgehilfen*. With the growth of larger commercial bureaucracies, labor specialization meant that the average *Commis* rarely acquired the skills needed to establish his own firm. And with the growing size and capital investment level of mercantile firms and with the increasing competition among larger firms it soon became an illusion for the typical *Commis* to hope to assemble the capital needed to own his own business. This development had numerous consequences which undermined the position of the *Commis*. The *Wiener Handelsakademie*, which required *Mittelschule* training and forced the applicant to pay high tuition rates, trained hundreds of the sons of wealthy Gentile and Jewish families to take over the family business or to serve as a senior employee in someone else's firm.[231] For the apprentices of the member firms, the time spent in gaining what was formerly a valued level of professional skills seemed increasingly in the 1880s to have been a bad investment.[232] Many *Commis* found themselves assigned to jobs within the merchant firms which involved manual labor, a serious infringement on the ideal of the nonworker status of the *Handlungsgehilfen*.[233] Most significantly, the numerical growth of the ranks of the *Commis* was far out of proportion to what the Viennese market could absorb, especially during the business depression of the 1870s and 1880s. The number of apprentices enrolled in the evening schools of the *Gremium* increased from 800 in 1885 to 1,700 in 1900, a growth which invited disaster for the group as a whole.[234] This disproportionate increase was true only for Vienna; other cities in the monarchy suffered from shortages of *Commis*.[235]

The attractiveness of the metropolitan center for young men seeking a secure road to bourgeois prosperity was overpowering. But so too was the disillusionment and frustration when the majority learned that the career of a *Commis* was a dead end. The possibilities of social mobility beyond the career seemed to close off just as the resources of bourgeois status respectability within the career seemed to disappear. That many of the young aspiring *Gehilfen* in the commercial world were poorer Jews desperately seeking a first tentative step toward economic integration into bourgeois society made the surge of antisemitism among Gentile *Handlungsgehilfen* intelligible.

The career of a *Commis* was not influenced, however, simply by the structures of great mercantile capital in the city. The second half of the century also saw the decline of open-air food markets in many sections of the city and the growth of hundreds of small- and medium-sized grocery and general goods stores.[236] There were 3,500 of these shops in the older ten districts of Vienna alone. Many of them prospered, but their prosperity was based on the exploitation of their small staffs of *Gehilfen* and apprentices, who were forced to work seventeen- or eighteen-hour days for very low wages. Many of the shopkeepers tried to avoid hiring *Gehilfen* at all, preferring to rely on the less expensive labor of apprentices. And when *Commis* did find employment in these shops, they knew that they had sunk to the lowest possible level of bourgeois respectability. Their jobs were little different from those of the *Handlungsdiener:* only a world of hope and illusion separated the two. And the ill treatment and exploitation extended to these men (they numbered in the thousands) made one very important political reality eminently clear to the *Handlungsgehilfen* by the later 1890s—a Christian Social grocery shop owner was no more sensitive to their aspirations than was a Liberal merchant.[237]

The organization of these lowest ranking commercial employees began in 1887–88 when the government forced the *Gremium* of merchants to organize the journeymen's association and the insurance society required by the reforms of 1883.[238] In late 1886 a group of antisemitic *Commis* under the leadership of Julius Axmann, Hermann Bielohlawek, and Heinrich Frass organized the *Verein österreichischer Handels-Angestellter* and waged a successful struggle to elect anti-Liberal candidates to the executive board of the *Gehilfen* association. Between 1887 and 1898, when Axmann lost control of the association to the Social Democrats, the anti-Liberals maintained a tight hold on the organizational resources of the *Gehilfen*.[239]

Axmann and his colleagues spent the first several years of their activity setting up the association as well as a fortnightly newspaper. In March 1890, however, they formulated a six-point reform program to which they hoped the *Gremium* would agree in an effort to better the situation of the majority of the *Commis*. This program included the limitation of the working day to fourteen hours for branches of commerce dealing with food provisioning and to eleven hours for other mercantile firms, the regulation of the use of apprentices in commercial establishments, the establishment of a certificate of competency as a prerequisite for operaing a mercantile trade (an attack on the privileged students of the *Handelsakademie* who might not have worked as *Commis* before entering the ranks of the management of a firm), and the prohibition of all Sunday labor. Both the program and the general strategy of Axmann's *Verein* betrayed a moderation which could be explained only in terms of the problematic social and ideological assumptions of the *Commis* themselves. Throughout the negotiations with the *Gremium* (indeed, well into the 1890s) Axmann and his colleagues insisted that they wanted peaceful cooperation and harmony with their *Chefs*. Although theoretically anti-semitic (many of these men worked for Jewish merchants—Axmann himself was employed by Leo Pollak, one of the wealthy Jewish leaders of the *Gremium*), there were functional limits to the reality of their antisemitism. Their political language tended to exceed social reality (or assist them in avoiding it), rather than reflecting operative social hatreds. Axmann repeatedly stated that "we in no way wish to injure the interests of our employers, but rather desire to cooperate with them, since we are very much aware that any injury to their interests would also affect our own interests in the most extreme fashion."[240] Axmann realized that the image of the *Commis* as "junior merchants" who belonged to a training group for the future Viennese Bürgertum could be sustained only if the *Commis* reaffirmed the customary patriarchal relationship which had once existed between the *Chefs* and *Commis*, even if the *Chefs* in this case happened to be Jews. For this reason the leaders of the *Verein* went to great lengths to avoid having their association viewed as a labor union—the rhetoric of their professional newspaper, the *Wiener Kaufmännische Blätter*, consistently emphasized the quasi-professional status of the *Commis* and the difference between them and the *Handlungsdiener*.[241] To make the image of a *Commis* as a proto-Bürger credible, the antisemitic *Handlungs-gehilfen* found themselves having to behave like Bürger. Illusion outran the reality of social immobility and for some years served as an uneasy substitute for it.

The *Gremium* did not reply for over a year to the memorandum of proposed reforms forwarded to it by the *Commis*. On 21 May 1891, a few months before the onset of the inflation of 1891, the executive board of the *Gremium* called a full assembly of its membership to consider the *Verein*'s requests. After some vigorous debate the *Gremium* rejected most of the *Verein*'s points.[242] Axmann met with little more encouragement among the general store owners: they too were unsympathetic with the *Commis*'s goals. With the inflation of 1891 Axmann felt more pressure from his constituents to win some meaningful concessions to improve their salary and work conditions, but the stubbornness of the *Gremium* made a con-ciliatory approach impossible. Not surprisingly, Axmann and his col-leagues eventually decided to exploit antisemitism as a way of expressing their frustration. Criticism of "big capital" and "dirty competition" soon found its way into the newspaper of the *Gehilfen*.[243]

The lack of cooperation by the merchants and the grocery shop owners with the *Handlungsgehilfen* in the early 1890s had fateful consequences for the history of all three of the major political movements in Vienna before 1900. The Christian Socials were able to coopt the *Handlungs-gehilfen* into a makeshift labor wing of their party during the mid-1890s, running both Axmann and Bielohlawek as successful Fifth Curia candi-dates against the Social Democrats in the national elections of 1897. The leadership of the *Verein,* unable to resolve its conflict with the *Gremium* with its own resources and unwilling to deny the theoretical possibility of labor cooperation (for to do otherwise would be to run the risk of being accused of Social Democracy), took the only course open to them: they joined that political party in Vienna which encompassed both Bürger and *Kleinbürger* interests with a language of social cooperation, a party an-chored in the votes of the lower and middle mercantile interests in Vienna, but which claimed to be able to reconcile in some magical fashion such Bürger interests with those of all employee groups which were first willing to deny that they would behave like workers. The Christian So-cials had no desire to pacify workers; but they could make a relatively convincing case for their interest in the fate of young, suffering proto-bourgeois types. By converting the *Commis* into the mythical likeness of the youthful social hopes and achievements of their own voters, the lead-ers of the Christian Social coalition sought to make them a credible part of that coalition. The *Commis* were allowed into this coalition of Bürger hope and illusion on borrowed time and on future credit, as it were, not for what they were, but for what they wanted to be and what they claimed to be. More than this Lueger asked of no man.

The problem with this political strategy was that it did not respond to the real, material interests of the *Commis* any more than did the attempt of Axmann to negotiate with the Liberal-controlled *Gremium* in the early 1890s. The first allegiances of the Christian Socials were always with the dealers, shopkeepers, and merchants of the city, not with their employees. For Axmann and his colleagues to follow the Christian Social prescriptions about social harmony and class conciliation meant that they would achieve little or nothing in concrete, material concessions. But for many in the ranks of the *Commis,* especially those who were better situated (a solid minority of the movement) or those who valued their self-conceptions as poor, yet respectable Bürger, Axmann's solution was a long-term possibility well beyond 1900.

Beginning in the early 1890s, however, a second option became available in the person of Fritz Austerlitz and his Social Democratic *Commis* movement. Austerlitz, who later became the fiery chief editor of the *Arbeiter-Zeitung,* preached a doctrine of class struggle among the Viennese *Gehilfen,* urging them to abandon their Bürger pretensions and accept the reality of their worker status.[244] It was significant, however, that the Social Democrats were able to take control of the *Gehilfen* association only in 1898 after they had won a court case allowing them to enroll the thousands of *Handlungsdiener* in the association. With the votes of the *Commis* alone, Austerlitz would never have won control of the assembly. The psychological privileges of the *Commis* were not easily abandoned, even in the face of material deprivations. What the Social Democrats and the Christian Socials had to learn after 1900 was that *Handlungsgehilfen* were neither Bürger nor workers, but rather an occupation with a new cultural mentality which was far more complicated than such traditional terms could do justice to. Even after the Socialists had succeeded in unionizing many of these men, they did not behave like and could not be treated like factory workers. The beginning of a modern employee mentality, which did not fit the preconceptions of the Social Democrats or the antisemites, dated from the early 1890s.

The years between 1890 and 1895 thus became for Viennese white collar groups of a variety of cultural traditions and economic bases a crucible of rapid social change from which they emerged in a radicalized and collectively organized state. Having reformed the political resources in the municipality of Vienna in conjunction with the formation of a great metropolitan area, the Liberal party committed itself to a more dangerous strategy among key voter groups from which there was to be no turning back. The elections of 1891 created in turn the clear preconditions for the evolution of a competitive, two-party political system in the city which invited the Christian Socials to win the political loyalties of Bürger voters within the privileged curias. Potential bourgeois voters such as the commercial employees, who could not yet vote but who might serve as an important buffer should the Christian Socials ever have to face the Social Democrats in open electoral competition, also merited cultivation.

The price inflation of 1891–92 upset Liberal political calculations and offered the antisemites a rich panorama of social unrest to exploit in the four years before the next Second Curia election in 1895. Overshadowing all of the calculations of both the Liberals and the antisemites lay the specter of a reformed and growing Social Democratic movement which made very clear by 1894 that the system of privileged political resources to which both the Liberals and the antisemites had become accustomed by 1890 was living on borrowed time.

The decade of the 1890s in Vienna was revolutionary precisely because it was the only period in modern Austrian political history in which the social resources, the cultural values, and the economic and political interests of three distinct, yet socially interlocked political movements came face to face in unrelieved political combat. That the Christian Socials overcame the hegemonic position of Viennese Liberalism (in 1895–96) immediately before Social Democracy broke through the first barriers of political privilege in the monarchy in 1897 left the antisemites with the awesome dilemma of defining the very nature and structure of their party both to match the energy of the Social Democrats and to preserve the valued Bürger traditions of the Austrian Liberals. After 1895 the Christian Socials were forced to play both roles—the privileged Bürger and the mass social—in a confused and confusing pattern of party-political behavior which was not clearly resolved even by 1914. The decision of the Christian Socials in 1899–1900 to retain the general concept of a curial municipal franchise structure in Vienna, with some rank modifications and with the addition of a small Fourth Curia which was little more than a sop to the proletariat, indicated how deeply committed the Christian Socials were to Bürger privilege in Viennese politics. The beginning of this process of ideological and political evolution for the anti-Liberals, who soon found themselves defending much of the Liberal heritage against a party which recognized neither *Stand* nor *Eigentum,* lay in the decisive economic and administrative events of 1890–91.

On the other hand, in assuming this mediatory role between mass social interest groups and the older traditions of Bürger privilege in the city, the Christian Socials did not sacrifice the primacy of party politics to a rigid, nonpluralistic interest-politics. Karl Lueger was neither the servant of the Imperial or city bureaucracy nor the lackey of the white collar or artisan interest groups. He cultivated these groups and earned their support, yet he insisted that his new movement continue to emulate the older tradition of petty notable and district club politics in Vienna in its exercise of political and administrative power. Well after 1900, when the Christian Socials had become the principal spokesmen for many of these groups in the Reichsrat and Landtag, a healthy tension was maintained between the organized interest groups and the party's political infrastructure. Each of the groups had identifiable representatives within the party, but none of these leaders could ensure the predictability of the party's performance on any given issue. And, more important, it was Lueger's custom to overlap such representation—Weiskirchner, who should have become the principal spokesman for the officials, ended up as the party's *Referent* on general economic and trade matters. Leopold Tomola, who initially represented the schoolteachers, eventually played a number of diverse and powerful roles within the *Stadtrat,* many of which had little to do with public education. Because municipal politics under the Christian Socials was still based on a local club structure of petty notables from a variety of occupations, the party maintained a certain if occasionally ambiguous distance from any single occupational interest group. That many of these interests were not exclusive or inclusive—a party leader could be a *Hausherr,* a *Stadtrat,* and an artisan or an official at the same time—lessened the separation between the groups themselves and reduced the effect of any single interest group on the party's general behavior. Ernst Schneider's schizophrenic attempt to be both the party's local czar of artisan affairs and its domestic advocate of a rabid brand of racial antisemitism tended to diffuse his impact in both areas. The success of Christian Socialism lay in its social pluralism and flexible political structure, which managed and directed but which was never absolutely controlled by any single element.

The problem of an inflexible, antipluralistic *Interessenpolitik,* which recent German political historians have seen as a crucial (and harmful) feature of later Imperial German politics on the national level (Dirk Stegmann, Heinrich A. Winkler, Hans-Ulrich Wehler, etc.) was not a critical issue in the new Christian Social political model.[245] In Vienna a relatively flexible tradition of club politics and party competition, in which political power was convertible into administrative control, led all competing political elites in the city's history to value their independence against any single occupational or economic interest group. In this sense, the Christian Socials under Lueger shared, almost without knowing it, in the older

Liberal notion of political universalism, just as the Liberals borrowed techniques of social interest representation from the Christian Socials.

The Christian Social party was a party which based itself on a middle class *Sammlungspolitik,* but Lueger and Gessmann never allowed the party's occupational constituencies to dominate its policy development after 1896 in an inflexible fashion. Once social interest had been articulated into political power through the electoral process, Lueger was not about to allow any group to dictate his political behavior. Even the powerful *Hausherren* associations found that the city government under the Christian Socials would not fulfill all of their preelection demands. The city avoided direct confrontation with the *Hausherren;* it rarely attempted policies which were directly injurious to their fundamental needs. But a review of the *Hausherren* electoral programs of the mid-1890s and city housing policy after 1896 would show that the Christian Socials were ultimately no more sympathetic than the Liberals had been to the most extreme demands of the property owners. If the Christian Social City Council was ruled after 1900 by an oligarchy controlled by a small party elite (which it was), it was an oligarchy of ward politicians and machine professionals, not of interest group representatives per se. This conclusion is altered (but not contradicted) only by the behavior of the growing force of agrarian representatives in the party after 1907. In Vienna itself, however, the City Council for all of its other imperfections never became what Max Weber once referred to as a *Banausenparlament,* serving interest groups on one side and meekly submitting to the entrenched power of a nonpolitical professional bureaucracy on the other. With Lueger the professionalization of party politics matured in the city, a politics all the more vital and all the more potent because of its simultaneous connection with *and* control over the rising wave of professional interest group politics.

6

The Collapse of the Liberals and the Antisemitic Conquest of Vienna, 1893–97

The city of Vienna after 1892 was dramatically influenced by the contingencies of national politics. During the 1870s the Liberal ministry had left the city in a state of protected (and protracted) isolation. It did little for the city in providing additional financial resources, but it did little to injure the city's political or internal administrative autonomy. The prestige of Mayor Cajetan Felder ensured Vienna against serious meddling in its affairs by the state and its bureaucrats. Vienna's role in national Liberal politics before 1879 was never sufficiently prominent for ministerial Liberals devising specific party-political strategies to give it more than secondary attention. Vienna was the bastion of Democracy, with the exception of the safe Liberal seats of the Innere Stadt and the Leopoldstadt; and the inherent regionalism of the Liberal party and its lack of a central party bureaucracy, which, if located in Vienna, might have enhanced the city's role within the party, made the city simply one reservoir of Liberal voters among many. Some high Liberals came from Vienna or Lower Austria (Glaser, Suess, Herbst later in his career, etc.), but the basic, formative control of the party was not in the hands of the Viennese delegation. Vienna and Lower Austria played a much more prominent role in the Progressive party movement, and had the Progressives survived the Liberal collapse in 1879, Vienna might have counted for something in orthodox Liberal terms. As it was, the iron-fisted control exercised by Felder over his *Mittelpartei* gave the Liberal ministry no excuse to worry about the reliability of the city. That Felder abstained from claiming a seat in the Abgeordnetenhaus (a practice his successors Uhl, Prix, and Grübl continued) meant that the local Liberals did not try to use the potentially powerful resources of the city to dominate Liberal politics or national policy. Liberal passivity toward Vienna is important in comprehending the fear which Karl Lueger inspired in 1895–96. For Lueger presented a novel assemblage of local, regional, and national power which would be sustained and operated simultaneously. For all their rhetoric of centralism, the Austrian Liberals were always a regionally organized party. There was some "Vienna versus the provinces" rhetoric in the party in the 1860s and 1870s, but this never had a fundamentally divisive effect on party affairs. The diffusion of Liberal organization to the *Land* level and below gave the Liberals tactical flexibility and ideological tolerance, but it also inclined them to select their top leaders because of the moral force and national prestige they possessed (Herbst, the younger Plener, etc.) and not because of the power they derived from a massive, local party-political base. Felder had such a base, and he dominated not only Viennese, but also Lower Austrian politics for two decades. But he deliberately refused to extend it to the national level and make Vienna the basis of Liberalism in an urban hegemonic mode. Vienna may have been *primus inter pares*—the debates on the *Verzehrungssteuer* illustrated the artificial affection which *all* Liberals displayed for Vienna against Dunajewski and Taaffe—but the city itself was not a bureaucratized force in national politics under the Liberals. When Lueger was forced into the opposition so early in his career, he had the opportunity to construct a political movement which began in Vienna, but which soon was prepared to exercise national claims to power as well, resting upon his Viennese base. Lueger's integration of the city as a definable political culture into the national system, through the mediation of the Christian Social party elite, was one of the most revolutionary aspects of his program after 1897.

Under the Taaffe regime the city's political culture gradually shifted to a more conflict-oriented variety of Mittelstand politics in which older Bürger political issues were fused with new social bourgeois interest demands. The change began with Taaffe's enfranchisement of the lower levels of the urban Bürgertum in 1882 and 1885. Taaffe's tolerance of movements which would disrupt the city's political equilibrium shifted the course of Viennese politics to a more competitive dimension. The government's concession to the German Liberals in 1890–91 of consumption tax reforms had equally disruptive and unpredictable effects. Metropolitan Vienna was still under their control after the crucial City Council elections of April 1891, but social issues had been raised and Bürger interest groups aroused which might very well return to haunt the Liberals *and* the government later in the decade. Under both the Liberal and the conservative regimes of the 1870s and 1880s Vienna reacted to a relatively stable and unified, if at times hostile, political direction from above. Politics at the national level, while not always sympathetic to the city's interests, was at least predictable and stable.

The period after 1892 saw quite the opposite development in Vienna's relations to the state. For the first time in fifteen years the city faced a ministry which was *overtly* politicized and which claimed active, ministerial responsibility in a multiparty coalition. The Liberal-Clerical coalition after 1893 surpassed Taaffe's Iron Ring in that it was not simply a parliamentary coalition, but a political ministry as well. For the Liberals especially, with their lack of experience in working within multiparty parliamentary coalitions, public accountability within a politicized ministerial framework was both a great opportunity and a grave danger. Unless the end justified the means they might pay dearly for their loss of anticlerical virtue. The inherent weakness of the coalition was that it allowed a wide range of national issues (from *Beamten* salaries to tax reform to franchise reform) to drift without meaningful direction or accomplishment. This left the Liberals with little to show for their ideological sacrifice of October 1893.

The relationship between the city and the state became more crucial during this period for two reasons: not only was the disorganization of political power on the national level an open invitation for social radicals in the city to pressure and embarrass the government on a variety of issues, but the city itself became by the early 1890s the center point for national attention on a vast range of explicit social and social-class issues which had little to do with the nationality question. The city's political life became an ongoing microcosm of larger social struggles throughout the monarchy which in other areas were obscured by the ideological potency of the nationality problem. Not only did Austria lack a variety of large urban political cultures for comparative purposes (Prague was so engulfed in the problem of nationalism that secular social issues tended to be less apparent), but the rise of a powerful Social Democratic movement within the state's only significant metropolitan center inevitably enhanced the role of the city in national policy affairs. Victor Adler's assumption of control of the Ring in November 1905 was vastly more important than SPD agitation in Berlin at the same time, at least in symbolic terms. The new street tactics of the Social Democrats in 1893–94 were merely the first installment of a movement to expose the ineptness and indecision of the coalition's leaders. For all of his sphinxlike calculations Taaffe had had the virtue of ostensible disinterest in party-political calculations. He was, as he constantly stressed, a *Kaiserminister*. But the leaders who dominated Austrian politics after his fall were men of deeply vested interests, whose political privileges were seriously threatened on the national level by the electoral demands of the Austrian Social Democrats. This piecemeal politicization of ministerial decision making after 1893 improved little with the fall of the coalition and the coming of Badeni. Indeed, the standard wisdom about the "depoliticization" of Austria after 1896 needs a serious reassessment. The whole period between 1897 and 1914 saw a new integration of party politics into the Imperial government, often in subtle and innovative ways. Although Badeni styled himself as the "strong man" who would stand above the parties—he would outdo Taaffe by not even assembling a permanent parliamentary majority behind him—Badeni quickly found himself pandering to the larger voting blocs in the Reichsrat on an issue-by-issue basis. Badeni's desperate moves in November 1895 and his ultimate concession of Vienna to Lueger were the actions of a man at a loss for meaningful options, a man caught between the residual power of the Liberals and others who represented the 1867 system and the new power of special interest forces in the city who revived the promises and illusions of 1848. The Christian Socials and the Social Democrats had this in common in 1895: both looked to cultural and ideological models which were deeply impressed on the Austrian political conscience in 1848, which the Liberals had refused to implement or implement properly.

In this political environment the rise of the Young Czech movement and the social disruptions which followed in Bohemia in 1891–93 played a crucial disequilibrating role. Not only was the government unable to respond effectively to Bürger unrest in Vienna, but its principal attentions were often deflected to the north—to Bohemia and Moravia, where the Liberals had such a great strategic and moral stake. Lueger and his movement in Vienna often seemed an annoyance, an untimely yet not mortal threat with merely a handful of delegates in parliament to cause trouble. The Liberal party swung between overconfidence and despair, relying on the traditional loyalties of Viennese Bürger voters to keep it in power in the capital while trying desperately to resolve the nationality question in Bohemia. Lueger not only represented the rise of bourgeois social protest in class and occupational terms, but also showed that the city of Vienna as a corporate entity did count for something in the dynamics of national politics. The older Liberals had been so concerned with protecting the city against the Imperial Verwaltung that they underestimated the potential of an aggressive urban politics. Lueger retained Liberal ideals of the city's autonomy, but he enhanced them by confronting and challenging the Imperial government, using Vienna itself as his weapon.

Given the opportunities offered by the decline of a stable ministry, the Christian Socials were perhaps bound to prosper. Any group with sufficient nerve, bravado, and financial backing might hope to win at least some public support by drawing comparisons between itself and the coalition parties. But the question is not simply why the Christian Socials won in 1895–96, but why they did so on such an impressive scale. How are we to account for the rapid and almost painless success which the Christian Socials achieved by April 1896, especially in view of the party's unspectacular performance in the local elections of 1891? Was this owing to a radical change in strategy and campaign organization, in leadership style and public opinion manipulation? Did Lueger's political language suddenly take on a certain demagogic word magic? Lueger's "charisma" was of little use to the party in the Council elections of 1891; did it suddenly become effective by 1895? Or were there other factors at work which enabled the party to pull off one of the truly stunning political feats in modern Austrian politics? If we may term the party a quasi-mass party by 1896, did this imply its complete abandonment of traditional Liberal political practices and cultural concepts?

The success Lueger and his colleagues achieved by 1896 hinged on factors which surpassed leadership style and campaign practices, although careful attention must be given to the innovations the party introduced into Viennese politics before the divisive campaign year of 1895 was over. Two other themes demand greater attention in this period: the relationship of the party to the new set of social issues generated in wider sectors of the Viennese Bürgertum, a Bürgertum shocked, as it was, by the rise of Adler's Social Democratic party and hungry for self-enhancing public policy adjustments; and, more important, the crucial relationship of the Imperial state to the whole system of competitive public politics in late-nineteenth-century Austria. The first set of issues provided the substance of Christian Social politics between 1892 and 1897, but the second gave to these issues a reasonable and, indeed, almost a predictable chance of success. Badeni's sudden reversal by April 1896 on the acceptability of Lueger as mayor of Vienna suggested important and far-reaching differences in Badeni's mode of rule from that of Taaffe and his predecessors, changes which were to have long-run ramifications on the future relationship between competitive politics and administrative rule in the late Imperial period. Because the demands of the two key Bürger voter groups which controlled the Second and First Curias, the officials and the *Hausherren,* were not absurdly inflated (as were those of the Third Curia artisans) and because they could not simply be dismissed as the product of demagogic irrationality, the period after 1892 assumed a very different real-political cast from that of the formative period of Viennese antisemitism in the mid-1880s. The Christian Socials were playing for higher stakes, and the government gradually realized that it was facing a massive revolt of bourgeois society against both Liberal inertia and Socialist egalitarianism. At the same time, it was precisely because the government was forced within two years to rearticulate and redesign its attitudes about administrative autonomy and party politics on local and regional levels that it could venture to greater gambles on the national level in 1897. Badeni's baptism of fire in public office was not his language ordinances, but the Lueger confirmation controversy. The Lueger controversy was more than a battle for Vienna. It was a test case of and a model for the workability of the Austrian political system.

The Coalition and Decline of Austrian Liberalism, 1893–95

The Liberal Dilemma

The fate of the Liberals between 1892 and 1895 must be considered on the national and municipal levels of politics. Long before October 1893 the leaders of the United German Left had wanted to establish links between their party and the Imperial government.[1] Following the elections of 1891 Ernst v Plener and other top Liberals had discussed the possibility of a revision of the parliamentary base of Taaffe's coalition. The Liberals' strategy was to pressure Taaffe to exclude the Czechs and to redesign his ministry to include Liberal representatives. Although the Liberals eventually sent Kuenburg into the Cabinet as *Landsmannminister* and offered Taaffe informal support in parliament up to December 1892, Plener's desire for a full share of ministerial power was never fulfilled. Neither the Clericals nor the Poles were interested in such an arrangement in 1891 or 1892, and Taaffe himself had grave doubts about the willingness of Plener to play a "nonparty" role.[2] When Taaffe intimated in November 1892 that he would not push the Bohemian *Ausgleich* through over the objections of the Czechs, he was also killing off any residual Liberal hopes that he would compromise with the German Liberals against Slavic political interests.[3] The Liberals were too accustomed to combine parliamentary and ministerial privilege, based on their experience from the 1870s, for Taaffe's taste.[4]

Taaffe was both prudent and correct, for the pre-1893 political situation did reflect a relative balance of power in national Austrian politics. Taaffe's attempt to rule above the parties on the ministerial level while seeking a firm support on the parliamentary level was appropriate for a political system operating on such narrow social terms and in the midst of such social and national turmoil. Although Plener would scarcely have admitted it, the role of oppositional virgin, attacked by the wicked Machiavellian, suited the Liberals rather well in the 1880s. Once the Liberals had relinquished power because of their own feuds in 1879, they lived in a self-created world of political deprivation, but one which easily sustained their illusions about themselves. Not until after 1890 did the truly desperate plight of the Austrian Liberals become apparent to the participants themselves. By returning to power in October 1893 (following the crisis provoked by the Steinbach-Taaffe franchise reform proposal), they placed themselves in a hopelessly defensive situation in which their pretense about the perfect harmony between their party and the state (the

Liberals as the *regierungsfähige Partei* par excellence) became both archaic and dangerous. Rather than dominating the government, the Liberals became simply one self-interested political group in a multiparty
competition after 1893. Rarely was the burden of discontinuity greater
than that experienced by the Austrian Liberals between 1879 and 1893.

The later Taaffe era was the great turning point for Liberalism in Austria. Not only did these years witness the rise of anti-Liberal bourgeois
parties and the collapse of the Bohemian *Ausgleich* negotiations, but they
witnessed the gradual loss of faith and mission among the Liberals themselves. The Liberals finally realized that the centralized state could exist
without the services of the party which had designed it, explaining
perhaps their willingness to accept a partial share of power in 1893. Karl
Lichnowsky, the German first secretary in Vienna and a perceptive observer of events, noted that the Liberals faced a crisis in self-definition:
the party no longer had an ideal for which to fight.[5] Their basic civil
libertarian and political-structural program of 1867 had largely been
fulfilled. Individual civil rights, within a general bourgeois environment,
were safely ensconced in the state political system. The Verwaltung had
come to accept the constitutional state and its parties. Liberals like
Herbst and the younger Plener never felt comfortable with the ideal of an
aggressive, strident German nationalism. To the extent that their more
traditional neo-Josephist statism was incompatible with such nationalism,
they were usually inclined to choose the former over the latter. Unlike
late-nineteenth-century Prussian Liberals, they had a very difficult time in
using the national question in a collective, self-definitional mode.
Nationalism (so many of them felt) meant federalism and "clericalism" at
best; at worst it might lead to the political fragmentation of the monarchy.
More pragmatically, a strident nationalism would put their own party in a
parity situation with other Austrian political groups, an intolerable situation for men who felt that in moral terms the Liberals were better than the
"others" of Hapsburg society.

The daring attempt of Taaffe in October 1893 to move beyond the
Bürgertum in an effort to bring flexibility into the increasingly polarized
electoral system was an important signal that his own strategy from the
1880s—enlarging the political bourgeoisie by enfranchising its lowest
elements—had failed its ultimate test. The reforms of 1882 and 1885 had
crippled the Liberals, but also enhanced movements like the Young
Czechs. Rarely did a successul tactical maneuver have such devastating
strategic implications.

The hysterical outrage felt by Plener and the Liberals in October 1893
cannot be properly understood unless the categorically anti-Bürger thrust
of Steinbach's reform bill is appreciated. The 1882 and 1885 suffrage

reforms did not undercut the unitary Bürgertum as an entity apart from the "masses" of society. Indeed, at least one party—the Christian Socials—emerged from these reforms still able to define itself in terms of the old Liberal Bürger ideal, albeit on somewhat broader and more generous terms. The projected reform of 1893 was, however, fundamentally different. Count Kálnoky, in sympathy with the interests of the Liberal party, realized this change immediately and angrily rebuked Taaffe for it.[6] When Taaffe sought to eliminate privileged curial voting in urban and rural areas and disassociate tax levels from voting rights, he was directly attacking the Bürgertum itself and calling into question thirty years of Liberal political existence. Even if the Liberals depended heavily upon the large landowners and the Chambers of Commerce for their power in parliament, the cities and small towns of the monarchy remained the core of the Liberal political ideal. Even Plener, as arrogant as he was, argued that the Liberals were the party of the "upper levels of the Mittelstand," not simply of the small capitalistic Hochbürgertum which Austria possessed by 1890.[7] The pride which this Bürger role had given the Liberals since 1861 was now declared bankrupt and shameful, not merely by the Social Democrats, but by Taaffe and Steinbach as well.

Taaffe's attempt to revise the Austrian political system by what amounted to quasi-administrative fiat found its more forceful and catastrophic parallel four years later when Badeni tried a similar attack from above, this time on the national question.[8] In both instances the behavior of the Austrian state was untraditional (one is almost tempted to say "Prussian-like"), and in both instances political autocracy failed. Both were typical of a decade of upheaval in which the higher Verwaltung was tempted to thrust beyond its conventional limits in restructuring the political system. Steinbach is typical of the 1890s, but not of Austrian administrative traditions. In part the Verwaltung's new activism was self-protective. If social radicalism and nationalist strife proceeded unimpeded, the higher service might find itself in a position toward the masses of state officials similar to that of the episcopate toward its errant clergy. Erich Kielmansegg's attempt to curb anti-Liberal Beamten politics by administrative fiat in August 1895 was an appropriate midpoint between Taaffe and Badeni.[9] It was not surprising that after 1901 the Verwaltung relinquished its hegemonic behavior and resumed a more conciliatory posture, while the political parties resumed their attempts to attract the support of the officials of their specific national backgrounds. Ernst v Koerber's regime differed from those of Bülow and Bethmann Hollweg in Germany precisely in its profoundly subjective sense of vulnerability and tentativeness—Koerber did not have the Germans' luxury of social imperialism or their false sense of manipulative power (which is the other side of a *Sammlungspolitik*). Appropriately, enaction of the last major franchise reform in Austria in 1905–7 was owing to a combination of Social Democratic power and personal intervention by the emperor, not to a semiautonomous strategy by the Verwaltung. Gautsch had learned Badeni's lessons only too well: the administration existed to mediate and to manage the system, not to dominate it.

That the Liberals had been the first to repudiate the ideal of the unitary Bürgertum by their discrimination against the lower bourgeoisie in 1849–50 was a blissfully forgotten point in their leaders' minds. October 1893 was a signal that even in areas of the monarchy where nationalism was not a viable issue the earlier irresponsibility of the Liberals toward their own political ideal was turning back on itself. Hence Karl Lueger's ambiguous on-again, off-again support for the 1893 reform. In moral and tactical terms it meant the end of Liberal rule, which he could only applaud. But in the long run it opened the door to masses of voters who might not tolerate any kind of Bürger hegemony, even one cast in an antisemitic mode. That Christian Socials like Liechtenstein and Pattai tried to becloud their uncertainty with utopian demands for a new corporate election system only indicated the Janus-like dilemma in which the antisemites were now caught.[10] Liechtenstein's ability to argue for suffrage reforms on the floor of the Abgeordnetenhaus and then hours later to turn around and lobby against them in the corridors of the parliament did not go unnoticed in the Liberal press. In criticizing such behavior, however, the Liberals were only showing their envy at not having that kind of moral flexibility.

A second consideration for the Liberals, aside from the lack of a definitional ideal, was the problem of effective party structure. Ernst v Plener's role in Austrian Liberalism was a controversial and ultimately unfruitful one. This was owing both to his personal political style and to the objective determinants of his situation. The United German Left Plener pulled together against Taaffe in the later 1880s comprised a myriad of segmented regional and social interests which in Germany would have been represented by distinct political parties. Karl von Lichowsky's frustration was hardly surprising when he tried to explain to Berlin the exact nature of Austrian Liberalism.[11] He finally suggested that they were an odd-lot combination of Free Conservatives, the National Liberals, and the more conservative sectors of the Prussian Progressives. Lichowsky's diagnosis by ideological division as superficially true, but the fact that the Austrian party represented such varied interests also reflected deep regional and curial loyalties, the latter phenomenon not being present in the German political system on the national level. On the extreme Right of the Austrian Liberals stood the Liberal large landowners and the delegates from the curia of the Chambers of Commerce and Industry; in its Center were the delegates from Moravia and the Alpine regions; on its Left, but only in their abrasiveness on the national question, were its Bohemian and Silesian delegations.[12] On many issues national and regional criteria were superimposed on more conventional political, ideological attitudes.

The Viennese and Lower Austrian delegation was traditionally less interested in national issues than were the delegates from the Bohemian lands or from provinces with a tradition of *Länder* autonomy, like Styria. Alpine Liberals, in turn, although they might share the northern Liberals' sensitivity to national affairs, were less impressed by the state as a central locus of sovereignty, a heritage of the days of Styrian autonomism in the 1860s and 1870s. Delegates from the city curial districts had slightly more ''progressive'' views on urban developments in the monarchy than had Liberals from the *Landgemeinden* (although the Liberals were not a true peasants' party even in these rural districts). On issues involving state intervention in the economy most urban and rural Liberals took note of the concerns of the Chamber of Commerce delegates (who sat with the party in the specific role of an economic pressure group for larger industrial and commercial interests). On questions of tariff reform and commercial protectionism the party was usually able to present a fairly united front, if only because the protectionists in the party were in the majority (there was not, as in Germany, a separate Liberal wing interested in free trade policies).[13] More important, the curial representation of ''big business'' in the party forced the Chambers of Commerce to discuss among themselves key commercial issues before demanding general policy statements from the party as a whole. Inevitably there were tensions within the party on a variety of issues (such as the distribution of tax revenues to urban and rural centers), but the Liberals were fortunate in always finding sufficient external enemies to distract them from their internal feuds—whether this be the decennial *Ausgleich* negotiations, Czech nationalism, or after 1880 the personality of Taaffe himself. The divisiveness of 1879 did not destroy the party in a permanent structural sense. Taaffe was neither so manipulative nor so oppressive nor the administration so hostile to the Liberals in the 1880s as to force them either into categorical opposition or to a Canossa. There was no Heidelberg program in Austrian Liberal history, just as there was no Eugen Richter.

The absence of a formal Progressive element in the national Liberal party was also owing to a technical omission. Unlike Eugen Richter and his German Progressives, the Austrian Liberals consciously refused to build Vienna into the national political system in a tight structural fashion. Whereas the Berlin mayor Forckenbeck habitually sat in the Progressive delegation in the Reichstag and the Berlin Progressive delegation used the financial resources of its city party for support, in Vienna fascination with local and regional political competitions distracted and diminished interest in national developments. The highly competitive nature of local and regional politics in Lower Austria consumed the energies of the Viennese Liberal leaders to the point where they had little interest in national commitments. Cajetan Felder's and Johann Prix's careers were classic examples of this point. Also, the more conservative nature of the local Viennese Liberals hardly qualified them to play a democratic-progressive role. Most Viennese Liberals did not feel so uncomfortable with the Bohemian and Alpine leadership of the party to try to challenge it—their watchdog on the northern Liberals in Vienna was their powerful press.

On the national level the Liberal party was essentially a parliamentary club. It had no central institutional organizations, aside from a few ancillary cultural groups like the *Deutschen Schulverein* (which was regionally and locally run) and the powerful Viennese press. The latter instrument was Vienna's unique contribution to national Liberal politics. Eduard Herbst's dependence upon the *Neue Freie Presse* may have been exaggerated by his later critics, but it was real nonetheless.[14] This dependence upon the press was a mixed blessing, since local and regional newspapers were keyed to the Viennese Liberal news-information system for their editorial policies as well as factual presentation in a way the regionally organized Liberal party itself was not. The famous attack on Plener launched by the *Neue Freie Presse* on Easter of 1895 was not limited to Vienna's readership alone. The political press of Vienna served as a surrogate political organization, not simply in spreading political ideas, but in providing value judgments upon such ideas.

During the oppositional period of the later 1880s Herbst and then Plener were able to hold the party together in a superficial way, but once Plener resigned from the club chairmanship in late 1893 (upon taking over the Finance Ministry) the party was unable to replace him. There was no single politician of equivalent moral stature or prestige who was also acceptable to the various regional and social factions in the party. After an experiment with a triadic structure, the club eventually created a nine-member executive board to govern its affairs by collegial vote. The Liberals in the Cabinet (Plener, Wurmbrand, and Bacquehem) encountered serious problems in trying to coordinate their policies with this unwieldly structure.[15] Six of the nine members were from urban curias, five of the nine from the Bohemian lands. Lower Austria had two delegates, Upper Austria and Carinthia one each.

Plener himself felt far more comfortable as a minister than as a parliamentary leader. This coldness and aloofness alienated many in his party, especially those who wanted interest group favors from the Finance

Ministry after 1893.[16] Plener also suffered from a bitter vendetta against him by the Viennese Liberal press, especially after March 1895. The *Neue Freie Presse* used Plener and his coalition politics as the scapegoat for the local Liberals' loss of the crucial spring elections, implying that the government was responsible for the catastrophe because of its refusal to repress the antisemites. Plener was contemptuous of the hysteria of the Viennese press, the situation soon degenerating into an intraparty feud.[17]

This period was not without Liberal efforts at self-renewal on a regional and local basis. In Lower Austria, for example, a group of Liberals led by Gustav Marchet and Eduard Suess pressed in 1892 for a stronger regional campaign organization.[18] Traditionally there was little consultation and no coordination between the Viennese Liberals and their rural and small town colleagues in the province. In November 1892 a rally held in Vienna for 1,200 party activists from all of Lower Austria created an executive committee to reorganize the provincial party. A permanent committee of sixty members, thirty from Vienna and thirty from the rest of the province, was to run future Landtag and Reichsrat campaigns, including funding and propaganda. The collegial nature of this arrangement revealed the lack of outstanding leadership among the local Liberals. Sixty-member committees are not effective instruments of political control. Although Raimund Grübl was delegated by the Viennese party to represent it to the new organization, Mayor Prix and other local Liberals continued to think in municipal terms in running their political campaigns.

The Coalition of 1893–95

Ernst v Plener once described some of the coalition's major policies to Philipp zu Eulenburg as his "children."[19] Had he known their destiny, he might have been less willing to admit paternity. Plener thought that the coalition of the Liberals, the Clericals, and the Poles which emerged in early November 1893 would endure at least until the 1897 general elections, that it would create an acceptable franchise reform without infringing on bourgeois political privileges, and that it would allow the Liberals to restore their prestige by pushing through a progressive program of tax and commercial reforms. Unfortunately, it accomplished none of these things.

The most important item on the coalition's agenda was electoral reform. In the emperor's mind, aside from getting the budget through, this was the coalition's only reason for existence. The three parties faced a gargantuan task of repressing mass social protest while retaining the kinds of comfortable electoral privileges from which the Liberals and Poles had profited for thirty years. The disharmonies over franchise reform which fragmented the coalition on the ministerial and the parliamentary level revealed much about its structural inadequacies. Each of the parties approached the issue with self-serving notions; but if this had been the only problem, some solution might have been found. Unlike the Poles, however, both Plener and Hohenwart were never entirely sure of the support of their respective Reichsrat delegations. The lack of support by Max Menger and Gandolf Kuenburg for the compromise proposals of June 1895 illustrated this kind of intraparty dissent.[20] Hohenwart's problem was greater still, since a powerful segment of his club, the Alpinists (led by Alfred Ebenhoch and Anton Dipauli), was hostile to the coalition and used every opportunity to undercut and embarrass the Liberals (their enthusiastic support for Lueger in 1895 was the best example). Hohenwart's isolation was significant in that the ostensible leader of the coalition, Prince Alfred Windischgraetz, refused to take any action on the franchise without Hohenwart's consent.[21] The coalition was not merely fractionalized, but leaderless.

The parties had three options for franchise reform: an isolated workers' curia; a fifth curia which would include newer voters but retain other, more reliable segments of the electorate; or a total reform of the system along corporate and federalist lines.[22] To these options were matched constituency favors. The Clericals wanted to avoid giving the rural working class the vote. Hohenwart's famous curial-corporate scheme of March 1894 was not simply an attempt to federalize the system (by giving 161 seats to delegates elected by the Landtage); it was also an attempt to deprive the rural labor force of the vote.[23] After he was forced to abandon his first plan as too utopian, Hohenwart returned to Plener's old *Arbeiterkammer* scheme of the 1880s, thus isolating the workers from the rest of the electorate.

The Liberals hesitated between the Fifth Curia option and the *Arbeiterkammer*, but most felt uncomfortable with the idea of a distinct workers' curia. They feared that the Social Democrats would use the *Kammer* as a base for proprietary political power. For most it would be preferable to create an additional general curia of very modest proportions, leaving the existing curial system (and its legitimacy) untouched.

After almost a year of fruitless negotiation on the ministerial level, the parties agreed in November 1894 to send the matter back to parliament, where a special subcommittee of the Committee on Electoral Reform was appointed to work out a compromise. In June 1895 the subcommittee presented its recommendations.[24] The proposals were a poorly designed compromise among all three of the structural options of 1894: a new curia was to be created, but then immediately divided into two distinct parts—one for workers enrolled in the sickness insurance system, the other for the members of the Bürgertum paying the lowest taxes (under 5 fl.), who could not vote under the 1882 franchise (who would then constitute a second, distinct section of existing urban and rural electoral curia). The workers' section received thirteen seats, the other section, thirty-four. The dual curia was in part a creature of the Clericals, in that all rural workers were automatically excluded (none were enrolled in insurance) and appropriate patronage was provided for the poorest sections of the rural and small town Bürgertum. The Liberals took satisfaction in the survival of the tax qualification principle, to which was added *Kranken-kasse* membership. In both cases the franchise resulted from some aspect of occupational status, not from inherent rights of universal citizenship, which might prove destructive of the unitary Bürgertum ideal.

Liberal press reaction to the plan was negative, following the lead of the *Neue Freie Presse*.[25] The new subcuria of *Kleinbürger* types would be prime material for Clerical and antisemitic recruitment—the Liberal Jews running the paper saw no reason why the Liberal party should squander its power to enhance anti-Liberal movements. The pressure of the Liberal newspapers was great enough to frighten large numbers of Liberal politicians from supporting the plan. Bacquehem tried in last-minute maneuvering in mid-June to achieve a compromise with the Clericals. The Liberals would accept the dual curial plan in parliament if, in return, the Hohenwart Club agreed to relocate the Slovenian gymnasium for Cilli to a less controversial place in Styria. In the end this also failed and the coalition collapsed under the weight of its own feuding and distrust, having accomplished nothing on the electoral reform issue after eighteen months of debate. Of equal significance, these years and this issue were the turning point for the Socialists in their new political tactics of mass street and parade protests. The Social Democrats used the *Wahlreform* issue in much the same way as the Christian Socials used the Lueger confirmation controversy—to generate new techniques of mass mobilization.

The Liberals had equally great expectations for their program of economic policy reforms. Plener controlled the most powerful ministry, Finance, while Wurmbrand, a less impressive figure, ran the Ministry of Trade. Aside from pushing through the final laws implementing the 1892 currency reforms, the most important legislation the Liberals sponsored was their comprehensive tax reform bill of March 1895. Plener built upon Emil Steinbach's proposals from February 1892, but the final version produced by the Tax Committee in parliament made some important adjustments in the original Steinbach plan.[26] Technically, the reform package was salutary in several ways. Not only was tax relief brought to smaller businesses and farms (in the form of *Nachlässe* or abatements on trade and land taxes), but a general, progressive income tax was instituted to help redress the enormous discrepancy between the distribution of wealth and the generation of tax revenues which existed in the monarchy. The Austrian revenue system before 1896, with its draconian and arbitrary tax rates, had worked at all only because of widespread tax cheating. Tax morality was never a high point in the Austrian public conscience in the nineteenth century.[27] Those occupational groups, like the *Staatsbeamten,* which had difficulty in cheating on their income taxes found their burdens particularly heavy. The 1895 laws, because they restored to the tax system a sense of realism and equity, made it possible to reeducate the Austrian public in tax honesty.

Plener saw the tax reforms as attractive in several ways. Not only would they distract attention from the hopeless negotiations on electoral reform, but they would provide what the Liberal press proudly touted as a "Christmas present" for the lower artisan Bürgertum in the form of tax abatements.[28] The reforms would weaken Lueger's accusation that the Liberals were a do-nothing party who were insensitive to bourgeois social reform. The timing of the tax package was clearly related to the crucial City Council elections in Vienna in the spring of 1895.

Unfortunately for the Liberals, their carefully conceived political strategy backfired. The political failure of the reforms resulted from inept management by the Liberals and from the explosive nature of several of the proposals. These reforms came at a decisive period of bourgeois interest group mobilization in Austria. Had parliament undertaken a comprehensive tax reform in 1885 rather than 1895, it might have had free rein to do what it wished. By 1895 Austria had too many mobilized interest groups for the ministry or parliament simply to write its own bill without provoking massive public reaction. Plener did not realize the full implications of this change. When Steinbach initially proposed the idea of rebates on the traditional land, rent, and trade taxes, he refused to set specific percentages. Plener, who had a Cartesian mind and liked his policy proposals in tight, logical packages, insisted that the level of the *Nachlässe* be made explicit in the law itself (with an elevator clause for possible increases, should tax revenue exceed projections).[29] Although reasonable in fiscal terms, this was a political error, for it opened a Pandora's box of special interest pleading by a variety of groups, all of whom were being courted by Lueger and the Christian Socials. No group of farmers, small businessmen, or property owners was satisfied with the level of rebates accorded to their particular group. Nor were the antisemites slow to charge that the new tax commissions which were to apportion the revised tax among the four levels of industrial producers were stacked against the *kleinen Mann.* What Plener thought would be a Christmas present turned by April 1895 into a politician's nightmare—

hundreds of angry petitions were sent to the Reichsrat from *Sparkassen,* property owners' associations, *Beamten* groups, and craft guilds demanding more generous treatment for their particular groups.

There were also serious discrepancies in the tax law in the way in which large, mobile capital investments were treated as opposed to other forms of capital investment, which may have been justified in terms of the successful operation of the new system and in spurring national economic growth, but which were difficult to explain to bourgeois voters anxious about their own economic self-enhancement. A classic case in point was the reaction of the various property owners' associations to the reforms. The new *Rentensteuer* (tax on interest) explicitly exempted from its purview all dividends and profits from capital investment in stock corporations, since these were to be taxed at the flat rate of 10 percent under the new *Actiensteuer* (which was a corporate and not an individual tax). Individual owners of real property, however, were still subject to drastic levels of taxation on their real estate (in Vienna over 40 percent of the gross rental income of an apartment building was taxed). The obvious difference between 10 percent and 40 percent was hard to explain to the angry *Hausherren* associations. Moreover, because under the provisions of the new trade tax *(Erwerbsteuer)* the profits of local *Sparkassen* which financed mortgages were now declared taxable at much higher rates than was previously the case, the *Sparkassen* were likely to raise their interest rates and credit costs to cover the new taxation, thus depriving new owners of buildings of any gain they might achieve by the modest rebates they received on their rent taxes. The *Hausbesitzer* thought that they were, in effect, placed under a system of double taxation. The government insisted that the tax increases would have a minimal effect on interest rates, but Lueger and the antisemites waged a vigorous propaganda campaign to persuade the *Hausbesitzer* that they were being cheated out of their rebates by the Liberals' decision to tax *Sparkassen* income.

A final point of contention was the way in which large industrial and commercial establishments would be taxed on the corporate level. This provoked a divisive feud between Plener and the local Viennese Liberals, and handed Lueger yet another issue to exploit in the spring of 1895. Formerly the city of Vienna enjoyed a majestic position vis à vis the other urban and regional tax centers of the monarchy in being able to claim itself as the administrative seat of commercial and financial institutions to be taxed. The new reforms differentiated, however, between the administrative center of a large bank (which might still be Vienna) and the localities in which the bank had branches and local business was actually performed. By a varying series of ratios, the right to tax these large conglomerates was now divided between Vienna and the rest of the monarchy.

Because tax revenue on the municipal level depended on the surtaxes levied on direct state taxation, a reduction in the share of Vienna's state taxation on a transport or insurance company, or a bank also meant that the city itself faced a loss of income.

Not only was Vienna facing, therefore, a decline in tax revenue (estimated by Plener himself to be nearly 400,000 fl. per year), but the reduction in the levels of taxation on the trade and rent taxes by means of the abatements reduced the city's surtaxes on these taxes as well. An official petition of protest to the Finance Ministry by the Liberal municipality in Vienna estimated the loss from these taxes to be another 800,000 fl. annually, a total loss of 1.2 million gulden. This was a grave threat to the financial future of a city with an annual deficit of nearly 4 million gulden.

This new division of revenue between Vienna and the rest of the state was in part a concession by the Liberals to the Clericals and the Poles, but it also reflected pressure from the Bohemian and Moravian Liberals to weaken Vienna's position in order to build up their own urban and rural tax bases. Although the Liberal party had supported the consumption tax reforms for Vienna in 1890, it was now divided over the distribution of corporate taxation. Indeed, this was one issue upon which German and Czech delegates from Bohemia could unite with ease and equanimity; in the 1860s and 1870s Eduard Herbst had joined with Bohemian Federalists and Czech Nationalists in urging a more equitable distribution of such revenue throughout the monarchy.[30] During the 1895 debates provincial Liberals or German nationalists representing other cities like Max Menger (Troppau, Silesia) and Otto Steinwender (Villach, Carinthia) found themselves on the same side as the federalists in rejecting the bitter accusations raised by Kronawetter and Lueger.[31]

The dispute placed the local Liberals in a quandary. Antisemitic newspapers raised a hue and cry that Plener was selling the city out to the agrarians, but it was clear that the "agrarians" in question were not simply the clerical or Polish variety. Plener claimed that he had tried to pressure the Tax Committee into a more moderate compromise, but these disclaimers were lost amid public outrage provoked by antisemitic propaganda—Joseph Strobach thundered in the City Council that the local Liberals were betraying their own city.[32] Mayor Grübl and his colleagues tried desperately to persuade Plener of the gravity of the situation,[33] but the minister refused to produce a counterproposal until weeks after the crucial Council elections for the Second Curia had taken place.

The Viennese Liberals paid dearly for Plener's timing. The political damage which this issue cost them clearly occurred during the early April elections, but Plener did not announce his "solution" to the problem until

29 April.[34] His response—to shift to Vienna a greater share of the government's proceeds from the *Verzehrungssteuer* to cover the 1.2 million fl. losses in tax revenue—might have defused the whole question and short-circuited the Christian Socials of an appealing issue. Instead, Plener left his Viennese colleagues in the lurch for nearly two months in order to preserve his freedom to maneuver within the parliamentary Tax Committee.

The confessional issue was the third source of weakness and instability within the coalition. The Alpinists in the Hohenwart Club were distrustful of Plener's assurances that the Liberal party would reduce its anticlerical profile for the sake of political accommodation. Plener honestly intended that this occur; but he had no way of controlling the powerful Viennese press, and it was to the Liberal press as much as to the Liberal party that the rural conservatives were reacting. One of the roles of the Polish Club in the coalition was to serve as a buffer between the two ideological parties. The coalition's minister of education, Stanislaus Madeyski, tried to bridge the gap between the Liberals and the Clericals by posing as a neutral intermediary. His conciliatory statements on education and religion were the subject of considerable debate in the Liberal and Catholic press, each side attempting to interpret Madeyski's views to fit its own ideological needs.[35] Plener hoped that as long as the Liberals retained good relations with the Poles, Hohenwart and the Clericals could be kept in line on cultural questions pertaining to religion and the schools.[36] On national questions (Cilli) this arrangement worked not at all, as Plener learned in June 1895.

Liberalism and the City, 1892–95

The Liberal regime which ran Vienna in the years before Lueger's takeover was a house divided against itself. It was also the victim of a series of policy and propaganda blunders which did nothing to enhance its reputation with the electorate. The Liberal Club in the Council was not nearly as homogeneous and cohesive as it was portrayed to be in antisemitic propaganda. Within the club there were a series of factions, ranging from the small group of Left Liberals led by Heinrich Friedjung and Adolf Daum to a less vociferous group of older Bürger politicians like Moritz Lederer, Joseph Schlechter, and Georg Boschan who were increasingly dissatisfied with the autocratic style of leadership which Mayor Johann Prix employed.[37] With the death of the first vice-mayor Franz Borschke in 1892 Albert Richter became the heir apparent of Prix. Whereas Borschke was an experienced local leader from the Alsergrund with a conciliatory manner and a willingness to listen to the complaints of the antisemites, if only in private, Richter was a wealthy lawyer from the Innere Stadt with a cold, formal demeanor and an inflexible manner. He was not only detested by the antisemites, but disliked by many in his own party as well. Richter was the local Viennese version of Ernst v Plener, but found himself in a political culture in which such extreme formalism was never acceptable. His rise to power owed a good deal to Prix's patronage as well as to the emphatic support of the Liberal press, especially the *Neue Freie Presse*.

The elections for the *Stadtrat* proved equally divisive. Prix adamantly refused antisemitic demands for one-third of the seats on the new Council, and the first slate of *Räthe* elected in May 1891 were all Liberals. Although the Liberal Club tried to spread the seats among the various *Bezirke* in an equitable fashion, eight of the twenty-five seats ended up in the hands of politicians from the Innere Stadt. Seventeen of the twenty-five had been elected in the First Curia, even though the Liberals controlled a good part of the Second and some of the Third Curia as well.[38] The *Stadtrat* itself was not representative of the Liberal party. When Prix finally relented in May 1893 and decided to concede two seats in the *Stadtrat* to the Christian Socials, he did so with mixed feelings. Lueger demanded five seats, and the *Bürgerclub* officially rejected the Liberal offer. The Liberals then rescinded the offer and prepared to reelect a pure Liberal slate to the committee. Surprisingly, however, when the actual voting occurred on 29 May, twenty-two Liberal delegates deserted their party to vote for Lueger against Theodor v Goldschmidt.[39] Lueger not only won a seat, but did so without the embarrassment of having made a "deal" with Prix. In Liberal circles consternation and outrage reigned for weeks after the vote. Many Liberals wanted sanctions imposed on the twenty-two heretics (whose names were protected by the secret ballot), but in the end the club failed to reestablish party discipline.[40]

The Lueger election fiasco was merely illustrative of Liberal intraparty bickering. This conflict cut across ethnic and class lines. Wilhelm Stiassny, for example, a wealthy Jewish architect from the Leopoldstadt, was among the most hostile to the new oligarchical tendencies manifest in the Liberal *Stadtrat* and to the way Prix and Grübl dealt with the Liberal Club. Some Liberals felt the antisemites should be given seats on various city commissions and boards. At the same time hostility was soon manifest in the Jewish community by those who felt that the Liberals were both laggard in their defense of the Jews and parsimonious in allocating to the Jewish community a fair share of the seats in various parliamentary bodies. Strong sentiment was evinced in the *Oesterreichische Union* to reexamine Jews' customary allegiance to the Liberal party. Social Liberals like Julius Ofner made political capital out of accusations against the orthodox Liberals of being "soft" on the antisemitism question.[41] Ultimately this kind of attitude revenged itself on the Liberals when significant segments of the Jewish electorate in the Innere Stadt and the Leopoldstadt sat out the elections of 1895 and 1896, refusing to vote for the Liberals, or even voted for antisemitic candidates out of frustration and bitterness. Prix and his colleagues found themselves in a cross fire between those who demanded repression of the antisemites and those who sought accommodation with them.

Prix also took a series of political missteps, some not his own fault, for which his party paid dearly in prestige. In late September 1892 the Lower Austrian School Council allowed the Viennese School Board to respond to a citizen's complaint and to implement an 1874 ordinance suggesting that a quiet tone of voice be used in the intonation accompanying making the sign of the cross in the schools.[42] On 10 October the School Board complied with this permission (which was given without the *Statthalter*'s knowledge), although Prix might have intervened to stop it. Realizing the explosive possibilities of the ordinance if the antisemites seized the issue, Erich Kielmansegg quickly revoked both the provincial and municipal instructions.[43] By this point it was too late, however, to prevent Lueger from using the ordinance as an example of the "anti-Christian" attitudes of the "Jewish-Liberals" running the city. Even though *Vaterland* admitted that the Jews had absolutely nothing to do with the affair (the original complaint had come from a local Protestant), the Christian Socials managed to exploit it artfully for several weeks, attacking both the Liberals and the episcopate for their hostility and weakness (respectively) toward "Christian" values in the classroom. The actual impact of the issue was not as great as its symptomatic value as an indicator of the quality of the city's Liberal leadership. One such incident would affect few votes, but a series of such issues might suggest unreliability and weakness on the part of the top municipal officers. Lueger was not interested in the truth value of any given accusation—if he could exploit Prix's faulty administrative decisions by blowing up the importance of a cluster of such minor issues, that might be sufficient to undermine confidence in the Liberals.

More significantly, the so-called *Wertpapier* affair in October/ November 1893 served to rock Liberal complacency. On his own authority Prix ordered in July 1893 the sale of 970,000 fl. in securities owned by the city to cover a temporary budgetary deficit during the summer months. This was a practice often used in the past, but since 1891 the Council as a whole had insisted that the *Magistrat* and the mayor obtain prior permission for such sales.[44] In particular the Council's Budget Committee was opposed to further sales of the city's capital investments and urged the *Magistrat* to cover budget shortfalls from the new, 35 million kronen water construction loan. Unfortunately for Prix, the loan had not yet been floated when he needed the money. He used the more traditional method of selling municipal securities, but did so without obtaining the consent of either the *Stadtrat* or the Council. The issue blew up when Prix insisted that the *Stadtrat* and City Council vote him indemnity in October 1893 for his actions. Not only did the antisemites scream for the mayor's head, but a strong minority within the Liberal Club itself disaffirmed Prix's discretionary action. Moritz Lederer, a rival of Prix and a Liberal with informal social connections to Lueger and some of the antisemitic leadership, went so far as to vote against the motion for indemnity in the *Stadtrat*.[45] By demanding a vote of confidence in the Council itself, Prix faced a variety of oppositional challenges, some from within his own party. When it appeared likely that some Liberals would secretly desert him or cast blank ballots, he abruptly resigned his office on 24 October 1893.

Prix's resignation came in the middle of the Steinbach-Taaffe crisis, and its immediate impact was somewhat obscured by national events. The Liberals were unable to replace him with anyone more competent, and the club soon decided to renominate him for the office, putting pressure on its members to fall into line. Early in November, Prix was reelected mayor by a straight party line vote of eighty-one to forty-five. Although Kielmansegg recommended that Prix not be reconfirmed and new elections to the whole Council be called to clarify the parties' respective public support, the newly appointed *Ministerrat* followed Plener's advice and consented to Prix's second term. But the episode showed how fragile the Liberal majority actually was, even with a relatively strong leader like Prix.

Upon Prix's death in February 1894 everyone in Vienna, including the antisemites, expected that Albert Richter would succeed to the post of mayor. Richter's selection was impeded by a scandal campaign waged against him by the antisemites for his having married a Jewish woman, but much more by prejudice in the Imperial Court itself against confirming a person in the office of *Bürgermeister* who was *konfessionslos* (Richter was a Gentile, but in order to marry he had to renounce his legal status as a Catholic under Austrian law).[46] Raimund Grübl, a far less abrasive personality than Richter, became mayor, and relations between the Liberal party and many of its voter constituencies, especially the *Hausherren*, improved somewhat. On the other hand, Grübl was clearly not the kind of strong party leader whom the Liberals needed to face Lueger in the 1895 elections.

The years 1891–95 were significant in the history of the administration of the city of Vienna; the many accomplishments of the Liberals should not be lost sight of. Prix engineered the smooth administrative integration of the newly incorporated suburban areas into the city, and initiated a program of massive capital expenditures to bring public services and public facilities in the suburbs up to a par with those of the city proper.[47] The new water construction loan was among the most farsighted and generous of these projects. At the same time the city's financial plight grew steadily more uncertain; outlays for suburban improvements added great burdens to an already overextended and underfinanced budget. By 1895 the city was anticipating a budgetary deficit of over 3 million fl., and it is in the context of this financial pressure that the Liberal party entered what was to prove its last series of election campaigns as the ruling force in Vienna.

Christian Socialism and the Coalition's Appeal to Rome

Between 1891 and 1895 the antisemites endured the most uncertain period of their history. Having made a push for power in 1891 and failing miserably, the party needed time to regroup and strengthen its internal structures before again assaulting the Liberal bastions in 1895. Before 1891 the crucial danger for the party had always been club fragmentation. After 1891 the more ominous problem for the Christian Socials was the internal stagnation that could result from playing a minority, oppositional role in the political system.

The thrust of the party's politics in this period was still largely reactive in nature, but unlike the pre-1891 situation, the Christian Socials gradually developed a sense of themselves as a programmatic force with an independent set of policy proposals, among the most prominent of which was the *Beamten* issue. Albert Gessmann made the latter the special proprietary possession of the antisemites by 1895. While Taaffe was in office the party was circumspect in its criticism of the government, but after November 1893 the antisemites found themselves with a ready-made target of inestimable value. Taaffe was of little use as an object of local criticism, but Plener and Wurmbrand were perfectly suitable for such a role. This meant opposing the Imperial government itself, however. Antisemitic politics between November 1893 and July 1895 assumed a much harsher, more uncompromising aura, precisely because the party's antagonist—the Liberals—held a significant share of state power.

The party found its greatest success in manipulating special interests of protesting Bürger groups, not only because such concerns followed logical lines and had specific goals, but because the Liberals had also promised to do something for these groups and could be held directly accountable for lack of success. When the antisemites tried to turn Steinbach's currency reform legislation of 1892–93 into a bimetallist crusade, they had much less success. Though controversial, currency reform did not have the mass appeal that tax reform had during the same period.[48] Many local Liberals also objected to the gold standard, so that the party could not claim a unilateral right to virtue on this issue.[49] The whole operation of conversion to the kronen was handled rapidly and successfully enough to deflate the issue by the time of the 1895 elections.

Franchise and tax reform were more attractive issues, but also more dangerous. The Christian Socials generally sided with the Young Czechs in opposing Plener's tax reforms. But they did not dare endanger the enactment of some kind of tax reduction for the lower Bürgertum. The party's pendulating behavior on electoral reform has been noted above. The last thing the Christian Socials wanted in 1893 was universal suffrage. A fifth curia with a limited number of seats in which voters from the older city and rural curias could also vote (a double vote) was immensely appealing, however. On the regional level, the pressure of the antisemites did contribute significantly to forcing the Liberals in the Lower Austrian Landtag to consent to a reform of the provincial suffrage, which instituted direct voting in the rural *Gemeinden* and redistributed the seats of the urban curia to reflect more equitably the population distribution of metropolitan Vienna. This reform was crucial to the majority control which the antisemites won in the 1896 Landtag elections.

Toward Schönerer the party maintained a distanced and ill-concealed suspicion. A police report in 1894 noted that Lueger and Gessmann feared that Schönerer might try to reenter Viennese politics, creating dissension and havoc among antisemitic voters.[50] When Schönerer did intervene, however, he only demonstrated the poverty and isolation of his position. On the eve of the 1895 Council elections he publicly demanded that Lueger repudiate Ernst Vergani or face his personal opposition in the elections. Lueger stalled for several weeks and maneuvered for a publicly acceptable compromise (showing the loyalty he had toward Vergani!), but was eventually forced to reject Schönerer's demands. Schönerer thereupon "ordered" nationalist voters to abstain from the elections, but by this time he was talking to shadows and phantoms.[51] Most Second Curia voters ignored him, to the extent that they were not simply amused by the situation.

The relationship of the party to the episcopate and the Clericals in the coalition became much more sensitive after 1893 and dominated the attention of the party during this period. With Vogelsang gone as a possible mediator and with Lueger forced to rely on Vergani's newspaper (until 1894–95) for much of his publicity, the latent feud with the conservatives soon became a scarcely concealed rivalry. After the Hohenwart Club entered the coalition, Lueger was forced to attack the Church establishment as an ally of the Liberals. As a "Christian" he now found "his" Church siding with his mortal enemies. The antiepiscopal and anticonservative rhetoric from this period reflects the defensive posture into which the Christian Socials were pushed. That some members of the Hohenwart Club, particularly the Alpinists under Ebenhoch, also had doubts about the coalition strengthened Lueger's resolve to attack the Liberals through their coalition partners. Having risked his prestige and political future on a party structure in which both religious symbolism and lower clerics played prominent roles, he could not afford to allow the conservatives to suggest that the Christian Socials were less "Christian" than the orthodox political Catholics.

The Third Catholic Congress held in Linz in August 1892 was the scene of the first preliminary confrontation between the two camps. The congress was organized by the Upper Austrian conservatives and placed under the patronage of Bishop Franz Doppelbauer, the authoritarian bishop of Linz who detested Lueger. Although most of the congress was relatively uncontroversial (Alois Liechtenstein showed up and gave a speech righteously proclaiming the Christian respectability of the antisemites and their refusal to be treated as second-class citizens by the conservatives), a group of radical lower clerics provoked trouble in the committee on press affairs.[52] Matthäus Bauchinger delivered a tough, uncompromising attack on *Vaterland,* demanding that the committee recommend the establishment of a new national Catholic newspaper in Vienna which would better reflect contemporary political developments. Other clerics joined in a chorus of complaints, and Franz M. Schindler, who chaired the press committee, was appointed head of a permanent committee to resolve the issue after the congress ended.[53] Schindler, a respected Viennese moral theologian and the Catholic adviser to Lueger since Vogelsang's death, saw two options: either *Vaterland* would be reformed, its circulation expanded, and its pages opened to a diversity of political opinion; or a new journal would have to be established. Schindler had already sought unsuccessfully during Vogelsang's lifetime to liberalize *Vaterland* by freeing it from Bohemian financial control. He thus had no illusions about the likelihood of the first option. By early 1893 Schindler's committee, in which the editor of the *Correspondenzblatt,* Roman Himmelbauer, played a leading role, decided to organize a new Catholic newspaper in Vienna.[54] This was the *Reichspost,* which along with the *Deutsche Zeitung* soon became an important rival of Vergani's *Volksblatt* for journalistic hegemony within the party. Funding for the *Reichspost* was obtained, as it was for the *Correspondenzblatt,* by a mass of voluntary contributions from common clerics and monks, in addition to some lay investments (Albert Gessmann invested a considerable sum to become a codirector of the paper). When the paper began its operations in December 1893, an important step forward in lower clerical independence from the episcopate had been taken. The *Reichspost* was the only major Catholic newspaper in the monarchy not under the patronage of a member of the episcopate. Even though Schindler tried to steer the paper away from the provocations of the

Hohenwart Club or the bishops, most conservatives saw the *Reichspost* as the sibling of Vergani's *Volksblatt,* which did not hesitate to throw mud at the Catholic Establishment. The *Reichspost* became the lightning rod for conservative distrust and hatred of the Christian Social party. Precisely because it represented the Clerical wing of the party, it drew down upon itself considerable enmity.

The party's relations to the episcopate worsened in October 1892 when Ernst Schneider delivered a vulgar, personal attack on elderly Cardinal Gruscha for not resisting the Liberal School Board's "sign of the cross" edict with more vigor.[55] Lueger intervened immediately and forced Schneider to issue a public apology to Gruscha, but the damage was done.[56] The conference of Austrian bishops prepared a public defense of Gruscha, issued to the daily press, supporting his integrity and his loyalty to the Church. This was an unusual, embarrassing action for the episcopate to have to take, and many bishops long remembered Schneider's vulgarity as *the* official position of the party (which it clearly was not).[57]

The most important event in the feud between the antisemites and the Clericals was the appointment of Antonio Agliardi as papal nuncio to Vienna in late 1893. Agliardi's behavior was soon a factor of constant provocation and irritation to the bishops and their Clerical allies. Although a relatively conservative diplomat in political terms (as nuncio in Munich he had sympathized with the conservative wing of the Center against the Rhenish progressive forces), Agliardi had an unconcealed contempt for the weakness and passivity of most of the Austrian episcopate.[58] He also had a penchant for political intrigue and closet politics which eventually proved his undoing. Soon after he arrived in Vienna he was introduced to Franz Schindler and asked the latter to prepare a memorandum on the Church's situation in the Bohemian lands. A personal relationship was established, and Schindler became the party's informal spokesman to Rome through Agliardi.[59] This was a turning point, since Lueger now had access to propaganda resources far more potent and dangerous than anything he had previously possessed.

Agliardi quickly decided that the Christian Socials were a safe and useful tool by which he might bring some movement into Catholic politics in the monarchy. That they were "Catholic" only in a subsidiary sense bothered him not in the least. He once remarked to a rather shocked Karl Lichnowsky that the antisemites were the "party of the future" for Austrian Conservatism.[60] In February 1894 he asked Schindler to prepare a party program for submission to Cardinal Rampolla, the papal secretary of state. This was an act of prudence and cunning—if Agliardi could obtain the support and approval of Rampolla for the antisemites before the government and the episcopate decided to act against them, their chances of survival might be enhanced.[61] Schindler and Liechtenstein drafted a declaration of electoral and social goals, assuring Rampolla of the party's conservatism and loyalty to the established order.[62] After Lueger approved it, Agliardi sent it to Rampolla, who in turn forwarded it in March 1894 to the Italian Catholic social organization, the *Unione cattolica per gli studi sociali*. Rampolla found nothing amiss in the substance of the program, although he did advise Schindler that the party should lower its antisemitic profile. Professor Giuseppe Toniolo of the Italian Union also approved of the program, although Toniolo, who was closer to Liberal Catholicism than to Vogelsang's neo-Romanticism, questioned Schindler's proposals for regulating the economy by establishing occupational corporations.[63]

Agliardi's behavior in Vienna was guided by a mixture of professional calculations and personal self-interest. His motives for supporting the Christian Socials have never been properly explained. Agliardi was *not* a political intimate of Rampolla; he did not share the latter's willingness to undermine the position of the empire in the European power system. At the same time Agliardi could not afford to contradict openly Rampolla's strategy of conciliating France and Russia while isolating and dividing the Central Powers.[64] Rampolla's well-known Slavophilism made Agliardi sensitive to the Hapsburg nationality problem on curial-political as well as ecclesiastical-pastoral grounds. He shared with Rampolla, however, a contempt for the Austrian episcopate's Josephist behavior toward the state. Like Rampolla, Agliardi was opposed to the decision of the Hohenwart Club to join the coalition with the Liberals in 1893.[65] That Cardinals Schönborn in Prague and Gruscha in Vienna approved of the coalition only made their loyalty to the true interests of Catholicism more doubtful in his eyes.

For Rampolla support for the Christian Socials underscored his dissatisfaction with the episcopate, while also registering his opposition to the ruling Austrian political coalition and thus the Austrian state itself. Rampolla, in other words, saw assistance for Lueger as an anti-Austrian action in a larger strategic sense, one which would weaken the internal stability of the Austrian ruling elites by encouraging radical oppositional parties. That he approved of the development of a vigorous, if only quasi-Catholic, political movement in Vienna was obvious, but this was merely subsidiary to his broader calculations.[66] Agliardi, in contrast, had a more positive evaluation of the party in terms of the empire's internal politics. He saw men like Lueger and Schindler as leaders of a movement which would not only rejuvenate Austrian conservatism, but also provide one possible key to resolving the nationality question in the monarchy on purely bourgeois social lines.

In 1888 Franz Schindler had suggested that political corporatism on occupational lines might be effective in a province like Bohemia to break the power of entrenched national parties.[67] Schindler was a German from Leitmeritz in northern Bohemia who shared none of Vogelsang's federalist ideals on the nationalities question.[68] His alternative proposal, made to Agliardi in 1893—to create two German dioceses and relinquish the other dioceses of Bohemia to the Czechs—was not greatly different from Liberal proposals to divide the land into German and Czech administrative areas, but Agliardi seemed to appreciate the effort at national equity inherent in Schindler's approach. Schindler's insistence that the Church face the nationality problem head-on (the episcopate proposed to ignore it) marked him as a man of shrewdness as well as courage.

Agliardi found this style of political rhetoric attractive.[69] To patronize a party which was both antiepiscopal and ostensibly nonnationalistic would enhance Rampolla's diplomacy and strengthen bourgeois politics in the monarchy in a way equitable to Czech, German, and Catholic interests. Doubtless the tactical cooperation between the Christian Socials and the Young Czechs in the Reichsrat in the early 1890s on issues like tax and franchise reform did not escape Agliardi's notice. The informal exchanges between the Fabian Liberals in Vienna and Czech Nationalist intellectuals in this period (the circle around Die Zeit) was yet another example of an attempt at Slavic-German cooperation using neutral social and economic issues which surpassed the narrow confines of the nationality problem. However illusory these expectations were, Agliardi was not the only one in Vienna entertaining them. Schindler's insistence that a renewed and nationally demarcated Church with stronger corporate institutions and with social reform programs could reduce national tensions must have contributed to Agliardi's long-term calculations. He dreamed of squaring Rampolla's circle: enhancing all non-Liberal bourgeois parties with a social reform program and thus strengthening the empire's political system, while striking out against both the episcopate and the Austrian Liberals. The additional benefit of isolating the Social Democrats made the strategy even more attractive. By supporting the Christian Socials he would meet Rampolla's demand that he embrace the latter's politics, but would do so with goals which may have differed considerably from Rampolla's. This conception had two dangers. It involved the nuncio in meddling in the internal politics of the state in ways which grouped together the Clericals and Liberals as the joint enemy of Rome; and it made a virtue out of the antiepiscopalism of the lower clergy, which had not formerly been sanctioned by any external source, especially Rome.

In 1894 a series of collisions between the Christian Socials and the coalition occurred which became more significant as the municipal elections of 1895 approached. In June 1894 the committee of conservative aristocrats responsible for organizing the next Catholic congress announced that the assembly would not be held in 1894 because of political disunity within the Christian camp. The move was a direct insult to Lueger's organization. To counter it, the Christian Socials decided to hold their own Lower Austrian congress in November. Although Cardinal Gruscha was extremely hostile to the idea of a congress (his approval for the gathering was never obtained by the party beforehand), he backed down when he realized that the antisemites would hold it even if he made his disapproval public.[70] He then refused to participate in the proceedings if Lueger or Gessmann were on the speakers' platform.[71] Schindler worked out a compromise with Albert Weiss, Gruscha's adviser (Lueger gave an unofficial welcoming speech and then left; Gessmann stayed away completely), and the congress went forward. The false unity displayed at the congress, however, scarcely veiled the fact that the Christian Socials had ignored the archbishop of Vienna and had simply appropriated for themselves the label "Catholic" to justify a propaganda festival which had little, if anything, to do with orthodox religious belief (some of the speeches were clearly political in nature). Even more disturbing was the fact that Alois Liechtenstein was able, through Agliardi, to procure a papal blessing for the assembly from Cardinal Rampolla. Both Kálnoky, the Austrian foreign minister with strong loyalties to the Liberal party, and Prince Windischgraetz were outraged over this Curial intervention in domestic politics.[72]

Even more disturbing was the mood of the Viennese clergy at the congress. At the session on press affairs they voted down a resolution which affirmed the "authority principle" in Catholic editorial practices—meaning loyalty to the local bishop. Less than two weeks after the congress the Austrian episcopate's Executive Committee met in Vienna under the chairmanship of Cardinal Schönborn. The Lower Austrian congress had convinced all of the bishops that something had to be done to curb lower clerical independence. But uncertainty still prevailed over the means and the timing of such an action. After deciding that a national Catholic political association to rival the Christian Socials was unfeasible, the committee voted to issue a special pastoral letter to the lower clergy of all Austrian dioceses, reaffirming episcopal authority over lower clerical political activities.[73] Schönborn was charged with drafting the document (with the assistance of Albert Weiss). Some sentiment may have been manifest for an intervention by Rome, but no definite decision was made about such a step, nor was a firm deadline set for the issuance of the letter. Schönborn's unenergetic personality let valuable time slip away.[74]

Two weeks after the bishops concluded their deliberations Joseph Scheicher delivered a diatribe against existing Church-state relations in the Austrian parliament. Until 1893, when Bishop Binder of St. Pölten died, Scheicher had been forbidden to run for election to the Reichsrat.[75]

When Johann Rössler was appointed as Binder's successor in 1894, Scheicher found a more sympathetic and congenial bishop, one who would tolerate his political indiscretions (the two men had been colleagues on the teaching staff of the local seminary). Scheicher was already a prime target of Liberal and Josephist abuse.[76] Even Franz Joseph himself ordered Rössler early in 1894 to warn Scheicher that his agitatorial behavior should cease.[77]

Scheicher's speech in December 1894 showed that he had no intention of moderating his views. He condemned the government's traditional use of the lower clergy as "servants of the state": "We demand that the Church, once and for all time, stand before the world as a church free of state domination." The clergy's use as a "tool of the police" damaged their pastoral (and political) effectiveness.[78] The language and ideas of the speech were a distillation of ten years of the rhetoric of the *Correspondenzblatt* circle, but never before had a simple priest uttered such harsh, abrasive words in parliament. Scheicher hit the coalition on its weakest and most sensitive nerve—the confessional question. In Scheicher's vitriolic language "freedom of the Church" now meant an end to the 1893 coalition and all those responsible for it.

Scheicher was fiercely independent, and it is doubtful that Lueger knew in advance what the priest would say (ostensibly the speech was supposed to deal with budgetary issues). Had he been consulted, Lueger would probably have urged a more moderate approach, but Scheicher now handed him and the rest of the party a fait accompli.

Stanislaus Madeyski would have been prudent to ignore Scheicher's bombast and let tempers cool down, but his personal arrogance and his ministerial position dictated a counterattack. Madeyski felt that his mediatory labors between the Liberals and Clericals had been insulted. In addition, the Christian Socials had given moral and political support to Stanislaus Stojalowski when the Polish agrarian radical had visited Vienna in 1893–94. Stojalowski's agrarian populism in Galicia was a direct threat to the privileges of the Polish gentry. In Madeyski's view Viennese Christian Socialism was comparably dangerous.[79] To allow Scheicher to get away with such language would undercut the hard-line, repressive stance of the Polish Club and the Polish episcopate vis à vis Stojalowski. Although the Christian Socials were not nearly as radical in intent or form as the Polish firebrand, conservative Poles saw the two as blood brothers.

Madeyski responded in the next session of the lower house. He claimed that he was shocked by Scheicher's language ("such speeches have never been heard in our parliament!") and piously proclaimed that his feelings "as a Catholic" had been deeply injured.[80] The real crux of his complaint came next: priests like Scheicher were undermining the principle of legitimate authority ("the destructive spirit of rebellion against authority") by attacking the system of Austrian Church-state relations. Authority was the idol Madeyski held up for adoration. In connecting political dissidence and criticism of the episcopate, however, Madeyski was showing how much it lay in the coalition's own interest to intervene against Lueger and his party.

The Pole's haughtiness forced Lueger to defend Scheicher. Rather than attack the merits of Madeyski's propositions, which would have been pointless, Lueger immediately went for the jugular. He wondered aloud how the minister could pontificate on the virtues of "authority" when Madeyski himself had abused the authority of his position to obtain appointments for relatives in the state bureaucracy.[81] Lueger's ad hominem assault left the hapless minister sitting in embarrassed silence, but it generated a bitterness which was long to influence the behavior of the Polish Club (as well as Casimir Badeni) towards Lueger's party.

Early in January 1895 the Christian Socials escalated matters further by playing their new Curial "card" in a dangerous fashion. Gessmann and Schindler wrote a long address to Leo XIII in the name of the *Reichspost*'s editorial board, declaring the importance of unanimity in the Austrian Catholic camp and asking for a papal blessing for the paper. The letter was a gamble, but with Agliardi's help the antisemites received their much wanted approbation two weeks later, with permission to publish it in the newspaper. In the interim Gessmann also decided to put the party on the offensive by invading the privileged sanctum of Upper Austria. Even though the conservative Upper Austrian *Volksverein* run by Alfred Ebenhoch had just celebrated its twenty-fifth anniversary in Linz on 2 January, Gessmann and Liechtenstein organized a Christian Social rally in the city for 20 January. Liechtenstein again used his family name and wrote to Rampolla asking for a second papal blessing for the agitation the party was about to conduct in Upper Austria. Owing to Agliardi's good offices, Liechtenstein received the desired response within forty-eight hours. As a result the party ended up with two papal blessings, both spread hawkishly over the front pages of the *Reichspost* (one on 20 January, the other on 25 January).[82]

The rally staged in Linz was an embarrassing flop. Most conservative Catholics in the city stayed away, and much of the audience, aside from the curious, consisted of 700 Social Democratic workers, whose attendance at the rally and disruption of it had been ordered by the local party leadership.[83] Lueger did not even bother to attend, leaving the task of facing the audience to his more masochistic colleagues. The effect of the rally was, however, far-reaching.[84] Bishop Doppelbauer had expressly forbidden the Christian Socials to enter "his" city. That they ignored him and even allowed their rally hall to be filled by Social Democrats (better them than empty seats) was the ultimate insult to the Austrian episcopate.

Rampolla's telegrams opened a hornet's nest of trouble. It was clear from the painfully defensive rhetoric in the *Reichspost* and the speeches at Linz that Gessmann and Liechtenstein saw their appeals to Rome as counterthrusts to the criticism heaped on the party by the newspapers and government in December, proving that the party was not simply the wild band of hooligans Madeyski and the Liberals had charged them with being. The antisemites sought to use the moral authority and prestige of Rome to show that they too enjoyed respectability and that they deferred to "authority," provided it was sympathetic to their interests. The party had nothing to gain by expanding its operations to Upper Austria, and Lueger knew it. From the Christian Socials' viewpoint these events were essentially self-justificatory and defensive. Papal blessings were not going to help the party win the Second Curia in Vienna, but by showing that some forms of public authority did respect it, the party would ease the burden of establishing its credentials as a *staatserhaltende Partei*. That such blessings also embarrassed the Clericals was an added benefit, but not the principal motive.

The bishops placed a different meaning on the actions of the Christian Socials. Not only did their clerical subordinates seem to be in open rebellion (Doppelbauer rightly suspected that many Upper Austrian clerics were admirers of Scheicher and Lueger), but their institutional authority was threatened by the extraordinary interventions of the papal nuncio in their home territories.[85] The bishops met in emergency session in Vienna late in January and confirmed their previous sense that intervention by Rome was necessary. Now, however, they acted with dispatch. The delegation to Rome carried with it three documents for which the bishops now sought official Vatican approval: a general pastoral letter, a programmatic series of disciplinary instructions for the clergy, and a long-winded commentary on the social question drafted by Weiss.[86] Cardinal Schönborn led the delegation, accompanied by Bishop Bauer of Brünn and Albert Weiss. Although the bishops might have simply issued such a letter on their own authority, the hard realities of Church politics forced them to turn to Rome. As long as the Viennese clergy could count on the support of Agliardi and the pro-Rampolla forces in Rome, the bishops would not be able to assert their authority effectively. Unless Schönborn could outmaneuver Rampolla or force him to back down, authoritarian statements at home were useless. Hence the ironic journey of quasi-Josephist bishops trying to get Rome to help them control their own clergy. The bishops faced a situation without parallel in Austrian ecclesiastical history. Shame was a powerful spur for their behavior. Conservative descriptions of the

Schönborn mission combine despair, outrage, and shame, in equal proportions. Schönborn had lost the struggle with Lueger before he ever left
Vienna, simply by having to go to Rome in the first place.

Before he departed, Schönborn had a private interview with the emperor and asked for the government's assistance in putting pressure on the
Curia.[87] After Lueger's insults Madeyski was only too happy to assist this
secondary line of attack. With the approval of the *Ministerrat* Madeyski
drafted and Kálnoky sent to the Austrian ambassador to the Vatican,
Count Revertera, a long memorandum condemning the Christian Socials
and urging Leo XIII to curb their activities.[88] Kálnoky, who had a low
opinion of Agliardi's diplomatic abilities, was enthusiastic about bolster-
ing Schönborn's mission. If Rome could tamper with Austrian domestic
politics, then Vienna could respond in kind.

The behavior of the Liberals was curiously passive. Plener supported
Madeyski in the *Ministerrat,* but does not seem to have been the source of
the idea of state intervention.[89] Given the willingness of others to do their
work for them, the Liberals could afford to sit back and watch hopefully.
Perhaps their investment in the coalition and their recent conciliatory
rhetoric toward the Church in several provincial Landtage would now produce some dividends.[90]

The Austrian negotiations in Rome were long, convoluted, and unsuccessful. Schönborn was isolated and virtually ignored throughout most
of the mission.[91] Several fruitless weeks spent in preliminary maneuvers
resulted in hundreds of rumors, but nothing concrete. The Liberal press
published some of the most incredible "wishful thinking" in the history of
Austrian journalism. Although Leo XIII appointed a Curial commission to
hear the bishops' complaints, the referee for the commission, Monsignor
de Cavagnis, was a protégé of Rampolla. Revertera stayed in the background for the first weeks, but by late February his patience wore thin. He
finally arranged a personal interview with Rampolla during which the two
men exchanged unusually bitter and acrimonious words.[92] In the interim
Rampolla had made known to Agliardi the accusations against which the
Christian Socials had to defend themselves. Schindler was again pressed
into service, writing a long defense of the party and taking it personally to
Rome for an interview with the pope.[93] Kálnoky's memorandum had, if
anything, a negative effect—Rampolla used it to argue that secular pressure was being brought to bear on affairs which were the internal concern
of the Church. The extensive coverage given to the mission in the Viennese Liberal press only handicapped the Austrians in Rome. A papal
condemnation of the antisemites, such as the *Neue Freie Presse* wanted,
grew more unlikely with each passing day.

The results of the commission's deliberations on 14 March were a qualified victory for Rampolla. The commission recommended that the antisemites publicly reaffirm their loyalty to the bishops, but the Austrian episcopate was to receive nothing in print to indicate papal displeasure with the Christian Socials.[94] With some last-minute modifications and adjustments, Leo XIII essentially followed the recommendations of his commission. Agliardi was instructed to ask the party leaders to make a public declaration of loyalty, while Schönborn was given a vague statement of sympathy to carry back to Vienna. Leo refused to approve a specific written condemnation of the Christian Socials. Schönborn did not leave Rome empty-handed, but the consensus on all sides was that, as Revertera put it, he had gotten "bloody little" for the seven tedious weeks he had spent in Rome. Philipp zu Eulenburg noted how depressed the cardinal was immediately after his return to Vienna.[95]

The failure of the Schönborn mission was of considerable moment for the Christian Socials. The behavior of the common clergy over the last eight years was now legitimated. The bishops could grumble and complain, but now they had to come to terms with the Christian Socials. The Liberals were perhaps the most disappointed of all. Plener himself may have expected little from the mission (or so he suggests in his autobiography), but the Liberal press was dumbfounded. Rather than embarrassing the party on the eve of the 1895 Council elections, the bishops' actions had given the antisemitic press new evidence of the conspiracy between Liberal and Clerical forces to undermine "Christian democracy" in Vienna. If the press thought that Leo would enhance Liberal election chances, it was sadly mistaken. The success of the Christian Socials in the April elections did not depend in a positive sense on the victory in Rome. Even with a papal condemnation it was likely that Lueger would have pulled off the victory. But legitimation from Rome was important later in the year, when Lueger was fighting desperately to prove his credibility as a responsible public figure deserving of confirmation as mayor. The abortive mission in March made it easier for the party to style Badeni's decision for nonconfirmation in November as an act of political vengeance rather than an act to "save the state" from revolutionary radicalism.

Lueger handled the party's response to the nuncio's instructions in a superb fashion. Although Agliardi received the order in early April, Lueger waited six weeks (until 16 May) to do anything about it. With the city elections safely out of the way, the party could afford to return to a slightly more "Catholic" stance. In a huge rally organized for the purpose in the *Musikverein*, the party leadership declared their loyalty to the established social order and their respect for all established authority, including that of the bishops.[96] The histrionic effect of the evening made the declaration almost a tour de force. Lueger had observed the letter of Agliardi's instructions, but hardly their spirit.

The Revolt of the *Beamten:* The Council Elections of April 1895

The cyclical election system of 1891 prescribed that the Second Curia would go to the polls in early April 1895. As noted above, this curia in most districts of the city was dominated by the state and municipal officials and by the public-school teachers, although a small number of lower ranking *Hausherren* also voted here. In the Josefstadt, for example, of the 1,366 enfranchised voters, 800 were *Staatsbeamten,* 50 were city officials, 80 were teachers, and 150 were *Privatbeamten.* The remaining 300 were smaller property owners.[97] The ratios for the Josefstadt were similar to those of other districts (in Währing the public employees constituted over 70 percent of the total electorate).[98] White collar voters living in the inner districts like the Landstrasse and the Josefstadt were likely to be more highly placed in their rank classifications on the average than those living in former suburban areas, if only because of the significantly higher cost of suitable rental housing in the inner districts.

The elections were nothing less than a catastrophe for the Liberal party. After the various runoffs were completed on 5 April the Christian Socials gained sixteen new seats in the Second Curia. Whereas in 1891 they had won only eight seats, they now had twenty-four, two more than the Liberals. The Liberal party lost nearly half of its seats in this crucial curia.[99] They lost districts like the Landstrasse, the Neubau, and the Josefstadt which had gone overwhelmingly Liberal in 1891. In 1891 the antisemites had barely managed to come up with 40 percent of the vote in the Landstrasse, but they now won 52 percent (Neubau 44 percent/52 percent, Josefstadt 45 percent/53 percent, Margarethen 40 percent/52 percent, etc.). In the few districts the Liberals salvaged, the results were no more encouraging. In Wieden, for example, the antisemites increased their share of the vote from 30 percent in 1891 to 46 percent in 1895, a clear indication of where voter sympathies were heading. Even in the Liberal bastions of the Innere Stadt and the Leopoldstadt the antisemites managed to increase substantially their relative share of the total vote.[100]

In part the shift to the antisemites reflected new voters entering the lists in the 1895 elections; 2,068 new voters used the opportunity to cast ballots in 1895.[101] But their presence was not the central reason for the Liberals' loss, as both Liberal and antisemitic newspapers pointed out. In fifteen of the nineteen districts of the city the Liberals won numerically fewer votes in 1895 than in 1891, even with the increase in the electorate as a whole.

The percentage of enfranchised voting (73.7 percent) was almost identical with that of 1891 (74.1 percent) so that the "stay-at-home" factor was similar for the two elections. More important, in most of the districts where the antisemites won former Liberal seats, the increase in the antisemitic vote in 1895 from that in 1891 surpassed the numbers of new voters in the district (in the Landstrasse, for example, the antisemites picked up 384 new votes, but the active district electorate increased by only 280). In addition, not all new voters would automatically have voted antisemitic. In fact it was likely that many of them would have voted Liberal, since private bureaucracies with Jewish white collar staffs were increasing their manpower levels faster in the 1890s than were the state and local bureaucracies or the school system. The Liberals had purposely put middle and upper level *Privatbeamten* in the Second Curia in 1891 to balance antisemitism in the public bureaucracies with a larger Jewish vote. During the Third Curia by-elections held in late March 1895 (to replace deceased or resigned councilmen) Jewish artisan voters in the Leopoldstadt had boycotted their party's candidates (out of resentment to Liberal indifference on the antisemitic question), with the result that an antisemitic baker, Lorenz Müller, defeated the Liberal candidate in this district.[102] Fearing a similar eruption in the Second Curia by Jewish voters, the Liberals worked desperately in the days between the Third and Second Curia elections to make certain that the Jewish private employees would not sit out the elections, with some success: there was no mass abstention of these voters reported either in the press or in the police reports on the elections.

All of the contemporary authorities and parties who monitored the election agreed that the Liberals' losses occurred from voting shifts among three groups of public employees: the state and communal officials, and the schoolteachers.[103] White collar disaffection was not restricted in 1895 to the lowest rank levels of the public bureaucracy, since districts were falling to the antisemites where officials of higher rank classifications were in the majority. Older teachers and officials seemed to be withdrawing their support from the Liberals, as well as officials with university educations.

The Liberal party's treatment of each of these groups between 1892 and 1895 showed much about the hapless, inept style of the party and its disordered sense of political priorities. In particular, Liberal ministerial behavior toward the state officials, the largest and most powerful of these groups, invited disaster in 1895. After the Liberals entered the coalition in October 1893, most Liberal voters among the state officials thought that at long last a major salary reform bill for the civil service would be brought before parliament. Indeed, those few Liberal politicians like Max Menger and Eduard Suess who did realize the implications of the growing impatience among the officials pleaded with Plener and Wurmbrand in 1894 to submit to parliament a comprehensive salary law.[104] *Beamten* complaints about the *Theuerung* which had begun in 1891 continued to grow. The professional newspapers of the officials published a series of exposés on the inadequacies of conventional white collar budgets for *Beamten* families.[105]

Plener chose to ignore the urgent advice of his party colleagues, however, believing that token measures would suffice to hold the state officials in line. He stalled on the salary problem for almost a year, giving meaningless assurances to a delegation of protesters in June 1894 that he would do what he could to alleviate their distress. Finally, in December 1894 Robert Pattai forced Plener's hand by submitting to parliament a bill which would have provided the four lowest rank levels in the bureaucracy with immediate raises of 200 fl. per individual.[106] Plener categorically rejected such an "extravagance," arguing the need to preserve the balanced budget. A comprehensive bill on the magnitude of Pattai's (which would have cost an additional 8 million fl. annually) would have to await new tax resources for the state. Instead, Plener proposed two stopgap measures to try to control the turbulence provoked by the antisemites.[107] Older officials who had served in the same rank level for more than fifteen to twenty years would receive an outright bonus of 100 to 200 fl. All other officials in the three lowest classes (XI–IX) would receive extraordinary *Subsistenzzulagen* (cost-of-living awards) which would vary between 60 and 100 fl. a year, depending upon rank and length of service. The total cost of Plener's proposals was slightly less than 3 million fl. per year.

That Plener was seriously interested in pushing through a complete salary reform in 1894–95, even if the government could have afforded it, was improbable. When Badeni and Bilinski attempted a comprehensive regulation in 1896 (at a projected cost of 11 million fl.), they met with serious resistance from the Clerical Conservatives and other agrarians who were unsympathetic to expensive special interest welfare programs for urban-based white collar voters.[108] Plener was more interested in using his limited patronage and intraministerial power on behalf of Liberal-sponsored tax reform programs and a sympathetic franchise reform than in squandering it on a *Beamten* salary bill. In the long run such "statesmanlike" action may have been sensible, but for the purposes of the April elections in Vienna it was disastrous.

The Viennese *Beamten* newspapers and the antisemitic press reacted to Plener's proposals with scorn. Not only was the first measure little more than tokenism (the total number of older officials affected was less than 2,000 out of a total work force of over 36,000), but Plener did not even bother to bring the second bill into parliament until mid-March 1895.[109] When the Viennese elections did occur, no significant parliamentary action had been taken on the second measure. Rather than cash in hand, the *Beamten* voters of the Second Curia had stale, four-month-old promises. Lueger reminded his voters of the *Beamten* congress of 1891, at which Guido Sommaruga had promised that a Liberal return to power would mean a salary reform for public employees. Lueger left it to his audiences to draw their own conclusions. Liberal propaganda to *Beamten* groups on the eve of the elections dredged up old arguments about Liberal "solidity" and "maturity," as well as the clerical menace, but now this kind of rhetoric found a much reduced impact. Not all *Beamten* deserted the Liberals, but a sufficient number within the lowest rank classes (as well as some from the higher classes, who were to get nothing from Plener's bills!) crossed over to the antisemites. That some of the antisemitic candidates for the Second Curia (thirteen out of the forty-six) adopted a nationalist stance (none were pure Schönerians) helped to salve the consciences of voters who could not bring themselves to vote "clerical," but who would vote "Christian-Nationalist."[110]

Unrest among the smaller group of city employees also led to some crossovers to the antisemites, although not on the scale of the state officials. When the Liberals on the *Stadtrat* pushed their reorganization of the *Magistrat* through in June 1892 to fit the new metropolitan area, they introduced a new *Rangclassen* system in which salary levels were raised over previous levels. In this the local party seemed to be making an honest attempt to fulfill its election promises to the communal employees. The problem came in November 1892, however, when the city bureaucracy had to be integrated into these new rank levels and when the Liberal politicians on the *Stadtrat* had to decide how many job positions would be allocated to each rank (this was the crucial factor rather than the improved salary levels themselves). Here Johann Prix's and Albert Richter's concern to balance the city budget and to cover the extraordinary expenses caused by the integration of the suburbs into the city led them to make an important tactical error. Rather than distributing the job positions in such a way as to facilitate promotion possibilities for younger employees, Richter and Prix placed an overproportionate share of the ratings in the lowest rank level and reduced the number of intermediate positions to which men might be promoted.[111] Many communal officials found themselves stuck in a rank level which did not reflect the actual work load and responsibilities they carried, since informal organizational patterns within the bureaucracy responded to task assignments and not to a theoretical organizational chart. The Liberals were engaging in a not so subtle form of political cheating—taking away from the city officials with one hand what had just been given to them with the other. Initial salaries were higher in the lowest two levels of the *Magistrat* than in parallel positions in the state bureaucracy, but promotion to higher levels was in many cases slower, because of the pattern of job distribution created in 1891–92.[112] Equally important, work loads in the local bureaucracy were relatively heavier, since the Liberals did not expand the *Magistrat* rapidly enough to cope with the new problems caused by metropolitan Vienna. In absolute terms the city employees were better off than their state cousins—they had a *Dienstpragmatik,* better pension rights, higher initial salaries—but in relative terms a considerable amount of bitterness took hold of the lower ranks of the *Magistrat* in the years 1892–94, which expressed itself in the voting of 1895. Professional mobility was a crucial issue here, since the Liberals seemed to be paying for the new metropolitan area by forcing austerity measures onto the city officials. Former suburban officials generally prospered by being brought into the metropolitan salary classification, but older and younger officials in the First through Tenth Districts looked at unification with ambivalence after 1892.

Perhaps the most striking change in political attitudes occurred among the 2,600 male schoolteachers in the city.[113] In 1891 most of these teachers had remained within the Liberal fold even when the state officials began to waver. Much more than the *Staatsbeamten* the schoolteachers depended upon a strident anticlericalism for their collective self-image. At the same time most schoolteachers (on the primary level) would not have found the nationalism issue in and of itself sufficient reason to abandon the Liberal party. A substantial minority of the Viennese teaching corps had been born in Bohemia or Moravia, but conventional assimilation into Viennese values and the absence in 1894–95 as yet of a strong Czech school movement in Vienna made the nationalism issue premature as a major determinant of voter choice.[114] In April 1895, however, a significant segment of the older and middle ranking teachers, especially in the inner districts, switched their allegiance and voted antisemitic.[115] Why did they sacrifice their historic anticlericalism to support a movement in which political clericalism played such a prominent, if admittedly subsidiary, role?

The revision in political behavior by many schoolteachers reflected several unfortunate policy decisions by the Liberal party in Vienna and Lower Austria. In December 1891 the Landtag passed the *Stadtrat*'s new salary bill, which brought the suburban teachers into a unified metropolitan framework and provided modest increases for the Viennese teachers. But in order to shore up the city's overextended education budget the Liberals decided to cut back on certain informal "fringe benefits" which had always gone with the position of tenured teacher in the city system.

Before 1891 most teachers taught between eighteen and twenty-four hours and were also expected to supervise recreational and sports periods and to teach extracurricular courses in their schools. The latter duties carried with them a flat rate of extra compensation which was rather generous—hundreds of teachers earned as much as 150–200 fl. in additional income by serving as sports supervisors and vocational instructors in their schools. The 1891 salary bill abolished all extra pay for such duties and made them mandatory for most teachers by raising the number of required hours to be taught each week. The result was to cut the net income of hundreds of middle and senior level teachers in the old ten districts of Vienna by as much as 50 fl. per year, even after the new salary raises went into effect.[116]

To add insult to injury, the Liberal politicians who approved the 1891 bill responded with blatant insults to the delegations of teachers protesting about the losses in their real income. One Liberal, Constantine Noske, a protégé of Albert Richter and a politician with little political common sense, angrily suggested that the teachers were lazy and took a week to do as much work as most people did in two days. He also accused them of greed and insensitivity to the needs of other taxpayers. Noske was not alone in such impolitic comments. Wenzel Lustkandl wondered aloud in the Landtag if the teachers who were signing protest petitions had actually bothered to read what they were signing.[117]

These political gaffes were illustrative of a deeper problem between the Liberal party and the teachers. Politicians like Noske and Lustkandl were not of the generation of Liberals who had created the 1869 school legislation. They simply inherited the public-school teachers, whom they mindlessly thought to be a reliable and complacent electoral group. Although the teachers were active in defense of their professional and political rights in the 1880s (against the clericalism drive by the Catholics), their material well-being was increasingly taken for granted by the Liberal party, largely because of the Liberals' overreliance on the anticlericalism issue. The Liberals thought they could buy off the teachers with ideological and political concessions. Even in staunchly Liberal teacher newspapers in the early 1890s the complaint was often voiced that the Liberals treated the teachers like *Stimmvieh*, men so stupid that they would always vote Liberal no matter what was done to them.[118] The Liberals had been extremely generous in their patronage of the teachers on ideological and cultural matters. As noted in chapter 5, it was largely because of Liberal patronage that the teachers came to possess an elevated self-image as *Bildungsbürger*. But the 1890s brought new, materialistic and more explicitly class concerns. *Bildung*, having been recognized, was no longer sufficient. Like the state officials the teachers gradually began to expect an absolute and relative increase in the material value of *Bildung,* both for themselves and for their children. Personal security and satisfaction were no longer defined in exclusively cultural and ideological terms. The kind of not so subtle material disabilities imposed on the Viennese teaching corps by the Liberal *Stadtrat* and Landtag simply invited renegade political responses.

Also many teachers began to question how serious the Liberals were in defending the Imperial school law on pure, anticlerical grounds. After all, it was Ernst v Plener who engineered the coalition of 1893 with the Clericals; it was also Plener who tried to reduce the anticlerical profile of the party. When Liberals like Lustkandl and Weitlof made conciliatory speeches to the bishops in the Lower Austrian Landtag in February 1895, pompously affirming their belief in religion as a stabilizing force in society, many teachers began to wonder what reality was left behind the old anticlerical facade of the Liberal party.[119]

Unlike the state officials the teachers also faced the first mass-based socialist challenge from various Austrian public service employees, providing older, antisemitic-minded teachers with an additional class-based motive for their voting choices. In the early 1890s Karl Seitz, a determined young provisional teacher *(Unterlehrer)* in Vienna who became the Socialist mayor of Vienna in the 1920s, organized his fellow *Unterlehrer* into a solid, aggressive movement. The *Unterlehrer* were the most exploited members of the teaching corps, often waiting as long as ten years before promotion to a regular position as teacher.[120] They had little job security and abysmally low salaries. The Liberals used them to fill positions which in theory should have gone to regular teachers, thereby saving money but also slowing down severely promotion opportunities for the provisionals. The *Unterlehrer* were in a vicious circle: by performing jobs which should have gone to fully tenured teachers, they were undermining their own careers. In the 1860s and 1870s the status of an *Unterlehrer* was no better, but the waiting period before promotion had been shorter. Especially after 1885 the city authorities purposely extended the apprenticeship period to five and often as much as ten years in order to stretch the education budget.

When Seitz first organized his movement, he began within the generally Liberal professional culture of the older teachers, even though his top colleagues in the movement all had a way of showing up later as prominent Socialist politicians (Otto Glöckel, Alexander Täubler, etc.). In 1894 Seitz moved to take over the older Liberal teacher association *Die Volksschule* by having 400 of his followers join it and elect a more radical leadership.[121] He planned on turning the association into a radical *Centralverein* for all teachers, regardless of rank or status, which would be used to urge both the city and the Imperial authorities to create better social welfare programs and grant professional rights for teachers. Prominent among Seitz's reforms was the elimination of the designation *Unterlehrer* and the creation of a common title for all teachers irrespective of age or service. Seitz also sought to eliminate political patronage in teacher appointments, making time in service and educational credentials the only valid criteria.

Rather than gaining the cooperation of the older teachers who controlled the Liberal association, Seitz encountered open hostility. Not only were the older, tenured teachers shocked at his aggressiveness and open disregard for political clientage, but they were disturbed by Seitz's intent to abolish internal rank designations, thereby devaluing their own long-sought and hard-won accomplishments. More important, by early 1895 Seitz and his associates were displaying an open commitment to Austrian Socialism and the Austrian proletariat, organizing in mid-1895 the first Socialist teachers' newspaper in Austria, the *Freie Lehrerstimme*. What had begun as a radical Democratic protest in 1890 was by 1895 an incipient crusade for egalitarian social rights. Seitz's use of Left Liberal social rhetoric, precisely the kind of Left Liberalism most Viennese bourgeois types had gladly abandoned in 1848, showed how easily radical Democratic rhetoric with an anticlerical base could be carried laterally into the Socialist movement. The Seitz group (the *Jungen*) replaced the older Liberal teachers as the most adamant and uncompromising anticlericals in the school system, combining Left Liberal ideology with Socialist values. Whereas older Liberal teachers increasingly tired of anticlericalism as a functional concern after 1895, hatred of Church and clergy gained a new lease on life in the hands of the Socialist *Unterlehrer*. This was, moreover, not simply a change in the advocates of anticlericalism, for the older anticlericalism of teachers in the 1870s and 1880s had always been narrowly bourgeois and cultural in orientation, closely affiliated with the theory of the unitary Bürgertum espoused by the Liberal party. Once the *Unterlehrer* adapted anticlericalism to a class orientation, replacing the Bürgertum with the proletariat as the object of their loyalties, the potency and danger of the issue increased geometrically.

This conjunction of class and cultural hatred in the hands of Seitz and his colleagues like Otto Glöckel immediately before the ascendancy of Karl Lueger and the Christian Socials was a fateful one for later Viennese politics. Not only did Lueger have a virtual revolt of the *Unterlehrer* on his hands when he took power in 1896, but these were teachers who were completely alienated from Christian Social bourgeois culture. That many older teachers voted antisemitic in 1895 as a way of expressing their anxieties and resentment over a "democratization" of the teaching corps by the *Jungen* was not unlikely. Perhaps as many as 40–50 percent of the older and intermediate teachers in the inner districts of the city repudiated the Liberals in favor of a party which seemed to take a more interest-oriented role toward their material rights, but which might also be more capable of controlling dissidence within the teaching corps itself.

An explanation for the ineptness of the Liberal party on the problem of white collar welfare rights in the mid-1890s is not easily boiled down into a few catch phrases. Some Liberals like Max Menger were capable, alert politicians who would have done well in any competitive system. Others, however, showed themselves to be completely hapless in dealing with Lueger. As different as the national Liberals and the local Viennese branch were, Ernst v Plener and Albert Richter shared certain political disabilities. Both allowed the aura of wealth and influence which the very highest levels of political power brought with them to corrupt their sense of political accountability to the Liberal Bürgertum. The classic example of this kind of insensitivity came in 1894–95 when on several occasions Albert Richter made remarks about the alleged greed and irresponsibility of the Viennese *Hausherren,* who were pressing the city administration for special favors. What Liberal politician in his right mind would attack the *Hausherren,* the core of the First Curia and the pillar of Liberal power in Vienna for nearly forty years? Yet Richter did so with a nonchalance which made his criticism seem almost normal and expected. The question was above all one of tact and style. Even if the Liberals could not do all that the *Hausherren* wanted, they at least could have made some effort to smooth ruffled feathers and calm unsettled emotions. Instead, Richter and many of his associates on the *Stadtrat* showed an uncanny ability to throw political kerosene on fires which in many cases were only beginning to smoke.

One might argue that men like Richter and Plener were influenced by "finance capitalism" to attack or ignore the traditional white collar and property-owning Bürgertum, and in part this may be correct. The highest placed notables of Liberal power in Vienna were in regular contact with the high bourgeois capitalist elites and their affiliated newspapers. Years of associating with the economic power elites of the city may have made politicians like Richter forget their political origins. With the ascendancy of Richter after 1890, the leadership of Viennese Liberalism ceased to be a local, *Vorstadt* phenomenon (which it had still been under Mayors Felder, Newald, and Uhl) and became more and more an appendage of the Chamber of Commerce and Industry and the *Neue Freie Presse.* Liberalism in general did not become purely "capitalist," but individual politicians clearly did as time passed after 1890.

More important, the oligarchical structure of the new statute of 1890

intensified these trends. Even under Felder, who was an administrative
autocrat more than a self-interested political oligarch, Viennese Liberalism consisted of a variety of factions and interest groups, which came
together against Lueger and the radical Democrats, but which enjoyed a
parity position against each other in the City Council and in the various
committees. Ater 1891 with the existence of the powerful new *Stadtrat*
the opportunities for self-enhancing political oligarchy increased tremendously. Prix and Richter purposely selected the majority of their *Stadträthe* in 1891 from the wealthy First Curia and allowed them to develop
private domains of patronage and financial interest which alienated them
from many in their own party. That this was a structural issue and not one
of individual morality was shown when the same thing happened to the
Christian Social *Stadträthe* ten years later. Political oligarchy was
perhaps more important than "capitalism" in alienating loyalist Liberal
voters. It was inconceivable that the Liberal party of the 1870s or early
1880s would have acted as nonchalantly about alienating key voter groups
like the teachers and the *Hausherren* as did Richter and his supporters on
the *Stadtrat* after 1891. Power on the executive council went to their
heads in a dizzying fashion. Rather than learning the lessons of interest
group politics articulated by the Christian Socials in 1891, these Liberals
simply took their election successes in 1891 for granted and proceeded to
ignore or abuse their constituents. Those Liberals who might have
stopped this trend were either isolated (Suess, Menger, von Billing,
Schlechter) or dead (Sommaruga) by 1895. Although Plener and the Viennese Liberal elite were on opposite sides on the Lueger confirmation
conflict and on the validity of the coalition of 1893, their *styles* of politics
were remarkably similar.

Equally characteristic for these late Liberals was their sluggish, unimaginative approach to municipal finance. The common Liberal explanation provided to all protesting white collar or propertied Bürger groups
demanding more special interest concessions was the need to shore up the
deficit-ridden budget of *Gross Wien*. But the Liberals never even considered the possibility of raising new income to finance white collar social
privileges. Richter's answer to the city's budgetary woes was essentially
that of Plener—belt tightening and selected cuts in expenditures. Only
with Lueger did a bourgeois party arrive on the scene which realized the
city's desperate need for additional discretionary income. Privileged
bourgeois politics after 1890 were inevitably and inexorably special interest politics in a collective mode which required additional revenue resources for the city and the province. Lueger realized this from the first
day of his accession to power. The only other alternative was a completely open, democratized political system, which neither the Liberals

nor the Christian Socials wanted. The Christian Social drive for profit-producing public utilities after 1896 must be seen in this light.

The final results of the spring elections of 1895 put the Liberals in an untenable position. Although on paper they still possessed a small majority in the Council, at least ten of the seventy-two remaining Liberals were known to harbor sympathies for the antisemites or were sufficiently hostile to Richter's and Grübl's oligarchical proclivities as to be unreliable. The core group on which Mayor Grübl could depend was no larger than the new antisemitic delegation—about sixty-two to sixty-three men. In an interview with the *Neue Freie Presse* immediately after the election, Grübl sketched several alternatives which were open to the Liberal Club: they could resign en masse from the city administration (including his own resignation as mayor) and force new elections in all three curias; they could compromise with the Christian Socials, handing over to Lueger the position of first vice-mayor and a parity position on the *Stadtrat;* or they could fight it out with their present weakened forces, refusing to resign or compromise.[122]

From the beginning of the crisis there was considerable disunity within the Viennese Liberals and a growing gap separating them from the national party represented in the *Ministerrat.* Although Grübl was the nominal leader, Albert Richter was the real force behind the party's strategy. Richter, in close alliance with the wealthy Liberal press, decided immediately after the election that Grübl's first alternative was the only acceptable, honorable way out.[123] The Liberals should resign their positions in the executive and on the *Stadtrat,* forcing the government to dissolve the City Council and summon new elections. If this meant a new surge of Christian Social victories (which no one could seriously doubt), at least the Liberals would be able to play a dignified oppositional role. Underlying this assumption was the arrogant belief that Lueger was completely unfit to rule the city and that if the emperor should confirm him, the antisemites would soon dig their own political graves by total administrative incompetence. Imperial confirmation would also lead to the breakup of the coalition, an event Richter and the *Neue Freie Presse* certainly would have welcomed.[124] As an alternative, if the emperor should decide not to confirm Lueger (or any other antisemite), perhaps the city could be placed under an Imperial bureaucratic directorate (a form of civil marshal law) for a sufficient length of time to allow the ministry to bring heavy pressure on the state officials to change their ways and vote Liberal. Richter's strategy was thus intimately related to the hysterical demands in the *Neue Freie Presse* that Plener and Wurmbrand should have insisted that the disciplinary authority of the state be brought to bear to "guide" bourgeois voter choices in the Second Curia.[125] In their desperation, the proponents of this view not only had sacrificed the idea of municipal autonomy (better a nonautonomous city than a free city under non-Liberal rule), but also were clearly willing to undercut one of the most sacred ideals of Liberalism, the individual's right to determine freely his own electoral choices.

For several weeks an uneasy peace reigned, with much intra- and inter-party discussion and speculation, but little concrete action. Lueger was clearly inclined to work for a compromise (Grübl's second option), provided that it could be accomplished quickly and without any embarrassments. The Liberal Club met on several occasions, and after some opposition Richter pushed through his strategy of a mass resignation. The new council met on 14 May to reelect Richter, whose term expired that month, as the first vice-mayor.[126] This led to the actual crisis. Richter was duly reelected by a seventy to sixty-four vote, but immediately refused to accept the renewal of his post. A second round of voting resulted in Lueger's election as first vice-mayor (several dissident Liberals deserted their party to vote with the antisemites). Lueger announced that he would accept the position. Since the post of vice-mayor was not subject to direct Imperial confirmation, Lueger immediately assumed the office. Within a day Raimund Grübl announced his resignation as mayor, noting that he could not remain as *Bürgermeister* with Lueger as his first chief assistant. Grübl recalled the Newald era as an example of a mayor governing with alleged "bipartisan" support, and he clearly did not consider that precedent an attractive one.[127] The Liberals also announced that they would boycott the upcoming elections for nine positions on the *Stadtrat*, thereby ensuring that all nine would go to the Christian Socials.

Grübl's resignation on 14 May left Lueger in temporary control of the city. He immediately summoned the representatives of all three of the political groups in the Council (Liberal, antisemitic, and unaligned) to a strategy session in which he proposed a grand compromise: the Liberals and antisemites would be free to compete for the position of mayor in open rivalry, but each would be accorded one vice-mayoral position and a proportionate share of the seats on the *Stadtrat*. The Liberals rejected the proposal out of hand, and when the elections for the new *Bürgermeister* were held on 29 May, Lueger was elected mayor on the third ballot with covert Liberal support.[128] The Liberals' tactic was to embarrass Lueger by handing him the office of mayor on a platter, with the implication that the Liberals would constantly harass and embarrass him, allowing minor administrative matters to go through the Council uncontested, but intervening to stop any major policy reforms the Christian Socials might attempt. Lueger saw through this plot and rejected the election, preferring to force new elections and obtain a stronger, majority position in the

Council before accepting the executive leadership of Vienna. After another fruitless round of voting the Council was dissolved by Erich Kielmansegg, who ordered a bipartisan *Beirat,* consisting of eight Liberals and seven Christian Socials, under the chairmanship of a Lower Austrian official, to administer the city until new elections could be called. If the Liberals were counting on a pure, nonpolitical control of the city by the civil service, they were sorely disappointed. The very fact that Kielmansegg had sufficient political sense to allocate nearly half the seats on the *Beirat* to the antisemites helped to legitimate the party's claim to administrative responsibility in the fall elections of 1895.

The behavior of the Imperial government during these events was curiously passive and ineffective. Most top officials and political figures seemed at a loss for viable alternatives, although all of them resisted as impractical and irresponsible the local Liberals' demands for direct administrative manipulation of the *Staatsbeamten* and other public employees. Plener for one opposed Richter's and Grübl's decision to resign.[129] After 14 May he worked hard to persuade the Liberal Club in the City Council to elect another, more moderate and flexible Liberal as mayor (like Moritz Lederer), instead of simply handing the city over to the antisemites. Richter and Grübl remained adamant, however, and Plener was forced to try another strategy. He approached several members of the Lower Austrian provincial government in an attempt to persuade them of the merits of emergency legislation to revise the 1890 *Gemeindeordnung* to create an appointive mayor. Again, Plener found little interest, since some of the Liberals on the provincial level (especially Eduard Suess and Josef Kopp), in contrast to their municipal colleagues, felt strongly about preserving the city's autonomy.

A crucial question which the *Ministerrat* considered but which Lueger's refusal of the post of mayor made unnecessary to resolve was the Imperial response to a Lueger confirmation request. Had Lueger accepted the election on 29 May, what would the coalition have done? Both Plener and Wurmbrand were against Imperial confirmation. The rest of the Cabinet (including Bacquehem, who was sympathetic to the Liberals on most matters) was for it, but only as the least of all possible evils.[130] Franz Joseph was undecided how to act, although he was personally against confirmation. On 20 May Kielmansegg was asked for his opinion and provided the *Ministerrat* with a detailed, thoughtful report which stressed the conservative and moderate political propensities of Lueger. Kielmansegg saw through Lueger's demagogic veneer to the calculating, professional politician below, and was confident that once in office Lueger would shed many of his "radical" trappings.[131] Kielmansegg recommended that Lueger be confirmed, provided that he resign his seat in the Reichsrat. Kielmansegg thus struck at the central concern of the German

Josephist bureaucracy (as opposed to the Liberal party per se): what would Lueger do if he could combine the political resources of a powerful Reichsrat delegation with the enormous institutional resources of the city of Vienna? Kielmansegg for one had no desire to find out, and his opposition to Lueger centered on the fundamental jurisdictional rivalry between city and state, which Lueger would only exacerbate by combining the offices of party leader and city executive of the *Residenzstadt*. The Imperial bureaucracy had never had to face a bourgeois party which used its control of Vienna in national policy confrontations with the state. The Liberals, as noted above, gave the city a low profile in the national political system, thereby paving the way for their classic detente with the high bureaucracy in the 1870s. Kielmansegg's report testified above all to his political realism. Personally Kielmansegg was sympathetic to the Liberals and would very much have preferred for them to retain control of the city (he strongly supported Plener's idea of a substitute for Grübl after 14 May). But he was sufficiently realistic to know that the government had to administer the 1890 statute in a fair and equitable fashion. Kielmansegg found it ironic that the same Liberals who were urging nonconfirmation were among those who had opposed his efforts to create an appointive mayor in the summer of 1890. But he was equally adamant about separating the offices of national party leader and chief executive of the capital, a position which led to a running feud between Lueger and himself as the autumn approached.

The September Elections and the Struggle for Confirmation: The Rise of a Mass Party

The Autumn Crisis

The events of April left both parties in a state of anxious waiting for the next round of elections. In theory the government should have called new elections within six weeks after the dissolution of the City Council, but Kielmansegg advised postponing the elections for as long as possible to allow tempers to cool down and to give the Liberals a chance to regroup. Precisely the opposite happened. Many Liberal politicians left town for their regular summer vacations, but Lueger and Gessmann ordered all Christian Social candidates to remain in the city and campaign throughout the summer. From its very inception this campaign became a very different kind of struggle. For the first time the antisemites sensed their proximity to power and were prepared to go to any lengths to attain it. Even though the elections were finally set for late September, the Christian Socials actually began their campaign in July. For nearly three months the city was the scene of increasingly bitter and hostile confrontations between the Liberals and the antisemites.

Each side pulled a predictable and normal share of dirty (and often illegal) tricks, and each side caught the other doing so with regularity. The Liberals tried to put pressure on small artisan tradesmen in various districts to vote Liberal by encouraging larger industrial and commercial wholesalers to threaten the artisans with withdrawal of business contracts.[132] The antisemites in turn spread lies about the Liberals' alleged generosity in donating money to the Czech Nationalist group which managed the Komensky school in Favoriten.[133] It was a season of frequent and entertaining libel trials on both sides—two antisemitic journalists were acquitted of printing slanders against the Jews, but a Liberal journalist was also acquitted in a jury trial of calling the radical clergy "dirty schemers."[134] The lawyer representing the Liberal newspaperman may have hit upon a singular truth when he defended his client by arguing that Viennese politicians and journalists never meant what they said in public and that everyone knew it. If the antisemites could insult the Jews, the Liberals had a similar right to insult the clergy. The jury, at least, seemed to agree.

The Liberal party was more disorganized than ever before and handicapped by the despondency their situation provoked. One new tactic the Liberals tried was to set up a front organization for dissident craft masters, the *Freie Gewerbepartei,* playing initially on the resentment of some ward-level artisan politicians against the treatment accorded by the Baumann organization in Währing to Johann Jedlička in July 1895.[135] Soon each district in the city had a small group of these masters, well financed by Liberal election money. A campaign of roughneck tactics, organized in response by the antisemitic members of the local District Committees, was clearly orchestrated by the central elite of the party: rallies set up by the Liberal tradesmen were invaded by dozens of antisemitic agitators and their speakers shouted down.[136] These tactics were not entirely new, but their central coordination and control *was* new, and it showed how determined the antisemites were that the Third Curia should remain their proprietary possession. The Liberals also funneled small amounts of money to renegade Czech Nationalist organizations, led by the journalist Wenzel Einert, to set up token Czech National election slates in the hope of drawing off some artisan support from the antisemites. In both cases the Liberals were wasting their money. Even without their bullying tactics the antisemites would have had little to worry about. When the elections were held, the regular antisemitic candidates easily crushed all opposition.

In the rallies for the Second and First Curia voters an entirely different tone prevailed, showing the new ability of the antisemites to develop propaganda to match the social pretensions and material interests of their various audiences.[137] The Liberals were at a natural disadvantage in the Second Curia, but in August 1895 an event occurred which compounded their problems. In late June the coalition ministry fell over the Cilli affair and Franz Joseph appointed Erich Kielmansegg to preside over a caretaker ministry until a new, permanent ministry could be arranged under Casimir Badeni in the autumn. Kielmansegg was a man of decided opinions and felt himself under no obligations to behave like a caretaker. Indeed, his ministry saw some important legislation passed by parliament, most notably the far-reaching reform of Austrian civil procedure in the judicial system. As *Statthalter,* Kielmansegg had been gravely concerned about the radical politicization of officials and teachers.[138] Since the Liberals were no longer in the Cabinet, he felt he could act to try to curb *Beamten* unrest without seeming to favor the Liberal party. On 10 August 1895 Kielmansegg issued his controversial *Beamtenerlass,* which sought to impose controls on the rights of public officials to organize public protests about political or professional matters.[139] The *Erlass* could be interpreted in several ways, but essentially covered three broad areas: it demanded an end to public electoral agitation by public officials in party contests; it required a toning down of professional, interest group protests (such as organizational petitions, professional rallies, *Beamten* congresses, and the like); and it urged that officials use regular hierarchical control channels to make their grievances known. Implicitly it suggested moderation by individual officials in their voting choices in the polling place, but the *Erlass* was explicitly directed to the first three areas, leaving the last to the individual discretion of the officials themselves. Unlike the Liberals, who simply wanted direct pressure brought on officials to vote Liberal, Kielmansegg sought a more indirect way to curb unrest. The *Erlass* was not so much pro-Liberal as it was pro-Verwaltung. Both Kielmansegg and the emperor were interested in tightening discipline within the ranks of the officials and limiting their professional radicalism. If this also benefited the Liberals (which Kielmansegg certainly hoped it would), that was acceptable as well. Not only did the *Erlass* apply to state-level employees, but *Land*-level administrative authorities were instructed to enforce similar guidelines against the public-school teachers.[140]

The Kielmansegg *Erlass* proved to be a colossal political blunder, a classic example of too little too late. Most *Beamten* and *Lehrer* organizations were outraged by the *Erlass* and refused to conform to its injunctions. They continued to meet and defend their rights of petition and protest.[141] Kielmansegg monitored *Beamten* political activity through the police, but there was little he could do to curb it. The antisemites seized on the issue, suggesting that the Liberals were behind the *Erlass* and urging officials to use the upcoming Council elections as a plebiscite on the document. Not only did most public officials not return to the Liberals in September 1895, but many of those who had remained Liberal in April now deserted to the antisemites in protest to the *Erlass*. Politicization among the officials had gone too far to be stopped by mere prohibitory injunctions, and unless the government was prepared to institute massive disciplinary controls (which it was not), the implementation of the *Erlass* was impossible. When Badeni took office in October, he acknowledged that the *Erlass* had been a mistake and would not be enforced literally.[142]

The fall 1895 campaign was the first in which the antisemites made a comprehensive propaganda effort in the First Curia. Assemblies were organized for property owners, urging them to consider Christian Social candidates for election. The rhetoric employed in these meetings was vastly different from that used in Third Curia rallies: the solidity, wealth, and even *Bildung* of property ownership were cited as reasons why the *Hausherren* should vote antisemitic.[143] Liberalism was not portrayed as "Jewish" exploitation in this curia; the antisemitism issue itself played a more secondary role in the party's agitation among the *Hausherren*. Instead, the Christian Socials reaffirmed the ideal of the Bürger property owner, once the basis for the patrician elite of the city but now threatened by "mobile" investment capital on the one side and by radical socialist egalitarianism on the other.

Beyond support for individual occupations and separate curias, however, another theme pervaded Christian Social rhetoric in this election. Precisely because the Christian Socials thought they had a decent chance to capture a significant number of First Curia seats, they could articulate a holistic vision of all three curias voting together for the first time in Viennese political history. Antisemitic propaganda to the *Hausherren* in the First Curia stressed this opportunity to unite the wealthier segments of the Bürgertum and Mittelstand with their less fortunate colleagues in the lower curias; hence Alois Liechtenstein's emphatic pleas in September 1895 that the *Hausherren* in the First Curia must "Hand und Hand gehen, mit dem kleinen Gewerbetreibenden, mit der Masse des kleinen Mittelstands einerseits, und mit den Classen der Intelligenz anderseits."[144] This notion of a new political front, a new unity of purpose and action, was a revival of older, pre-1848 conceptions of Bürger unity, placed in a new class situation. Liechtenstein's rhetoric showed that the party elite had transcended its Third Curia origins and now intended to launch a crusade to recast and reunite the whole traditional Bürgertum in a new age of political defensiveness. Officials were urged to vote antisemitic as a *Bürgerpflicht;* the victory of the antisemites would mean that once again the old *Bürgerschaft* controlled the city, not the state Verwaltung.[145] Kielmansegg noted this appeal when he reported to Badeni in late October that Lueger not only had the support of the "gesamte Kleinbürgertum" in the Third Curia, but also enjoyed the loyalty of many in the "höheren und höchsten Ständen" in Vienna as well.[146]

The campaign showed that the Christian Socials had made substantial progress in improving the efficiency of their party organization, a fact noted in the police reports on the party from late 1895.[147] Before 1895 much of the party's methodology was still indebted to the older voluntaristic, small-notable tradition of politics developed by the Liberals. As a result of the need for a concentrated period of political maneuvering, however, Gessmann and Lueger began to experiment with more coherent and disciplined political methods, which would supplement (but not replace) the older, district-level, notable tradition. Early in June 1895, for example, Gessmann instituted central scheduling and planning of district rallies.[148] Henceforth rallies were to be coordinated with the central committee, which would approve and help to fund them and try to find appropriate "name" speakers for them. Gessmann also imported outside agitators from smaller German cities in northern Bohemia and Moravia in the weeks before the election. Politics ceased to be a purely local phenomenon in some wards, with outsiders helping in the final push before election day.[149] New funding procedures were also developed in the course of 1895. Beyond purely voluntary contributions, the party began a twofold campaign to supplement its income.[150] Pressure was brought to bear on Church dignitaries to contribute (Gessmann badgered old Cardinal Gruscha into giving 1,000 fl. in December 1895), but more significantly, contributions were solicited door-to-door by local ward-level agitators from private homes and individuals. The clergy were extremely active in these solicitations, as were some of the small Christian Social family associations organized in the early 1890s.[151] As the police noted, these tactics surpassed the former voluntarism of party funding: informal coercion was openly employed on individuals and local businessmen to contribute to the party's election chest. The door-to-door approach was also extended to candidate presentation, going beyond the older tradition of rallies as the center point of party discussions. Candidates of the party and their supporters went up and down streets, knocking on doors of tenement houses and private homes, soliciting votes for themselves and their colleagues. This was not a comprehensive street and parade politics as the Socialists were to develop it, but it was clearly a step beyond the older rally politics of the Liberals and Democrats.[152]

The central committee also played a larger strategic role in the campaign than it had before. The furious attacks on the Liberal artisan group, the *Freie Gewerbepartei,* were led by Christian Social district committeemen from the *Bezirksausschüsse* who had been ordered to "invade" the Liberal rallies and disrupt them. Again, what was new here was not the rowdiness, which had always been a part of Third Curia politics, but the fact that it was being planned and coordinated on a larger level. In general the party tried to keep such tactics in hand and not provoke extreme illegalities, but the tone of the campaign was a harsh one.

These months also saw the evolution of the famous personality cult of Karl Lueger. This was both the product of and a response to the tensions of the confirmation campaign. Before 1895 Lueger had been an extremely popular figure, but the apparatus of his cult—pictures, medallions, songs, posters, matchbooks, rallies with young girls dressed in white gowns presenting him with flowers—had never been a central concern of the party.[153] The autumn 1895 and spring 1896 Council campaigns focused much more on his person, however, as a result of its being clearly a mayoral, and not simply a Council, election year. Lueger the mayoral candidate became larger than life, a living symbol of the "oppression" of the Christian *Volk* by the Jews and Liberals. Though the Liberal and Hungarian press attacked him with ad hominem arguments, accusing him of "madness" and "extreme egotism," such rhetoric simply enhanced his personal importance. Lueger the martyr was a superb tool for anti-semitic propagandists, and they exploited it to the hilt.[154] The Council elections of March/April 1895 were essentially interest group oriented, but those that followed became more personalized and cultic. The cult was less a conscious creature of Lueger and his fellow elite members than it was the product of external circumstances. The government and the press did as much to create it as did Lueger or Gessmann.

The problem with the cult, as the police noted, was that it raised expectations which could not be satisfied. If the party could not obtain the office of mayor for Lueger in a legal way, how could this "defeat" be justified in terms of the theatrical exaggerations of the cultism?[155] The personal audience which Badeni was forced to arrange for Lueger with Franz Joseph in April 1896, before Lueger relinquished the mayoralty to his colleague Joseph Strobach, was a response to the party's need to confirm the public image of Lueger as a cultic, political titan who would not back down to ministerial or Liberal intimidation, but who would honor a "personal" request from the emperor himself.

The cult around Lueger was expressively theatrical but not "irrational": this is the key to understanding its impact in Viennese Bürger circles. Lueger's image became a clever way to heighten voter interest by supplementing the narrow organizational demands of the various curial groups, giving them a more universal significance and a general moral justification. By supporting Lueger, not only would the state officials fight for better salaries, but they would help "Christianity" and the city against its "enemies." The personality cult would never have worked without a rational, interest-based core, but its dramatic qualities were immensely useful to enliven, expand, and justify the selfish professional demands of the voter groups involved. Rather than having problems of conscience about the self-serving nature of Viennese politics, Bürger voters could now enjoy the best of both worlds. They could enrich themselves and save society from the Red menace as well.

Lueger's personality cult was supplemented by other kinds of political theatricality. In the winter of 1895–96, for example, the Christian Socials organized political dramas in various *Gasthäuser* throughout the city in which antisemitic ward leaders performed simulated City Council sessions before interested spectators, some taking Liberal, others antisemitic roles. Not only was this a relatively inexpensive form of entertainment, but it relieved the endless tedium of rally-hall speeches without forcing the party into radically different kinds of political aesthetics.[156] Political drama was hardly new to Vienna, but this sort of coordinated theatricality was a novel instrument in the hands of the Christian Socials.

The new organizational momentum and aggressiveness of the party in the autumn of 1895 had a lasting effect on its structure and ideology. Precisely because the party had begun to operate with the rudiments of coherent central control and with some level of disciplined subordination, as a party and not as a collection of random clubs and individuals, it was prepared to cope successfully with the Socialist challenge in the 1897 general parliamentary elections. Small improvements became major achievements. The antisemites were able to match the Socialists' astonishing ability to hold massive rallies and demonstrations because they learned to coordinate their resources on an interdistrict level, instead of letting each district and each club decide how it would use its own limited propaganda and financial resources, as was usually the case before 1895.[157]

It is possible to assert, therefore, that by late 1895 the Christian Social party was adopting some of the attributes of a "mass" party. This term is one of the most confusing and troublesome in the political rhetoric used to analyze this period. The term was rarely used by contemporary Austrian commentators, except in the form of *massenhaft* to describe the quantitatively larger audience and constituency size of the Social Democrats.[158] Generally the term may convey several descriptive meanings, which may or may not be compatible with one another. It may mean the massive audience to which the party directs itself, an audience which surpasses the narrow strata of the higher bourgeoisie to include a larger constituency (in either class or professional group terms). Or it may refer to a style and method of politics: "mass" in the sense of the subordination of individual notability to formal and central bureaucratic control. It also may suggest a new emphasis on political effectivity: "mass" in the sense of the new personalism and "irrationalism" which has sometimes been seen as characterizing fin de siècle politics in Vienna. Finally, it may suggest a more ambitious, interest group structure on which the party is constructed, a structure which is more conscious of itself as a collection of interest groups and which attempts to control the party which allegedly represents it.

As noted throughout this book the Liberal party was never simply a party of the higher bourgeoisie, nor did it lack some measure of central control, at least on local and regional levels (although the control may have been of a voluntaristic, cooperative nature, without coercion and centralized discipline). The Liberals and especially the Democrats never lacked popular political leaders capable of some manipulation of colloquial Viennese German to entertain and persuade their audiences. Nor were the Liberals totally oblivious to the social groups which underpinned their coalition. But it was apparent that the Christian Socials were slowly evolving into a party within which all of these qualities were placed in a more coordinated, coercive framework. The Christian Socials were an excellent example of a transitional party, rooted in an age of voluntarism and district notability but gradually evolving attributes of central control and direction as well. Perhaps this evolutionary quality itself was the most notable thing about the party: "mass" bourgeois politics in Vienna were not born overnight. They did not suddenly appear in the wake of the collapse of the Liberals, foisted on the Austrian public by Lueger's charismatic powers. Nor did they break categorically and totally with their own past, a past in which the history of the Christian Socials owed much to the Liberal and Democratic traditions. The Christian Socials may have been the bastards of Austrian Liberalism, but they were its heirs in class and in political-structural terms nonetheless.

The term "mass" party may be justifiably used in Austrian politics when the following criteria are present and functioning at a meaningful level:

1. When the party has achieved a regular, predictable structure for voter mobilization and recuitment which surpasses the older antisemitic-Liberal rally-club framework (in the case of the antisemites, the new door-to-door campaign tactic, the use of professional outsiders paid to do the work, the use of patronage employees in the larger city bureaucracies after 1896—such phenomena suggest a movement beyond the older tradition).
2. When the party has achieved a level of central direction and control

which makes possible effective coordination of scarce resources, either through a regular party bureaucracy or by a strong, dominant core group of professional leaders in the elite who function as a kind of political oligarchy qua directorate (in the case of the Christian Socials, the latter was more the case than the former).

3. When the party has established a more effective, comprehensive means of fund raising than simply relying on voluntary contributions by sympathetic businesses or individuals. This could occur by membership revenue, by secret subsidies from larger institutional entities provided on a regular and sustained basis, or by effective, ward-level coercion of individuals and businesses anxious for contracts from the city or employment in city agencies and bureaucracies. The important thing here is that contributions become regular and semicompulsory. All modern political machines rely on semicompulsory revenue disguised as voluntary contributions (in the case of the Christian Socials, the latter two methods were increasingly utilized with success). Also, the boycott of Jewish businesses was a kind of negative funding vehicle, used to deprive a rival party of campaign contributions—depriving one's opponent of funds by coercive means is almost as useful as obtaining them for one's own party. It might be noted here that the Social Democrats also adopted the technique of mass boycotts.

4. When the party is able to differentiate between its audience as a whole and as a collection of parts, knowing when to utilize holistic rhetoric to portray the party as representing "all" of society and when to stress the particularistic role which the party will play as interest group advocate (the Christian Socials did this in a masterful fashion, interweaving holistic, pan-curial visions of a new social order, based on very traditional social values and institutions, with particularized social sponsorship of each segment of the party's base constituency).

5. When the party is able to employ new aesthetic devices going beyond older propaganda and control techniques (in Vienna this was not difficult to do, since so much of the political culture was based on a sense of political theatricality, but the Christian Socials did make considerable progress in the use of political drama).

6. When new segments of the nonvoting population are brought under the party's purview for possible exploitation in electoral maneuvering or social protests (the best examples for the Christian Socials would be the commercial *Angestellten* and the politicized women, the first group used as a potential barricade against the dangers of universal suffrage in the city; the second used as an alternative source of public political controversy, without any serious consideration given to the women themselves).

7. When the party evolves institutional methods for underpinning party support, whether this be through an extensive network of secondary and voluntary organizations, or, as occurred in Vienna under

Lueger, through a frank politicization of the resources of the municipal and provincial bureaucracies.

8. When the party begins to develop well-defined positions on important national and regional issues beyond simple interest group complaints, and when the party obtains regular channels of communication with the government on ministerial or subministerial levels (this can occur formally or very informally, as often happened with the Social Democrats in Vienna). The Christian Socials never had this kind of comprehensive policy stance before 1895, and their ability to work with the Imperial bureaucracy after 1897 was a heritage of their successful confrontation between 1895 and 1897 with Kielmansegg and Badeni. This comprehensive programmatic emphasis must be compulsory for all party members, once the final policy stance has been arrived at.

The central theme of all of these characteristics is a shift beyond local notability and voluntarism to a more coercive, disciplined style of politics in which the party ceases to be a collection of individuals and becomes an entity surpassing individual discretion or deference. In the case of the Christian Socials some progress had been made by late 1895/early 1896 in each of these areas, although the party never abandoned the heritage of anarchic localism and district independence which characterized its early days. The Christian Social party never achieved the level of bureaucratic control and subordination which the Social Democrats made famous. Discipline was achieved, and central control was imposed by the party elite; but beneath the veneer of this particular "mass" party lay a good deal of ward-level bargaining and interchange with the leaders of the Christian Socials. Informal consensus determined much of the behavior of the party's leadership structure, rather than routinized control or subordination to ideological dictates. The "mass" party was attractive to previously unenfranchised segments of the electorate after 1897 (such as the *Commis*) precisely because of its insistence on defending traditional, small group values and older cultural norms. This was a party which used "mass" techniques to preserve a society and a culture which found the "masses" antithetical to its own best interests. Inevitably the form began to work at cross-purposes to the function after 1897.

When the Council elections were finally held in September, the fate of the Viennese Liberals was sealed forever. In the Third Curia the Christian Socials retained all of their seats and even managed to conquer the seats of the First District, largely a result of intense campaigning by the Catholic clergy.[159] The Second Curia followed suit, giving the party uniform and widespread support.[160] Most officials and teachers were still not "antisemitic" in the artisan sense of the word—the police reports from late 1895 insisted that white collar protest was still interest group oriented rather than ideological, but they were interested in protecting their new-found rights to political expression.[161] The Kielmansegg *Erlass* was a disastrous move which the Liberal press was incapable of dealing with.

Most surprisingly, however, was the response of the First Curia, formerly the bedrock of Liberal support.[162] After the voting was over, the antisemites had fourteen seats in this curia and came away with a very respectable 32 percent of the vote. They swept most First Curia seats in the newly incorporated districts and gained respectable minorities in several of the older districts as well.[163] This was a crucial trend in local politics which had fateful consequences for the party and the city. In the February 1896 elections the party actually picked up four more First Curia seats, two of them in inner districts (Margarethen and Neubau), and soon began to make inroads into First Curia seats on some of the district committees. Not all *Hausherren* were deserting the Liberal party, but it was clear that a significant minority had already done so and it seemed likely that more would soon follow.

In all, the Christian Socials now possessed ninety-two seats in the newly elected City Council, giving them a quorum for important financial legislation. Even if the Liberals abstained from attending Council sessions, they would be unable to block Lueger's reform plans. When Lueger proudly proclaimed that he represented the Christian *Volk* in its entirety, he was not incorrect. His party was now obtaining support from all those whom the party understood as covered by this rubric—the enfranchised Bürgertum and its subordinate client groups, like the commercial employees (which was the conventional usage for the term *Volk* in the party elite).[164]

Although the elections ended in late September, the Council did not meet to elect the new mayor until 29 October. In the interim Count Casimir Badeni assumed the office of minister-president. The Lueger confirmation question was one of the first crises to confront the new leader of the Imperial government.

This decision has become part of the lore of Austrian political history, and a careful review of the proceedings seems justified, especially in view of Badeni's later equivocation and final surrender to the antisemites.[165] Badeni came to Vienna from his post as *Statthalter* of Galicia, where he had cultivated a reputation for ruling with an "iron hand." He liked to present himself as the strong man who would stand above interparty feuds and bickering to bring order to national politics.[166] Badeni had, however, some serious political weaknesses. Like most provincials, Badeni depended for his knowledge of Viennese politics before October (when he finally arrived in the city to stay) almost exclusively on what he read in the *Neue Freie Presse* and on his conversations with visiting Liberal politicians, like Ernst v Plener. His close contacts with members of the Polish Club (especially Madeyski) did nothing to deflect the view of Lueger as a petty, street-corner demagogue which Badeni derived from high Liberal sources. Also, Badeni had no sense of the complexities and malleability of western Austrian politics. He was accustomed to a much more corrupt and yet more simple political system based on personal clientage and patronage, such as existed under gentry rule in Austrian Galicia.

Badeni's chronic need to style himself as a forceful leader who would outdo even Taaffe contained a strong element of self-deception and pose. Badeni has traditionally been seen from several critical views: as the uninformed, stupid blusterer who overextended himself politically and meddled in situations so complex that only his naiveté saved him from immediate humiliation; as the inept, incompetent place-saver who wanted to be loved by everyone, but whose dissimulation and exaggerations ended up losing him the confidence of all; or as the cunning, overly crafty tactician who confused short-term advantage with long-term, enduring strategy. In spite of the overly negative press which the man received in the aftermath of his 1897 fiasco, each of these views merits some attention, and they are not mutually exclusive. Badeni had neither the political skill nor the imagination of Taaffe. The range of his political artistry was remarkably narrow, from arrogant pose to surface outrage with little in between. His rule lacked consistency and timing above all else. He had an uncanny ability to throw his support behind the right party at the wrong time, and an equally disconcerting tendency to misjudge the real strength of the parliamentary parties and their respective social and cultural constituencies. Rather than preaching coercion and using consensus, the traditional Austrian tandem, he reversed the logical order of these categories, announcing to all that he favored conciliation and peace, but used overtly coercive and ill-prepared bureaucratic intervention to achieve his ends. He wound up losing the confidence of all political groups in the system, not only for his specific decisions but also on account of the unpredictability of his behavior. Not only did the western Austrians (of a number of political and national persuasions) dislike him as the arrogant, naive Pole, but they distrusted his political judgment as well.

When he arrived in Vienna, Badeni was uncertain how to respond to the Lueger problem. His personal inclinations led him to oppose Lueger in spite of Lueger's popular power, but he would not have been averse to recommending the confirmation of some other antisemite as mayor if Lueger had been willing to step aside.[167] The problem initially for Badeni was how to humiliate Lueger and embarrass the antisemites—another Christian Social as mayor would (so Badeni thought) hopelessly discredit the party by ruining the city administration within a few months. It was as if Badeni confronted a wild, disorganized group of antisemitic Polish peasants or illiterate Ruthenian radicals, and he produced a typical gentry solution—isolate their leader and give them the rope with which to hang themselves.

On 29 October the newly elected City Council met to vote for the new *Bürgermeister*. On the first ballot Lueger was elected mayor by a ninety-three to forty-one margin. Lueger immediately announced that he would accept the election.

The *Ministerrat* requested that Kielmansegg (who had resumed the office of Lower Austrian *Statthalter*) provide another report on the question of confirmation. Kielmansegg met with Lueger on 30 October and made it clear that he had no problems with Lueger's alleged demagogy. What really impeded a favorable recommendation was the administrative problem created by the fact that Lueger would hold a Reichsrat seat and the office of mayor simultaneously. Lueger replied with some equivocation, but later reported to Kielmansegg that he was unwilling to resign from parliament.[168] Badeni later disputed that Kielmansegg had made a favorable recommendation contingent upon Lueger's resignation of the seat, but Lueger clearly thought that he had, explaining much of the bitterness in antisemitic circles toward Kielmansegg after November.[169] Finally, after much soul-searching Kielmansegg decided to swallow his scruples and recommend Lueger's confirmation. Kielmansegg saw that Lueger was the most competent anti-Liberal to run the city administration and saw no reason to prolong the uncertainties of the interim leadership which the city endured under the *Beirat*. He was especially opposed to Badeni's idea of the appointment of a straw man in place of Lueger as mayor. Kielmansegg rightly sensed that Lueger would still control municipal affairs, but would be totally beyond the reach of public accountability; the *Statthalter* was not anxious to cope with the problem of nonresponsible power. As a realist Kielmansegg knew that the Christian Socials were not going to disappear, even without Lueger as mayor, and that the Verwaltung would have to live with the antisemites. He was especially concerned with curbing the image of Lueger as martyr and wanted to keep the crown out of popular political struggles. But the Josephist in him refused to die—the report which he submitted on 1 November was not unequivocally in favor of confirmation, but supported it only as the least of all possible evils.

Had Badeni followed Kielmansegg's advice and recommended confirmation to the emperor, he might have saved himself considerable embarrassment later on. But other factors came into play. Badeni himself was little concerned with the question of Lueger's Reichsrat mandate. He even told Lueger privately that he would prefer that Lueger keep it.[170] Political rather than administrative concerns soon came to the fore in

Badeni's calculations. The Liberal party reacted to the possibility of Lueger's confirmation with a surface indifference which masked deep intraparty turmoil. The Liberal press was openly antagonistic to Lueger and strongly disposed against confirmation. The Liberal party leadership was equally opposed, but more discrete in making its views known. Finally, the Liberal president of the lower house, Johann Chlumecky, who controlled the more conservative aristocratic and commercial wing of the party, let it be known to Badeni on 5 November that if Badeni recommended confirmation, he could not guarantee the support of the conservative Liberals for Badeni's legislative programs.[171] Chlumecky also threatened to resign from the presidency if Lueger were confirmed.

Powerful Hungarian interests were also deployed against Lueger. On several occasions in 1895 Baron Bánffy, the Hungarian minister-president, had protested to Franz Joseph about the insults against Hungary which had become a standard element of Christian Social propaganda.[172] To confirm Lueger on the eve of the new *Ausgleich* negotiations and at the beginning of the Hungarian millennial celebration (1896 marked the thousand-year anniversary of the conquest of Hungary by the Magyars) would embarrass the Hungarian leadership and compromise the upcoming interministerial negotiations. Badeni, as a Pole, was not particularly sympathetic to these arguments and even admitted to the German ambassador that he found the Hungarian-Jewish press campaign against Lueger tasteless and crude.[173] But in the balance Magyar pressure when combined with that of the Liberals—the two constitutional partners of 1867 who felt threatened by new bourgeois political ventures anywhere in the monarchy—did have a decisive influence on Badeni (Bánffy and several other Hungarian dignitaries just "happened" to be visiting Vienna on 4–5 November for the installation of a new minister of agriculture).[174]

On 4 November the *Ministerrat* was held to decide the Lueger question. A majority of the new Cabinet, led by the defense minister Welsersheimb, accepted Kielmansegg's arguments and favored confirmation. Baron Gautsch and Count Gleispach, who were covert supporters of the German Liberals, voted against the motion for confirmation, but the recommendation passed by a strong majority.[175] Badeni decided, however, to ignore the vote in the Cabinet and make his own recommendation to the emperor for nonconfirmation. Since Lueger had flatly refused to go along with the idea of a substitute mayor, Badeni felt free to bow to Liberal and Hungarian pressure. Although the crown prince, Franz Ferdinand, urged Franz Joseph to confirm Lueger, the emperor preferred Badeni's advice and officially rejected Lueger's candidacy.[176]

Badeni's decision reflected external political pressure, but also his psychological need to pose. He remarked to the German first secretary, Lichnowsky, that he had now "shown" the Viennese political community what a strong leader he was, as if insulting Lueger would accomplish this end. Nonconfirmation in November resulted as much from Badeni's profound personal insecurity as it did from pressure from the Liberals and the Magyars. Lueger happened to provide the first test case for Badeni's pose as the iron man—Lichnowsky was impressed with how much Badeni had personalized the whole affair into a battle between the demagogue Lueger and the man of power and integrity Badeni.[177] Lueger was not the only one trying to push a personality cult in Vienna in 1895. But in Badeni's case, unlike Lueger's, there was no broader political movement which made this pose a rational, effective tool.

The decision was in all respects an unfortunate one. Had Badeni ignored the Liberals and followed the majority of his own Cabinet, there would have been grumbling and short-term outrage, but the Liberals would have had to go along. Far too much was at stake in the upcoming electoral reform bill for the Liberal party to simply "walk out" over the Vienna question. Local Viennese Liberals and the press might have tried to force a secession against the government, but they did not control national Liberal policy. The Liberal delegations from Bohemia, Moravia, and the Alpine lands had other concerns and problems than Karl Lueger. Also, the Liberal party as a whole was to a certain extent accustomed to being abused. Through its inclination to self-pity the party actually expected a certain amount of ministerial hostility. More important, a positive recommendation on Lueger would have placed the Liberals in a more favorable position for later and more meaningful struggles. Liberalism was politically dead in Vienna, and all the nonconfirmation decisions in the world were not going to revive it. But the party might have argued that Badeni now "owed" it something; instead, he wasted its credit early in his regime on a lost cause.

As for the Hungarians, their bellicose threats were even more absurd. The negotiations for the *Ausgleich* would have been little affected by Lueger's sitting in the *Rathaus*. Hungarian policy on the *Ausgleich* always asserted maximal national self-interest, even during the Liberal era. A Lueger confirmation could not have increased what had already been attained at its own natural extreme. When the negotiations for the *Ausgleich* did stall in August 1896, this was not because the antisemites had finally gained control of Vienna; both the Liberals and the Hungarians had other tactical motives in mind in delaying the final settlement until after the 1897 Reichsrat elections.[178] Badeni also managed to antagonize the Clerical Conservatives with his decision, since they saw the move against Lueger as a sign that the new ministry would be hostile to clerical and agrarian interests. Other middle bourgeois parties, especially the Young Czechs, saw the issue in terms of a clear violation of urban autonomy which would only assist the more radical German National movements. Confronted with Lueger or with Schönerer and Steinwender, the Young Czechs had no trouble in supporting a party which claimed to be social reformist and to favor municipal and provincial autonomy, as opposed to one which emphasized post-Liberal German Nationalism.

The Antisemitic Response: Badeni versus Lueger

The Imperial decision for nonconfirmation, announced late in the afternoon of 6 November, took Lueger by complete surprise. Lueger thought that he had a reasonably good chance to secure the mayoralty in November. The negative decision stung his pride and filled him with ominous forebodings. Would the government continue to block his election in future confrontations? If so, what kinds of options did his party realistically have?

On 8 November Robert Pattai brought an angry motion before the lower house of parliament demanding to know the reasons behind the nonconfirmation.[179] Badeni could have remained silent and would have been prudent to do so. Instead, he announced arrogantly that the government could not recommend someone for mayor who lacked "objectivity" and rationality.[180] The personal insult against Lueger provided more material for the cult of Lueger, the Christian martyr. The party elite met with the full *Bürgerclub* and decided to challenge Badeni by again electing Lueger mayor. To Kielmansegg this was a direct challenge to the prerogatives of the crown itself. When the Council again met and elected Lueger, Kielmansegg ordered its immediate dissolution and the reinstallation of the *Beirat* under Hans v Friebeis. Henceforth Kielmansegg became an intractable opponent of Lueger's confirmation, seeing such a step as a concession by the crown to popular political force.[181]

Immediately after the announcement of the second dissolution on 13 November, angry crowds gathered in front of the *Rathaus* and the parliament and then surged through the streets, yelling "Down with Badeni" and "Down with the Jews."[182] Lueger and his closest advisers made no effort to encourage the crowds, and after a few hours the police brought the disturbances under control. The "riotous" (but not riotlike) behavior of these Lueger sympathizers was not the work of the party elite, but merely a collective expression of popular emotions.[183] Immediately after his election on 29 October some of Lueger's more enthusiastic followers had wanted to organize an *Illumination,* a display of fire and light in windows and on sidewalks and street corners to celebrate his victory. The Liberal party had set a precedent for such an act with its *Illumination* after the abrogation of the Concordat. Lueger forbade this pageant of lights, however, fearing public unrest and possible rowdiness.[184] The elite was committed to a policy of nonviolence and overt legality.

Legality did not mean, however, compliance with Badeni's efforts to ignore the party. The central committee of the party reconstituted itself immediately after the Council's dissolution and decided upon a strategy of continuous pressure on and legal confrontations with the government until the new Council elections were called. Rather than tamely back down, Lueger and Gessmann sought to bring new social forces to bear while keeping their own voters in an emotionally charged state. As Lueger put it in a rally held in Margarethen, he was an "old fox" who had waited twenty-five years for the mayoralty and could easily afford to wait a few more. He had no intention of surrendering to Badeni.[185]

The party chose two different tactics to keep public emotions charged and ready for the next round of elections, which Kielmansegg scheduled for mid-February 1896. The new mass campaign tactics utilized in the fall of 1895 (door-to-door campaigning, coercive money solicitation, etc.) were renewed on a more intensive basis. Lueger's personality cult grew by leaps and bounds. The language of the party became particularly hostile and aggressive, using direct, ad hominem attacks on individual ministers and officials. Hostile words rather than hostile deeds—this was an appropriately bourgeois Viennese response to the crisis. That the radical clergy played key roles in a number of districts in organizing intensive precinct- and parish-level agitation was noted by the police with grave suspicion. Sermons during church services became open political diatribes, to an extent not before seen in the city.[186]

More interesting, the party opened a second front with a coordinated effort to bring the wives of antisemitic Third and Second Curia voters into political assemblies. Beginning in mid-November dozens of rallies of the "Christian women" were organized, often drawing as many as 1,500 to 2,000 women at a time. This was a novel development in Austrian bourgeois politics. Never before had the party concentrated so much attention on bourgeois females.[187] In part this effort was a tactical device to allow the male audience of the party a period of rest—during these weeks the party refrained from holding rallies for its regular, male voters, fearing that they would tire of political controversies before Council elections arrived and the campaign would "peak" too soon.[188] The women functioned as a substitute audience before which spokesmen could use their most ferocious language against the government and the press. A prime theme in the rallies was the organization of an effective boycott of Jewish merchants in retribution for the alleged influence of the Jewish community in preventing Lueger's confirmation. Previous attempts at a *Kauft nur bei Christen* campaign organized by the "Christian Family" associations had met with marginal success at best, but contemporary reports from late December 1895 indicated that this time the party's boycott was seriously injuring a number of Jewish-owned businesses.[189] This was a cruel, harsh tool to pressure the government. Lueger used it as a last resort (the boycott was lifted after the February 1896 elections); but it showed how desperate the party was by late 1895.

Most important, Lueger was setting his female cadres up to play a shadow role to the Social Democrats. Several of the women's rallies got out of hand, and angry women marched from the rallies in small groups screaming at passersby and local shopkeepers, some of them Jewish.[190] The party elite would never have tolerated this kind of behavior from its male voters, but covertly encouraged such street and sidewalk rowdiness from the females (who quickly earned the designation "Lueger's Amazons" in the daily press). The police were totally baffled by these disturbances and felt uncertain how to deal with them; they were hardly riots in any conventional sense of the word, but small groups of angry women marching down the sidewalks swinging umbrellas and chanting "Hoch Lueger!" were hardly to be tolerated. The dramatic entrance of the Christian Social women on the political scene was intended by Lueger and Gessmann to suggest to the government that the antisemites could also bring the women out onto the streets if they so desired. Implicitly they were telling Badeni and Kielmansegg that women belonged in the home and that the party would gladly keep them there, but that, to prove a point, they were also willing to use them to disrupt the traditional pattern of retail commerce and local consumption, as well as to embarrass the government. Lueger played the Christian Social women like a talented musician would play a cheap violin. After 1896, when the government conceded the city to the Christian Socials, the women returned to the political obscurity from whence they had come. The Christian Socials were never really interested in developing strong women's organizations for the sake of the women's own social and occupational rights. Lueger wanted to be able to use them on an ad hoc basis to suggest that the party was a mass party when it cared to be, but that it was also willing to behave itself along traditional neo-Liberal lines, if the government cooperated. No political device better showed the transitional, half-mass, half-traditional bourgeois nature of the party by 1896 more clearly than this contrived use of women in local politics.

The police were extremely uneasy about the new style of confrontation politics. Franz Stejskal, the police president for Vienna, took an unusually negative view of Lueger's behavior, characterizing it to Kielmansegg as "perfidy" and "dangerous to the public order."[191] On several occasions Stejskal tried to bring indictments against Lueger for using "dangerous" language in the women's assemblies (such as accusing Badeni of behaving "with great stupidity" or asserting that the ministry was under "Jewish control"), but the Justice Ministry killed the indictments before any official action was taken on them.[192] Obviously there was considerable disagreement within the government on how to respond to the popular unrest the Christian Socials were inciting. The party was careful to swear its undivided loyalty to the emperor each time it castigated Badeni or Kielmansegg, but more and more the crown seemed to be dragged into partisan political conflict. For Lueger it was important to get the message across that loyalty to the crown was a two-way street. In a constitutional monarchy (which was Lueger's view of the Austrian political system, all surface *Hapsburg-treu* rhetoric aside), the crown had to respect fundamental political institutions such as urban autonomy.

The new Council elections were set for late February 1896. Kielmansegg now argued that the government should hold fast to its rejection of Lueger and let the antisemites make the next move; any other plan would weaken the theoretical sovereignty of the crown. Kielmansegg regretted that Badeni had dragged the emperor into a situation of political partisanship. But since it had happened, the monarch's right to confirm or not to confirm Viennese mayors had to be kept sacrosanct.

Badeni, however, gradually began to adopt a different view of the situation. In mid-December 1895 he reported to Philipp zu Eulenburg that personally he found much that was attractive in the Christian Social program and implied that he rued the disruptions and bad publicity the whole episode had brought.[193] Rather than winning the gratitude of the Liberals, he seemed no closer to a workable, informal majority in parliament than he had been in October. By attacking Lueger, he had alienated important segments of the Alpine Conservatives under Ebenhoch and Dipauli. Badeni was shocked by the bitter attacks on Kielmansegg which the antisemites launched in late January 1896 when the Lower Austrian Landtag convened.[194] Badeni felt himself trapped in an impossible situation: not to confirm Lueger yet a third time might lead to more explosive agitation in Vienna at a time when Badeni was hoping to push through his electoral reform bill in parliament (in April 1896). Personally Badeni was anything but the strong man of his self-created legend. He hated the bruising, tough style of urban politics in which he now found himself trapped. When an opportunity arose to design a compromise agreement in early February 1896, he quickly seized it as a way of extricating himself from the corner into which Lueger had painted him.

Just as he had ignored Kielmansegg's earlier view of the Lueger situation, Badeni now ignored the *Statthalter*'s insistence on keeping the crown out of politics. Through his son Louis, Badeni opened a secret channel of communication with Lueger, using a personal friend of Lueger, Johann Zacherl, as contact man. Zacherl arranged a secret, after-dark meeting between the two early in February in Badeni's offices.[195] Lueger came and had a long discussion with Badeni on possible ways to avoid yet another crisis on the confirmation question. Finally, the two reached an agreement whereby Badeni's original proposal of October 1895, that Lueger bow to a substitute Christian Social as mayor, was accepted, but modified on three crucial points. First, Lueger insisted that he would occupy the position of first vice-mayor during this period of expediency and that the substitution would last not longer than a year; the government, in other words, was buying itself a year's grace by the compromise, but nothing more. Second, Lueger insisted that the election of his straw man replacement (he specifically mentioned Joseph Strobach, the Christian Social *Hausherren* leader) would occur only after Lueger himself had been elected mayor once again. Third, Lueger insisted that, immediately after his election and his acceptance, the emperor would issue a public request that Lueger come to a private audience, at which Franz Joseph would request as a personal favor that Lueger stand aside for the public good and take the position of vice-mayor until such time as it might be opportune for him to move up to the mayoralty.

Badeni had a great deal of trouble persuading Franz Joseph to go along with this strategy. For what Lueger was in fact demanding was that the crown itself admit that Vienna's political autonomy had been violated and that the regular, competitive political system had to be restored, even if this occurred on the basis of non-Liberal rule. Eventually, however, Badeni got his way and Franz Joseph agreed to the audience. The deal was worked out and confirmed by all parties concerned before the Third Curia elections began on 28 February, although the antisemitic press was silent about the arrangement so as not to disrupt the party's propaganda front during the actual voting.[196]

Badeni's decision to reverse himself and compromise with Lueger was masked by bravado and bluster—he tried to impress Eulenburg with the clever "trick" he had played on Lueger by getting him to accept the substitute mayor arrangement, but Eulenburg rightly suspected that this was a mere cover-up.[197] In a more honest and sober mood, Badeni later admitted to Kielmansegg that he was the one who had been tricked. The Imperial audience was what Lueger had really wanted, and the "old fox" was willing to wait a year for the mayoralty if he got it.[198]

The decision also encouraged Badeni's enormous capacity for self-deception. Once he had conceded Vienna to the antisemites, he decided that his role as a medical doctor to the German Liberals and other German groups should be expanded. He justified his change of policy to Eulenburg with the curious argument that Lueger was a kind of bad medicine which the Liberals would have to take if they did not want to find themselves permanently disabled. That is, doing harmful things to the Liberals was in their own best interest. It was hardly accidental or surprising that the same kind of logic governed Badeni's justification for his speech ordinances a year later.[199] Badeni was subconsciously trying to turn his defeat and humiliation of 1896 into an ersatz victory in 1897 by attacking the Liberals and Germans in the name of their own best interest. That the Liberals had seemingly accepted the Lueger confirmation—after all, they still voted for the electoral reform bill in May 1896 even though Strobach had been confirmed—was yet another reason for Badeni to believe that they were as weak and as easy to intimidate as Lueger seemed to suggest. From one extreme, overestimating Liberal power in 1895, Badeni moved to the other in 1897, underestimating German-speaking political and cultural interests in the monarchy as a whole. The confirmation episode magnified (although it did not create) in Badeni's imagination the wrong kind of role for a nonparty minister-president in the Austrian system. In a nonparty ministry, the only valid function of a regime would be one of mediation and negotiation, not a mentality of a forced *Staatsstreich,* such as occurred in 1897. By placing himself in the position of a demigod by fiat (ignoring his advisers repeatedly on the confirmation question and involving the crown in domestic political squabbling), he began an unfortunate pattern of political meddling which soon became dangerous.

The February Elections and the Antisemitic Takeover

The City Council elections for February/March 1896 brought no surprises for either party, except that the antisemites won more seats in the First Curia. The Liberals approached the election in a totally disorganized state.[200] Liberal attempts to coerce antisemitic artisans in September 1895 were now superseded by antisemitic pressure on Liberal businessmen and other local notables not to join the Liberal ticket. The Liberal party had difficulty in finding suitable volunteers to stand for office in many districts, since businessmen feared the antisemitic boycott launched after the nonconfirmation decision in November.[201] The Christian Socials now profited from the role of a winner—the police reported that they had accumulated an unusually large campaign chest for this election. As the campaign progressed, the kind of intrarally violence associated with the autumn of 1895 was absent. The Liberals expected to lose and did little to prevent the inevitable.

What was novel in 1896, however, was a series of confrontations with the Social Democrats. The Socialist leadership under Victor Adler decided that the 1896 Council campaign would be an appropriate moment to begin a systematic electoral agitation on the municipal level. The Social Democrats had no hope of winning any Council seats, but they saw such electoral work as valuable experience and training for the greater effort they hoped to make in the upcoming 1897 parliamentary elections in Vienna. Incidents of Socialist disturbance of bourgeois voter rallies—Liberal and Christian Social—increased as the spring campaign wore on.[202] On 2 February 1896 the *Arbeiter-Zeitung* published the Socialists' first comprehensive municipal reform program, a landmark document which argued that the city's institutional power should be used to curtail the traditional privileges of *all* forms of bourgeois wealth, whether this involved the removal of the city's contractual business from large-scale industrialists or the creation of smaller monopoly consumer goods industries (such as city-owned bakeries and meat markets).[203] Neither large capitalist wealth nor small- and medium-scale property owners and merchants were exempt from Socialist attack. Articles appeared in the *Arbeiter-Zeitung* with increasing frequency attacking the *Hausherren* and urging the city to build its own municipal housing to force private tenement owners to lower rents.[204] The Christian Socials had a new enemy in this campaign. Liberalism as a credible political force in the city was dead, but, given the radical programs and efficient electoral methods the Socialists employed, the antisemites were moving toward a more ominous confrontation. Lueger had conquered the Liberals, only to find himself forced to defend all kinds of established wealth—capitalist and noncapitalist—against Adler's cohorts.

On 18 April the newly elected Council assembled for the third mayoral election which the city was to endure within less than a year. Lueger was elected (ninety-two to forty-two), as planned, and immediately announced his acceptance. On 24 April Lueger officially informed the *Bürgerclub* of the deal he had made with Badeni (although most members knew of it unofficially long before).[205] A small group of Nationalist councilmen led by Paul v Pacher objected to the settlement, but the great majority, led by Gessmann, were in favor of it. Finally, on 27 April Lueger was received by Franz Joseph and the prearranged scenario played out. Lueger took a day to "think over" the emperor's request, and on 28 April he notified Hans v Friebeis that he was withdrawing from the race for mayor.[206] Lueger told the club the same day that Badeni had promised him that he would move up to the position of mayor by January 1897 at the latest.[207]

The Imperial audience was by all accounts a masterful political ploy. Nothing served to confirm the *staatserhaltende* pretensions of the party more than this event. The Christian Socials now had a private relationshp with the emperor, even if it was against Franz Joseph's will. More important, the party had not bowed to ministerial pressure but to a special personal request of the emperor, which was clearly extraconstitutional. The antisemites' claim to be the staunchest defenders of the city's political autonomy seemed to have been vindicated.

With Lueger's withdrawal a minor conflict broke out within the party over the distribution of the three executive offices of the city. Lueger was ensured the post of first vice-mayor, but no one was certain whom Lueger would support for the second vice-mayoral slot. In February Lueger had chosen Strobach for the mayoral position, both because of his experience in urban administration as a member of the *Beirat* and his respectability as a *Hausherren* leader. The party elite had not announced this decision, however, in order to keep suspense building during the first part of April. When it was made public, there were a number of ambitious politicians in the party who envied Strobach's luck and who coveted the post of second vice-mayor.

Immediately after Lueger withdrew the pan-Germanists, led by Karl Wolf, organized several protest rallies, screaming that Lueger had betrayed the city by not refusing to resign.[208] Wolf represented a pitifully small constituency with nothing to gain from a peace settlement between Lueger and the government. In the *Bürgerclub* the Wolfian refrain was taken up by Paul v Pacher, a wealthy factory owner who had entered the Council in September 1895 from Wieden. A friend of Wolf and a former ally of Schönerer, Pacher had long envied and distrusted Lueger.[209] Pacher persuaded a small number of nationalist-minded Council delegates (especially those from Wieden and Favoriten, including the members of the Hauck Club from the latter district) to demand that the *Bürgerclub* nominate him, Pacher, for the second vice-mayoral slot. Neither Lueger nor Gessmann had any intention of allowing this, since both feared the repercussions of having an independent nationalist as an executive officer of the city.

Lueger arranged for a special committee to be organized within the *Bürgerclub* which would nominate the new slate, placing Gessmann in charge. Various contenders emerged, among them Joseph Schlesinger of *Volksgeld* fame, whom Ernst Vergani pushed for the mayoral position in his *Deutsches Volksblatt*. Instead of Pacher, Gessmann was willing to offer the third spot on the slate to Josef Neumayer, a moderate nationalist lawyer from the Innere Stadt, conditional on Neumayer's repudiating any connection with Schönerer or Wolf.[210] On 4 May the *Bürgerclub* met in plenary session and approved of Gessmann's slate of Strobach, Lueger, and Neumayer as the new municipal officers. Strobach issued a statement indicating that he was prepared to step down as mayor and give the position to Lueger at any time the party so desired.

Finally, on 6 May Strobach was elected mayor. His confirmation followed on 16 May, and he was officially sworn in by Kielmansegg on 19

May 1896.[211] The temporary administrative directorate under Friebeis which had run the city for a year was disbanded and the municipal political system again restored as the autonomous agent responsible for the control of the city. After fifteen years of bitter and often fruitless struggle, having endured many uncertain and uneasy episodes, the Christian Social coalition took control of the capital of the Hapsburg Empire. For the first time in the modern urban political history of Central Europe, a major metropolitan area had fallen to non-Liberal rule.

Kielmansegg, formerly hostile to the idea of any straw man as mayor, had no alternative but to fall in line and recommend Strobach's confirmation.[212] Kielmansegg found much that he could support about Strobach, noting in his report that although the latter had no formal *Bildung* (Strobach was an autodidact who owned a lucrative textbook sales and supply house), he was an intelligent, self-made man with considerable native intelligence who would not simply be a dupe for Lueger. Kielmansegg found Strobach's insistence that upon Lueger's becoming mayor, he would take up the position of first vice-mayor, to be a good sign that the *Hausherren* leader would act with some degree of independence. That Strobach was known for his militant hostility to Schönerer did not injure his candidacy in ministerial circles.

The *Hausherren* in Politics: The Completion of the Christian Social Coalition, 1895–96

The election of Strobach as mayor illustrated the new prominence of the *Hausherren* in the affairs of the Christian Social party elite, since Strobach owed his political prominence almost entirely to his position as vice-chairman of the Central Association of Viennese Property Owners. Once the municipal elite of the party began to be recruited from the ranks of the *Hausherren,* as occurred in 1895–96, the party finally arrived at a position where it was roughly comparable in its social constituency to the earlier Liberals. It had become, in other words, a Bürger party. But the property owners of the First Curia who gradually began to throw their support to the Christian Socials did not lack professional organizations by 1895 to guide them in their political views. Hence, the trend toward anti-semitism among First Curia voters must be analyzed in the context of the evolution of a professional interest group mentality among the Viennese *Hausherren*.

Organizational History

The rise of an independent political consciousness among the Viennese property owners dated from the later 1880s, when several events occurred which shook at least some of the *Hausherren* out of their former political complacency. In October 1886 the Austrian parliament passed a revised version of the Austrian *Executionsordnung*,[213] the regulations governing distraint of personal property by creditors in bankruptcy proceedings. Touted by the Iron Ring as a piece of humanitarian social reform, this legislation was directed to the needs of poorer peasants and small industrial artisans, who found themselves deprived of basic occupational necessities after bankruptcy proceedings (such as the loss of a plow, in the case of a peasant, or a set of tools, in the case of a master shoemaker). Several Viennese politicians noted, however, that the wide-ranging and indiscriminate concessions the new *Ordnung* gave to all borrowers might also be applied to other kinds of contractual credit arrangements. Ferdinand Kronawetter angrily suggested that unscrupulous tenants in rental apartments in larger cities might exploit the new *Ordnung* by refusing to pay their rent on time (or at all), knowing that the new regulations could also be used to protect their personal property and furniture from legal confiscation by landlords.[214] Guido Sommaruga agreed with Kronawetter that the new *Ordnung* would encourage the growth of class warfare between property owners and their tenants by allowing the older informality which had traditionally governed tenant-landlord relations in Austria to be upset. The liberality of the new *Ordnung* would encourage credit abuses, forcing the owners to adopt a much harsher view of their poorer tenants.[215]

The ministry's spokesman (and the author of the law) Emil Steinbach dismissed the warnings of the Viennese as groundless.[216] He was confident that the law would have little effect on public behavior in credit matters. Property owners might have to be more careful about whom they allowed to live in their buildings, and the new *Ordnung* would have a positive effect in discouraging loans and leases to unreliable persons in the first place. Kronawetter countered by characterizing Steinbach's assertions as naive and dangerous (how could an owner know in advance if the tenant in question would cheat on his rent?), but the Iron Ring passed the law over Viennese objections. The agrarians and the Clericals in the coalition were only interested in the law's promised beneficence for small farmers and handwork artisans. Steinbach for his part dreamed of launching a new era of conservative, government-led social reform, the *Executionsordnung* being merely one small step in the reconstruction of Austrian society.

Unfortunately for the government and, ironically, for the Liberals as well, Kronawetter's fears soon proved to have a very real basis in fact. In the two years following the publication of the law in June 1887 hundreds of complaints were heard in property owners' circles in Vienna and the suburbs about the increasing incidence of rent cheating in tenancy relationships. In late 1887 groups of *Hausherren* began to organize defense associations in several districts of the city (Leopoldstadt was among the first).[217] A petition circulated by these clubs and submitted to the Reichsrat in April 1888, requesting the abolition of the new *Executions-ordnung* or its revision to exempt rental leases from its purview, was signed by 2,000 owners. By mid-1888 each of the districts in the city (with the exception of the Innere Stadt) had a *Hausherrenverein*. Leaders of the district clubs met in June 1888 to establish the *Centralverband der Hausbesitzer-Vereine* in order to coordinate the clubs' lobbying activities. In 1888 the *Hausherren-Zeitung* was also founded, the first professional newspaper for property owners in the monarchy.[218] The Viennese own-ers, almost inadvertently, now found themselves equipped with a tightly coordinated and well-funded cadre group to articulate their views on a wide range of public policies. A seemingly innocuous revision in a minor law, by provoking the angry protests of thousands of *Hausherren,* re-sulted in the mobilization of the collective opinion of a group of voters with a powerful position in the municipal electoral system.

Because the *Ordnung* impaired the ability of owners to hold or sell personal property to cover unpaid rents, it placed many apartment house owners in a problematic situation vis à vis the Austrian tax administra-tion. The largest single source of direct tax revenue in Vienna, for both city and state, was the *Mietzinssteuer,* or tax on tenant rents, paid by the owners to the government as a percentage of the gross rental revenue of their buildings. The *Mietsteuer* accounted for 12.6 million fl. of the 16 million fl. raised by the city in direct taxes in 1893.[219] Set at extremely high rates (26 percent of gross rents for national taxation, plus provincial and city surtaxes, all of which totaled approximately 42 percent of the rental income of a building, unless the house enjoyed a special tax-free status), the tax was based on rental income projections set by the gov-ernment at the beginning of each fiscal year and *not* on the basis of actual rental income received by the *Hausherr* at the end of the year. Many property owners now found themselves having to pay taxes on unpaid rents *(uneinbringlicher Mietzins)* out of their own pockets, since the Aus-trian revenue service adamantly refused to give rebates or credits on taxes assessed and paid on the basis of projected rents in cases in which the tenant had refused (or was financially unable) to pay the actual rent.

Since the new *Ordnung* made it difficult to confiscate or hold personal property until the rent was paid (or the owners reimbursed by the sale of the goods), the *Hausherren* felt that the government had placed them in an impossible situation. They were compelled to pay assessed taxes, even if their tenants absconded without paying their fair share of the rent. In spite of the overtly selfish and closed aura of *Hausherren* politics and their clear aspiration to class hegemony, one cannot help but recognize the justice of at least some of their frustrations. Most owners did not want to confiscate their tenants' property (which was a troublesome and time-consuming process, even before 1887), but they felt that as long as the government refused to grant rebates on taxes based on unpaid rents, they needed a harsh bankruptcy law to use against errant renters, if not as a real then at least as a symbolic constraint.

The struggle over the *Executionsordnung* inaugurated public expression of other matters which had long angered local property owners. The *Centralverband* energetically exploited old and new grievances to legitimate itself among the thousands of Viennese *Hausherren* as a tough, uncompromising representative of their interests. Because it affected the ability of owners to cover taxes on unpaid rents, the *Ordnung* immediately shifted the attention of the *Centralverband* to larger questions involving tax reform and the operation of the Austrian revenue system. More important, once the movement was launched, wealthier and more prosperous owners were drawn into it, since the *Verband* was able to raise issues of interest to owners of all income and tax levels. Suburban owners also organized clubs, and after the unification of the city and suburbs in 1891 these also joined the *Centralverband*. By the mid-1890s most of the clubs had developed a vigorous associational life, with monthly meetings and regular social gatherings supplemehted by city-wide rallies held by the *Centralverband* on key political and economic issues.[220] By 1895 over 6,000 owners had joined the various district clubs as dues-paying members. These were not simply poorer and middle-level owners who were directly affected by the *Executionsordnung* because they rented to *Arbeiter* tenants, but "sehr viele vermögende Haus-eigenthümer" as well.[221] Of all the bourgeois interest organizations in Vienna by 1895 the *Centralverband* was probably the most powerful and most effective. Its executive secretary, Paul v Duniecki, was a wealthy lawyer who specialized in real estate; the editor of its newspaper was Johann Dötzl, a clever but cautious publicist who was able to mediate between the Liberal and Christian Social factions within the *Verband*. Each year the *Verband* proudly touted its accomplishments in dealing with various governmental agencies on behalf of individual owners; and compared to the often sparse results the early *Beamten* and *Lehrer* organizations obtained, the *Hausherren* were often able to make their collective weight felt.

By 1895 the profile of the *Verband* as a leading interpreter of bourgeois rights and privileges in the city had also made it one of the most ferocious opponents of political Socialism in Vienna. Each issue of the *Haus-herren-Zeitung* brought attacks on or rebuttals to the *Arbeiter-Zeitung* and its schemes for state-sponsored public housing projects.[222] The hysteria of the *Verband* on the public housing issue was a reaction not simply to fears of competition or rent controls, but to the larger issue of social and political egalitarianism itself. Property for the *Hausherren* was sacred both in cultural and political terms. Upon individual ownership rested the whole system of curial voting privileges which the *Verband* repeatedly glorified. Public management of real estate would not only limit private housing profitability, but destroy the unique distinction between *Staatsbürger* and *Stadtbürger* which the *Hausherren* used to justify their political superiority.[223] Only men of solidity and propertied wealth were *Stadtbürger,* and only they could qualify for political rights in the city and regional government. The hostility of most *Hausherren* to Socialist politics paralleled the built-in tensions between poorer tenants on monthly or even weekly leases and owners in suburban or inner city areas who rented to working-class families. Together such cleavages formed the basis for the enormous conflict surrounding property ownership which marked the first years of the Austrian First Republic in Vienna. The tensions and hatreds of 1920–27 had a long prehistory in the singularly privileged political position and the narrow, self-serving cultural assumptions of the Viennese *Hausherren* in the Imperial period.

Although it would be inaccurate to postulate a direct, unilateral connection between the *Centralverband* and all *Hausherren* political behavior in 1895–96, it was likely that the opinions of many First Curia voters were influenced by the issues raised by the association. This was, in fact, the important role of the *Verband* and its subordinate clubs. In theory the *Verband* remained nonpartisan on electoral matters, and although individual clubs could choose to endorse the slates of a given party in their district, most clubs had Liberal and antisemitic factions by 1895–96, coexisting with each other in relative tolerance and peace.[224] They were bound together by too many common social interests to allow politics to destroy their internal unity. What the *Verband* did do was to raise a series of issues in the voters' minds to which each of the parties was then forced to respond. Before the September 1895 elections, for example, each candidate of the Liberal and Christian Social parties in all three curias received a copy of the program of the *Hausherren* clubs in the mail, with the "request" that he announce his unconditional, public support for the whole list of demands. For obvious tactical reasons—they were in the opposition, without the responsibility of governing—the Christian Socials found it much easier to respond convincingly to such confrontations.

The importance of house ownership for the Christian Social party elite by 1895 may be gauged by the fact that of over one hundred candidates chosen to run for the City Council on the three antisemitic slates in September, sixty-nine were *Hausherren.*[225] Thirty were members of one of the executive committees of the district clubs of the *Centralverband.* The properties they owned varied greatly in size and value: from the four-story apartment building of Joseph Strobach in Margarethen, which produced almost 7,000 fl. in rents, or the house of Karl Schuh in Alsergrund, which was even more valuable (10,050 fl. per year), to the smaller, suburban property owners in Hernals and Währing, like Franz Eigner of Hernals, who owned two three-story buildings which produced a total rental of 4,000 fl. per year.[226] In general, the Christian Social property owners tended to be owners of medium-sized buildings producing rents on the average between 2,500 and 5,000 fl. per year. These holdings were hardly *Zinspalais* on the Ringstrasse (no owner of a Ringstrasse building ever served on the executive board of a district *Hausherrenverein*—they would hardly have needed the services of such associations), but they were sufficient to give many of these candiates the right to vote in the First Curia, even if they chose to stand for office in a lower curia. Among suburban owners the party had its greatest support from those who owned buildings which served a primarily working-class clientele. In the inner districts, with their more affluent populations and higher rent levels, the Christian Socials and Liberals competed for the votes of a diversity of owners with more complex tenant populations. There is no evidence, at least on the basis of available data about the leaders of the nineteen district associations, that Christian Social *Hausherren* were necessarily poorer or less prosperous than Liberal *Hausherren* within a given district. Between districts, of course, typical house and land values varied greatly. Although conservative, the Christian Social *Hausherren* politicians were not unambitious; later housing data indicated that many of them used their newly won political prominence after 1896 to arrange for new mortgages on their buildings in order to remodel or rebuild them, producing higher rent levels. Karl Hallmann, for example, Strobach's colleague in Margarethen, expanded and modernized his house in 1896–97, achieving an annual gross rental level of nearly 15,000 fl.[227]

Social Composition and Cultural Views

The *Hausherren* clubs consisted largely of owners of income-producing properties, usually on a scale large enough to cause them to worry about their rental income. In 1900 Vienna had approximately 30,000 buildings devoted to residential or rental use.[228] Many of these buildings were small one- or two-story suburban units producing little rental income, and still others were single-family residences on the outskirts of the city. Data on rent levels in 1900 indicated that over 12,000 buildings in the city produced less than 2,400 fl. in rents, the level an owner would have to reach before he could seriously expect to vote in the First Curia.[229] The *Hausherren* clubs appeared to have been dominated by owners of medium and large buildings, if the composition of their district boards reflected their general membership (which there is no reason to doubt). For the Second through Tenth Districts (Leopoldstadt through Favoriten), of the 149 local leaders whose rental income could be ascertained from contemporary tax reports, only 15 percent (22) owned buildings with an annual rental income under 2,400 fl.[230] Even in the suburbs a similar trend occurred. For the Sixteenth through Eighteenth Districts (Ottakring through Währing), which had the most active suburban clubs, the 55 owner-leaders had among them only 21 with rent levels below 2,400 fl., and many of those men were within 200 to 300 fl. of the mark. Given the lower rent levels in the suburbs on a relative scale, the larger number below 2,400 fl. was not surprising.

Data on the occupations of those owners who did not rely on their rental income as their only source of livelihood (probably 65–70 percent of the total) are difficult to assemble from contemporary census materials, since not until 1910 did the Austrian census survey in detail the occupational breakdown of house ownership. Even the 1910 data are unreliable, as a number of owners refused or neglected to indicate their occupation, perhaps out of fear of investigations by the Austrian tax service. Of the 26,000 houses owned by individuals or married couples in 1910, 6,878 were listed as owned by people in industry (owners or senior employees) and another 4,841 were owned by commerce and transportation owners and employees.[231] About 1,300 were owned by government employees (teachers, professors, government officials) and another 5,700 by individuals who classified themselves as *Rentner,* which could have meant several things to the census takers of the time. Many of the latter were probably living off their investments in real estate, or were retired and living off a combination of rental income, securities, and pensions. But a final category—over 7,400—were listed as "without occupational designation." Obviously, such data are of limited utility in determining the social status of owners, but they do suggest several trends: white collar members of the intelligentsia were not likely to own an apartment house, unless they did so in the status of a retiree. Most of those owning houses who were employed in industry or commerce were *selbständige,* independently employed merchants, factory owners, and wealthier artisans and shopkeepers who ran or owned their own businesses. The total share of these commercial types was probably far higher than the 1910 data would suggest, since many of the *Rentner* category were probably former *Industrie* and *Handel* persons who had first invested in a house before their retirement.

A survey of the occupations of the leadership of the various *Hausherren* district clubs would confirm, in reliable proportions, the assumption that most owners were middle bourgeois types and that the majority were self-employed in industry, trade, or one of the free professions such as law or medicine. Of the 368 members of the nineteen district executive boards of the clubs, 67 percent were men employed ·in industry, commerce, or construction, the remainder being either *Rentner* (20.9 percent) or white collar types (free professions and government officials together constituted 12.1 percent).[232] Most appear to have been modestly well off persons who invested in housing as a source of personal security and long-term economic growth. Few were representatives of big wealth in the city (there were no bankers or industrialists among them). Of the 75 men whose occupations could be designated as commercial, only 11 could be considered to be individuals in upper bourgeois work positions in industrial or modern commercial firms or bureaucracies (6 senior railroad employees, 3 senior insurance officials, 2 banking employees). The great majority were mid-scale merchants (*Gemischtwarenhändler* with firms listed in the trade register), restaurant owners, and middle-level commercial employees.

A survey of the property these men owned provides some interesting insights. Most of the local leaders owned one house (or in rarer cases two houses), typically registered under joint ownership with their spouses for those who were married. Their properties usually occupied a place in the middle to upper middle range of the distribution of rents used by the Austrian housing census in 1900 (the middle range was 2,000–6,000 fl., the upper middle was 6,000–12,000 fl., with the total number of buildings in both categories 14,549, or over 50 percent of the residential buildings in Vienna with known rental levels). Housing in Vienna varied greatly in quality and value, as did land value appreciation and rent profits after expenses. But within the boards of each district club, most owners had houses of broadly comparable size and value. Even though membership in the clubs may have itself led to this comparability by a process of self-selection, the lack of fundamental disjunction in housing ownership within each district club may help to explain the relative unanimity with which both Christian Social and Liberal owners, together with nonpartisan members, in the same district could support the *Verband* on a broad range of tax and policy questions. From contemporary reports, it was clear that virtually all of the clubs had factions loyal to each party, but there was sufficient similarity among all politically active *Hausherren* in each district to make it possible to pose a common front to the outside world, especially the Socialist world of Victor Adler.

Traditionally, before the 1870s at least, the *Hausherr* was the preeminent "capitalist" in Viennese society. The tensions between poorer artisans and their *Hausherren* in 1848 have already been noted. Artisan resentment against the property owners for charging excessively high rents for business premises was still apparent in the testimony at the

1873–74 trade *Enquête* held by the Chamber of Commerce in Vienna.[233] A classic portrait of the *Hausherr* from this period, which still reflected pre-1848 values of the owner as a patrician figure in local society, occurred in Ludwig Anzengruber's *Das vierte Gebot* (1878), in which Hutterer, the avaricious, money-grubbing *Hausherr,* ruins his daughter's future happiness in search of personal power and gain. At the same time, the image of the wicked, evil *Hausherr* was only one side of a dual persona in the popular perception of property holding. For as much as master artisans might resent their local *Hausherr* on an individual basis, they wanted nothing more than to emulate him, to be like him, someday to own a piece of the Viennese *Heimat.* Thus, although feared and sometimes hated, the *Hausherr* was inevitably a figure of respect and petty dignity as well. For many he was the first and most ominous representative of the state, since the bulk of direct taxation in the city had to be paid via the *Hausherr* to the *Magistrat.* In his person he combined high social status and quasi-official public power which transcended and overshadowed the prestige which his other occupation might bring with it. This dualism of fear and respect was felt toward owners of all levels.

The ideal of the *Hausherr* as the Bürger patrician to whom all local glory and dignity were owing, as the best representative of "good" wealth in the city, persisted long after 1880 in *Hausherren* circles themselves. The *Hausherren-Zeitung* in the 1890s was filled with self-enhancing, self-descriptive language which insisted that the owners were the heart of the *Wiener Bürgerschaft,* the *verlässlichste* Bürger who were the pillars of economic and social integrity in the community.[234] *Hausherren* were the equivalent neither of the artisans, nor of the *Kapitalisten;* rather they were the ideal *mittlere Leute,* the *besserer Mittelstand* who really made the city work.[235] Because most had other occupations, also of social value, they contributed twice over to the stability and productivity of municipal society. The image of the *Hausherr* was a curious fusion of older notions of the owner as "house" holder, as one whose patriarchal authority constituted a basic unit of Viennese society, and modern notions of the *Hausherr* as a capitalist investor whose relations with his tenants were purely rational and goal-instrumental, based on hard cash. Authoritarian patriarchy and capitalist property accumulation combined in one unstable model to give later-nineteenth-century owners a broad spectrum of arguments with which to defend their political and social privileges.

As the city's economy gradually reflected the broader industrialization and large-scale commercialization of the later nineteenth century, however, other bourgeois elites slowly began to challenge the singular dominance of the *Hausherren* (as well as older early commercial and mid-scale industrial occupations in general), more in cultural and economic terms than in effective political curial terms. The increasing numbers of university graduates and students, the concentration of banking and insurance bureaucracies in the city, the growth of large-scale retail and wholesale commerce, the rise of powerful new artistic and literary institutions (the high Liberal press), the expansion of the state bureaucracy—all these trends resulted by 1895 in an upper bourgeoisie, materially or intellectually or both, which in some respects overshadowed the cultural prominence of the older, property-owning patriciate of the Vormärz (although with some interchange and overlap between the two strata). Two factors must immediately be noted, however, about this new putative *Hochbürgertum:* its relatively modest size and its limited political-electoral effectiveness.

If the new elites of Viennese society (what some have referred to as the ''second'' society of the city, below the court and highest aristocracy) were gauged by purely their wealth and numbers, they did not amount by 1900 to more than 5,000 households in the city (in a city with over 350,000 household units). Data from the personal income tax instituted in 1898 suggested that the number of households reporting aggregate incomes of 6,000 fl. per year or more was not more than 4,900 for all commercial, industrial, and private white collar occupations, including the free professions.[236] The total number of households reporting income between 3,600 and 6,000 fl. per year (surely an absolute minimum for inclusion in upper bourgeois rank groups) was less than 9,000, many of them probably consisting of wealthier merchants and property owners running traditional businesses or aristocrats involved in city business ventures who decided to report their income in Vienna rather than in a rural tax district.[237] The actual number of truly ''modern'' industrial and commercial occupations was therefore smaller. Allowing for the inadequacies of the figures for the first years of the personal income tax and for an assumed level of tax cheating and underestimation of income, the size of the highest strata in bourgeois society was still small.

If the ''second'' society of high elites is measured in qualitative terms as well, by adding to the above totals the academic and artistic elites and the high state bureaucracy, who had education and power but often a lower financial status, the aggregate would increase by not more than 3,600 households, so that the total number of households in a city of over 1.6 million people which could realistically be described as *Hochbürger* would be at the most 17,000 and probably somewhat less.[238]

More important, the political power of the new bourgeois elites was fragmented by the Viennese curial election system. To the extent that the new industrial and commercial *Hochbürgertum* voted, much of it would vote after 1890 in the Second Curia. All upper ranking members of the political intelligentsia, including free professionals, high state officials, university and gymnasial professors, and high-level commercial and industrial employees on the management level who paid an income tax of 30 fl. or more annually, automatically voted in the Second Curia. As a result, they were eliminated from the First Curia, and equally significant, in the Second Curia their votes were overwhelmed by those of the municipal schoolteachers and lower and middle ranking state and local officials. Thus, the high intelligentsia was at a serious disadvantage in the municipal electoral system.

Although some big industrialists and commercial capitalists voted in the First Curia, the general culture of this curia was not industrial-capitalist in nature either. An exact determination of personal investment patterns for Vienna would be, on the basis of existing data, impossible, but the attitudes expressed in the high Liberal press and other contemporary reports suggested that property owning, especially after 1880, was not a desirable way to invest money for short-term income gain.[239] As Ludwig v Mises noted in his autobiography, "Most [house] owners were small businessmen who invested their savings in a house which savings banks financed at 50% of a customarily over-appraised valuation."[240] House ownership was another form of personal savings, not an income-producing venture of the most opportune sort. The enormous property taxes in the city made real estate unattractive, unless one valued the cultural status of being a *Hausherr* or unless (and this was much rarer) one had the good fortune to find a house whose land value would appreciate rapidly because of its geographical situation. Since house ownership was within the reach of many in the "better" Mittelstand, by means of first and even second mortgages (a common practice in the later nineteenth century), the housing culture of the city was not dominated by high bourgeois types who were "capitalist" in their personal values.

As a result, the growth of a small, but economically and culturally powerful, capitalist bourgeoisie in the city did not much influence the composition of the city's First Curia, at least outside the Innere Stadt, since unlike Berlin taxation was not an indiscriminate qualification for voting in the First Curia in Vienna. Only special kinds and levels of taxation would gain one entrance. In 1895 the city employed the provisions of the 1890 *Gemeindeordnung* for the First Curia, which consigned to the curia all who paid 500 fl. in rent taxes or a personal income or trade tax of 200 fl. Because of the gradation of rates for the latter two taxes, a substantial annual income (over 3,000 fl.) would be required before a man would pay such a high personal tax. Although some of the First Curia was high bourgeois in a modern sense, all contemporary reports agree that the majority of the First Curia still consisted of *Hausherren* who used their tenants' rent taxes as their own for political purposes.[241] If anything, inflation in rents between 1850 and 1890 opened the curia to more middle bourgeois owners, since the 500 fl. line was never raised.

The upshot of this dualism was that although the city's high culture by 1890 was dominated by a narrow, European-style high bourgeoisie, its local politics was still firmly entrenched in the hands of the "model" bourgeoisie of 1850—the upper middle Bürger-type voter who managed to save sufficient funds to buy an apartment house in the city. Until the later 1880s the relations between the two strata, at least in political terms, were harmonious. The Liberal party drew support from both groups. The *Neue Freie Presse* and *Wiener Tagblatt*, as well as the academic elite from the university, gave the party its ideological pretensions, while more socially traditionalist voters qua *Hausherren* loyally followed along with solid support in the First Curia. This mixture of *Bildung* and *Besitz* was typical of many Liberal party groups in Central Europe at the time.

In the early 1890s, however, the alliance began to unwind and eventually collapsed, under the impact of the new aggressiveness and self-assertiveness of the *Hausherren* clubs. Many local Liberal politicians felt comfortable with the clubs' goals and supported them loyally, but the top party elite in the *Rathaus* after 1891 felt that its freedom of movement was increasingly constrained by the "upstart" *Hausherren,* formerly passive types who now dared to dictate municipal policy to the leaders of the party. The high Liberal press reacted sharply to the new wave of *Hausherren* independence, often printing derogatory or unsympathetic commentaries on them. Equally important, the *Hausherren* were now threatened by an ominous force in local politics, one which recalled the Left Liberal defenses of tenant rights against *Hausherren* "cruelty" which had taken place in 1848—the Viennese Social Democrats. The Liberal party seemed increasingly unable or unwilling to provide the kind of class leadership necessary to curb Socialist agitation. Many younger Liberals and university academics, influenced by Fabians like Professor Eugen v Philippovich, even began to show sympathy for the ideals (if not the goals) of Austrian Social Democracy. Nothing served to divorce the property owners from Viennese Liberalism after 1895 so much as the development of Left Liberalism in the city espousing social reform ideas like land and housing reform projects which were anathema to traditional First Curia voters.[242]

Hausherren Politics, 1891–96

Virtually all of the issues raised by the *Hausherren* involved demands for tax concessions and rebates from the government. Since the Liberals ran the municipal government between 1891 and 1895 and since they also controlled the powerful Finance Ministry between 1893 and 1895, they inevitably became the targets for the owners' lobbying efforts. On the national level the Steinbach-Plener tax reforms, finally considered by parliament in 1895, formed the crystallization point of *Hausherren* complaints. The *Centralverband* argued that Plener was favoring the lower artisan Mittelstand and the capitalist bourgeoisie against the needs and interests of the middle and upper middle sectors of urban society.[243] The master artisan got his rebate on the trade tax, the capitalist got a relatively low rate for his dividends, but little seemed to change for owners of real estate in the city. Although owners were to receive a rebate of 10 percent on the rent tax, this was substantially less than that accorded to the artisans. Equally noteworthy, Plener adamantly refused to raise the level of allowable deductions for repairs and upkeep on apartment buildings from 15 percent to 30 percent, even though house owners in smaller cities and towns in the monarchy enjoyed the 30 percent rate. Also, Plener refused to do anything about the *Centralverband*'s demand for rebates or credits on taxes paid on projected rents in cases where the tenant did not actually pay the rent. Not until later in the decade did the government finally concede this point to the *Hausherren* and bring in legislation to protect house owners against rent cheaters.

The *Verband* also complained bitterly about the insolent, arbitrary behavior manifested toward the *Hausherren* by Austrian tax officials. Their complaints about their role as unpaid tax collectors for the Austrian government paralleled similar grumblings among the Catholic lower-order clergy. Both groups now decided that they wanted to revise their formerly "etatist" roles in favor of more Liberal social roles which would retain their political privileges but permit them to escape from the unpleasant duties accompanying those privileges. In the case of the *Hausherren* their self-centered duplicity was obvious: they wanted to be rid of the role of tax collector (this was never explicitly stated, but the propaganda of the *Verband* was clearly heading in this direction); at the same time they still wanted to have their tenants' rent taxes credited to them personally for the purpose of voting rights. Clerics and house owners shared a desire to move beyond the traditional Austrian symbiosis of state and society by obtaining for their own privileged *Stand* a more independent, politically anchored social role. But neither ever saw this strategy as leading to a genuine liberalization of political society in Austria. Rather, a new conglomeration of special interest bourgeois pressure groups would find greater tolerance by supporting an ostensibly antistatist party designed to accommodate their privileged expectations.

Had the *Hausherren* restricted themselves to grumbling about the 1893–95 tax reforms, their later political dissidence might never have moved so far in support of the antisemites. But other problems soon arose. On the regional level Erich Kielmansegg decided in 1894 to crack down on what he thought to be a minor, but still significant, abuse by the owners—their refusal to clear the sidewalks in front of their buildings of snow during the winter and refuse during the summer. The *Central-verband* argued that since the sidewalks were the property of the city (how easily their proprietary rhetoric about being the true "owners" of the city was forgotten when financial questions arose!), it was the city's responsibility to clear them. In the autumn of 1894 Kielmansegg instructed the police to bring citations against any owners whose sidewalks were found to be inadequately cleaned. This was clearly a tempest in a teapot. The whole affair had an aura of petty absurdity about it which might have made it simply humorous, if it had not been for the angry reaction which Kielmansegg's order produced in all of the district clubs, even those with prominent Liberals as members. Like Kielmansegg's *Beamtenerlass* the important feature was the symbolic value of the act more than its actual content. The government seemed to be harassing the "innocent" Bürger by introducing regulatory guidelines to force him to behave in a more publicly responsible fashion toward the general population.

The most controversial area of policy and regulatory disputes between the owners and the government involved the city in its capacity as the first level of national tax administration (the *übertragener Wirkungskreis* of the city of Vienna). Here the potentiality for acrimonious dealings with the Liberal elite in the newly constituted *Stadtrat* increased geometrically. Not only did the owners' dealings with the *Magistrat* (which collected all direct taxes in the city) lead to hundreds of petty disputes and arguments, but the *Centralverband* initiated a campaign in 1892 to force the city to collect the so-called *Zinskreuzer* directly from individual tenants, rather than using the *Hausherren* as the city's local tax agents. The *Zinskreuzer* was a 9 percent direct tax on tenant rents which Vienna levied to pay the costs of the municipal school system and other communal services. Technically, it was not a surtax on the *Mietzinssteuer*, but a local tax controlled solely by the city government. Since the 1860s the *Magistrat* had required the *Hausherren*, for reasons of administrative convenience, to collect the *Kreuzer* along with their regular direct taxes. Like the state, the city refused to grant rebates on taxes which tenants later refused to pay.[244]

The *Verband* initiated a pressure campaign to force the city to assume the responsibility for collecting the *Zinskreuzer*, or at least to revise its policy about tax rebates. The equity of the first alternative was questionable indeed, since the owners adamantly refused to promise that they would reduce their rent levels if the city began to collect the *Kreuzer*.

Clearly no *Hausherr* would have done this—the real losers would have been the tenants, who would have been forced to pay the value of the tax twice over. In late 1894 the *Centralverband* did win an important concession on its second alternative (its real tactical goal). The *Ministerium des Inneren* issued an administrative decision ordering all municipal governments which collected the *Zinskreuzer* through the agency of individual owners to issue tax credits to owners who paid the *Zinskreuzer* on behalf of tenants who then refused to pay their rent taxes. The Liberals disliked this decision intensely, since it was both a political embarrassment and an administrative imposition. Both Johann Prix and Albert Richter did nothing to disguise their feelings that the *Zinskreuzer* affair was a cheap trick designed by the *Centralverband* to embarrass the city and rob poorer tenants as well. On several occasions in 1893 and 1894 both Prix and Richter bluntly informed the representatives of the *Verband* that they were unsympathetic to such special interest tactics and would do nothing to support them.[245] It would be a mistake to see in this hostility a genuine social welfare stance by the high Liberal elite. For the Liberals the *Hausherren* demands were first and foremost a threat to the oligarchical powers of the *Stadtrat,* and only secondarily a class-oriented attempt to exploit the poor in favor of the Mittelstand.

The *Zinskreuzer* was merely the most prominent point of contention between the city administration and the owners. Dozens of other, more petty issues contributed to the crescendo of discontent, from complaints about the correct rates for water provisioning to squabbles between individual owners and city housing inspectors over water mains and sewer lines between houses and the street. Before 1890 many owners may have resented municipal policy on such issues, but their protests and grievances counted for nothing, since they had no collective voice and presence. With the rise of the *Centralverband,* an association which went out of its way to raise controversial issues, the city now had a serious troublemaker on its hands.

This period of rising *Hausherren* protests saw the Liberal leaders becoming less adept and less careful in the way they treated their traditional supporters. Indeed, the *Stadtrat*'s behavior toward the *Hausherren* threw caution to the winds. The *Centralverband*'s pressure campaign for more privileges and favors came precisely at the time of the enormous budgetary pressures on the city after 1891. Johann Prix felt, quite understandably, that for the city to hire additional personnel to collect local taxes would simply create one more deficit in a budget already dripping with red ink. Other prominent Liberals were equally hostile to the *Centralverband.* Albert Richter accused the whole *Hausherren* movement of being a covert appendage of the antisemites (which it clearly was not) and simply interested in greedy self-aggrandizement.

More circumspect Liberals, like Sommaruga and Kronawetter (both of whom were also owners), made every effort to placate the owners, even when they could not entirely support their demands. Ultimately the question devolved to one of political style. Granted that the owners' politics was self-serving and self-centered, they were long-term Liberal loyalists who had stood with the party for forty years. If a Social Democrat or a Liberal Fabian had spoken of *Hausherren* ''greed,'' no one would have been surprised, but for a conservative ''capitalist'' Liberal like Richter to talk about these voters in this way led to massive resentment on the part of many First Curia voters. Given the resentment many suburban *Hausherren* still harbored over the terms of the 1891 unification, the *Stadtrat* should have made every effort to placate them. Instead, precisely the opposite occurred. The willingness of some wealthy Liberal financiers in the *Niederösterreichischen Gewerbeverein* to sponsor working-class housing projects after 1890 only served to antagonize the owners still further.

The conflict between the owners and the older Liberals was part of a much larger cluster of issues in late-nineteenth-century urban politics. After 1890 the city desperately needed more financial resources to cover its growing administrative and welfare responsibilities. The shortage of tax revenue led many short-sighted Liberal leaders to behave in an inflexible way toward traditional Liberal voting groups now agitating for tax concessions and social bourgeois privileges to enhance their own lifestyles. The Christian Socials, with a more imaginative sense of municipal funding and budgeting, saw that new sources of revenue had to be found to circumvent this kind of intrabourgeois feuding and cannibalism. Not surprisingly, the *Hausherren* clubs were extremely enthusiastic supporters of municipalization schemes to improve the city's financial base.[246] Strobach and his antisemitic *Hausherren* took the lead in demanding a city-owned gas works, a city electrical plant, a city *Sparkasse,* and a municipal insurance and mortgage company. In all of these ventures the narrow, self-serving class orientation of the *Hausherren* was manifest. The owners wanted municipalized utilities neither for social welfare purposes nor to improve public services, but simply to create a new source of tax revenue which would then allow the city to cut their property taxes (or at least stabilize them) by reducing surtax on the *Mietzinssteuer.* A municipal *Sparkasse* would also provide lower interest rates for mortgages (so they hoped) than did commerical institutions. The enthusiasm of the Christian Social elite for municipalization schemes both complemented and in a sense derived from the presence of so many property owners in the elite by 1896. Of all the interest groups in the party coalition the owners thought that they would profit the most from municipalization. When the party demanded a gas works in 1896, it did so on behalf of a private interest group which just happened to be coordinate with much of the political leadership of the party itself. And unlike public housing, municipalized utilities would not threaten the owners' cultural justifications for privileged voting positions, since there was no tradition in Vienna of private *local* ownership of public service utilities and transportation companies. Traditional notions of *Eigentum* simply did not apply to institutions like a city electrical works, because real estate in its traditional form was not at stake here.

To many *Hausherren* after 1891 the Liberals in the *Stadtrat*, with their personal and ideological connections with the high Liberal press, seemed to betray the older traditions of Bürger politics in the city. Even Liberal *Hausherren* stressed their desire for a return to the days when the property owners were respected as the main embodiment of the city's probity and cultural importance, rather than the new university elites and the editorial staffs of the high Liberal newspapers usurping that function. In spite of the arrogance of the older Liberals and the modernistic progressiveness of the younger Fabians (and the two were not altogether dissimilar on some points—many of the Fabians applauded Plener's personal income tax reforms as a step toward social equity), the property owners were very conscious of the fact that they still controlled the First Curia. The Liberal Fabians might join with the Socialists in inventing new housing reform programs, but as long as *Besitz* dominated city politics such ideas were stillborn. This was a hard, cruel, immovable fact which many of the younger academic Liberals of the 1890s inevitably encountered. *Hausbesitz* maintained its stranglehold on the political system long after the city's culture and economy had shifted to more progressive and cosmopolitan styles. To the extent that the Fabians found Koerber's new etatism in municipal government attractive after 1900 it was because of their hostility to the power of traditional property in local politics, and not necessarily to the threat of rival nationalities in such politics.

In 1891 most property owners voted Liberal as a matter of course. The antisemites did not run a serious slate of candidates for the Council in the First Curia that year. Those antisemites who tried to run for seats on the district committees in the inner districts in the First Curia were easily crushed by huge Liberal majorities. Because of the irreverent and at times hostile behavior of Prix and his group in the Council between 1891 and 1895, *Hausherren* political attitudes began a slow but certain shift toward the antisemites. By 1896 the party controlled eighteen seats in the First Curia, including two from inner districts, with significant minorities in several of the other inner-Bürger districts as well. Not all *Hausherren* immediately became antisemites, but a clear trend was apparent in favor of the Christian Socials by the time of Strobach's election.

The newspaper of the *Centralverband,* which remained neutral throughout 1895–96, repeatedly stressed the need to restore peace to the city administration and to reclaim the control of the local polity from the Imperial state. City autonomy was the perfect setting for maintaining the dignity and stability of the ideal *Hausherr* voter.[247] The Christian Socials refrained from using heavy antisemitic rhetoric on First Curia voters, and instead approached these men with the argument that they should support the party which would restore autonomy and propertied virtue to the municipal regime. The whole Bürgertum, with the *Hausherren* at the lead, would regain its lost unity and patriarchal power in the new urban society. These were the themes which governed Strobach's speeches. For the owners the Christian Socials were not so much an antisemitic party as they were a traditionalist Bürger party, a party which recognized their caste pretensions and petty privileges and sympathized with their anti-Socialist paranoia. Not surprisingly, many *Hausherren* found the Christian Socials' revival of the older ideal of the unitary Bürgertum, uniting voters of all three curias into one grand Bürgertum, very attractive. The Christian Socials argued that old, Vormärz tensions between Third and First Curia voters (master artisans against *Hausherren*) were both absurd and critically dangerous in the context of the new political situation created by the collapse of Liberalism and the rise of Austrian Social Democracy. What was needed was a common front of all honest Bürger, whatever their curial membership, against the forces of social change and egalitarianism. Big capitalists on the one side, the Reds on the other— only a political *juste milieu* of the traditional middle-Bürgertum could defend against these dangers. That the real enemy lay on the Left no one could doubt; even the *Hausherren-Zeitung* differentiated between the sniping resentment of the *Neue Freie Presse* and the categorical hatred of the *Arbeiter-Zeitung*. In a situation of pressure no one could doubt where ultimate alliances would be formed.

The inclusion of the *Hausherren* in the Christian Social coalition proved, thus, to be the last stage in an ascending hierarchy of Bürger interest groups upon which the party based its electoral strategies. The party could style itself as a real, if admittedly vulgarized, version of the *allgemeinen Bürgerstand*, formerly claimed by the early Liberals as their ideal. Artisans and property owners did not cease being at odds—the barbed comments by the *Hausherren-Zeitung* about lower artisan types who sometimes cheated on their taxes to the detriment of the "better middle class" of property owners in the city showed that earlier tensions between the two groups still endured.[248] But the Christian Socials made a concerted effort to get the groups to vote together in a single, multi-interest coalition by forcing these traditional intra-Bürger tensions into subordinate roles. Given the hostility of the Social Democrats to both the master artisans and the property owners, the success of the antisemites' tactic was assured, at least in the short term.

More important, political antisemitism itself began to play a more diverse and yet less emphatic role as the party sought to entice the voters of the First Curia. First Curia voters may have resented the arrogance of *Grosskapital,* but they clearly were not ready to respond favorably to the vulgar street-corner antisemitism of Ernst Schneider. With the rise to power of men like Strobach in the ranks of the *Hausherren* the power of the artisan antisemites like Schneider decreased in party affairs. The presence of the *Hausherren* did not destroy antisemitism in the party as a functional device for political mobilization, but it did lessen the dependence of the elite upon Jew hatred as an issue. Recent scholarship on late-nineteenth-century German antisemitism has noted the decline (or, as Richard Levy has suggested, the "downfall") of radical political antisemitism in late Imperial Germany. In Vienna political antisemitism in a formal sense never disappeared since by their very nature the Christian Socials were an "antisemitic" party. But the real effectiveness of the antisemitism issue did suffer a decline nonetheless, which was ultimately similar to what occurred in Germany. Antisemitism became a mere subsidiary issue, directed more against the Social Democrats than against the Jewish community as such. After 1897 the Christian Socials concentrated most of their energies on effective interest group representation for their Bürger client groups.[249] The presence of higher and more stable Bürger occupational groups within the coalition, like the senior schoolteachers and the *Hausherren,* made this dilution of artisan antisemitism possible. Ironically, antisemitism declined not because of the weakness of the supporters of the coalition, but because of their residual stability and strength.

The Final Victory: Lueger's Accession to Power

The year following Strobach's election as mayor was one of great moment in the history of the Christian Social party. The party immediately gained a hegemonic position within the *Stadtrat,* since all of the Liberal members resigned and refused to accept a minority allotment of seats on the committee. The new *Stadtrat* was designed to reflect the various constituencies and interests within the party (Catholics, Nationalists, teachers, property owners, artisans, etc.).[250] Unlike the Liberals the Christian Socials selected their committee in proportion to the relative size of the three curias (two, First Curia; eight, Second Curia; fifteen, Third Curia). They also tried to provide each district with at least one representative on the body. In theory the party was committed to the abolition of the *Stadtrat*, but events soon showed the party elite the advantage of retaining it as an executive directorate of municipal policy.[251]

An analysis of the first year of Christian Social rule in Vienna properly belongs with a more systematic examination of the administrative and political history of the party between 1897 and 1920, which will be the subject of the companion volume to this study. It might be noted, however, that Lueger's decision to press ahead immediately with his plans for a city-owned gas works was not an·act merely of political acumen, but also of administrative necessity. The new gas works was the first installment of Lueger's promise to revitalize Vienna's financial structure and thereby enhance its administrative and political independence. Municipal socialism in Vienna was far less ''social reform'' than it was an act of aggressive urban autonomy, providing the city with significant revenue resources for discretionary budget expenditures on white collar and artisan protectionism. Its history in Vienna must be viewed within the context of the general political and social history of the party after 1896, as well as in connection with the party's relationship with the Verwaltung after 1897. But the timing of municipalization was also set by administrative determinants: the deadline for the city's decision on whether to build a new gas works or buy out the older English-owned concern was 31 October 1896. Lueger had no choice but to push immediately for a decision on the question as soon as the party took control of the *Rathaus*.[252]

In November 1896 the party mounted a comprehensive campaign for the Lower Austrian Landtag elections and easily achieved a majority position within that body (forty-six Christian Socials and nationalists versus twenty-eight Liberals).[253] These were the first Landtag elections conducted under the franchise reform of August 1896, which opened rural electoral districts to direct voting. Not surprisingly, the party swept all rural seats and made drastic inroads into remaining Liberal seats in the smaller towns and cities in the province. Henceforth Lueger would not have to worry about having a hostile regional political authority overseeing his decisions in Vienna (increases in surtax rates on direct state taxes in the city and the issuance of large, construction-oriented loans for municipal improvements were subject to prior approval by the Landtag). Since the majorities in the Council and the Landtag were now controlled by one party elite, Lueger could move ahead without delay. Control of the *Landesausschuss* (the elected executive directorate which ran provincial affairs as they pertained to agendas outside of the city of Vienna) provided the party with a substantial increase in high ranking, salaried administrative positions which could be allotted to party functionaries who were not given paid positions within the city executive or the *Stadtrat*. Albert

Gessmann, Leopold Steiner, and August Kupka, among others, were appointed as officials of the *Landesausschuss* in 1897, each responsible for a specific area of provincial administration (Gessmann took the portfolio for school administration, giving him enormous patronage powers in Lower Austria).[254] This integration of the party elite into high-level functionary status was the beginning of a powerful drive toward bureaucratization, which had fateful consequences after 1897.

The path to hegemony in the Landtag was made possible by an extremely effective campaign in rural areas. In September 1896 the party staged the First Lower Austrian Peasants' Congress, in part organized by radical Catholic clerics.[255] More than in the city itself, the radical clergy proved a tool of immense political value in rural electoral districts in motivating peasants to exercise their franchise and support the antisemites. Only gradually did endogenous peasant politicians begin to make their way into the party elite. None of the antisemitic members of the *Landesausschuss* in 1896 was a peasant (Scheicher, who joined it in 1897, represented the peasantry, but was a cleric).[256] For the time being the Viennese elite ran provincial affairs as well, although this imbalance was not tenable in the long run.

The Landtag elections were also an opportunity for Lueger and Gessmann to settle accounts with the extreme nationalists, like Paul v Pacher and Wilhelm Hauck. In October 1895 a small group of moderate nationalists from small towns and cities in Lower Austria led by Franz Richter, a gymnasial professor from Krems, united to form the *Deutsche Volkspartei* of Lower Austria, hoping to start a local variant of Otto Steinwender's moderate German National movement in the province.[257] In August 1896 Richter made a deal with the Christian Socials at the antisemitic party congress held in Vienna whereby the two parties would support a joint slate of candidates for the Landtag elections.[258] In most instances this agreement worked smoothly, although the pan-Germans under Wolf screamed treachery. Twelve *Volkspartei* members and thirty-four Christian Socials were elected in November, giving the antisemites an absolute majority. All of the *Volkspartei* seats came from outside Vienna, in smaller urban communities where traditional fears of "clericalism" still prevented complete Christian Social rule, but where Liberalism was equally unacceptable.[259]

In Vienna Lueger decided to end the nominal independence of the few remaining Nationalists, whatever their coloration. Joseph Schlesinger was nominated to run against Hauck in Favoriten, and Josef Bärtl against Pacher in Wieden. When the final tabulations were in, both Christian Social candidates had won, depriving the Nationalists of any influence in the Viennese delegation.[260]

The decision to oppose Pacher and Hauck led to a secession within the *Bürgerclub* by a small number of Nationalists. Pacher himself resigned from the Council in July, allegedly in protest to the promotion of a baptized Jew, Victor Tachau, as *Magistratsdirektor,* but in fact out of bitterness over his slighting by Gessmann.[261] In late October 1896 eleven of his supporters announced that they were abandoning the *Bürgerclub* as well.[262] The majority of Nationalist-minded Councilmen issued a declaration reaffirming their membership in the club, and, indeed, within a few years they were indistinguishable from regular Christian Social party members. Several occupied leading positions on the *Stadtrat* (Theodor Wähner, the Nationalist editor of the *Deutsche Zeitung,* became a trusted confidant of Lueger on financial matters in the *Stadtrat*).[263] The rewards of political conformity were great indeed.

Having achieved unity within the antisemitic camp, Lueger was immediately forced to reckon with the imposing problem of the Social Democrats. The first major confrontation with the Viennese Socialists came in the hotly contested campaign for the five new Fifth Curia seats allotted to Vienna in the general elections of March 1897. On purely organizational terms the antisemites were no match for the disciplined, systematized cadre organization of the Socialists.[264] The Socialists even turned the tables on Lueger and Gessmann by exploiting the technique of rally disruption which the antisemites had used against the Liberals in 1895. Now it was Lueger's turn to scream for police protection on election day for his party, an ironic shift which the high Liberal press noted with considerable satisfaction.[265] This was perhaps the most bitter political campaign Vienna had ever experienced, marked not so much by antigovernmental rhetoric as it was by arguments drawn from class considerations. The year 1897 saw the first purely class political struggle in Viennese politics since the chaotic days of 1848. The flow of police reports to the *Statthalterei* and Interior Ministry stressed the new polarity which had come to characterize popular politics in Vienna. A small Social Liberal party tried to revitalize Liberal politics, but this movement amounted to nothing in dynamic, power terms.[266]

The results of the Fifth Curia competition showed, however, that Lueger's political finesse was still intact. All five Socialist candidates, including Victor Adler and Franz Schuhmeier, went down in humiliating defeat before the Christian Socials. In part this was due to Badeni's gerrymandering of election districts for the Fifth Curia: none of the potentially Socialist districts, like Ottakring or Favoriten, was left alone or combined with others of similar social makeup. Rather, each was joined with several Bürger districts (Favoriten was combined with the Landstrasse and Wieden, instead of with Meidling), leaving a preponderance of

Christian Social voters in each of the five areas. Of the 216,809 men who voted, nearly 57 percent (117,102) voted antisemitic. In the 1896 Landtag elections, under the privileged curial franchise, the Christian Socials had won 39,862 out of a total of 58,967 votes cast. In the general parliamentary elections under limited universal suffrage Lueger was able to come up with over 70,000 new voters. If the Christian Socials were a mass party only to a limited extent, where and how did they assemble such impressive support from nonprivileged voters?

Christian Social success in the Fifth Curia in 1897 astounded everyone in the city. The Social Democrats bitterly complained that Gessmann had tampered with the election lists, pushing hundreds of "dummy" voters in who would automatically vote for the Christian Socials, while deregistering hundreds of Social Democratic voters on petty and often illegal technicalities. Doubtless these tactics played a role in Lueger's success, but it would be absurd to attribute the success which all five antisemitic candidates enjoyed to such manipulations. The Imperial government issued instructions to Kielmansegg and the police that the elections were to be as honest as possible, so as to prevent the Socialists from blaming possible losses on the political system itself.[267] Although vote manipulations later became a serious problem in Viennese politics, the Christian Socials were not yet experienced enough in 1897 to be able to make thousands of dead men vote.

The key lay, rather, in the ability of the party to find candidates who would appeal to both older Bürger voters, who had the chance to vote twice (once in the Fifth Curia and once in the privileged urban curia), and those newer voters who were not interested in styling themselves as "workers." Hence, the selection as candidates of commercial employees like Julius Axmann, Hermann Bielohlawek, and Julius Prochazka and service industry workers like Karl Mittermayer (who was a restaurant waiter) was a clever, successful tactic.[268] As noted earlier, the antisemitic *Commis* in Vienna provided thousands of potential voters whom the party had begun to cultivate since the early 1890s. The restaurant waiters were another group who traditionally thought of themselves as involved in a cooperative, patrimonial relationship with their employers and who disdained the label "worker."[269] The restaurant workers' association was controlled throughout the 1890s by the antisemites, not by the Socialists. Equally important, Vienna had thousands of petty service attendants in governmental and private commercial and retail service (*Staatsdiener, Amtsdiener, Briefträger,* etc.), men whose whole life was centered on subservient codes of behavior before any legitimate authority and whose political attitudes, when they had any, were often very conservative.[270] By appealing to the social conservatism and hopes of petty bourgeois

security among these voters, the Christian Socials were able to put together enough older and newer voters to match the Social Democratic
masses (it is also possible that some artisan journeymen voted antisemitic
in industries like printing and jewelry production that were still controlled
by the Liberals).[271] Unfortunately for the Socialists, the light industrial,
governmental, and service orientation of the city's economy, together
with its generally conservative social culture, worked in favor of a
pseudo–mass party like the Christian Socials. There were nearly as many
commercial employees in the city as there were heavy industrial factory
workers, a situation which put the Social Democrats at a disadvantage.
That many voters also supported the antisemites because of Lueger's
personal popularity cannot be denied, at least in the 1897 elections.

Much of the Christian Social vote, to the extent that it relied on lower
commercial employees or the ranks of the city and provincial bureaucracy
and subordinate service personnel, was "soft" in nature. That is, with an
intensive program of political education and with a series of attractive
issues, the Social Democrats might yet hope to win a majority in some of
the Fifth Curia districts, especially in the Third, Fourth, and Fifth. As
time passed the initial popularity of Lueger inevitably became more
routinized and less immediate as a force for voter motivation. But the
results of 1897 showed that Adler and his lieutenants had a long road
ahead of them before they could win control of the city's Reichsrat delegation, especially if the city's economy remained stable and prosperous.
This election did not prove that the Christian Socials were the equals of
the Social Democrats either in organizational prowess or ideological
force. But it did show that the peculiar attractiveness of the Christian
Socials—their cultivation of struggling nonbourgeois types who wanted
desperately to be accorded recognition as Bürger in the city—was a
powerful lever in winning electoral support. Paradoxically, the Christian
Socials won precisely because they were not a classic mass party. They
did not attempt to reduce their constituency to the lowest common denominator, but instead held up a vision of a higher rank and status level to
which subordinate voters might aspire. Nor did they abandon the kinds of
class and caste pretensions which had so long survived in Viennese politics. Rather, they tried to make these accessible to a wider section of the
voting population.

Badeni had insisted that Lueger wait until after the parliamentary elections for elevation to the office of mayor. With its new prominence in
regional affairs and with its obvious role as defender of bourgeois life
against the Social Democrats, Lueger felt the party strong enough by the
late spring of 1897 to demand that Badeni finally honor his promise and
allow him to move up to the mayoralty. Badeni was about to plunge the

Hapsburg state into political turmoil over his language ordinances, and it was a calculated assumption on both sides that making Lueger mayor would earn the minister-president at least the passive support of the party on the language issue. Lueger was frank about this, and the Christian Socials did hold off as long as possible from a categorical break with Badeni's regime.

On 31 March 1897 Joseph Strobach abruptly resigned as mayor.[272] The City Council met on 8 April and elected Lueger to the post for the fifth time in two years. Kielmansegg went through the motions of raising objections about Lueger's national political aspirations and defiance of the crown, but had to give way and concede to Badeni that the government had no alternative but to confirm Lueger.[273] Badeni needed no such prompting in any event: Lueger now led a party delegation in parliament of over twenty members, not extremely large, but significant enough in close votes to be worth courting.

Accordingly on 20 April 1897 Karl Lueger was sworn in as *Bürgermeister* of Vienna.[274] Lueger used his inaugural address to provide an overview of the kinds of programs he wanted for the city: municipalized utilities, improved poor care, more efficient city government. Lueger emphasized that all of his ideas would cost money and asked the Imperial government for a greater share of the consumption tax revenues for the city. He also made a direct connection between the profits from city-owned utilities and the improvement of white collar job benefits in the city bureaucracy. The speech scarcely touched on political issues, leaving both the Jews and the Socialists unmentioned. But Lueger did speak out against extreme nationalism, insisting that nationalist strife could not be allowed to disrupt peaceful social reform projects and that no German-speaking party should exploit the nationalities issue for its own advantage. Lueger managed to adopt a sympathetic, but openly independent position to the Verwaltung. He urged cooperation with the Imperial administration, noting that his programs for municipalization would be impossible to implement without state assistance. But he also noted that he had been elected freely by the Christian people and represented them, not the Verwaltung. This tension between power in and out of relation to the national state was to be a crucial issue in the next quarter century of Christian Social rule.

Some of Lueger's loyalists tried to organize an *Illumination* for the evening of his inauguration. They met with partial success at best. In those districts and areas which were strongly Bürger in social composition (such as the Landstrasse and Margarethen), the party was able to get a respectable (and peaceful) showing of lights in windows, fires, and other celebratory acts. But in the populous working-class areas of the city, like

Ottakring and Rudolfsheim, the streets remained corridors of darkness. Even in its aesthetics the city was now divided into two camps, not antisemitic and Liberal, but antisemitic and Socialist. For the first time since 1848 Vienna stood on the brink of a profound ideological and cultural dualism which would mark all of its politics after 1897. Not only had bourgeois politics returned to its original ideal of the unitary Bürgertum, albeit on very different cultural and ideological terms, but also the general framework of secular politics had come full circle since 1848. The efforts of the early Liberals to impress upon the city's political culture a unity of power, class, and taste had failed. When those efforts were revived and restored by the anti-Liberals, using a different set of cultural assumptions, a new epoch of bourgeois politics opened, but one in which the Viennese Bürgertum was no longer the only actor in the general political system.

Lueger's succession to power revolutionized the Austrian political system. Lueger presided over a party in the midst of structural turmoil and ideological confusion. For here was a man who combined the most repressive and reactionary features of Liberal-notable politics with some of the most enterprising and expansive aspects of mass social politics. Lueger juxtaposed the best features of charismatic personalism with a hard commitment to parliamentary power and responsible constituency organization. Like Victor Adler he was intent on making the Imperial government, in whatever form it constituted itself, responsible to mass political power in a structured, parliamentary framework. He distrusted the uncontrolled politics of the street, although he was willing to use the streets occasionally to accomplish his larger policy ends. At the same time Lueger's cultural and social blinders were severe and immovable. Although he conceived of his party in a modern, representational sense, with central control and coordination, the party itself was deeply indebted to older Liberal forms of notable politics in its local and regional operations. More important, the basic cultural goal of the party was not to open all of adult society to political action, but to limit both politics and political society to fit the needs of the circle of bourgeois interests the Christian Socials represented. Under Christian Social leadership the traditional German-speaking Bürgertum found a much more effective and powerful spokesman for itself than under the Liberals, but the cultural cost was high indeed. Antisemitism and clericalism remained until 1918 as substantive themes of the party's propaganda, even if both concepts became more diffuse and opportunistic over time.

Conclusion

The great and abiding goal of Karl Lueger's political life was the reunification of the fragmented bourgeoisie into a more imposing, effective political party which would cope both with the demands of Mittelstand extremism and with the challenge of Austrian Social Democracy. That Lueger came to this goal in a fully conscious sense only through a process of trial and error, and that it was not until after 1891 that he and his fellow party leaders realized the essentially middle bourgeois requirements of any successful Mittelstand movement, was no denigration of his accomplishment. Lueger's career was a fascinating example of informal pragmatism gradually returning to basic political traditions. For Lueger's accomplishment by 1897 was nothing less than a new, albeit much revised, version of the consensus politics which had eluded the moderate Liberals of the Viennese political community in the anarchic months of 1848. In 1848 master artisans and small shopkeepers were denouncing *bürgerlichen Hausherren* and *bürgerlichen Honoratioren* in Vienna in a divisive split which undercut all efforts at bourgeois political unity. By 1897, through the efforts of Lueger, both groups had learned to live with each other in a new, revised Bürger political culture. If this was "reactionary" politics, it was nonetheless both effective and impressive for its time and place. What was impossible in the ideologized culture of 1848 was a necessity in the fundamentally socialized culture of 1898. If in accomplishing this restoration Lueger was forced to utilize political antisemitism and political clericalism to disarm and destroy Viennese Liberalism, these were devices which were tightly controlled and which, at least for Lueger, did not repudiate the idea of a Liberal *Rechtsstaat*. That the Christian Socials presented and instilled models of political behavior which in other hands and in a different time period could destroy the Liberal state became a historical burden that Lueger and his movement must inevitably carry.

Revival of bourgeois political unity owed much to the fundamentally different role the urban working classes played in Vienna in 1848 and 1895. During the Revolution of 1848 the novelty of political liberty and the holistic ethical sense of early Liberal politics made it essential that the lower orders of Viennese society be treated with respect and decorum

411

worthy of potential citizens of the new state. Thus, master craftsmen serving in the suburban National Guard supported and sympathized with worker protests not simply out of a sense of tactical utility, but because the political virtue of the "others" of Austrian society—the workers— assured a mutually supportive linkage between Bürger society and the working class. The disruptive effects of industrial modernization were not yet so extreme in Vienna in 1848 as to break completely the nexus of master-journeyman loyalty which was still a part of Vormärz society. And even among the more distinctively proletarian strata of workers—the factory workers of the outlying suburbs—the level of political self-consciousness was so low and so disorganized that it was easy for Left-oriented activists and younger university academics to impute to these workers goals and interests common with those of the Viennese bourgeoisie.

By 1895 the rise of Austrian Social Democracy guaranteed that the political and ethical power of the working classes would be isolated from and turned against the interests of all of the strata within the Viennese Bürgertum. The Socialists' ghetto mentality only paralleled, moreover, an ongoing social and cultural estrangement within traditional sectors of the craft trades and smaller factories of Vienna. In 1848 master craftsmen might still look upon their workers as possible political allies (even if they did so with overt status reservations); by 1895 the same master craftsmen (three generations later) were trying to cope with the strike activity of industrial labor unions intent on destroying their economic independence and cultural superiority. The *Gehilfe* in Vienna by 1895 was not merely an economic antagonist of the artisan master, but a clear cultural rival as well. Socialist demands that the journeymen be made coresponsible for guild affairs along with the masters reflected something of the normative revolution in Viennese working-class culture which had occurred between 1848 and 1895. That the Socialists decided to accept the traditional craft trades structures and work within them to achieve cultural and economic parity with the Viennese Bürgertum was far more threatening for the lower bourgeoisie than if the Socialists had maintained their isolated social anarchism of the early 1880s. The worker was not only a Red political danger by 1895, but an agent for cultural egalitarianism as well. That the threshold of political tolerance and experience within the Austrian Bürgertum was low was a historically demonstrable fact—many of these voters had not been enfranchised until the 1880s under the Taaffe regime. That they should react with near hysteria to the intrusion of Austrian Socialism into their newly won political privileges was not therefore surprising.

Karl Lueger's naiveté on the national question was both disarming and illusory, but the party's attempt during the later 1890s to stand above the nationalities problem only demonstrated his professional concern to concentrate all possible emotional and technical resources on the primacy of a social bourgeois politics which would transcend national enmities. His manifest hostility to the Magyars can hardly be called a feature of the nationalities problem.

The question of Lueger's relationship to a hypothetical protofascist tradition of politics cannot be ignored, but his book has argued (as will the second volume, dealing with Vienna and the party from 1897 to 1920) that Lueger's model for competitive social politics in the bourgeois mode was deeply rooted in nineteenth-century traditions and values. Lueger sought not to surpass and destroy the traditional state, but to work more effectively within it; he asked not that law be ignored or misused, but that its potentially conservative and anti-Socialist implications be fully exploited; he sought not the role of a demagogic and authoritarian *Führer,* but rather that of a patrimonial and patriarchal *Vater.* The political mode employed was, if anything, baroque, not fascistic.

Lueger and the Modernization of Austrian Politics

For all of his cultural and political traditionalism, however, Lueger did revolutionize Austrian politics in several distinct, yet interrelated ways. Lueger was one of the first party politicians in Imperial Austria to take the profession of politics seriously. This went beyond his willingness to sacrifice his law practice to demands of political agitation; it encompassed the idea of total immersion of the self in the genre of public political behavior. Lueger had no personal life; indeed, he consciously styled himself as having no personal needs. The self-gratification he required and eventually received came totally from the successful exercise of competitive political power. Lueger needed no bribes or graft because money was not an end value in his professionalization of political power. Money for Lueger had merely utilitarian functions—it could buy printed propaganda, it could fund party newspapers and rallies, it could ease the burdens of sub-elite recruitment; but it was not a goal in and of itself. Precisely this total dedication to his political endeavors, in the context of the traditional, strife-ridden Viennese political club culture, made Lueger such a valuable and successful manager. As noted previously, Lueger differed from his colleagues like Robert Pattai in his refusal to engage in personal feuds. Lueger's conception of personal *Ehre* was far more modern than Pattai's. For Lueger a duel was the mark of petty self-indulgence and self-gratification in an arena of life which demanded that the self be absorbed by wider strategic concerns. Pattai was a dilettantish amateur who brought private values of neocorporate society into public political issues. This was precisely the reason for his second-rate status within the party elite. As a professional Lueger realized that personal emotions and motives had to play a subordinate role in situations demanding a public political rationality.

Lueger modernized the use of language in political action. Sensitive to the popular forms of Viennese speech, he was hardly the first urban politician in Austria to use language in quasi-demagogic forms on selected occasions. But he was the first to appreciate the inherent flexibility and time-related opportunities a careful use of language offered. Not only did Lueger provide language purists like Karl Kraus with evidence for the increasing disjunction between words and ideas and institutions, but he did so gladly and with enormous confidence in the salutary benefits of such a new, essentially *political* language. Lueger saw that fin de siècle social culture in Austria encompassed far too many contradictory demands and needs for the political institutions of the state to be able to deal with each one of them in an absolute, literal, and inflexible fashion. The political system of Imperial Austria was not hopeless, nor was it completely antiquated, but it needed time and discretionary opportunities to slow down and drag out the divisive social and national inputs being introduced into its structures. Given the polarities within the social and ethnic foundations of the political system, direct elite bargaining on a consociational model was a distant possibility as a mode of conflict resolution, but not one which was immediately workable. For consociational elite decision making implies that the leaders of or spokesmen for the conflicting national and social interests be able to manage and control the emotions and social demands of "their" constituents and that they themselves accept the slow, progressive, and evolutionary time frames in which public policy must take shape. Lueger was one of the first to realize the need in Austria for a new culture of political language which would control and manage public demands from diverse social and cultural sectors, allowing partisan decision makers and allegedly neutral state officials the necessary time to play out antinomies and polarities within more circumscribed and tightly controlled small groups. This was a role which only the parties could play, not the Verwaltung itself. He realized that the apparent "irrationality" of public language was itself a highly rational instrument for achieving social equilibrium within the traditional Hapsburg state. If others who followed him in the twentieth century distorted and misused the popular control features of this new language in an effort to destroy the privileged traditions of Bürger society and the Imperial state, this can hardly be blamed on Lueger. For Lueger, language, like money and honor, was an instrument to stabilize and to reunite bourgeois society in a traditional, patrimonial mode. It was not a tool for the creation of a "new society" of new values and new men, most of whom had been torn out of traditional social matrices by the events of 1914–25.

Lueger was also responsible for the development of a new style of high-tension, issue politics in which dramatic social and economic problems were used as mobilization devices both to manipulate public sentiment and, if necessary, to create it. Both Lueger and Gessmann combined the traditional respect which earlier Liberal politicians had brought toward their local district constituencies with a sense of the malleability and tentativeness of voter opinion on issues in which the collective self-enhancement of larger, city-wide interests groups might take place. This does not mean that they lied to their electorate or that they consciously misled and betrayed them in a wild, demagogic fashion. Lueger was far too much a local Viennese politician not to respect the inherent accountability built into the Viennese political system. But he did make the operational distinction between the use value of an issue in explicit political terms and its probable consequences in policy and administrative terms, whereas the older Liberals tended to equate the two. This resulted from Lueger's sharper differentiation of public politics on one hand and administration and governmental policymaking on the other. Unlike the early Austrian Liberals, who still hoped that a government (namely, *their* government) could perform both roles simultaneously, Lueger had learned that policy changes could be designed and effectively implemented only when a powerful external political momentum based on social mobilization had first been achieved outside government. Austrian society had become too diverse and strife-ridden to tolerate an absolute congruence between politics and Verwaltung—hence Lueger's insistence that Austrian political systems were coequally political-electoral and administrative-economic in nature. Lueger's modernity was illustrated by his perception that in a political system in which social (and national) issues played a critical, disequilibrilizing role in voter motivation, interest aggregation between political groups had to precede appeals to the Verwaltung for policy responses. Lueger never placed much faith in doctrinaire demands for explicit ministerial government in Austria; he viewed national politics as a conflict in which social interest and privilege, once articulated and aggregated by popular politics, would move through the channels of governmental deliberation and find an equilibrium point of partial satisfaction.

The Austrian Liberals had attempted to control the Verwaltung by politicizing it in an internal cultural fashion by obtaining the individual allegiances of *Staatsbeamten* as participants in the electoral system. They had no ready grasp of, and felt uncomfortable with the idea of parties in permanent rivalry with the Verwaltung, since their first experiences in national government in the years 1867–79 placed them in the happy position of being both the party of government and the government itself. Unlike the Prussian Liberals, the Austrians had been *too* unfortunate in their early career. When Taaffe came and deprived them of this happy internalist accommodation, they were shocked into immobility and despair. The rise of the nationalities issue compounded this problem, since it increased the disjunctiveness between party politics and the Imperial administration, leaving the Liberals as simply one group among many courting the administration for favors and privileges. Lueger in contrast dispensed with the Liberals' pathos-ridden ideal of a unanimity between political mobilization and administrative policy and sought to reaffirm on explicit social terms the class consciousness and internal social homogeneity of the Austrian Bürgertum as a means to sustain social privilege. By creating a strong externalist constituency, he could then confront the Verwaltung with his demands.

Political parties became more functionally important and more self-willed in Austria than in Wilhelmine Germany because the level of potent social and national conflict in Austria was so much greater. The crucial issue in Austria was not the domination of parties by organized interest groups and thus the abortion of an idealized "pluralist" society (as younger German historians have tried to argue), but the fact that Austrian society was *too* plural to begin with. Austria required more from her political parties than did Germany, since, as hapless and incompetent as they often were, they were the only viable buffers between explosive social unrest and rational administrative decision making. Parties thus played a rather different and more multifaceted role in the Austrian political system. The last thing the system needed was doctrinaire demands for complete congruence between political parties and administrative power—this could have destroyed it. The proper and meaningful role for parties after 1880 was to serve as intermediate channels of social and national interest in a multinational, political culture. Lueger was one of the first politicians in Austria to realize the implications of this development and to exploit it for his own purposes. By emphasizing the power and the vitality which a united Bürgertum could have in its national interest demands, Lueger legitimated his strategies on the municipal level as well. The ultimate "interest group" for Lueger was the Viennese Bürgertum itself, as a social and cultural entity. At the same time, Lueger had a close appreciation of the need to dominate society through politics—in an overly pluralist and disruptive society, parties needed to control social interests rather than be dominated by them.

Finally, Lueger's greatest achievement was a superbly traditional one, but one which also placed his party in grave danger by 1914. By re-establishing the old Viennese Bürgertum on a new set of conceptual terms, by providing it with a new set of additional occupants who learned to live in tenuous coexistence with former intrabourgeois rivals (e.g., artisans versus *Hausherren*), and by securing his system through a remarkable combination of traditional Liberal and new mass political practices Lueger had restored an old Liberal political ideal on very new terms, using conventional as well as novel means. The common denominator of his party's strategy was, however, the notion of the fundamental disjunction within the *Volk* of the lower orders from the Bürgertum. Precisely because Lueger stressed so often his dedication to the whole of Viennese society could he treat the whole as less than the sum of its parts. If Lueger served the "people," it was in defense of the Bürgertum, not the other way around. The problem inherent in this tactic was that it postulated a rather rigid and inflexible notion of what the "people" were, and assumed that the political privileges enjoyed by the Bürgertum in Austrian regional and local political systems would always be tolerated by those deprived of such privileges. Here Lueger's modernity came to a sudden and uncompromising halt. In order to sustain the privileges necessary to allow his party to behave in a "modern" fashion on the national level, Lueger employed biased and exclusionist means on the local and regional levels. Whereas politics and administration in the national government for Lueger could be kept distinct, on the municipal level politics and bureaucratization gradually merged. The history of this collision of mass-traditionalist politics and municipal bureaucracy in Vienna and *its* detente with the Imperial state in defense of Bürger privilege after 1897 must constitute the central theme of the party's history after 1897.

One conventional view of nineteenth-century Austrian history has always assumed that the words "Liberal," "bourgeois," and "capitalist" were synonymous. Within Viennese society in this century it is clear by now that each of these terms comprehended a distinct and often dissimilar entity. The peculiarities of the Viennese political system were such that a Bürger ethos on a pre- or at best early industrial social base became normative for all of nineteenth-century political society. For nearly seventy years (from 1850 to 1918) a franchise and electoral structure and a party system were imposed on the city which were clearly not typical of a grand bourgeoisie, either in financial resources or in ideology. The ideal heroes of the 1850 franchise were the property owners, prosperous artisans and merchants, and mid-century *Intelligenz*, not the Ringstrasse bankers or great industrial plutocrats. Solidity, honor, and Bürger respectability were the valued norms of this society, not extreme wealth or power. Well into the twentieth century the city was afflicted with this heritage from the mid–nineteenth century.

At the same time the specific determinants of Viennese political history made it possible for a non-Liberal bourgeois movement to advance by 1896 to control the most populous and vital city in all of the Hapsburg Empire. Precisely because the lower and middle reaches of the city's political system were always pre- or nonindustrial, even during the Liberal era (but not necessarily premodern—the schoolteachers were an excellent example of a group which found its self-conception revolutionized during the Liberal era), it was possible for a group of daring, enterprising politicians to build upon the discontent of the Third Curia artisans to achieve political hegemony within the upper two curias as well.

The idea of the unitary Bürgertum in 1848 was the great contribution of the Liberals to Austrian political history. Critics like Ferdinand Kronawetter and Victor Adler might mock it in their efforts to achieve universal suffrage, but in its most generous and literal form it was an impressive idea. The problem for the Austrian Liberals was that they were not faithful to their own ideal. Rather than insisting that all of bourgeois society be politicized in the 1850s and 1860s, they gladly bowed before the wishes of the neo-absolutist regime and expelled thousands of their fellow *Mitbürger* from the political system in an act of stupidity and arrogance. The lower ranking artisans might have been socialized into Liberal values, but instead by 1880 they were an angry mass susceptible to new and different kinds of cultural appeals which denigrated Liberal humanitarian sympathies while insisting upon full Bürger political rights. The poorer artisans became the force which set in motion a profound reconstruction of the Viennese political system by 1900. Their enfranchisement by Taaffe on the local and regional level in 1885 forced all Viennese politicians to cope with a new set of radical social interest issues. Once an appropriate ideology had been found to neutralize Liberal anticlericalism—i.e., antisemitism—the Liberals found themselves on the defensive for the first time since 1848. The Liberal party was not the party of the Jews, as the antisemites were wont to charge. As noted in chapter 2, much of the local Liberal party was openly and staunchly Gentile. The press may have been staffed by Jewish editors, but the Jewish vote and Jewish candidates were not the major forces behind Viennese Liberalism. That the Liberal party was punished for its alleged subservience to the Jews was one of the great ironies of Austrian history; no party in the monarchy's history was more zealous in avoiding appointing Jews to any level of government.

Unlike Berlin and the Stöcker movement political antisemitism spread upward, but the very meaning of the term shifted and expanded as it encountered new political clients. First Curia voters were loath to style themselves as "antisemites," but their traditional self-conception as property-owning Bürger whose interests the Liberals seemed unable or unwilling to protect could be exploited to win their political support. Antisemitism became the first step to encourage non-artisan bourgeois groups like the state officials, the priests, the senior schoolteachers, and other such strata to rethink their attitudes about the state and contemporary politics. The very locus of opportunity provided by Lueger's oppositional politics encouraged all of these groups to define themselves in a more aggressive, interest-group way. Group self-interest merged with and was stimulated by competitive electoral rivalries.

What had begun in the early 1880s as a movement of the artisans paying the lowest taxes became by the mid-1890s a widespread revolt of middle bourgeois society in Vienna, manipulated by Lueger in the name of the Bürgertum as an idol of righteousness and virtue. Defining the unitary Bürgertum in 1848, the Liberals then proceeded to divide and fragment it; Lueger reversed the process, beginning with the men excluded in 1848–50, but ending with older notions of Bürger unity against the Austrian Social Democrats. By 1900 Lueger's political machine in Vienna represented both politically and culturally the ideal of the unitary Bürgertum in pre- and early industrial terms, not simply the lower artisans of the Third Curia. From this point an accommodation with the Austrian capitalist establishment, which became the hallmark of the party after 1907, was easily achieved.

The curial structure of Vienna made these operations possible in a way which the more oligarchical and rigid three-class systems of Prussia would not have allowed. The Christian Socials were able to capitalize on the more stable and predictable nature of the three curias in Vienna. They were able not only to recruit new voters into their party, but also to convert many older voters of known occupations who had voted in the same curia year after year. They had, in other words, a flexible, yet predictable constituency to which to appeal.

The decision of Lueger and the other secular politicians in the movement to adopt a quasi-religious facade for their party was an act of the highest prudence. Not only did the priests and Vogelsang provide important cadre-level resources and valuable political propaganda, but the association of a vague Christian motif with the movement helped to tone down its state-political radicalism and differentiate clearly between native Viennese Bürger antisemitism and the more categorical varieties of racial and national hatred preached by Schönerer. Once antisemitism had neutralized anticlericalism to an initial degree, the pragmatic example of priests engaged in ward-level political agitation and organization helped to push the political issue of anticlericalism into oblivion.

For many years Lueger and Gessmann were relatively unimaginative in developing new technical resources and methods. Early Christian Social political techniques did not differ fundamentally from those of the Liberals or Democrats, aside from Lueger's more creative language and the more adventurous fashion in which the antisemites played upon occupational issues. But by 1895–96 the party was well on the way to developing a "mass" side in its organization, its funding, and its party programs. Crucial to this trend was the availability of the enormous financial and administrative resources of the city of Vienna itself. Much of the history of the party after 1897 must be seen in the context of the symbiosis that came to exist between a mass party eager for national power and the growth of significant public bureaucracies in the city which helped to underpin and sustain the party's momentum.

By struggling with the Verwaltung in 1895–96 and winning, Lueger not only forced Badeni and the crown to recognize the idea of non-Liberal politics as an acceptable basis for administrative power, but may have inadvertently encouraged Badeni to play upon the weakness of the German Liberals in his attempt to push through his speech ordinances in 1897. Badeni tried to turn his defeat of 1896 into a victory in 1897 by taking Lueger at his word—that Liberalism was dead and its former constituents ready to be manipulated. Unfortunately, what Badeni failed to realize was that the interest group power demonstrated by the Christian Socials in Vienna in 1896 could also be brought to bear in defense of national, as well as social, issues. He also failed to accept the more passive, regulatory role prescribed for the Verwaltung in the Austrian system. Lueger saw the Imperial administration as a mediator and broker between divergent interests, not as the provocateur of radical national change.

The history of the Christian Socials after 1897 is necessarily a part of the larger institutional and political development of the monarchy as a whole. By consolidating its power in Vienna, by harnessing bureaucracy and machine politics into a workable model of political efficiency, the party gradually became a major bourgeois political force in the empire after 1900. Lueger's municipal socialist projects, beginning with the new gas works in 1896–97, provided the city with a new level of financial autonomy against the state. Unlike similar projects in Germany, the Viennese municipalization model was implicitly antistatist in its politics. City ownership was not a new variant of state intervention in society, but rather the attempt to protect Viennese autonomy against the state by buttressing the city's proprietary financial base. Municipal socialism was not an act of "social reform" for Lueger so much as it was an act of party-political autonomy against the central state. By 1910 a substantial share of the city budget depended upon the profits derived from the network of municipal utilities and services. At last the city had a source of discretionary revenue over which the state had no direct control. With the revenues and the enormous patronage opportunities represented by the thousands of new jobs in city industries, Lueger and his elite were in a position to forge a political machine of unparalleled power in Austrian history. The party's detente with the Viennese aristocratic and capitalist establishments, largely in place and functioning by 1900, helped ease the way for its acceptance of ministerial power between 1907 and 1911. The history of the party's bureaucratization of mass politics in the city and its extension of local and regional power to the national level, using Vienna as a power base, will be the principal themes of the second volume of this work.

Abbreviations

AHY   *Austrian History Yearbook*
AHZ   *Allgemeine Handwerker Zeitung*
AKBMS   *Archiv für Kirchengeschichte von Böhmen-Mähren-Schlesien*
AÖG   *Archiv für österreichische Geschichte*
AÖZ   *Allgemeine Österreichische Zeitung*
ARWP   *Archiv für Rechts- und Wirtschaftsphilosophie*
ASGSS   *Archiv für Soziale Gesetzgebung und Statistik*
ASLW   *Archiv der Stadt- und des Landes Wien*
ASWSP   *Archiv für Sozialwissenschaft und Sozialpolitik*
AVA   *Allgemeines Verwaltungsarchiv*
AZ   *Arbeiter-Zeitung*
BHGK   *Berichte der Handels- und Gewerbekammer, Wien*
BSWG   *Berichte über die Sitzungen des Wiener Gemeinderathes*
BZ   *Beamten-Zeitung*
CB   *Correspondenzblatt für den katholischen Clerus Österreichs*
CEH   *Central European History*
CON   *Die Constitution*
CR   *Contemporary Review*
CSAZ   *Christlich-soziale Arbeiter-Zeitung*
DEZ   *Demokratische Zeitung*
DGZ   *Deutsche Gewerbe-Zeitung*
DNR   *Das Neue Reich*
DÖLZ   *Deutsch-Österreichische Lehrer-Zeitung*
DV   *Deutsches Volksblatt*
DZ   *Deutsche Zeitung*
EBDA   *Erzbischöfliches Diözesanarchiv*
EE   Joseph Scheicher, *Erlebnisse und Erinnerungen* (6 vols., Vienna and Leipzig, 1906–12)
F   *Fortschritt*
FH   *Freiheit*
FLS   *Freie Lehrerstimme*
FN   *Friedrich Funder Nachlass (HHSA)*
FPB   *Freie pädagogische Blätter*
FR   *Der Freimüthige*

GA Gerad' aus
GG Geschichte und Gesellschaft
GN Cardinal Gruscha Nachlass (EBDA)
HHSA Haus-, Hof-, und Staatsarchiv
HHZ Hausherren-Zeitung
HPB Historisch-politische Blätter
HZ Historische Zeitschrift
JGVV Jahrbuch für Gesetzgebung, Verwaltung, und Volkswirtschaft
JIDG Jahrbuch des Instituts für Deutsche Geschichte
JLG Jahrbuch der österreichischen Leogesellschaft
JLN Jahrbuch für Landeskunde von Niederösterreich
JMH Journal of Modern History
JNS Jahrbücher für Nationalökonomie und Statistik
JVGSW Jahrbuch des Vereins für Geschichte der Stadt Wien
KP Kaufmännische Post
KVZ Konstitutionelle Vorstadt-Zeitung
KZ Kaufmännische Zeitschrift
KZSS Kölner Zeitschrift für Soziologie und Sozialpsychologie
LBY Leo Baeck Yearbook
MCSR Monatsschrift für christliche Sozialreform
MIÖG Mitteilungen des Instituts für österreichische Geschichts-
   forschung
MÖIU Mitteilungen der Oesterreichisch-Israelitischen Union
MÖSA Mitteilungen des Österreichischen Staatsarchivs
MP Morgenpost
MVGSW Mitteilungen des Vereins für Geschichte der Stadt Wien
NFP Neue Freie Presse
NO Neue Ordnung
NÖB Neue österreichische Biographie
NÖLA Niederösterreichisches Landesarchiv
NPZ Neue Preussische Zeitung
NWT (A) Neues Wiener Tagblatt (Abendblatt)
ODP Ost-Deutsche Post
ODR Ostdeutsche Rundschau
ÖGL Österreich in Geschichte und Literatur
ÖR Oesterreichischer Reformer
ÖRD Österreichische Rundschau
ÖSBZ Oesterreichische Staatsbeamten-Zeitung
ÖSZ Österreichische Schul-Zeitung
ÖV Oesterreichischer Volksfreund
ÖW Oesterreichische Wochenschrift
PAAA Politisches Archiv des Auswärtigen Amtes (Bonn)

PAPS   *Proceedings of the American Philosophical Society*
PJ   *Pädagogischer Jahresbericht*
PN   *Pichl Nachlass (AVA)*
PP   *Past and Present*
PR   *Die Presse*
PV   Gustav Kolmer, *Parlament und Verfassung in Österreich* (8 vols.,
       Vienna and Leipzig, 1902–14)
RGBl   *Reichsgesetzblatt*
RHM   *Römische Historische Mitteilungen*
RP   *Reichspost*
RQ   *Römische Quartalschrift für christliche Altertumskunde und*
       Kirchengeschichte
SB   *Der Staatsbeamte*
SJ   *Statistische Jahrbücher der Stadt Wien*
SM   *Statistische Monatschrift*
SML   *Stimmen aus Maria-Laach*
SP   *Stenographische Protokolle über die Sitzungen des Hauses der*
       Abgeordneten
SPB   *Sprechsaal des Beamtentages*
SPNÖLTG   *Stenographisches Protokoll des Landtages für das Erzher-*
       zogtum Österreich unter der Enns
SVSP   *Schriften des Vereins für Sozialpolitik*
TPQS   *Theologisch-praktische Quartalschrift*
TQ   *Theologische Quartalschrift*
UDW   *Unverfälschte Deutsche Worte*
V   *Vaterland*
VN   *Vogelsang Nachlass* (Bibliothek der katholisch-theologischen
       Fakultät, Wien)
VO   *Vorwärts*
VSWG   *Vierteljahrschrift für Sozial- und Wirtschaftsgeschichte*
VT   *Volkstribüne*
VW   *Volkswohl*
VZ   *Vossische Zeitung*
WD   *Wiener Diözesanblatt*
WFFZ   *Wiener Fleischhauer- und Fleischselcher Zeitung*
WG   *Wiener Geschichtsblätter*
WGGT   *Wiener Gewerbe Genossenschaftstag*
WKB   *Wiener Kaufmännische Blätter*
WW   *Wort und Wahrheit*
WZ   *Wiener Zeitung*
Z   *Die Zeit*
ZABV   *Zeitschrift des Allgemeinen Beamtenvereins*

ZGSW   Zeitschrift für die gesamte Staatswissenschaft
ZKG   Zeitschrift für Kirchengeschichte
ZKSB   Zeitschrift des Königlich preussischen statistischen Bureaus
ZÖR   Zeitschrift für öffentliches Recht
ZP   Zeitschrift für Politik
ZSSR   Zeitschrift der Savigny-Stiftung für Rechtsgeschichte, Kanonistische Abteilung
ZVSV   Zeitschrift für Volkswirtschaft, Sozialpolitik, und Verwaltung
ZWN   Zeitung für die Wiener Nationalgarde

Notes

Preface

1. The leading American historian of this view is Klemens v Klemperer. See his important biography *Ignaz Seipel* (Princeton, 1972), chap. 1. In Austria the work of Erika Weinzierl-Fischer and Reinhold Knoll has generally maintained similar assumptions.

2. See Peter G. J. Pulzer, *The Rise of Political Anti-Semitism in Germany and Austria* (New York, 1965), a lucid account of the Christian Socials, stressing their connections to European antisemitism.

3. See Lothar Gall, "Liberalismus und 'bürgerliche Gesellschaft.' Zu Charakter und Entwicklung der liberalen Bewegung in Deutschland," *HZ* 220 (1975): 324–56; James J. Sheehan, "Liberalism and the City in Nineteenth-Century Germany," *PP* 51 (1971): 116–37; idem, "Liberalismus und Gesellschaft in Deutschland, 1815–1848," in L. Gall, ed., *Liberalismus* (Cologne, 1976), pp. 208–23; W. J. Mommsen, "Der deutsche Liberalismus zwischen 'klassenloser Bürgergesellschaft' und 'Organisiertem Kapitalismus.' Zu einigen neueren Liberalismusinterpretationen," *GG* 4 (1978): 77–90. My general interpretation of both Austrian Liberalism and Austrian Christian Socialism owes a great deal to the recent work on German Liberalism by Gall, Sheehan, and Mommsen, among others.

4. See Carl E. Schorske, "Politics in a New Key: An Austrian Triptych," *JMH* 39 (1967): 343–86. My comments on Schorske's work do not suggest that his argument about Lueger is wrong in and of itself. But the analysis of Christian Socialism must try to anchor the man in the social and group context in which he worked. On the whole, Schorske's articles on fin de siècle Vienna are the most impressive and suggestive pieces of research done since the days of Otto Brunner and Heinrich Ritter v Srbik. This book is not a "rejection" of Schorske's arguments, but rather a different view which, I think, is ultimately complementary to his arguments, employing different analytical categories.

5. See Ludwig Jedlicka and Rudolf Neck, eds., *Österreich 1927 bis 1938* (Munich, 1973), pp. 44–45.

Chapter 1

1. See Reinhart Koselleck, *Preussen zwischen Reform und Revolution* (Stuttgart, 1967); Mack Walker, *German Home Towns: Community, Estate, and General Estate, 1648–1871* (Ithaca and London, 1971); Leonard Krieger, *The German Idea of Freedom* (Boston, 1957); Sheehan, "Liberalism and Society in Germany, 1815–1848," *JMH* 45 (1973): 583–604; idem, *German Liberalism in the Nineteenth Century* (Chicago, 1978); Wolfgang Köllmann, *Bevölkerung in der industriellen Revolution* (Göttingen, 1974).

2. Friedrich Walter, *Die österreichische Zentralverwaltung*, II Abt., 1.Bd./2. Halbband, Teil 2, *Die Zeit Franz II. (I.) und Ferdinands I (1792–1848)* (Vienna, 1956), pp. 1–25.

3. See Gerhard Oestreich, "Strukturprobleme des europäischen Absolutismus," *VSWG* 55 (1968): 344ff. For the immobility of the Austrian administrative structure in the Vormärz, see Harm-Hinrich Brandt, *Der österreichische Neoabsolutismus. Staatsfinanzen und Politik, 1848–1860* (2 vols, Göttingen, 1978), 1:12–129; 2:999–1001. This is not to suggest that

there was no economic growth or social-urban development before 1848, but that the growth which did occur often did so in spite of rather than because of rational, aggressive attempts by the state to achieve social modernization. On Austrian economic growth before 1848, see Nahum Gross, *Industrialization in Austria in the Nineteenth Century* (diss., University of California, Berkeley, 1966), pp. 18–19, 32–37, 84–85; Richard Rudolph, "The Pattern of Austrian Industrial Growth from the Eighteenth to the Early Twentieth Century," *AHY* 11 (1975): 3–25; and Brandt, 1:25–47. The existence of individuals within the Verwaltung who subscribed to administrative and economic reform, often with extreme caution and with self-contradictory methods, must be acknowledged, but does not render the general impression of bureaucratic and social immobility in the Vormärz inoperative. For a more positive view of the "liberalism" of the state service, see Alois Brusatti, "Die Staatsgüterveräusserungen in der Zeit von 1780–1848," *MÖSA* 11 (1958): 252–74. But see also Brandt's more recent, and I think insightful, comments on the ambivalent reformism of men like Kübeck, in *Der österreichische Neoabsolutismus,* 1:126, note 61.

4. On Vormärz censorship, see Julius Marx, *Die österreichische Zensur im Vormärz* (Vienna, 1959). On the borrowing of foreign political and social models by native Austrians, see Sebastian Brunner, *Woher? Wohin? Geschichten, Gedanken, Bilder und Leute aus meinem Leben* (5 vols., 3d ed., Regensburg, 1891), 2:145–46 and passim; Ernst Violand, *Die sociale Geschichte der Revolution in Oesterreich* (Leipzig, 1850), pp. 58, 62–67; and Wolfgang Häusler, "Hermann Jellinek im Vormärz. Seine Entwicklung zum revolutionären Demokraten," in Heinrich Fichtenau and Erich Zöllner, eds., *Beiträge zur neueren Geschichte Österreichs* (Vienna, 1974), pp. 345–62; and Hans Lentze, *Die Universitätsreform des Ministers Graf Leo Thun-Hohenstein* (Vienna, 1962), pp. 28–29. Ignaz Kuranda's *Die Grenzboten,* published in Leipzig, was important in this process, since it was read in Vienna in the later 1840s. For the Saxon influence, see Häusler, "Hermann Jellinek im Vormärz," pp. 351–52, 357–58. See also W. Alexis, *Wiener Bilder* (Leipzig, 1833), pp. 371ff., who noted that the Viennese could read whatever they liked, but not do anything about it. Ordinary areas of public life became deeply privatized in the Vormärz. On Vormärz culture, see William M. Johnston, *The Austrian Mind: A Social and Intellectual History, 1848–1938* (Berkeley and Los Angeles, 1972), pp. 11–29; Ferdinand Leopold Graf Schirnding, *Oesterreich im Jahre 1840* (4 vols., Leipzig, 1840–44), vols. 1 and 2.

5. On the *Leseverein* and Guizot, see Anton Springer, *Geschichte Oesterreichs seit dem Wiener Frieden, 1809* (2 vols., Leipzig, 1863–65), 2:181. On Vormärz political life in general, see ibid., vol. 1; Ignaz Beidtel, *Geschichte der österreichischen Staatsverwaltung, 1740–1848* (2 vols., Innsbruck, 1896–98), 2: 38–76, 213–36, 315–24, 341–44, 428–34; Eduard Winter, *Frühliberalismus in der Donaumonarchie* (Berlin, 1968), pp. 55–82, 164–85; Victor Bibl, *Die niederösterreichischen Stände im Vormärz* (Vienna, 1911); Matthias Koch, *Oesterreichs innere Politik* (Stuttgart, 1847); Wolfgang Häusler, "Ernst von Violand. Der Lebensweg eines österreichischen Demokraten," *JIDG* 6 (1977); 185ff.; F. E. Pipitz, *Verfall und Verjüngung. Studien über Oesterreich in den Jahren 1838–1848* (Zurich, 1848).

6. See Hans Lentze, *Die Universitätsreform des Ministers Graf Leo Thun-Hohenstein,* pp. 24–28, 33–39. For Prussia, see John R. Gillis, *The Prussian Bureaucracy in Crisis, 1840–1860* (Stanford, 1971), pp. 37ff., 50ff., 200ff., 212ff.; and Koselleck, *Preussen zwischen Reform und Revolution.* For a perceptive contemporary analysis, see "Oesterreich und seine Beamten," *Die Grenzboten* 7 (1848): 189–96 ("Das System hat dafür gesorgt, durchaus nur von Mittelmässigkeiten umgeben zu sein; was darüber herausragt, wird abgesondert, beseitigt . . . kein Wunder also, dass Mittelmässiges nur Mittelmässiges, oft Schlechtes erzeugt" [p. 190]).

7. See the suggestive comments of Grete Klingenstein in her "Einige Überlegungen zum politischen System des aufgeklärten Absolutismus," in *Les Lumières en Hongrie, en Europe*

centrale, et en Europe orientale: Actes du Troisième Colloque de Matrafüred 28 septembre–2 octobre 1975 (Budapest, 1978), pp. 37–38. Also, Schirnding, *Oesterreich im Jahre 1840*, 1:86–87, 275–76. For statistics on Austrian *Neuadel* in the nineteenth century, see Paul Ghelardoni, *Die feudalen Elemente in der österreichischen bürgerlichen Gesellschaft von 1803 bis 1914* (diss., University of Vienna, 1961), pp. 3–20. Ghelardoni found that over 40% of the higher diplomatic service in Austria by 1900 was either *Beamtenadel* or pure bourgeois. In the course of the nineteenth century over 2,000 higher officials received various patents raising them into the lower or middle nobility. On the absence within the Austrian social structure of a Junker-type lower nobility, see Erich Kielmansegg, *Kaiserhaus, Staatsmänner, und Politiker* (Vienna, 1966), p. 201.

8. Beidtel, *Geschichte*, 2:44–48, 234–36, 269. Beidtel wanted to disparage the high aristocracy, but had to admit (p. 269) that nonnobles were increasingly filling important posts in the higher Verwaltung (of the 400 top posts reserved for the aulic and sub-aulic aristocracy in 1770 about 40 were still in their hands by the mid-Vormärz). See also Nikolaus von Preradovich, *Die Führungsschichten in Österreich und Preussen, 1804–1918* (Wiesbaden, 1955), pp. 59–72. For a sensitive comparative analysis of the Austrian and Prussian civil services under enlightened absolutism and the different role of each state's nobility in the higher service, see Otto Hintze, "Der österreichische und der preussische Beamtenstaat im 17. und 18. Jahrhundert," in Gerhard Oestreich, ed., *Staat und Verfassung. Gesammelte Abhandlungen zur allgemeinen Verfassungsgeschichte* (Göttingen, 1962), pp. 350–52.

9. See Friedrich Schütz, *Werden und Wirken des Bürgerministeriums* (Leipzig, 1909), pp. 68ff.; Friedrich Uhl, *Aus meinem Leben* (Stuttgart, 1908), pp. 98–119; Julius Bunzel, *Der Lebenslauf eines vormärzlichen Verwaltungs-Beamten* (Vienna, 1911), passim. Ghelardoni's arguments about the "feudalization" of Austrian society are unconvincing, as is his inclusion of the civil service in a "feudal-aristocratic" as opposed to a "bourgeois" occupational group in nineteenth-century Austria. He fails to differentiate between the Austrian and the Prussian nobility and between comparative modes of political behavior (simply because one became a *Neuadel* in Austria did not mean one abandoned one's Liberal politics). Also, the evidentiary basis for his cultural arguments (*Neuadel* as "feudal" because of land ownership or hunting) is based on extremely small numbers of individuals. See Ghelardoni, *Die feudalen Elemente*, esp. p. 169, where he admits that all new nobles did not simply mimic the old aristocracy. A more convincing argument has been offered by Heidemarie Ortner, *Das Eindringen des Wiener Bürgertums und Geldadels in den landtäflichen Grundbesitz Niederösterreichs, 1815–1895* (diss., University of Vienna, 1968), who argues that the "new wealth" and new nobles who bought smaller estates in Lower Austria after 1848 (virtually all of the big estates remained in the hands of the *Hochadel* throughout the century) brought radically different, capitalist investment mentalities to the countryside, rather than simply mimicking the lassitude of the older aristocracy. Most higher civil servants in Vienna who became *Beamtenadel* did not buy land (only 11% of the estates in Lower Austria purchased between 1848 and 1900 were bought by public officials). See ibid., pp. 143–48, 194, 200–201.

10. Gall, "Liberalismus und 'bürgerliche Gesellschaft,'" pp. 324–56. See also Dirk Blasius, "Bürgerliches Recht und bürgerliche Identität," in Helmut Berding, ed., *Vom Staat des Ancien Regime zum modernen Parteienstaat. Festschrift für Theodor Schieder* (Munich and Vienna, 1978), pp. 213–24; Koselleck, *Preussen zwischen Reform und Revolution*, pp. 379ff., 387ff., 557ff.

11. For an important evaluation of Gall's arguments, see Mommsen, "Der deutsche Liberalismus zwischen 'klassenloser Bürgergesellschaft' und 'Organisiertem Kapitalismus,'" pp. 77–90. Characteristic of the Viennese situation was the value which the *Magistrat* placed on the privileges of the artisan guilds, which, according to Karl Weiss, were seen

as the "Schwerpunkt der Fortentwicklung des alten Wiener Bürgertums." See Weiss, *Rückblicke auf die Gemeindeverwaltung der Stadt Wien in den Jahren 1838–1848* (Vienna, 1875), p. 90. The Bürgertum here was not a model of political opportunity, but a defense against social change and mobility. For the pre-1848 Bürgertum, see also Friedrich Walter, *Wien. Die Geschichte einer deutschen Grossstadt an der Grenze* (3 vols., Vienna, 1941–44), 3:37–45, 73–74, 124ff., a book marred by blatent racism but still useful for some empirical observations.

12. *Aemtliche Verhandlungs-Protokolle des Gemeinde-Ausschusses der Stadt Wien vom 25. Mai bis 5. Oktober 1848*, pp. 54–56. Pre-1848 Bürger also had the right to participate in the *Bürgergarde*, which was organized into two regiments, but whose military value was minimal. For pre-1848 conflicts between the guild artisans (the *bürgerlichen Meister*) and the *Freimeister* or *Dekretisten*, see Heinz Zatschek, *Handwerk und Gewerbe in Wien* (Vienna, 1949), pp. 49–55, 71–81; idem, *550 Jahre Jung Sein. Die Geschichte eines Handwerks* (Vienna, 1958), pp. 24–34, 136–38. See also the report in *CON*, 26 Apr. 1848, pp. 456–57, Weiss, *Rückblicke*, pp. 93–94, and Birgit Frieben, *Die Sozialstruktur Wiens am Anfang des Vormärz* (diss., University of Vienna, 1966), esp. pp. 66–68.

13. On associational life in the Vormärz, see Friedrich Engel-Janosi, "Der Wiener juridisch-politische Leseverein," *MVGSW* 4 (1923): 58–66; Uhl, *Aus meinem Leben*, pp. 111–20; Heinrich Reschauer and Moriz Smets, *Das Jahr 1848. Geschichte der Wiener Revolution* (2 vols., Vienna, 1876), 1:16–20, 64–68, 90–141; Julius Marx, "Polizei und Studenten. Ein Beitrag zur Vorgeschichte des 13. März 1848 in Wien," *JVGSW* 19/20 (1963–64): 218–50. Marx shows that attempts to find in the Vormärz a deeply rooted student associational system are fables. There were informal discussion groups, however.

14. On the significance of early associational activity as a characteristic of a developing political society, see Thomas Nipperdey, "Verein als soziale Struktur in Deutschland im späten 18. und frühen 19. Jahrhundert. Eine Fallstudie zur Modernisierung I," in his *Gesellschaft, Kultur, Theorie* (Göttingen, 1976), pp. 259–78.

15. On Vormärz legal training, see Lentze, *Die Universitätsreform des Ministers Graf Leo Thun-Hohenstein*, pp. 43–79, 134–36; Alfred Fischer, *Das österreichische Doktorat der Rechtswissenschaften und die Rechtsanwaltschaft* (Innsbruck and Munich, 1974), pp. 57–80; Schütz, *Bürgerministerium*, pp. 80–96 (on the young Eduard Herbst). See also Beidtel, *Geschichte*, 2:55; Häusler, "Ernst von Violand," pp. 185–89; and Friedrich Engel-Janosi, "Die Theorie vom Staat im deutschen Österreich, 1815–1848," *ZÖR* 2 (1921): 360–94.

16. See Schuselka's speech in *Verhandlungen des österreichischen Reichstages nach der stenographischen Aufnahme* (Vienna, 1848–49), 4:328. See also *HPB* 23 (1849): 526. On Schuselka, see Richard Charmatz's essay in *ÖRD* 28 (1911): 264–75; Hans Kudlich, *Rückblicke und Erinnerungen* (3 vols., Vienna and Leipzig, 1873), 2:64–69; and Schuselka's memoirs, *Deutsche Fahrten*, vol. 2, *Während der Revolution* (Vienna, 1849).

17. See Heinrich Heffter, *Die deutsche Selbstverwaltung im 19. Jahrhundert* (Stuttgart, 1950), pp. 322–403, esp. pp. 331–32.

18. See chap. 6.

19. For the early structure of the Christian Social party, see chap. 4.

20. On 1848 in general, see R. John Rath, *The Viennese Revolution of 1848* (Austin, 1957); Reschauer and Smets, *Das Jahr 1848*, vol. 1; Springer, *Geschichte*, vol. 2; (Franz Hartig), *Genesis der Revolution in Österreich im Jahre 1848* (Leipzig, 1850); and the various articles by Wolfgang Häusler.

21. See Reschauer and Smets, *Das Jahr 1848*, 1:134–35. On Rudolf v Arthaber, see Josef Mentschl, "Rudolf von Arthaber, ein Textilgrosshändler und Verleger der Biedermeierzeit," *OGL* 13 (1969): 395–98. For a discussion of property owning in the Vormärz, which

later became the basis for important political rights, see Winfried Bammer, *Beiträge zur Sozialstruktur der Bevölkerung Wiens auf Grund der Verlassenschaftsakten des Jahres 1830* (diss., University of Vienna, 1968), esp. pp. 36ff., 152ff.

22. *ZWN*, 1 June 1848, p. 2; 10 June 1848, p. 30; 17 June 1848, pp. 50–51; 6 July 1848, pp. 88–94; 22 Aug. 1848, p. 204; 31 Aug. 1848, pp. 219–20. The pre-1848 Bürger regiments maintained a separate subidentity within the National Guard, but were under its administrative and political leadership.

23. See *Aemtliche Verhandlungs-Protokolle*, esp. pp. 22ff., 39ff., and 43–56.

24. The constitution of the *Bürgergarde* before 1848 illustrated the relatively integrated relationship between the higher- and middle-level *Bürgerstände* in Vienna. The enlisted ranks of the First Regiment were recruited from regular masters in the industrial or commercial guilds, while its officers were generally wealthier merchants or wholesalers in the city. See Schirnding, *Oesterreich im Jahre 1840*, 1:290–91; *CON*, 27 Mar. 1848, p. 37; 26 Apr. 1848, pp. 456–57.

25. Johann Michael Häusle, *Die Majorität im gegenwärtigen Wiener Gemeinderath* (Vienna, 1849), pp. 9–10, 16–20; Franz Müller, *Die Wahlkörper des Wiener Gemeinderathes* (Vienna, 1849), pp. 9–10.

26. On the Democratic movement, see the memoirs of Kudlich and Schuselka (above, note 16) and Violand, *Die sociale Geschichte;* also, Ernst Victor Zenker, *Die Wiener Revolution 1848 in ihren socialen Voraussetzungen und Beziehungen* (Vienna and Leipzig, 1897), pp. 131–79; Richard Charmatz, *Adolf Fischhof* (Stuttgart and Berlin, 1910); Paul Molisch, "Die Wiener Akademische Legion und ihr Anteil an den Verfassungskämpfen des Jahres 1848," *AÖG* 110 (1924): 1–208; and the conservative commentaries of Freiherr v Helfert, *Die Wiener Journalistik im Jahre 1848* (Vienna, 1877), and *Aufzeichnungen und Erinnerungen aus jungen Jahren. Im Wiener konstituierenden Reichstag, Juli bis Oktober 1848* (Vienna, 1904), passim. For a modern evaluation, see Wolfgang Häusler, "Hermann Jellinek (1823–1848). Ein Demokrat in der Wiener Revolution," *JIDG* 5 (1976): 125–75; and idem, "Ernst von Violand," pp. 185ff. There were, of course, factions within the movement, but most participants shared a commitment to radical political democracy, if not to complete social democracy.

27. See, for example, *CON*, 28 March 1848, pp. 50–51; 22 Aug. 1848, p. 1269; 25 Aug. 1848, pp. 1293–94; 27 Aug. 1848, p. 1309; 2 Sept. 1848, p. 1349; 3 Sept. 1848, p. 1360; *FR*, 21 Apr. 1848, pp. 1–2; 23 Apr. 1848, pp. 86, 88; 28 Apr. 1848, pp. 97–98; 2 May 1848, p. 111; 12 May 1848, p. 145; 5 Sept. 1848, p. 530; 27 Aug. 1848, p. 501; 6 Sept. 1848, p. 536; *AÖZ*, 23 Aug. 1848, p. 1; *GA*, 14 May 1848, p. 1; 16 May 1848, p. 3; 13 June 1848, pp. 2–3; 11 July 1848, p. 1. These papers and others like them contained hundreds of similar criticisms of the privileged Bürgertum mentality. For a classic Democratic critique of the National Guard, see Andreas v. Stift's comments, cited in Häusler, "Hermann Jellinek," pp. 135–36.

28. *ZWN*, 22 Aug. 1848, p. 204; 24 Aug. 1848, pp. 205–6; 31 Aug. 1848, pp. 219–20; *PR*, 23 Aug. 1848, p. 193, 29 Aug. 1848, p. 213; *Aemtliche Verhandlungs-Protokolle*, pp. 39–40, 63ff.; Reschauer and Smets, *Das Jahr 1848*, 2:494–96. Häusler, "Ernst von Violand," p. 193, properly notes that even within the Security Committee unity was often dramatically absent among the various radical factions and views.

29. For labor views of society in 1848, see Herbert Steiner, *Karl Marx in Wien. Die Arbeiterbewegung zwischen Revolution und Restoration 1848* (Vienna, 1978), esp. pp. 185ff.; Ernst Hanisch, *Der kranke Mann an der Donau. Marx und Engels über Österreich* (Vienna, 1978), pp. 119–27.

30. See Leopold Engländer, *Offener Brief an jene Hausherren, welche unerschwingliche Zinsen verlangen* (Vienna, 1848); *CON*, 18 Apr. 1848, pp. 372–73; 25 Apr. 1848, pp. 449–50; 3 May 1848, p. 578; Steiner, *Karl Marx in Wien*, pp. 48, 50.

31. Reschauer and Smets, *Das Jahr 1848*, 2:88–89; Violand, *Die sociale Geschichte*, pp. 88–90; Zenker, *Die Wiener Revolution*, pp. 129–31.

32. See esp. *FR*, 23 Apr. 1848, p. 86; 2 May 1848, p. 111; 12 May 1848, p. 145.

33. Steiner, *Karl Marx in Wien*, pp. 21, 31, 53; Violand, *Die sociale Geschichte*, pp. 142–43.

34. Violand, *Die sociale Geschichte*, pp. 82–83; Theodore Hamerow, *Restoration, Revolution, and Reaction: Economics and Politics in Germany, 1815–1871* (Princeton, 1958), pp. 137–55; Heinrich Reschauer, *Geschichte des Kampfes der Handwerkerzünfte und der Kaufmannsgremien mit der österreichischen Bureaucratie* (Vienna, 1882), pp. 206–10.

35. See Zenker, *Die Wiener Revolution*, pp. 150–54, 215–19; Reschauer and Smets, *Das Jahr 1848*, 2:506–7; Violand, *Die soziale Geschichte*, pp. 92–95. On Swoboda's later plan, see August Swoboda, *Statuten des Privat-Darlehen-Vereins* (Vienna, 1848), and *AÖZ*, 15 Sept. 1848, pp. 1179–80.

36. For the Sept. riots, which did not involve any workers and which were a purely bourgeois political struggle, see *FR*, 14 Sept. 1848, pp. 557–58; 16 Sept. 1848, p. 568; *GA*, 15 Sept. 1848, pp. 1–2; 17 Sept. 1848, pp. 1–2. Swoboda managed to obtain thousands of subscribers for his loan shares, including members of the court and higher bureaucracy.

37. Wenzel Dunder noted the radical significance of the Sept. riots when he wrote that it was "das erstemal die Gelegenheit herbeigeführt wurde, dass Garde gegen Garde, Bürger gegen Bürger sich feindlich gegenüber standen. . . ." See his *Denkschrift über die Wiener October-Revolution. Ausführliche Darstellung aller Ereignisse* (Vienna, 1849), p. 12. The National Guard was bitterly divided during the riots, since many of the suburban guards either sided with or participated in the protests.

38. See Rudolf Till, "Die Mitglieder der ersten Wiener Gemeindevertretung im Jahre 1848," *WG* 5 (1950): 61–72. See also the commentaries in *Aemtliche Verhandlungs-Protokolle*, pp. 62–64, and *ZWN*, 14 Sept. 1848, pp. 247–48.

39. On the May 1848 municipal franchise, see Reschauer and Smets, *Das Jahr 1848*, 2:248–50, and the criticism in *CON*, 27 Aug. 1848, p. 1309. Men holding the *Bürgerrecht* were also entitled to vote.

40. For the text of the Aug. 1848 franchise, see *Aemtliche Verhandlungs-Protokolle*, pp. 43–47. For Democratic critiques, cf. *FR*, 5 Sept. 1848, p. 530, and *CON*, 3 Sept. 1848, p. 1360.

41. *Aemtliche Verhandlungs-Protokolle*, p. 43.

42. Ibid., pp. 42–43. Dr. Glickh summarized this mentality of the unitary Bürgertum well when he argued that "Wer die Lasten trägt, muss auch an den Rechten Theil nehmen können. . . ." Since the proletariat did not pay direct taxes, it could not claim the rights of the Bürgertum. Glickh was careful to insist, however, that of all who did pay direct taxes there must be "nur eine Klasse von Individuen in der Gemeinde" who had "gleiche Rechte"—this was the total Bürgertum, including the *Kleingewerbe*. Ibid., p. 55. Potentially this would include nonguild masters as well, as long as they paid their trade taxes.

43. Ibid., pp. 52–53.

44. See Wolfgang Häusler, "Nachwort," in Steiner, *Karl Marx in Wien*, p. 195. Companies of the Guard from the Leopoldstadt, the Landstrasse, and the Alsergrund remained conservative, so that the usual claim that all suburban companies supported the Democrats and the workers is not entirely accurate. The *Stadtgarde* in the Innere Stadt was extremely conservative. By Oct. 1848 the size of the Guard had dropped to 18,000 from an original 40,000 in May, owing to desertions and emigration from the city. Perhaps 6,000 of the 18,000 were solidly conservative (Dunder's estimate). For a conservative critique of the radical suburban companies, see Dunder, *Denkschrift*, pp. 6–7, 13–14, 33, 92–93 and passim. See also Anton Schütte, *Die Wiener Oktober-Revolution. Aus dem Tagebuche des Dr. Schütte* (Prague, 1848), pp. 15–26, 51–54. There does not appear to be any easy correlation between

pre-1848 bourgeois status and political behavior in 1848. Many of the *befugte* masters who joined Guard companies behaved conservatively, while others were remarkably radical. It might well be, however, that younger artisans and state officials were potentially more sympathetic to social radicalism than were the older guild members and officials.

45. Häusle, *Die Majorität*, pp. 6–7; Häusler, "Nachwort," pp. 202–4.

46. See Karl Weiss, *Entwicklung der Gemeinde-Verfassung der Stadt Wien (1221–1850)* (Vienna, 1867), pp. 100–101. For the opposition to Zelinka's proposal, see the protest statement lodged by a minority of delegates led by Johann Häusle in the *Sitzungs-Protokolle des Gemeinderathes* (*ASLW*, 11 June 1849, pp. 370–71).

47. *PR*, 10 July 1849, p. 1. For the opposing Democratic view, see *ODP*, 14 June 1849, p. 1; 15 June 1849, p. 1 (attacking the proprietary idea of "ownership" of the *Gemeinde* as being in the hands of the taxpayers). The *Post* specifically attributed the genesis of the curial idea to the higher bourgeois reaction against the revolutionary behavior of some of the lower-*Bürgertum* in October 1848. See ibid., 17 June 1849, p. 1.

48. See Weiss, *Entwicklung*, pp. 125–29. Exclusion by tax level as opposed to social category would have affected both older guild and newer *befugte* masters, although the latter would have been far more likely to suffer. After 1859 and the liberalization of the *Gewerbeordnung*, this distinction was meaningless.

49. See *PR*, 29 Mar. 1850, p. 1; Weiss, *Entwicklung*, p. 130; and Gustav Strakosch-Grassmann, *Das allgemeine Wahlrecht in Österreich seit 1848* (Leipzig and Vienna, 1906), p. 11. The ministerial *Akten* on this decision were not available, because of their status as *Brandakten*.

50. Schmerling thought highly of the conservatism and bourgeois moderation of the Viennese *Bürgerausschuss* in 1848. See Paul Molisch, "Anton v Schmerling und der Liberalismus in Österreich," *AÖG* 116 (1943): 11–12. For the 1861 franchise arrangements, see ibid., pp. 22–25; Josef Redlich, *Das österreichische Staats- und Reichsproblem* (2 vols., Leipzig, 1920–26), 1:783–85 (who stresses the influence of Bach's earlier ideas on the 1850 *Landesstatuten* on Schmerling). For a modern evaluation, see Robert A. Kann, *The Multinational Empire* (2 vols., New York, 1950), 2:115–25. On the 1871 adjustment in the Lower Austrian Landtag franchise, see Walter Rogge, *Oesterreich von Villagos bis zur Gegenwart* (3 vols., Leipzig, 1872–73), 3:309, 445; Sigmund Mayer, *Ein jüdischer Kaufmann, 1831 bis 1911* (Leipzig, 1911), pp. 238ff.; Gustav Strakosch-Grassmann, *Das allgemeine Wahlrecht in Österreich*, p. 39. On the background to the 1861 patent, see Fritz Fellner, "Das 'Februarpatent' von 1861. Entstehung und Bedeutung," *MIÖG* 63 (1955): 549–64; and Brandt, *Der österreichische Neoabsolutismus*, 2:964–96.

51. Friedrich Walter, *Die österreichische Zentralverwaltung*, III Abt., Bd. 3, *Die Geschichte der Ministerien vom Durchbruch des Absolutismus bis zum Ausgleich mit Ungarn und zur Konstitutionalisierung der österreichischen Länder, 1852 bis 1867* (Vienna, 1970), pp. 96–97.

52. See esp. the brilliant study by Brandt, *Der österreichische Neoabsolutismus*, 1:246–69; 2:995–1028; Helmut Rumpler, *Einleitungsband: Ministerrat und Ministerratsprotokolle, 1848–1867. Die Protokolle des österreichischen Ministerrats, 1848–1867* (Vienna, 1970, pp. 41, 74; Waltraud Heindl, "Probleme der Edition," in *Die Protokolle . . .*, III Abt., *Das Ministerium Buol-Schauenstein*, Bd. 1 (Vienna, 1975), pp. xxviii–lxiii; Christoph Stölzl, *Die Ära Bach in Böhmen* (Munich and Vienna, 1971), esp. pp. 306–14.

53. See Lentze, *Die Universitätsreform*, pp. 30, 84, 88–89, 136; Helmut Böhme, *Deutschlands Weg zur Grossmacht* (2d ed., Cologne, 1972), pp. 14–17, 22–29; Brandt, *Der österreichische Neoabsolutismus*, 1:253ff., who stresses the need for competition with Prussia as an essential motive in Austria's forced-pace modernization. Competition is a form of emulation and flattery, however.

54. On Schwarzenberg's program, see Heindl, "Probleme der Edition," pp. xxxiv–xxxv;

Heinrich Friedjung, *Österreich von 1848 bis 1860* (2 vols., Stuttgart and Berlin, 1912), 2:155–70; Kann, *The Multinational Empire*, 2:68ff.; Brandt, *Der österreichische Neoabsolutismus*, 1:247ff.

55. Heindl, "Probleme der Edition," pp. xlvii–xlviii. See also Lorenz Mikoletzky, "Karl Freiherr von Krauss (1789–1881)," *ÖGL* 14 (1970): 57–71.

56. Brandt, *Der österreichische Neoabsolutismus*, 2:1025–28.

57. On the Concordat in general, see Erika Weinzierl-Fischer, *Die österreichischen Konkordate von 1855 und 1933* (Vienna, 1960); Max v Hussarek, "Die Verhandlung des Konkordats vom 18. August 1855. Ein Beitrag zur Geschichte des österreichischen Staatskirchenrechts," *AÖG* 109 (1922): 447–811; idem, "Die Krise und die Lösung des Konkordats vom 18. August 1855. Ein Beitrag zur Geschichte des österreichischen Staatskirchenrechts," *AÖG* 112 (1932): 211–480; Karl Vocelka, *Verfassung oder Konkordat? Der publizistische und politische Kampf der österreichischen Liberalen um die Religionsgesetze des Jahres 1868* (Vienna, 1978).

58. Arthur Skedl, ed., *Der politische Nachlass des Grafen Eduard Taaffe* (Vienna, 1922), pp. 44–46. This is not to suggest that the expansive militarist regime of the fifties was not a cause in provoking Liberal opposition to the neo-absolutists, for it clearly was. See Brandt, *Der österreichische Neoabsolutismus*, 1:264–67; 2:971–75. But in emotional and in symbolic terms the Austrian Church provided a much more convenient and obvious target for the Liberals than did the hapless Austrian army. The first decennial compromise legislation on the army, that of 1868, was the product of a solidly Liberal ministry. Although there were complaints about military expenditures in the 1870s, it was not until 1878–79 that the party divided over the army in a tactical sense. The differences between the Liberal position of 1878–79 and that of the Prussian Progressives of 1860–64 were marked. The Prussian conflict did not involve the issues of financial expenditures so much as it did more basic constitutional and especially antimilitarist ideological issues, both of which were much less present in the Austrian Liberal dilemma of 1879. The Austrian struggle over the 1879 Defense Law was primarily political-national (anti-Taaffe in a short-term tactical sense) and fiscal in nature, and only secondarily constitutional. Hence the fact that conservative and progressive Liberals could vote against the final law but bitterly divide on other issues. Also noteworthy was the fact that the 1879 struggle had no long-range impact in the development of a renewed progressive Liberalism—most of the Progressives who voted against the bill (Kopp, Menger, Sturm, Reschauer, etc.) became prominent centrist or conservative Liberals by the early 1890s. For typical Progressive speeches, emphasizing the fiscal issue above all else, see *SP*, IX, 1879, pp. 553ff. (Fux); and pp. 562ff. (Menger).

59. For the final text, see Weinzierl-Fischer, *Die österreichischen Konkordate*, pp. 250–58.

60. See Hans v Perthaler, *Auserlesene Schriften*, Ambros Mayr, ed. (2 vols., Vienna, 1883), 2:207–10. For the later portrait of Joseph II in the nineteenth century, see Johanna Schmid, *Der Wandel des Bildes Josephs II. in der österreichischen Historiographie von den Zeitgenossen bis zum Ende der Monarchie* (diss., University of Vienna, 1972).

61. On Austrian Liberalism there is no satisfactory, comprehensive work, and those studies which do exist are far below the quality level of current work on German Liberalism. See Georg Franz, *Liberalismus. Die Deutschliberale Bewegung in der Habsburgischen Monarchie* (Munich, 1955); Karl Eder, *Der Liberalismus in Altösterreich* (Vienna and Munich, 1955); Josef Schöffel, *Erinnerungen aus meinem Leben* (Vienna, 1905); Richard Charmatz, *Deutsch-österreichische Politik* (Leipzig, 1907); Hans Hartmeyer, *Die führenden Abgeordneten des Liberalismus in Österreich* (diss., University of Vienna, 1949); Ernst v Plener, *Erinnerungen* (3 vols., Stuttgart and Leipzig, 1911–21); Elisabeth Wymetal, *Eduard Herbst, sein Werdegang und seine Persönlichkeit vornehmlich auf Grund seiner selbstbio-*

graphischen Aufzeichnungen (diss., University of Vienna, 1944); Elfriede Hummel, *Der Liberalismus in seiner Relation zur Wiener Presse mit besonderer Berücksichtigung der ideengeschichtlichen Entwicklung* (diss., University of Vienna, 1953).

62. See esp. Heinrich August Winkler, "Vom linken zum rechten Nationalismus: Der deutsche Liberalismus in der Krise von 1878/79," *GG* 4 (1978): 5–28; Michael Stürmer, *Regierung und Reichstag im Bismarckstaat, 1871–1880. Cäsarismus oder Parlamentarismus* (Düsseldorf, 1974); Alan Mitchell, "Bonapartism as a Model for Bismarckian Politics," *JMH* 49 (1977): 181–99, and the comments following Mitchell's article; and Michael Gugel, *Industrieller Aufstieg und bürgerliche Herrschaft* (Cologne, 1975), pp. 137–52. It might be possible to view Schwarzenberg as a "Caesarist" and interpret the early 1850s in a Bonapartist mode (see Brandt, *Der österreichische Neoabsolutismus*, 1:255), but the important difference between Schwarzenberg and Bismarck is, of course, that the former's regime lasted a scant four years, whereas the latter's endured to make a fundamental impact on later German political culture. For the absence of a Bismarckian figure in Cisleithanian politics in the 1860s, see also the insightful comments of Friedrich Engel-Janosi in his "Einleitung," *Die Protokolle des österreichischen Ministerrates, 1848–1867. VI. Abteilung. Das Ministerium Belcredi.* Vol. 2 (Vienna, 1973), p. xxxii.

63. For Auersperg's claim to independence, see Auersperg to Julius Andrassy, 14 Jan. 1876, in Paul Molisch, ed., *Briefe zur deutschen Politik in Österreich von 1848 bis 1918* (Vienna, 1934), pp. 185–86. But see also the comments of Erich Kielmansegg in his *Kaiserhaus, Staatsmänner, und Politiker* (Vienna, 1966), pp. 190–91, and Plener, *Erinnerungen,* 2:13. For the emperor's concern with preserving political continuity, see Molisch, *Briefe,* pp. 235–42 (Weeber's interview with Franz Josef, which may be stylized in Weeber's account, but probably took the lines which he described). See also, Alois v Czedik, *Zur Geschichte der k. k. österreichischen Ministerien, 1861–1916* (4 vols., Teschen and Vienna, 1917), 1:304ff.

64. See Plener, *Erinnerungen,* 2:130–31; Molisch, *Briefe,* pp. 211–33; Kielmansegg, *Kaiserhaus,* p. 193; Heinrich Pollak, *Dreissig Jahre aus dem Leben eines Journalisten. Erinnerungen und Aufzeichnungen* (3 vols., Vienna, 1893–98), 3:224–29. On Herbst's doctrinaire behavior in 1868 at the ministerial council of 8 Nov. 1868, see Skedl, ed., *Der politische Nachlass,* pp. 47–63.

65. The literature on the early Liberals is potentially enormous, but extremely diffuse. On Schmerling, see Molisch, "Anton v Schmerling"; Alfred v Arneth, *Anton Ritter v Schmerling* (Vienna and Leipzig, 1894); Redlich, *Staats- und Reichsproblem,* 2:369–72. On Ignaz v Plener, see Mechthild Wolf, *Ignaz von Plener, Vom Schichksal eines Ministers unter Kaiser Franz Joseph* (Munich, 1975), and Fritz Fellner, "Kaiser Franz Josephs Haltung in der Krise des Bürgerministeriums. Nach Aufzeichnungen und Briefen Ignaz von Pleners," *MÖSA* 6 (1953): 327–37. Lasser has no adequate modern biography, but his essential conservatism may be observed in his speeches in the 1848 Reichstag. See also Josef v Kalchberg, *Mein politisches Glaubensbekenntniss* (Leipzig, 1881), and Czedik, *Zur Geschichte,* 1:17–303.

66. See Josef Redlich, "Lasser und Schmerling (nach ihren Briefen)," *ÖRD* 19 (1909): 79–93.

67. The best analysis of the relations between the crown and the Liberals is that of Fritz Fellner. See his "Kaiser Franz Joseph und das Parlament. Materialien zur Geschichte der Innenpolitik Österreichs in den Jahren 1867–1873," *MÖSA* 9 (1956): 287–347. Helmut Rumpler's attempt to portray the period after 1867 as one of undifferentiated, personalist absolutism on the part of Franz Joseph, based on his examination of the formal structure of the *Ministerrat* as an institution before 1865, is a subtle and interesting thesis, but one with which I profoundly disagree. The Cisleithanian political system (in a modern functionalist sense) after

1867 was far more complex than that of a simple autocratic absolutism. See Rumpler, *Einleitungsband*, pp. 66, 106–8.

68. Redlich, *Staats- und Reichsproblem*, 1:715–33, 786–89. On Gneist, see Heffter, *Die deutsche Selbstverwaltung*, pp. 373–402.

69. See Mayr, ed., *Auserlesene Schriften*, 2:145.

70. On second-generational Austrian Liberalism, see Schütz, *Bürgerministerium*, passim; Plener, *Erinnerungen*, 1:6–23; 2:5–26; Heinrich Pollak, *Dreissig Jahre aus dem Leben eines Journalisten. Erinnerungen und Aufzeichnungen.* For a modern evaluation of this generation of Liberals, see Gerald Stourzh, "Die österreichische Dezemberverfassung von 1867," *ÖGL* 12 (1968): 1–16.

71. See Ludwig Bergsträsser, ed., *Das Frankfurter Parlament in Briefen und Tagebüchern* (Frankfurt, 1929), pp. 174, 177, 182, and Giskra's speech in favor of German national unity in *Stenographischer Bericht über die Verhandlungen der deutschen constituirenden Nationalversammlung*, IV, pp. 2791–98.

72. These data were computed on the basis of regular and significant committee and plenary work in the Reichsrat. They are admittedly arbitrary and selective; but many delegates did little or nothing in terms of meaningful legislative work, and it is important to see the shift in the actual leadership cadres of the Liberal party in its delegation in parliament.

73. On the history of Viennese Democracy, see Cajetan Felder, *Erinnerungen eines Wiener Bürgermeisters*, Felix Czeike, ed. (Vienna, 1964); Paul Molisch, "Die Stellung Wiens in der deutschösterreichischen Politik von 1848 bis 1918," *JVGSW* 3/4 (1942): 149–227, esp. 170–82; Gertrude Hahnkamper, *Der Wiener Gemeinderat zwischen 1861 und 1864* (diss., University of Vienna, 1973), pp. 111–283. See also chap. 4.

74. See Diethild Harrington-Müller, *Der Fortschrittsklub im Abgeordnetenhaus des österreichischen Reichsrats 1873–1910* (Vienna and Cologne, 1972).

75. See Kronawetter's heated denunciation of the Liberals on the issue of universal manhood suffrage, in which he presented an excellent summary of the idea of the unitary Bürgertum as something exclusive of the whole of Austrian society (which he then proceeded to denounce) in *SP*, XI, 1893, pp. 11368–85. On the absence of a "bourgeois-democratic" ideology within Austrian Liberalism, see Redlich, *Staats- und Reichsproblem*, 2:648–49.

76. These data were assembled from Sigmund Hahn's *Reichsrats-Almanach* from 1867 and 1873, from the *Wiener Zeitung* for 1867 and 1873, from the biographical data in the index for the 1873–79 session, and from Oswald Knauer's *Das österreichische Parlament von 1848–1966* (Vienna, 1969).

77. On the 1873 franchise reforms, see Gustav Adolf Schimmer, "Vergleichende Statistik der direkten Reichsratswahlen in Oesterreich, 1873," *SM* 3 (1877): 249ff.

78. For the program of the Progressives, see Harrington-Müller, *Der Fortschrittsklub*, pp. 159–63. See also Walter Rogge, *Oesterreich seit der Katastrophe Hohenwart-Beust* (2 vols., Leipzig and Vienna, 1879), 1:201 (the Progressives as "meist wenig bedeutende Leutchen").

79. A good example of this process was the case of Heinrich Reschauer. See chap. 2.

80. See Winkler, "Vom linken zum rechten Nationalismus: Der deutsche Liberalismus in der Krise von 1878/79," p. 10; Gustav Schmidt, "Die Nationalliberalen—eine regierungsfähige Partei? Zur Problematik der inneren Reichsgründung, 1870–1878," in Gerhard A. Ritter, ed., *Die deutschen Parteien vor 1918* (Cologne, 1973), pp. 208–23.

81. Rudolf Till, "Die Anfänge der christlichen Volksbewegung in Österreich," *JLG*, 1937, pp. 98–103.

82. See Weinzierl-Fischer, *Die österreichischen Konkordate*, pp. 121–22.

83. *PV* 2:237ff.; 3:12ff. Richard Charmatz, *Deutsch-österreichische Politik* (Leipzig, 1907), pp. 165, 173. When the Bohemian Feudals returned to the Reichsrat in 1879, they sat with the Czechs, but they still functioned as ersatz "political" Catholics.

84. *PV* 3:222–23.
85. See Vocelka, *Verfassung oder Konkordat*, pp. 17–18, 95–103, 177–79.
86. *SP*, VIII, 1873, pp. 115–19. On the moderate, guarantist version of Liberal anti-clericalism, see Plener, *Erinnerungen*, 2:5–26; Mikoletzky, "Karl Freiherr von Krauss," pp. 61–65; Kielmansegg, *Kaiserhaus*, pp. 193–94. The Austrian Liberals refused to be drawn into the Prussian *Kulturkampf* (at least on the ministerial level), a fact which Rome recognized and responded to. See Weinzierl-Fischer, *Die österreichischen Konkordate*, pp. 120–21. For the opposition between Herbst and Muhlfeld in 1868 on modes of overturning the Concordat, see Vocelka, *Verfassung oder Konkordat*, pp. 56–64.
87. For typical Progressive speeches, see *SP*, VIII, 1874, pp. 951ff., 854ff. A moderate statement of the issues behind the 1874 legislation, which summarizes well the compromise-oriented view of the Liberal ministry, may be found in Karl v Lemayer's *Referat* in *SP*, VIII, 1874, Beilage Nr. 40, pp. 221–74, the commentary on this text in Vocelka, *Verfassung oder Konkordat*, pp. 171–74, and Plener, *Erinnerungen*, 2:19–20.
88. See Harrington-Müller, *Der Fortschrittsklub*, pp. 58–60; *SP*, VIII, 1873, pp. 95–99 (Haase); 1874, pp. 867–69 (Fux); 1874, pp. 894–95 (Dittes).
89. *SP*, VIII, 1874, pp. 445–48; 884 (Eduard Suess).
90. For Lienbacher's critique, see ibid., pp. 873–75, 880–81.
91. On the attitude of Franz Joseph to the Liberal campaign against the Church, see Fellner, "Kaiser Franz Joseph und das Parlament," pp. 310–19. Fellner has described very well the consensus-type compromise arrived at by the two sides as a "Kompromiss auf mittlerer Linie," a designation which could be expanded to cover the whole relationship between the Liberals and the crown. For a similar evaluation, see Vocelka, *Verfassung oder Konkordat*, p. 176.
92. See Redlich, *Staats- und Reichsproblem*, 1:716–32; 783ff. Schmerling himself was responsible for the provincial self-governmental institutions created in the 1861 *Landesordnungen*, a concession which Redlich rightly attributes both to principle and to tactical necessity. Ibid., pp. 796–99.
93. See Hugo Preuss, "Verwaltungsreform und Staatsreform in Österreich und Preussen," *ZP* 5 (1912): 219–35.
94. Redlich differentiated between Schmerling and Lasser in 1861–62 in the *Gemeinde* debates, suggesting that Lasser was more authoritarian than Schmerling, but see the discussion in Carl Brockhausen, *Die österreichische Gemeindeordnung* (Vienna, 1905), pp. 1–40, which suggests that Schmerling was not so flexible on the municipal level. It was perhaps more than accidental that one of Eduard Herbst's most influential early patrons was Count Franz Stadion, the author of the 1849 *Gemeinde* law. See Schütz, *Bürgerministerium*, pp. 86–88. On Lorenz v Stein's views on municipal autonomy, see Heffter, *Die deutsche Selbstverwaltung*, pp. 449–52, and Karl Lamp, *Das Problem der städtischen Selbstverwaltung nach österreichischem und preussischem Recht* (Leipzig, 1905), pp. 43ff.
95. See Herbst's speech in *SP*, IV, 1867, p. 1093. See also Redlich, *Staats- und Reichsproblem*, 2:646–47 ("Vom diesem Ursprung haftete dem österreichischen Liberalismus jener Tage ein eigentümlicher kleinbürgerlicher Zug an").
96. *WZ*, 22 June 1879, p. 2.
97. See Taaffe's comments on the neutrality of the state bureaucracy toward the Liberals and the need to prevent "collisions" with them, in Skedl, ed., *Der politische Nachlass*, pp. 36–37. See also Redlich, *Staats- und Reichsproblem*, 2:742, note 5.
98. See chap. 6.
99. Uhl, *Aus meinem Leben*, p. 98.
100. Max Weber recognized, if only in an informal, impressionistic way, this difference in the styles of aristocratic leadership in Prussia and Austria and, more important, its wider implications for the respective civic cultures of both states. When Weber wrote in 1917 that

the "Deutschösterreicher" was influenced in his bourgeois political behavior by the "wirkliche Aristokratie durchgeformten Art des Auftretens...," he was suggesting an extremely important hypothesis: that bourgeois politics in Austria owed much in its cultural values to the more elevated and latitudinarian traditions of the high Austrian aristocracy, who, Weber realized, possessed a cultural tradition quite distinct from that of the Prussian middle and lower gentry (the Junkers). Not only did the Austrian Liberals find it easier to "settle" with the higher Verwaltung in Austria, but they did so because many of the top aristocratic policymakers in the civil service manifested a style of aristocratic-Josephist leadership which was not as incompatible with Liberalism as was that of the Prussian Junker-caste mentality. See Max Weber, "Wahlrecht und Demokratie in Deutschland," in *Gesammelte politische Schriften* (Munich, 1921), pp. 312–13. To the extent, therefore, that the Austrian bourgeoisie was "feudalized," this process resulted in a very different kind of end product than in Prussia, one which was not necessarily antithetical to the class or cultural interests of the bourgeoisie in a modern industrial or parliamentary sense. Arguments which simply present the process of "feudalization" as a monolithic experience (see above, note 9) miss the mark by a wide margin.

101. On Hügel, see Alfred Loibl, *Die Stellung der 'Konstitutionelle Vorstadt-Zeitung' zur sozialen Frage, 1855–1878* (diss., University of Vienna, 1950), and chap. 4.

102. *DEZ*, 29 May 1875, pp. 1–3.

Chapter 2

1. For the crisis of 1878–79, see Czedik, *Zur Geschichte*, 1:272–315; Pollak, *Dreissig Jahre*, 3:224–72; *PV* 3:26–62; Molisch, *Briefe*, pp. 207–43; Walter Rogge, *Oesterreich seit der Katastrophe Hohenwart-Beust*, 2:442ff., 477–516.

2. See *SJ*, 1883, pp. 24–26. The ratio of males to females in industry was 4:3, 24,719 males to 18,773 females. In commerce there were 17,700 males to only 4,920 females. These statistics include Viennese peddlers who did not operate from a permanent location. The data reflect the social reality of the city's economy, but not the legal reality, since not all of the businesses calling themselves independent in the census were, in fact, owned by master craftsmen. Many of these "independents" were the *Pfuscher* or journeymen without a master's certificate employing other journeymen in their own shops.

3. Ibid., pp. 269, 274. These data include some service jobs not included in the 1880 census.

4. See Eugen Schwiedland, *Kleingewerbe und Hausindustrie in Oesterreich* (2 vols., Leipzig, 1894), 1:188–89; Ludwig Schüller, "Die Wiener Enquête über Frauenarbeit," *ASGSS* 10 (1897): 408–9; and Walter Schiff, "Die ältere Gewerbestatistik in Oesterreich und die Entstehung der Betriebszählung vom Jahre 1902," *SM* 33 (1907): 501ff., 613ff.

5. *SJ*, 1883, p. 133. On the Austrian commercial tax system, see Emil v Fürth, *Die Einkommensteuer in Österreich und ihre Reform* (Leipzig, 1892), chap. 1; Alois Gratz, "Die österreichische Finanzpolitik von 1848 bis 1948," in Hans Mayer, ed., *Hundert Jahre österreichische Wirtschaftsentwicklung, 1848 bis 1948* (Vienna, 1949), pp. 222–71; a convenient summary in English may be found in U.S. State Department, *Consular Reports on Commerce, Manufactures, Etc.: Reports from the Consuls of the United States*, nos. 99 and 100 (Washington, 1888), pp. 260–89.

6. See *Ergebnisse der gewerblichen Betriebszählung vom 3. Juni 1902 in Niederösterreich* (Vienna, 1909), pp. 294–95. These statistics exclude laborers working for private associations, and state and local government.

7. A classic work for the decline of the "old" middle class in America, which is still of value for similar trends in Austria, is C. Wright Mills, *White Collar* (New York, 1951), esp. pp. 3–62; also, Ralf Dahrendorf, *Class and Class Conflict in Industrial Society* (Stanford,

1959). See also Emil Lederer, "Mittelstandsbewegung," *ASWSP* 31 (1910): 970–1026; idem, "Die Bewegung der öffentlichen Beamten," ibid., pp. 660–709; idem, "Privatbeamtenbewegung," ibid., pp. 215–54; and H. Herkner, "Über Erhaltung und Verstärkung der Mittelclasse," *ZVSV* 2 (1893): 209–27.

8. The literature on the artisan problem is enormous. For some important contemporary discussions, see Schwiedland, *Kleingewerbe;* Heinrich Waentig, *Gewerbliche Mittelstandspolitik* (Leipzig, 1898); Emanuel Adler, *Über die Lage des Handwerks in Oesterreich* (Freiburg i. B., 1898); *Untersuchungen über die Lage des Handwerks in Österreich, SVSP* 71 (1896); *Untersuchungen über die Lage des Hausiergewerbes in Oesterreich,* ibid. 82 (1899); *Verhandlungen der am 23., 24., 25. September 1897 in Köln abgehaltenen Generalversammlung des Vereines für Sozialpolitik* (Leipzig, 1898); Emil Sax, "Die österreichische Gewerbenovelle von 1883," *JGVV* 7 (1883): 867–908; Richard Schüller, "Die österreichische Handwerker-Gesetzgebung," *ASGSS* 11 (1897): 381–401; Otto v Zwiedeneck-Südenhorst, "Die Bedeutung des Bedarfes für die Entwicklung der gewerblichen Betriebssysteme," *ZVSV* 7 (1898): 15–74; Rudolf Kobatsch, "Das österreichische Gewerberecht und seine bevorstehende Reform," *JNS* 66 (1896): 785–847; Josef Kaizl, "Die Reform des Gewerberechts in Österreich vom Jahre 1883," ibid. 42 (1884): 593–604; Victor Mataja, "Die gewerblichen Genossenschaften in Oesterreich," ibid., 66 (1896): 718–38; Eduard Popper, "Der Abänderungs-Entwurf zur österreichischen Gewerbe-Ordnung," ibid., 39 (1882): 404–17. For recent analyses of the *Kleingewerbe* in Austria, see Herbert Matis, *Österreichs Wirtschaft, 1848–1913* (Berlin, 1972); Kurt Rothschild, "Wurzeln und Triebkräfte der Entwicklung der österreichischen Wirtschaftsstruktur," in Wilhelm Weber, ed., *Österreichs Wirtschaftsstruktur* (2 vols., Berlin, 1961), 1:1–158; and esp. Stefan Koren, "Die Industrialisierung Österreichs—Vom Protektionismus zur Integration," in ibid., 1:235–36, 305, 344, 373–74, 491–502.

9. See *Entwicklung von Industrie und Gewerbe in Österreich in den Jahren 1848–1888* (Vienna, 1888), pp. 74–75.

10. For a description of the solid existence the older silk manufacturers lived in Vienna before 1848, see the first volume of Sebastian Brunner's autobiography, *Woher? Wohin?* Brunner's father was a wealthy *Seidenzeugmacher*.

11. Both mechanized production and the house-industrial system had long traditions in Austria before 1848. But the period from 1848 until 1873 was decisive for getting centralized business and financial structures established and functioning. For the industrialization of the textile industry, see Schwiedland, *Kleingewerbe,* 1:127–28, and Matis, *Österreichs Wirtschaft,* pp. 182–83; on the metal, iron, and machine trades, see ibid., pp. 179–80, and Philippovich's "Referat" in the *Verhandlungen,* p. 77. The large clothing dealers sometimes started as old clothes dealers and then expanded their capital investment. For the expansions of large wholesale and retail firms in the clothing industry in Vienna, see Friedrich Leiter, "Die Männerkleider-Erzeugung in Wien," *Untersuchungen,* 1896, pp. 493–99. Also Sigmund Mayer, *Die Wiener Juden* (Vienna and Berlin, 1918), pp. 338–40, 414–27.

12. Gustav Schmoller, *Zur Geschichte der deutschen Kleingewerbe im 19. Jahrhundert* (Halle, 1870), p. 660.

13. Matis, *Österreichs Wirtschaft,* p. 368.

14. For complaints on the low level of retail and wholesale commerce, see the *BHGK* for the years 1874–95. Matis argues on the basis of the researches of Heinrich Rauchberg and Th. Drapala that the fall in prices and wages hurt the producers far more than it did the consumers—in this case the urban proletariat and salaried employees and officials. Real wages actually rose during the depression period, although artisan masters, as independent businessmen, would not have profited from this trend. See Matis, *Österreichs Wirtschaft,* p. 289, also p. 426.

15. See *Stenographisches Protokoll der im k. k. Arbeitsstatistischen Amte durchgeführten Vernehmung von Auskunftspersonen über die Verhältnisse im Schuhmachergewerbe* (Vienna, 1904), pp. 402–26. Fränkel's export business was also hurt by the refusal of French customs officials to admit his products in France, since they carried a false label reading "made in Paris." By 1891 Austrian shoe exports sank to less than 50% of the pre-1886 levels, primarily because of the unsuccessful tariff policy. See Richard Schüller, "Die Schuhmacherei in Wien," *Untersuchungen*, 1896, p. 52. In an examination of another large Viennese industry, the clothing industry, which employed 25,000 workers, Friedrich Leiter reported a similar clash between exporters seeking to enter the domestic market and small tailoring shops. See Leiter, "Die Männerkleider-Erzeugung," p. 498. Eugen Schwiedland, "Die Entstehung der Hausindustrie mit Rücksicht auf Oesterreich," *ZVSV* 1 (1892): 146–70.

16. Fränkel obviously paid other taxes—since his income was many times that of an artisan, he was obligated to pay a personal income tax. But the fact remained that his business taxes were extraordinarily low on a relative and absolute scale.

17. Koren, "Die Industrialisierung Österreichs," p. 270; Alois Brusatti, *Österreichische Wirtschaftspolitik vom Josephinismus zum Ständestaat* (Vienna, 1965), pp. 84–86. The 1896 tax reform provided some relief for the masters, although in antisemitic circles this aspect of the legislation was minimized and ridiculed. See *RP*, 1 July 1897, p. 9; 18 July 1897, p. 9; 27 July 1897, pp. 9–10.

18. This consumer situation was especially prevalent in the clothing business, where fashions began to change with greater rapidity than before 1848 and where even lower class men and women desired new clothes with some degree of fashionability. See *Entwicklung von Industrie und Gewerbe*, pp. 136–37.

19. Schwiedland, *Kleingewerbe*, 1:126–55. For a detailed description of this threat of mechanization, see V. Kienböck, "Die Gürtler und Bronzearbeiter in Wien," *Untersuchungen*, 1896, pp. 620, 633; R. Weiskirchner, "Das Hutmachergewerbe in Wien," ibid., p. 38; idem, "Die Zuckerbäckerei und die mit derselben verwandten Gewerbe in Wien," ibid., pp. 4–8. Mechanization was also in an advanced stage in the linen and clothing industries. See *Die Verhältnisse in der Kleider- und Wäschekonfektion* (Vienna, 1906), pp. 5–58.

20. For the history of *Heimarbeit* in Austria, see Schwiedland, *Kleingewerbe*, 1:1–121; Fritz Winter, "Die Heimarbeit in der österreichischen Konfektionsindustrie," *ASGSS* 15 (1900): 725–39; Stephan Bauer, "Die Heimarbeit und ihre geplante Regelung in Oesterreich," ibid. 10 (1897): 239–67; Schwiedland, "Die Heimarbeit und ihre staatliche Regelung," *Das Leben* 1 (1897): 123–34; idem, "Die Entstehung der Hausindustrie," passim.

21. A *Stückmeister* or *Zwischenmeister* was a master artisan with a *Befugnis* to practice his given trade, for which he was taxed. There were many nonlicensed individuals who practiced in the *Hausindustrie* system, avoiding the taxation and the legal regulations placed on the *Meister*.

22. Leiter, "Die Männerkleider-Erzeugung," pp. 546–47, 501; L. Schüller, "Die Wiener Enquête," pp. 408–9.

23. A. Ascher, "Das Schirmmachergewerbe in Wien," 1896, *Untersuchungen*, pp. 127–67.

24. R. Schüller, "Die Schuhmacherei," pp. 56–57. Many journeymen worked directly for factories, creating more bitterness among the master artisans.

25. See the 1900 housing census in *SJ*, 1902, p. 40.

26. Schwiedland, *Kleingewerbe*, 1:118–22; J. Herrdegen, "Das Pfaidlergewerbe in Wien," *Untersuchungen*, 1896, p. 125; Schwiedland, "Die Heimarbeit und ihre staatliche Regelung," p. 123; Zwiedeneck-Südenhorst, "Die Bedeutung," pp. 18, 46–54; Philippovich, "Referat," *Verhandlungen*, pp. 77–78; Kobatsch, "Das österreichische Gewerberecht," p. 807.

27. In some industries, such as *Wäschekonfektion*, house industry and factory manufac-

turing were indistinguishable in terms of the technical methods employed. The difference between the two lay in the legal status of the business and its layout. See Hedwig Lemberger, *Die Wiener Wäscheindustrie* (Vienna, 1907), p. 7.

28. Schwiedland, *Kleingewerbe,* 1:67–77, 156.

29. In many industries master craftsmen faced competition not only from Vienna-based firms, but, as in shoemaking, from factories located in Bohemia and Hungary, whose exports to Vienna were often cheaper than similar Viennese goods because of lower production costs. See *Verhältnisse im Schuhmachergewerbe,* pp. 212, 269, 392.

30. *Verhältnisse in der Kleider- und Wäschekonfektion,* p. 55; L. Schüller, "Die Wiener Enquête," p. 410; Winter, "Die Heimarbeit," p. 735; Kamilla Theimer, *Frauenarbeit in Österreich* (Vienna, 1909), p. 211.

31. See Ernst Schneider's speech on *Heimarbeit,* in *WGGT,* Mar. 1896, p. 5.

32. Bauer, "Die Heimarbeit," p. 241; R. Schüller, "Die österreichische Handwerker-Gesetzgebung," p. 390.

33. In 1895 the government presented a bill which would have regulated a few of the unseemly aspects of *Heimarbeit,* but it died in parliamentary committee. The law of 23 Feb. 1897 attempted to regulate the apprentice system, without great success. H. Herkner correctly predicted in 1893 that if the *Verlag* system was replaced by anything, economic necessity would dictate that the factory would triumph over the handwork shop, as it had done in Western Europe and America. See Herkner, "Über Erhaltung und Verstärkung der Mittelclasse," *ZVSV* 2 (1893): 216.

34. See *Verhältnisse im Schuhmachergewerbe,* pp. 148, 162–63, 170–75, 190, 201, 208, 212.

35. Kobatsch, "Das österreichische Gewerberecht," pp. 802, 805, 812. Some of the clothing and shoe dealers whom Kobatsch classified as *Händler* were actually *Konfektionäre*. A *Konfektionär* was, however, not necessarily a *Händler,* since the latter restricted his distribution to the city itself and usually controlled a smaller capital investment than the *Konfektionär.*

36. The *Gemischtwarenverschleisser* could sell practically anything, including low quality, cheaply produced articles from incompetent artisans or provincial producers. There were a series of complaints and demands on the part of other petit bourgeois artisans and shopkeepers to restrict and control these stores. See *KP,* 10 Mar. 1892, pp. 2–3; 10 May 1892, pp. 1–2. Ironically, the shopkeepers, led by Johann Pabst, became one of the strongest supporters of Lueger, thereby earning the right to make certain demands within the party for some measure of support of their position. Small stores had natural enemies in the department stores, the warehouses, the cooperative societies, and similar organizations. Thus, although the artisan and the shopkeeper might feel animosities toward each other, they had common opponents to supply a rationale for tactical unity.

37. See *SP,* IX, 1886, p. 634.

38. Kobatsch, "Das österreichische Gewerberecht," pp. 806, 831.

39. Weiskirchner, "Das Hutmachergewerbe in Wien," p. 26; see also Herrdegen, "Das Pfaidlergewerbe," pp. 86, 125, and Ascher, "Das Schirmmachergewerbe," pp. 134–35.

40. Schwiedland, *Kleingewerbe,* 1:158–59: "Heute ist Wien mehr eine Stadt der Zwischenhändler denn der Erzeuger.... Der Kundenverkehr ist dem Handwerk zum namhaftesten Teile entwunden; das Publikum befriedigt seinen Bedarf zumeist in Verkaufsläden, welche alle Gegenstände führen, seien diese von Fabriken hergestellt, von Handwerkern fertig gekauft oder direkt im Lohne des Magazines angefertigt."

41. Philippovich, "Referat," pp. 78–79.

42. Mayer, *Wiener Juden,* pp. 412, 414, 424; Kobatsch, "Das österreichische Gewerberecht," p. 803; *BHGK,* 1882, pp. 281–82.

43. See *DGZ,* 20 Oct. 1888, p. 1.

44. For the overflow of dealers in Vienna and their price wars, see Schwiedland, *Kleingewerbe*, 1:166–67; F. Leiter, "Die Männerkleider-Erzeugung," pp. 497–98; *BHGK*, 1882, pp. 281–82. The accusation of business fraud was one of the most serious of the day, especially since it had strong antisemitic overtones. One must distinguish, however, between actual frauds, such as accusations by some Viennese watch dealers that their competitors were offering false guarantees, and the clever opportunism of already established dealers who broadcast false accusations to ward off competitors from intruding on their "territory." Craftsmen tended to include new business practices, such as clearance sales, in those to which they objected. Although some dealers practiced shady business policies during such sales and a law was passed by the Reichsrat in 1895 regulating such sales, even honest clearance sales might encounter accusations of "dishonest competition" merely because the scale of operations in artisan workshops or stores did not permit sales of any type. Novel and superior business practices also came to be described as "dirty competition." The willingness of some retailers to work longer hours or to use split working shifts or to keep their stores open longer (through the sacred Viennese lunch and coffee breaks) were all viewed as characteristics of "dishonest competition."

45. The annual report of the Chamber of Commerce for 1880 assumed a connection between efforts to cut production costs and the attempt to provide customers with goods, even if of low quality, at a lower cost. *BHGK*, 1880, p. xiii. It is interesting to note that, while masters expected consumers to pay higher prices for their wares (owing to less efficient methods, the high cost of raw materials, etc.), they refused to buy high priced tools for their own workshops, demanding cheaper instruments. See ibid., p. 76. Also, there is some evidence that most customers were well aware of the low quality wares which they received for low prices. See ibid., 1893, p. 313; Zwiedeneck-Südenhorst, "Die Bedeutung," pp. 54, 57. Thus, it was less a case of the deception of consumers by "trickery" than of the inability of individuals to purchase better quality goods at higher prices.

46. Kobatsch, "Das österreichische Gewerberecht," pp. 802–13. The number of tailors increased from 2,716 to 3,181 between 1880 and 1890; the shoemakers grew from 2,492 in 1885 to 2,680 in 1890. Other trades shared similar growth trends. Many service trades, aside from retail sales and smaller artisan shops which did repair work, were also overpopulated. There were too many restaurants and *Gasthäuser* in the city—one for every 211 persons. See *BHGK*, 1890, p. 245.

47. The revolutions in production and distribution were accompanied by a slow, but perceptible revolution in consumer taste. The lack of credit for artisan masters was a chronic cause of their inability to demand better prices for their work. See *BHGK*, 1891, p. xxv.

48. For the *Kaufmannstag*, see *ÖV*, 17 Aug. 1884, pp. 1–2.

49. The larger food provisioners who organized the first *Kleinhandel* movement belonged to the *Gremium der Wiener Kaufmannschaft*, the guild organization of Viennese merchants. However, they were generally treated with ill-concealed indifference by the larger mercantile and commercial firms which controlled the *Gremium*.

50. Ernst Schneider thought of exploiting the discontent among the *Händler* for his own political purposes, but neither he nor the other leading antisemitic artisan politicians ever seriously considered them a major part of the anti-Liberal movement. See Schneider to Vogelsang, 8 Aug. 1884, *VN*, Mappe 12, Nr. 174.

51. That the populace often confused the *Greissler* or *Verschleisser* and the *Gemischtwarenhändler* was the subject of complaints in the latter's newspaper, *KP*, 10 Mar. 1892, pp. 1–3.

52. These statistics are based on a comparative examination of the statistical reports of the annual reports of the Chamber of Commerce from 1877 to 1883. The trend could be demonstrated for many other trades, but the trades cited were among the largest and politically the most influential.

53. This interpretation is given support by statistics cited by Schwiedland, *Kleingewerbe*, 1:144–47, comparing factories paying over 42 fl. per year in trade taxes and those paying less (one determination of what actually was a factory). Between 1880 and 1890 the largest machine factories increased their numbers by 83%, while the smaller shops increased by only 17%. The unprofitability of the smaller shops as defined by their tax base may be demonstrated by the fact that in 1880, 3,373 small shops paid 21,805 fl., while in 1890, 3,944 shops paid only 23,506 fl. The average yearly tax per workshop had obviously declined.

54. See *V*, 25 Nov. 1887, p. 2.

55. *Nachtragsbericht ... betreffend die Abänderung und Ergänzung der Gewerbe- ordnung, SP*, IX, 1882, Nr. 580, p. 3; Kobatsch, "Das österreichische Gewerberecht," p. 799. This shift was also owing to the increase in the number of independent shops set up by master journeymen after 1859, but still reflected the greater *political* reservoir of small master artisan disenchantment.

56. See *BHGK*, 1882, pp. i–vi. Matis, *Österreichs Wirtschaft*, pp. 415–16. A broad number of Viennese crafts were adversely affected by the ups and downs of the Viennese construc- tion industry, which had been in the economic doldrums in 1877–78. In 1880–83, owing in part to the new tax exemption granted to owners of newly constructed houses and to the lower cost of building materials, as well as to a decline in the interest rates for mortgage and commercial loans, construction picked up. See the *BHGK* for 1881–83.

57. *BHGK*, 1890, pp. xxvii–xxix.

58. Schwiedland, *Kleingewerbe*, 1:144–45.

59. Emanuel Adler, *Über die Lage des Handwerks*, pp. 21–25.

60. *Verhältnisse im Schuhmachergewerbe*, p. 71.

61. Philippovich, "Referat," p. 79.

62. For an illuminating discussion of work and labor discipline in Berlin, see Jürgen Kocka, *Unternehmensverwaltung und Angestelltenschaft am Beispiel Siemens* (Stuttgart, 1969).

63. The drama by C. Karlweis, *Der kleine Mann*, first performed in 1894, captured this point of view. See also the comments by Sigmund Mayer in *Ein jüdischer Kaufmann*, p. 251. However, the term *Spiessbürger* was also used by antisemitic leaders in a half-humorous, half-derogatory sense to refer to their own voters. See Schneider to Vogelsang, 23 Feb. 1883, *VN*, Mappe 12, Nr. 6.

64. See *AZ*, 30 Oct. 1895, p. 1; 7 Nov. 1895, p. 1; 8 Nov. 1895, p. 1.

65. See below, pp. 67–88.

66. Bernard Berelson et al., *Voting: A Study of Opinion Formation in a Presidential Campaign* (Chicago, 1954), p. 322.

67. On the apprentices, see Johann Pollitzer, *Die Lage der Lehrlinge im Kleingewerbe in Wien* (Tübingen, 1900); Waentig, *Mittelstandspolitik*, pp. 228–76; Karl Metschl, *Wiener Lehrlings-Elend* (Vienna, 1907). The number of apprentices registered with the trade guilds in Lower Austria in 1894 was 52,123. Most apprentices entered their service between the ages of fourteen and sixteen and worked for three to four years. Rural youth from Bohemia and Moravia were especially recruited by professional "apprentice dealers," who spe- cialized in such matters.

68. Pollitzer, *Die Lage*, p. 7.

69. The legislation regulating the apprentice system rested on sections of the laws of 8 March 1885 (*RGBl*, Nr. 22, 1885) and 23 Feb. 1897 (*RGBl*, Nr. 63, 1897). The first law, which dealt in a summary fashion with protection of factory labor, offered some general in- structions on the duties of the master toward his apprentice, most of which were ignored in social reality. Other questions concerning the apprentices during the 1880s were left to the discretion of the guilds, which interpreted the laws in a manner favorable to the artisans.

70. See *AZ*, 10 Nov. 1895, p. 3.

71. In trades where the journeymen and the day laborers had forced through union representation and had succeeded in obtaining better working conditions and a shorter work day, such concessions were never automatically granted to the apprentices as well. See Pollitzer, *Die Lage*, p. 86. The average working day of apprentices in the baking trade was one to two hours longer than that of any other category of worker, although the apprentices were the youngest.

72. See Pollitzer, *Die Lage*, pp. 58–60; Waentig, *Mittelstandspolitik*, pp. 239–40.

73. The training of apprentices in Vienna tended to be worse than that in rural areas, since there specialization of labor had not proceeded to such a great degree. Pollitzer, *Die Lage*, p. 72.

74. On vocational training in Austria, see R. v Klimburg, *Die Entwicklung des gewerblichen Unterrichtswesens in Oesterreich* (Tübingen, 1900). Also, Pollitzer, *Die Lage*, pp. 94–114, and Waentig, *Mittelstandspolitik*, pp. 241–63. There were various categories of vocational schools: the *Allgemeinen gewerblichen Fortbildungsschulen*, the *gewerblichen Vorbereitungsschulen*, and the *gewerblichen Fachschulen*. The last were the most comprehensive, but of the 126 guilds in Vienna in 1898, only 36 had organized such institutes. Many of the larger trades refused to do so.

75. Waentig, *Mittelstandspolitik*, pp. 247–48.

76. For the 1870s, see Ernst v Plener, "Referat," *SVSP* 11 (1875): 81.

77. For a range of opinions on the *Handwerkerfrage* in 1897, most of which were relatively pessimistic about its ability to survive, see the *Verhandlungen*, esp. Bücher's comments on pp. 16–33, Voigt's comments on pp. 97–103, Werner Sombart's comments on pp. 103–5, and Schmoller's concluding remarks on pp. 131–32. See also Karl Kautsky, *Das Erfurter Programm in seinem grundsätzlichen Theil* (Stuttgart, 1892), pp. 1–30.

78. Emanuel Adler, *Über die Lage des Handwerks*, pp. 19–20.

79. Eduard Bernstein, *Evolutionary Socialism*, trans. by Edith Harvey (New York, 1899), pp. 60–62.

80. The question was not whether some shoe repair shops would survive (Bernstein postulated that some would, and no one seriously questioned this), but whether, in view of the growth of mechanized shoe production and large shoe retailers, all of the 2,500 master shoemakers in Vienna could survive on repair work or in producing luxury shoes or shoes for individuals with anatomical deformities.

81. Bernstein suggested (p. 61) that in trades like shoemaking or tailoring, when production or repair work failed to provide a groundwork for subsistence, the small workshop might be converted into a small retail store. Although this transfer was in progress in some Viennese crafts, the prospects of these small retailers, many of whom had little capital and no knowledge of sales techniques or bookkeeping, were not very bright. The central question remains, however: Was mere subsistence at proletarian wage levels an acceptable sociopolitical situation for these ex-artisan masters who despised and resented the proletariat?

82. *BHGK*, 1872–74, p. xix. For a representative Liberal statement of this view, see Wilhelm Frankl, *Zur Reform der Gewerbegesetzgebung* (Vienna, 1876).

83. Waentig, *Mittelstandspolitik*, pp. 40–62.

84. *RGBl*, 1859, Nr. 227. Also, Kobatsch, "Das österreichische Gewerberecht," pp. 794–95.

85. For the pre-1859 guilds, see Heinrich Reschauer, *Geschichte des Kampfes der Handwerkerzünfte und der Kaufmannsgremien mit der österreichischen Bureaucratie* (Vienna, 1882), pp. 1–201; Heinz Zatschek, *Handwerk und Gewerbe in Wien* (Vienna, 1949), esp. pp. 49–90; idem, *550 Jahre Jung Sein. Die Geschichte eines Handwerks* (Vienna, 1958). The last book is an important study of the carpenters' guild in Vienna and is noteworthy for

its attempt to plot the ethnic origins of the carpenters over three centuries. Zatschek shows how the German dominance of the guild gradually gave way in the mid–nineteenth century to a preponderance of Bohemian and Moravian immigrants (pp. 144–48). Waentig estimated that of those individuals who should have been members of a guild in the 1850s not more than 50% were actually enrolled (*Mittelstandspolitik*, p. 359).

86. Thus, if an individual exercised several trades at the same time, he could belong to several guilds simultaneously (section 107).

87. *Sitzungsbericht der Wiener Kammer*, 1 (1868): 271; cited in Waentig, *Mittelstandspolitik*, p. 365.

88. *RGBl*, 1859, Nr. 227, section 126.

89. Attendance rates at general guild meetings were low. Even after 1883 the quorums necessary to conduct business were set low in relation to the total membership of the guild. In 1869 the master tailors in Vienna voted to request the government to allow them to loan 5,000 fl. to a local shoe cooperative to establish a sales hall. The total number of men present and voting was only 37, out of a total membership of over 2,000. For a commentary on the lack of a collective spirit on the part of the artisans, see Zwiedeneck-Südenhorst, "Die Bedeutung," p. 71.

90. H. Ehrenberger, "Die Entwicklung der Erwerbs- und Wirtschaftsvereine in Oester-reich während der letzten 12 Jahre," *SM* 5 (1879): 372–74.

91. Schwiedland, *Kleingewerbe*, vol. 1; Kobatsch, "Das österreichische Gewerberecht," p. 797.

92. Mayer, *Wiener Juden*, pp. 333, 408–14.

93. For the history of the *Tag* before 1880, see *V*, 25 Nov. 1887, p. 2; *DGZ*, 18 Dec. 1887, p. 2; Sigmund Mayer's memoir in *Z*, 27 Aug. 1897, pp. 131ff.; and *WGGT*, 23 Mar. 1894, p. 1. In 1871 a small trade association, the *Kleingewerbebund*, was organized in Vienna, but its impact on local politics was not very impressive. Much of its rhetoric was "free-cooperative" in nature. See *KVZ*, 22 Apr. 1871, p. 2; 26 Apr. 1871, p. 2.

94. *WZ*, 25 November 1873, p. 712. The *Tag* tried to reorganize itself in May 1876, but it was not until 1879–80 that it began to act in an aggressive fashion as the leader of the Viennese artisans on behalf of a protectionist program. The *Tag*'s first chairman, Adolf Streblow, was a Democrat and occasionally showed up at Democratic political rallies, but the political posture of the *Tag* as an institutional entity was relatively neutral and non-political. See *KVZ*, 18 Apr. 1870, p. 3.

95. For the 1871 petition, drafted by Streblow, see *KVZ*, 26 Apr. 1871, pp. 1–2. For socialist resistance against the *Tag* and its assemblies, see *V*, 25 Nov. 1887, p. 2; Reschauer's comments in *SP*, IX, 1882, p. 8590; *KVZ*, 1 Apr. 1870, p. 2; 29 Mar. 1872, p. 2. See also R. Schüller, "Die österreichische Handwerker-Gesetzgebung," p. 383.

96. For early union activity in the craft trades, see Deutsch, *Geschichte*, pp. 42–80; Klenner, *Die österreichischen Gewerkschaften*, 1:60–88; Ludwig Brügel, *Geschichte der österreichischen Sozialdemokratie* (5 vols., Vienna, 1921–25), 1:158–64, 185–86, 223, 234–54.

97. For early strike activity, see Herbert Steiner, *Die Arbeiterbewegung Österreichs, 1867–1889* (Vienna, 1964), pp. 52ff. The workers were very hostile to the *Zwangsgenossen-schaften*. Many of their strikes were clearly political in character.

98. On early Liberal-Democratic flirtations with the worker movement, see Deutsch, *Geschichte*, p. 37; Steiner, *Die Arbeiterbewegung*, p. 55; Brügel, *Geschichte*, 1:115ff., 190; 2: 77–80; Klausjürgen Miersch, *Die Arbeiterpresse der Jahre 1869 bis 1889 als Kampfmittel der österreichischen Sozialdemokratie* (Vienna, 1969), pp. 13–21. Eduard Hügel, who tried to steer the early labor movement into Liberal-bourgeois, self-help lines with his *Konstitionelle Vorstadt-Zeitung*, was effectively isolated from the movement by late 1869. A few other

Democrats, like Kronawetter, continued Liberal patronage into the 1870s, but others believed that the Democratic movement had been greatly injured in the eyes of its Bürger voters by its free assistance for the *Arbeiter* and that such patronage should cease immediately. See *DEZ*, 29 May 1875, p. 3.

99. *Enquête der niederösterreichischen Handels- und Gewerbekammer über die Wünsche des Handels-, Gewerbe-, und Arbeiterstandes im Kammerbezirke bezüglich der Revision des Gewerbegesetzes vom 20. Dezember 1859* (Vienna, 1868), esp. pp. 5–7, 10–17.

100. *Protokolle der allgemeinen öffentlichen Enquête über die Lage des Kleingewerbes in Nieder-Österreich*, Bd. 1 (Vienna, 1874).

101. Ibid., esp. pp. 156–238, 305–22, 445–66, 556–58. On the relative moderation of pre-1874 artisans in Vienna, see *Z*, 1 June 1895, p. 130.

102. See Waentig, *Mittelstandspolitik*, pp. 85–86. Waentig was a late-nineteenth-century German Liberal with a scarcely concealed contempt for the artisans' movement. His book must be used with caution. Also, Sax, "Die österreichische Gewerbenovelle," p. 871.

103. *Entwicklung von Industrie und Gewerbe in Oesterreich*, pp. 73, 206, 267; and the various articles on the state of the Viennese craft trades in the *DGZ*, 1888.

104. See Rudolf Kobatsch, "Wien und das übrige Niederösterreich," in *Untersuchungen über die Lage des Hausiergewerbes in Oesterreich*, *SVSP* 82 (1899): 6–9, also xxxiv.

105. See J. Pizzala, "Der Consum Wiens in den Jahren 1871–1880," *SM* 7 (1881): 396–406, esp. 401–2; Matis, *Österreichs Wirtschaft*, p. 425. The aggregate decline for the mid-1870s may have been illusory, however, in view of the smuggling across the *Verzehrungssteuer* lines.

106. In general, see *BHGK*, 1880, pp. 38–39; *BHGK*, 1882, pp. 37–38.

107. These conclusions are based on an examination of quarterly retail price reports for the food items listed in the *BHGK* for the years 1871–88. Beginning in 1883 the city published its comprehensive *SJ*, which also contained retail price data. For the years 1883–88 both sources were used.

108. Potato prices declined after 1874 but rose again in 1879–80 (from 3.5/4 fl. for 100 kilos in 1878 to 5/6 fl. for 100 kilos in 1880 and in 1881—September prices showed a similar trend). Bread also declined after 1874 but rose again in 1880–81. (For *Weissbrot*, from 12/27 [the minimum-maximum rates, computed quarterly] in 1879 to 16/27 in 1889 and 15/29 in 1882–83. *Schwarzbrot* revealed a similar rise.) For beef, pork, and mutton there were similar rises between 1879 and 1881, although pork prices did not really rise until 1881. For beef, for example, the quarterly prices for March of 1877 and 1878 were 36/76, but by 1880–81 they had reached 42/80. This was true for the other three quarterly reports in these years as well, in terms of relative price increases. Meat prices declined after 1884 until the *Teuerung* of 1890–92, as did other common food products.

109. For example, *KVZ*, 9 May 1880, p. 2; *ÖV*, 1881–82, passim.

110. Waentig, *Mittelstandspolitik*, p. 101; *WZ*, 30 Sept. 1879, p. 5.

111. *SP*, IX, 1882, pp. 8493–94. These comments were in reference to the 1877 draft proposals of the government. See *Gutächtliche Aeusserungen über den Entwurf einer neuen Gewerbeordnung* (Vienna, 1879).

112. See Josef Kaizl, "Der Regierungsentwurf eines Gesetzes zur Abänderung und Ergänzung der Gewerbeordnung in Oesterreich," *JNS* 34 (1879): 294–309.

113. For artisan protests, see *SP*, IX, 1879–82, pp. 328, 910–13, 1416, 2000, 3457, 3878, 4334, 6730, 7047, 7560, 7697, 7725, 7738, 7740, 8079, 8281, 8384. For Kronawetter's comments, ibid., 1880, pp. 897–98.

114. *SP*, IX, 1880, Beilage Nr. 124; also pp. 1191–92.

115. See Heinrich Reschauer, *Das Wort des Kaisers und die Bedürfnisse des Gewerbestandes* (Vienna, 1873). Reschauer wrote a long position paper in late 1879 for the committee

that the *Tag* and the Conservatives found unacceptable. See *SP*, IX, 1880, pp. 3308–9; 1882, p. 8551. Also, Kurt Ebert, *Die Anfänge der modernen Sozialpolitik in Österreich* (Vienna, 1975), pp. 123–25.

116. For the political maneuvering within the committee and the dominance of Belcredi and Zallinger, see Ebert, *Die Anfänge*, pp. 138–45; *KVZ*, 4 Mar. 1880, p. 2. Belcredi was a noble landowner from Moravia. For his politics, see the collection of letters to Rudolf H. Meyer in Meyer, ed., *Hundert Jahre conservativer Politik und Literatur* (Vienna, 1895), pp. 305–36.

117. For the moderate pro-artisan stance of the Center party, see Karl Bachem, *Vorgeschichte, Geschichte, und Politik der deutschen Zentrumspartei* (9 vols., Cologne, 1927–32), 4:120–21, 128; and Emil Ritter, *Die katholisch-soziale Bewegung Deutschlands im neunzehnten Jahrhundert* (Cologne, 1954), pp. 120–26. For artisan unrest in Germany, see Shulamit Volkov, *The Rise of Popular Antimodernism in Germany: The Urban Master Artisans, 1873–1896* (Princeton, 1978). For the Center's later position on artisan protectionism, see the pragmatic speeches of Hertling and Hitze on the 1897 compulsory guild legislation in the *Stenographische Berichte über die Verhandlungen des Reichstags*, 9/IV, 1897, pp. 5984–92, 6168–69.

118. On Meyer, see Adalbert Hahn, *Die Berliner Revue. Ein Beitrag zur Geschichte der konservativen Partei zwischen 1855 und 1875* (Berlin, 1934); Kurt Feibelmann, *Rudolf Meyer* (Jena, 1931); Robert Michels and Ernst Ackermann, eds., *Carl Rodbertus-Jagetzow. Neue Briefe über Grundrente, Rentenprinzip, und soziale Frage an Schuhmacher* (Karlsruhe, 1926), pp. 66–74; and Meyer's memoir in *Z*, 3 Oct. 1896, pp. 4–5. Meyer claimed that he alone was responsible for advising Belcredi, which was probably an exaggeration. Belcredi was also in contact with Schneider by mid-1882, and Schneider also commented on Belcredi's draft. See Belcredi to Meyer, 22 July 1882, *Hundert Jahre*, p. 324. Belcredi admitted to Meyer that he knew little or nothing about social reform. Ibid., pp. 315, 317.

119. See *Z*, 3 Oct. 1896, p. 4. It is probable that Belcredi and Thun financed the September 1879 *Gewerbetag* in Prague. See Waentig, *Mittelstandspolitik*, p. 99.

120. Alois Liechtenstein, *Über Interessenvertretung im Staate mit besonderer Beziehung auf Österreich* (Vienna, 1877). The pamphlet was based on a lecture Liechtenstein delivered before a small group of Catholics in the autumn of 1875.

121. Liechtenstein, *Interessenvertretung*, pp. 8–10. See also *Verhandlungen des allgemeinen österreichischen Katholikentages* (Vienna, 1877), pp. 216–43, esp. pp. 239–40.

122. See Liechtenstein to Vogelsang, 21 June 1878, *VN*, Mappe 15, Nr. 20.

123. This was clearly apparent in the testimony at the 1883 *Arbeiterenquette*, where high nobles represented the Austrian sugar and glass industries, and took a very uncertain and indifferent attitude to labor protection as it pertained to the industrial labor force. See *Stenographisches Protokoll über die im Gewerbeausschuss des Abgeordnetenhauses stattgehabte Enquête über die Arbeitergesetzgebung* (Vienna, 1883), pp. 28–30, 155–57, 227–29.

124. See Reschauer's comments in *SP*, IX, 1882, pp. 8027–28. For Liberal attempts to exploit the Iron Ring's defensiveness on this issue, see ibid., p. 6602 (Mauthner), and pp. 7956–67 (Kronawetter).

125. *KVZ*, 28 Sept. 1880, pp. 2–3; 3 Oct. 1880, p. 2; 10 Oct. 1880, p. 3. Throughout the 1870s the Democratic clubs in the City Council had offered various bills to assist the artisans on the municipal level. See, for example, *WZ*, 11 Nov. 1873, p. 543; 13 Dec. 1873, p. 987. This involved tax credits, public grants, public contracts, and such.

126. The police prohibited an artisan assembly in Aug. 1880. *KVZ*, 26 Aug. 1880, p. 3. This may have reflected police unease over worker unrest, since 1880 saw a wave of police confiscations of worker newspapers (see Deutsch, *Geschichte*, p. 102). By 1881 the situation had quieted down enough to allow the government to differentiate between the workers and

the protesting master artisans. No attempt was made to prohibit Löblich's 1882 congress. See police report P3 ad 7316/1882, *NÖLA*.

127. On Buschenhagen, see his testimony before the 1883 *Enquête, Stenographisches Protokoll . . . über die Arbeitergesetzgebung*, pp. 311–16.

128. The *DV* published an apocryphal story of Buschenhagen's motives in organizing the antisemitic rallies in 1880. See 12 October 1890, Beilage I, pp. 5–6.

129. *KVZ*, 12 Oct. 1880, p. 4.

130. *KVZ*, 26 Oct. 1880, p. 3.

131. *KVZ*, 14 Nov. 1881, p. 1; 15 Nov. 1881, pp. 3–4; 16 Nov. 1881, p. 1; *ÖV*, 12 Nov. 1881, pp. 1–2; 19 Nov. 1881, pp. 2, 4.

132. For the congress proposals, *KVZ*, 16 Nov. 1881, p. 1; *JGVV*, 6 (1882): 346–50.

133. Mayer, *Wiener Juden*, p. 381; idem, *Ein jüdischer Kaufmann*, p. 250.

134. *SP*, IX, Beilage Nr. 253; *KVZ*, 17 Jan. 1882, pp. 1–2; Ebert, *Die Anfänge*, pp. 133–38.

135. See the *Nachtragsbericht* in Beilage Nr. 580.

136. *Nachtragsbericht*, p. 2. Belcredi's proposals dealt only with five sections (I–IV, VII) of the *Gewerbeordnung*. The remaining sections were left until 1885, indicating the order of priorities of the Clericals. See *Hundert Jahre*, pp. 320–31, and Ebert, *Die Anfänge der modernen Sozialpolitik*, pp. 115–61.

137. *RGBl*, 1882, Nr. 142. The actual legislation was passed by parliament in Mar. 1882. The government estimated that the new suffrage would increase the Viennese voting lists by 13,000 men (from 24,000). The final tally produced, however, an absolute increase against 1879 of 21,862 men (*SJ*, 1885, p. 38), with a total electorate of 46,226. A report in 1884 in the *Gemeinde-Zeitung* offered an occupational breakdown of some of the new voters in the city: 7,591 were artisan masters, 2,833 were officials or employees, 472 were teachers, and 358 were municipal employees. See Gertrud Stöger, *Dr. Karl Lueger*, p. 106. It should be noted, however, that in municipal elections the voting power of the artisans in the Third Curia was actually greater than these statistics would suggest, since after 1885 both the teachers and the middle and lower ranking state and local officials were permitted to vote in the Second Curia. The government's projected increase of 7,591 artisans was set too low, since in 1881 nearly 21,000 artisans in Vienna paid a trade tax of 5 fl. The number of females in this category was probably not 14,000. Liberal control of the city voting machinery and the nature of Viennese voter registration procedures (which were very haphazard and inaccurate) may have had something to do with this discrepancy.

138. The resolutions of the congress were printed in *SP*, IX, 1882, pp. 8485–86. See also *KVZ*, 13 Nov. 1882, pp. 1–2.

139. *SP*, IX, 1882, p. 8566.

140. Ibid., pp. 8593–94.

141. Ibid., p. 8592.

142. See Mayer, *Wiener Juden*, p. 394.

143. *RGBl*, 1883, Nr. 39.

144. The law did not specify what was meant by a "factory." Later administrative regulations from the Ministry of Trade established several guidelines which might be used individually or collectively to designate a business to be a factory. According to the decree of 18 July 1883 a factory was an enclosed place of production in which twenty or more workers were employed and in which machines were used as vital components of the production process. Other criteria such as extensive division of labor, high tax rates, etc., were also mentioned.

145. This provision would seem to have been directed against the *Konfektion* system itself. The provision could be avoided by hiring a straw man as a manager or co-owner. Other *Konfektion* houses, especially those founded before 1883, were usually owned by men

who had once been skilled artisans themselves or had at least possessed a master's certificate. The provision might not have affected retail merchants who simply purchased finished products from artisan masters for sales, although this was a legal point of some controversy.

146. *Motivenbericht,* p. 5.

147. See Belcredi to Meyer, 22 July 1882, *Hundert Jahre,* p. 324.

148. Koren, "Die Industrialisierung Oesterreichs," pp. 491–92. Koren was minister of finance from 1966 to 1970 and is now president of the Austrian National Bank.

149. *Stenographisches Protokoll der Gewerbeenquête* (Vienna, 1893), pp. 91–92.

150. *ÖV,* 29 Jan. 1882, p. 3.

151. See Georg Simmel, *Conflict and the Web of Group Affiliations,* trans. by Kurt H. Wolff and Reinhard Bendix (Glencoe, 1955).

152. This was especially the case because the Austrian Socialists chose to make the curial franchise system the central issue of the early 1890s, an issue on which ultimately the Christian Socials were as vulnerable as the Liberals. As early as 1891 the Socialists were supporting Left Liberal candidates in runoffs against the antisemites. See Brügel, *Geschichte,* 4:157. For a comprehensive overview of the strategy of the Socialists in the 1890s, see Hans Mommsen, *Die Sozialdemokratie und die Nationalitätenfrage im Habsburgischen Vielvölkerstaat. I. Das Ringen um die supranationale Integration der zisleithanischen Arbeiterbewegung (1867–1907)* (Vienna, 1963).

153. For these statistics and those following which relate to the personal income tax, see Friedrich Leiter, *Die Verteilung des Einkommens in Österreich* (Vienna and Leipzig, 1907), pp. 233–76.

154. Occupational data of the 1900 census may be found in *SJ,* 1901, pp. 74, 96.

155. Those who did pay the income tax were probably the elite of the artisans. Voting rights to the parliament and Council were based on any direct tax. Before 1896 this was largely the trade tax *(Erwerbsteuer),* which all businesses had to pay, regardless of their gross or net profits. Businessmen viewed it as a business expense, and sales prices were adjusted to cover it. Since the lowest rate of the trade tax in Vienna was 5 fl., before 1895–96 all artisans in Vienna paid at least that much. Some artisans in the Third Curia, therefore, were likely not to be represented in the lists of those paying a personal income tax in addition to their trade tax, although the precise discrepancy was never calculated at the time and it is now impossible to estimate with precision.

156. Matis, *Österreichs Wirtschaft,* pp. 423–24.

157. *SJ,* 1899, p. 759. It was probable that some foreigners or non-Viennese Austrians owned passbooks, and that some individuals (or families) possessed two or more books at the same *Sparkasse.* However, there was no financial advantage to be gained from the latter practice. It is true that some of the *Sparkassen* paid higher interest rates for smaller accounts (to attract customers), but most institutions treated several small accounts owned by one person as one large account for interest purposes, permitting them to use the lower interest schedules.

158. See Leiter, *Verteilung,* p. 185.

159. This was especially true in view of the fact that individual income reports tended to minimize actual earned income.

160. *SP,* XI, 1895, pp. 21414, 21443–44; *AZ,* 12 Nov. 1895, p. 1.

161. G. Bingham Powell, *Social Fragmentation and Political Hostility: An Austrian Case Study* (Stanford, 1970).

162. Kurt Steiner, *Politics in Austria* (Boston, 1972), p. 185.

163. Robert Dahl, *Who Governs? Democracy and Power in an American City* (New Haven, 1961), pp. 96–97.

164. See, for example, N. H. Tur-Sinai, "Viennese Jewry," in Josef Fraenkel, ed., *The Jews of Austria* (London, 1967), p. 316.

165. Ernst Waldinger, "Darstellung einer jüdischen Jugend in der Wiener Vorstadt," ibid., p. 266.

166. Paul Molisch, *Geschichte der deutsch-nationalen Bewegung* (Jena, 1926), p. 145.

167. It is possible that the newer, less integrated Jewish migrants from Galicia and Hungary first settled in the Leopoldstadt, but then moved out into the city as they gained economic stability and more independence from the Jewish community per se. Of a total Jewish population in 1900 of 146,926, 63,777 lived in the Leopoldstadt and Brigittenau. If one adds the Jewish population of Alsergrund and the Innere Stadt, the total is still only 92,326, leaving over 54,000 Jews living in the older Bürger districts and in the newer suburban districts. Housing segregation, while it doubtless did occur, was not a major problem for Viennese Jews, in the way in which it became one for the American black in the twentieth century. Immediately after the National Socialist occupation in 1938 a large number of Jewish families were found to be renting apartments in Gentile-owned buildings, much to the dismay of the local Nazi elite. See Gerhard Botz, *Wohnungspolitik und Judendeportation in Wien 1938 bis 1945* (Vienna, 1975), p. 165. By late 1939, 24,000 apartments remained occupied by Jews (out of an original 60,000 in early 1938), and 12,000 of these units were owned by Gentiles.

168. See the important essay by Gary B. Cohen, "Jews in German Society: Prague, 1860–1914," *CEH* 10 (1977): 28–54.

169. *V,* 25 Feb. 1892, p. 6.

170. *WFFZ,* 5 April 1895, p. 1. For a similar example, involving the *Drechsler* guild, see *V,* 20 Oct. 1892, p. 5.

171. The rights of the *Händler* to do this were affirmed by the decision of the *Verwaltungsgerichtshof* in Feb. 1888.

172. See *Stenographisches Protokoll der Gewerbeenquête,* pp. 18–20, answering questions 9, 10, and 11 of the questionnaire.

173. For the general history of Austrian antisemitism, see Peter G. J. Pulzer, *The Rise of Political Anti-Semitism in Germany and Austria* (New York, 1964); Dirk van Arkel, *Antisemitism in Austria* (Leiden, 1966); and Wolfgang Häusler, "Toleranz, Emanzipation, und Antisemitismus. Das österreichische Judentum des bürgerlichen Zeitalters (1782–1918)," in Nikolaus Vielmetti, ed., *Das österreichische Judentum* (Vienna and Munich, 1974), pp. 83–140. For pan-German antisemitism, see the important study by Andrew Whiteside, *The Socialism of Fools* (Berkeley and Los Angeles, 1975).

174. Eulenburg to Hohenlohe, 31 May 1895, *PAAA,* Öst. 86/Bd. 8, A5972.

175. *MÖIU,* Nr. 58, Feb. 1894.

176. The persistence of latent antisemitism among Gentile Austrian Liberals was (and still is) a touchy, sensitive topic which many would have preferred to forget about. But as progressive a social Liberal as Michael Hainisch harbored clear antisemitic attitudes, even though he freely associated with Viennese Jews. See Friedrich Weissensteiner, "Michael Hainisch—Persönlichkeit und Werk," in Michael Hainisch, *75 Jahre aus bewegter Zeit. Lebenserinnerungen eines österreichischen Staatsmannes* (Vienna, 1978), pp. 13–14. There was, of course, some intermarriage between wealthy Jews and Gentiles, which often worked to the advantage of the Gentiles. Raimund Grübl, for example, who became Lueger's great antagonist in the Landstrasse, was of humble social background but married a relation of Heinrich Jacques, a notable Jewish lawyer and politician in the city. Working as Jacques's law clerk and enjoying his strong and generous patronage, Grübl's career took a very different course from that of Lueger.

177. See the *MÖIU,* Nr. 60, Apr. 1894; Nr. 69, Mar. 1895; Nr. 71, May 1895. The same

theme was present in Bloch's *ÖW*. Indeed, Bloch eventually came to see the Viennese Liberals to be as bankrupt as Lueger did. Their "cowardice" in being unwilling to speak out aggressively against antisemitism was one of Bloch's persistent themes. Julius Ofner remarked with some truth that the Liberals only began to worry about antisemitism and feel outrage when the anti-Liberals began to exploit the issue successfully against them. *MÖIU*, Nr. 60, Apr. 1894.

178. See Austriacus, *Oesterreich ein Juwel in jüdischer Fassung* (Berlin, 1880), pp. 5–12, 15–17, 21–24. For an early defense of the Jews, see J. W-m-r, *Der Judenhass* (Vienna, 1873). Also Heinrich Jacques, *Denkschrift über die Stellung der Juden in Oesterreich* (Vienna, 1859).

179. Ernst Vergani, *Die Judenfrage in Oesterreich* (Leipzig, 1892), pp. 5–9, 34–41.

180. This was brought out in the various libel trials which Vergani and his editors fought in the early and mid-1890s. See *ÖW*, 7 Apr. 1893, pp. 260–61.

181. *AZ*, 19 July 1903, p. 5.

182. Ibid., 15 Mar. 1908, pp. 4–5.

183. Pattai and Liechtenstein both made threatening speeches against the Jews in the later 1880s, but Lueger and Gessmann set the tone of the party elite in dealing with the issue.

184. *SP*, X, 1890, p. 13400; Bloch, *My Reminiscences*, passim.

185. *MÖIU*, 1893–95; *ÖW*, 1 Dec. 1893, pp. 931–32.

186. Early Jewish demographic statistics are unreliable, because younger male Jews associated the census with military conscription (as did other ethnic groups in the monarchy) and are therefore underrepresented in the aggregate totals. For 1854, see G. Wolf, *Geschichte der Juden in Wien*, p. 159. For the Jewish population in the monarchy in 1869 and 1880, see *Die Juden in Oesterreich. Veröffentlichungen des Bureaus für Statistik der Juden*, Heft 4 (Berlin, 1908), pp. 6–9.

187. See Gustav Schimmer, "Die Juden in Oesterreich nach der Zählung vom 31. Dezember 1880," *SM* 7 (1881): 489ff.

188. Ibid., 492–93. The Viennese census of 1900 (*SJ*, 1901, pp. 32–115) did not correlate religion with place of birth or with current *Heimatrecht* status. It is difficult to estimate, therefore, how many members of the Viennese Jewish community were first- or second-generation immigrants and to isolate the source of their emigration. Given the large numbers of individuals in the Leopoldstadt in 1900 whose *Heimatrecht* was registered in Bohemia (20,537), Moravia (23,261), and Hungary (24,098), it is clear that a significant proportion of the Jewish ghetto in Vienna was from the north and east. The 1880 census, which was the most explicit in the nineteenth century in terms of dealing openly with Jewish demographic data, reported that over one-fourth of the Jewish community in Vienna in 1880 had been born in Hungary. Approximately 10% had been born in Galicia and Bukowina, with an additional 20% born in Bohemia and Moravia. Vienna had the largest share, with nearly 30%. See Stephan Sedlaczek, *Ergebnisse der Volkszählung vom 31. Dezember 1880* (3 vols., Vienna, 1884–87), 2:130ff. Anson Rabinbach's contention in his "Migration of Galician Jews to Vienna, 1857–1880," *AHY* 11 (1975): 44–54, that most Jews coming to Vienna were from Galicia, is not correct.

189. See Heinrich Rauchberg, "Die Alters- und Familienstandsgliederung der Israeliten in den im Reichsrathe vertretenen Königreichen und Ländern," *SM* 19 (1893): 273–77. Jews had surprisingly lower illegitimacy rates than Gentiles (in 1900 there were 404 illegitimate births to 2,762 legitimate births among the Jews, whereas among the Catholics the ratio was 16,932 to 33,849). This may have resulted from the earlier marriage age among Jews, as well as the absence within the Jewish community of a large working-class segment per se.

190. For the early cultural rivalries between Orthodox and Reformed within the community, see G. Wolf, *Geschichte der Juden in Wien*, pp. 164–70; Max Grunwald, *Vienna*

452   Notes to Pages 79–81

(Philadelphia, 1936), pp. 417–18; and more recently Wolfgang Häusler, "'Orthodoxie' und 'Reform' im Wiener Judentum in der Epoche des Hochliberalismus," *Studia Judaica Austriaca* 6 (1978): 29–56.

191. On the structure of the July 1867 statute, see G. Wolf, *Geschichte der Juden in Wien*, pp. 165–69. When the Viennese community was forced to revise the statute to bring it into conformity with the new law of 1889 regulating the external relations of the Jewish communities in Austria, the Liberal elite within the community went to great extremes to preserve its power and authority. For the 1896 statute, see *ÖW*, 31 July 1896, pp. 617–28; and the critique of the new ordinance by Hermann Fialla, ibid., 25 Sept. 1896, pp. 765–66. Fialla noted that the leaders of the community refused to lower the minimum census level to 5 fl., for fear that the Jewish *Kleinbürgertum* would come to dominate the *Gemeinde*.

192. *ÖW*, 15 Dec. 1893, p. 974.

193. For some suggestions on the wealthier structure of urban German Jewry, see Reinhard Rürup, "Emanzipation und Krise—Zur Geschichte der 'Judenfrage' in Deutschland vor 1890," in Werner E. Mosse, ed., *Juden im Wilhelminischen Deutschland, 1890–1914* (Tübingen, 1976), pp. 48ff.; Werner E. Mosse, "Die Juden in Wirtschaft und Gesellschaft," ibid., pp. 80–81. But see also the comments of Jakob Segall in *Die beruflichen und sozialen Verhältnisse der Juden in Deutschland* (Berlin, 1912), pp. 72–75. More convincing evidence on wealth levels may lie in the comparative income resources of respective *Gemeinde* organizations. For example, in 1895 Vienna had 133,397 Jews but only 12,797 contributors to the Jewish community, producing an income of 190,979 fl. In contrast, Berlin with a community of 86,152 Jews had 17,261 contributors with an income of 564,362 fl. The total budget for the Berlin community (allowing for revenues obtained outside of regular contributions) was 2,339,217 fl. as opposed to 529,185 fl. for the Vienna community, a difference of over 400%. Of course, a "wealthy" community might be defined in several ways (i.e., one having a large number of very poor and a small number of very rich persons), but the aggregate statistics suggest that communities like Berlin with a less dramatic influx of terribly poor eastern Jews were generally more prosperous than those like Vienna. See *SJ*, 1895, p. 285, and *Statistisches Jahrbuch der Stadt Berlin, 1896*, p. 54.

194. *Die Juden in Oesterreich*, pp. 112–13.

195. Ibid., p. 113.

196. Thus, the Jews were granted special privileges by the Austrian government in 1810 to trade in grain and other agricultural products, partly in the hope that they would not attempt to establish handwork artisan businesses. See Victor Heller, *Der Getreidehandel und seine Technik in Wien* (Tübingen, 1901), p. 11.

197. Mayer, *Wiener Juden*, pp. 417–23.

198. Ibid., pp. 412–15.

199. See, for example, *ÖV*, 10 Nov. 1889, p. 5.

200. *Die Juden in Oesterreich*, pp. 140–41; Goldhammer, *Die Juden Wiens*, pp. 45–48.

201. Grunwald, *Vienna*, p. 425.

202. See Johann Haker, *Cornelius Vetter, der Volksmann aus Trencsin* (Vienna, 1890), pp. 6–7. On Schneider's corruption, see Bloch, *My Reminiscences*, pp. 273, 287–88, 294. On the general corruption in the party, see Marianne Beskiba, *Aus meinen Erinnerungen an Dr. Karl Lueger* (Vienna, 1911). Father Joseph Deckert, Bloch's bête noire in the 1890s, began his confrontations with the law in 1890 when he ran a fraudulent parish lottery. See Bloch, *My Reminiscences*, p. 373.

203. See the biographical statement of J. Leb, Ms. 91, Schindler Papers, *FN*. Some insurance companies, in order to ensure their artisan investments, refused to allow Jews to sit on their boards of directors. It was particularly embarrassing when Gentile-dominated

insurance firms, like the "Austria" in 1895, almost went bankrupt because of accounting mistakes by its management. See *ÖW*, 14 June 1895, p. 440; *AZ*, 10 June 1895, p. 3.

204. The works of Stefan Zweig, Jakob Wassermann, Max Brod, and more recently Harry Zohn and William Johnston have discussed in detail the contributions to imaginative writing of the Austrian Jews and the dilemmas they faced in the monarchy before 1914. It should only be noted that the way in which any single individual writer or scientist, such as Sigmund Freud, experienced antisemitism and the methods by which he sought to make such experiences intelligible to himself were probably quite distinct from the ordinary experiences of the poorer, less articulate Jews who constituted the bulk of the Viennese Jewish community. To cite Freud's encounters with antisemitism as evidence of the oppressed nature of pre-1914 Viennese Jewry is not tenable. On Jewish journalists in Vienna, see Richard Grunberger, "Jews in Austrian Journalism," in Josef Fraenkel, ed., *The Jews of Austria* (London, 1967), pp. 83–95; on Jewish lawyers, see Franz Kobler, "The Contribution of Austrian Jews to Jurisprudence," ibid., pp. 25–40; on Jewish physicians and surgeons, see Moshe Atlas, "Grosse jüdische Ärzte im neunzehnten und zwanzigsten Jahrhundert," ibid., pp. 41–66.

205. *Die Juden in Oesterreich*, p. 100; Goldhammer, *Die Juden Wiens*, p. 40 (based on a recalculation of Goldhammer's statistics).

206. See Berthold Windt, "Die Juden an den Mittel- und Hochschulen Oesterreichs seit 1850," *SM* 7 (1881): 442ff.

207. The increase in practicing attorneys may have reflected a normalization of the pre-1861 practice of a licensed lawyer employing a large staff of *Koncipienten*, most of whom had their law degrees or were in the last stages of their university training, and who did in fact much of the preparatory work on a client's case.

208. Windt, "Die Juden," pp. 452–53.

209. See Friedrich Kübl, *Geschichte der österreichischen Advokatur* (Graz, 1925), p. 126.

210. *ÖV*, 4 June 1881, p. 1.

211. Mayer, *Ein jüdischer Kaufmann*, p. 251.

212. Windt, "Die Juden," pp. 442, 448–52. For data on Jewish attendance after 1885, see the *SJ*, 1885, p. 176; 1899, p. 405; 1901, p. 453; 1911, p. 394; and *Die Juden in Oesterreich*, pp. 93–98 ("In Niederösterreich ist sicherlich die relative Abnahme der jüdischen Schüler nur dar auf zurückzuführen, dass die Vermehrung der Bevölkerung hauptsächlich durch die Zuwanderung erfolgt und unter der zuwandernden Bevölkerung sich in verhältnissmässig geringer Zahl Familien mit Mittelschulen besuchenden Knaben befinden"). Tuition costs for the gymnasien and *Realschulen* were generally the same.

213. Bloch, *My Reminiscences*, pp. 289ff. See also Ernst Schneider's vulgar remarks on Jewish doctors made during the committee hearings on the reform of the *Gewerbeordnung* in 1905 in *RP*, 27 Aug. 1905, p. 6.

214. Antisemitism did not prevent leading Christian Social politicians from using Jewish doctors for their personal situations. See *UDW*, Nr. 22, 1901, p. 265.

215. Mayer, *Wiener Juden*, p. 377; *ÖW*, 31 Aug. 1894, p. 673. Jews were discouraged from entering the judicial system even before the rise of antisemitism, that is, under the Liberal era. The majority of Jewish instructors at the university level were not at the rank of ordinarius. The antisemite Türk charged in 1886 that there were fifty-five Jewish professors in the law and medical faculties at Vienna. According to Bloch, however, twenty-one of these men were baptized, and of the remaining twenty-four only two were full professors. Bloch, *My Reminiscences*, p. 246.

216. The number of male converts to Christianity between 1868 and 1903 among the Jews in Vienna was 5,097. Of the 7,401 converts of both sexes between 1886 and 1903, 75% were single, perhaps suggesting that marriage to a Gentile or a job prospect may have been

frequent motives. Fifty percent of the conversions occurred between the ages of twenty and thirty. See *Die Juden in Oesterreich*, p. 70. It is impossible to determine with any accuracy the number of converts wanting jobs in the state service. Schneider wrote to Vogelsang insisting that 60% of the state factory inspectors were Jewish, but there is little evidence to support or refute this assertion. Schneider to Vogelsang, 19 Feb. 1890, *VN*, Mappe 12, Nr. 3.

217. *Z*, 23 Mar. 1895, p. 180.

218. Ibid., 21 Sept. 1895, p. 188.

219. Mayer, *Wiener Juden*, p. 471.

220. Ibid., p. 452. This would also include such jobs as clerk in a store. The *Commis* were split into two factions, antisemitic and Liberal, with much of the latter faction consisting of Jews.

221. *ÖW*, 9 Oct. 1896, p. 805 (on discrimination against Jews in the *Nordbahn*).

222. Bloch, *My Reminiscences*, p. 333. For Germany, see Mosse, "Juden in Wirtschaft und Gesellschaft," pp. 73–74, who estimates that Jews constituted 25% of members of corporate boards.

223. See Sedlaczek, *Ergebnisse der Volkszählung vom 31. Dezember 1880*, 3:56. These data, which correlated occupation to religion, were based on the principal occupation. Thus, the rubric *Hausbesitzer* as used here indicated those whose principal occupation was that of property owner. It is likely, however, that the relative distribution was similar for all *Hausbesitzer* in the city, since the issue of antisemitism never arose in the context of the *Hausherren* movement before 1900. Had there been a large minority of Jewish property ownership, it would certainly have come to light, but even such stalwart antisemites as Joseph Strobach never bothered to use it in the campaigns of the 1890s. Karl Türk in a frank admission noted that Jews did not dominate Viennese property ownership. *SP*, X, 1890, p. 13458. The *ÖW* estimated the number of houses owned by Jews in Vienna in 1893 to be not more than 5%, which is clearly too low. See *ÖW*, 15 Dec. 1894, p. 974. Later reports on the city in the national census avoided correlations of religion with occupation. For Jewish property holding in the 1930s, see Botz, *Wohnungspolitik*, pp. 171–72.

224. Mayer, *Wiener Juden*, pp. 376–78; Hugo Gold, *Geschichte der Juden in Wien* (Tel Aviv, 1966), p. 36. For the higher participation rate in Germany, see Peter Pulzer, "Die jüdische Beteiligung an der Politik," in Mosse, ed., *Juden im Wilhelminischen Deutschland*, pp. 177–96. The difference between Germany and Austria may have reflected the wealthier structure of the German Jewish communities (more Jews paid higher taxes there) as well as the more oligarchical nature of the Prussian three-class municipal election system relative to Vienna's curial system (see chap. 5).

225. Even in the Leopoldstadt the number of enfranchised Jews was not more than 35% of the total electorate. The *Österreichische Union* had the right to send several delegates to the Liberal *Centralcomité*, which ran elections for the party in the city and the province, but they were in an embarrassing minority. The Liberals showed in 1894, when they selected a Gentile (Constantine Noske) to fill Heinrich Jacques's seat in the Innere Stadt, that they were unwilling to allocate a permanent "Jewish" seat for the Innere Stadt. Julius Ofner played on this tension between the older Liberals and the Jews when he ran for the Reichsrat and Landtag in 1895–97 as a social Liberal. See *MÖIU*, Nr. 60, Apr. 1894; *AZ*, 6 Apr. 1894. Even the *Union*, the Jewish political club, was forced to admit in its tenth-anniversary report in 1896 that its influence was not very impressive, on the Liberals or on the electorate in general. See *ÖW*, 1 May 1896, pp. 350–51. Similar feuding between Liberal Jews and Gentiles occurred in Oct. 1895, when the party had to select a candidate for a by-election to the Landtag in the Innere Stadt. See *NPZ*, 13 Oct. 1895, Beilage, p. 1.

226. Pulzer, "Die jüdische Beteiligung," pp. 186–93; Adolf Wermuth, *Ein Beamtenleben* (Berlin, 1922), pp. 333–34.

227. For the structure of the 1850 and 1890 franchises, see chap. 5.

228. *Die Juden in Oesterreich*, p. 112. Occupational statistics on Jews in the nineteenth century are extremely unreliable before 1890. Goldhammer (*Die Juden Wiens*, p. 68) rightly points out that Jewish workers usually entered the craft trades rather than factories.

229. On the history of the *Verein*, see Wolf, *Geschichte der Juden in Wien*, pp. 143, 216; Hugo Gold, *Geschichte*, p. 124; Schwiedland, *Kleingewerbe*, 2:241–44; *WZ*, 22 Mar. 1868, p. 989; *MP*, 4 Mar. 1873, p. 3.

230. Wolf, *Geschichte der Juden in Wien*, p. 216, note 1. When first founded in 1841, the *Verein* had serious difficulties with the government, since the authorities did not want Jewish apprentices living in Vienna. Only after 1859, with the new commercial regulations, was the way opened for a more successful program.

231. Schwiedland, *Kleingewerbe*, 2:241–42.

232. Ibid., p. 242. Also, *NFP*, 20 Apr. 1887 (M), p. 5. When the *Verein* celebrated its fiftieth anniversary in 1890, many prominent Jews and Gentiles showed up at the official celebrations. David Ritter v Gutmann gave the association 14,000 fl. to increase the scope of its training programs. *WZ*, 30 Nov. 1890, p. 3.

233. *SJ*, 1891, p. 475.

234. For Hirsch's philanthropy in Austria in the 1880s and 1890s, see S. Adler-Rudel, "Moritz Baron Hirsch," *LBY* 8 (1963): 40–41; Kurt Grunwald, "A Note on the Baron Hirsch Stiftung in Vienna, 1888–1914," ibid., 17 (1972): 227–36.

235. There were several other Jewish organizations in Vienna which supported artisan craftsmen, such as the *Verein zur Unterstützung israelitischer Handwerker und Gewerbetreibender*.

236. See "Die Zukunft des Handwerkes," *ÖV*, 20 Jan. 1889, pp. 5–6. For other hostile articles, ibid., 19 Jan. 1890; 12 Mar. 1893; 20 Aug. 1893; 3 Sept. 1893. See also Schneider's attack on Jews involved in handwork trades: "In Bezug auf das Handwerk, wollen wir auf die mittelalterlichen Zustände zurückkommen, wir wollen dass die Juden im Handwerk nichts mehr zu thun haben und dann wird das Handwerk wieder einen goldenen Boden haben." *AZ*, 24 Jan. 1896, p. 3. When the antisemites realized that the *Gewerbe* reforms of 1883 did not prevent Jews from entering the trades, they increased their demands that the guilds should have the power to administer tests for competency among the journeymen, a mode which might have led to numerous discriminations against younger Jewish artisans.

237. *RP*, 12 Dec. 1894; 28 Apr. 1894; 16 Dec. 1894; 19 Apr. 1895; *V*, 2 Feb. 1890.

238. Schwiedland, *Kleingewerbe*, 1:242.

239. Mayer, *Wiener Juden*, p. 452.

240. *ÖV*, 20 Jan. 1889, p. 5.

241. For German antisemitism, see Pulzer, *Political Antisemitism*, passim; Richard S. Levy, *The Downfall of the Anti-Semitic Political Parties in Imperial Germany* (New Haven, 1975); Reinhard Rürup, *Emanzipation und Antisemitismus. Studien zur 'Judenfrage' der bürgerlichen Gesellschaft* (Göttingen, 1975); and the essays in Mosse, ed., *Juden im Wilhelminischen Deutschland*.

242. Kuppe, *Lueger*, p. 98; *ÖV*, 21 May 1882, pp. 4–5. See also Louis Greenberg, *The Jews in Russia*, Mark Wischnitzer, ed. (2 vols, New Haven, 1944–51), 2:19–25.

243. Marr later wrote a column for the *ÖV* in the 1880s.

244. See the report on the trial in Bloch, *My Reminiscences*, pp. 81–135. Rohling's work had its first great impact in Germany in the 1870s.

245. Billroth's antisemitism has been somewhat distorted. According to Pulzer Billroth was responsible for having "drawn attention to the dangers of Jewish predominance in medicine." Pulzer, *Political Antisemitism*, p. 252. This is slightly misleading. A careful reading of Billroth's book, *Über das Lehren und Lernen der medicinischen Wissenschaften*

(Vienna, 1876), would show that Billroth was a sociocultural elitist more than he was an antisemite. He disliked the Hungarian-Jewish students for three reasons: their poverty, their urgent quest for social mobility, and the low level of their previous educational training. He did not call, however, for prohibiting Jewish enrollments in Vienna or even for a *numerus clausus.* Many of the students whom Billroth received at Vienna were products of low quality secondary schools which did not adequately prepare them for the rigorous training programs Billroth wanted enforced at Vienna. Billroth believed that many of these students had been forced by their parents to study medicine for reasons of family prestige, although they were intellectually unprepared to do so and even did not want to in some cases. He was concerned, moreover, with the flood of students at Vienna, who could not be properly trained given the shortage of facilities. To alleviate this situation, Billroth later suggested (in 1886) that all students in medicine be required to show a *Maturitätszeugnis* from an Austrian secondary school, as opposed to one from a Hungarian or foreign school. This would have excluded Hungarian Jews (along with Hungarian Gentiles), but would not have affected Galician, Bohemian, or Viennese Jewish students. In 1892 Billroth contributed money to the *Verein zur Abwehr des Antisemitismus* and repudiated any of the remarks in his earlier book which sounded anti-Jewish. See Albert Fuchs, *Geistige Strömungen in Österreich* (Vienna, 1949), p. 177.

246. Paul Molisch, *Die deutschen Hochschulen in Oesterreich* (Munich, 1922), p. 118; Whiteside, *Socialism of Fools,* pp. 43–63.

247. Carl Lent, "Die deutsche und die österreichische Burschenschaft," *Burschenschaftliche Blätter,* 5 (1890/91): 97.

248. Bloch, *My Reminiscences,* p. 249; Waldinger, "Darstellung," p. 266; Mayer, *Ein jüdischer Kaufmann,* p. 290.

249. See, for example, *MÖIU,* Nr. 68, Feb. 1895. The Schönerians organized a *Schulverein für Deutsche* in the mid-1880s which catered to the antisemitic interests of what was probably a small minority of schoolteachers (but a vociferous minority!) in its secondary and upper primary schools.

250. See "The Jewish Background of Victor and Friedrich Adler," *LBY* 10 (1965): 273, 275.

251. For these events, see *NWT,* 1 Dec. 1887, pp. 1–2; 13 Jan. 1888, pp. 3–4; Mayer, *Ein jüdischer Kaufmann,* pp. 290–92. The order was issued by Gautsch, but the Liberals approved of it. The government was especially interested in harassing Josef Fiegl and used his participation in a duel as an excuse to bring disciplinary proceedings against him, a sure sign of political persecution. Steinwender was a not formal pan-German, but was a nationalist who taught in a Viennese city gymnasium.

252. Pichl, *Schönerer,* 2:1–16; Whiteside, *Socialism of Fools,* pp. 43–63; Molisch, *Hochschulen,* pp. 123–24. As early as 1879 Schönerer had attacked the "semitic domination of money." Molisch argues, probably with justification, that the students offered their antisemitism as a model to Schönerer, rather than the reverse. Once Schönerer had adopted antisemitism, however, he became the undisputed hero of the clubs. See also Lent, "Die deutsche und die österreichische Burschenschaft," p. 64.

253. On Zerboni, see *NWT,* 28 Feb. 1886, p. 4; Bloch, *My Reminiscences,* pp. 27–29; Karl Hron, *Wiens antisemitische Bewegung* (Vienna, 1890), p. 51. Zerboni fled to Hungary in 1886 to escape his creditors.

254. The paper had 780 subscriptions in 1882. *ÖV,* 15 Jan. 1882, p. 4. Three hundred were from artisans, the rest from wealthier tradesmen, teachers, and a number of army officers and state officials. The paper depended upon secret subsidies. Belcredi implied in a letter to Vogelsang in 1887 that he was arranging for Ludwig Psenner, the later editor, to get a regular subsidy. Belcredi to Vogelsang, 28 Oct. 1887, *VN,* Mappe 7, Nr. 94; and *ÖR,* 30 Sept. 1886, p. 2 (accusing the paper of taking subsidies from the *Nordbahn*).

255. The first members of the *Verein* were not poor artisans, but somewhat more prosperous pan-German types. *ÖV,* 19 Feb. 1882, pp. 1–2; 6 Mar. 1882, p. 2. Also, Pichl, *Schönerer,* 2:25–43; Kuppe, *Lueger,* pp. 93–97; Hron, *Bewegung,* pp. 51–52; and the police reports P3 ad 1009/1882 and P3 ad 1728/1882, *NÖLA.* The *Statuten des politischen Vereins 'Oesterreichischen Reformvereines' in Wien* are in the *PN,* Karton 37.

256. Pattai's father had been a moderate Liberal delegate from Styria to the Frankfurt Assembly in 1848. Pattai himself attended the University of Graz in the 1870s and then settled in Vienna, where he tried to break into local Liberal politics by joining the local Liberal political club. See *KVZ,* 4 Dec. 1880, p. 2; 12 Dec. 1880, p. 3; and the testimony in the Hron-Pattai libel trial in Apr. 1890 in *WZ,* 25 Apr. 1890, pp. 5–6, and *NWT,* 25 Apr. 1890, p. 8, 25 Apr. 1890 (A), pp. 1–3, 26 Apr. 1890 (A), p. 1. For a hostile view of Pattai's opportunism, see Pichl, *Schönerer,* 2:43–56.

257. *NWT,* 25 Apr. 1890 (A), p. 2.

258. *ÖV,* 27 Apr. 1884, pp. 2–3, 5.

259. *KVZ,* 21 Mar. 1882, p. 2; *ÖV,* 26 Mar. 1882, pp. 1–2; *Fremdenblatt,* 22 Mar. 1882, p.1; *V,* 25 Mar. 1882, pp. 1–2; *NWT,* 21 Mar. 1882, p. 4.

260. See the comments in *KVZ,* 7 Mar. 1880, p. 2, and 13 Mar. 1880, p. 4, on the radical style of the United Left under Lueger in 1880. Mandl's association, the *Eintracht,* was long noted for its rowdy assemblies.

261. *SP,* IX, 1882, pp. 8246–47; also, 823, 8281, 8303.

262. *ÖV,* 9 Apr. 1882, pp. 1–3; *KVZ,* 5 Apr. 1882, p. 3; *MP,* 5 Apr. 1882, p. 2; *NFP,* 5 Apr. 1882 (M), p. 6.

263. For Holubek's program, see *KVZ,* 6 Apr. 1882, p. 1. Holubek tried to hold a third antisemitic rally on Apr. 24, but the police intervened and prohibited it on the grounds of public order. See police report P3 ad 2730/1882, *NÖLA.*

264. See *ÖV,* 2 Oct. 1882, pp. 1–2, and Bloch, *My Reminiscences,* pp. 61–63, for Holubek's later prosecution by the government for his disruption of public order.

265. On Holubek's later career, see Pichl, *Schönerer,* 2:38.

266. For Buschenhagen's later opposition to Lueger in 1884, see *UDW,* 1 Apr. 1884, pp. 12–13.

267. For Schönerer's speeches, see Pichl, *Schönerer,* 2:33ff.

268. The *Deutschnationaler Verein* was not originally intended by Schönerer to be an open rival to the *Reformverein,* but that was what soon happened. Ibid., pp. 73ff.

269. The *Deutschnationaler Verein* voted to exclude Jews from its meetings in July 1882. Ibid., p. 73. The crucial break with Pernerstorfer, which had long-term ramifications on the history of Social Democracy in Vienna, came in June 1883. See Whiteside, *Socialism of Fools,* pp. 101–2; Pichl, *Schönerer,* 2:74–75, 161–63.

270. For example, Pichl, *Schönerer,* 2:30–32; Whiteside, *Socialism of Fools,* pp. 87–88. See also *ÖV,* 10 Dec. 1882, pp. 2–4.

271. The government, especially on the provincial level, was concerned about the spread of such antisemitic materials and monitored this trend closely. See the instructions to the mayors and provincial officials of Lower Austria from the *Statthalterei* in 1882, P11 ad 4363, 4366, 6860/1882, and the reports back to the *Statthalter* from local officials, Nr. 4463, 6723, 8148, *NÖLA.*

272. The *Reformverein* rarely held consecutive meetings in the same district of the city. The constant shifts in meeting places demonstrated that this club was not in the tradition of local Viennese politics, based on district loyalties and having a stable constituency.

273. Schneider to Vogelsang, 14 Mar. 1883, *VN,* Mappe 12, Nr. 164; Molisch, *Geschichte,* p. 143.

274. For Schneider's campaign speech in Hernals, see *MP,* 5 Apr. 1882, pp. 1–2. For biographical data on Schneider, see *ÖV,* 12 Feb. 1893, pp. 1–2. Schneider claimed that he

had picked up his interest in antisemitism during an extended visit to Paris. He depended heavily on Catholic aristocratic money to finance his various intrigues and plots. See Gustav Blome to Vogelsang, 15 Sept. 1889, in Wiard v Klopp, ed., "Briefe des Grafen Gustav Blome an den Freiherrn Karl von Vogelsang," *JLG*, 1928, p. 294 ("Schneider ist keine unbedenkliche Persönlichkeit. Die reichen Geldmittel unseres Freundes [Alois Liechtenstein] fänden wahrlich angemessenere Verwendung als für hochfliegende Pläne unter solchem Einfluss"). Schneider became heavily involved in absurd conspiracies with several minor Viennese anarchists in 1883–85, reports on which fill his letters to Vogelsang in the *VN*. See also Bloch, *My Reminiscences,* pp. 295–97. Once the party came to power in 1896 Schneider's financial status improved substantially, but his position in the party elite was always secondary in nature, if only because of chronic alcoholism and his psychological imbalance.

275. See the letters of Schneider to Schönerer, 4 Apr. 1882 and 16 June 1882, *PN*, Karton 40.

276. See Leopold Hollomay, *Der Mechaniker Schneider und sein Antisemitismus* (Vienna, 1886), pp. 12–14. Lueger is alleged to have said something similar: "You must be careful in the presence of Schneider because you never know whether the man is an agent of the Vaterland party or a paid provocateur of the police." Bloch, *My Reminiscences,* p. 272. Lueger told Vogelsang that the latter was the only person whom Schneider would listen to and asked him for help in keeping Schneider under control. Lueger to Vogelsang, 12 Oct. 1888, *VN*, Mappe 22, Nr. 271.

277. Schneider to Vogelsang, 14 Mar. 1883, Nr. 164, and 22 Mar. 1883, Nr. 166, *VN*, Mappe 12.

278. Schneider explained his conspiracies to Vogelsang in his letter of 7 July 1884, Nr. 43, and 8 Aug. 1884, Nr. 174, *VN*. He often went to absurd extremes to avoid Schönerer, such as refusing to sit at the same table with him in a beer hall. Schönerer in turn had only contempt for Schneider.

279. Schneider to Vogelsang, 11 June 1884, *VN*, Nr. 173. He also revealed an inflated ego in his assumptions about the extent to which he could control other politicians' behavior—in this instance he reported to Vogelsang that he was having Pattai "trailed" by one of his spies to "keep some controls on him" and make sure that Pattai avoided the pan-Germans.

280. Schneider bragged to Vogelsang about his ability to attract newer, less affluent artisans to join the association. Schneider to Vogelsang, 7 July 1884, *VN*, Nr. 43, esp. p. 6, where he claimed that he had recruited 107 new members into the *Reformverein*.

281. See *Tribüne,* 14 Nov. 1882, p. 2. For the status and organization of Viennese Czechs in master artisan roles, see the excellent analysis by Monika Glettler, *Die Wiener Tschechen um 1900. Strukturanalyse einer nationalen Minderheit in der Grossstadt* (Munich and Vienna, 1972), pp. 64–68, 182–224, 486–87. Glettler notes that the bourgeois Czechs in economic-independent categories were extremely slow in organizing specifically Czech professional or political organizations. Ibid., pp. 127, 206–7.

282. *ÖV,* 9 Mar. 1884, pp. 4–5; 16 Mar. 1884, pp. 4–5; *KVZ,* 11 Mar. 1884, p. 3; 13 Mar. 1884, p. 4. For a report on Schneider's negotiations, see Schneider to Vogelsang, 8 Apr. 1884, *VN*, Mappe 12, Nr. 39.

283. Pattai's rhetoric on the *Nordbahn* a month later compensated for his political obfuscations. See *ÖV,* 27 Apr. 1884, pp. 2–3.

284. *UDW,* 1 Apr. 1884, pp. 12–13; 16 May 1885; *ÖV,* 30 Mar. 1884, p. 4.

285. Pattai to Schneider, 28 May 1884, *VN*, Mappe 12, Nr. 220. Schneider reported to Vogelsang as early as Mar. 1884 that Pattai was looking for a way to resign from the presidency of the *Reformverein*. Schneider to Vogelsang, 21 Mar. 1884, *VN*, Nr. 33.

286. *UDW,* 1 June 1884, p. 1. Some pan-German leaders were suspicious of Pattai's

opportunism and fence-sitting as early as 1884. See the letter of A. Kautschitsch to Schönerer warning him against giving Pattai money for the 1884 election campaign, 10 June 1884, *PN*, Karton 37.

287. The protocols of the sessions of the executive committee of the *Deutschnationalen Verein* from 13 May and 16 May 1884, in which the funding for Pattai's campaign was agreed upon, are in *PN*, Karton 37.

288. When Pattai was elected to parliament in 1885, he refused to join Schönerer's club leading to violent accusations on the part of the pan-Germans about Pattai's "treachery." Pattai in turn insisted that the promise of 1884 was moot and void in 1885 and that he owed Schönerer nothing. *ÖR*, 10 Jan. 1886, pp. 1–2; *ÖV*, 22 Nov. 1885, pp. 2–3; *UDW*, Nr. 22, 1885, p. x.

289. *UDW*, Nr. 2, 1885, pp. vi–vii. W. Ph. Hauck established a pan-German district club in Favoriten the year before, but this remained isolated within the broader dynamics of the city's Bürger politics.

290. Pichl, *Schönerer*, 2:45–46; Hron, *Bewegung*, pp. 54–55; *V*, 8 Feb. 1885, p. 5.

291. *UDW*, Nr. 10, 1886, pp. 100–101; Schneider to Vogelsang, 9 Feb. 1885, *VN*, Mappe 12, Nr. 177.

292. See *ÖR*, 10 Jan. 1886, p. 1; 25 Apr. 1886, pp. 1–2; *DV*, 25 Apr. 1890 (M), p. 4.

293. *ÖR*, 25 Apr. 1886, p. 2; Cornelius Vetter, *Nur für Mechaniker Schneider. Eine Erwiderung* (Vienna, 1886), pp. 4–18. The *ÖR* was controlled by Vetter after Oct. 1886. Vetter hated Schneider for personal as well as political reasons. Interestingly, one of Hollomay's accusations against the *Reformverein* was that Schneider was too dependent upon Vogelsang and the *Vaterland* party, but correspondence in the *VN* shows that Belcredi was also giving Vetter a subsidy in 1886–87, probably mediated through Pattai and Vogelsang. See Belcredi to Vogelsang, 28 Oct. 1887, *VN*, Mappe 7. Vetter's secession also resulted from the poor showing the antisemites made in the 1886 City Council elections, winning only one seat in Mariahilf. Vetter and Pattai thought that Schneider had to be isolated for the future good of the antisemitic movement.

294. Schneider's self-defense, in an offprint dated Apr. 1886, is in the *PN*, Karton 37.

295. *UDW*, Nr. 8, 1886, p. 81; Nr. 10, 1888, p. 101. The pan-Germans resented the fact that Pattai had supported a countercandidate to Hauck in the 1885 parliamentary elections as well. Hauck lost the election.

296. *ÖR*, 31 Oct. 1886, p. 1. Yet a third was created in Alsergrund in May 1887. *V*, 29 May 1887, pp. 9–10.

297. Schneider to Vogelsang, 2 Sept. 1885, *VN*, Nr. 177. A report in 1892 from the Chamber of Commerce commented on the situation of the artisan carpenters: "Die kleinen Meister leiden überaus schwer unter dem Druck der Grosstischlereien mit maschinellem Betriebe, und wird neuerlich erklärt, dass sie mit denselben, wenn ihnen nicht in irgend einer Weise Schutz oder Hilfe geboten wird, nicht concurrieren können." *BHGK*, 1892, p. 354. For polemical literature on the post–1883 period, see Ludwig Psenner, *Die neueste Gefahr für den österreichischen Mittelstand* (Vienna, 1895); Alois Naske, *Die gewerbepolitische Bewegung in Oesterreich und ihre Schlagworte* (Brünn, 1896).

298. *BHGK*, 1890, p. xxvii.

299. The growth in the number of artisan businesses which occurred in 1883–84 in many crafts may be attributed to the rush of journeymen to register as master artisans before the provisions of the 1883 *Gewerbeordnung* went into effect.

300. Weiskirchner, "Das Hutmachergewerbe," p. 38.

301. In 1895, when the *Magistrat* was still controlled by the Liberals, the guild of the turners tried to use 500 fl. of guild funds to set up a pre–Christian Social newspaper. Some of this money came from membership contributions by journeymen, who protested the plan

vigorously. The *Magistrat* refused to permit the guild to go ahead with the expenditure. Once the Christian Socials had control of the city bureaucracy, such a decision was very unlikely. *AZ*, 19 Jan. 1895, p. 5.

302. For the decision, *DGZ*, 1 Apr. 1888, pp. 3–4.

303. These disputes and the Chamber of Commerce's recommendations, which were usually accepted by the Ministry of Trade, were collected in Friedrich Frey and Rudolf Maresch, eds., *Sammlung von Gutachten und Entscheidungen über den Umfang der Gewerberechte* (2 vols., Vienna, 1894–97).

304. *AZ*, 3 May 1895; 11 May 1895; 8 Aug. 1895.

305. *SJ*, 1894, p. 502.

306. Philippovich, "Referat," p. 81; Waentig, *Mittelstandspolitik*, pp. 401–19.

307. *AZ*, 10 Sept. 1896, p. 2.

308. *BHGK*, 1895, p. xlviii.

309. Ibid., p. lxix; *Verhältnisse im Schuhmachergewerbe*, pp. 67, 1087.

310. See Rudolf Kobatsch, "Das österreichische Gewerberecht," p. 834.

311. Even before 1896 several guilds were active in channeling military contracts to their members and in delivering the finished products to army supply centers. In 1894 the shoemaker guild arranged for orders involving over 4,000 pairs of shoes, distributed among 286 artisans. *BHGK*, 1895, p. lii.

312. *RGBl*, 1888, Nr. 33.

313. There were over ninety journeymen's *Krankenkassen* in 1891, including most of the larger craft trades. Members of the craft trades where no guild *Kasse* existed joined one of the district *Krankenkassen*.

314. *SJ*, 1891, p. 451.

315. *AZ*, 5 July 1896, p. 4. Many of the chairmen in the guilds came from modest economic backgrounds. For them, therefore, guild administration was a route to social mobility and local prestige in the community. See Schwiedland, *Kleingewerbe*, 2:89.

316. In 1890 four guilds had their own newspapers, but by 1900 the number had increased to sixteen, including the larger guilds like the tailors, the bakers, and the plumbers.

317. *BHGK*, 1895, p. xlvii; 1896, p. lxi.

318. In the 1891 municipal elections the antisemites claimed that they had the active support of the majority of the larger and many of the smaller craft guilds. During the crucial 1895 elections, Josef Bitza of the shoemakers' guild and Georg Hütter of the butchers' guild used their own guilds to help artisans running on the Christian Social ticket in the Third Curia, in addition to relying on the party's other local clubs. Usually guild political propaganda was more diffuse, however, concentrating on issues like the peddlers and on the reform of the *Gewerbeordnung*.

319. See Gabriel Almond and G. Bingham Powell, *Comparative Politics: A Developmental Approach* (Boston, 1966), p. 175.

320. The antisemitic coalition ran ten officials (seven of them chairmen) associated with the Viennese guilds during the 1891 City Council elections.

321. *KVZ*, 29 May 1885, p. 4.

322. Schneider to Vogelsang, 8 Aug. 1884, *VN*, Mappe 12, Nr. 174.

323. *UDW*, 16 Sept. 1884, pp. 5–7.

324. This decision was explicitly confirmed by Schneider in 1889: *DV*, 8 Mar. 1889 (M), p. 3. See also Schneider to Vogelsang, 21 Jan. 1889, *VN*, Nr. 192–93: "Ich habe weiter gearbeitet, habe meine Thätigkeit in anderer Weise entfaltet…und im Stillen eine neue gewerbliche Organisation geschaffen."

325. The *Tag* rarely intervened in district-level politics directly. Its function was primarily that of a coordinating cadre group which bridged the nebulous gray area between explicit

electoral politics and pure internal guild affairs. As such, it was invaluable in mobilizing and coordinating the political work of the individual chairmen of the various guilds.

326. Schneider to Vogelsang, 22 June 1890, *VN*, Nr. 208.

327. *DGZ*, 17 Mar. 1887, p. 1; 17 July 1887, p. 1; 24 July 1887, p. 3; *ÖR*, 25 July 1886, p. 3 (the ÖR occasionally printed summaries of the *Tag*'s meetings); *V*, 16 Oct. 1886, p. 7; 23 Oct. 1886, pp. 6–7; 5 Nov. 1886, p. 6.

328. *DGZ*, 2 Oct. 1887, pp. 2–3; *NWT*, 22 Oct. 1887, p. 5. The number of guilds participating in the *Tag* sank from fifty-three in 1886 to thirty-four in 1887, a fact that the Liberal trade newspapers tried to use to show the thinness of Schneider's constituency within the artisan movement. However, this argument failed to consider that the guilds which remained in the *Tag* were among the largest and most powerful in the city, such as the carpenters and the shoemakers. By 1899 the *Tag*, under its new name as the *II. Wiener Genossenschaftsverband*, claimed a membership of sixty-three guilds. See *WGGT*, Apr. 1899, p. 2.

329. This process began in the summer and autumn of 1885. In Oct. 1885 the antisemitic faction in the tailors' guild won control of the vice-chairmanship in a by-election. See *ÖR*, 11 Oct. 1885, p. 3 (they won the full leadership in 1889). Schneider already dominated the mechanics' guild. The antisemites won control of the shoemakers in 1888 and the carpenters in 1887. In some cases existing leaders simply converted to antisemitism and carried their guilds with them. See *NWT*, 17 Jan. 1888, p. 3; 11 Oct. 1887, p. 5.

330. This process was filled with personal enmities and feuds. Schneider was behind most of the plots in individual guilds, giving money and advice to men like Jedlička in the carpenters' guild and Bitza in the shoemakers'. His correspondence with Vogelsang is filled with details about his conspiratorial activities.

331. *WFFZ*, 1 Jan. 1895, p. 2; *NFP*, 30 Mar. 1894 (M), p. 5.

332. See the extreme protectionist demands put forth by the bakers' guild in the *Bäckermeisterzeitung*, 19 June 1892, pp. 1–2. Liberal guild leaders were as hostile to the peddlers as were the antisemites. See *DGZ*, 18 Mar. 1888, p. 4. They were, however, more ambivalent about the proof of competency.

333. The restaurant waiters of the *Gastwirthe* guild were antisemitic, not socialist, playing upon the traditional distinction in Viennese society of a waiter as occupying a social position "above" that of a mere worker.

334. *DGZ*, 5 June 1887, p. 4.

335. Ibid., 24 July 1887, p. 2.

336. *AHZ*, 5 Aug. 1888, p. 6. Even Cornelius Vetter, although outraged over Schneider's attempt to turn the *Reformverein* into a "Czech" club, strongly supported the election of Josef Bitza as chairman of the shoemakers. See *ÖR*, 8 Jan. 1888, p. 6.

337. *BSWG*, 1888, pp. 719ff., 754ff.

338. In point of fact there was little the government or the city could do to prevent Fränkel from establishing retail sales stores and selling his shoes. The judge who heard the Hamburger–Fränkel libel trial in Oct. 1888 concluded that although Fränkel was selling cheaply made shoes, most of them were of sufficient quality to avoid government intervention on the grounds of fraudulent sales or advertising practices. See *DGZ*, 10 Oct. 1888, pp. 1, 5.

339. Schneider's motives in organizing the congress, which was a very expensive venture, were heavily censured by a Liberal artisan writer, Oskar Hein, who accused Schneider of wasting thousands of gulden of the various guilds' financial reserves in what amounted to an attempt at personal glorification. See *Ein offenes Wort an die Gewerbetreibenden Oesterreichs!* political pamphlet, *PN*, Karton 37.

340. See *Bericht über die Verhandlungen des vierten allgemeinen österreichischen Gewerbetages* (Vienna, 1890).

341. Ibid., pp. 152–61. Alois Liechtenstein submitted Schneider's 1890 program to the Reichsrat in Mar. 1893 as a proposed revision of the *Gewerbeordnung*. See *Stenographisches Protokoll*, pp. 1081–87.

342. For a commentary on the 1890 program, see Philippovich, "Referat," pp. 83–84.

343. *SP*, XI, 1891, pp. 845–53.

344. Ibid., p. 848.

345. See *RP*, 29 Nov. 1893, for a later version of Liechtenstein's views.

346. See Rudolf Kobatsch, "Die Gewerbegesetznovelle vom 5. Februar 1907," *ZVSV* 17 (1908): 276–315.

347. Liechtenstein to Vogelsang, 22 May 1889, *VN*, Mappe 15, Nr. 5.

348. See Theodor Wähner's critical review of Schlesinger's theories in *DZ*, 30 July 1896, pp. 1–2. Wähner was a powerful Christian Social *Stadtrat* of moderate German national proclivities on whom Lueger depended for advice on economic policy questions.

349. Emil Lederer, "Die Bewegung der öffentlichen Beamten," *ASWSP* 31 (1910): 707, note 19.

350. Schwiedland, "Die Heimarbeit," p. 127.

351. This discrepancy in attention is apparent in the number of police reports submitted to the Lower Austrian *Statthalter* on the labor and artisan movements in the years 1880–85. For every report on an antisemitic artisan assembly, there were at least twenty for the workers.

352. *ÖW*, 22 Dec. 1893, pp. 990–92.

353. *SP*, IX, 1882, p. 8590.

354. Ibid., XI, 1891, p. 850.

355. *AZ*, 27 Sept. 1889, p. 7; 3 Jan. 1890, p. 9; 10 Jan. 1890, pp. 1–2. Initial worker reaction to the guild system of 1883 was negative, and many workers refused to join the *Gehilfen* associations. By the later 1880s, however, the Socialists realized that these associations were a valuable area for proselytization and voter recruitment. Distrust of the *Gehilfenversammlungen* was never eliminated entirely, but the craft workers began to exploit the obvious opportunities for organization which they offered. Schwiedland, *Kleingewerbe*, 2:89–93.

356. Schwiedland, *Kleingewerbe*, 2:92. With good reason, since Franz Juraschek reported that tuberculosis rates and general mortality rates were often far higher in the artisan shops than in factory work places. See his "Zur Statistik der Sterblichkeit der arbeitenden Classen," *SM* 19 (1893): 425–26, 433.

357. *AZ*, 17 Apr. 1891, p. 3. Blaschek was an ex-socialist and a competitor of Ernst Schneider in the artisan movement. He represented a more clerical, orthodox Catholic view than Schneider and put more emphasis on corporatism. He never enjoyed much power or respect in Vienna. He was also a correspondent of Vogelsang in the 1880s and a great admirer of Lueger. Lueger's photograph appeared on the cover of the first issue of Blaschek's *Oesterreichische Gewerbezeitung* in 1888.

358. Klenner, *Gewerkschaften*, 1:164ff. For an example of the hostility of the journeymen toward the masters, see *Protokoll über die Verhandlungen des IV. österreichischen Schuhmacher-Tages der Gehilfen* (Vienna, 1890), pp. 49ff.

359. For the separation of work and home in Austria, see Michael Mitterauer and Reinhard Sieder, *Vom Patriarchat zur Partnerschaft. Zum Strukturwandel der Familie* (Munich, 1977), pp. 133ff., 160ff.; Mitterauer, "Auswirkungen von Urbanisierung und Frühindustrialisierung auf die Familienverfassung an Beispielen des österreichischen Raums," in Werner Conze, ed., *Sozialgeschichte der Familie in der Neuzeit Europas* (Stuttgart, 1976), pp. 55–56, 112–13, 128–30; and the initial results of the important project undertaken by

William Hubbard, "Forschungen zur städtischen Haushaltsstruktur am Ende des 19. Jahrhunderts. Das GRAZHAUS-Projekt," in ibid., pp. 283–91. For worker associationalism as a form of semipublic sociability, see Tony Judt, *Socialism in Provence* (Cambridge, 1978).

360. Mitterauer has noted that even when laborers and apprentices continued to live within the artisan household, patterns of cultural interaction changed radically. See Mitterauer, "Auswirkungen," p. 79.

361. Ironically the state of *Sitzgesellenwesen*—independent journeymen working apart from masters—was often favored by workers precisely because it offered greater levels of personal freedom in terms of time and sexual relationships, although it may have been less economically stable. See the comments in the *Verhältnisse im Schuhmachergewerbe*, p. 166.

362. Informal cooperation between "capitalists" and "anticapitalists" was especially apparent in the behavior of Christian Social artisans who were elected to the Viennese Chamber of Commerce after 1897. See *AZ*, 13 May 1903, p. 3.

363. *RGBl*, 1885, Nr. 22.

364. Ibid., 1888, Nr. 1. Employees paid 10%, employers 90% of the premiums.

365. *AZ*, 24 Sept. 1895, p. 4. For opposition against Sunday rest, see ibid., 31 May 1895; 8 Aug. 1895; 11 Sept. 1895.

366. *WGGT*, Mar. 1896, pp. 4–6; *RP*, 9 Mar. 1896, p. 2; *AZ*, 9 Mar. 1896, p. 3.

367. *AZ*, 8 July 1896, p. 6; *DZ*, 5 July 1896, p. 5.

368. *DZ*, 24 July 1896, p. 3.

369. After Taaffe had the *Tag* dissolved (see *SP*, XI, 1891, p. 1051), its leaders tried to get it reestablished under the 1883 *Gewerbeordnung* as the official representative of all guilds in Lower Austria. The government preferred, however, to allow a Liberal trade organization run by Joseph Schlechter to pose as the official representative of the masters (the *Niederösterreichischer Gewerbegenossenschaftsverband*). The *Tag* was allowed to reorganize itself in 1892 under the Associations Law of 1867 as an independent *Verein*, which deprived it of any official status under the 1883 *Ordnung*, but which made it possible by later 1892 for it to resume operations. By 1894 a substantial number of the 127 guilds in Vienna were still controlled by Liberal factions (certainly over 50), but these were generally the smaller and less endangered crafts. See *WGGT*, 23 Mar. 1894, pp. 1–2; 31 Dec. 1894, p. 2.

370. Ibid., July 1897.

371. Pichl, *Schönerer*, 3:100, 104, 353. The theme of "practical Christianity" remained in the antisemitic vocabulary well beyond 1900.

372. Johannes Moritz, *Dr. Ludwig Psenner—von der antisemitischen Volksbewegung zur christlichsozialen Reform* (diss., University of Vienna, 1962), pp. 57–59.

373. Ibid., p. 70: "War Psenner überzeugt, dass dem Antisemitismus ein positiver Grund, ein sittliches Ziel gesetzt werden müsste."

374. *ÖV*, 20 Oct. 1889, pp. 1–4.

375. *V*, 30 Apr. 1887, Beiblatt, p. 3; *ÖV*, 13 Mar. 1887, p. 1. See also the *Statuten des Christlichsozialen Vereins* in *VN*, Mappe 20, Nr. 240. The smaller Catholic clerical clubs in the city, which had vegetated throughout most of the 1880s, were initially hostile to the new association. See Kuppe, *Lueger*, p. 160. The association gained some of its membership from individuals interested in Pattai's political *Bezirksvereine* in Vienna.

376. *V*, 12 May 1887, p. 6.

377. Pattai to Schneider, 28 May 1884, *VN*, Mappe 21, Nr. 220.

378. Schneider to Vogelsang, 14 Mar. 1883, *VN*, Nr. 164; 28 May 1887, Nr. 181 ("liberalen und liberalsten Pfaffen"); 31 Dec. 1886, Nr. 24; 9 Jan. 1888, Nr. 185. See also the letters in *ÖV*, 3 Apr. 1887, pp. 5–6, criticizing priests for associating with Jews.

379. See the interview of Stefan Grossmann with Bielohlawek in *Z*, 19 Feb. 1898, p. 124. Grossmann tried to embarrass Bielohlawek by asking him loaded questions, but the natural political ability and shrewdness of the latter is what is really apparent in the interview. Bielohlawek came off rather well. See also *Das Echo*, 7 Mar. 1897, p. 1, and Robert Ehrhart, *Im Dienste des alten Österreich* (Vienna, 1958), p. 225.

380. The listings in the public *Schwarzbuch* which the *HHZ* published after 1894 contain the names of many master artisans as well as journeymen and industrial factory workers who did not pay their rents and who were therefore considered to be unreliable tenants.

381. The Socialists also used political-cultic devices. In their hands, however, such devices were exploited in a more systematic and powerful fashion than in the antisemites'. Both parties had special songs devoted to their movements, but not until the work of Richard v Kralik did the Christian Socials begin to match the mass, aesthetic spectacles of the Socialists. This occurred after 1895. Pattai was a devotee of Richard Wagner's music, but Lueger certainly was not interested in political musicology. Politics for Lueger was a business that was occasionally pleasurable, not the reverse, as was the case with many Viennese politicians.

382. See Franz Eichert, "Mein Lebenslauf," in *Sänger und Prophet. Gedenkblätter zum 70. Geburtstage des Dichters Franz Eichert* (Innsbruck, 1927), p. 41. Eichert was a protégé of Heinrich Abel and a later collaborator of Richard v Kralik in the *Gral* movement.

383. On Lueger's claim that he would fill the churches (and the synagogues as well), see Mayer, *Wiener Juden*, p. 464.

384. *WD*, 1901, pp. 241–42.

385. Abel's pilgrimages to Maria-Zell and elsewhere (sometimes to Klosterneuburg) began in 1893 and continued through 1914. He also organized a series of Catholic congregations for special occupation groups in Vienna, most of which were oriented to artisan and lower bourgeois constituents. The most famous of these was the *Marianische Kaufmanns-kongregation*, established in 1890. Abel was often annoyed at Lueger and other party dignitaries for the indifference with which they treated religion in their private lives. Abel, in turn, was slightly too "clerical" for many Christian Social politicians. See Josef Leb, *P. Heinrich Abel* (Innsbruck, 1926), p. 68, and *Pater Abel S. J. und die Wiener Männerfahrten nach Maria-Zell* (Vienna, 1907), p. 91. For a humorous example of Abel's sermons, see Peter Rosegger, "Ein Reichsdeutscher über das katholische Leben in Österreich," *Heimgarten* 25 (1900): 195–208. Leb, *P. Heinrich Abel*, p. 46, suggested parallels between Abel and Abraham a Sancta Clara and Klemens Maria Hofbauer.

386. *Pater Abel S. J.*, pp. 22–23.

387. Leb, *P. Heinrich Abel*, pp. 51–52. Lest this format of political ritual be used to see in these events some sort of nineteenth-century protofascism, it should be noted that Abel styled himself as a *Vater*, not a *Führer*. The cultural referents employed were baroque, not fascistic.

388. There was a tradition of women's groups within the Liberal party, but these were usually small philanthropic and charitable associations. The Jewish community also had such groups. The Christian Family clubs were not more rigidly organized, but their appeal was more directed toward the manipulation of consumer purchasing in favor of Gentile shopkeepers. For an example of the kind of pietistic literature distributed to these women, see the *St. Angela Blatt*, the journal of the apostolate of the "christlichen Töchter."

389. For the Christian Social women's movement, see its newspaper, the *Christliche Wiener Frauen-Zeitung*.

390. Waentig, *Mittelstandspolitik*, p. 115.

391. *ÖV*, 13 July 1890, p. 1. For a similar view in the artisan movement, see *WGGT*, 26 Feb. 1895, p. 2.

Chapter 3

1. For the early ecclesiastical reforms, see Rudolf Reinhardt, "Zur Kirchenreform in Österreich unter Maria Theresia," *ZKG* 77 (1966): 105–19; Peter Hersche, "Erzbischof Migazzi und die Anfänge der jansenistischen Bewegung in Wien," *MÖSA* 24 (1971): 280–309; Elisabeth Kovács, *Ultramontanismus und Staatskirchentum im Theresianisch-Josephinischen Staat* (Vienna, 1975), pp. 7–55; Heinrich Benedikt, "Der Josephinismus vor Joseph II," in *Österreich und Europa. Festgabe für Hugo Hantsch zum 70. Geburtstag* (Graz, 1965), pp. 183–201; Ferdinand Maass, *Der Frühjosephinismus* (Vienna, 1969); Eduard Winter, *Der Josephinismus. Die Geschichte des österreichischen Reformkatholizimus, 1740–1848* (Berlin, 1962), pp. 22–99; Grete Klingenstein, *Staatsverwaltung und kirchliche Autorität im 18. Jahrhundert* (Munich, 1970), pp. 88–130.

2. Klingenstein, *Staatsverwaltung,* pp. 97ff.; Peter Hersche, "War Maria Theresia eine Jansenistin?" *ÖGL* 15 (1971): 14–22; idem, "Die österreichischen Jansenistien und die Unionsverhandlungen der Utrechter Kirche mit Rom," *ZKG* 82 (1971): 314–43; Hans Wagner, "Der Einfluss von Gallikanismus und Jansenismus auf die Kirche und den Staat der Aufklärung in Österreich," *ÖGL* 11 (1967): 521–34; Adam Wandruszka, *Leopold II* (2 vols., Vienna, 1963–65), 2:111–39. For the effect of the late Theresian and Josephist reforms on clerical education, see especially Kovács, *Ultramontanismus.* The best sources for Joseph's reforms remain Paul Mitrofanov, *Joseph II* (2 vols., Vienna and Leipzig, 1910), and Ferdinand Maass, *Der Josephinismus. Quellen zu seiner Geschichte in Österreich* (5 vols., Vienna and Munich, 1951–61). See also Elisabeth Kovács, "Kirchliches Zeremoniell am Wiener Hof des 18. Jahrhunderts im Wandel von Mentalität und Gesellschaft," *MÖSA* 32 (1979): 109–42, an important and suggestive essay.

3. On Rautenstrauch, see Josef Müller, *Der pastoraldidaktische Ansatz in Franz Stephan Rautenstrauchs "Entwurf zur Einrichtung der Theologischen Studien"* (Vienna, 1969); idem, "Zu den theologiegeschichtlichen Grundlagen der Studienreform Rautenstrauchs," *TQ* 146 (1966): 62–97.

4. On the civil responsibilities of the lower clergy under Joseph, see Eduard Winter, *Josephinismus,* pp. 123–33, 176–91. For the general problem of clerical education in the late eighteenth century, see Eduard Hegel, "Die Situation der deutschen Priesterausbildung um Wende von 18. zum 19. Jahrhundert," in Georg Schwaiger, ed., *Kirche und Theologie im 19. Jahrhundert* (Göttingen, 1975).

5. On the semi-independent legal status of the lower clergy, see Beidtel, *Geschichte,* 1:229, 284, 299–300, and Maass, *Josephinismus,* 3:85.

6. Staffs of the general seminaries were often recruited from the lower clergy, offering younger clerics routes of professional mobility. Other clerics, like Lorenz and Jüstel, ended up as high ranking civil administrators of clerical affairs.

7. Compare Joseph's statements on the ideal cleric in Eduard Winter, *Josephinismus,* pp. 123, 134, with his ideal portrait of a lower state official in his "Hirtenbrief" in Friedrich Walter, ed., *Die österreichische Zentralverwaltung,* II/4, pp. 123–32. In both cases public virtue is the implicit concern of each professional group, beyond the differentiating features of external roles. Both groups were allied with the process of what Gerhard Oestreich has called the "Sozialdisziplinierung" of corporate society. See his "Strukturprobleme des europäischen Absolutismus," pp. 344–45. Both groups were responsible for maintaining that level of self-regulation and autonomous self-management which Joseph thought necessary for the professionalized rationalization of the eighteenth-century state.

8. For the reaction of the clergy in Vienna, see Franz Wehrl, "Der 'Neue Geist.' Eine Untersuchung der Geistesrichtungen des Klerus in Wien von 1750–1750," *MÖSA* 20 (1967): 36–114; Ernst Wangermann, *From Joseph II to the Jacobin Trials* (2d ed., Oxford, 1964), pp. 7–9, 16ff.; and Charles H. O'Brien, "Jansenists and Josephinism: 'Nouvelles ecclésias-

tiques' and Reform of the Church in Late Eighteenth Century Austria," *MÖSA* 32 (1979): 143–64.

9. See Eduard Hosp, *Kirche Österreichs im Vormärz, 1815–1850* (Vienna and Munich, 1971), pp. 91, 162, 181, and passim. Sebastian Brunner's autobiography, *Woher? Wohin? Geschichten, Gedanken, Bilder und Leute aus meinem Leben* (3d ed., Regensburg, 1891), is filled with portraits of men of Josephistic pietistic dispositions.

10. See the important new study by Peter Hersche, *Der Spätjansenismus in Österreich* (Vienna, 1977), pp. 376–90, 179–95; and O'Brien, "Jansenists and Josephinism," pp. 159ff.

11. Kovács, *Ultramontanismus*, pp. 80–121; Wangermann, *From Joseph II*, pp. 12–15.

12. See the "Aktenstücke zur Geschichte des österreichischen römisch-katholischen Kirchenwesens unter Kaiser Leopold II," in *Archiv für Kunde österreichischer Geschichts-Quellen*, 4 (1850): 83, 86, 96–99, 107.

13. See esp. Kovács, *Ultramontanismus*, pp. 28, 74, 78, 80, 85, 105–6, 114–16; A. Fournier, *Gerhard van Swieten als Censor* (Vienna, 1876), pp. 432–41.

14. Wandruszka, *Leopold II*, 2:130ff.

15. For eighteenth century France, see Edmond Préclin, *Les Jansénistes du XVIIIe siècle et la constitution civile du clergé* (Paris, 1929).

16. Klingenstein, *Staatsverwaltung*, pp. 83–87, for a similar process in the ranks of the Imperial civil service.

17. For Leopold II's adjustments in ecclesiastical legislation, see Beidtel, *Geschichte*, 1: 429–39, and the literature cited in Wangermann.

18. For the Franciscan clergy in general, see Hosp, *Kirche Österreichs;* Beidtel, *Geschichte*, 2; Martin Brandl, "Theologie im österreichischen Vormärz," in Martin Schmidt and Georg Schwaiger, eds., *Kirchen und Liberalismus im 19. Jahrhundert* (Göttingen, 1976), pp. 126–42.

19. Eduard Winter, *Josephinismus*, pp. 222–97; idem, *Frühliberalismus in der Donaumonarchie* (Berlin, 1968), pp. 30ff., 83ff., 150ff.; idem, "Die katholische Restauration in Österreich, 1808–1820," in *Katholischer Glaube und Deutsches Volkstum in Österreich* (Salzburg, 1933), pp. 149–59; Eduard Hosp, *Zwischen Aufklärung und katholischer Reform. Jakob Frint, Bischof von St. Pölten* (Vienna and Munich, 1962); Josef Wodka, *Kirche in Österreich* (Vienna, 1959), pp. 312–24.

20. On the episcopate in the Vormärz, see the studies of Hosp, *Kirche Österreichs*, pp. 21–185; and the documents and commentary in Maass, *Josephinismus*, 5:134–41, 683–721. Also, Weinzierl-Fischer, *Die österreichischen Konkordate*. For the Josephist ideal of a bishop, see Knut Walf, *Das bischöfliche Amt in der Sicht Josephischer Kirchenrechtler* (Cologne and Vienna, 1975). See also Beidtel, *Geschichte*, 2:159–64.

21. Eduard Winter and Maria Winter, *Der Bolzanokreis, 1824–1833* (Vienna, 1970), p. 13.

22. See Erika Weinzierl-Fischer, "Visitationsberichte österreichischer Bischofe an Kaiser Franz I (1804–1835)," *MÖSA* 6 (1953): 240–311, esp. 288–94.

23. For continued restrictions on pietistic revivals in the Vormärz, see Hosp, *Kirche Österreichs*, pp. 159, 163, 293, 299ff., 349ff.

24. Ibid., pp. 63, 181; Weinzierl-Fischer, "Visitationsberichte," pp. 264–67, 282–87; Brunner, *Woher? Wohin?* 1:123ff.; 2:115ff.

25. Beidtel, *Geschichte*, 1:439; 2:156, 162–63; Anton Springer, *Geschichte Österreichs seit dem Wiener Frieden, 1809* (2 vols, Leipzig, 1863–65), 1:562; 2:610–11; Fritz Valjavec, *Der Josephinismus* (Brunn, 1944), pp. 65–68, 75–76, 100.

26. For this mode of argument, see Hosp, *Kirche Österreichs*, pp. 332ff.

27. Weinzierl-Fischer, "Visitationsberichte," pp. 287–93; Berthold Auerbach, *Tagebuch aus Wien* (Breslau, 1849), pp. 42–43; Beidtel, *Geschichte*, 2:163, 287; Hosp, *Kirche Öster-*

reichs, pp. 100, 117–18, 120, 150, 174; Kovács, "Kirchliches Zeremoniell am Wiener Hof," p. 138.

28. Hosp has shown how the Franciscan regime took great pains to ensure good order within the Church and the clergy, occasionally blaming the bishops if public effectiveness was not manifest. See *Kirche Österreichs,* pp. 82, 119, 165ff., 177.

29. On Hofbauer, see Rudolf Till, *Hofbauer und sein Kreis* (Vienna, 1951); Eduard Winter, "Die katholische Restauration in Österreich"; Thomas W. Simons, "Vienna's First Catholic Political Movement: The Güntherians, 1848–1857," *Catholic Historical Review* 55 (1969/70): 173–85.

30. Simons, "Vienna's First Catholic Political Movement," p. 178.

31. On Bolzano, see Eduard Winter, *Bernard Bolzano und sein Kreis* (Leipzig, 1933); idem, *Frühliberalismus,* pp. 157–62; idem, ed., *Wissenschaft und Religion im Vormärz. Der Briefwechsel Bernard Bolzanos mit Michael Josef Fesl, 1822–1848* (Berlin, 1965); William M. Johnston, *The Austrian Mind: An Intellectual and Social History, 1848–1938* (Berkeley and Los Angeles, 1972), pp. 274–78.

32. The best source for Bolzano's early ideals of piety and social ethics is his *Erbauungsreden,* which he delivered at the University of Prague in 1813.

33. See Bernard Bolzano, "Das Büchlein vom besten Staate," in Jan Berg and Jaromír Loužil, eds., *Sozialphilosophische Schriften* (Stuttgart, 1975), pp. 31–70.

34. Johnston, *The Austrian Mind,* p. 277.

35. See Fesl's autobiographical statement, composed on 10 Apr. 1848 for Franz v Sommaruga, the minister of education in the revolutionary government, in Eduard Winter and Maria Winter, *Der Bolzanokreis,* pp. 41–48.

36. Eduard Winter, *Der Josephinismus,* pp. 218–22 and passim.

37. Eduard Winter and Maria Winter, *Der Bolzanokreis,* pp. 7–17; Eduard Winter, *Der Josephinismus,* pp. 240–46, 254–56.

38. For Leo Thun's connections with Bolzano, see Christoph Thienen-Adlerflycht, *Graf Leo Thun im Vormärz* (Graz, 1967); and Eduard Winter, *Frühliberalismus,* pp. 261ff.

39. On Günther, see Paul Wenzel, *Das wissenschaftliche Anliegen des Güntherianismus* (Essen, 1961); Eduard Winter, *Die geistige Entwicklung Anton Günthers und seiner Schule* (Paderborn, 1931); Joseph Pritz, *Glauben und Wissen bei Anton Günther* (Vienna, 1963); Ernst Karl Winter, "Anton Günther. Ein Beitrag zur Romantikforschung," *ZGSW* 88 (1930): 281–333.

40. Simons, "Vienna's First Catholic Political Movement," pp. 183ff.; Pritz, *Glauben und Wissen,* pp. 26–35.

41. For Günther's philosophy, see Wenzel, *Anliegen,* pp. 152–72; Pritz, "Anton Günther," in Heinrich Fries and Georg Schwaiger, eds., *Katholische Theologen Deutschlands im 19. Jahrhundert* (3 vols., Munich, 1975), 1:370ff.

42. Compare the anthropocentrism of Rautenstrauch and the man-oriented Christology of Günther in Müller, "Zu den theologiegeschichtlichen Grundlagen der Studienreform Rautenstrauchs," p. 93, and Alois Dempf, "Die letzte Vollanthropologie: Dem Andenken Anton Günthers (+ 1863)," *Wissenschaft und Weltbild* 15 (1962): 184–92.

43. For Günther's stance on the Church, see Joseph Pritz, "Zur Lehre Anton Günthers der Kirche," *Wiener Beiträge zur Theologie* 10 (1965): 275–336.

44. For Günther's political theory, see Joseph Pritz, *Mensch als Mitte. Leben und Werk Carl Werners* (Vienna, 1968), pp. 56–57, and Anton Günther, "Die doppelte Souveränität im Menschen und in der Menschheit," *Aufwärts* 1 (1848): 54–57, 84–88, 132–34, 225–29, 233–37, 242–46.

45. Erwin Mann, "Die philosophisch-theologische Schule Anton Günthers," in Victor

Flieder, ed., *Festschrift Franz Loidl zum 65. Geburtstag* (3 vols., Vienna, 1970), 2:242–44; and Pritz, *Mensch als Mitte*, pp. 59–61, 73–74.

46. Simons, "Vienna's First Catholic Political Movement," pp. 182–83. On Veith, see Johann Heinrich Löwe, *Johann Emanuel Veith. Eine Biographie* (Vienna, 1879).

47. See Veith's essay on Hofbauer in Sebastian Brunner, *Clemens Maria Hofbauer und seine Zeit* (Vienna, 1858), pp. 267–80.

48. See Brunner, *Woher? Wohin?* 2:145–48.

49. Pritz, *Glauben und Wissen*, pp. 42–43. Günther's sectarianism, both before and during the Revolution of 1848, was not simply owing to the lack of a public civic culture in Vormärz Vienna, although this fact doubtless encouraged his exclusivist views.

50. On the revolution and the Church, see Eduard Hosp, *Kirche im Sturmjahr: Erinnerungen an Johann Michael Häusle* (Vienna, 1953); Till, *Hofbauer*, chap. 3; Simons, "Vienna's First Catholic Political Movement" (an excellent survey); Cölestin Wolfsgruber, "Die Haltung des Wiener Klerus in den Märztagen 1848," *JLN* 13 (1914–15): 483–94; Gustav Otruba, "Katholischer Klerus und 'Kirche' im Spiegel der Flugschriftenliteratur des Revolutions-Jahres 1848," in *Festschrift Franz Loidl* 2:265–313; Wolfgang Häusler, "Konfessionelle Probleme in der Wiener Revolution 1848," *Studia Judaica Austriaca*, Bd. I, *Das Judentum im Revolutionsjahr 1848* (Vienna and Munich, 1974), pp. 64–77.

51. Hosp, *Kirche im Sturmjahr*, pp. 34–35.

52. Ibid., p. 38; Simons, "Vienna's First Catholic Political Movement," pp. 379–80.

53. On Milde and the revolution, see Otruba, "Katholischer Klerus," pp. 271–73; for Schwarzenberg, see Cölestin Wolfsgruber, *Friedrich Kardinal Schwarzenberg* (3 vols., Vienna and Leipzig, 1906–16), 1:259–98.

54. Till, *Hofbauer*, p. 99; Wolfsgruber, *Schwarzenberg*, 1:284–87,»298–99; Springer, *Geschichte*, 2:609–10; Erika Weinzierl-Fischer, "Die Kirchenfrage auf dem österreichischen Reichstag, 1848/49," *MÖSA* 8 (1955): 171–74.

55. Only Friedrich Schwarzenberg represented the Austrian episcopate at the conference of German bishops in Würzburg. On the conference, see Rudolf Lill, "Die ersten deutschen Bischofskonferenzen," *RQ* 59 (1964): 136–78.

56. On Gärtner, see the short sketch in E. Gierach, ed., *Sudetendeutsche Lebensbilder* (Reichenberg, 1930).

57. See Otruba, "Katholischer Klerus," pp. 268–69.

58. Simons, "Vienna's First Catholic Political Movement," pp. 383–84.

59. See Rudolf Till, "Theologen in der Wiener Stadtverwaltung," *JVGSW* 13 (1957–58): 203ff.

60. Simons, "Vienna's First Catholic Political Movement," pp. 380–81. For a moderate clerical view of the revolution rejecting the clergy's political involvement, see Franz Rieder, "Der katholische Klerus in Oesterreich und die Constitution," *TPQS* 1 (1848): 120ff.

61. Pritz, *Mensch als Mitte*, pp. 51–52.

62. Eduard Winter, *Josephinismus*, pp. 331–32; idem, *Frühliberalismus*, p. 218.

63. Eduard Winter, *Josephinismus*, pp. 315–34; idem, *Bernard Bolzano*, pp. 233–42.

64. For Gärtner's obsequious behavior toward Milde, see Simons, "Vienna's First Catholic Political Movement," p. 380.

65. Rudolf Till, "Die Anfänge der christlichen Volksbewegung," pp. 59–83.

66. See Veith's letter to Carl Werner, 2 Aug. 1848, cited in Pritz, *Mensch als Mitte*, pp. 62–63; Simons, "Vienna's First Catholic Political Movement," pp. 388, 617.

67. On German Catholicism in Vienna, see Andreas Posch, "Die deutschkatholische Gemeinde in Wien," in Leo Santifaller, ed., *Festschrift zur Feier des zweihundertjährigen Bestandes des Haus-, Hof-, und Staatsarchivs* (Vienna, 1951), 2:269–82; Eduard Winter,

Frühliberalismus, pp. 162–64, 221; Hosp, *Kirche,* pp. 61–64; Erika Weinzierl-Fischer, "Österreichs Clerus und die Arbeiterschaft," *WW* 10 (1957): 618.

68. Till, "Die Anfänge der christlichen Volksbewegung," pp. 83–87.

69. Wolfsgruber, *Schwarzenberg,* 2:44–51, 453–67; Eduard Winter and Maria Winter, *Domprediger Johann Emanuel Veith und Kardinal Friedrich Schwarzenberg. Der Günther-prozess in unveröffentlichten Briefen und Akten* (Vienna, 1972), pp. 8–40.

70. Hosp, *Kirche im Sturmjahr,* pp. 78, 85–92; Till, *Hofbauer,* pp. 119–20; Cölestin Wolfsgruber, *Joseph Othmar Cardinal Rauscher* (Freiburg i. B., 1888), pp. 348–57, 442–57.

71. See Rauscher's attack on Günther in 1852, Wolfsgruber, *Schwarzenberg,* 2:375–76.

72. For the decline in seminary enrollments in this period, see F. Franke, "Der Säcular-Clerus Oesterreichs im Jahre 1875," *SM* 3 (1877): 277. Enrollments dropped from 2,669 in 1870 to 1,754 in 1875, a decrease of 35% in five years.

73. Anton Erdinger's comments in *TPQS* 29 (1876): 283.

74. For a similar development in France, see Roger Magraw, "The Conflict in the Villages," in Theodore Zeldin, ed., *Conflicts in French Society: Anticlericalism, Education, and Morals in the Nineteenth Century* (London, 1970), pp. 169–227.

75. See *TPQS* 35 (1882): 1–15.

76. See Veith to Schwarzenberg, 5 Mar. 1858, in Eduard Winter and Maria Winter, *Der Güntherprozess,* pp. 148–49.

77. See Johann Prammer, *Konservative und christlichsoziale Politik im Viertel ob dem Wienerwald* (diss., University of Vienna, 1973), pp. 65ff., 72–85.

78. On Opitz, see Augustin K. Huber, *Ambros Opitz, 1846–1907. Ein Bahnbrecher der katholischen Bewegung Altösterreichs* (Königstein, 1961).

79. Statistics on circulation may be found in the *CB,* 1884, *Literaturblatt,* Nr. 1, p. 1; 1886, p. 778; 1887, p. 781. The size of the secular clergy in Austria in 1895 was 16,894. The size of the regular clergy was more difficult to determine, since the statistics included both priests and nonordained members of the male orders. The total membership of the male orders was 8,530. See Julius v Twardowski, *Statistische Daten über Österreich* (Vienna, 1902), pp. 45–46.

80. *EE,* vol. 2, illustrates the openness and relative flexibility of the seminaries after 1855, compared with the Vormärz system.

81. On the legal status of the Augustinians in Austria, see Floridus Röhrig, "Die Gründung der österreichischen Chorherren-Kongregation und ihre Vorgeschichte," in *Festschrift Franz Loidl,* 2:320–40.

82. See Barbara Schmid-Egger, *Klerus und Politik in Böhmen um 1900* (Munich, 1974), pp. 31–32; and A. K. Huber, ed., "Franz Kordačs Briefe ins Germanikum," *AKBMS* 1 (1967): 162–64, 170–72.

83. On Scheicher, see *EE;* Hedwig David, *Joseph Scheicher als Sozialpolitiker* (diss., University of Vienna, 1946); Josef Kendl, *Joseph Scheicher* (diss., University of Salzburg, 1967); and Josef Wagner, "Joseph Scheicher," *Hochland* 24 (1926–27): 406–16. The general of the Jesuit order in Rome in 1940 noted that Scheicher had been the most influential Austrian priest in the monarchy during his lifetime (David, *Scheicher,* p. 115). For a social evaluation of Scheicher, see *AZ,* 26 Aug. 1892, pp. 2–3. For a detailed analysis of his career, see John Boyer, "Conservatism and Modernism in Austrian Christian Socialism: Joseph Scheicher and Franz M. Schindler," unpublished manuscript (Chicago, 1977).

84. *SPNÖLTG,* 7 Wahlperiode, I, 1890, p. 498.

85. *EE* 1:151; 2:9–16.

86. On Werner, see Pritz, *Mensch als Mitte.*

87. *EE* 2:497–516.

88. See Joseph Scheicher, *Sebastian Brunner. Ein Lebensbild* (Würzburg, 1888), esp. pp. 151–84, 188–218, for his own appreciation of Brunner. Scheicher noted in this book that "Ein Josephiner kennt ja keine kirchliche Hierarchie" (p. 133), an ironic comment with some relevance to himself.

89. For the history of the *Clerustag,* see Joseph Scheicher, *Der österreichische Clerustag* (Vienna, 1903); *RP,* 2 Sept. 1902, p. 2; and Boyer, "Conservatism and Modernism in Austrian Christian Socialism."

90. This is not to suggest that the opinions of the *CB* were shared by every cleric in Lower Austria. But it is clear that the *CB* had a large and loyal constituency and was able to guide the attitudes of the mass of the clergy by serving as the voice of the activist cadre of priests who engineered the clerical involvement in the Christian Social movement. Its powerful influence may be gauged by the fact that after 1892 many bishops tried to prevent their seminarians from reading it, prohibiting their seminary libraries from purchasing subscriptions. It was not until after 1906, however, that the episcopate was able to enforce a prohibition on their clergy from newspaper involvement without the written consent of the local bishop. See the *Protokoll der bischöflichen Versammlung in Wien vom 11. bis zum 18. Oktober 1906,* pp. 7–10, *EBDA.* Franz Doppelbauer tried to establish official guidelines for editors of Catholic papers in 1894, but these were largely ignored in the turbulence of the mid-1890s. See *Protokoll der bischöflichen Versammlung in Wien vom 2. bis zum 10. April 1894.*

91. For the political aspects of episcopal appointments, see Edith Sauer, *Die politischen Aspekte der österreichischen Bischofsernennungen, 1867–1918* (Vienna, 1968).

92. Even during the Concordat period there was latent dissatisfaction with the policies of the episcopate. See Weinzierl-Fischer, *Die österreichischen Konkordate,* pp. 97–98.

93. Friedrich Engel-Janosi, *Österreich und der Vatikan, 1846–1918* (2 vols., Graz, 1958–60), 1:276.

94. For the Tyrol situation, see Richard Schober, "Die Tiroler Konservativen in der Ära Taaffe," *MÖSA* 29 (1976): 258–314.

95. For the problem of clerical incomes in general, see Julius Bombiero-Kremanać, "Die Entwicklung der staatlichen Kongrua-Gesetzgebung in Österreich," *ZSSR,* Kanonistische Abteilung, 12 (1922): 110–67; and the articles "Kongrua" and "Religionsfonds" in the *Österreichisches Staatswörterbuch* (4 vols., Vienna, 1905–9). See also Ferdinand Anheil, *Caritative und soziale Unternehmungen in der Wiener Erzdiözese von 1802 bis 1918* (diss., University of Vienna, 1968).

96. The *Religionsfond* comprised sixteen different units, since each province was treated as an administrative entity. By 1885, because of inept management and rising costs, the fund was incapable of meeting its responsibilities.

97. The rates elsewhere were lower. Josephist legislation also made a distinction between "old" and "new" parishes, the former receiving a lower guaranteed income. This distinction was dropped in the 1885 bill. See Bombiero-Kremenać, "Die Entwicklung," pp. 126–34.

98. *PV* 2:250ff.; Rogge, *Oesterreich von Vilagos bis zur Gegenwart,* 3:417–18.

99. See *SP,* VII, 1872, pp. 34–36.

100. *PV* 3:305–9.

101. *CB,* 1884, Beilage, following p. 408.

102. *CB,* 1884, pp. 441–42, 457–58.

103. *CB,* 1884, pp. 293–94.

104. *CB,* 1885, p. 52; 1884, p. 427; 1883, pp. 347, 436.

105. See "Die materielle Lage des Arbeiterstandes in Oesterreich," *MCSR* 1 (1879): 481–82. These data reflected 1878–79 costs for housing, clothing, food, heating, and voluntary sickness insurance.

106. *RGBl*, 1885, Nr. 47, pp. 131–36. This was termed "provisional" at the insistence of the episcopate, who still awaited a definitive settlement of the question of Church wealth.

107. Ibid., p. 135.

108. *SJ*, 1895, pp. 616–18. These data were based on labor disputes involving 41,266 workers over a two-year period. Some categories of workers fell above or below these norms, but the overwhelming majority were within these parameters. This comparison assumes a maximal 48- 50-week work period per year (allowing for unemployment, sickness, and seasonal downturns in production). For a skilled worker earning 13–14 fl. per week, this would result in approximately 650 fl. a year. Allowing for another 200–250 fl. from additional family income (child labor, semiskilled labor by wives, etc.), the total family income of a better placed working-class family might reach 800–850 fl. per annum. According to Johann Hagenhofer (*Die soziale Lage der Wiener Arbeiter um die Jahrhundertwende* [diss., University of Vienna, 1966] pp. 73–74), wages in Vienna remained relatively stable between 1889 and 1905, rising only after 1906 in response to the sharp rise in consumer products.

109. An official entering Rank XI of the civil service (according to the law of 1873) would receive 900 fl. per year, including *Aktivitätszulagen*. In Rank X he would receive 1,200 fl. a year. The younger clerics thus fell between the two civil service ranks, but since their housing was often free, their salaries were closer to Rank X than XI.

110. See W. G. Runciman, *Relative Deprivation and Social Justice* (Berkeley and Los Angeles, 1966), pp. 21–22.

111. *CB*, 1886, pp. 198, 215, 254, 366, and passim.

112. *CB*, 1894, pp. 812–15.

113. *CB*, 1896, pp. 730–34, 908–10.

114. *CB*, 1886, pp. 706–7; 1887, pp. 789–91.

115. *RGBl*, 1888, Nr. 99, p. 348. The additional income was not to be included in the Congrua; thus, it served as additional salary for the younger clerics. *CB*, 1898, p. 19. In Vienna clerics had to teach ten hours a week gratis, with each weekly hour taught thereafter compensated at the rate of 30 fl.

116. *CB*, 1894, pp. 813–14, 855–56; 1895, pp. 95–99.

117. *CB*, 1896, pp. 274–75, 307–11, 731–34; 1897, pp. 10–13, 133–36.

118. *CB*, 1884, pp. 293–94; 1893, pp. 381–84; 1894, p. 855; 1896, pp. 911–12.

119. *CB*, 1894, p. 855. Many clerics in Vienna also took summer vacations, traveling in the empire and in Germany, a custom dating to the Vormärz.

120. Beidtel (*Geschichte*, 1:233) presented a bleak picture of the lower clergy everywhere and argued that most clerics dependent on the Congrua had to pay all of their salaries to the pastor for room and board. Various random reports in the *CB* indicate that the customs of many dioceses such as Vienna and Prague did not recognize this practice. If the clerics had had to pay all of their salaries over to their pastors (thereby obviating the point of the 1885 salary reforms to begin with), the *CB* would have been filled with complaints about such a practice, which it was not. See *CB*, 1886, p. 290; 1887, p. 284; 1889, p. 282.

According to a survey published in *V* in 1889, 104 *Cooperatoren* taught in the public schools in Vienna in 1888–89, earning a total of 24,930 fl., or an average of 240 fl. over and above their minimum Congrua of 500 fl. Forty priests taught in the *Bürgerschulen*. *V*, 13 Nov. 1889, Beiblatt, p. 1. In 1888 there were 157 secular clerics and 54 regular priests permanently stationed in the city, so that the great majority were probably engaged in some kind of school teaching. *SJ*, 1888, pp. 79–80. We may assume that most of the radical antisemitic clerics complaining about their salaries earned at least 700 fl. and possibly as much as 800–850 fl. per year. Given that the cleric's personal living expenses were lower than those of a typical white collar family, his salary was comparable to that of a middle echelon civil servant of younger years. The extraordinary interest of the *CB* in the pension question was an indirect index that most clerics actually lived long enough to worry about a pension.

121. *CB*, 1884, pp. 293–94.

122. *CB*, 1883, pp. 269–70; 1888, pp. 679–80; 1894, pp. 161–63; 1896, p. 733.

123. *SP*, IX, 1882, pp. 1261–63.

124. *CB*, 1892, p. 583; 1887, p. 254; 1894, pp. 812, 206.

125. *CB*, 1894, p. 162; 1896, p. 179.

126. *CB*, 1896, pp. 734, 865; 1897, p. 18.

127. *CB*, 1896, pp. 862–63.

128. *CB*, 1896, pp. 734, 865. On the uncertain feelings of many clerics toward the urban working class, see Heinrich Swoboda, *Grossstadtseelsorge* (Regensburg, 1909), p. 11.

129. *CB*, 1892, p. 332; 1896, pp. 731–33.

130. *CB*, 1894, p. 856.

131. The great majority of the Lower Austrian and Viennese clergy came from urban Bürger or *Kleinbürger* and peasant social backgrounds. Clerics from the working class (in Austrian terms) were rather rare. See Gustav Müller, *Die Erhabenheit und Bedeutung des katholischen Priestertums* (Vienna, 1890); *CB*, 1900, p. 143; Weinzierl-Fischer, "Österreichs Klerus und die Arbeiterschaft," p. 617.

132. See the important distinction between status as a characteristic of social rank and status as a characteristic of traditional cultural expectations, in Peter Stearns, "Introduction," Peter Stearns and Daniel J. Walkowitz, eds., *Workers in the Industrial Revolution* (New Brunswick, N.J., 1974), p. 8.

133. *CB*, 1889, p. 350.

134. *CB*, 1889, p. 564.

135. *CB*, 1890, p. 133.

136. *CB*, 1888, p. 99; 1893, p. 520.

137. There is no satisfactory history of the administrative and policy development of the Austrian public-school system. But see Gustav Strakosch-Grassmann, *Geschichte des österreichischen Unterrichtswesens* (Vienna, 1905); Ferdinand Frank, *Die österreichische Volksschule, 1848–1898* (Vienna, 1898); Ernst Papenek, *The Austrian School Reform* (New York, 1962), pp. 21–41; William Jenks, *Austria under the Iron Ring* (Charlottesville, Va., 1965), pp. 122–40. A German educational journal, *Pädagogischer Jahresbericht*, contained a convenient summary of political and legal developments pertaining to the Austrian school system.

138. For the 1883 legislation, see *PV* 3: 102–6, 284–97; Jenks, *Iron Ring*, pp. 122–40; *PJ*, 1883, pp. 664–782.

139. *PV* 3:285.

140. Proclerical school laws were enacted in Upper Austria (1884), in Tyrol (1892), in Vorarlberg (1899), and in Lower Austria itself (1904). For the shift of administrative and political power to the Landtage, see Ferdinand Schmid, *Finanzreform in Oesterreich* (Tübingen, 1911), pp. 3–93.

141. A secret report drafted by the episcopate and submitted to the Ministry of Education in late 1892 made this shift from political to administrative maneuvering explicit. The bishops recognized that the parliament would not pass additional clerical school legislation, and asked that the Imperial bureaucracy use its considerable powers to pressure the various *Land*-level school authorities to conform more closely to the Church's desires. See the "Eingabe an das k. k. Gesamt-Ministerium in Betreff der beklagenswerten Zustände der Volksschulen," in *Protokoll der bischöflichen Versammlung in Wien vom 2. bis zum 10. April 1894, EBDA*. See also *WD*, 1897, p. 26.

142. The parliamentary debates over the anticonfessional laws are filled with references to Joseph II, illustrating the Liberal party's self-understanding in terms of Joseph's administra-

tive statism. Richard Charmatz, *Oesterreichs innere Geschichte* (2 vols., Leipzig, 1909), 1:83–84.

143. *CB*, 1892, pp. 214–15.

144. *CB*, 1888, p. 239.

145. *CB*, 1894, p. 206; 1890, p. 597.

146. See the complaints in *TPQS* 37 (1884): 955ff.

147. For teacher education, see Ludwig Battista, "Die pädagogische Entwicklung des Pflichtschulwesens und der Lehrerbildung von 1848–1898," in *100 Jahre Unterrichts Ministerium, 1848–1898. Festschrift des Bundesministeriums für Unterricht* (Vienna, 1948), pp. 149–51; Rudolf Gönner, *Die österreichische Lehrerbildung von der Normalschule bis zur Pädagogischen Akademie* (Vienna, 1967). The intensity of anticlericalism among teachers in the 1870s and early 1880s may be seen in the national congresses they held to discuss their professional interests. Much of the early "professionalism" rhetoric of the teachers was curiously dependent upon the Church for its logic and substance. The teachers styled themselves as independent educated professionals precisely because they saw their historic role as the "conquerors" of the clerical "fiend." Professionalism was defined by negativistic criteria. See *Protokolle des VII. allgemeinen österreichischen Lehrertages* (Vienna, 1879).

148. In 1887 a Catholic School Association was founded in Vienna, which soon spread throughout Austria. It was well financed and well supported by most of the episcopate and lower clergy, although in Vienna it became an ancillary tool of the Christian Socials after the early 1890s (a fact which some Clerical conservatives found disturbing—see Albert Weiss's comments to Cardinal Gruscha in his letter, 3 April 1894, *GN*). See also Bloch, *My Reminiscences*, p. 168, and *WD*, 1887, pp. 129–31, 139–42, 199. The association established a teacher training institute *(Seminar)* in Vienna in 1888 to provide an alternative to the government's training colleges. By 1905 the Catholic institute, together with the institute run by the provincial government of Lower Austria (controlled by Albert Gessmann), produced the majority of new public-school teachers for Vienna and Lower Austria each year.

149. *FPB*, 1889, pp. 49ff., 234, 238ff.

150. *CB*, 1888, pp. 637–40.

151. *FPB*, 1889, p. 104; *PJ*, 1889, p. 643.

152. *CB*, 1889, pp. 41–44, 117–19, 143, 597. For an extreme clerical statement, see Franz Stauracz, *Der Schlachtengewinner Dittes und sein Generalstab, oder. Ein Jammerbild österreichischer Schulzustände* (Vienna, 1889).

153. *CB*, 1886, p. 446, also, 544–46; 1887, p. 690.

154. *PV* 4:174–75. Also, *CB*, 1890, pp. 635–36. The nationalism prevalent in the ranks of the primary-school teachers was less sectarian and virulent than that found among the gymnasial teachers and younger state officials, by and large, since the teachers were not indoctrinated with Schönerianism at the university as the latter groups were. The teacher training institutes discouraged, in the Liberal and in the Christian Social eras, student groups devoted to pan-Germanism. To the extent that the schoolteachers were "nationalistic," this was a more diluted, secular concept which largely meant that they were anticlerical but that they also wanted a more respectable and more politically acceptable way of sustaining their anticlericalism under the Christian Socials. There was a small core group of Schönerer partisans, but most eventually conformed to the views of the mother Christian Social party after 1898, as did their nominal spokesman in the party elite, Leopold Tomola. For the shift in teacher political views away from the Liberal party to the Christian Socials, see chap. 6. None of the teachers felt comfortable with their new priestly allies after 1897, but class considerations held most in the coalition.

155. For the spread of socialism among the *Unterlehrer*, see chap. 6 and the *Stenographisches Protokoll der Versammlung vom 7. Jänner 1897 des Central Vereins der Wiener Lehrerschaft* (Vienna, 1897); J12 ad 238, Nr. 436/1897, *NÖLA*.

156. *CB*, 1893, pp. 341–42.

157. *CB*, 1894, pp. 11–15.

158. *CB*, 1890, pp. 3, 531–32.

159. *CB*, 1886, pp. 444–46; 1888, pp. 137–38. The *CB* was confiscated on a number of occasions.

160. Scheicher confirmed the importance of Schönerer for many clerics in stimulating an interest in antisemitism. *EE* 4:167–72. Sebastian Brunner was also an important influence on the antisemitism of priests like Scheicher. See Erika Weinzierl-Fischer, "On the Pathogenesis of the Anti-Semitism of Sebastian Brunner," *Yad Vashem Studies* 10 (1974): 217–39.

161. See Stanislav Andreski, *The Uses of Comparative Sociology* (Berkeley and Los Angeles, 1965), p. 295.

162. Hans Schmitz, "Aus P. Abels Erinnerungen an die christlichsozialen Frühzeit," *VW* 14 (1923): 342–43. On Abel, see Ernst Karl Winter, "Abel," in *Staatslexikon* (5 vols., Freiburg i. B., 1926), 1:1; *Die Fackel*, Nr. 22, 1899, pp. 10–20.

163. For Deckert, see J. W. Boyer, "Catholic Priests in Lower Austria: Anti-Liberalism, Occupational Anxiety, and Radical Political Action in Late Nineteenth Century Vienna," *PAPS* 118 (1974): 337ff. Most of Deckert's pamphlets were first published in his journal, the *Sendboten des heiligen Joseph*.

164. See Joseph Deckert, *Türkennoth und Judenherrschaft* (Vienna, 1894), pp. 12–15, esp. p. 15.

165. Ibid., pp. 15–19. Also, idem, *Kann ein Katholik Antisemite Sein?* (Dresden, 1893), pp. 3–4.

166. Deckert, *Türkennoth*, pp. 19–24; *Kann ein Katholik*, p. 40.

167. For the history of the Deckert trial of Sept. 1893, see Bloch, *My Reminiscences*, pp. 361–540, and the articles in *ÖW*, 12 May 1893, pp. 355–63; 19 May 1893, pp. 375–79; 26 May 1893, pp. 395–98; 2 June 1893, pp. 415–19. The 1893 trial recalled another such event in Vienna ten years earlier, when Rabbi Joseph Bloch had vindicated himself against August Rohling, the author of the scurrilous *Der Talmudjude*.

168. *CB*, 1886, pp. 286–87; 1887, pp. 3–5.

169. *CB*, 1894, p. 12; 1892, pp. 434, 439–40.

170. *CB*, 1886, pp. 287, 735.

171. On the Ehrhard affair, see Alois Dempf, *Albert Ehrhard* (Kolmar, 1946); Norbert Trippen, *Theologie und Lehramt im Konflikt* (Freiburg i. B., 1977), pp. 110–84; Oskar Schroeder, *Aufbruch und Missverständnis. Zur Geschichte der reformkatholischen Bewegung* (Graz and Vienna, 1969), pp. 393–401; and Boyer, "Conservatism and Modernism." Cardinal Gruscha, Joseph Scheicher's nemesis, was behind the *fronde* against Ehrhard. See Gruscha to Johann Rössler, 27 Nov. 1902, and Georg Kopp to Gruscha, 17 Jan. 1903, *GN*.

172. For nineteenth-century descriptions of the specific roles attributed to the role-set of the Catholic priest, see Wolfgang Dannerbauer, *Praktisches Geschäftsbuch für den Curat-Clerus Oesterreichs* (Vienna, 1896).

173. "Man darf im Priesterstande nicht die Grundsätze der Bürokratie zur Anwendung bringen... Es hängt das mit der Verstaatlichung unseres Kirchentums zusammen." *CB*, 1889, p. 723.

174. *CB*, 1891, p. 755.

175. *CB*, 1891, p. 310; 1896, pp. 1–3; 1888, pp. 522–23.

176. Joseph Scheicher, *Der Clerus und die soziale Frage* (Innsbruck, 1884), esp. p. 12.

177. *CB*, 1888, p. 523; 1889, pp. 513–15; 1894, pp. 13–14.

178. *EE* 4:47; idem, "Kirchliche Zeitläufe," *TPQS* 38 (1885): 687; Prammer, *Konservative Politik*, pp. 140–46.

179. *CB*, 1890, p. 2.

180. *CB*, 1890, p. 629; 1891, p. 310.

181. *CB*, 1888, pp. 3–4.

182. *RP*, 24 Oct. 1894, p. 5.

183. See J6 ad 7723/1895 (Nr. 8096 and 8396) and B2 ad 7831/1895, *NÖLA*. For a competent, interesting survey of the clergy in the Catholic wing of the movement up to 1907, which appeared too late for the present chapter, but which largely (with a few minor points of debate) confirms the argument in my 1974 article on the clergy, see the dissertation by Gavin Lewis, *Kirche und Partei im politischen Katholizismus* (Salzburg, 1977). My own views on the relationship of the party to the episcopate and the clergy for the period 1897–1920, as well as the role of *Los von Rom* and the conflict with the Socialist teachers' organizations in the urban and national policy considerations of the Christian Social elite, will be considered in detail in the second volume of the present history. For the involvement of Joseph Scheicher and Franz Schindler in the Austrian modernism crisis, the *Clerustag*, and the Ehrhard affair, see Boyer, "Conservatism and Modernism."

184. On Piffl, see Erika Weinzierl-Fischer, "Friedrich Gustav Piffl," *NÖB* 9 (1956): 175–87; for his private journal, see the "Personal Diary of Gustav Piffl, 1894–1901," entry of 27 Oct. 1894, *EBDA*. For a similar statement, see Karl Hilgenreiner, "Lebenserinnerungen," *KK* 32 (1938): 160, cited in Schmid-Egger, *Klerus und Politik*, p. 69. Piffl also noted his concern that Lueger made little effort to even play the role of being a genuine Catholic. Piffl for one was under no illusions about the seriousness or depth of Lueger's "Catholicism," realizing that Lueger's lifework in politics was designed to achieve party political hegemony for himself and the secular side of his movement, not for the Church or the clergy.

185. *ÖV*, 21 Sept. 1890, p. 2. See also Josef Dittrich's defensive propaganda when he ran for the Reichsrat from the Leopoldstadt in 1897: *Das Echo*, 20 Mar. 1897, p. 1.

186. From the confidential transcripts of the bishops' assemblies and Executive Committee meetings, it is clear that the issue of the hierarchy's personal and professional authority over their clerics was the most critical problem in creating hostility to the Christian Socials. The bishops were aware of wider social and economic controversies, and they certainly did not enjoy being subject to public insults from antisemitic hawkers like Ernst Schneider, but the radicalism of the clergy itself challenged their professional status in authority relations, and as good "Josephists" (in their internal relationships with their clergy), they worried first about their own bureaucratic hegemony and only then about the wider concerns of civil society. The bishops disliked the *vages Christentum* which was undermining their official authority. See *Protokoll der bischöflichen Versammlung...1894*, pp. 96–98. Catholic editors had to be loyal to their bishops. Cardinal Schönborn admitted openly at the 1894 Executive Committee meeting that he liked *Vaterland* because it stressed the "authority principle." *Protokoll der Conferenz des bischöflichen Comités vom 29. bis zum 31. März*, p. 8. The episcopate was equally suspicious of the new cult of quasi-political pilgrimages, fearing *Missbräuche* in the relations of authority. *Protokoll der bischöflichen Versammlung...1897*, pp. 11–15, 63–64. In contrast, the party's social and economic policies received very little attention, aside from a rather resentful grumbling in Jan. 1896 that the episcopate disliked the *Gebahren* of the Christian Socials. The most specific comments made at the conferences in reference to the social question were a series of harsh evaluations of the Social Democrats and the need to bolster the Mittelstand. By 1897 the bishops were already moving to a position where logically they had to tolerate Lueger and the Christian Socials, since Lueger was the best guarantee the Church had against the extraordinary anticlericalism of the Socialists. See especially *Protokoll der bischöflichen Versammlung...1897*, pp. 6–7. For a similar view, see Albert M. Weiss, *Lebensweg und Lebenswerk* (Freiburg i. B., 1925), p. 413.

187. *CB*, 1887, p. 35; 1888, pp. 67, 675; 1889, p. 43; 1891, pp. 310–11, 626, 754–55; 1893, pp. 305–9, 341–43, 581–84.

188. *PV* 5:6.

189. *WD*, 1891, pp. 37–41.

190. The transcripts of the episcopal assemblies between 1891 and 1895 contain few references to the Christian Socials, aside from affirmations of loyalty to *Vaterland* under its new, post-Vogelsang editorship. Most bishops were probably waiting for Cardinal Gruscha to act before proposing a collective response.

191. *WD*, 1892, p. 97; 1893, p. 48.

192. On Gruscha, see Otto Posch, *Anton Gruscha und der österreichische Katholizismus, 1820–1911* (diss., University of Vienna, 1947); and Ferdinand Bischof, *Kardinal Gruscha und die soziale Frage* (diss., University of Vienna, 1959). Also, Weiss, *Lebensweg*, pp. 370–92; Kielmansegg, *Kaiserhaus*, pp. 380, 413; and Johann Bruckner, *Der Arbeiterapostel von Wien P. Anton Maria Schwartz* (Vienna, 1935), pp. 65–66. Weiss noted to Bishop Aichner in 1895 that Gruscha was incapable of managing the Viennese situation and reported that he had urged the Cardinal to take on a coadjutor bishop for the archdiocese to assist him. Gruscha refused to do so. Weiss to Aichner, 16 Jan. 1895, in Norbert Miko, ed., "Zur Mission des Kardinals Schönborn, des Bischofs Bauer, und des Pater Albert Maria Weiss OP im Jahre 1895," *RHM* 5 (1961/62).

193. Aside from the transfer of Rudolf Eichhorn to a rural parish in Lower Austria, which seems to have been done with Eichhorn's agreement, there were few explicit disciplinary actions taken against individual Viennese clerics. Several clerical activists even obtained promotions to pastor in the mid-1890s, such as Adam Latschka in Alsergrund.

194. See chap. 6. Agliardi told Eulenburg that Schönborn's mission was doomed because of the publicity generated about it in the Liberal-controlled Viennese press. Rome could hardly give the *NFP* the satisfaction of condemning Lueger. *PAAA*, Öst. 90/Bd. 3, A6237, 8 June 1895.

195. The best example of this kind of secular, semipolitical synodalism was the "Social Course" which Franz Schindler and Albert Gessmann organized for the lower clergy in Vienna in Aug. 1894, where hundreds of clerics participated in sessions designed to assist them in applied social theory and in practical political organization. See Franz M. Schindler, ed., *Soziale Vorträge, gehalten bei dem Wiener socialen Vortrags-Curse 1894* (Vienna, 1895); *AZ*, 14 Aug. 1894, p. 1. Gessmann urged the clerics to adopt organizational procedures which would surpass those of the Socialists, implying the weakness and debility of extant Catholic labor organizations such as the various *Gesellenvereine*.

196. René Rémond, *Les deux congrès ecclésiastiques de Reims et de Bourges, 1896–1900* (Paris, 1964); Adrien Dansette, *Religious History of Modern France* (2 vols., New York, 1961), 2:112–37; Emil Ritter, *Die katholisch-soziale Bewegung Deutschlands im neunzehnten Jahrhundert* (Cologne, 1954); August Pieper, *Volksbildungsbestrebungen. Ihre Noth und ihr Mittel* (Munich and Gladbach, 1899); Giampiero Cappelli, *Romolo Murri: Contributo per una biografia* (Rome, 1965); Francesco Cecchini, *Murri e il murrismo* (Urbino, 1973); Sergio Zoppi, *Romolo Murri e la prima Democrazia cristiana* (Florence, 1968). In general, see the important new study by Emile Poulat, *Catholicisme, démocratie, et socialisme* (Paris, 1977).

197. For the *Jednota*, see Ludwik Němec, "The Czech Jednota, the Avant-Garde of Modern Clerical Progressivism and Unionism," *PAPS* 112 (1968): 74–100; Schmid-Egger, *Klerus und Politik*, pp. 32–33, 40–49. The *Jednota*'s newspaper, the *Vestnik* (1900–), was modeled on the *CB*. Many of the *Jednota* priests attended Scheicher's *Clerustag* in 1901, a year before the group was established.

198. Erich Kielmansegg paid careful attention to the radicalization of the clergy, as did the police. But without the cooperation of the archdiocesan authorities, there was little they could do to curb the clergy's political agitation. See J6 ad 7723/1895 (Nr. 8096 and 8396); B2 ad 7831/1895, *NÖLA*.

199. *PAAA*, Öst.75/Bd. 5, A8131, 6 Sept. 1894.

200. Sauer, *Die politischen Aspekte,* pp. 39–40 (on the appointment of Bishop Rössler in 1894); *PAAA*, A8131, 6 Sept. 1894 (on the appointment of Archbishop Puzyna in 1894).

201. Scheicher openly admitted his debt to Vogelsang: "When I joined the Christian Social camp, the social program—I might even say the social system—of Vogelsang guided me." *EE* 4:80. For Schindler's appreciation of Vogelsang, see Franz M. Schindler, "Karl Freiherr von Vogelsang," *MCSR* 13 (1891): 1–8.

202. On Vogelsang, see Wiard v Klopp, *Leben und Wirken des Sozialpolitikers Karl Freiherr von Vogelsang* (Vienna, 1930); Johann Christoph Allmayer Beck, *Vogelsang* (Vienna, 1952); Hans Rizzi, "Karl von Vogelsang," *NÖB* 2 (1925): 186–95; Marie Freiin von Vogelsang, "Aus dem Leben des Sozialpolitikers Karl von Vogelsang," *DNR* 7 (1924): 43–46, 64–66; Josef Schwalber, *Vogelsang und die moderne christlich-soziale Politik* (Munich, 1927); Ernst Karl Winter, "Die beiden Schulen des mitteleuropäischen Katholizismus (Karl von Vogelsang und Heinrich Pesch, S.J.)," *NO* 3 (1927): 121–26; August M. Knoll, "Karl von Vogelsang und der Ständegedanke," in *Die soziale Frage und der Katholizismus. Festschrift zum 40. jährigen Jubiläum der Enzyklika "Rerum Novarum"* (Paderborn, 1931), pp. 64–85; and Reinhold Knoll, *Zur Tradition der Christlich-Sozialen Partei* (Vienna, 1975), which contains a useful section on Vogelsang. For Catholic social thought in the nineteenth century, see August Knoll, *Der soziale Gedanke im modernen Katholizismus* (Vienna, 1932); Theodor Brauer, "Der deutsche Katholizismus und die soziale Entwicklung des kapitalistischen Zeitalters," *ARWP* 24 (1930–31): 209–54; Clemens Bauer, "Wandlungen der sozialpolitischen Ideenwelt im deutschen Katholizismus des 19. Jahrhunderts," in *Die soziale Frage und der Katholizismus,* pp. 11–46.

203. For the cultural values of the pre-1848 German aristocracy, see Robert Berdahl, "Prussian Aristocracy and Conservative Ideology: A Methodological Examination," *Social Science Information* 15 (1976): 583–89.

204. Klopp, *Leben,* pp. 4–11; Marie von Vogelsang, "Aus dem Leben," p. 44.

205. Klopp, *Leben,* p. 16.

206. Marie von Vogelsang, "Aus dem Leben," p. 44.

207. Vogelsang was merely one of a number of distinguished converts to Catholicism in this period (Gustav Blome, Emil v Bülow, Onno Klopp, etc.), for all of whom Catholicism after 1848 seemed to offer a more viable, historically rooted religious culture to defend against unwarranted social change.

208. Klopp, *Leben,* pp. 229–30.

209. "I took it upon myself to create at least an external unity among the feuding Catholic factions. . . . I chose for that purpose the idea of social reform, which would unite all that was conservative and bring disunity to the enemy." Cited in Beck, *Vogelsang,* p. 63.

210. For a favorable response of conservative Protestant Germans to Vogelsang's ideas, see *MCSR* 5 (1883): 410.

211. See the collection of Blome's letters to Vogelsang in "Briefe des Grafen Gustav Blome an den Freiherrn Karl v Vogelsang," *JLG,* 1928; and Gertrude Hartel, *Graf Gustav Blome* (diss., University of Vienna, 1952).

212. On Belcredi's politics, see Rudolf Meyer, *Hundert Jahre conservativer Politik,* pp. 305–36. On Liechtenstein, see chap. 2. On Pergen, see Erika Weinzierl-Fischer, "Aus den Anfängen der christlichsozialen Bewegung in Österreich. Nach der Korrespondenz des

Grafen Anton Pergen," *MÖSA* 14 (1969): 464–86. Vogelsang also befriended several Dominican priests in Vienna, whose political views differed from his but who shared his radical views on usury. See Weiss, *Lebensweg*, p. 357; Andreas Walz, *Andreas Kardinal Frühwirth* (Vienna, 1950), pp. 106–8.

213. Erika Weinzierl-Fischer, "Aus den Anfängen der 'Österreichischen Monatsschrift für Gesellschaftswissenschaft und christliche Sozialreform,'" in *Im Dienst der Sozialreform. Festschrift für Karl Kummer* (Vienna, 1965), pp. 51–61; Klopp, *Leben*, pp. 147–54; Beck, *Vogelsang*, pp. 65–73. For the first two years, the journal appeared anonymously. From 1881, Vogelsang was identified as its editor.

214. Wiard v Klopp, ed., *Die socialen Lehren des Freiherrn Karl von Vogelsang* (St. Pölten, 1894), pp. 488–92; *MCSR* 3 (1881): 284; 5 (1883): 40–41.

215. See Rudolf Kuppe, *Pfarrer Eichhorn zur Arbeiterfrage* (Vienna, 1925), pp. 6ff.

216. Association with Schneider forced Vogelsang to clarify his own position on antisemitism. Vogelsang's antisemitism was both nonracial and nonviolent. He used the Jew mainly as a symbol for the "materialism" to which Christians so easily succumbed. He rejected, however, special legislation against the Jews or any form of persecution. Klopp, *Leben*, pp. 121, 158; *MCSR* 3 (1881): 316; 2 (1880): 311; 4 (1882): 68–69; *V*, 16 May 1881, 1; Klopp, ed., *Die socialen Lehren*, pp. 187–94.

217. When Vogelsang began to meet regularly with Lueger, Gessmann, and Scheicher in 1888 in Hietzing, both Lueger and Gessmann arrived and departed incognito for fear of being tagged "clericals." For a movement which ultimately valued publicity and image manipulation so highly, the Christian Socials began their collective existence in the most hesitant of ways—sneaking to meetings under the cover of darkness hardly became Karl Lueger's reputation, but such covert behavior was inevitable until ways could be found to defuse the anticlericalism of the voters. See Marie von Vogelsang, "Aus dem Leben," p. 65; *CB*, 1904, pp. 733–36.

218. See Vogelsang's comment that most peasants and artisan masters acted like better aristocrats than did the nobility. *MCSR* 8 (1886): 204. His later correspondence suggests despondency over the aristocracy's passivity and selfishness. Klopp, *Leben*, pp. 294–96.

219. Vogelsang defended the lack of religious uniformity in the Christian Social alliance, recognizing the agnosticism of many of its leaders: "One must be satisfied now if they call themselves Christian. In the face of the word Catholic they would be very hesitant." Weiss, *Lebensweg*, p. 382.

220. Liechtenstein to Vogelsang, 25 Sept. 1888, *VN*, Mappe 15, Nr. 6.

221. Klopp, *Leben*, pp. 192, 239, 278–79, 291–92. Belcredi complained to Vogelsang as early as 1884 that among the conservative majority on the *Gewerbe* committee in parliament he found little sympathy for additional worker legislation ("auch im Gewerbeausschuss lassen mich Zerfahrenheit und Unverstand der Majorität immer mehr am Erfolge zweifeln." Ibid., p. 279. See also Hans Rosenberg, *Grosse Depression und Bismarckzeit* (Berlin, 1967), pp. 248–52.

222. Schneider to Vogelsang, undated, 1886, *VN*, Mappe 12, Nr. 127.

223. See, for example, *V*, 11 Jan. 1890, p. 1; 26 Oct. 1890, p. 1.

224. See, for background, Paul Siebertz, *Karl Fürst zu Löwenstein. Ein Bild seines Lebens und Wirkens* (Munich, 1924), pp. 214ff.; August Knoll, *Der soziale Gedanke*, pp. 132–43; Friedrich Novotny, *Die Vorarbeiter der Enzyklika Rerum Novarum* (diss., University of Vienna, 1954).

225. For the Haid theses and Vogelsang's commentary on them, see *MCSR* 5 (1883): 337–51. See also Weiss, *Lebensweg*, pp. 353–54, and the balanced evaluation in Ritter, *Die katholisch-soziale Bewegung*, pp. 81–87.

226. See Karl Bachem, *Vorgeschichte, Geschichte, und Politik der deutschen Zentrumspartei,* 4:125–31. Even the *Germania* in Berlin, otherwise sympathetic to social conservatism, attacked Vogelsang, an event which Karl Löwenstein realized did not bode well for the committee. See his "An die geehrten Mitglieder des Comité der katholischen Sozialpolitiker," 19 Oct. 1883, *VN,* Mappe 6, Nr. 47.

227. Klopp, *Leben,* pp. 235–39; August Knoll, *Der soziale Gedanke,* pp. 139–43; *MCSR* 5 (1883): 410–25. For criticism of Vogelsang by German Catholics and theologians, see *MCSR* 5 (1883): 543–59; A. Lehmkuhl, "Zur Arbeiterfrage," *SML* 25 (1883): 225–49; idem, "Zur Verständigung in der socialen Frage," ibid. 25 (1883): 457–67.

228. See Franz M. Schindler, "Neun Jahre Entenabende," *VW* 14 (1923): 304–10, esp. 308. The membership lists of the *Ente,* which show a gradual decline in the numbers of conservatives and higher clericals attending after 1890, are located in the *Handschriftensammlung* of the *Wiener Stadtbibliothek.* The lists of lecture topics for the meetings are in the Schindler Papers, *FN.*

229. Wiard v Klopp, "Eine sozialpolitische Gesellschaft vor dreissig Jahren in der 'Goldenen Ente,' " *DNR* 9 (1926): 1183–86.

230. Klopp, *Leben,* p. 307; idem, "Eine sozialpolitische Gesellschaft," p. 1185; on Orel, see Dorit Weinberger, *Die christliche Sozialreform Anton Orels* (diss., University of Vienna, 1966).

231. Franz Sommeregger, "Die Wege und Ziele der österreichischen Agrarpolitik seit der Grundentlastung," in *Die Soziale Woche. Bericht über den vom 'Katholischen Volksbund für Österreich' unter dem Namen 'Sociale Woche' veranstalteten sozialwissenschaftlichen Kursus vom 3. bis 10. September 1911* (Vienna, 1911), pp. 117–19.

232. See Alfred Diamant, *Austrian Catholics and the First Republic* (Princeton, 1960), pp. 48, 50, 63–64.

233. For discussions of this mentality, see Heinrich A. Winkler, "Der rückversicherte Mittelstand: Die Interessenverbände von Handwerk und Kleinhandel im deutschen Kaiserreich," in Walter Rüegg and Otto Neuloh, eds., *Zur soziologischen Theorie und Analyse des 19. Jahrhunderts* (Göttingen, 1971), pp. 163–79; Rosenberg, *Grosse Depression,* passim.

234. *MCSR* 1 (1879): 71–75, 121–32.

235. Karl v Vogelsang, *Zins und Wucher* (Vienna, 1884), pp. 3, 22.

236. Vogelsang's essays were collected in 1886 as the *Gesammelte Aufsätze* (Augsburg, 1886). The other principal sections of his work are two editions edited by Wiard v Klopp, *Die socialen Lehren des Freiherrn Karl von Vogelsang* (St. Pölten, 1894; 2d ed., Vienna, 1938). Since Klopp's selections were very arbitrary and frequently distorting, however, it is preferable to use the original texts as they appeared in the *MCSR.*

237. See Helge Pross, "Bürgerlich-konservative Kritik an der kapitalistischen Gesellschaft. Zur Theorie Lorenz von Steins," *KZSS* 18 (1966): 137. Vogelsang was influenced by Stein's theory of a social kingship, but never pursued the idea systematically. Vogelsang's social king would have been a categorical attack on modern bourgeois society, not, as it was for Stein, a mode of social adjustment and modification.

238. *MCSR* 2 (1880): 1–4.

239. *Gesammelte Aufsätze,* p. 421; *MCSR* 6 (1884): 402–6.

240. The literature on the usury question by conservative European intellectuals in the second half of the nineteenth century is immense. See, for example, Freiherr v Mirbach-Sorquitten, *Zur Währungs- und Wucherfrage* (Berlin, 1880); M. Klonkavius, *Die Wucherfrage* (Amberg, 1878); Ernst Barre, *Der ländliche Wucher. Ein Beitrag zur Wucherfrage* (Berlin, 1890). The *Verein für Sozialpolitik* conducted hearings on the agrarian usury question in 1888.

241. *MCSR* 5 (1883): 342–43.

242. See John T. Noonan, *The Scholastic Analysis of Usury* (Cambridge, Mass., 1957), pp. 401–2.

243. In the discussions preceding the Second Catholic Congress (1889), Lueger ordered any reference to usury eliminated from the program. Klopp, "Eine sozialpolitische Gesellschaft," p. 1185. In 1887 Pattai criticized Vogelsang's views on this question as well. *MCSR* 9 (1887): 63–66.

244. *MCSR* 6 (1884): 134–35; 5 (1883): 342; Wiard v Klopp, "Vogelsangs Lehre über Zins und Wucher," *NO* 4 (1928): 106.

245. *MCSR* 8 (1886): 197–206; 12 (1890): 57–62, 288–308; 6 (1884): 607–12, 636ff.

246. See Thienen-Adlerflycht, *Graf Leo Thun*, pp. 104–38, 170.

247. *MCSR* 12 (1890): 287, 304; 4 (1882): 281–91.

248. The most problematic aspect of Vogelsang's thought was his view of the state. He never achieved a satisfactory balance between the strong state and a social and political structure which would surpass governmental centralization. The former Lutheran with Josephist proclivities fought with the former *Rittergutsbesitzer* steeped in Romantic corporatism—no topic was more appropriate than the idea of the state to bring out all of the internal antinomies in Vogelsang's thought. If he failed to resolve the dilemma of state power versus corporate right, it was not for want of effort, but because the intensely autobiographical nature of Vogelsang's work did not permit an easy, unilinear solution. His view of the state was partially dependent upon Adam Müller's superimposition of the state on civil society. But the state for Vogelsang was less a summation of society (as it was for Müller) and more a subsidiary mechanism which, Vogelsang insisted, he disliked, but which he was forced to accept. The ultimate goal of the state was to create a new corporate society and thus surpass the need for itself, not unlike the attempt of Marx to insert the state into the evolutionary course of European history and then remove it when the "end days" of the classless society came about.

Diamant (*Austrian Catholics*, p. 50) charged that Vogelsang merely "gave lip service to the idea of social pluralism" and was "more interested in establishing the claims of the state over all sectors of society." This view minimizes, however, the obvious tension in Vogelsang's work between the state and corporate systems of authority.

249. See Schindler's comments at the *Arbeitsbeirat* in 1899 in *Sitzungs-Protokolle des ständigen Arbeitsbeirathes,* 5. Sitzung, 4 Nov. 1899, pp. 313–20. For Schindler's corporatism, see his *L'organisation corporative des professions libérales selon des États* (Fribourg, 1890); idem, *Die soziale Frage der Gegenwart* (Vienna, 1905); idem, "Organisation der Volksstände," *Austria Nova* 2 (1916): 227–34. For his opposition to interest prohibitions, see "Das Kapitalzinsproblem," *Die Kultur* 4 (1902): 595–610.

250. *MCSR* 2 (1880): 32; 5 (1883): 66; 6 (1884): 133, 135; 10 (1888): 79, 287; 11 (1889): 598; 12 (1890): 303; *V,* 20 Sept. 1889, p. 1; 20 June 1888, p. 1.

251. See Adler's comments in *AZ,* 14 Nov. 1890, p. 4. Also, Victor Adler, *Aufsätze, Reden, und Briefe* (11 vols., Vienna, 1922–29), 8:353ff.; *MCSR* 11 (1889): 353–58.

252. It would be naive to assume that some manifest and even more latent antisemitism was not present in the ranks and leadership of the Center party, but the profound difference between the Center and the Austrian Christian Socials hinged in part on the absence within the Center of a definable locus of antisemitism as a public policy issue. Within the more oligarchical political franchise systems of German cities and provincial areas, antisemitism as an electoral strategy would have made little sense to the Center. On the national level, with universal suffrage, the Center was immediately set into competition with the Social Democrats and the Left Liberals, against whom antisemitism was never an effective political issue, even in Vienna. Also, German Jewish communities were qualitatively different from the burgeoning, impoverished Viennese Jewish *Gemeinde,* and this may have played a role

as well. The most important reason for the Center's avoidance of this issue was, however, the fact that it had religion itself as a force for social cohesion and control and did not need to use Jew hatred. This was a strategic, not an ethical, decision. For the issue of antisemitism among German Catholics, see Hermann Greive, "Die gesellschaftliche Bedeutung der christlich-jüdischen Differenz. Zur Situation im deutschen Katholizismus," in Mosse, ed., *Juden im Wilhelminischen Deutschland*, pp. 349–88; Werner Jochmann, "Struktur und Funktion des deutschen Antisemitismus," in ibid., pp. 398–99, 435, 456.

    253. Ernst Karl Winter, "Abel," p. 1.

Chapter 4

    1. The literature on Lueger is enormous. For basic biographical data, see Rudolf Kuppe, *Karl Lueger und seine Zeit* (Vienna, 1933); Kurt Skalnik, *Dr. Karl Lueger* (Vienna, 1954); Heinrich Schnee, *Karl Lueger* (Berlin, 1960); idem, "Die politische Entwicklung des Wiener Bürgermeisters Dr. Karl Lueger," *Historisches Jahrbuch*, vol. 76 (1956); Benno Ninkov, *Die politischen Anfänge Dr. Karl Luegers im Lichte der Wiener Presse* (diss., University of Vienna, 1946); Gertrud Stöger, *Die politischen Anfänge Luegers* (diss., University of Vienna, 1941); Gertrud Schmitz, *Die Entwicklungsgeschichte der christlichen Volksbewegung in Österreich* (diss., University of Vienna, 1938); Margot Kunze, *Dr. Karl Lueger als Gemeinderat von 1875–1896* (diss., University of Vienna, 1968); Carl Schorske, "Politics in a New Key: An Austrian Triptych," *JMH*, vol 39 (1967). Literature written by Christian Social or antisemitic partisans includes: Richard Kralik, *Karl Lueger und der christliche Sozialismus* (Vienna, 1923); Franz Stauracz, *Dr. Karl Lueger. Zehn Jahre Bürgermeister* (Vienna, 1907); idem, *Die Entwicklung der christlich-sozialen Partei und deren Hausfeinde* (Vienna, 1901); Marianne Beskiba, *Aus meinen Erinnerungen an Dr. Karl Lueger* (Vienna, 1911); Alfred Berger, "Doktor Lueger," *ÖRD*, vol. 23 (1910); Robert Ehrhart, *Im Dienste des alten Österreich* (Vienna, 1958); Friedrich Funder, *Vom Gestern ins Heute* (3d ed., Vienna, 1971); and the articles in the *RP*, 23 Oct. 1904 and 10 Mar. 1910. For contemporary comments or reflections on Lueger, see the autobiographies or diaries by Stefan Zweig, Karl Renner, Franz Brandl, Rudolf Sieghart, Ernst v Plener, Eduard Suess, Arthur Schnitzler, Erich Kielmansegg, Michael Hainisch, Joseph Bloch, Sigmund Mayer, Alexander Spitzmüller, Eduard Leisching, and Josef Redlich (for publication data, see the bibliography). For the pan-German viewpoint, see Pichl's multivolume biography of Schönerer. See also Karl Hron, *Wiens antisemitische Bewegung*. Social Democratic commentaries on Lueger may be found in the daily commentaries in *AZ* from 1896 to 1910 and in the party's theoretical journal, *Kampf,* after 1907.

    2. See Harold Lasswell, *Power and Personality* (New York, 1948), p. 47.

    3. Lueger once honored Josef Nikola with words which revealed his own high valuation of personal mobility: "Er ist einer der jenen Wenigen denen es gegönnt war, durch eigene Kraft und Tüchtigkeit sich beinahe auf allen Gebieten des menschlichen Lebens eine Achtung gebietender Stellung zu erringen." *KVZ,* 17 July 1880, p. 3.

    4. Stauracz, *Lueger,* pp. 16–18.

    5. Kuppe, *Lueger,* p. 15. In Dec. 1870, Lueger sided with the Austrian faction among the university students in the debates on the role of Austria in the Franco-Prussian war. See Eduard Leisching, *Ein Leben für Kunst und Volksbildung, 1858–1938* (Vienna, 1978), p. 28. A former student associate of Lueger recalled in 1895 that Lueger disrupted the German National rally of the *Burschenschaft Silesia* in 1871 by calling the German flag a product of "despotic arbitrariness." *NFP,* 18 Apr. 1895 (M), p. 3.

    6. *RP,* 10 Mar. 1910, Beilage, p. 2; Kuppe, *Lueger,* p. 18.

    7. *RP,* 10 Mar. 1910, Beilage, pp. 3–4.

    8. Kuppe, *Lueger,* p. 71; Lasswell, *Power and Personality,* pp. 50–51.

    9. Kielmansegg, *Kaiserhaus,* pp. 384, 389–91, 404, 407.

10. Lueger maintained an extremely close relationship with his mother, vowing at her deathbed never to marry so as to be able to take care of his two sisters who were unmarried spinsters. Lest this be construed to suggest that he suffered from problems of sexual maladjustment, it should be noted that he enjoyed a normal sex life, having a string of mistresses, with some of whom he maintained close emotional relations.

11. Kuppe, *Lueger*, pp. 20ff.

12. For Viennese history in the 1860s and 1870s, see Czeike, *Wien und seine Bürgermeister;* Rudolf Till, *Geschichte der Wiener Stadtverwaltung in den letzten zweihundert Jahren* (Vienna, 1957); Gertrude Hahnkamper, *Der Wiener Gemeinderat zwischen 1861 und 1864* (diss., University of Vienna, 1973); Brigitte Fiala, *Der Wiener Gemeinderat in den Jahren 1879 bis 1883* (diss., University of Vienna, 1975).

13. See Felder, *Lebenserinnerungen*, pp. 282–84; Till, *Geschichte*, pp. 72ff. After 1882 the party changed its name to the *Fortschrittsclub*, reuniting various minor factions along with it.

14. The quality of Liberal delegates to the Council declined over time, as the appeal of serving in the body declined. See Felder, *Lebenserinnerungen*, p. 174; Mayer, *Ein jüdischer Kaufmann*, p. 249; Kielmansegg, *Kaiserhaus*, p. 381.

15. The *Linke* was the club of Josef Kopp, Josef Nikola, Eduard Pichl, and other moderate Liberals. After the rise of Lueger's and Mandl's political radicalism many of these men returned to the main body of the Liberals.

16. In 1874 the *Äusserste Linke* had thirty members, twenty of whom were artisans or merchants, the rest either free professionals or officials. *DEZ*, 2 May 1874, p. 2. For the history of the Democratic movement, see ibid., 3 Jan. 1874, p. 2; 13 June 1874, p. 2.

17. See, for example, the reports of local Liberal associations such as the *Bericht über die Thätigkeit des politischen Vereins "Eintracht" im VIII. Bezirke in den Jahren 1873–1884* (Vienna, 1884) and *Der Verein der Verfassungsfreunde im VII. Bezirke von 1873–1888. Eine Vereins-Chronik* (Vienna, 1888).

18. For the Democratic program, see *MP*, 27 Apr. 1873, pp. 2–3. For Democracy as an heir to Mar. 1848, see *DEZ*, 14 Mar. 1874, p. 1. The local Democrats' anticlericalism was unusually bitter, perhaps in an attempt to outdo the main-line Liberals. See, for example, *KVZ*, 17 Apr. 1872, p. 2 (against the Jesuits).

19. For examples of artisan-journeyman confrontations, which left the well-meaning Democrats bewildered about their course of action, see *MP*, 9 Apr. 1873, pp. 2–3; 20 Apr. 1873, p. 3. See also Klausjürgen Miersch, *Die Arbeiterpresse*, pp. 13–22.

20. See *DEZ*, 3 Jan. 1874, p. 2; *KVZ*, 13 Apr. 1873, pp. 2–3.

21. *MP*, 13 Apr. 1873, pp. 2–3.

22. Felder, *Lebenserinnerungen*, p. 214. On the party's organizational problems, see *MP*, 6 Mar. 1873, p. 2; 12 Mar. 1873, pp. 1–2; *F*, 23 Jan. 1881, pp. 1–3; 19 Mar. 1882, p. 1. For the decline in voter participation and the increase in voter apathy, see *KVZ*, 29 Sept. 1880, p. 2 ("Statistisches über die Wiener Gemeinderaths-Wahlen"), and *Statistik der Wahlen für den Gemeinderath der Reichshaupt- und Residenzstadt Wien in den Jahren 1861 bis 1880* (Vienna, 1880), pp. 12–14.

23. *DEZ*, 29 May 1875, pp. 3–4; *NWT*, 22 Apr. 1875, pp. 2–3.

24. *NWT*, 3 Jan. 1874, p. 3; *NWT*, 22 Apr. 1876, p. 4; (A), p. 2.

25. See the *Gedenkblatt zum vierzigjährigen Bestande des politischen Fortschritts-Vereins 'Eintracht' im 3. Bezirke, 1872–1912* (Vienna, 1912), pp. 1–2.

26. Kuppe, *Lueger*, pp. 100, 190–92.

27. See the commentary on Lueger's behavior in *NWT*, 7 Sept. 1876, p. 3; and Felder, *Lebenserinnerungen*, pp. 152, 215.

28. For Mandl's opposition to Friedrich Dittes in the Landstrasse, see *MP*, 2 Oct. 1873, p. 3; 22 Nov. 1873, p. 3.

29. Felder, *Lebenserinnerungen*, pp. 215, 289.

30. *NWT*, 15 Oct. 1875, p. 2; 29 Oct. 1895, pp. 2–3; 30 Oct. 1875, pp. 3–4.

31. Felder, *Lebenserinnerungen*, pp. 226ff.

32. *MP*, 14 Oct. 1876, pp. 2–3; *F*, 20 May 1877, pp. 1–2.

33. *NWT*, 5 Dec. 1875, p. 3; 10 Dec. 1875, p. 3.

34. *MP*, 9 Dec. 1875, p. 2; *NWT*, 30 Dec. 1875, p. 3.

35. Felder, *Lebenserinnerungen*, pp. 296–97.

36. *NWT*, 6 Sept. 1876, p. 3; Felder, *Lebenserinnerungen*, p. 296; Kuppe, *Lueger*, pp. 36–37.

37. *NWT*, 17 Oct. 1876, p. 3; 21 Oct. 1876, p. 3.

38. *MP*, 5 Mar. 1878, pp. 2–3.

39. Mayer, *Ein jüdischer Kaufmann*, pp. 253–55.

40. For Neurath's work, see Wilhelm Neurath, *Volkswirtschaftliche und Socialphilosophische Essays* (Vienna, 1880).

41. *KVZ*, 6 Feb. 1882, pp. 1–2.

42. *MP*, 4 Mar. 1878, p. 3.

43. See, for example, *F*, 16 Jan. 1881, pp. 2–3; 15 May 1881, pp. 2–3; 28 Aug. 1881, p. 1; 25 Sept. 1881, p. 1.

44. See Mandl's personal account of his early career in *F*, 22 Feb. 1885, pp. 1–6, esp. p. 3; Mayer, *Ein jüdischer Kaufmann*, p. 254.

45. *F*, 23 Jan. 1881, p. 3; Lueger criticized the Gas Company in harsh terms as early as 1878 (*MP*, 14 Nov. 1878, p. 2), but did not demand municipalization. See also Kunze, *Lueger*, pp. 147–49.

46. See Felder, *Lebenserinnerungen*, pp. 224–27; *MP*, 6 Mar. 1875, p. 2. When Julius Hirsch suggested the idea of municipalization of the gas works in 1875, many Democrats opposed the plan, fearing financial unprofitability. *MP*, 13 Mar. 1875, p. 2; 15 May 1875, p. 2. For a review of the history of the gas controversy, see the historical section of the report by Heinrich v Billing in *BSWG*, 1885, pp. 1317–32.

47. Felder, *Lebenserinnerungen*, pp. 175–76, 191–93, 228, 287–89.

48. *MP*, 14 Mar. 1878, p. 2.

49. *NWT*, 17 Mar. 1878, p. 2; *MP*, 12 Apr. 1878, p. 2.

50. *NWT*, 10 Feb. 1878, p. 3.

51. Felder did not resign from the Lower Austrian Landtag, however. He continued to serve as an effective defender of the curial franchise system in the Landtag in the 1880s.

52. On Newald, see Czeike, *Wien und seine Bürgermeister*, pp. 321–28, and Helmut Kretschmer, *Dr. Julius Newald. Bürgermeister von Wien* (diss., University of Vienna, 1971).

53. The first chairman was Johann Schrank. Lueger served as one of the vice-chairmen initially.

54. For Lueger's program, modified in Aug. 1880, see *KVZ*, 12 Sept. 1880, pp. 1–2; *F*, 12 Sept. 1880, pp. 1–2; Kuppe, *Lueger*, pp. 51–52, 56–57.

55. *KVZ*, 26 May 1880, p. 2.

56. *F*, 23 Jan. 1881, pp. 1–3. Lueger fought with Johann Prix in Dec. 1880 over putting tougher demands on the Tramway Company. *KVZ*, 8 Dec. 1880, p. 2.

57. *KVZ*, 6 Mar. 1883, p. 3; *F*, 23 Jan. 1881, pp. 1–3.

58. See the commentary in *KVZ*, 7 Mar. 1880, p. 2.

59. Ibid., 1 Oct. 1880, p. 4.

60. Ibid., 3 July 1881, p. 2; Kuppe, *Lueger*, p. 61. Some Liberals, bitter about Newald's politics, seceded from the *Mittelpartei* to form the *Wiener Club*, led by Johann Prix.

61. The main support for the United Left came from the Third Curia, but it enjoyed considerable resources in the Second Curia as well. For the Council elections, see *NWT*, 11 Mar. 1879, p. 3; 14 Mar. 1879, pp. 2–3; 20 Mar. 1879, pp. 2–3; *KVZ*, 16 Mar. 1880, pp. 1–2; 18 Mar. 1880, p. 2. Following the 1880 elections the *Mittelpartei* was left with a narrow majority, which often slipped away when issues arose on which the Liberals themselves were disunited. In 1880 the United Left employed a central *Wahlcomité* system for its slate, a precedent in anti-Liberal politics.

62. *F*, 23 Jan. 1881, pp. 1–2; Kuppe, *Lueger*, pp. 59–60.

63. For the fire and its consequences in general, see Fiala, *Gemeinderat*, pp. 211ff., and Czeike, *Wien und seine Bürgermeister*, pp. 327ff.

64. *KVZ*, 15 Dec. 1881, p. 3.

65. Ibid., 7 Jan. 1882, pp. 1–2.

66. Ibid., 23 Dec. 1881, pp. 1–2.

67. Ibid., 18 Jan. 1882, p. 2.

68. Ibid., 31 Jan. 1882, p. 2; 2 Feb. 1882, p. 3. Even Mandl's *Fortschritt* wished Newald had adopted a stronger and more aggressive position in defense of himself (22 Jan. 1882, p. 1; 29 Jan. 1882, p. 1).

69. See Kuppe, *Lueger*, pp. 60–61. For characterizations of Lueger's behavior under stress and anger, see Mayer, *Ein jüdischer Kaufmann*, p. 256, and *EE* 4:416.

70. *KVZ*, 6 Feb. 1882, pp. 1–2; *F*, 12 Feb. 1882, pp. 1–2.

71. Kielmansegg, *Kaiserhaus*, pp. 364–65, 374. Also, *F*, 25 Sept. 1881, pp. 1–2.

72. For the history of the construction and finances of the *Stadtbahn*, see Gustav Gerstel, *Der Betrieb der Wiener Stadtbahn* (Vienna, 1898), and Hugo Koestler, "Die Wiener Stadtbahn," in *Geschichte der Eisenbahnen der oesterreichisch-ungarischen Monarchie* (4 vols., Vienna, 1898–1919), 1/2:429–66. For the early political controversy, see *Verwaltungsbericht der Reichshaupt- und Residenzstadt Wien für das Jahr 1883* (Vienna, 1884), pp. 157–63; and *Verwaltungsbericht . . . für das Jahr 1884* (Vienna, 1885), pp. 180–83.

73. *KVZ*, 17 Nov. 1881, p. 2.

74. Von Goldschmidt was the president of the *Allgemeine Österreichische Baugesellschaft* and had been accused on several occasions of illegal, conflict of interest involvements. See *F*, 12 Feb. 1882, pp. 1–2. The Fogerty libel question was merely symptomatic of a culture in which bribery was a rampant and daily political fact, but one which neither the government nor any of the major political parties were prepared to deal with.

75. *KVZ*, 2 Mar. 1882, pp. 1–2; 3 Mar. 1882, p. 3; 2 Apr. 1882, p. 7. Lueger's fine of 100 fl. was remitted by an appellate court.

76. Stöger, *Lueger*, p. 79. The later history of the Fogerty project is notable. Under Lueger's pressure and with the general consensus of the Council, so many restrictions and objections were placed in the way of the Fogerty project that by 1885 the English withdrew from the affair entirely. Eventually the goverment built the *Stadtbahn* with public funds and operated it in Vienna as a state railway. Had the Liberals really wanted the *Stadtbahn* in 1882–83, they could have pushed it through the Council, but many Liberals, themselves property owners in the inner districts, probably shared Lueger's misgivings.

77. *KVZ*, 7 Mar. 1882, pp. 2–3; Kuppe, *Lueger*, pp. 71–72.

78. Ibid., 26 Nov. 1880, p. 3.

79. *F*, 12 Feb. 1882, p. 2.

80. See Pattai's criticism of the establishment of maximum limits on personal wealth in *SP*, X, 1888, p. 9909.

81. Renner, *An der Wende*, p. 233; Bloch, *My Reminiscences*, p. 233.

82. The best source for Lueger's political speeches before 1890 is *V*, thereafter the *DV* and *RP*. The *AZ* is an important corrective to all of the above, since many of the speeches of Christian Social leaders were "edited" by their own papers. Some of the more embarrassing and controversial remarks never found their way into print.

83. *SP*, X, 1887, p. 5766.

84. Bloch, *My Reminiscences*, p. 230.

85. Kielmansegg, *Kaiserhaus*, pp. 366, 382, 385–86.

86. *KVZ*, 8 Apr. 1882, pp. 2–3; 20 Apr. 1882, p. 2.

87. Ibid., 18 April 1882, p. 3; *NWT*, 22 Apr. 1882, p. 3. Even Mandl's newspaper, *Fortschritt*, noted the distaste many voters had for political controversies that seemed to denigrate the city itself.

88. *KVZ*, 6 Mar. 1883, p. 3. For examples of "scandalous" behavior by the Democrats, see *MP*, 12 Mar. 1873, p. 3; *KVZ*, 19 Mar. 1870, p. 3; 30 Mar. 1870, p. 2; *MP*, 15 Nov. 1873, p. 2 (the Democrats as "Petroleure").

89. A good example of this cult of the city as an autonomous entity occurred at the banquet held to celebrate the opening of the new water supply system in 1873. See the speeches in *MP*, 25 Oct. 1873, pp. 2–3.

90. *KVZ*, 13 Mar. 1883, p. 1.

91. See Mandl's historical survey of the Democratic movement in *F*, 22 Feb. 1885, pp. 1–6. On Gessmann, see Edeltrude Binder, *Doktor Albert Gessmann* (diss., University of Vienna, 1950), pp. 12–23, 39.

92. Kunze, *Lueger*, passim, and the *BSWG*, 1882–85.

93. *BSWG*, 1884, pp. 567–68. A number of prominent Liberals voted with Lueger—Ludwig Vogler, Johann Steudel, Karl Vaugoin, Joseph Schlechter, etc. Steudel and Vogler also supported Mandl's city mortgage bank proposal, which was defeated by a very close vote (forty-eight to forty-six). *KVZ*, 1 May 1883, p. 2.

94. In spite of the fact that a Liberal (von Billing) presented a report recommending immediate municipalization in 1885, the *Magistrat* suggested holding off until 1899 to take control of the gas works. See *KVZ*, 31 May 1885, p. 2, and Franz Borschke's critique of von Billing's report in *BSWG*, 1885, pp. 1335–47.

95. For the history of the contract negotiations with the Gas Company, which dated back to Felder's administration, see *BSWG*, 1885, pp. 1317–31, 1348–59, 1717–30.

96. For Liberal financial policy in the 1880s, see Felix Czeike, *Liberale, Christlichsoziale, und Sozialdemokratische Kommunalpolitik (1861–1934)* (Vienna, 1962), pp. 33–48.

97. *NFP*, 5 Mar. 1895 (M), p. 7.

98. See Richard Charmatz, *Adolf Fischhof. Das Lebensbild eines österreichischen Politikers* (Stuttgart, 1910), pp. 377–99; and the Clerical Conservative critique of Fischhof, suggesting Taaffe's secret support in Molisch, *Briefe*, pp. 277–80.

99. For the *Volkspartei*'s program, see Charmatz, *Adolf Fischhof*, pp. 388–89; *KVZ*, 24 May 1882, pp. 1–2.

100. See the attacks on the new party in *ÖV*, 23 July 1882, pp. 1–2, and *NFP*, 18 July 1882 (M), p. 1.

101. *KVZ*, 18 Apr. 1882, p. 3; 20 Apr. 1882, p. 3–4; 7 Nov. 1882, p. 3. Kronawetter resigned his parliamentary seat and challenged the Liberals to run a candidate against him in a new election to determine voter preferences. When the election was held in Nov. 1882, Kronawetter lost by a narrow margin. He regained his seat in the 1885 elections, however, once the new artisan voters had been enfranchised.

102. Bloch, *My Reminiscences*, p. 87.

103. *KVZ*, 16 June 1883, p. 3; *F*, 8 May 1883, pp. 1–2. Lueger defended himself against accusations of clericalism in *MP*, 22 May 1883, pp. 2–3.

104. *F*, 27 July 1883, pp. 1–2. Joseph Porzer, a Catholic leader in Vienna, defended Lueger during the Fogerty trial.

105. Lueger proposed a resolution of the Council calling for the nationalization of the *Nordbahn* in Oct. 1883 and held protest meetings on the issue in Apr. 1884 and Feb. 1885.

106. *ÖV*, 9 March 1884, pp. 4–5; 16 Mar. 1884, pp. 4–5.

107. *SJ*, 1885, p. 38.

108. *MP*, 4 July 1884, p. 3; Stöger, *Lueger*, p. 95.

109. *KVZ*, 2 June 1885, p. 1. The Democrats ran in the Third, Fifth, Seventh, and Eighth Districts; the antisemites ran in the Second and Sixth Districts. The parties won in all but the Second and the Third.

110. Pattai to Vogelsang, 21 Sept. 1885, *VN*, Mappe 21, Nr. 213.

111. For the speech, see *KVZ*, 28 Apr. 1885, p. 3; Kuppe, *Lueger*, pp. 123–26.

112. Kuppe, *Lueger*, p. 128.

113. Kunze, *Lueger*, pp. 89–91. Kunze, who is extremely sympathetic to Lueger, questions why Lueger suddenly stopped fighting for suffrage reform after 1886, having posited beforehand that Lueger was actually interested in additional reforms. The obvious answer is that the original assumption was erroneous. Lueger was totally opposed to universal suffrage on local and regional levels of government.

114. *SJ*, 1885, p. 38. Lueger ran from Margarethen in this election.

115. *SJ*, 1887, p. 54. The upward trend was most significant in the Third Curia, where the majority of new voters were registered. In 1885, 7,183 out of a possible 20,611 voters exercised their votes in the municipal elections, but in 1886 (the first year the new tax level applied to city elections), 15,874 out of a possible 31,994 chose to vote.

116. For a survey of election statistics in the early 1880s, by district and by curia, see Fiala, *Gemeinderat*, pp. 33ff.

117. See the *Bericht über die Thätigkeit des politischen Vereins "Eintracht" im VIII. Bezirke in den Jahren 1873–1884*, pp. 13–14; *Der Verein der Verfassungsfreunde im VII. Bezirke von 1873–1888. Eine Vereins-Chronik*, pp. 2–6.

118. *KVZ*, 4 Mar. 1885, p. 2.

119. *SP*, X, 1886, p. 830.

120. Ibid., pp. 3374–76, 4410–12, 4413, 4415–16.

121. Ibid., p. 4292.

122. Ibid., pp. 831, 2537.

123. Ibid., pp. 2532–37, 2733–35, 2737–38.

124. Ibid., pp. 2662ff.

125. Ibid., pp. 2906–16, 2950–51; Kuppe, *Lueger*, p. 156.

126. *SP*, X, 1886, pp. 3899–3901, also p. 5087; *KVZ*, 19 Oct. 1886, p. 4.

127. Schneider to Vogelsang, 7 June 1884, *VN*, Mappe 12, Nr. 43.

128. *ÖR*, 28 Mar. 1886, pp. 1–2; *WZ*, 30 Mar. 1886, p. 5.

129. Kuppe, *Lueger*, p. 142.

130. *NFP*, 30 Mar. 1886 (M), pp. 6–7. Two-thirds of the members of the "Democratic Left" were master artisans of one variety or another, but none of them was particularly poor or on the borderline of proletarianization. All could afford to serve in the Council without a salary.

131. *KVZ*, 21 Jan. 1886, p. 2.

132. *UDW*, Nr. 8, 1886, p. 81; Kuppe, *Lueger*, p. 144.

133. Pulzer, following Kuppe, asserts that Lueger's first antisemitic speech was given in Sept. 1887. This is not correct chronologically, and even this speech may be called "antisemitic" only in a qualified sense.

134. *V*, 15 June 1887, pp. 4–5.

135. *ÖV*, 11 Sept. 1887, pp. 2–3.

136. For the speech, see *V*, 25 Sept. 1887, Beiblatt, pp. 1–2.

137. For the diffusion of the artisan movement to other parts of Austria, see Waentig, *Mittelstandspolitik*, pp. 378–400.

138. *V*, 25 Sept. 1887, Beiblatt, pp. 1–2.

139. For a similar speech the following month, ibid., 11 Oct. 1887, p. 5.

140. Ibid., 6 Jan. 1889, Beiblatt, pp. 1–2.

141. Ibid., 11 Oct. 1887, p. 5.

142. Ibid., 24 Nov. 1887, pp. 5–6.

143. On Ursin's election, see *ÖR*, 9 Oct. 1887, pp. 1–3; *V*, 15 Oct. 1887, p. 1; and the official reports to Kielmansegg from the local *Bezirkshauptmann*, 14 Oct. 1887, P2 ad 121, Nr. 5622/1887, *NÖLA*. Ursin was a merchant by profession and, according to the official report, a rather hapless local politician who was totally dominated by Schönerer's authoritarian personality. Schönerer began early in the autumn of 1887 to plan a vigorous political strategy for these elections, using local affiliates of the *Schulverein für Deutsche* to organize political agitation. See B3 ad 4873/1887, *NÖLA;* and Erhard Unterberger, *Liberalismus in St. Pölten (1870–1918)* (diss., University of Vienna, 1966), pp. 59–64.

144. *V*, 15 Oct. 1887, p. 1; 26 Nov. 1887, p. 1.

145. *EE* 4: 167–72.

146. *V*, 30 Nov. 1887, p. 5.

147. The *UDW* abandoned the pretense of United Christian unity when Rudolf Eichhorn dared to challenge Schönerer in the by-election held in Oct. 1888 for the latter's parliamentary seat. See *UDW*, Nr. 20, 1888, pp. 249–50.

148. At a Democratic rally in early Oct. 1887 Kreuzig announced his opposition to Schönerer's antisemitic legislation, urging other Democrats to do the same. *ÖR*, 9 Oct. 1887, p. 5. See also Binder, *Albert Gessmann*, pp. 41–42.

149. *ÖV*, 27 Nov. 1887, p. 4.

150. *ÖR*, 8 Jan. 1888, p. 4; *V*, 19 Jan. 1888, p. 3. The term *Bürgerclub* was an obvious play on the older Liberal *Bürgervereine*, which Felder had organized in 1871–73, revealing the effort of the antisemites to mimic the Liberals' posture as a party of the total Bürgertum.

151. *ÖV*, 12 Feb. 1888, pp. 5–6.

152. *NWT*, 22 Jan. 1888, p. 3; 28 Jan. 1888, p. 3; 15 Feb. 1888, p. 2; *KVZ*, 15 Feb. 1888, p. 3; 19 Feb. 1888, p. 1.

153. *KVZ*, 20 Mar. 1888, p. 1; and the police report P10 ad 1185, Nr. 2055/1888, *NÖLA*.

154. See *Gedenkblatt*, pp. 7–11.

155. For the history of this incident, see Hellwig Valentin, "Der Prozess Schönerer und seine Auswirkungen auf die parteipolitische Verhältnisse in Österreich," *ÖGL* 16 (1972): 81–97; Whiteside, *Socialism of Fools*, pp. 132–44.

156. *SP*, X, 1888, pp. 7391–94.

157. For this action see chap. 6.

158. Pattai to Vogelsang ("streng vertraulich"), 25 Mar. 1888, *VN*, Mappe 21, Nr. 196. Pattai tried to persuade Vogelsang that he should intercede with Clerical party leaders for Schönerer, but this had little effect. As Pattai himself admitted, Taaffe wanted Schönerer's head.

159. Vogelsang admired Lueger's willingness to strike a position on the school issue which, while not clerical, was fiercely anti-Liberal. See *V*, 22 June 1888, p. 4. In a speech to the Reichsrat in 1888 Lueger styled himself as a defender of teacher rights against the "oppressive" Liberals. He also insisted that the whole school system needed reform and that more emphasis should be placed on simple reading and writing. By insisting that the "rich Jews" were responsible for the inadequacies of the educational system, Lueger was

obviously playing for the anti-Liberal vote without having to move into a clearly clerical position, which would have been suicidal. *SP*, X, 1888, pp. 8237–41.

160. See Schindler, "Neun Jahre Entenabende," p. 306; Vogelsang to Pergen, 30 Nov. 1887, reprinted in Weinzierl-Fischer, "Aus den Anfängen der christlichsozialen Bewegung in Österreich," pp. 483–84.

161. See Maria v Vogelsang, "Aus dem Leben," p. 65, and Scheicher's comments in *CB*, 1904, pp. 733–36. Vogelsang's daughter emphasized the nonideological character of this early meeting. It occurred to discuss "die Verständigung über gemeinsames Vorgehen in politisch-gemeinnützigen Dingen." This was apparently the meeting where Lueger and Gessmann came and left in disguise.

162. "Aus P. Abels Erinnerungen," p. 342.

163. Lueger to Vogelsang, 30 Aug. 1888, *VN*, Mappe 22, Nr. 268.

164. Lueger to Vogelsang, 5 Oct. 1889, *VN*, Mappe 22, Nr. 281.

165. Vogelsang to Lueger, 10 Dec. 1888, Handschriftensammlung, Stadtbibliothek, I.N. 40959. Vogelsang also noted that it was easy for him to write about social theory from the comfort of his study, but that Lueger had to "throw his breast against the enemy" in public confrontations (11 Dec. 1890, I.N. 40960).

166. See the private diary of Gustav Piffl, entry of 17 Oct. 1894, unpublished, *EBDA*. Lueger once quipped to Joseph Scheicher that laymen had no business worrying about religious problems: "Don't think about it, don't speculate about it. If we laymen do that, we will involve ourselves in endless problems. Love the Lord and trust him and then nothing bad can happen to us." *EE* 5: 406–7. This view reflected Lueger's sense of secular, Vormärz theism as a last bastion of religious observance. Traditional Austrian culture needed religion as a force for social stabilization, Lueger felt, making the post-1861 period of Liberal anticlericalism both historically atypical and historically anachronistic. Religion itself need not involve any positive changes in one's behavior or one's life-style. It certainly did not mean "clericalism," in the sense of the dominance of the clergy over matters of public policy— Lueger was far too Josephistic for that. Lueger's willingness to leave religious speculation (and, it should be noted, religious intolerance) to the professionals (the clergy) had another implication as well. Lueger's Manichaean division of labor meant that the priests could participate in politics, just as laymen could join in religion, but that elite political control belonged to the laymen, not to the clerics. This view of party-political Josephism governed all of Lueger's relations with the Church.

167. See Ernst Karl Winter, *Arbeiterschaft und Staat* (Vienna, 1934), p. 18.

168. See, for example, Lueger's comments on religion as the only power which could ultimately eliminate social inequality (thereby excusing the Christian Socials from any serious effort to try to do so), in *RP*, 5 Jan. 1897, p. 3; *AZ*, 5 Jan. 1897, p. 1.

169. Klopp, *Leben und Wirken*, p. 346, note 13, quoting an article by Abel in the *Neuigkeits-Weltblatt* of 19 Sept. 1926. This meeting has been the subject of some controversy. Kurt Skalnik confused the fact that *two* birthday celebrations were held for Vogelsang, one in September and one in December, the latter a public banquet for propaganda purposes. Lueger was unable to attend the December affair because of the death of his mother. Skalnik therefore concluded that Vogelsang could not have made his suggestion about a "Christian Social coalition to Lueger at any point except in Feb. 1888, when both men attended the public banquet of the United Christians." Skalnik was incorrect, however, since Abel was careful to emphasize that a meeting between the two men did take place in Sept. 1888. The comment by Vogelsang only makes sense in relation to Schönerer's new predicament. Vogelsang would have had no reason to make such a suggestion before Apr. 1888. See Skalnik, *Lueger*, p. 65. See also *ÖV*, 16 Sept. 1888, p. 1.

170. *V*, 16 May 1888, p. 4; 4 June 1888, Beiblatt, p. 4; 20 June 1888, p. 5.

171. *ÖV*, 25 Nov. 1888, p. 1.

172. Klopp, *Leben und Wirken*, p. 342; and ibid., p. 324, for Bülow's letter to Vogelsang of 11 Oct. 1888 concerning fears of conservatives that antisemitic rhetoric and shouting might occur at the congress.

173. On Vergani, see Adelmaier, *Vergani*, passim; Pichl, *Schönerer*, 2: 106–7, 152–60, 4:315–28. Funder, *Vom Gestern ins Heute*, pp. 96–97, 349–57; and the testimony in the Hron-Pattai libel trial in Apr. 1890.

174. *UDW*, Nr. 10, 1890, p. 100; Nr. 17, 1890, p. 200; Nr. 21, 1890, pp. 241–42.

175. See the police reports on the 1888 elections, P10 ad 1185, Nr. 2055/1888, *NÖLA*.

176. Lueger to Gessmann, 21 Jan. 1889, *VN*, Mappe 22, Nr. 273. Lueger told Gessmann that Vetter and Hollomay were so hostile to Mandl that they were behaving like "madmen."

177. Lueger to Vogelsang, 9 Feb. 1889, *VN*, Mappe 21, Nr. 275.

178. Kuppe, *Lueger*, pp. 190–92; *DV*, 20 Feb. 1889 (M), p. 5. On the plotting which preceded this meeting, see the later recollections of Leopold Hollomay at the meeting of the pan-German *Deutschen Volksverein* on 23 Sept. 1890 in *DV*, 25 Sept. 1890 (M), p. 3; *UDW*, Nr. 19, 1890, pp. 222–24.

179. Schneider to Vogelsang, 21 Jan. 1889, *VN*, Mappe 12, Nr. 192.

180. *V*, 27 Feb. 1889, p. 5; 18 Mar. 1889, p. 4; Pichl, *Schönerer*, 2:107–8, 136.

181. For the election results, see *V*, 19 Mar. 1889, p. 1; 22 Mar. 1889, p. 5; 27 Mar. 1889, p. 6; and P10, Nr. 2187/1889, *NÖLA*.

182. *Verhandlungen des II. Allgemeinen österreichischen Katholikentages* (Vienna, 1889), pp. 39–42. Lueger also spoke in the Social Committee of the congress (ibid., pp. 148–53, 169–78), supporting labor protection legislation for workers in large industry, but ignoring the situation of apprentices and journeymen in the small artisan shops. He also cautioned the Catholics against utopian expectations that social reform of any kind could be produced overnight, an implicit rejection of Vogelsang's holistic theorizing.

183. Plener, *Erinnerungen*, 2:372; *SP*, X, 1889, pp. 12200, 12203; Pichl, *Schönerer*, 2:106.

184. In a confidential memoir in the *VN*, Liechtenstein explained his reasons for resigning both the chairmanship of his club and his seat. Originally he held back from giving up his parliamentary seat. Then he realized that it might look as if he wanted to retain parliamentary influence without bearing the responsibilities of leadership, and this calculation led him to resign from the Reichsrat in the fall of 1889. See *VN*, Mappe 15, Nr. 2, dated autumn 1889.

185. Kuppe, *Lueger*, pp. 197–98. Liechtenstein had known Lueger personally at least since 1886, when both men had served on the *Gewerbe* committee of the Abgeordnetenhaus.

186. Pichl, *Schönerer*, 3:399–400; Whiteside, *Socialism of Fools*, p. 142.

187. Valentin, "Der Prozess Schönerer," p. 83.

188. Schnee, *Lueger*, p. 50; Valentin, "Der Prozess Schönerer," p. 84.

189. Kielmansegg to Taaffe, 8 Aug. 1890, Nr. 5538/1890, Min. d. Inneren, AVA.

190. *WZ*, 3 Oct. 1890, p. 3.

191. See the police report J12 ad 2627, Nr. 7458/1893 (12 Nov. 1893), *NÖLA*. The by-election held in Zwettl in Oct. 1888 to fill Schönerer's vacated seat in parliament was occasion for his followers to organize a sympathy campaign on his behalf and write his name on the ballot, even though such votes were clearly null and void. Schönerer received 185 votes out of the total 436 cast, hardly an impressive plurality. See the report of the *Bezirkshauptmann* in Zwettl to Kielmansegg, 10 Oct. 1888, P2 ad 234, Nr. 6309/1888, *NÖLA*.

192. Kielmansegg to Taaffe, 6 Oct. 1890. Nr. 4231/1890, Min. d. Inneren, AVA.

193. Valentin, "Der Prozess Schönerer," pp. 87–88; Hron, *Bewegung*, p. 62; *V*, 15 Oct. 1889, p. 6. The *Deutschnationaler Verein* was replaced by the *Deutschen Volksverein* in

Jan. 1890, which was organized by Karl Iro, a lieutenant of Schönerer. See *UDW*, Nr. 3, 1890, pp. 28–30.

194. Cited in Valentin, "Der Prozess Schönerer," p. 89, note 106.

195. He was not alone. Many within the German National movement itself were shocked by the new radicalism, some of whom, like Josef Fiegl, were soon expelled from the party. See Whiteside, *Socialism of Fools*, pp. 142–43.

196. Plener, *Erinnerungen*, 2:234, 359; *PAAA*, Öst. 70/Bd. 24, A10931, 3 Oct. 1890.

197. Plener, *Erinnerungen*, 2:322.

198. Ibid., 382–83. The emperor commented on the new Czech party: "Eine ganz eigentümliche Gesellschaft erscheint an der Oberfläche, degegen muss energisch eingeschritten werden." For the rise of the Young Czech movement, see the important new study by Bruce M. Garver, *The Young Czech Party, 1874–1901, and the Emergence of a Multi-Party System* (New Haven, 1978), pp. 123ff.

199. Jenks, *Iron Ring*, pp. 239–40, 274–75.

200. Funder, *Vom Gestern*, pp. 65–66; Jenks, *Iron Ring*, p. 235; Kielmansegg, *Kaiserhaus*, p. 239.

201. For a survey of the Feb. 1891 elections, which confirmed the growth of radical politics in German and Czech lands, see *PV* 5:6–13.

202. Schneider to Vogelsang, 19 Feb. 1890, *VN*, Mappe 12, Nr. 3.

203. Taaffe to Kielmansegg, 7 Nov. 1890, J2 ad 8047, Nr. 8047/1890, *NÖLA*. This new concern may have come in response to pressure by the emperor. See Kielmansegg, *Kaiserhaus*, pp. 40–41.

204. For a relatively objective view of these disturbances, see *AZ*, 11 Apr. 1890, pp. 1–2; *NWT*, 9 Apr. 1890, pp. 4–5; *WZ*, 9 Apr. 1890, pp. 7–8; and *DV*, 9 Apr. 1890, Beilage, p. 1. The government also used the riots as an excuse to prohibit the meetings of several Socialist associations.

205. *WZ*, 19 Apr. 1890, p. 2.

206. See Franz Joseph's comments on street disturbances at a session of the *Ministerrat* on 31 Jan. 1894 in Brügel, *Geschichte*, 4:244ff.

207. Lueger to Kielmansegg, 16 Sept. 1890, M1889–90, Stadterweiterungsakten, 2962b, *NÖLA*.

208. See Plener, *Erinnerungen*, 3:242–43.

209. Renner, *An der Wende*, pp. 201–2, also p. 234.

210. For Pattai's speech see *ÖR*, 20 Oct. 1889, pp. 1–2. In Dec. Pattai and a group of his cronies invaded a pan-German political rally in Mariahilf and took control of the podium. It was on this occasion that Pattai was alleged to have cried out "pereat Schönerer" in reply to taunts by Schönerer's supporters. Pattai later denied that he had said it, but it was clear that even if he did not say it, he certainly felt like saying it and that his supporters knew this. See *DV*, 17 Dec. 1889 (M), p. 6, and *Deutsches Montagsblatt*, 16 Dec. 1889, pp. 4–5.

211. Pattai admitted to Vogelsang that Lueger had intervened to try to persuade him to bury the dispute with Schönerer and Vergani, but that his personal "honor" prevented him from doing so. Pattai to Vogelsang, 20 Nov. 1889, *VN*, Mappe 21, Nr. 216.

212. Valentin, "Der Prozess Schönerer," p. 86.

213. *V*, 3 Oct. 1889, p. 5.

214. Ibid., 23 Nov. 1889, Beiblatt, p. 3.

215. *SP*, X, 1890, p. 13384.

216. *DV*, 8 Oct. 1889 (M), p. 7 ("Ich habe nichts degegen, dass das 'Deutsches Volksblatt' gegen tschechische Bestrebungen ankämpft. Das 'Deutsches Volksblatt' möge aber nicht das tschechische Volk als solches beschimpfen"). See also 4 Sept. 1895 (A), p. 2.

217. Pichl, *Schönerer*, 4:241–44.

218. Ibid., pp. 235–40.

219. Ibid., p. 52.

220. Cajetan Felder tried to force a heavy regime of discipline and club unanimity onto the *Mittelpartei* before 1870, but this fell apart in the 1870s and was never restored. See *Lebenserinnerungen*, pp. 203, 287.

221. For representative lists of members of several Christian Social *Wahlcomités* in the 1891 Reichsrat elections, see *DV,* 4 Mar. 1891 (M), pp. 3–4. These committees were generally not permanent organizations before 1896. Thus, they were similar to local Liberal groups of voluntary notables who did their work and then went home. They were, of course, more disciplined and more effective than their Liberal counterparts.

222. See Thomas Nipperdey, "Die Organisation der bürgerlichen Parteien in Deutschland vor 1918," in Nipperdey, *Gesellschaft, Kultur, Theorie. Gesammelte Aufsätze zur neueren Geschichte* (Göttingen, 1976), pp. 293–94. From the confidential police reports submitted to Kielmansegg in late 1895 and early 1896 it was clear that the Christian Socials had no more of a central party bureaucratic apparatus than did the Liberals. Much of the tactical and strategic planning in both parties was handled in private discussion between local party leaders, often in private homes and apartments. The Christian Socials did possess, however, a more disciplined style of elite decision making, since Lueger and Gessmann were able to dictate general party policy by 1896 in a way rarely accomplished within the Liberal party. Both parties' *Centralwahlcomité* structure was not a ruse or a "front," but it was used only when a previous level of consensus on important policy issues had already been arranged on most matters. This was especially the case with the Christian Socials. Exceptions did, of course, occur, and the party often had vigorous discussions on party policy in the sessions of their *Bürgerclub* meetings. But most decisions on tactics in elections were taken informally by the elite leaders concerned. See, for example, Stejskal to Kielmansegg, 14 Feb. 1896, B2 ad 452, Nr. 1108, *NÖLA.*

223. *DV,* 1 Mar. 1891 (M), p. 9; 4 Mar. 1892 (A), p. 4.

224. Liechtenstein owed his election to his name, but also to the extensive local-level campaigning done on his behalf by other Christian Social leaders.

225. *UDW,* Nr. 13, 1895, p. 155.

226. *DV,* 3 Sept. 1895 (M), p. 6.

227. B2 ad 452, Nr. 1773/1896, *NÖLA.*

228. See the *NFP*'s reports on the election agitation on 18, 19, 22, and 24 Sept. 1895. For an example of one vigorous Liberal political organization, which at its zenith was as effective as most of those the Christian Socials created, see Sigmund Mayer's description of his Leopoldstadt machine in *Ein jüdischer Kaufmann,* pp. 284–85. Mayer himself admitted, however, that even his level of preparation was unable to stop the antisemitic surge among the Gentile voters (Jews comprised less than 35 percent of the Leopoldstadt's total electorate).

229. See Stejskal to Kielmansegg, B2 ad 452, Nr. 1108/1896, *NÖLA.*

230. These personal connections with Liberal politicians were clearly manifest during the Lueger–Alexander Scharf libel trial in 1890. See *NFP,* 27 Nov. 1890 (A), p. 2; 28 Nov. 1890 (M), pp. 6–8.

231. Schneider to Vogelsang, 22 June 1890, *VN,* Mappe 12, Nr. 208.

232. *EE* 5:265–68; 6:373–74 (for Gessmann's authoritarianism after Lueger's death).

233. The following occupational and social data were derived from a wide variety of sources, including the police reports on the newly elected candidates to the Council for the years 1887 to 1891 (Statt. Präs., *NÖLA*), the *Lehmann's Allgemeiner Wohnungs-Anzeiger* for 1888 to 1891, the *HHZ* for 1889 to 1891, and the dissertation by Martha Helmbe, *Die Tätigkeit des Wiener Gemeinderates von 1889–1892* (University of Vienna, 1974). My data

were arrived at largely independent of Helmbe, but in most cases we agree on occupational and social designations and rank.

234. For aggregate data on ages of City Council members for the period 1884–88, but not broken down by party affiliation, see Eduard Hausner, *Die Tätigkeit des Wiener Gemeinderates in den Jahren 1884–1888* (diss., University of Vienna, 1974), pp. 436–43. The mean age of the Council as a whole in 1887 was fifty-two, so that the Liberals must have been slightly older as a group than the antisemites.

235. Hausner found that 67% of all the Council members in 1888 had been born in Vienna, but he did not break this down by party affiliation. It is likely that more Liberals than antisemites were natives of Vienna and Lower Austria. There is no substantial correlation among the antisemites themselves between place of birth and personal material prosperity. Some of the wealthiest antisemitic politicians, like Karl Stehlik and Andreas Weitmann, had not been born in Vienna.

236. The police report of 1888 indicated that three antisemitic politicians, Cornelius Vetter, Josef Hawranek, and Leopold Slama, had run afoul of the law at some time in their lives on charges of disorderliness and fist-fighting, but these infractions were not serious enough to warrant their disqualification from public office. Vetter and Slama left active political life in 1891–92; Hawranek went on to become a respectable and influential local leader and a very wealthy man. The majority of the antisemites were men with no skeletons in their closets.

237. For Knoll's argument, see *ÖGL*, 16 (1972): 75–78. A rather different argument which attempts to explain the early conservatism of the Mittelstand groups in terms of their early commercial as opposed to late industrial capitalism, such as that offered by Wolfgang Sauer in his 1967 *AHR* article, must be seriously qualified. The Christian Socials were never entirely out of sympathy with industrialism even before 1896, and some of the party's voter cadres, like the private employees, depended upon capitalist and industrial bureaucracies for their jobs. It is seriously debatable whether one can characterize the Christian Social elite or sub-elite as similar to the down-and-out types who later surfaced to occupy central positions in the *NSDAP* between 1919 and 1932. Many were successful lawyers and businessmen, as well as respected, secure property owners. They did not operate with a mode of debased humiliated hopelessness, nor did they have any inclinations toward active political violence. Ernst Schneider was *not* typical of most Christian Social leaders.

238. See Hansjoachim Henning, *Das westdeutsche Bürgertum in der Epoch der Hochindustrialisierung, 1860–1914* (Wiesbaden, 1972), pp. 483–91.

239. Henning, *Bürgertum*, p. 486.

240. For an insightful analysis of the white collar and *Beamten* wing of the party, with which Lueger himself felt the most affinity, see *PAAA*, Öst. 74/Bd. 12, A18340, 15 Oct. 1905.

241. In 1891, during the Liberal era, of the 342 men serving as members of the nineteen district committees, 225 were men who owned small or medium businesses. Nearly 200 were *Hausherren*. *WZ*, 7 May 1891, pp. 1–2.

242. B2, Nr. 2490/1890, *NÖLA*.

243. See Schindler, "Neun Jahre Entenabende," p. 305.

Chapter 5

1. *PAAA*, Öst.70/Bd. 24, A4358, 22 Mar. 1889.

2. On the history of the 1850 city statute for Vienna, see Rudolf Till, *Geschichte der Wiener Stadtverwaltung in den letzten 200 Jahren* (Vienna, 1957); Karl Weiss, *Entwicklung der Gemeinde-Verfassung der Stadt Wien (1221–1850)* (Vienna, 1867); and Cajetan Felder, *Erinnerungen eines Wiener Bürgermeisters* (Vienna, 1964), pp. 120–33. Also, Erich Scheithauer,

Beiträge zur Sozialstruktur der Wiener Aussenbezirke, Entwicklung im Zeitraum 1850–1910 an Hand der Volkszählungsergebnisse (diss., University of Vienna, 1954); Erika Wodak, *Die Selbstverwaltung der Stadt Wien von 1848 bis 1861* (diss., University of Vienna, 1936). For a general discussion of the legal status of the municipalities in Austria in the nineteenth century, see Jiři Klabouch, *Die Gemeindeselbstverwaltung in Österreich, 1848–1918* (Vienna, 1968).

3. Till, *Stadtverwaltung*, pp. 51–56; Wodak, *Selbstverwaltung*, pp. 11–16.

4. For the *Vororte* before their incorporation into Vienna, see J. Franz-Ferron, *Neu-Wien. Rückblick auf die Geschichte der am 21. December 1891 zur Commune Wien einverleibren Vororte-Gemeinden* (Korneuburg, 1892); and Fred Deters, *The Role of the Suburbs in the Modernization of Vienna* (diss., University of Chicago, 1974). On demographic development, see G. A. Schimmer, *Die Bevölkerung von Wien und seiner Umgegung nach dem Berufe und der Beschäftigung* (Vienna, 1874). Many of these communities functioned as places of summer residence for the Viennese bourgeoisie during the Vormärz.

5. *SJ*, 1892, pp. 30–50; Stephan Sedlaczek, *Die definitiven Ergebnisse der Volkszählung vom 31. December 1890 in der k. k. Reichshaupt- und Residenzstadt Wien* (Vienna, 1891), pp. 17–91.

6. See Stephan Sedlaczek, *Die Wohn-Verhältnisse in Wien. Ergebnisse der Volkszählung vom 31. December 1890* (Vienna, 1893), pp. 28–32.

7. For the history of housing development in Vienna after 1848, see Josef Pizzala, "Die Bautätigkeit in und um Wien in den Jahren 1843–1881," *SM* 8 (1882): 170–80; Hans Bobek and Elisabeth Lichtenberger, *Wien. Bauliche Gestalt und Entwicklung seit der Mitte des 19. Jahrhunderts* (Vienna, 1966); Eugen v Philippovich, "Wiener Wohnungsverhältnisse," *ASGSS*, vol. 7 (1894); Paul Schwarz, "Die Entwicklung der städtischen Grundrente in Wien," in *Neue Untersuchungen über die Wohnungsfrage in Deutschland und im Ausland*, *SVSP*, 94 (1901); Rudolf Eberstadt, "Wiener Wohnverhältnisse," in *Neue Studien über Städtebau und Wohnungswesen* (Jena, 1912); the extensive discussion of housing development in Vienna in the 1860s and 1870s in Franz Baltzarek, Alfred Hoffmann, and Hannes Stekl, *Wirkschaft und Gesellschaft der Wiener Stadterweiterung* (Wiesbaden, 1975), pp. 217–51, 259–343; and Peter Feldbauer, *Stadtwachstum und Wohnungsnot. Determinanten unzureichender Wohnungsversorgung in Wien, 1848 bis 1914* (Vienna, 1977).

8. See Bobek and Lichtenberger, *Wien*, p. 26.

9. See Schwarz, "Die Entwicklung," pp. 74–83, 85–143.

10. See Friedrich Schnierer, "Die Steigerung der Mietzinse in Wien, 1881–1907," in *Mitteilungen der Zentralstelle für Wohnungsreform in Oesterreich*, Nr. 20 (Aug. 1911), pp. 9–14; Schwarz, "Die Entwicklung," pp. 66–74; Franz Juraschek, "Das Wachstum des Territoriums, der Bevölkerung, und des Verkehrs von Wien, 1857–1894," *SM* 22 (1896): 330–36.

11. Schwarz, "Die Entwicklung," p. 66. Between 1869 and 1895 the Austrian *Staatsbeamten* received one major salary increase (in 1873), which increased their net income by approximately 15%. Rents in Vienna, in contrast, rose by as much as 40% in the same period.

12. On the basis of the tax's 1889 levels, Vienna received 1,691,666 fl. from surcharges on the government's tax. This amount was 12% of the yearly tax income the city of Vienna enjoyed. *SJ*, 1889, pp. 73–74.

13. Vienna's financial situation was unenviable compared with that of many German cities. See Leo Munk, *Die Steuerbelastung der Reichshauptstädte Wien und Berlin in vergleichender Darstellung* (Vienna, 1889), pp. 131–43. This was in contrast to and, in a sense, because of the kind of political freedom the municipality of Vienna enjoyed, which was more exten-

sive than that of many Prussian cities. See Josef Redlich, *Das Wesen der österreichischen Kommunalverfassung* (Leipzig, 1910), pp. 9–12; Hugo Preuss, *Die Entwicklung des Deutschen Städtewesens* (Leipzig, 1906), 1:337–40.

14. See the comments of Ferdinand Kronawetter and Max Menger, *SP*, X, 1889–90, pp. 13973–87, 14027–28.

15. Leopold Berg, *Wien und die Vereinigung der Vororte* (Vienna, 1876), pp. 1–15.

16. The history of the negotiations between the city and the suburbs was a very long and thorny one. For an early statement of the city's negotiating position, see the *Vorlagen der Kommission zur Berathung der Reform der Verzehrungssteuer und der Vereinigung der Vororte mit Wien*, Nr. 1–7 (Vienna, 1880–89), prepared by the *Magistrat* for the commission. For the unsuccessful course of the negotiations, see the *Verwaltungsbericht der Stadt Wien für das Jahr 1883* (Vienna, 1884), pp. 1–5; *Verwaltungsbericht der Stadt Wien für das Jahr 1884* (Vienna, 1885), pp. 1–3; *Verwaltungsbericht der Stadt Wien für das Jahr 1885* (Vienna, 1886), pp. 1–2. Also, *NFP*, 26 Feb. 1884 (M), pp. 4–5. For a general defense of the suburbs' position, see *Denkschrift der Vororte Wiens über die Folgen einer eventuellen Hinausrückung der Verzehrungssteuer-Linien* (Vienna, 1884).

17. For general background, see Till, *Stadtverwaltung*, pp. 92–94; and Kronawetter's speech of 22 Mar. 1890 in *SP*, X, 1889–90, pp. 13973–87. Also, *NFP*, 22 Mar. 1890 (M), p. 2.

18. See Menger's account of his subcommittee, in *SP*, X, 1889–90, p. 14028.

19. *PV* 4:274; Kielmansegg, *Kaiserhaus*, pp. 233, 236.

20. Till, *Stadtverwaltung*, p. 93.

21. Erich Kielmansegg, *Beiträge zur Geschichte der Vereinigung der Vororte mit Wien, 1890*, handwritten memoir, Ostern, 1891, M1889–90, Stadterweiterungsakten, 2962a, pp. 2–3, *NÖLA*. For the events of 1888–89, see *Die Gemeinde-Verwaltung der Stadt Wien für die Jahre 1889–1893. Bericht des Bürgermeisters Dr. Raimund Grübl* (Vienna, 1895), pp. 2–5; *PV* 4:461–62; *PAAA*, Öst.70/Bd. 24, A4846, 10 Apr. 1890. See also Kielmansegg, *Kaiserhaus*, pp. 226–36.

22. Kielmansegg, *Beiträge*, pp. 8–10.

23. For the bill, *SP*, X, 1890, Beilage Nr. 949. For the committee's report which accompanied the bill, see ibid., Beilage Nr. 987.

24. See, for example, *SP*, X, 1890, pp. 13034, 13739–43. See *NFP*, 6 Mar. 1890 (M), p. 5; ibid., 13 Mar. 1890 (M), p. 8.

25. See the comments of Wrabetz and Herbst in *SP*, 1890, pp. 13969–73, 14019–27.

26. Kielmansegg, *Beiträge*, pp. 3–4.

27. Elisabeth Uhl, *Eduard Uhl. Bürgermeister der Stadt Wien, 1882–1889* (diss., University of Vienna, 1950), pp. 48–53; on Prix and his administration, see Birgit Harden, *Das Amt des Bürgermeisters der Stadt Wien in der Liberalen Ära, 1861–1895* (diss., University of Vienna, 1967), and Felix Czeike, *Wien und seine Bürgermeister. Sieben Jahrhunderte Wiener Stadtgeschichte* (Vienna and Munich, 1974), pp. 328–37.

28. Kielmansegg, *Beiträge*, p. 5.

29. That Prix might entertain such fears was demonstrated by Kielmansegg's attempt to revise the city statute along more authoritarian lines so that the *Bürgermeister* would be appointed by the crown, rather than elected by the City Council. The Liberals managed to avoid Kielmansegg's plan. See *NFP*, 11 July 1890 (M), p. 6.

30. See the emperor's comments against the Young Czechs, *PAAA*, Öst. 86/Bd. 5, A4731, 28 May 1891; *PV* 5:319.

31. Kielmansegg, *Beiträge*, pp. 5–6.

32. Ibid., pp. 6–9. Also, idem, *Kaiserhaus*, pp. 40–41, 229. Kielmansegg was so determined to see his ideas through to a successful conclusion that he even instructed his assistants in the *Statthalterei* to write anonymous articles for leading Liberal newspapers

attacking the government's (meaning Taaffe's and Dunajewski's) slowness in dealing with the unification question. See his *Beiträge*, pp. 5–9. Dunajewski was forced by the pressure of events to go along with Kielmansegg, but the true feelings of the *Finanzministerium* were probably represented by Dunajewski's *Sectionschef*, Freiherr v Baumgartner, who was *ganz entsetzt* when he heard the news. Ibid., p. 9; idem, *Kaiserhaus*, pp. 233, 236.

33. See the summary of the various positions articulated in the June debates in the *WZ*, 28 June 1890, pp. 4–5, and *NFP*, 28 June 1890 (M), pp. 5–6. The transcripts of the *Enquête* are in M1889–1890, 2962a, *NÖLA*.

34. *WZ*, 2 July 1890, pp. 6–8; *NFP*, 2 July 1890 (M), pp. 1, 7–8; Kielmansegg, *Beiträge*, pp. 9–10. When informed on 2 July by Taaffe of Kielmansegg's intentions to transform the *Enquête* into one dealing with unification, the emperor approved.

35. *WZ*, 8 July 1890, pp. 4–5; 24 July 1890, p. 4; *NFP*, 8 July 1890 (M), p. 5.

36. See his comments in the *NFP*, 10 July 1890 (M), p. 6.

37. For the official text of the results of the hearings, ibid., 24 July 1890 (M), pp. 3–4.

38. Till, *Stadtverwaltung*, p. 96.

39. *WZ*, 10 Sept. 1890, pp. 5–6; *NFP*, 10 Sept. 1890 (M).

40. For the debates in the Council, see *BSWG*, 1890, pp. 1040–1447.

41. For the political allegiances of the antisemitic candidates, see Pichl, *Schönerer*, 4:61–67.

42. On Schneider's propaganda journey to Bohemia, see *Der politische Nachlass des Grafen Eduard Taaffe*, Arthur Skedl, ed. (Vienna, 1922), pp. 617, 625, 635, 637–38.

43. For the problematic stance of the loyal Schönerians toward the rest of the antisemitic coalition, see the various speeches given 23 Sept. 1890 at a meeting of the *Deutschen Volksverein* in Vienna by disgruntled Schönerian loyalists. *DV*, 25 Sept. 1890 (M), p. 3. Karl Türk tried to persuade his listeners to abstain from any support for Lueger in the Landtag elections.

44. One relatively accurate measure of the prosperity of artisan and small shopkeeper businesses in any given *Bezirk* in Vienna was the number of such businesses in arrears in their taxes. In the Leopoldstadt 73% of the 1894 *Erwerbsteuer* was unpaid by 31 Dec. 1894. Margarethen and Mariahilf had 51% and 55% in arrears. The Josefstadt, in contrast, had only 44% in arrears (as a percentage of projected returns).

45. *SJ*, 1892, p. 202. The total number of businesses paying either 5 or 10 fl. in trade taxes *(Ordinarium)* in the Josefstadt was 2,616 in 1892 (the first year the tax data were broken down by district). If one estimates the number of these businesses owned by women who could not vote at 20% of the total (which would be extremely conservative), the number of male-owned *Gewerbe* in 1892 would be 2,092. The number would have been somewhat lower in 1889, given the gradual expansion of the Viennese economy beginning in the later 1880s. Even 1,900 such men would be numerically less than half of the total registered voters in the district in Oct. 1890. Also, it is interesting to note that in the City Council elections in the Josefstadt in 1891 the First and Second Curias made up over 44% of the total enfranchised groups of voters in the district, whereas in poorer districts, like Mariahilf and Margarethen, the first two curias constituted only 35% of the total electorate.

46. In 1890 (according to the census) the Josefstadt had 1,397 men working in the capacity of *Beamten* or *Lehrer* for some level of the national, regional, or local government. It also had 420 individuals who were registered by the census in the category of "other free professions" and 1,910 who were registered as employees of industrial or commercial firms. Some of the latter group would have been the commercial clerks *(Commis)* and not likely to be able to vote. The majority of the other groups would have been eligible to vote according to the privileged franchise. *SJ*, 1892, p. 58; *NWT*, 8 Apr. 1891, pp. 6–7.

47. *SPB*, 13 Dec. 1885, p. 198. This estimate is based on 1885–86 voter registration data

(and includes teachers), but the relative proportion of officials in the Viennese electorate would not have changed significantly between 1887 and 1890.

48. For the history of the *Beamten-Verein*, see Rudolf Schwingenschögl, *Der erste allgemeine Beamten-Verein der österreichisch-ungarischen Monarchie. Geschichte seiner Gründung, Entstehung, und Tätigkeit während der ersten 25 Jahre seines Bestehens (1865–1890)* (Vienna, 1890). The policy and structure of the *Verein* is best studied through its newspaper, the *Beamten-Zeitung*. The *Verein* was dominated by higher ranking, university-trained *Beamten* in the employ of the state. On the history of the officials in Austria, see Alfred Hoffmann, "Bürokratie insbesondere in Österreich," in *Beiträge zur neueren Geschichte Österreichs*, Heinrich Fichtenau and Erich Zöllner, eds. (Vienna, Cologne, and Graz, 1974), pp. 13–31.

49. *ZABV*, 23 Jan. 1873, pp. 26–28. Also, *MP*, 10 Feb. 1873, p. 2, and *BZ* 21 (1890): 7.

50. The petition campaign of the late 1860s and early 1870s did not leave any permanent organizational imprint on the collective consciousness of the *Staatsbeamten*. See the comments of Josef Eissert, the editor of *Der Staatsbeamte*, in the *Protokolle der Enquête über Personalcredit und Wucher* (Vienna, 1904), VI, pp. 5–12. According to Eissert, the modern *Beamten* movement in Austria did not begin until after 1885. For the social situation of the *Beamtentum* in the Bach era, see Christoph Stölzl, *Die Ära Bach in Böhmen* (Munich, 1971), pp. 112–19.

51. There is no modern history of wages and prices for nineteenth-century Austria or nineteenth-century Vienna. These conclusions are based on the data in Matis, *Österreichs Wirtschaft*, pp. 289, 421, 424–25. The salary improvements made in 1873 had a definite effect on the recruitment of university graduates to the state service, since the career became more attractive and prestigious. See Franz v Juraschek, "Der Besuch der österreichischen Universitäten in den Jahren 1861–1875," *SM* 2 (1876): 332. Juraschek reported that the rise in university enrollments in the 1870s in the legal and administrative faculties of Austrian universities was attributable to the "neuerdings verbesserten und gesicherten Lage der Staatsbeamten."

52. *SPB*, 3 Feb. 1884, pp. 17–19; 3 Aug. 1884, p. 121; 7 Sept. 1884, p. 141; 17 Oct. 1884, p. 170.

53. *SPB*, 17 Oct. 1884, pp. 170–71; 7 June 1885, p. 89; 21 June 1885, p. 99.

54. For the early history of the *Verband, SPB*, 12 Apr. 1885, p. 57; 19 Apr. 1885, p. 61; 14 June 1885, p. 96; 21 Mar. 1886, p. 45; 4 Apr. 1886, pp. 53–54; 20 June 1886, p. 98.

55. *SPB*, 27 Mar. 1887, p. 49.

56. Ibid., 4 Jan. 1891, pp. 1–2.

57. *DV*, 24 Feb. 1889 (M), p. 5.

58. The ambivalence of governmental (and Liberal) policy toward the full active political rights of the officials was most clearly demonstrated in the 1880s in the half-hearted attempts of the government to control agitation among the schoolteachers, who were the most politically mobilized group among the middle-Bürgertum in this period.

59. Government harassment of the political activities of individual schoolteachers tended to ease up once the political party involved had gained access to a measure of public power. After 1897 the government was very lax in its dealings with Christian Social sympathizers among the schoolteachers.

60. Victor Schidl, "Die österreichische Staatsbeamtenorganisation. Ihre Ziele und Methoden," *Dokumente des Fortschritts* 4 (1911): 92–96.

61. Thus, the Viennese *Beamten* did not suffer from the dilemma of the Prussian *Beamten* in being left in a relatively depoliticized status in the pre-1914 period, just as the Austrian artisan Mittelstand was not left in a noneffective, neofeudal status in Vienna. Heinrich August Winkler's conclusions in his study of the German Mittelstand are not applicable to

Vienna, since in Vienna privileged Bürger voting rights, the competitive sponsorship of the nationality groups, and the development of an effective Mittelstand movement under Lueger gave the Mittelstand a relatively stable political home.

62. The gradual shift of *Beamten* voter support away from the Liberals after 1889 may have been due to the increasing willingness of such men who resided in the suburbs but worked in the city to vote in the municipal elections. By the 1885 franchise reforms, such men were entitled to vote in the district in which they were employed, but the antisemites had a great deal of difficulty in overcoming their apathy. Many felt, according to a report in the *DV*, that the Viennese municipal elections had no meaning for their lives, and so they ignored them. In 1891, of course, these men would have become citizens of the city and would thus have had more interest in local political affairs. *DV,* 7 Feb. 1889 (M), p. 4; 16 Feb. 1889 (M), p. 5.

63. In 1889 the antisemites had picked up three seats in the Second Curia of the Council; in 1890 they won an additional six. However, this was done on a very ad hoc basis with little formal organizational appeal to white collar voters as such. The antisemites were almost as surprised as the Liberals were shocked at their early successes among *Beamten* voters. It was not until the crucial elections of Mar.–Apr. 1891 that the antisemites mounted a consistent, well-organized campaign to appeal to the *Beamten*.

64. *DV,* 21 Mar. 1890 (A), p. 4.

65. *SP,* X, 1889, pp. 12946–47.

66. *BSWG,* 1890, pp. 1108–10, 1113, 1121–22.

67. During a police investigation of this matter, which Kielmansegg ordered because of his suspicions that a security leak had occurred in his office, Polzhofer admitted that he was given the secret franchise proposal by Robert Pattai, who, in turn, had obtained it from Joseph Schöffel. Schöffel was a renegade Lower Austrian Democrat from Baden who, during his long career in the Landtag, often took delight in embarrassing the ruling Liberal party. He eventually voted for the unification bill, however. See the police interview with Polzhofer, 14 Sept. 1890, in M1889–90, Stadterweiterungsakten, 2962a, Nr. 6584, *NÖLA.*

68. Gautsch to Kielmansegg, 3 Oct. 1890, B2 ad 4110, Nr. 7116/1890, *NÖLA.*

69. *NFP,* 13 Sept 1890 (M), p. 5; 17 Sept. 1890 (M), p. 5.

70. *DV,* 25 Sept. 1890 (M), p. 5.

71. Ibid., 28 Sept 1890. The concern of the teachers was manifested in a petition demanding the passive franchise which they drafted and submitted to Kielmansegg (27 Sept. 1890), B2 ad 4110, Nr. 7116, *NÖLA*).

72. *NFP,* 17 Sept. 1890 (M), p. 5.

73. Ibid., 16 July 1890 (M), p. 3; 17 July 1890 (M), p. 3.

74. Schnabl was able to force Grübl into a runoff because the Schönerians ran a third candidate and deprived either of the two major candidates of an absolute majority. In the runoff many of the voters attracted to the Nationalists voted for Schnabl.

75. The Liberals themselves realized the importance of toning down their traditional anticlericalism after 1890, especially under the prodding of Ernst v Plener. See esp. *V,* 2 Feb. 1895, Beilage Nr. 1; *PV* 5:484.

76. *SPB,* 29 Mar. 1891, p. 1.

77. For the rank structure of the Austrian state bureaucracy, see Josef Eissert, "Die persönlichen Bezüge im Staatshaushalte Oesterreichs," *BZ* 21 (1890), pp. 509–12, 526–28. In 1890 the state employed 33,857 tenured *Beamten* at all ranks (including 3,700 in the state railway systems). This statistic does *not* include the *Staatsdiener* or the part-time clerks *(Diurnisten),* who were paid a daily wage but who often ended up doing the same tasks as regular officials because of the government's failure to provide sufficient staff or to utilize the staff which it did have in an efficient manner. Of the 33,857 individuals, 39.8% had some

kind of university or higher technical training, 8.6% had completed a *Mittelschule*, 28.8% had attended a *Mittelschule* or an *Untergymnasium* of some kind for a period of years without gaining an *Abitur*, and 11.7% had only *Volksschule* training on their records. Another 11% had special technical education credentials. For a clear description of the three broad status levels within the bureaucracy, see also the comments of Hans Mayer in *Protokolle der Enquête über Personalcredit und Wucher*, VII, pp. 3–7. Mayer, who was an official with the Lower Austrian provincial government, believed that most of the debts accumulated by these men were largely owing to their family responsibilities. The time when an individual would be likely to feel the greatest financial pressure was, however, different for each of the three ranks. The *Zertifikatisten*, who were usually thirty-two to thirty-four years old upon entering the state bureaucracy, often found themselves in debt because their civil appointments were delayed for months or even years beyond the expiration date of their enlistments in the army. Also, the government did not provide them with an allowance for the costs of relocation from one part of the monarchy to another. For the *Mittelschule* types, many of whom ended up in the government's financial and communications services, and who began their careers between eighteen and twenty years of age, financial problems beset the whole course of their careers. Most of these men were married by the age of thirty, and few of them ever rose byond Rank VIII salary. They were also the largest numerical group of the three. For the *Juristen*, who had university credentials, marriage was usually deferred until after the *Praktikanten* probationary period. Mayer estimated that as many as 50% of these higher ranking officials, having delayed doing so in their youths, chose never to marry. Precise statistics on the number of men who worked in the Viennese metropolitan region itself are not readily available, but a safe estimate would be approximately 25% of the whole.

78. See the correlation between rank achievement and occupational designation and educational background in Eissert, "Die persönlichen Bezüge," p. 527.

79. One of the criticisms raised frequently by the *Beamten-Verein* against the 1873 salary law for state officials was that it failed to provide a separate rank and salary subsection within the XI *Rangclasse* for men with *Mittelschule* educational backgrounds. See *BZ* 21 (1890): 41–42.

80. Ibid., 15 (1884): 146–48; and esp. *SB* 1 (1896): 119 ("Der Standard of life, die der socialen Stellung des Beamten entsprechende Entlohnung kann demnach unter allen Umständen nur dann gesichert erscheinen, wenn jeder Staatsbeamte im Laufe seiner Dienstzeit zeitgemäss eine Rangclasse erreicht, welche ihm eine Lebenshaltung gestattet, die nicht nur vor Nahrungssorgen schützt, sondern auch die Würde und die Ehre der staatlichen Berufsstellung nach aussen kenntlich macht").

81. This fundamental psychological distinction in Viennese society between intermediate level *Beamten* and *Kanzlisten*, for whom the term *subaltern* was usually used, was of crucial importance in understanding the political behavior of the Austrian Mittelstand. One sees the same phenomenon in the young Hitler's adulation of his father as a "senior Imperial customs official" (even though his father never advanced beyond an advanced intermediate rank), which, as Joachim Fest has pointed out, reveals the curiously Austrian origins of Hitler's sense of social stratification and social prestige among the various levels of the Austrian and Viennese Bürgertum. The Viennese did not think of the Mittelstand or the Bürgertum as divided simply between a grande bourgeoisie and a petite bourgeoisie. In relative, self-evaluative terms there existed a broad *Mittelbürgertum* and upper Mittelstand in Vienna which both the Liberals and the Christian Socials depended upon for voting support. See Joachim Fest, *Hitler*, trans. by Richard and Clara Winston (New York, 1975), pp. 32–37. For the three rank levels of the Austrian state bureaucracy, see also Alfred Hoffmann, "Bürokratie insbesondere in Österreich," p. 20.

82. Hansjoachim Henning, *Das westdeutsche Bürgertum in der Epoche der Hoch-industrialisierung, 1860–1914. Soziales Verhalten und soziale Strukturen* (Wiesbaden, 1972).

83. *PAAA,* Öst.70/Bd. 24, A10931, Nr. 292, Bericht aus Wien, 3 Oct. 1890. The *NFP* confirmed Reuss's analysis when it complained on 18 Sept. 1890 that with the elections less than two weeks away the Liberals had done very little in way of preparation. See *NFP,* 18 Sept. 1890 (M), p. 1.

84. Till, *Stadtverwaltung,* p. 97. Kielmansegg reported on 13 Oct. that the Imperial government had attempted to take into consideration the desires of the city of Vienna in drafting the final version, which meant in effect that the government had given the Liberal party what it wanted and needed. *NFP,* 14 Oct. 1890 (M), pp. 2–3.

85. The antisemitic delegates walked out of the Landtag before the final vote. Lueger would not vote against unification, but he could not vote for it.

86. Till, *Stadtverwaltung,* pp. 86, 96, 98. Adolf Daum, *Zur Reform der Wiener Gemeindeordnung* (Vienna, 1890).

87. For a discussion of the operations of the Prussian *Magistrat* system, see H. Kappelmann, "Die Verfassung und Verwaltungsorganisation der preussischen Städte nach der Städteordnung vom 30. Mai 1853," *Verfassung und Verwaltungsorganisation der Städte, SVSP,* vol. 117 (1906). Also, Otto Most, ed., *Die deutsche Stadt und ihre Verwaltung* (3 vols., Berlin, 1912). On Rudolf Gneist's conservative attitudes toward systematic party control of municipalities, see Heinrich Heffter, *Die deutsche Selbstverwaltung im 19. Jahrhundert* (Stuttgart, 1950), pp. 372–403, 731–47, and Rudolf Gneist, "The Government of Berlin," *CR* 46 (1884): 769–94, which provides a concise statement of Gneist's views on the idea of municipal government.

88. Adolf Daum, a Viennese Liberal who was often at odds with the regular Liberal organization in Vienna, argued for a revised *Gemeindeordnung* which would be similar to that used by Prussian and Bavarian cities, in that the powers of the appointive *Magistrat* would have been enhanced. Daum's ideas found little support in Vienna, however. See Daum, *Zur Reform,* pp. 18–19.

89. Till, *Stadtverwaltung,* p. 99; Daum, *Zur Reform,* pp. 10–15. It was not surprising that the professional civil servants employed in the *Magistrat* reacted with hostility to this attempt to exert more political control over their careers. In mid-Oct. 1890, the *Club der Conceptsbeamten* voted to send a delegation to Kielmansegg to protest the powers which the new statute gave to the *Stadtrat* and to ask that control over the *Magistrat* be retained by the office of the mayor. Later in the month they backed down, fearing disciplinary action against them by Prix and the Liberals. See *BZ* 21 (1890): 519, 587–88. Even after 1890, when in most larger German cities the processes of bureaucratization and professionalization were placing greater limits on the powers of the *Stadtverordnetenversammlung* to control the city *Communalbeamten* in German municipalities (a trend which enhanced the powers of the Bavarian and Prussian *Bürgermeister,* most of whom claimed to be "nonpolitical"), in Vienna a tradition of power distribution evolved which was very different. The *Bürgermeister* of Vienna was a local party-political leader and not a trained administrator. It was not surprising that the local officials reacted to this situation by organizing a professional pressure group to defend their interests against all political parties. For developments in Germany, which were distinct from the pattern of development in Vienna, see James J. Sheehan, "Liberalism and the City in Nineteenth-Century Germany," *PP* 51 (1971): 116–37.

90. Till, *Stadtverwaltung,* pp. 98ff.

91. Prix was the leader of the *Mittelpartei* by 1889. Like Lueger, however, he had started his political career in the 1870s as an opponent of Felder's political hegemony. After the Newald catastrophe he shifted his loyalties to the Right within Viennese Liberalism. See *Z,* 1 June 1895, p. 130, and Felder, *Erinnerungen,* pp. 199–200.

92. *PV* 5:322.

93. Theoretical discussions of the idea of municipal autonomy and the function of the free community within the monarchical or constitutional monarchical state did not begin in any systematic fashion until after 1848. During the *Stände* movement of the 1840s, however, especially in Lower Austria and in Bohemia, the notion of municipal autonomy was a much vaunted concept.

94. I use the concept of subordination here only in a dynamic power sense and not as a theoretical objection to Hugo Preuss's arguments in favor of the original and immediate autonomy of the free *Gemeinde* against the sovereign state.

95. See esp. Hugo Preuss, "Verwaltungsreform und Staatsreform in Österreich und Preussen," *ZP* 5 (1912): 219–35.

96. See, for example, the lead article in the *NFP*, 12 Sept. 1890 (M), p. 2, admiring the city of Berlin for its ability to suppress political agitation and radicalism. Ernst v Plener had doubts about the free, competitive system of Vienna, but he could not persuade the Liberals to restructure the city's politics along the Prussian model. Plener, *Erinnerungen*, 3:258–59.

97. Lueger was extremely frank about the need the antisemites felt for having annual election campaigns: "Die alljährigen Ergänzungswahlen sind ein Glück, weil der Gemeinderath doch wenigstens sich einmal im Jahr gelegentlich der Wahlen mit den Wählern ins Einvernehmen setzen kann, und die Wähler wenigstens einmal im Jahr das Glück haben, ihre Gewählten von Angesicht zu Angesicht sehen zu können." *BSWG*, 1890, p. 1182.

98. The population of the inner districts was 817,299, that of the suburbs 524,598. On an exact proportional basis, the suburbs should have received fifty-three seats rather than forty-five. Also, the Liberals gave the First and Second Districts an overproportional representation because of their reliability.

99. The First through Ninth Districts had a Jewish population of 99,441 in 1890, as opposed to 18,387 for the suburbs.

100. *WZ*, 18 Sept. 1890, p. 3; 28 Nov. 1890, p. 2; 4 Dec. 1890, pp. 2–3. For the final debates in the Lower Austrian Landtag on the unification legislation, see *SPNÖLTG*, 7 Wahlperiode, I, 1890, pp. 504–830.

101. *PV* 5:317.

102. The text of the 1850 *Gemeindeordnung* for Vienna is in the *WZ*, 23 Mar. 1850, pp. 1–3. Each of the curias received forty seats, but those of the First Curia were distributed by tax performance among the districts, whereas in the Second and Third Curias each district received a fixed allocation of seats. In 1861 the First Curia in the First District ended up with eighteen seats, but by 1890 this had declined to twelve, owing to the increasing prosperity of other districts in the city. For a discussion of the operations of the early franchise system, see Hahnkamper, *Der Wiener Gemeinderat*, esp. pp. 123–97.

103. Income taxes for government employees were regulated by the Imperial Patent of 29 Oct. 1849. Cf. *RGBl*, 1849, Nr. 439.

104. For the Aug. 1849 draft, see Weiss, *Entwicklung der Gemeinde-Verfassung*, pp. 104–25.

105. For Bach's adjustments, ibid., pp. 127–30; J. Prochazka, *Die provisorische Gemeindeordnung für die Stadt Wien* (Vienna, 1850), pp. 56ff.

106. For a defense of the curial system, see *PR*, 22 June 1849, p. 1; for a critique of the curial idea, see *ODP*, 14 June 1849, p. 1; ibid., 15 June 1849, p. 1.

107. The provisional City Council had enacted in late Aug. 1848 a temporary municipal franchise in order to conduct new elections for the City Council in the autumn of 1848. This *Ordnung* provided for the complete enfranchisement of the unitary Bürgertum—all 5 fl. men were enfranchised and included with the rest of the Bürgertum in a noncurial assembly. From the debates in the Council in Aug., it is clear that many delegates wanted as many

officials as possible included in the *Intelligenz* section of the *Ordnung* in order to offset the weight and influence of the *Kleinbürger* artisans, not because they actually wanted the officials to get the vote.

108. *ZWN*, 30 June 1848, pp. 78–79; also, *CON*, 29 Mar. 1848, pp. 64–65 (a more radical viewpoint).

109. In general, for Prussia, see Reinhart Koselleck, *Preussen zwischen Reform und Revolution* (Stuttgart, 1967). Vienna's political traditions before 1848 were not so restrictive as those of many Prussian cities in terms of limiting political participation in the city assembly to Bürger types. To belong to the *Äussere Rath* after 1790 did not necessarily require ownership of a house. Rather, "personal capacities" might be taken into consideration. However, because Austria did not enjoy the kind of urban reforms enacted by Stein in Prussia, municipal political institutions had very little significance in Vienna before 1848. Generally, service as an *Armenvater* or as a *Gerichtsbeisitzer* was all that was required by the government before a man might be appointed to the *Äussere Rath*. The 1850 franchise for Vienna still reflected in its language something of the older social distinction between a *Stadtbürger* and a member of the *Intelligenz* (or, more specifically, the *Honoratioren*), since it divided voters into two groups—*Gemeindebürger* and *Gemeindeangehörigen*. The members of the former group would in general be those who practiced a trade or owned a house in the city before 1850 and who had been admitted to the *Bürgerschaft* under pre-1848 regulations. The *Angehörigen* were in part individuals owning no *Besitz* or *Gewerbe*, such as officials, clerics, teachers, academics, and certain categories of military officers. But the law also acknowledged that in the future men buying a house or setting up a trade would not necessarily be covered by pre-1848 conceptions of the *Bürgerschaft*, and therefore created a special category of *Angehörigen* who owned a business and a trade and who paid at least 10 fl. in direct taxes, who might now be able to vote. In time the number of *Angehörigen* in the city far surpassed the number of the *Bürgerschaft*. Thus, the older distinction of voting rights being limited to the *Bürgerschaft* and the *Bürgerschaft* including most of the stable *Besitz* and business in the city exploded. Henceforth the title of Bürger was a purely honorific one awarded by the ruling political party in Vienna (whether Liberal or Christian Social) to older artisans and businessmen or to property owners who had distinguished themselves in their careers. Ludwig Spiegel examined the legal meanings of the term Bürger in 1907 and concluded that urban social and administrative legislation in Austria had evolved so far beyond that of the Vormärz in complexity that the term could not be defined in any single legal sense. See Ludwig Spiegel, "Das Heimatrecht und die Gemeinden," *Verfassung und Verwaltungsorganisation der Städte*, SVSP 122 (1907): 20–29; also, Karl Weiss, *Entwicklung der Gemeinde-Verfassung*, p. 98.

110. *SPB*, 6 July 1884, p. 105.

111. Felder, *Lebenserinnerungen*, pp. 140–41.

112. Legislation passed in Jan. 1867 eliminated the discrimination in the 1850 statute against those in arrears in their taxes. The law of Oct. 1868 made it possible for taxpaying residents of Vienna who were not permanent residents and who thus did not qualify for Bürger or *Angehörige* status to vote. See Gustav Schimmer's summary in *SM* 6 (1880): 536–38.

113. *SJ*, 1886, p. 51; *DV*, 7 Feb. 1889 (M), p. 4.

114. See the speeches of the Liberals who sponsored the Mar. 1873 salary legislation, in *SP*, VII, 1873, pp. 1256–1321.

115. *RGBl*, 1873, Nr. 47, pp. 221–24. The Liberal *Beamten-Zeitung* never failed to point out to its readers that they owed the 1873 salary reforms to the Liberal party. For example, see *BZ* 21 (1890): 7–8, 41–42.

116. For Thun's reforms, see Hans Lentze, *Die Universitätsreform des Ministers Graf*

Leo Thun-Hohenstein, passim. After taking power in Austria, the early Liberals tried to denigrate Thun's work and to emphasize the revolutionary creativity and liberality of their own reforms in the early 1870s, but later Liberals adopted a more balanced judgment of Thun's reforms. See ibid., pp. 283–94, and H. Schrutka v Rechtenstamm, "Rechts- und Staatswissenschaftliche Facultät," *Geschichte der Wiener Universität von 1848 bis 1898* (Vienna, 1898). The effect of Thun's reforms on the development of modern Liberalism in Austria remains an unexamined topic for future research. The introduction of a legal history/common law program of juridical training for Austrian lawyers and *Staatsbeamten* after 1850–55 must have had an important effect on the development of the third generation of Austrian Liberalism (those men who received their university legal training between 1860 and 1875) and on the first generation of anti-Liberal politicians who were also trained in the law, such as Karl Lueger and Robert Pattai.

117. See the speech of Friedrich Dittes, the Liberal, Protestant school reformer, when he ran against Lueger in the Landstrasse in 1890. *NFP,* 4 Mar. 1890 (M), p. 4. Ernst v Plener expressed these Liberal assumptions in a surprisingly explicit sense in Mar. 1891. He argued that "Alle Massregeln zur Hebung des Beamtenstandes sind theils von unserer Partei durchgeführt, theils wenigstens angeregt worden.... Die ganzen Traditionen des Beamtenstandes, wenn sie ernstgenommen und hochgehalten werden, weisen dieser Wählerclasse keinen anderen Platz an als die Zugehörigkeit zu unserer Partei." *SPB,* 5 Apr. 1891, p. 2. See also *MP,* 16 Mar. 1873, pp. 2–3.

118. *PV* 1:315.

119. *SP,* VII, 1872, pp. 495–99.

120. See the comments in *MP,* 16 May 1873, pp. 2–3; 22 Oct. 1873, p. 2; and *DEZ,* 2 May 1874, p. 2. The Democrats in Vienna often complained about the propensity of *Beamten* voters to support the Liberals. The 1873 salary law cost the state 9.7 million additional gulden in budgetary outlays. For that kind of money, the Liberals expected something in return—to wit, political cooperation.

121. Joseph Schöffel, *Erinnerungen aus meinem Leben* (Vienna, 1905), pp. 8–11.

122. *Tafeln zur Statistik der Österreichischen Monarchie/Neue Folge I* (Vienna, 1856), Heft 8, pp. 10–11, 53; *Statistiches Jahrbuch für das Jahr 1881* (Vienna, 1884), pp. 10–13, 42–43; *SJ,* 1884, pp. 154–56. These statistics are based on winter semester enrollments. In the case of both the enrollments and the juristic exams, the great increase took place after 1861, that is, during the constitutional era in Austria. See also Franz v Juraschek, "Der Besuch der österreichischen Universitäten in den Jahren 1861–1875," pp. 303–37. Enrollment data for the Vormärz are more difficult to evaluate, but the enrollment level in the legal faculty of the University of Vienna seems to have stabilized with approximately 1,462 students registered in 1847. By 1880, therefore, the number of students enrolled in law at the University of Vienna had increased by 35% from the later 1840s. See *Tafeln zur Statistik der Österreichischen Monarchie für die Jahre 1847 und 1848* (Vienna, 1953), Zweiter Teil, A, section 11, p. 1. In respect to university enrollments I have used the data from 1851, rather than from 1847, to show how far the reformed and modernized higher educational systems had developed from the nadir of the revolutionary period. The absolute increase in students was much greater for intermediate schools than for the universities.

123. Cf. *Tafeln...Neue Folge I,* Heft 8, pp. 20–21, 34; *Neue Folge II,* Heft 9, p. 3; *Statistisches Jahrbuch...1881,* pp. 92–93, 104–5, 110–11. For the development of intermediate educational institutions in Vienna, see Wilhelm Löwy, *Das Unterrichtswesen in Wien,* part 2, *Mittel- und Hochschulen* (Vienna, 1891), pp. 3–15; Joseph Hain, *Handbuch der Statistik des österreichischen Kaiserstaates* (2 vols., Vienna, 1853), 2:667, who estimated a 22% decline in secondary enrollments between 1841 and 1851. Even allowing for this drop,

however, the growth after 1851 was formidable (from 2,700 in 1841 to over 5,000 in 1881). It is certain that some graduates of Austrian *Realschulen* eventually found careers as *Angestellten* in Austrian commercial and industrial bureaucracies, a pattern quite similar to developments in Germany. See Jürgen Kocka, *Unternehmensverwaltung und Angestelltenschaft am Beispiel Siemens, 1847–1914* (Stuttgart, 1969), pp. 466–73. Available statistics do not reveal the source of *Mittelschule* training for the 37% of the state *Beamten* who claimed such training in 1890. It is likely that many of these men had attended an *Untergymnasium* or an *Unterrealschule* for some period of time before trying to obtain full-time employment in the government. Many of the middle sectors of the state and private railway bureaucracies were recruited from the ranks of such men.

124. This partial Slavicization of the Austrian state bureaucracy occurred in several stages. Its pace and success varied in terms of the specific national group involved, the location of the conflict (whether in the central ministries in Vienna or in local units of administration in the provinces), the rank and salary levels at stake, and the climate of national politics at any given point in time. For the slow, but steady penetration of Czechs into the Viennese central ministries by 1900, see Glettler, *Die Wiener Tschechen*, pp. 70–72.

125. The *Beamten* newspapers of the late 1880s and early 1890s in Vienna emphasized the unique worth and prestige of the career of the state official and of the usefulness of the official to civil society. Important here was the careful articulation of such notions, which stressed performance-oriented behavioral criteria, as well as the fact that officials felt that making such ideas explicit in a public context was both tactically useful and psychologically necessary. One *Beamten* newspaper called for the renewal of the old *Corpsgeist* of the state officials as a way of encouraging their collegiality. This in turn would raise the *Ehre* of their occupation in the eyes of late-nineteenth-century society. The paper proved that it did not want a return to older, neo-*ständisch* values for their own sake, however, by then arguing that the heightened collegiality and increased honor of the officials would give them an excellent justification for requesting more salary raises from the government. Older values and newer utility would combine to justify in a hard functional sense the prerogatives and rewards owed to the officials. See *ÖSBZ*, 15 Feb. 1895, p. 1.

126. See the complaints of the *Kanzleibeamten* in the administrative service that they deserved respect and "decorum" appropriate to their *Stand*, and following from this, that they deserved a salary raise, a *Dienstpragmatik*, better pensions, and a reduced service time before retirement, in *SPB*, 15 Nov. 1885, p. 181. Other articles complained about the miserable treatment and contempt the *Kanzlisten* received from the higher and intermediate ranking officials in the *Verwaltungsdienst*. See *ÖSBZ*, 1 Jan. 1892, p. 10; 15 Jan. 1892, p. 17; 15 Feb. 1892, p. 7; 1 Aug. 1892, p. 10. The *Diurnisten* question was one of the most troublesome and difficult personnel issues facing the government and the parliament. Most of these men were qualified to be enrolled in the second status category of the *Mittelschule* type (and some even had university training), and most were forced to do the same work as tenured officials for considerably lower financial and psychological rewards. Since *Diurnisten* could be hired and fired at will (they were paid on a per diem basis with no job security), their existence gave the government some flexibility in managing both the administrative and the political aspects of personnel decisions. On the *Diurnisten* problem, see *BZ* 21 (1890): 116–17, 290, 514–15.

127. In the German-language *Beamten* newspapers, Dunajewski was portrayed in the most unfavorable light. See, for example, *SPB*, 8 Feb. 1891, p. 1.

128. *ÖSBZ*, 1 June 1895, p. 6; *SPB*, 15 Feb. 1891, p. 1.

129. See the comments of J. Havranek in *Die nationale Frage in der Österreichisch-Ungarischen Monarchie, 1900–1918* (Budapest, 1966), pp. 329–30.

130. *AZ,* 17 June 1898, p. 3.

131. Data on the outstanding loans of the *Verein* were published in an annual report attached to the *BZ.* The data cited here are based on the 1889 reports.

132. *Protokolle der Enquête über Personalcredit und Wucher* (Vienna, 1904).

133. The fact that many Austrian university graduates and, in turn, that a number of the young men who managed to survive the relative penury of the *Praktikanten* stage (in Austria *Praktikanten* were paid a small subsistence allowance) of the state bureaucracy were men who came from very humble family backgrounds made this discrepancy between what they thought they ought to achieve in monetary rewards and the consumption such rewards would allow them all the more intolerable. For them, the position of state official was one resulting from the most extraordinary personal and familial sacrifice, a sacrifice which in many cases seemed to go unnoticed and unrewarded. A similar process of disenchantment, using relative status criteria designed in terms of the antinomy family poverty/personal achievement, was also to be found among the middle ranks of the state bureaucracy. The humble backgrounds of the Austrian university graduates and the lack of "culture" of many Austrian state officials were often used by higher ranking state officials as an explanation for the alleged corruption in the Austrian civil service. Although the arrogance implied in such interpretations was obvious, they were often not far from the truth. See esp. Friedrich v Schulte, "Bureaucracy and Its Operation in Germany and Austria-Hungary," *CR* 37 (1880): 455–56, 439–42. The university student population in Austria was less representative of major wealth resources than was that of Germany. Prussian salaries for civil servants were, in turn, more generous than those offered for similar rank and status positions in Austria.

134. Gerd Hohorst, Jürgen Kocka, and Gerhard A. Ritter, *Sozialgeschichtliches Arbeitsbuch. Materialien zur Statistik des Kaiserreichs, 1870–1914* (Munich, 1975), pp. 96–99, 115.

135. The drive of many Viennese white collar families to maintain appropriate levels of personal material consumption was often subject to bitter and ultimately unfair ridicule in contemporary periodicals like *Die Fackel.*

136. Dittes was an extreme supporter of the demand for including the teachers in the Second Curia in the 1870s. See *DEZ,* 8 Nov. 1873, p. 2; 15 May 1875, pp. 1–2.

137. This change in occupational claims was well illustrated in the new conception of the teacher as a *Volksschullehrer* as opposed to the older *Schulmeister.* See Rudolf Gönner, *Die österreichische Lehrerbildung von der Normalschule bis zur Pädagogischen Akademie* (Vienna, 1967), p. 144; Peter Ladinger, *Die soziale Stellung der Volksschullehrer vor und nach dem Reichsvolksschulgesetz* (diss., University of Vienna, 1975); Hubert Teml, "Die Lehrerbildung nach dem Reichsvolksschulgesetz," in *Österreichische Bildungs- und Schulgeschichte von der Aufklärung bis zum Liberalismus. Jahrbuch für österreichische Kulturgeschichte* 4 (1974):92–93.

138. On the effect of the *Wiener Pädagogium,* see Hermann Schnell, *100 Jahre Pädagogisches Institut der Stadt Wien* (Vienna, 1968), pp. 44–56; Gönner, *Die österreichische Lehrerbildung,* pp. 183–85, 193. Gönner reports that by the end of the nineteenth century the *Lehrerschaft* was "nun der Bedeutung ihres Berufes und seiner grossen ideellen und materiellen Aufgaben stärker bewusst geworden."

139. A similar upgrading occurred in the profession of *Mittelschule* professor, which before 1850 was not considered to be a career of significant prestige. By the 1890s the situation had changed dramatically. See *NFP,* 3 Mar. 1890 (M), p. 6. For parallels in Germany, see Henning, *Das westdeutsche Bürgertum,* pp. 125, 142, 182, 486.

140. A central association of German-speaking schoolteachers in Austria, the *Deutschösterreichischer Lehrerbund,* was established in Nov. 1885, but already by the late 1870s the province of Lower Austria and the city of Vienna had twenty-one different teacher associations. Teachers had a greater social opportunity to organize themselves into an interest

group, since professional organizations seemed appropriate and vital to their regular work—they helped in disseminating new pedagogical methods, they served as the basis for provincial evaluations of the school system, etc. Also, the spread of teacher organizations was greatly intensified by the attack on the public-school system which the Clerical Conservatives began in the late 1870s and the early 1880s.

141. "Communallehrer und Magistratsbeamte," in *SPB*, 19 Apr. 1885, p. 61. Also, the frank comments of Johann Prix, who admitted in 1890 that the teacher appointment process had become politicized. *NFP*, 2 Dec. 1890 (M), p. 3.

142. The rising self-esteem which occurred first among the schoolteachers and only later among the *Beamten* was apparent in the debates of the various teacher congresses held in the 1870s and 1880s. See, for example, the *Protokolle des VII. allgemeinen österreichischen Lehrertages* (Vienna, 1879), pp. 27–28, in which one speaker insisted that the teachers had as much *Intelligenz* as did the university graduates and demanded that their *Ehrgefühl* as professionals be respected by giving them the *Einjährig-Freiwilligen-Recht*.

143. *SPB*, 13 Feb. 1884, p. 19; 19 Apr. 1885, p. 61; 21 Mar. 1886, p. 45.

144. The Liberals in the Landtag had tried on two previous occasions to get the vote for the teachers, once in 1875 and again in 1883, but on both occasions the Imperial government refused to sanction the bills. Only when the 5 fl. men were put in the Third Curia did Taaffe see fit to open the Second Curia to the officials and teachers. It is clear, however, that these groups' own self-image, which had changed drastically since the Vormärz, played a significant role in the willingness of the Liberals to support and endorse such legislation. For the earlier attempts, see *SPNÖLTG*, 6 Wahlperiode, Beilage Nr. 74, pp. 7–8.

145. *SPB*, 13 Dec. 1885, p. 198; 4 Apr. 1886, pp. 53–54.

146. *SP*, XI, 1891, pp. 2144–52, and *PV* 5:137. In Feb. 1891 a senior jurist in the Austrian appellate court system in Styria issued a warning to judges in the province against antisemitic attitudes. See *NFP*, 24 Feb. 1891 (M), p. 1.

147. *PAAA*, Öst. 70/Bd. 28, A3841, 11 Apr. 1895 ("Graf Kalnoky sagte mir dass die Beamten seines Ressorts ohne Ausnahme für die Antisemiten gestimmt hatten").

148. *Protokolle der Enquête über Personalcredit und Wucher*, VII, p. 6.

149. There was a clear parallel here between the motives of the Catholic priests, who felt resentful over the unwillingness of secular Austrian bourgeois society to recognize the value of their educational attainments, and the middle levels of the state bureaucracy, which found that their educational credentials bought very little in terms of market value.

150. *SPB*, 4 Jan. 1891, p. 2. The police reported to Kielmansegg that "Das Gros der mit den Antisemiten gehenden Staatsbeamten ist wohl noch jetzt nicht ganz als antisemitisch zu betrachten." B2, Nr. 7831/1895, *NÖLA*.

151. See the *Allgemeines Beamten Program* in the *SPB*, 15 Feb. 1891, p. 1, which provides a convenient summary of the current complaints.

152. The number of small *Hausherren* transferred out of the Second Curia was not more than 1,796 for the Second through Tenth Districts. For this estimate, see Boyer, "Veränderungen im politischen Leben Wiens," note 182.

153. *SJ*, 1891, pp. 84–85.

154. The relative size of each of these components in each district is very difficult to estimate. Some of the districts had a high proportion of lower ranked *Staats-* and *Communalbeamten*, such as Währing, where nearly two-thirds of the Second Curia came from their ranks. In the older districts of the city the percentage of these voters in the Second Curia would not have been as high. In each of the districts the *Hausbesitzer* constituted a significant segment of the electorate, but because they were divided between the Second and the First Curias, their representation in the Second Curia is difficult to estimate precisely. The *NWT* reported that the Second Curia in the Josefstadt contained approximately 800

state officials out of a total electorate in the curia of 1,366. There were also 150 *Privat-beamten* and 80 teachers. The remaining 300 voters were largely *Hausherren*. See *NWT*, 8 Apr. 1891, pp. 6–7. Under the 1890 statute an individual voted in the district in which he lived. The office of the mayor was responsible for preparing and opening to public inspection the voting lists at least four weeks before the election. Voters received official ballots and legitimation cards about two weeks prior to voting.

155. Eduard Suess pointed to this uneasiness as early as 1882 in Reichsrat debates on the national suffrage reform legislation of that year. Suess's views were not shared at the time, however, by most Austrian Liberals.

156. "Wiener Patriot" to Erich Kielmansegg, 5 Nov. 1890, M1889–90, Stadter-weiterungsakten, *NÖLA*.

157. Lueger's respect for private property and personal investment was clearly revealed during the testimony at the famous libel trial which he instigated against Alexander Scharf, the editor of the *Sonn- und Montagszeitung*, in Nov. 1890. Lueger had been the legal counsel for the *Rudolfsheimer Spar- und Vorschussverein* from 1874 to 1881. When given the task of prosecuting delinquent debtors or mortgagees of the *Verein*, Lueger proceeded with a ruthlessness and an efficiency which later came back to haunt him in 1890. Many of the delinquent debtors were impoverished artisans and petty shopkeepers! See *NFP*, 27 Nov. 1890 (A), p. 2; 28 Nov. 1890 (M), pp. 6–8.

158. For Lueger's advocacy of the abolition of the curial system, see *SPNÖLTG*, 7 Wahl-periode, I, 1890, pp. 736–38, 754–58. For the Liberal response by Nicholas Dumba, see ibid., pp. 758–59. For Lueger's admission of the desirability of having a "curia of the in-telligentsia," see ibid., pp. 781–82. Lueger was also against transferring *Hausherren* into the Third Curia, demonstrating that he too was sensitive to the fact that many voters in the city *liked* the idea of privileged curias.

159. *DV*, 7 Apr. 1891.

160. Pichl, *Schönerer*, 4:87–94. The Liberals were weakened in the Fifth, Eighth, and Ninth Districts by having Democratic candidates run against them, making for three-way races.

161. "New voters" in this instance refers to newly registered voters or voters who had been previously registered but who had not participated in the 1890 Landtag election. In Mariahilf the antisemites picked up 486 new votes, the Liberals only 53. In Neubau and in Josefstadt the antisemitic-Liberal ratios were 605:331 and 240:164, respectively. In the Landstrasse and in the Alsergrund, on the other hand, the Liberals fared somewhat better. In the Landstrasse the Liberals won 684 new votes, whereas the antisemites lost 420. (The Anti-semites ran two candidates—these data are based on a consolidated total.) In the Alsergrund the Liberals won 212 new votes, while the antisemites lost 851. The voting in the Land-strasse proved that the Liberals were also able to attract former antisemitic voters, since some of the 684 "new" votes here were doubtless those of the voters who had deserted the antisemites and *not* those of newly registered voters. In the Alsergrund the Liberals profited largely from transfers and not from any new voters as such.

162. Reichsrat elections offered the antisemites the opportunity to run their highest pro-filed candidates. A good example of the criteria for successful candidate selection on the national level was the case of Professor Joseph Schlesinger, who ran for the antisemites in the Josefstadt.

163. It is interesting to note that large numbers of Czech artisans voted for the Christian Social/antisemitic coalition in this election, even though the antisemitic voter club in Favor-iten was markedly German nationalist and pro-Schönerer. This phenomenon of Slavs voting for German candidates (or Jews voting for antisemitic candidates) was not untypical of the variable and often unpredictable nature of Viennese politics. In this case a vote for an

antisemite might be a step toward assimilation into the city's residually German culture, while it was also a convenient way of repudiating both the nationalism and the wealth resources of the Liberals. Czech artisans, therefore, when faced with limited options on the nationality question (on which the local Liberals and the Christian Socials differed very little when all was said and done), tended to *behave* like artisans and selected their candidates on the basis of sociocultural and economic compatibility. See *NWT*, 8 Mar. 1891, p. 2. For their own part the various antisemitic politicians in Vienna took great pains to stress their amiability and friendship toward the Viennese Czech community, as long as the assimilated Czechs accepted the right of the Viennese Germans to maintain political control. The heavy reliance of the antisemites on the Jewish issue in the city can be explained only by their desire to avoid stirring up unnecessary nationalistic enmity between various segments of the Third Curia, artisan electorate. For examples of antisemitic cultivation of the Viennese Czechs, see *DV*, 17 Mar. 1890 (M), p. 2; 1 Mar. 1891 (M), p. 9.

164. The *NFP* remarked that Sommaruga and his lieutenants had organized a campaign in the Landstrasse marked by a "seltene Bravour." *NFP*, 6 Mar. 1891 (M), p. 2. Baron Guido Sommaruga was a long-time resident of the Landstrasse and a prominent member of the Viennese Liberal party since the 1870s. He was an older Liberal who learned to adapt his rhetoric and tactics to counter the attractiveness of the antisemites. Had the Liberals had more candidates like him in 1895, Lueger might have failed in his attempt to take control of the city.

165. *SPB*, 29 Mar. 1891, pp. 1–2. The *NFP* noted that the schoolteachers and the petty officials in the Landstrasse had decided to vote Liberal in the Reichsrat election, as opposed to their behavior in Oct. 1890.

166. *DV*, 8 Apr. 1891 (A), pp. 1–3.

167. The occupational designations and the information on house ownership presented here are based on data derived from a variety of sources, including Lehmann's *Allgemeine Wohnungsanzeiger* for 1890 and 1891; the *DV*; the *NFP*; the *HHZ*; the dissertation by Martha Helmbe, *Die Tätigkeit des Wiener Gemeinderates von 1889–1892* (University of Vienna, 1974); and the following police reports in *NÖLA: Präs. Akten*, P10 ad 1287, Nr. 1748/1887; P10 ad 1185, Nr. 2055/1888; P10, Nr. 2187/1889; B2, Nr. 2490/1890; and B3 ad 2536, Nr. 2800/1891.

168. It was not unusual for the Liberal party to nominate chairmen of the larger craft guilds in the 1880s for City Council posts. The antisemites were simply continuing a Liberal tradition.

169. This disjunction in wealth between the Liberals and the antisemites did not always hold true, however. Many of the early antisemitic political figures were men of considerable personal wealth. Men like Karl Stehlik, Theodor Trambauer, Josef Bärtl, Wigo Zeller-Schömig, A. Melziuschek, and Johann Garber had personal fortunes well above the 20,000 fl. line, not including their annual income.

170. For the occupational background of *successful* antisemitic candidates between 1886 and 1891, see Boyer, "Veränderungen im politischen Leben Wiens," note 200.

171. The government was concerned that there might be disturbances on the election days, in view of the high stakes involved for both parties. The elections were held, however, without any serious disturbances. B3 ad 2536, Nr. 2651/1891, and B3 ad 2536, Nr. 2800/1891, *NÖLA*.

172. *DV*, 8 Apr. 1891 (M), p. 3.

173. *SPB*, 29 Mar. 1891, p. 1; *PAAA*, Öst.70/Bd. 24, A4358, 22 Mar. 1889.

174. *NWT*, 4 Apr. 1891, p. 9; 7 Apr. 1891, pp. 6–7; and the political reports in the *NFP* for 2–9 Apr.

175. See his comments in the *NFP*, 3 Mar. 1891 (M), p. 5.

176. *SPB*, 29 Mar. 1891, p. 1; *NFP*, 2 Apr. 1891 (M), p. 6.

177. *SPB*, 5 Apr. 1891, pp. 1–2.

178. *BZ* 21 (1890): 109–10, 150–51.

179. *SPB*, 15 Mar. 1891, p. 1. For the program of the municipal officials, ibid., 22 Mar. 1891, pp. 1–2.

180. Prix assured the *Staatsbeamten* that "Es wird Sache der deutschfortschrittlichen Partei im Parlament sein, dahin zu wirken, dass seiten des Staates für seine Beamten dasselbe geschieht." *NWT*, 1 Apr. 1891, p. 5.

181. The Liberals in the suburbs were also helped by the fact that, with the exception of Hernals and Währing, the antisemites had not yet built up ward organizations which were any more effective than (or any different from) those the Liberals relied on.

182. The *DV* estimated the membership of the various *Hausherrenvereine* at 4,000 in 1891: 8 Apr. 1891 (M), p. 3.

183. Ibid., 9 Apr. 1891 (M), p. 1.

184. *NWT*, 9. Apr. 1891, p. 2.

185. *NFP*, 3 Mar. 1891 (M), p. 5.

186. I follow the customary usage of most Austrian social scientists and historians in defining the word *Mittelstand* to include a slightly broader social representation than merely the lowest levels of the *Beamtentum* and handwork artisans. Thus Bobek and Lichtenberger: "der Mittelstand setzte sich einerseits aus der breiten Schicht der Gewerbetreibenden,...anderseits aus der Masse der Angehörigen der freien Berufe sowie dem mittleren Beamtentum zusammen" (*Wien*, p. 38). For similar examples, see Heinrich Rauchberg, *Die Bevölkerung Österreichs auf Grund der Ergebnisse der Volkszählung vom 31. Dezember 1890* (Vienna, 1895); Elisabeth Lichtenberger, *Wirtschaftsfunktion und Sozialstruktur der Wiener Ringstrasse* (Vienna, 1970), p. 37; Bammer, *Beiträge*, p. 353. This distinction is of linguistic/sociological importance, since in Vienna the word *Mittelstand* usually referred to more groups than simply the classic petite bourgeoisie or the subaltern white collar employees—it included members of the free professions, moderately wealthy merchants, and wealthy *Hausherren* as well. It also referred to rank levels within occupations that were slightly more prominent than those of the *Kleinbürgertum*. In a sense this is a highly relativistic distinction, based as it is on the lack of a large, numerically significant *Grossbürgertum* in the city before 1900. Less than 8% of the full-time employed population in the city of Vienna earned more than 3,600 fl. in taxable wealth. Less than 4% earned over 6,000 fl. per year. Even allowing for some discrepancy between reported income and actual income, the thinness of the top elites is very apparent. See F. Leiter, *Verteilung*, pp. 177–84. For the various meanings of the term *Mittelstand* in nineteenth-century Prussia, see Frederick D. Marquardt, "Sozialer Aufstieg, sozialer Abstieg, und die Entstehung der Berliner Arbeiterklasse, 1806–1848," *GG* 1 (1975): 44–47.

187. The police noted that "von dieser Strömung ist nicht nur der sogenannte kleine Mann, der Gewerbestand, erfasst, sondern sie hat auch in weiteren Kreisen, in dem mittleren Bürgerstande sowie insbesondere auch in dem Beamtenstande platzgegriffen." B2, Nr. 7831/1895, *NOLA*.

188. *DV*, 11 Apr. 1891 (M), pp. 1–2.

189. For an excellent survey of the political development of German cities in the nineteenth century, see Sheehan, "Liberalism and the City in Nineteenth Century Germany," pp. 116–37. On the city of Berlin, see Hans Herzfeld, ed., *Berlin und die Provinz Brandenburg im 19. und 20. Jahrhundert* (Berlin, 1968), pp. 82–116, 231–50; Annemarie Lange, *Das Wilhelminische Berlin* (Berlin, 1967), pp. 65–106, 151–215. On Cologne, see *Die Stadt Cöln im ersten Jahrhundert unter preussischer Herrschaft, 1815–1915* (2 vols., Cologne, 1916), 2:354–89.

190. On the idea of political resources as criteria for and determinants of social rank, see Jürgen Kocka, "Theorien in der Sozial- und Gesellschaftsgeschichte. Vorschläge zur historischen Schichtungsanalyse," *GG* 1 (1975): 39, 41–42.

191. Cf. the political propaganda for municipal elections in Berlin, from the Socialist and Liberal parties, in Eduard Bernstein, *Die Berliner Arbeiter-Bewegung, 1890–1905* (Berlin, 1924), pp. 213–40. Contemporary reports on the elections in the Third Class, as discussed in *Vorwärts*, reveal a similar mix of voters: *VO*, 13 Nov. 1893, Beilage Nr. 1; 9 Nov. 1895, Beilage Nr. 1; 9 Nov. 1897, Beilage Nr. 1; also, *VZ*, 7 Nov. 1895, pp. 1–2; and the important analysis in *NPZ*, 18 Oct. 1895 (M), p. 1.

192. On the Prussian three-class municipal franchise, see Preuss, *Städtewesen*, chap. 5; Gneist, "The Government of Berlin"; P. Hirsch and H. Lindemann, *Das Kommunale Wahlrecht* (Berlin, 1905); Helmuth Croon, *Die gesellschaftlichen Auswirkungen des Gemeindewahlrechts in den Gemeinden und Kreisen des Rheinlandes und Westfalens im 19. Jahrhundert* (Cologne, 1960); and *AZ*, 13 Nov. 1895, p. 2. Unlike Vienna, the city of Berlin did not publish complete election statistics in its *Statistische Jahrbücher.* The data cited for Berlin were computed on the basis of the distribution of voters in the 1893 and 1895 elections. See *Statistiches Jahrbuch der Stadt Berlin, 1893* (Berlin, 1895), p. 466, and *Statistisches Jahrbuch der Stadt Berlin, 1895* (Berlin, 1897), p. 546. For a similar distribution for 1891, see Robert C. Brooks, "City Government by Taxpayers: The Three-Class Election System in Prussian Cities," *Municipal Affairs* 3 (1899): 429. The relative percentile distribution is only meaningful, however, in regard to the comparability of the voter populations of each of the cities. The population of Vienna in 1891 was 1.34 million, that of Berlin was 1.579 million (as of 31 Dec. 1890 in both cases). The total number of enfranchised citizens in Vienna was 79,215. In contrast, Berlin had 271,019. The larger number of voters in Berlin was owing to the inclusion of large numbers of workers who paid a small amount of direct income tax or other direct tax. In Vienna, where there was no general direct tax on incomes until 1898, such men were intentionally excluded from the vote. On the basis of percentages alone, therefore, the presence of so many workers in the Berlin data might be seen as distorting the comparative distribution in Vienna's favor. However, if one looks at the numerical distribution of voters in Vienna and Berlin in 1891, it is apparent that the Second Class in Berlin was far more plutocratic and far smaller than the Second Curia of Vienna. In Vienna the First Curia had 5,409 voters, the Second Curia 22,236 voters, and the Third Curia 51,570 voters. In Berlin, in contrast, in 1891 the First Class had 3,555 voters, the Second 18,030, and the Third 239,132. In 1892 the Berlin statistics became even more lopsided because of the effect of the Prussian tax reforms of 1891: 1,892 for the First Class, 12,546 for the Second, and 264,812 for the Third. See Georg Evert, *Die Staats- und Gemeindewahlen im preussischen Staate. XVII. Ergänzungsheft zur Zeitschrift des Königlich-preussischen statistischen Bureaus* (Berlin, 1895), pp. 164–65. See also the *Verhandlungen des preussischen Landtages. Stenographische Berichte des Hauses der Abgeordneten*, 1899, Anlagen, Aktenstück Nr. 194, pp. 2646–48, 2666. Municipal voting in Vienna was direct, whereas in Berlin it was indirect. These statistics remain suggestive rather than definitive, since an exact comparative review of the two cities would have to survey the relative numerical distribution of key voter groups in each of the cities, a task which would be extremely difficult to accomplish given the current state of the historiography on both cities. However, even on a purely impressionistic basis, the decline of a significant level of political antisemitism in Berlin can be explained only in terms of the relative smallness of the Second Class in the city, which forced many of the middle income artisans and smaller *Beamten* into the Third Class, where they were overwhelmed after the mid-1890s by the Social Democratic majorities in Berlin. See esp. the interview with the *Oberbürgermeister* of Berlin, Robert Zelle, who noted that the Liberal party in Berlin faced a different kind of social and political constituency in its Third Class

elections, in *NFP,* 6 Oct. 1895 (M), p. 5. The conservative *Kreuzzeitung* noted in 1893 the new antinomy in Berlin politics, which had eliminated political antisemitism as an effective alternative: "Der schlimmste Feind der freisinnigen Partei ist jetzt nicht mehr die konservative Bürgerpartei, sondern die Sozialdemokratie. Aber die Erfolge der letzteren sind begrenzt, sie werden niemals über die dritte Wählerabteilung hinausgehen." *NPZ,* 9 Nov. 1893 (A), p. 1.

193. For the data on Cologne, see Evert, *Die Staats- und Gemeindewahlen . . . ,* p. 164, and *Statistisches Jahrbuch der Stadt Cöln für 1914* (Cöln, 1915), p. 127. A survey of voting districts in the First and Second Classes (Curias) in Berlin and Vienna shows the difference between the two systems. In 1897 the average First Class electoral district in Berlin had 90 voters, whereas that in Vienna had 303. Eight of Vienna's top curial districts had voter registrations substantially larger than the largest district in Berlin, even though Vienna's districts were geographically and demographically smaller than those in Berlin.

194. Nor were the Viennese mayors unwilling to fight the Imperial bureaucracy in defense of the rights and prerogatives of the city of Vienna as a political and administrative entity. During the negotiations concerning the amount of money the city of Vienna would contribute annually to the cost of maintaining the police in the new, enlarged metropolitan region, Johann Prix adamantly refused to concede to Erich Kielmansegg the 750,000 fl. per year which Kielmansegg wanted to require of the city. Even with Count Taaffe's personal intervention in the negotiations, Prix refused to back down, and the Imperial government was eventually forced to compromise for an amount considerably lower. See the correspondence between Taaffe and Kielmansegg in M1889–90, Stadterweiterungsakten, 2963b, esp. 14 Nov. 1890, P2 ad 4110, Nr. 8188, *NÖLA.* On the nonpolitical role of German mayors during the later decades of the nineteenth century, see Sheehan, "Liberalism and the City," pp. 125–26. In their willingness to defend the essentially competitive nature of the Viennese political system, Liberals and anti-Liberals of the generation of the 1860s and 1870s were quite alike.

195. Data on the movement of monthly food prices in Vienna from 1885 to 1896 are available in the *SJ* of the city from 1887 to 1897 and in the *BHGK* from 1885 to 1896. The rise in beef prices began in the third quarter of 1891 (from 40/70–60/90 to 44/90–64/95). Horse meat increased from 24/28–28/32 to 24/32–28/36. Mutton increased in the third quarter from 40/80, where it had been for the previous four years, to 46/80, but then jumped again in the summer of 1891 to 46/90. The prices of pork and fish also changed significantly. The prices of potatoes and of two of the four common forms of bread rose significantly between 1890 and 1891. The prices of dairy products remained, however, unchanged. There were also severe shortages of coal and wood for domestic fuel during the winter of 1891–92. See *WZ,* 10 Jan. 1892, p. 11; and Herbert Matis, *Österreichs Wirtschaft,* p. 421. Matis's data (in the form of a graphic presentation of price movements in Austria since 1867) indicate that food prices were relatively stable in the monarchy as a whole from the mid-1880s until the crisis years of 1891–92.

196. *BHGK,* 1891, pp. xii–xiv.

197. *BHGK,* 1890, pp. iii–xxxvii; 1891, p. xxiv. A serious problem for the metropolitan region was increasing competition from the burgeoning Hungarian economy, esp. the city of Budapest. Also, German goods were increasingly beating the Viennese products for the Hungarian import market. See *PAAA,* Öst. 70/Bd. 24, A4358, 22 Mar. 1889.

198. *BHGK,* 1892, pp. vii–viii. For data on levels of poverty in Vienna in 1890–91, see Karl Theodor Inama-Sternegg, *Die persönlichen Verhältnisse der Wiener Armen* (Vienna, 1891).

199. *WZ,* 23 Feb. 1892, pp. 3–4. For strike activity in 1891, see "Die Arbeitseinstellungen in den Jahren 1891 und 1892," *SM* 19 (1893): 298–300.

200. *WZ*, 8 Mar. 1892, p. 5.

201. *PAAA*, Öst. 70/Bd. 25, A2233, 11 Mar. 1892.

202. *AZ*, 27 Nov. 1891, pp. 5–6. Taussig refused them the money, and they went away empty-handed.

203. *SPB*, 18 Oct. 1891, p. 1; 5 Nov. 1891, p. 1; 13 Dec. 1891, p. 1; *NFP*, 11 Dec. 1891 (M), p. 6. One major point of controversy between Prix and his communal officials was the way in which he intended to implement his promise of a new, more federalized administrative structure of the metropolitan area. To fill the personnel needs of the system, he announced that he wanted to hire new *Praktikanten* to help take up the slack. At the same time, he stated that he was hesitant about promoting already tenured *Communalbeamten* to higher rank and salary grades. All of these decisions created considerable animosity against him—the hiring of the new *Praktikanten* meant that Prix had no intention of appointing additional tenured officials in higher ranks in the near future, and that officials working in the system would become overburdened with more work responsibilities since the *Praktikanten* would not be able to perform at the same level of competence as an experienced official. Prix also delayed the enactment of the new salary regulations and the new *Rangclassen* structure until late 1892. A final source of friction was Prix's personality. His *Beamten* accused him of rude behavior toward their delegations, once the Liberals had won the election. See *NFP*, 14 Nov. 1891 (M), p. 6.

204. The leaders of the new association explicitly stated that the *Teuerung* and the financial pressures on their members in 1891 were the major reason behind the organization's establishment. *SPB*, 13 Dec. 1891, p. 1.

205. The City Council had already prepared a list of reforms in Feb. 1891, which, if enacted, would have ameliorated the meat shortage in the city. See *BHGK*, 1891, pp. 70–71. Also, *WZ*, 23 Feb. 1892, pp. 3–4.

206. *WZ*, 26 Jan. 1892, p. 2; 20 Mar. 1862, p. 3.

207. *SP*, XI, 1891, pp. 3811–19, 3864–74.

208. *WZ*, 15 Dec. 1891, pp. 3–5.

209. On the origins of the inflation, see *BHGK*, 1891, pp. 32–33, 67–71. For a general overview of the decline of Austrian exports in 1891, see J. Pizzala, "Österreich-Ungarns Aussenhandel im Jahre 1891," *SM* 18 (1892): 134–46, esp. 136.

210. *BHGK*, 1891, pp. 32–33.

211. Ibid., pp. 47–51.

212. *BHGK*, 1892, pp. v–vi, 71–72; *BHGK*, 1893, pp. iv–vii. The monthly retail food prices published by the city of Vienna in the *SJ* indicate that relief from the excessively high prices gradually took effect by late 1892–early 1893. By mid-1893 meat and cereal prices had returned to their pre-1891 levels. Naturally there was no relief from increased rental costs. For the drop in wholesale cereal prices after 1892, see Hermann v Schullern-Schrattenhofen, "Die Bewegung der Getreidepreise in Österreich," *SM* 21 (1895): 219–40, esp. 224–27.

213. *BHGK*, 1892, pp. 71–72; *WZ*, 4 Aug. 1892, p. 6; Kielmansegg, *Kaiserhaus*, pp. 370–72.

214. *Petition der Wiener Beamtenversammlung vom 15. März 1892, betreffend die Verbesserung der materiellen Lage der Beamten*, in *SP*, XI, 1892, p. 5501.

215. *SPB*, 10 May 1891, p. 1.

216. The four major petitions were printed in the *SP*, XI, pp. 405–6, 5497–5500, 5501–2, 11148–52.

217. *NFP*, 1 Dec. 1891 (M), p. 6; *BZ* 23 (1892): 251.

218. *BZ* 23 (1892), pp. 278, 460–61; *SPB*, 18 Oct. 1891, p. 1.

219. Schidl, "Die österreichische Staatsbeamtenorganisation," pp. 92–93.

220. For the later history of the *Staatsbeamtenbewegung* in Austria, see the articles of

Emil Lederer in the *ASWSP* 31 (1910): 681–709; 33 (1911): 975–84; 35 (1912): 895–913. Lederer emphasized, without adequately explaining, the more radical nature of the Austrian *Beamtenbewegung* compared with that of the German Reich. This character can be accounted for only in part by the successes the Social Democrats enjoyed in the period after 1900 among the officials. It also resulted from the early and strong patronage accorded to the officials by the Liberals and from the similar patronage given to sections of the bureaucracy by other national political groups. Lederer noted that even the conservative *Beamten-Verein* in Vienna was more independent and more self-assertive than similar associations in Germany. This occurred precisely because of the greater influence which Liberalism had on public life in Austria in the 1860s and 1870s than it had in Bismarck's Germany. When Austrian ministers like Erich Kielmansegg tried to formulate Puttkamer-like policies for controlling the Austrian officials in the mid-1890s, even before the chaos produced by the Badeni crisis, they found that these curbs simply could not be enforced. No national group, including the Austro-Germans, would tolerate such chicanery and pressure leveled against "its" officials. Because in a rather perverse, yet effective, way the nationality conflict in Austria made the Imperial government sensitive to issues which might invite national explosions, the Austrian officials as a *social* collectivity had more latitude and more flexibility in their public collective behavior than their colleagues in Prussia.

221. *SB* 1 (1896): 287–88.

222. *SP*, XI, 1892, pp. 5501–2. For the Christian Social railway employees movement, see Leopold Kunschak's newspaper, *Freiheit*, and the party railway employees' newspaper, *Das Signal*, 1896–. For the early history of the Social Democratic railway employees' movement, see Julius Deutsch, *Geschichte der österreichischen Gewerkschaftsbewegung* (Vienna, 1908), pp. 216–17; *Verhandlungen des sechsten österreichischen Sozialdemokratischen Parteitages* (Vienna, 1897), pp. 150–54. See also Leo Verkauf's speech on the life situations of railway employees in *SP*, XII, 1897, pp. 380–93.

223. The Social Democratic success in winning the loyalties of vast numbers of railway employees and workers was owing to the simple fact that the party was the only serious and fully committed supporter of the *Eisenbahner*. Count Badeni's attempt in Apr. 1897 to crush the Social Democratic unionization of the railroads, and thus set a precedent for a general prohibition of unions among governmental employees, was a failure. Badeni stated openly that one of the prime reasons for the government's action against the Social Democratic railway organizations in 1897 was that they were beginning to win converts among railway officials as well as railway employees. This process did not cease in 1897. See *SP*, XII, 1897, p. 394. During the tense weeks of Nov. 1905 the passive resistance of the Social Democratic railway workers was important in pressuring the government to move toward enacting universal suffrage. See Deutsch, *Geschichte*, pp. 304–9.

224. The *Gremium*'s journal was the *Bericht des Gremiums der Wiener Kaufmannschaft*. For the factions within the *Gremium*, see *DV*, 20 Feb. 1890 (M), p. 6. For the history of the *Gremium*, see *Chronik des Gremiums der Wiener Kaufmannschaft* (Vienna, 1903), pp. 67–125.

225. A general discussion of the problem of the *Gemischtwarenverschleisser* and their attempt to resist governmental restrictions on the number of goods they might sell in their shops may be found in the *Bericht betreffend die Regelung des Gemischtwarenverschleisses*, Beilage Nr. 1 (29 Mar. 1893), *Sitzungsprotokolle der Handels- und Gewerbekammer, Wien* (Vienna, 1893), including the extensive report by Rudolf Kitschelt. The distinction between a *Händler* and a *Verschleisser* depended upon the trade tax the firm paid. Only larger firms listed in the trade register were called *Handlungen*. In 1891 in the older ten districts of Vienna plus the village of Floridsdorf there were 636 *Händler* and 3,292 *Verschleisser*. Of the latter,

approximately 800 paid a tax of at least 20 fl. annually. About two-thirds dealt exclusively with food products; the rest functioned as general stores. The statute of the *Gremium* from 1863 provided that *Gemischtwarenverschleisser* were also to be members, regardless of tax level, but the latter eventually obtained their own guild. See *Chronik*, pp. 77–78.

226. Marie v Vogelsang, "Die Handlungsgehilfen in Österreich," *MCSR* 13 (1891): 302.

227. The membership of the association in 1894 was listed by name, rank, and employer in the *KZ*, 15 Oct. 1894, pp. 159–66. Most of the ranks were those of middle or higher level *Privatangestellten* positions. There were very few *Commis* in the list.

228. For a survey of *Privatbeamten* salaries in Austria, see "Ständeverhältnisse der Privat-Angestellten," *WZ*, 20 Feb. 1898, pp. 1–2. Also, *Die Ergebnisse der über die Standesverhältnisse der Privatangestellten im Jahre 1896 eingeleiteten amtlichen Erhebungen* (Vienna, 1898).

229. *Petition der Privatbeamtenschaft in Wien um Errichtung eines allgemeinen Pensionsinstitutes der Privatbeamten im Wege der Gesetzgebung, SP*, XI, 1892, pp. 6823–24.

230. Contemporary polemical discussions of the *Handlungsgehilfen* problem are multitudinous; good analytical discussions are somewhat rarer. More attention was given to the problem in German social science literature than in the Austrian journals. See, for example, Karl Oldenberg's study of the Berlin *Commis* in *JGVV*, vol. 16 (1892); Georg Adler, *Die Sozialreform und der Kaufmannstand* (Munich, 1891); and Wilhelm Lexis's article on *Handel* in *Schönbergs Handbuch der Politischen Ökonomie* (4th ed., 1898). In terms of Lexis's distinction between a higher and a lower class of *Gehilfen*, depending upon income and occupational rank situation, most *Commis* in Vienna would have fallen into the second category. In terms of modern German scholarship on the *Angestellten* question, Jürgen Kocka's path-breaking study of the *Angestelltenschaft* at the Siemens works is fundamental to any serious consideration of the question. On the Austrian situation, see Marie v Vogelsang's articles in the *MCSR*, vol. 13 (1891), and the newspaper of the antisemitic Viennese *Commis*, the *WKB*. The *AZ* under Victor Adler's and especially under Friedrich Austerlitz's direction took a great interest in the process of the Socialist *Gehilfen* in taking control and in managing the affairs of the *Commis*'s *Gehilfenversammlung*.

231. Enrollments at the *Handelsakademie* nearly doubled between 1885 and 1910. Jews constituted nearly 45% of the full-time student body. The annual tuition for the *Akademie* was 160 fl., which put it beyond the reach of most *Kleinbürger* families. The program's utility was increased by the fact that students enrolled in the *Akademie* enjoyed the *Einjährig-Freiwilligen-Recht*. The completion of a gymnasium was not an absolute requirement for attendance, but the student was required to have had at least four years of a *Mittelschule*.

232. An indication of the consciousness of many of the *Commis* that their educational backgrounds in commercial subject areas were marginal was the fact that the association of the *Commis*, Julius Axmann's *Verein österreichischer Handels-Angestellter*, made a great effort to set up its own evening vocational courses for students who wished to study stenography, English, French, and several other subjects. The choice of subjects indicated that the *Verein* sought to give the *Commis* the skills which they could use in finding placement in subordinate clerk positions in the larger business bureaucracies of the city, rather than in sales techniques.

233. *WKB*, 25 Oct. 1891, p. 6.

234. The total membership of their *Krankenkasse* in 1891, which was part of the merchants' *Gremium*, was approximately 13,500. There were several thousand *Commis* in the city, however, not registered in the *Krankenkasse*. Apprentice statistics may be obtained

from the *SJ*. The total number of *Gehilfen* in the city, in all occupational situations, was approximately 16,000.

235. Marie v Vogelsang, "Die Handlungsgehilfen in Österreich," pp. 300–301.

236. Rudolf Kitschelt, *Bericht betreffend die Regelung des Gemischtwarenverschleisses.*

237. See the antagonism toward the *Gemischtwaren* shops in the *WKB*, 25 June 1891, p. 2; 25 Oct. 1895, pp. 3–4. Also, *FH*, 15 Dec. 1898, p. 1.

238. *WKB*, 25 Jan. 1891, pp. 1–3.

239. Axmann's association was a merger of various anti-Liberal *Gehilfen* groups, including Catholic, German National–antisemitic, and the simply discontented (which was probably the largest segment). Unlike Germany, the German National *Gehilfen* never played a prominent role in the politics of the *Commis* in Vienna. Axmann's *Verein*, which had a membership of 3,697 in Nov. 1895, never adopted a specific position on clericalism or nationalism. It was much closer in its behavior and ethos to the quasi-secular, a-nationalistic stance of the main body of the Christian Social coalition, which helps to explain why Lueger and Gessmann tolerated them and even assisted them—the party did not like extremists of any kind, unless the extremism was hatred for the Social Democrats. The German National merchants and shopkeepers in Vienna had their own commercial association, the *Zukunft*, as did the Catholic merchants in their *Handelscasino*. These were of minor importance, however.

240. *WKB*, 10 Apr. 1891, p. 3.

241. Ibid., 25 Oct. 1891, p. 2: "Wer wird wohl wünschen, dass das Verhältnis zwischen Handels-Angestellten und Principialen sich durchwegs so gestalte, wie zwischen gewerblichen und industriellen Arbeitern und Arbeitnehmern?" Although Axmann and several other leaders in the *Verein* joined Leopold Kunschak's *Christlichsoziale Arbeiterpartei*, they never conceived of themselves as "labor leaders" in the strict sense. Their speeches at the meetings of the Kunschak party tended to dwell on banal generalities concerning the "arbeitenden Stände," which could have meant almost anyone in Vienna. See, for example, *FH*, 15 Jan. 1896, pp. 1–2. After the Social Democrats won control of the *Gehilfenversammlung* in 1898, Axmann and his colleagues moved to regular bourgeois positions within the party, accepting salaried sinecures in governmental or party posts which Lueger and Gessmann gave them. See *EE* 5:311–14.

242. *WKB*, 25 Feb. 1891, p. 2; 25 Mar. 1891, pp. 2–4; 10 June 1891, pp. 1–2.

243. Ibid., 10 May 1891, pp. 6–9; 25 July 1891, pp. 1–2; 10 Aug. 1891, pp. 3–4; 25 Jan. 1895, p. 1.

244. Austerlitz founded the socialist *Fachverein der Handelsangestellten* in 1892. For his position, see his comments in the *Gewerbe Enquête* of 1893 in *Stenographisches Protokoll der Gewerbe-Enquête* (Vienna, 1893), pp. 6–9, 34–41.

245. Dirk Stegmann, *Die Erben Bismarcks. Parteien und Verbände in der Spätphase des wilhelminischen Deutschlands* (Cologne and Berlin, 1970); Heinrich August Winkler, *Pluralismus oder Protectionismus? Verfassungspolitische Probleme des Verbandswesens im deutschen Kaiserreich* (Wiesbaden, 1972); Hans-Ulrich Wehler, *Das Deutsche Kaiserreich, 1870–1918* (Göttingen, 1973).

Chapter 6

1. Joseph M. Baernreither, *Der Verfall des Habsburgerreiches und die Deutschen. Fragmente eines politischen Tagebuches, 1897–1917* (Vienna, 1938), pp. 9–11; Plener, *Erinnerungen*, 3:63ff.; *PAAA*, Öst. 70/Bd. 25, A11236, 17 Dec. 1891. In the crisis of 1878–79 Plener disagreed with Herbst and sought to preserve Liberal ministerial power.

2. Plener, *Erinnerungen*, 2:448ff.; 3:24–28, 57–69; *PAAA*, Öst. 70/Bd. 25, A11236, 17 Dec. 1891; Jenks, *Iron Ring*, pp. 275–89.

3. *NFP*, 24 Nov. 1892 (M), p. 1; *SP*, XI, 1892, pp. 7973–74; *PV* 5:82–86.

4. On Franz Joseph's personal dislike of Plener, see Plener, *Erinnerungen*, 3:108, and Reuss's report of 17 Dec. 1891 (above, note 1).

5. *PAAA*, Öst. 70/Bd. 29, A8868, 20 Aug. 1896.

6. Skedl, ed., *Der politische Nachlass des Grafen Eduard Taaffe*, p. 309.

7. Plener, *Erinnerungen*, 3:91.

8. See Baernreither's portrait of Badeni in *Der Verfall*, pp. 3–7, 26–28 (Badeni as a "gewalttätige Natur"). Also, Hans Mommsen, *Arbeiterbewegung und Nationale Frage. Ausgewählte Aufsätze* (Göttingen, 1979), pp. 161–64.

9. "Verordnung des Justizministeriums von 10. August 1895," in *Verordnungsblatt des k. k. Justizministeriums*, 14 Aug. 1895, pp. 138–40.

10. For Christian Social response to Taaffe's electoral reform in 1893, see *SP*, XI, 1893, pp. 11453–63 (Pattai) and 11498–11504 (Gessmann).

11. *PAAA*, Öst. 70/Bd. 28, A4661, 29 Apr. 1895 (this report is one of the most insightful Lichnowsky produced during his tenure in Vienna).

12. *NFP*, 24 Nov. 1892 (A), p. 2; 25 Nov. 1892 (M), pp. 2–3; *PAAA*, Öst. 70/Bd. 29, A8868, 20 Aug. 1896.

13. Karl Heinz Werner, "Österreichs Industrie- und Aussenhandelspolitik 1848 bis 1948," in Hans Mayer, ed., *Hundert Jahre österreichische Wirtschaftsentwicklung, 1848–1948* (Vienna, 1949), pp. 396–428; Franz Geissler, "Die Entstehung und der Entwicklungsgang der Handelskammern in Österreich," in ibid., pp. 103–8; Matis, *Österreichs Wirtschaft*, pp. 349, 367ff . 371–72. It should also be noted that many Liberals elected from the provinces also maintained residences and occasionally even practiced occupations in Vienna, so that their *political* distance from Vienna was somewhat mitigated by social contacts and social loyalties in the city itself.

14. Plener, *Erinnerungen*, 2:7, 150.

15. Ibid., 2:372; 3:114–15, 203, 211, 283.

16. *PAAA*, Öst. 70/Bd. 28, A4661, 29 Apr. 1895.

17. *NFP*, 14 Apr. 1895 (M), pp. 1–2; Plener, *Erinnerungen*, 3:243.

18. For Lower Austrian Liberal reforms, see *NFP*, 21 Nov. 1892 (A), pp. 2–3.

19. *PAAA*, Öst. 70/Bd. 27, A10650, 20 Nov. 1894; Plener, *Erinnerungen*, 3:98.

20. *AZ*, 8 June 1895, pp. 2–3.

21. *PAAA*, Öst. 88/Bd. 2, A8099, 4 Sept. 1894; Öst. 70/Bd. 27, A10650, 20 Nov. 1894. In July 1895 Plener sought to oust Windischgraetz and replace him with Badeni, while retaining the coalition itself. Unfortunately, Plener's strategy backfired—Badeni came, but the Liberals left. *PAAA*, Öst. 70/Bd. 28, A7426, 6 July 1895.

22. For the background to 1893–95 electoral reform politics, see Brügel, *Geschichte*, 4:235–51.

23. *AZ*, 16 Mar. 1894, pp. 2–3, for Hohenwart's plan.

24. On the June 1895 compromise, *AZ*, 4 June 1895, pp. 1–3; 5 June 1895, pp. 1–2.

25. For press reaction to the 1895 compromise, see *AZ*, 5 June 1895, pp. 2–3.

26. On 1895–96 tax reforms, see Rudolph Sieghart, "The Reform of Direct Taxation in Austria," *Economic Journal* 8 (1898): 173–82; Friedrich v Wieser, *Die Ergebnisse und die Aussichten der Personaleinkommensteuer in Österreich* (Leipzig, 1901); Emil v Fürth, *Die Einkommensteuer in Österreich und ihre Reform* (Leipzig, 1892).

27. Franz v Myrbach, "Die Reform der direkten Steuer in Österreich," *JGVV* 22 (1898): 517–21. Myrbach's article presents a comprehensive summary of the final edition of Plener's original legislation.

28. See Kaizl's critique of Liberal propaganda on the tax reform in *SP*, XI, 1895, pp. 17144–45.

29. Plener, *Erinnerungen*, 3:166, 169.

30. For Herbst's federalist sympathies in the 1860s and 1870s, see Kronawetter's speech in *SP*, XI, 1895, pp. 18417–31.

31. Ibid., pp. 18443–48 (Lueger); 18448–52 (Menger); 18441–43 (Steinwender).

32. *Amtsblatt der Stadt Wien*, 1895, pp. 343ff.

33. See Grübl's petition of 21 Apr. 1895 to parliament against the government's proposals in *SP*, 1895, pp. 18260–64.

34. Ibid., pp. 18436–41.

35. See, for example, Madeyski's speech in *SP*, XI, 1894, pp. 13302–6, and the analysis of the speech in *PAAA*, Öst. 75/Bd. 5, A6591, 17 July 1894.

36. *PAAA*, Öst. 88/Bd. 2. A8099, 4 Sept. 1894. Plener visited Poland in an attempt to build support for the Liberal-Polish collaboration within the coalition.

37. On the fragmentation of the Liberals in Vienna, see *V*, 23 Apr. 1892, p. 5; 16 May 1892, pp. 4–5; *NFP*, 25 Oct. 1893 (A), pp. 1–2; 3 Oct. 1893 (M), p. 6. In 1892 a group of dissident Liberals, belonging to Left Liberal and anti-Richter factions, signed a statement of protest demanding that Mayor Prix open the sessions of the *Stadtrat* to other city councilmen and that the Council's right to supervise the *Stadtrat* be recognized. They felt that Prix was using the autocracy of the *Stadtrat* not only against the Christian Socials, but against them as well. See also Kielmansegg, *Kaiserhaus*, p. 369, for Prix's arrogant behavior after 1891.

38. *Die Gemeinde-Verwaltung der Stadt Wien in den Jahren 1889–1893*, pp. 50–51; *V*, 5 Jan. 1892, p. 5. It was characteristic of the post-1890 Liberal Club that when Raimund Grübl became mayor in 1894 (on Prix's death), he was replaced as second vice-mayor by Joseph Matzenauer, who, like Richter, came from the Innere Stadt. This meant that two of the three executive officers of the city were from the First District, leaving most of the *Vorstädte* unrepresented in the city executive. Matzenauer's election provoked resentment on the part of Liberals like Georg v Billing and Adolf Daum, who considered Matzenauer too typical of First District "big wealth" for the good of the Liberal party as a whole. *NFP*, 5 Apr. 1894 (M), p. 6.

39. *NFP*, 28 May 1893 (M), p. 6.

40. Ibid., 9 June 1893 (M), p. 6; 16 June 1893 (M), p. 6.

41. *ÖW*, 29 Mar. 1895, pp. 235–37; 5 Apr. 1895, p. 249; 2 Oct. 1896, pp. 785–88. For Ofner's race against another Liberal, Constantine Noske (who was not Jewish), for the seat formerly held by Heinrich Jacques, see *NFP*, 16 Mar. 1894 (M), p. 3; 30 Mar. 1894 (M), pp. 2–3.

42. *NFP*, 19 Oct. 1892 (M), p. 6.

43. *V*, 26 Oct. 1892, pp. 1–2; 15 Nov. 1892, p. 3.

44. *NFP*, 21 Oct. 1893 (M), pp. 6–7.

45. Ibid., 24 Oct. 1893 (A), pp. 2–3; 25 Oct. 1893 (A), p. 1; Plener, *Erinnerungen*, 3:117–18.

46. *NFP*, 13 Mar. 1894 (M), p. 1. As late as 11 Mar. the *NFP* was insisting that Richter would be the mayoral candidate. The Liberals thought that Liechtenstein and the nuncio, Agliardi, were responsible for turning the Court against Richter.

47. For a summary of the institutional developments in the city during the Prix administration, see *NFP*, 1 Mar. 1895 (M), p. 6.

48. *V*, 23 Nov. 1892, p. 5, for antisemitic attacks on the gold standard.

49. For Liberal views of the currency question, see Plener, *Erinnerungen*, 3:158–63; Carl Menger, *Der Übergang zur Goldwährung* (Vienna, 1892); Josef v Neupauer, *Die Schäden und Gefahren der Valutaregulirung* (Vienna, 1892). Eduard Suess was the most prominent Liberal opponent of the gold standard.

50. See the report of Stejskal to Bacquehem, 10 Feb. 1894, Nr. 575/793, Min. d. Inneren, *AVA*. In Nov. 1894 Stejskal informed Kielmansegg that Schönerer's efforts to regain support in Vienna were failing miserably. J12 ad 7376/1894, *NÖLA*.

51. *UDW,* Nr. 7, 1895, pp. 75–78.

52. *Bericht über den 3. allgemeinen österreichischen Katholikentag in Linz* (Wels, 1892); *V,* 9 Aug. 1892, p. 3.

53. On Schindler, see Funder, *Aufbruch,* passim, and idem, *Vom Gestern,* pp. 44, 53–54, and passim, 73. Schindler was a respected moral theologian whose intellectual orientation, in contrast to Vogelsang's, was neoscholasticism. See Rudolf Weiler, "Katholische Sozial-lehre unterwegs," in *Festschrift Franz Loidl,* 2:354, 368. See also "Franz Kordačs Briefe ins Germanikum," pp. 98, 176.

54. Schindler to Vogelsang, 26 Jan. 1889, Nr. 25, and 8 Feb. 1889, Nr. 31, *VN,* Mappe 23; and Schindler's proposal to liberate *Vaterland* from Leo Thun: ("Vertraulich") 15 Feb. 1889, Handschriftensammlung, Stadtbibliothek, Nr. 63526. After 1890 the bishops were forced increasingly to subsidize *V*'s deficit, which by 1892 was around 40,000 fl. a year. See the "Schreiben der 'Vaterland' Gesellschaft," in *Protokoll der bischöflichen Versammlung in Wien vom 2. bis zum 10. April 1894,* pp. 92–96. By 1895–96 even the episcopate was uneasy about the paper's lethargic state, seeing the need for a more aggressive editorial posture. See the *Protokoll der Conferenz des bischöflichen Comités in Wien vom 19. bis zum 28. November 1895,* pp. 6–7.

55. *NFP,* 23 Oct. 1892 (M), p. 3; 24 Oct. 1892 (A), p. 2; *V,* 19 Oct. 1892, p. 5; *ÖW,* 20 Dec. 1895, pp. 939–40.

56. *V,* 23 Oct. 1892, pp. 1–2; *NFP,* 24 Oct. 1892 (A), p. 2. The police noticed that Schneider's vulgarity was disturbing to Lueger, but that there was little he could do to control Schneider. See Stejskal to Bacquehem, 10 Feb. 1894, Nr. 575/793, Min. d. Inneren, *AVA.*

57. *Protokoll der bischöflichen Versammlung in Wien vom 2. bis zum 10. April 1894,* p. 38.

58. On Agliardi, see Christoph Weber, *Quellen und Studien zur Kurie und zur Vatikan-ischen Politik unter Leo XIII* (Tübingen, 1973), pp. 152–59, 401–5, pp. 46–47, note 100. Also, Francesco Vistalli, "Il cardinale Antonio Agliardi," *La Scuola Cattolica* 43 (1915): 139–54, 272–91. Eulenburg had known Agliardi when both were stationed in Munich in the early 1890s and was shocked by the nuncio's support for the Christian Socials and by his hatred of the Austrian episcopate. See *PAAA,* Öst. 75/Bd. 5, A1657, 10 Feb. 1895. In 1893 Eulenburg had a long conversation with Agliardi on the relationship of the Vatican to the Center party and had impressed on Agliardi the need to support the right wing within the Center. Agliardi seemed to agree with Eulenburg (see Weber, *Quellen und Studien,* pp. 539–41) on the need to curb the "democratization" of the Center under Ernst Lieber (a pet idea of Eulenburg himself). However, once he arrived in Vienna and comprehended the different composition and behavior of the Austrian episcopate, as opposed to the German, Agliardi soon adopted a more aggressive, hostile stance toward the Austrian clerical Right.

59. Funder, *Aufbruch,* p. 103.

60. *PAAA,* Öst. 75/Bd. 6, A5085, 9 May 1895.

61. Funder, *Aufbruch,* p. 105. Agliardi seems to have initiated this on his own. He may have been anticipating an action by the Austrian bishops against the Christian Socials in the spring of 1894. There were rumors to this effect in Vienna in Mar. and Apr. Albert Weiss discussed a possible letter to the clergy in his correspondence with Cardinal Gruscha (see Weiss to Gruscha, 28 Feb. 1894, *GN*), and the episcopal conference held in Mar. discussed the possibility of a letter (see *Protokoll der Conferenz des bischöflichen Comités in Wien vom 29. bis zum 31. März 1894*). This represented a change in Weiss's views, since in 1893 he had opposed a joint action by the episcopate against the antisemites. See Weiss to Gruscha, 6 Jan. 1893; 14 June 1893, *GN.*

62. The program is preserved in the Schindler Papers, *FN.* It is partially reprinted in Funder, *Vom Gestern,* pp. 104–8.

63. Rampolla's reply is in Funder, *Vom Gestern,* pp. 109–11, dated 17 Mar. 1894. On

Toniolo and the Italian Union, see Fernand Mourret, *L'église contemporaine* (Paris 1925), 9:431–32; Eduardo Soderini, *Il Pontificato di Leone XIII* (Milan, 1932), 1:383–84. For Toniolo's reply, see Toniolo to Agliardi, 24 May 1894, in Giusepe Toniolo, *Lettere I, 1871–1895*, Guido Anichini and Nello Vian, eds. (Vatican City, 1952), pp. 328–31.

64. For Rampolla, see Weber, *Quellen und Studien*, pp. 156–59, 411–14, 477–78. When Agliardi was appointed to Vienna, he received instructions from Rampolla that he should adopt a more sympathetic posture toward his, Rampolla's, diplomatic goals. See *PAAA*, Öst. 86/Bd. 6, A4941, 7 May 1895. Agliardi fulfilled these instructions with enthusiasm.

65. Agliardi did not conceal his contempt for Hohenwart's alliance with the Liberals. See *PAAA*, Öst. 98/Bd. 2, A4077, 19 Apr. 1895; Öst. 75/Bd. 5, A1657, 10 Feb. 1895. Also, Weiss, *Lebensweg*, pp. 418–19.

66. Rampolla's hostility to the Austrian Clericals paralleled his unwillingness to help the eastern Centrists against Lieber and the main body of the Center party. See Weber, *Quellen und Studien*, pp. 541–42, and Rampolla's memorandum on the Center party in *PAAA*, Deutschland 125, Nr. 1/Bd. 3, 14 July 1893.

67. *Nordböhmisches Volksblatt*, 16 Nov. 1888, p. 2.

68. Schindler to Vogelsang, 24 Dec. 1888, *VN*, Mappe 23, Nr. 33.

69. Funder, *Aufbruch*, p. 104. After the debacle of his visit to Hungary in May 1895 a more humble Agliardi tried to argue that he had never favored lower clerical independence and that he had been forced into supporting the Christian Socials by Rampolla. See *PAAA*, Öst. 90/Bd. 3, A6237, 8 June 1895. This was doubtful, and even Eulenburg was not convinced by it. It was similar to another kind of explanation for Leo XIII's support for Lueger, namely, that Rampolla had "tricked" the pope and prevented him from seeing the full story—a weak, meager, and unconvincing argument which hardly did justice to the perspicacity of Leo XIII.

70. Gruscha may also have been angry over the controversy stirred up at the Social Course organized by Franz Schindler in Aug. 1894 for several hundred radical clerics, where Albert Gessmann made some remarks about the inactivity of the local Catholic *Gesellenvereine*, which were Gruscha's pride and joy (ironically, Joseph Scheicher, the principal Catholic critic of these pietist clubs, was not allowed to speak at the Social Course). Gessmann's suggestion that the clerics ought to learn to compete with the Socialists by emulating their methods must have been rather hard for the old man to tolerate. See *AZ*, 14 Aug. 1894, p. 1; *RP*, 11 Aug. 1894, pp. 2–6; Weiss, *Lebensweg*, pp. 375–80, 409.

71. *PAAA*, Öst. 75/Bd. 5, A1816, 15 Feb. 1895; Funder, *Aufbruch*, pp. 107–10; idem, *Vom Gestern*, pp. 81–82.

72. See Kalnoky to Revertera, 2 Feb. 1895, *HHSA*, pol. Archiv, IX/262, Rome-Varia, reprinted in Miko, ed., "Zur Mission," pp. 190–91. See also *RP*, 14 Nov. 1894, pp. 1–3; 15 Nov. 1894, pp. 4–5.

73. *Protokoll der Conferenz des bischöflichen Comités . . .20. November bis 1. Dezember 1894*, pp. 8–9; Weiss to Aichner, 24 Jan. 1895, in Miko, ed., "Zur Mission," p. 188.

74. See the comments on Schönborn's lack of energy and even laziness in *PAAA*, Öst. 75/Bd. 5, A1657, 2 Feb. 1895; A2377, 6 Mar. 1895; Bd. 6, A5281, 13 May 1895.

75. On Scheicher, see chap. 3.

76. Franz Joseph was openly critical of the Viennese clerics. See Eulenburg's report, Öst. 75/Bd. 5, A8131, 6 Sept. 1894.

77. See the private diary of Bishop Rössler in the *Rössler Nachlass*, St. Polten Diocesan Archive, cited in Kendl, *Scheicher*, pp. 76–77.

78. *SP*, XI, 1894, pp. 16363–65.

79. On Stojalowski, see *ÖV*, 13 May 1894, pp. 1–2; 28 Jan. 1894, p. 2; *Z*, 19 Oct. 1895, p. 33; and *Der Prozess Msgr. Stojalowski in Krakau, 20–29 Juni 1893* (Vienna, 1893). Stojalowski had himself transferred in 1893 from Lemberg to the diocese of Antivari in order to obtain the protection of the metropolitan of Montenegro, Milinović. His status in the monarchy

therefore was that of a foreign missionary. See Eduard Winter, *Russland und die slaw-ischen Völker in der Diplomatie des Vatikans, 1878–1903* (Berlin, 1950), pp. 111–15. Winter argues that Rampolla dealt with Stojalowski in the same way he handled the Christian Socials, dragging his feet to enhance the status of the errant priest. However, the evidence Winter presents indicates that the Curia's position on Stojalowski was not identical to their view of Lueger. Both Rampolla and Leo XIII did act against Stojalowski, but their efforts were undercut by Milinović and Bishop Strossmayer. See Eduard Winter, *Russland*, pp. 111–15, 159–65; idem, *Russland und das Papsttum* (2 vols., Berlin, 1961), 2:496. The famous papal blessing Stojalowski received for his radical journal was actually an accident. The Vatican received thousands of congratulatory telegrams for Leo XIII's jubilee and responded with thousands of "standard" papal blessings for the organizations or individuals sending messages. Stojalowski's blessing was not the same as those engineered for the Christian Socials by Agliardi.

80. *SP*, XI, 1894, pp. 16422–23.

81. Ibid., p. 16453; *EE*, 5:223–46.

82. *RP*, 20 Jan. 1895, p. 1; 25 Jan. 1895, p. 1.

83. *V*, 22 Jan. 1895, pp. 1–2; *AZ*, 21 Jan. 1895, pp. 1–2. The party had submitted to the Upper Austrian *Statthalterei* a request for approval of the statute of a Christian Social Association in Linz in late 1894, but no action had as yet been taken. That this meant, however, that Lueger intended to expand into Linz on a large scale was very doubtful.

84. Schönborn made the final decision to intervene against the Christian Socials only after the Linz rally. See *PAAA*, Öst. 75/Bd. 5, A1657, 2 Feb. 1895.

85. The bishops tried to negotiate with Agliardi on an individual basis but got nowhere. Schönborn then realized that only Rome could stop the nuncio. See Weiss to Aichner, 16 Jan. 1895 and 24 Jan. 1895, in Miko, ed., "Zur Mission," pp. 186–89.

86. For the purpose of the mission, see the detailed and informative report in *PAAA*, Öst. 75/Bd. 5, A2892, 18 Mar. 1895; and Kalnoky to Revertera, 2 Feb. 1895, in Miko, ed., "Zur Mission," pp. 190–92. For the documents carried with the delegation, see Weiss, *Lebensweg*, pp. 420–21; *AZ*, 29 Jan. 1895, p. 1 (an edited version of the pastoral letter); and *VT*, 10 Feb. 1895, pp. 5–6. For the origins of the documents, see *NPZ*, 3 Feb. 1895 (M), p. 2. The interesting study by Lewis, *Kirche und Partei* (Salzburg, 1977), which arrived after this chapter was drafted, contains a good account of the Schönborn mission and the tensions between the bishops and the party. See ibid., pp. 320–50. Lewis made no use, however, of the important German diplomatic documents in *PAAA* or of the materials in the *VN*.

87. Eulenburg learned of this audience in May (*PAAA*, Öst. 75/Bd. 6, A5281, 13 May 1895). It was likely that Schönborn was the one who initiated the idea of a government *demarche* in Rome, since he realized that the bishops alone would not accomplish much. In making his request, however, the Cardinal was able to fall back upon earlier inferences given to him by Prince Windischgraetz that the government would not be unsympathetic to an episcopal action in Rome. See *NPZ*, 3 Feb. 1895 (M), p. 2.

88. "Memorandum der österreichischen Regierung an den Heiligen Stuhl," Feb. 1895, *HHSA*, pol. Archiv, IX/262, Rome-Varia, reprinted in Miko, ed., "Zur Mission," pp. 192–94.

89. Plener, *Erinnerungen*, 3:219.

90. In Jan. 1895 Cardinal Kopp made some conciliatory gestures to the Liberals in the Silesian Landtag. This, together with similar events in the Lower Austrian Landtag, gave rise to speculation that the Liberals were ready for a compromise with the Church.

91. Weiss noted to Gruscha on several occasions that Schönborn was being ignored in Rome. Weiss to Gruscha, dated Feast of Saint Joseph 1895 and 9 Mar. 1895, *GN*.

92. Revertera to Kalnoky, 25 Feb. 1895, in Miko, ed., "Zur Mission," pp. 202–4; Weiss to Gruscha, 20/21 Feb. 1895, *GN*.

93. Funder, *Aufbruch*, pp. 111–12. For the complete text of Schindler's defense, see F. Funder, "Aus den Anfängen christlichsozialer Programmarbeit," *VW* 14 (1923): 7–10.

94. *PAAA*, Öst. 75/Bd. 5, A2892, 18 Mar. 1895; Revertera to Kalnoky, 20 Mar. 1895 and 30 Mar. 1895, in Miko, ed., "Zur Mission," pp. 216–19; Weiss to Gruscha, 16 Mar. 1895, *GN*.

95. *PAAA*, Öst. 75/Bd. 6, A5281, 13 May 1895; Weiss, *Lebensweg*, p. 433. Weiss admitted publicly in July that the Schönborn mission had failed. See his "Persönliche Glossen über die gegenwärtige Lage," *TPQS* 49 (1895): 978–91.

96. *RP*, 18 May 1895, pp. 1–2; Funder, "Aus den Anfängen," pp. 10–11.

97. *NWT*, 8 Apr. 1891, pp. 6–7. Out of 888 voters in Hietzing, there were 440 state officials and 100 teachers. *NFP*, 23 Sept. 1895 (M), pp. 5–6.

98. *DV*, 21 Mar. 1895 (M), p. 4.

99. *NFP*, 2 Apr. 1895 (M), pp. 5–6; *AZ*, 2 Apr. 1895, pp. 1–4; 4 Apr. 1895, p. 4.

100. For the official statistics, see *SJ*, 1891 and 1895. In the Leopoldstadt the Christian Socials got 28% of the vote in 1891, but 37% in 1895; in the Innere Stadt they received 17% in 1891, but 30% in 1895. These data for both parties were calculated on the basis of an average return for the party slate in a given district. Because a voter could choose to cast fewer than the maximum number of names, individual candidates on a slate might receive slightly different totals. Most voters seemed to have voted straight party slates. Since my calculations were for both parties for all nineteen districts, the resulting "average" number, used in a relative and comparative framework, does represent typical voter support for the two parties.

101. By "new voters" I mean either those men who were newly enfranchised or voters who had been enfranchised in 1891, but who had chosen not to vote. Contemporary political reports give no hint of which group was predominant, but it is likely that the former group made up the vast majority of new voters. The 1891 elections were as well advertised and as interesting as those of 1895. A voter not interested in voting in 1891 would have had no greater motive to do so in 1895.

102. For Müller's election, see *NFP*, 30 Mar. 1895 (M), pp. 5–6; 29 Mar. 1895 (M), p. 7; 31 Mar. 1895 (M), pp. 3–4, 10. Albert Richter made a special appearance before a rally of the *Oesterreichische Union* to plead with Second Curia Jewish voters not to abstain from voting. Most Jewish leaders supported this appeal.

103. For police reports on the elections, see B2 ad 1349 (Nr. 1781, 2195, 2402), *NÖLA*, 1895. See also *NFP*, 2 Apr. 1895 (M), pp. 1–2, 5, for the teachers and officials as giving the *Ausschlag* in the election.

104. *NFP*, 1 Oct. 1895 (M), p. 4.

105. *ÖSBZ*, 1 Feb. 1895, pp. 3–4; 1 Mar. 1895, p. 8; 15 Sept. 1895, pp. 6–8; *BZ* 26 (1895): 99–100, 152–53.

106. For Pattai's motion, see *SP*, XI, 1894, pp. 16178–79.

107. Ibid., pp. 16182–84.

108. Ibid., XI, 1896, pp. 27317–23, 27344–47.

109. *ÖSBZ*, 1 Mar. 1895, p. 3; 15 Mar. 1895, p. 3; *ÖSZ*, 1 Jan. 1895, pp. 3–10. The raises were to be retroactive to 1 Jan., but Plener failed to realize that paper promises in this case would not win votes. *BZ* 26 (1895): 99–101; *DV*, 17 Mar. 1895 (M), pp. 1–2; *DZ*, 17 Mar. 1895, pp. 1–2.

110. For a list of antisemitic candidates in this election, with notations as to which of the forty-six were "nationalist" (there were thirteen persons, distributed throughout the city), see *DZ*, 27 Mar. 1895, pp. 4–5.

111. *BZ* 23 (1892): 533–34; *SPB*, 18 Oct. 1891, p. 1; 13 Dec. 1891, p. 1; *NFP*, 10 Nov. 1892 (M), p. 6; 11 Nov. 1892 (M), p. 6.

112. *AZ*, 3 July 1896, pp. 1, 3; *ÖSBZ*, 1 Feb. 1895, pp. 3–4.

113. There were 1,597 male teachers with tenure in the First through Tenth Districts; 1,042 in the Eleventh through Nineteenth Districts.

114. Approximately 50% of the male *Bürgerschullehrer* (the more senior and coveted jobs) in Vienna in 1895 were born in Bohemia, Moravia, or Silesia. I have not been able to get similar data for the *Volksschullehrer*, but the percentage there was probably similar. See *ÖSZ*, 1895, pp. 577–78. These data do not indicate whether these teachers were of German or Czech descent. The Germans were probably in the majority, but it is possible that some were upwardly mobile Czechs whose parents had moved to the city after 1860 as artisans or petty shopkeepers. And simply because a teacher was born in Bohemia does not mean that he would necessarily incline to a harsher nationalist stance, especially if his later adolescence and educational socialization took place in Vienna. "Nationalism" in Vienna was an extremely diverse and often vacuous phenomenon; easy stereotypes must be avoided in using the concept.

115. For the shift in voting among the teachers to the antisemites, see *DZ*, 6 Apr. 1895, p. 1; *ÖSZ*, 10 Apr. 1895, pp. 236–37 ("Die grosse Mehrheit der Lehrer hat für die Partei Lueger-Liechtenstein gestimmt"); *DÖLZ*, 15 Mar. 1896, pp. 61–62.

116. For a comparison of teachers' salaries before and after the 1891 law, see *DV*, 1 Mar. 1895 (M), p. 4. See also *PJ* 44 (1891): 227–29; *NFP*, 26 Nov. 1891 (M), p. 7.

117. For Noske's insult against the teachers, see *BZ* 23 (1892): 113; *ÖSZ*, 24 Mar. 1892, pp. 193–94.

118. For complaints about being taken for granted, see *ÖSZ*, 24 Mar. 1892, pp. 185–86; 3 Jan. 1895, pp. 11–12.

119. Criticism of the Liberals' new sympathy for the Clericals in the coalition was frequently voiced in teachers' newspapers. *ÖSZ*, 20 Feb. 1895, p. 127; 10 Apr. 1895, p. 241; 17 Apr. 1895, p. 272; *DÖLZ*, 1 Mar. 1896, p. 54; 15 Mar. 1896, pp. 61–62.

120. A provisional *Unterlehrer* in Vienna was paid an annual rate which amounted to about 33 fl. a month, during the months when school was in session. Such teachers had little job security and often worked on a one-day-at-a-time basis. They received the worst class assignments and were often placed in working-class areas where discipline was nonexistent and the children were half-starving. It is hardly surprising that they should have served as the basis for a Socialist teachers' movement. See the description of Otto Glöckel's teaching assignment as an *Unterlehrer* in Oskar Achs and Albert Krassnigg, *Drillschule-Lernschule-Arbeitsschule. Otto Glöckel und die österreichische Schulreform in der Ersten Republik* (Vienna and Munich, 1974), pp. 47–49; and *AZ*, 16 Jan. 1896, p. 4. An *Unterlehrer* with tenure had a slightly better salary but received few of the benefits usually given to the regular teachers. In 1892 there were 1,182 *Unterlehrer* in the school system, out of a total of 4,050 teachers.

121. For Seitz's tactics, see *ÖSZ*, 3 Jan. 1895, pp. 10–11; 6 Mar. 1895, p. 160; Otto Glöckel, *Selbstbiographie* (Zurich, 1939), pp. 40–47; *FLS*, 1 July 1895, pp. 1–3. Seitz finally created a *Centralverein* for younger teachers in mid-June 1896, using it to attack the Christian Socials.

122. For Grübl's options, see *NFP*, 2 Apr. 1895 (M), p. 2.

123. For this view, ibid., 4 Apr. 1895 (A), p. 2; 5 Apr. 1895 (M), pp. 6–7.

124. Plener, *Erinnerungen*, 3:256–57.

125. *NFP*, 14 Apr. 1895 (M), p. 1; 18 Apr. 1895 (M), p. 1, and Alfred Lenz's comments on p. 3. The isolated, arrogant posture Viennese Liberalism had assumed by 1896 was exemplified by Lenz, a man whom many voters even in his own party detested for his attempt to pressure *Beamten* into voting Liberal.

126. B2 ad 3131/1895, *NÖLA*.

127. See *NFP*, 2 Apr. 1895 (M), p. 2; 4 Apr. 1895 (A), p. 2; *PAAA*, Öst. 70/Bd. 28, A5393, 15 May 1895. (In an interview with Grübel, Eulenburg declared that he was profoundly tired of political competition and that he was more than willing to resign his seat.)

128. For the maneuvering on 29 May, see *DZ*, 30 May 1895, pp. 1–2; *AZ*, 30 May 1895, p. 1.

129. Plener, *Erinnerungen*, 3:258; *DZ*, quoting the *Fremdenblatt*, 31 May 1895, pp. 1–2.

130. Plener, *Erinnerungen*, 3:257. Kalnoky told Eulenburg that he expected that Franz Joseph would follow the wishes of the majority of the *Ministerrat* and confirm Lueger, if Lueger accepted the office. *PAAA*, Öst. 70/Bd. 28, A3841, 11 Apr. 1895.

131. For Kielmansegg's report to the *Ministerrat*, see B2 ad 6847, Nr. 6967/1895, *NÖLA*.

132. *DV*, 4 Sept. 1895 (A), p. 2. Stejskal to Kielmansegg, B2 ad 5936, Nr. 6008, *NÖLA*, 15 Sept. 1895; *AZ*, 15 Sept. 1895, p. 1.

133. *NFP*, 5 Sept. 1895 (M), p. 5.

134. Ibid., 9 Oct. 1895 (A), p. 3; 15 Oct. 1895 (A), p. 2.

135. *NFP*, 4 Sept. 1895 (M), p. 5; 7 Sept. 1895 (M), p. 6. After the elections the Liberal group fell apart, having no reason to continue to function.

136. *NFP*, 3 Sept. 1895 (M), p. 5; 6 Sept. 1895 (M), p. 6; 10 Sept. 1895 (M), p. 7; and the insightful comments in *AZ*, 6 Sept. 1895, pp. 2–3; 7 Sept. 1895, p. 2.

137. *DV*, 13 Sept. 1895 (A), pp. 2, 4; 20 Sept. 1895 (A), pp. 1–2; *RP*, 13 Sept. 1895, p. 1; 22 Sept. 1895, p. 9.

138. Kielmansegg, *Kaiserhaus*, pp. 47–48.

139. *DZ*, 11 Aug. 1895, p. 3; *PV* 5:537.

140. *DÖLZ*, 15 Jan. 1896, pp. 15–16; 1 Apr. 1896, pp. 73–74.

141. *NFP*, 3 Dec. 1895 (M), pp. 5–6; and the defense in *ÖSBZ*, 1 Dec. 1895, p. 8. A careful examination of the various teachers' and officials' newspapers from late 1895 and 1896 revealed no decline in white collar political and organizational activity. Kielmansegg monitored *Beamten* political activity, while recognizing that he could not stop it. See the interviews of the police with officials who were suspected of singing the "Lueger March" at a political rally, J12 ad 1416, Nr. 2193/1896. The officials involved denied doing so —what could Kielmansegg do? Also, see B2 ad 1225, Nr. 1471/1895, and J12, Nr. 5868/1895, *NÖLA*.

142. *NFP*, 20 Dec. 1895 (M), p. 4; Kielmansegg, *Kaiserhaus*, p. 49.

143. See esp. *DV*, 25 Sept. 1895 (A), p. 1; *RP*, 26 Sept. 1895, p. 1.

144. *DV*, 25 Sept. 1895 (A), p. 4.

145. *DV*, 13 Sept. 1895 (M), p. 3; 14 Sept. 1895 (M), p. 7. The Liberal party used the same kind of rhetoric, glorifying itself as the only real representative of the Bürgertum. See *NFP*, 13 Sept. 1895 (M), p. 7; 18 Sept. 1895 (M), p. 1; 19 Sept. 1895 (M), p. 5. See also Strobach's assertion that the *Bürgerschaft* needed to be defended against the Jews. *DZ*, 17 Sept. 1896, p. 2.

146. B2 ad 6847, Nr. 6967/1895, *NÖLA*.

147. J6 ad 7723, Nr. 8396/1895; B2 ad 452, Nr. 452/1896; B2, Nr. 7831/1895, *NÖLA*.

148. *DZ*, 2 June 1895, pp. 2–3.

149. *NFP*, 10 Sept. 1895 (M), p. 8.

150. J6 ad 7723, Nr. 8396/1895, *NÖLA*.

151. J6, Nr. 7723/1895, *NÖLA*. See also Funder, *Vom Gestern*, p. 62.

152. *NFP*, 18 Sept. 1895 (M), p. 6; 23 Sept. 1895 (A), p. 5

153. See *PAAA*, Öst. 70/Bd. 29, A12159, 13 Nov. 1895; *NFP*, 24 Sept. 1895, p. 1; B2 ad 452, Nr. 452/1896, *NÖLA*.

154. For a description of a typical social event devoted to Lueger personally, see B2 ad 452, Nr. 777/1896, *NÖLA*.

155. B2 ad 452, Nr. 1773 and 3238/1896, *NÖLA*.

156. B2 ad 452, Nr. 1773/1896, *NÖLA*.

157. *DV*, 11 Sept. 1896 (M), p. 6; E5 ad 872, Nr. 1005/1897, *NÖLA*.

158. The most insightful analysis of the problem of mass politics in late-nineteenth-century Europe is still that of Max Weber. See his "Politik als Beruf" and "Wahlrecht und Demokratie in Deutschland" in *Gesammelte politische Schriften* (Munich, 1921), esp. pp. 415–35; and Weber's *Wirtschaft und Gesellschaft* (4th ed., Tübingen, 1956), as well as Robert Michels, *Political Parties*, trans. by Eden and Cedar Paul (Glencoe, 1949). For Weber the essential characteristics of a mass as opposed to a notable politics are a heightened level of coercion and regimentation, which would usually be associated with the development of a widespread intraparty bureaucracy. In elucidating the requirements for mass politics in Vienna, I have attempted to make more specific the kinds of criteria by which mass politics must be judged. The second volume of this study will focus more closely on the way in which Lueger and the mature party may be seen as representing a model of Weber's classic formulation of the nature of Central European party politics—a politics controlled on one hand by the *Beamtenstaat* and intraparty bureaucratization, and on the other by demagogic, interest group politics, while also having some features of the modern, personalized system of political leadership in a parliamentary framework.

159. For the election results, see *NFP*, 18 Sept. 1895 (M), p. 6; *ÖW*, 2 Oct. 1895, pp. 721–22; B2 ad 5936, Nr. 6069/1895, *NÖLA*.

160. *NFP*, 24 Sept. 1895 (M), pp. 6–7; *AZ*, 24 Sept. 1895, p. 4. The party won thirty-two of the forty-six seats in the Second Curia.

161. B2, Nr. 7831 (dated 5 Dec. 1895), *NÖLA; NFP*, 12 Sept. 1895 (M), p. 5; 19 Dec. 1895 (M), pp. 6–7; *ÖSBZ*, 1 Oct. 1895, p. 3.

162. *NFP*, 27 Sept. 1895 (M), pp. 6–7; *AZ*, 27 Sept. 1895, p. 1. By Apr. 1896 the party controlled eighteen seats in the First Curia.

163. The antisemites also picked up some support from the powerful butchers' guild in 1894–95, and many butchers may have been house owners, since they were usually among the wealthiest artisans. See Kielmansegg, *Kaiserhaus*, pp. 371–72, and *WFFZ*, 5 Apr. 1895, p. 1.

164. For an example of this usage, see the comments of Joseph Schlesinger in the police report B2, Nr. 25541/1895, for a rally held on 11 Nov. 1895, *NÖLA*.

165. For background to the controversy, see Erwin Burger, *Die Frage der Bestätigung der Wahl Dr. Karl Luegers zum Bürgermeister von Wien* (diss., University of Vienna, 1952). My analysis of the 1895–96 *NÖLA* materials was done independently of that in Burger.

166. For Badeni, see Berthold Sutter, *Die Badenischen Sprachenverordnungen von 1897* (2 vols., Graz and Cologne, 1960–65), 1:128–33; Plener, *Erinnerungen*, 3:279–80; Sieghart, *Die letzten Jahrzehnte*, pp. 410–11; Karl v Grabmayr, *Erinnerungen eines Tiroler Politikers, 1892–1920* (Innsbruck, 1955), pp. 43–45. For a favorable, pro-Czech view of Badeni, see Garver, *The Young Czech Party*, pp. 218–20.

167. *PAAA*, Öst. 70/Bd. 29, A12159, 13 Nov. 1895; *NPZ*, 8 Nov. 1895 (A), p. 1.

168. B2 ad 6847, Nr. 6967 (dated 1 Nov. 1895), *NÖLA*.

169. B2 ad 6847, Nr. 7210/1895, and the attached *Erinnerung* written by Kielmansegg.

170. Kielmansegg, *Kaiserhaus*, p. 376.

171. Ibid., pp. 377–78; Leon Bilinski, *Wspomnienia i dokumenty* (2 vols., Warsaw, 1924–25), 1:91–93.

172. Kielmansegg, *Kaiserhaus*, p. 62.

173. *PAAA*, Öst. 70/Bd. 29, A12159, 13 Nov. 1895.

174. Badeni visited Budapest in mid-October for a three-day visit; Banffy came to Vienna in early November. It is utterly inconceivable that the Lueger question was not discussed.

175. Kielmansegg, *Kaiserhaus*, p. 377.

176. Ibid., pp. 62–64, 377–78.

177. See above, note 173.

178. See Sutter, *Die Badenischen Sprachenverordnungen*, 1:134, who suggests Liberal concern with the upcoming national elections in 1897 as the principal reason for the deadlock.

179. *SP*, XI, 1895, pp. 21380–81, 21382–83.

180. Ibid., pp. 21381–82.

181. Kielmansegg, *Kaiserhaus*, pp. 63–64; and Kielmansegg's report, B2 ad 6847, Nr. 7266/1895, *NÖLA*.

182. *NFP*, 14 Nov. 1895 (M), pp. 7–8.

183. B2 ad 4847 (Nr. 5801 and 5696), *NÖLA*.

184. *NFP*, 29 Oct. 1895 (M), p. 4.

185. B2, Nr. 25541, *NÖLA*, 12 Nov. 1895.

186. J6, Nr. 7723, *NÖLA*, 4 Dec. 1895; and J6 ad 7723, Nr. 7630, *NÖLA*, 16 Dec. 1895.

187. For the novelty of this device, see B2 ad 452, Nr. 64/1896, *NÖLA*.

188. B2, Nr. 7831/1895, *NÖLA*.

189. *ÖW*, 10 Jan. 1896, pp. 35–36.

190. *NFP*, 3 Dec. 1895 (M), p. 6; 4 Dec. 1895 (M), p. 6; *ÖW*, 6 Dec. 1895, p. 901. For the police reports on the women's rallies, see J12 ad 7425 (Nr. 7633, 7593, 7700, 7752, 7776, 7857, 7858, 7945, 7993, 7994, 8025, 8098), *NÖLA*, 1895.

191. See, for example, B2 ad 6847, Nr. 7281/1895; B2, Nr. 7831/1895, *NÖLA*.

192. J12 ad 37 (Nr. 650, 1526, 1522, 1333), *NÖLA*, 1896.

193. *PAAA*, Öst. 70/Bd. 29, A13204, 7 Dec. 1895.

194. Kielmansegg, *Kaiserhaus*, p. 64.

195. Ibid., pp. 64–65.

196. *PAAA*, Öst. 70/Bd. 29, A2209, 28 Feb. 1896; B2 ad 452, Nr. 1108/1896, *NÖLA*. The police reported that Lueger was under pressure from Ebenhoch and the Alpine Conservatives to find a way out of the confrontation.

197. *PAAA*, Öst. 70/Bd. 29, A4734, 1 May 1896.

198. Kielmansegg, *Kaiserhaus*, p. 65. Eulenburg thought that Badeni had been intimidated by Lueger when he realized the extent of Lueger's popularity in the city. *PAAA*, Öst. 70/Bd. 29, A4546, 28 Apr. 1896.

199. Sutter, *Die Badenischen Sprachenverordnungen*, 1:137, 143, 181.

200. B2 ad 452, Nr. 1773/1896, *NÖLA*.

201. B2, Nr. 1203 ("Vertraulich"), *NÖLA*, 1896.

202. B2 ad 452 (Nr. 1108, 2140, 2504), *NÖLA*, 1896.

203. *AZ*, 2 Feb. 1896, pp. 1–2.

204. For example, ibid., 30 Jan. 1896, p. 7.

205. B2 ad 2104, Nr. 2870/1896, *NÖLA*.

206. Ibid., Nr. 2921/1896, *NÖLA*.

207. Ibid., Nr. 2952/1896, *NÖLA*. Lueger missed the Jan. deadline by four months, since Badeni later insisted that it would be better to wait until after the 1897 parliamentary elections in Mar. before allowing Lueger to take over. Lueger agreed, since this gave him more free time to devote to the 1897 electoral campaign.

208. *DV*, 1 May 1896 (M), pp. 1–2; *ÖW*, 3 Apr. 1896, p. 269; *ODR*, 28 Apr. 1896, p. 1. The *ODR* published the famous attack on Ernst Vergani by Franz Arnoscht in April.

209. Pacher had authored a scurrilous pamphlet attacking Lueger in the mid-1880s from a Schönerian point of view *(Die demokratische Caricatur des V. Bezirkes)*. He was allowed on the 1895 election slate as a gesture to the more moderate nationalists, but neither Lueger nor Gessmann trusted him.

210. See Gessmann's public response to Pacher's accusation in *DV*, 10 May 1896 (M), pp. 2–3; also, Lueger's attack on Wolf and Pacher in *DV*, 13 May 1896 (M), pp. 9–10.

211. B2 ad 2104, Nr. 3156/1896, *NÖLA*. On Strobach, see the police report B2 ad 2104, Nr. 2176/1896.

212. B2 ad 2104, Nr. 3156 and 3460/1896, *NÖLA*. Kielmansegg noted in an addendum to his records for the report, which he did not send along to Badeni, that some higher officials in the *Magistrat* resented Strobach for his "rough demeanor" and his lack of juristic training.

213. *RGBl*, 1887, Nr. 74; *PV* 4:305–6.

214. *SP*, X, 1886, pp. 3453–60.

215. Ibid., pp. 3465–68.

216. Ibid., pp. 3468–71.

217. *NWT*, 6 Jan. 1888, p. 4; 28 Jan. 1888, p. 4.

218. For the early organizational history of the *Centralverband*, see HHZ, 1 Jan. 1890, pp. 2–3, 6; 15 Jan. 1890, pp. 1–3; 1 Feb. 1890, pp. 1–2; *NWT*, 2 June 1888, p. 3; 4 June 1888, p. 3; 5 June 1888, pp. 5–6.

219. *SJ*, 1893, pp. 163, 166. For the relevant tax data on Vienna's contribution to national revenue, see *HHZ*, 1 Jan. 1893, pp. 2–7.

220. Each district club elected five delegates to the *Centralverband*'s executive committee. Each club retained, however, operational sovereignty, discussing and voting upon policy statements independently of the *Centralverband*. By the mid-1890s many of the local clubs had rented headquarters and some were even planning to construct permanent headquarters.

221. *HHZ*, 15 Apr. 1895, p. 5. In view of the *Centralverband*'s hostility to further tax exemptions for new buildings constructed in Vienna, it is probable that many of the *Hausherren* owned older properties, subject to the full tax rate.

222. For sample attacks on the *AZ*, see *HHZ*, 1 Sept. 1895, pp. 3–4.

223. For the *Stadtbürger* versus *Staatsbürger* distinction, ibid., 15 Dec. 1895, p. 6.

224. There were occasional outbursts of ill-temper and petty infighting among the opposing factions, such as the ousting of Thomas Mück as the local chairman of the Ottakring Club (Mück was a Liberal who found it difficult to get along with the antisemitic majority) or the federalist pretensions of the Landstrasse Club, which had a Liberal majority. But most of the clubs seemed to keep their internal peace relatively undisturbed.

225. The attributions of property ownership and membership in the *Verband* on the part of the Christian Social politicians are from notations in the *HHZ*, the *DV*, the *DZ*, and *Lehmanns Allgemeiner Wohnungsanzeiger*. The party did not run serious candidates in the First or Second District.

226. These data on gross rental income levels, as well as age and size of buildings, came from Joseph Lenobel, ed., *Häuser-Kataster der k. k. Reichshaupt- und Residenzstadt Wien* (17 Hefte, Vienna, 1905). These data are in *Kronen* and had been converted. Each district was surveyed by Lenobel, using tax data from 1903 provided by the Imperial and municipal tax authorities. Although average rents would have risen by approximately 15% between 1895 and 1903, the relative distribution of rental income among politically active owners is the important fact in this context, and the inflationary rises in rents tended to move across the

spectrum of apartment rentals in the city, except for areas where the age of the building or a drastic shift in the human ecological environment caused rents to decline or remain stable.

227. Lenobel, *Häuser-Kataster,* Heft 5.

228. For the 1900 housing census, see *SJ,* 1902, esp. p. 22.

229. See Prochazka, *Die provisorische Gemeindeordnung,* p. 69 (Prochazka estimated that 2,343 fl. in rental income would be required, using the 1850 tax rate of 21%). In 1895 the rate was 26.6%, but one must first allow for the 15% credit against gross taxable income which could be deducted as house maintenance costs. On this basis the estimate of 2,400 fl. in gross rent would result in approximately 500 fl. in state taxes. Since the data on rent levels come from 1903, however, by which time a probable increase in rents of 10–15% would have taken place, I have further adjusted the 1903 data by an additional 15% in estimating 1895 values. Lenobel correctly omitted the *Zinskreuzer* from his rental income estimates.

If the First Curia contained only 5,500 voters in 1895, how does this statistic compare with the 15,000 buildings in the city with rents over 2,300 fl.? A relatively large number of buildings constructed after 1874 still enjoyed in 1895 some kind of tax exemption status under laws passed in the 1870s and 1880s providing a significant reduction in direct taxes for a period of twelve to twenty-five years for new or reconstructed buildings. Those owners would have paid a reduced tax (5 percent direct rental tax, plus city and provincial surcharges) and may have sacrificed their First Curia voting rights for the period of their exemption, regaining them after the tax exemption period expired. Also, since the census did not differentiate between the sexes of owners, it is impossible to know how many buildings were owned by females. But a reasonable number certainly were, and this would have had an effect on voter registration in the curia. Another factor influencing the composition of the curia was the large number of buildings (5,380) under the joint ownership of several persons (not married couples). In such cases each shareholder was credited, for the purpose of voting rights, with a relative percentage of the rental taxes on his building. Many of these co-owners were probably excluded from the top curia, since their partial share of taxes did not surpass the minimum 500 fl. level needed to vote in the First Curia. Certainly the propaganda and rhetoric of the various district clubs between 1891 and 1896 assumed that most of their members were enfranchised First Curia voters. See *HHZ,* 1 Apr. 1890, p. 4; 15 May 1893, pp. 2–3; *NFP,* 22 Sept. 1895 (M), p. 2; *AZ,* 25 Sept. 1895, p. 1; 26 Sept. 1895, p. 2.

For the variety of tax exemptions and their implications for the Viennese market, see Paul Schwarz, "Die Entwicklung der städtischen Grundrente in Wien," pp. 42ff. For recent literature on the history of housing in nineteenth-century Vienna, see Peter Feldbauer, "Die Wohnungsverhältnisse der Unterschichten im Franzisko-Josephinischen Wien. Thesen und Probleme," *JVGSW* 34 (1978): 358–89. Feldbauer has noted the problem of the shift in support of the *Hausherren* to the Christian Socials as a crucial feature of late-nineteenth-century housing history, arguing correctly that the owners became a crucial electoral support group for the Christian Socials after 1897. Ibid., pp. 385–88.

230. The data on rental income for these owners derive from Lenobel, *Häuser-Kataster,* adjusting for the rise in rents between 1896 and 1903. Each district had a local board, numbering anywhere from 15 to 25 members (it varied from club to club). Each board usually included the district's delegates to the *Centralverband* (although this was not required), as well as other prominent local owners. The names of the members of each board were printed from time to time in the *HHZ.* Information on these men came from comparing the data in the *HHZ* with citations in Lehmann and Lenobel. Although there were 203 leaders on these boards, I was able to obtain data on rent levels for only 149. For Vienna as a whole there were 368 men on the nineteen district boards.

231. *Die Ergebnisse der Volkszählung vom 31. Dezember 1910*, vol. 4, Heft 1, *Häuser, Wohnungs-, und Haushaltungsstatistik* (Vienna, 1914), pp. 77–78.

232. On the 368 men of the boards, see above, note 230. Leiter notes that over 70% of the retirement income of state and local officials came from state pensions, not from investments. See Leiter, *Die Verteilung*, p. 480.

233. *Protokolle der allgemeinen öffentlichen Enquête über die Lage des Kleingewerbes in Nieder-Österreich* (Vienna, 1874), 1:166ff.

234. *HHZ*, 1 May 1895, pp. 2–3; 15 July 1895, p. 2; 1 Aug. 1895, p. 2; 15 Dec. 1895, p. 6.

235. *HHZ*, 1 May 1894, pp. 2–3; 15 May 1894, p. 6. For the *Hausherr* as a patriarchal "house-holder" in pre-modern societies, see Mitterauer and Sieder, *Vom Patriarchat*, pp. 188–90.

236. If one includes pensioners and retirees, this figure would rise to 6,600, but some of the latter would be older women of uncertain status. These data are tabulated on the basis of the statistics in Leiter, *Die Verteilung*, pp. 205–408.

237. Extant statistics on the personal income tax offer only general occupational categories which are not broken down to a level where specific occupations might be ascertained. In using these data, I am assuming that personal income is a relatively accurate index to levels of personal consumption and family prosperity, as well as a crude index to social class positioning. Obviously, other data (such as capital investments not listed on the income tax returns) or outright tax cheating would force revisions of the argument in individual cases. That in all cases personal income may not be congruent with class positioning and *relative* social rank is of course obvious. Also, although Vienna reported 88% of all income returns for all of Lower Austria, it is possible that some individuals lived in the city, but had their principal residence outside Vienna and paid their taxes there.

238. The number of "high bourgeois" academic types in the city was remarkably small. For all institutions of higher learning in 1902, including the university and the technical *Hochschule*, there were only 262 individuals occupying full or associate professorships in the city. There were an additional 323 *Dozenten*, but many of these individuals would hardly qualify in a top status rank group. For gymnasial professors there were 382 regular faculty members for all thirty-one gymnasial and *Realschule* institutions in the city.

239. Rudolf Eberstadt, *Neue Studien über Städtebau und Wohnungswesen* (Jena, 1912), pp. 160, 189–200; Emil Lederer, "Ein Vorschlag zur Reform der Gebäudesteuer," *ZVSV* 18 (1909): 238–40; Leo Munk, *Die Steuerbelastung*, p. 28.

240. See Ludwig von Mises, *Notes and Recollections* (South Holland, Ill., 1978), pp. 20–21.

241. See above, note 229.

242. For a personal view of the social Liberal movement, see Hainisch, *75 Jahre aus bewegter Zeit*, pp. 124–65. Emil Fürth was a crucial figure in the Fabians' housing reform movement.

243. *HHZ*, 15 Jan. 1895, p. 2; 15 Mar. 1895, pp. 1–2; *SP*, XI, 1895, pp. 17652–53.

244. On the *Zinskreuzer* controversy, see *HHZ*, 1 Jan. 1893, pp. 10–11; 15 Feb. 1895, p. 12; and *DV*, 26 Nov. 1892 (M), p. 4. Kielmansegg, *Kaiserhaus*, pp. 373–74, insists that until 1891–92 the city collected the *Zinskreuzer* and only then demanded that the owners collect it, but numerous essays in *HHZ* argued that this was not the case—that since the 1870s the owners had been forced by the city to collect the tax.

245. *HHZ*, 15 Feb. 1893, pp. 5–6; 1 May 1893, pp. 2–3; 15 May 1894, p. 6; 15 Apr. 1895, pp. 3–4.

246. Ibid., 1 Mar. 1895, p. 7; 15 Nov. 1895, pp. 3–4. Suburban owners found Lueger's plans for an expanded, municipalized tramway particularly attractive, since better trans-

portation in their districts would enhance the market value of their houses. This was merely one reason for the enthusiastic support given the party by suburban owners. Resentment against the higher property tax rates as a result of the 1891 unification and more direct hostility to the Socialists qua tenants were obviously other important motives.

247. *HHZ,* 15 Aug. 1895, pp. 6–7.

248. See esp. *HHZ,* 1 May 1895, pp. 2–3.

249. See Richard S. Levy, *The Downfall of the Anti-Semitic Political Parties in Imperial Germany* (New Haven, 1975). See Feldbauer, "Die Wohnungsverhältnisse der Unterschichten," pp. 385–88, for the long-range significance of the assimilation of the owners into the party.

250. *DV,* 28 May 1896 (M), p. 4.

251. The Christian Socials retained the *Stadtrat* when they reformed the *Gemeindeordnung* in 1899–1900. For this reform, see vol. 2 of this study.

252. For Lueger's report to the Council on 21 Oct. 1896, see *Amtsblatt der Stadt Wien,* 1896, pp. 1612–16.

253. For the elections, see *NFP,* 5 Nov. 1896 (M), pp. 1–3; *RP,* 5 Nov. 1896, p. 7; 6 Nov. 1896, p. 3; *DZ,* 6 Nov. 1896, pp. 3–4.

254. *AZ,* 11 Apr. 1897, p. 2. For the Landtag franchise and the operations of the provincial administration, see Friedrich Kant, *Der niederösterreichische Landtag von 1902 bis 1908* (diss., University of Vienna, 1949).

255. *RP,* 15 Sept. 1896, pp. 1, 3–6; *AZ,* 14 Sept. 1896, p. 1. The antisemites claimed 11,000 showed up, but the *AZ* reported that about 6,000 men had actually attended, two-thirds of whom were rural property owners and peasants. A special committee of the party, which coordinated electoral agitation in Vienna and in the rural areas, sent letters to Catholic priests in Lower Austria asking for cooperation in the election work. Many priests were invited to come to Vienna for a day in order to discuss election tactics with members of the central committee. For a sample letter to the clergy, see *AZ,* 12 Sept. 1896, pp. 1–2.

256. For agrarian politics in Lower Austria, see Therese Kraus, *Die Entstehung des 'Niederösterreichischen Bauernbundes'* (diss., University of Vienna, 1950), esp. pp. 56–80, 99–170; Ernst Bruckmüller, *Landwirtschaftliche Organisationen und gesellschaftliche Modernisierung, Vereine, Genossenschaften, und politische Mobilisierung der Landwirtschaft Österreichs vom Vormärz bis 1914* (Salzburg, 1977). The history of the agrarian wing of the party will be discussed in vol. 2, since its major growth occurred after 1897.

257. *DZ,* 28 Sept. 1896, pp. 1–2. The *DZ* was the moderate nationalist paper in Vienna until the later 1890s, when it became more orthodox in support of the Christian Socials.

258. *RP,* 24 Aug. 1896, pp. 1–2; *DZ,* 24 Aug. 1896, pp. 1–2.

259. For Lower Austrian politics in this period, see Karl Gutkas, *Geschichte des Landes Niederösterreich* (3 vols., St. Pölten, 1955–59), 3:153–64.

260. *DV,* 29 Oct. 1896 (A), p. 2; 4 Nov. 1896 (A), pp. 1–2; Pichl, *Schönerer,* 4:69–83. Baumann broke openly with the pan-Germans in this election.

261. See Pacher's self-justification in *ODR,* 26 July 1896. Also, *DV,* 23 July 1896 (A), p. 2.

262. *DZ,* 20 Oct. 1896, p. 4. The eleven were Fochler, Gruber, Hipp, Migl, Pollak, Rader, Rissaweg, Sauerborn, Schrabauer, Tomanek, and Wieder. A few, like Hipp, later made their peace with Lueger.

263. For the majority declaration, see *DV,* 21 Oct. 1896 (A), p. 1.

264. This is an obvious conclusion from the police reports on both movements in 1896–97. See, for example, E5 ad 872 (Nr. 1325, 1005), *NÖLA,* 1897. Also B2 ad 452, Nr. 1108/1896.

265. *NFP,* 10 Mar. 1897 (M), pp. 1–4; also 9 Mar. 1897 (M), pp. 1–2.

266. E5 ad 1431, Nr. 2240/1897, *NÖLA;* Eva Holleis, *Die Sozialpolitische Partei* (Vienna, 1978); and Boyer, "Freud, Marriage, and Late Viennese Liberalism." The Left Liberals

were important, however, in helping to provoke a new wave of anticlericalism in Vienna.

267. See Badeni to Kielmansegg, E5 ad 1098, Nr. 1309/1897, *NÖLA*. For Socialist complaints about vote fraud and registration irregularities, see *AZ*, 8 Mar. 1897, pp. 1–2; 12 Mar. 1897, pp. 4–5; 13 Mar. 1897, pp. 4–5. The *AZ* also claimed that the antisemites had urged *Hausherren* to threaten their working-class tenants with eviction if they voted Socialist.

268. The fifth candidate was Lueger, who put his reputation on the line to run in the Fifth Curia. Axmann, Bielohlawek, Prochazka, and Mittermayer were also candidates of Leopold Kunschak's fledgling Christian Social Workers' Party, which had been organized in Jan. 1896. Most of Kunschak's party consisted of master artisans and other antisemitic voters interested in organizing an anti-Socialist front group to undercut Socialist election success in journeyman circles. See J1, Nr. 7671/1896, *NÖLA*. On Kunschak, see his own *Steinchen vom Wege* (Vienna, 1937) and *45 Jahre Christlichsozialer Arbeiterverein* (Vienna, n.d.); and esp. "Aus dem Werden der christlichen Arbeiterbewegung Österreichs," *VW* 14 (1923): 246–53, 279–84. The propaganda of the party consisted of outraged protests against the "terrorism" of the Socialists. See *FH*, 5 Mar. 1897, pp. 1–2. The Mar. 1897 victory was achieved by the mother party, not Kunschak's organization, and Lueger never let Kunschak forget this point. See also VI, 26 Mar. 1897, pp. 1–3.

269. On Mittermayer, who later disgraced the party when it was discovered that he was a thief, see *AZ*, 26 Mar. 1897, p. 1; 20 June 1897, p. 5. The other three Fifth Curia candidates proved to be men of political reliability and eventually occupied important leadership positions in the party elite.

270. The Austrian census included the *Diener* in the more general category of workers, so it is difficult to estimate precisely how many petty service types there were in the city. Contemporary estimates agree that there were thousands of these men in Vienna in 1897. For interesting propaganda during the 1897 election, stressing Hermann Bielohlawek's "respectability" and his image as a self-made man within the Bürgertum, see *Das Echo*, 7 Mar. 1897, pp. 1–2; 14 Mar. 1897, p. 2.

271. Although the Socialists hated to admit it, there were minorities in each of the major craft trades who were sympathetic to the antisemites. Their numbers were often small, but as an aggregate in a general election they might have had an impact. Lueger's personal popularity may have played a role also. See *FH*, 15 May 1896, p. 2.

272. B2, Nr. 2653/1897, *NÖLA*.

273. B2 ad 2653, Nr. 2834/1897, *NÖLA*. For Baden's presentation to the Emperor, see *HHSA*, Kabinettskanzlei, Vortrag Nr. 1503, 15 Apr. 1897.

274. For a complete transcription of Lueger's speech at the ceremony, see *NFP*, 20 Apr. 1897 (A), pp. 2–3.

Bibliography

Archival Materials

Haus-, Hof-, und Staatsarchiv, Vienna *(HHSA)*
  Friedrich Funder Nachlass
  Franz Martin Schindler Papers
  Akten des Politischen Archivs, Rome-Rapports, and Rome-Expeditions-
    Varia, 1895
  Akten der Kabinettskanzlei, Vorträge
Allgemeines Verwaltungsarchiv, Vienna *(AVA)*
  Eduard Pichl Nachlass
  Akten des Ministeriums des Inneren, 1880–94
  Präsidialakten des Ministeriums für Kultus und Unterricht, 1887–90
Niederösterreichisches Landesarchiv, Vienna *(NÖLA)*
  Präsidialakten, Statthalterei, 1880–97
  Stadterweiterungsakten, 1888–91
Bibliothek der katholisch-theologischen Fakultät, Universität Wien, Vienna
  Karl v Vogelsang Nachlass
Erzbischöfliches Diözesanarchiv, Vienna *(EBDA)*
  Cardinal Gruscha Nachlass
  Protokolle der bischöflichen Versammlungen, 1891–1907
  Protokolle der Conferenzen des bischöflichen Comités, 1891–1907
  Tagebuch, Friedrich Gustav Piffl, 1894–1901
Wiener Stadt- und Landesarchiv, Vienna *(WSLA)*
  Gemeinderatsprotokolle, 1848–49
Handschriftensammlung, Wiener Stadtbibliothek, Vienna
  Karl Lueger Nachlass
Politisches Archiv des Auswärtigen Amtes, (Bonn *(PAAA)* (National Archives
    Films–UCI, ACP, and UM Series)
  Österreich 70, 74, 75, 86, 88, 90, 91
  Deutschland 125, Nr. 1.
  Päpstlicher Stuhl 1, 2, 5, 6

Newspapers

Allgemeine Handwerker Zeitung
Allgemeine Österreichische Zeitung
Arbeiter-Zeitung

NOTE. Newspapers published in Vienna unless otherwise noted.

Beamten-Zeitung
Bericht des Gremiums der Wiener Kaufmannschaft
Christlich-soziale Arbeiter-Zeitung
Die Constitution
Correspondenzblatt für den katholischen Clerus Österreichs
Demokratische Zeitung
Deutsch-Österreichische Lehrer-Zeitung
Deutsche Gewerbe-Zeitung
Deutsche Schulzeitung
Deutsches Volksblatt
Deutsche Zeitung
Das Echo
Fortschritt
Freie Lehrerstimme
Freies Blatt: Organ zur Abwehr des Antisemitismus
Freiheit: Organ für die christliche Arbeiterschaft Österreichs
Der Freimüthige
Gerad' aus
Hausherren-Zeitung
Kampf
Kaufmännische Post
Konstitutionelle Vorstadt-Zeitung
Mitteilungen der Oesterreichisch-Israelitischen Union
Monatsschrift für christliche Sozialreform
Morgenpost
Neue Freie Presse
Neue Preussische Zeitung (Berlin)
Neues Wiener Tagblatt
Nordböhmisches Volksblatt (Warnsdorf)
Oesterreichischer Reformer
Oesterreichischer Volksfreund
Oesterreichische Staatsbeamten-Zeitung
Oesterreichische Wochenschrift
Ost-Deutsche Post
Österreichische Schul-Zeitung
Pädagogischer Jahresbericht (Leipzig)
Politische Fragmente
Die Presse
Reichspost
St. Angela Blatt
Sendboten des heiligen Joseph
Das Signal
Sprechsaal des Beamtentages
Der Staatsbeamte
Theologisch-praktische Quartalschrift (Linz)
Tribüne

Unverfälschte Deutsche Worte
Vaterland
Volkstribüne
Vorwärts (Berlin)
Vossische Zeitung (Berlin)
Währinger Bezirks-Nachrichten
Wiener Diözesanblatt
Wiener Fleischhauer- und Fleischselcher Zeitung
Wiener Gewerbe-Genossenschaftstag
Wiener Zeitung
Die Zeit
Zeitung für die Wiener Nationalgarde

Government Publications

*Aemtliche Verhandlungs-Protokolle des Gemeinde-Ausschusses der Stadt Wien
vom 25. Mai bis 5. Oktober 1848.* Vienna, 1848.
Amtsblatt der Stadt Wien. Vienna, 1892–1911.
*Berichte über die Industrie, den Handel, und die Verkehrsverhältnisse in
Nieder-Österreich.* Vienna, 1874–96.
*Denkschrift der Vororte Wiens über die Folgen einer eventuellen Hinausrückung
der Verzehrungssteuer-Linien.* Vienna, 1884.
*Enquête der niederösterreichischen Handels- und Gewerbekammer über die
Wünsche des Handels-, Gewerbe-, und Arbeiterstandes im Kammerbezirke be-
züglich der Revision des Gewerbegesetzes vom 20. Dezember 1859.* Vienna,
1868.
*Ergebnisse der gewerblichen Betriebszählung vom 3. Juni 1902 in Niederöster-
reich.* Vienna, 1909.
*Die Ergebnisse der über die Standesverhältnisse der Privatangestellten im Jahre
1896 eingeleiteten amtlichen Erhebungen.* Vienna, 1898.
Die Ergebnisse der Volkszählung vom 31. Dezember 1910. Vol. 4, Heft 1.
Häuser-, Wohnungs-, und Haushaltungsstatistik. Vienna, 1914.
Erkenntnisse des k. k. Verwaltungs-Gerichtshofes. Vienna, 1889–93.
Lenobel, Joseph, ed. *Häuser-Kataster der k. k. Reichshaupt- und Residenzstadt
Wien.* 17 Hefte. Vienna, 1905.
*Protokolle der allgemeinen öffentlichen Enquête über die Lage des Kleingewerbes
in Nieder-österreich.* Vienna, 1874.
Protokolle der Enquête über Personalkredit und Wucher. Vienna, 1904.
Reichsgesetzblatt. Vienna, 1880–1907.
Sedlaczek, Stephan. *Die definitiven Ergebnisse der Volkszählung vom 31. De-
zember 1890 in der k. k. Reichshaupt- und Residenzstadt Wien.* Vienna, 1891.
———. *Ergebnisse der Volkszählung vom 31. Dezember 1880.* 3 vols. Vienna,
1884–87.
———. *Die Wohn-Verhältnisse in Wien. Ergebnisse der Volkszählung vom 31.
Dezember 1890 in der k. k. Reichshaupt- und Residenzstadt Wien.* Vienna,
1891.

Sitzungs-Protokolle des ständigen Arbeitsbeirathes. Vienna, 1899–1903.

Statistik der Wahlen für den Gemeinderath der Reichshaupt- und Residenzstadt Wien in den Jahren 1861 bis 1880. Vienna, 1880.

Statistische Jahrbücher der Stadt Wien. Vienna, 1883–1911.

Statistische Monatschrift. Vienna, 1877–1911.

Stenographische Berichte über die Verhandlungen des Reichstags. Berlin, 1897.

Stenographische Protokolle des Landtages für das Erzherzogtum Österreich unter der Enns. Vienna, 1875–97.

Stenographische Protokolle über die Sitzungen des Hauses der Abgeordneten. Vienna, 1867–1911.

Stenographischer Bericht über die Verhandlungen der deutschen constituierenden National-Versammlung. Frankfurt a. M., 1848.

Stenographische Sitzungs-Protokolle der Delegation des Reichsrathes. Vienna, 1894–98.

Stenographisches Protokoll der Gewerbe-Enquête. Vienna, 1893.

Stenographisches Protokoll der im k. k. Arbeitsstatistischen Amte durchgeführten Vernehmung von Auskunftspersonen über die Verhältnisse im Schuhmachergewerbe. Vienna, 1904.

Stenographisches Protokoll über die im Gewerbeausschuss des Abgeordnetenhauses stattgehabte Enquête über die Arbeitergesetzgebung. Vienna, 1883.

Tafeln zur Statistik der Österreichischen Monarchie. Vienna, 1850–59.

U.S. Department of State. *Consular Reports on Commerce, Manufactures, Etc. Reports from the Consuls of the United States.* Washington, 1888.

Veränderungen im Stand der Gewerbe während der sieben Jahresperioden 1900/01–1906/07. Vienna, 1909.

Die Verhältnisse in der Kleider- und Wäschekonfektion. Vienna, 1906.

Verhandlungen des österreichischen Reichstages nach der stenographischen Aufnahme. Vienna, 1848–49.

Verhandlungen des preussischen Landtages. Stenographische Berichte des Hauses der Abgeordneten. Berlin, 1899.

Verordnungsblatt des k. k. Justizministeriums. Vienna, 1896.

Verwaltungsberichte der Reichshaupt- und Residenzstadt Wien. Vienna, 1880–95.

Vorlagen der Kommission zur Berathung der Reform der Verzehrungssteuer und der Vereinigung der Vororte mit Wien. Nos. 1–7. Vienna, 1880–89.

Contemporary Printed Materials

Adler, Victor. *Die Arbeiterkammern und die Arbeiter.* Vienna, 1886.

———. *Aufsätze, Reden, und Briefe.* 11 vols. Vienna, 1922–29.

"Aktenstücke zur Geschichte des österreichischen römisch-katholischen Kirchenwesens unter Kaiser Leopold II." *Archiv für Kunde österreichischer Geschichtsquellen* 4 (1850).

Alexis, W. *Wiener Bilder.* Leipzig, 1833.

Arneth, Alfred von. *Anton Ritter v Schmerling.* Vienna, 1894.

Auerbach, Berthold. *Tagebuch aus Wien.* Breslau, 1849.

Austriacus. *Oesterreich ein Juwel in jüdischer Fassung.* Berlin, 1880.

535   Bibliography

————. *Wählet keinen Juden. Ein Mahn- und Warnungsruf an die Völker Oesterreich-Ungarns*. Berlin, 1881.

Baernreither, Joseph M. *Der Verfall des Habsburgerreiches und die Deutschen. Fragmente eines politischen Tagebuches, 1897–1917*. Vienna, 1938.

Barre, Ernest. *Der ländliche Wucher. Ein Beitrag zur Wucherfrage*. Berlin, 1890.

Bauer, Otto. "Der Tod des christlichen Sozialismus." *Der Kampf* 4 (1911).

Berger, Alfred. "Doktor Lueger." *ÖRD* 23 (1910).

Bergstrásser, Ludwig, ed. *Das Frankfurter Parlament in Briefen und Tagebüchern*. Frankfurt a. M., 1929.

Bericht betreffend die Regelung des Gemischtwarenverschleisses. Sitzungsprotokolle der Handels- und Gerwerbekammer, Wien. Beilage Nr. 1 (29 Mar. 1893). Vienna, 1893.

Bericht über den 3. allgemeinen österreichischen Katholikentag in Linz. Wels, 1892.

Bericht über den vierten allgemeinen österreichischen Katholikentag in Salzburg. Salzburg, 1896.

Bericht über die Thätigkeit des politischen Vereins "Eintracht" im VIII. Bezirke in den Jahren 1873–1884. Vienna 1884.

Bericht über die Verhandlungen des dritten allgemeinen österreichischen Gewerbetages. Vienna, 1884.

Bericht über die Verhandlungen des vierten allgemeinen österreichischen Gewerbetages. Vienna, 1890.

Bernstein, Eduard. *Evolutionary Socialism*. Trans. by Edith Harvey. New York, 1899.

Beskiba, Marianne. *Aus meinen Erinnerungen an Dr. Karl Lueger*. Vienna, 1911.

Billroth, Theodor. *Über das Lehren und Lernen der medicinischen Wissenschaften*. Vienna, 1876.

Bloch, Joseph Samuel. *My Reminiscences*. Vienna and Berlin, 1923.

Blome, Gustav Graf. "Briefe des Grafen Gustav Blome an den Freiherrn Karl v Vogelsang." *JLG* (1928).

Bolzano, Bernard. *Sozialphilosophische Schriften*. Ed. by Jan Berg and Jaromír Loužil. Stuttgart, 1975.

Brandl, F. *Kaiser, Politiker, und Menschen*. Vienna, 1936.

Bruckner, Johann. *Der Arbeiterapostel von Wien. P. Anton Maria Schwartz*. Vienna, 1935.

Brunner, Sebastian. *Clemens Maria Hofbauer und seine Zeit*. Vienna, 1858.

————. *Woher? Wohin? Geschichten, Gedanken, Bilder und Leute aus meinem Leben*. 5 vols. 3d ed. Regensburg, 1891.

Bunzel, Julius. *Der Lebenslauf eines vormärzlichen Verwaltungs-Beamten*. Vienna, 1911.

Chronik des Gremiums der Wiener Kaufmannschaft. Vienna, 1903.

Dannerbauer, Wolfgang. *Praktisches Geschäftsbuch für den Curat-Clerus Österreichs*. Vienna, 1896.

Deckert, Joseph. *Kann ein Katholik Antisemite sein?* Dresden, 1893.

————. *Türkennoth und Judenherrschaft*. Vienna, 1894.

Dunder, W. G. *Denkschrift über die Wiener Oktober-Revolution. Ausführliche Darstellung aller Ereignisse.* Vienna, 1849.

Ehrhart, Robert. *Im Dienste des alten Österreich.* Vienna, 1958.

Eichert, Franz. "Mein Lebenslauf." In *Sänger und Prophet* (qv).

Eichhorn, Rudolf. *Die weissen Sklaven der Wiener Tramwaygesellschaft.* Vienna, 1885.

Engländer, Leopold. *Offener Brief an jene Hausherren, welche unerschwingliche Zinsen verlangen.* Vienna, 1848.

Entwicklung von Industrie und Gewerbe in Österreich in den Jahren 1848–1888. Vienna, 1888.

Felder, Cajetan. *Erinnerungen eines Wiener Bürgermeisters.* Ed. by Felix Czeike. Vienna, 1964.

Funder, Friedrich. *Aufbruch zur christlichen Sozialreform.* Vienna, 1953.

————. "Aus den Anfängen christlichsozialer Programmarbeit." *VW* 14 (1923).

————. "Die katholische Presse." In *Der Katholizismus in Österreich,* ed. by Alois Hudal. Innsbruck, Vienna, and Munich, 1931.

————. *Vom Gestern ins Heute.* 3d ed. Vienna, 1971.

Gedenkblatt zum vierzigjährigen Bestande des politischen Fortschritts-Vereins "Eintracht" im 3. Bezirke, 1872–1912. Vienna, 1912.

Gesellige Vereinigung "Freundschaftsverband Lueger," 1896–1908. Vienna, 1906.

Glöckel, Otto. *Selbstbiographie.* Zurich, 1939.

Grabmayr, Karl von. *Erinnerungen eines Tiroler Politikers, 1892–1920.* Innsbruck, 1955.

Grossmann, Stefan. *Ich war begeistert.* Berlin, 1930.

Günther, Anton. "Die doppelte Souveränität im Menschen und in der Menschheit." *Aufwärts* 1 (1848).

Gutächtliche Aeusserungen über den Entwurf einer neuen Gewerbeordnung. Vienna, 1879.

Hahn, Sigmund. *Reichsrats-Almanach.* Vienna, 1867 and 1873.

Hainisch, Michael. *75 Jahre aus bewegter Zeit. Lebenserinnerungen eines österreichischen Staatsmannes.* Ed. by Friedrich Weissensteiner. Vienna, 1978.

Haker, Johann. *Cornelius Vetter, der Volksmann aus Trencsin.* Vienna, 1890.

Hansen, H. *Gefühlsantisemiten. Ein Wiener Zeitbild.* Zurich, 1898.

Harden, Maximilian. *Köpfe.* Berlin, 1911.

[Hartig, Franz, Graf v]. *Genesis der Revolution in Österreich im Jahre 1848.* Leipzig, 1850.

Häusle, Johann Michael. *Die Majorität im gegenwärtigen Wiener Gemeinderath.* Vienna, 1849.

Helfert, Joseph Alexander, Freiherr von. *Aufzeichnungen und Erinnerungen aus jungen Jahren. Im Wiener konstituierenden Reichstag Juli bis Oktober 1848.* Vienna, 1904.

————. *Die Wiener Journalistik im Jahre 1848.* Vienna, 1877.

Hertling, Georg von. *Kleine Schriften zur Zeitgeschichte und Politik.* Freiburg i. B., 1897.

Hollomay, Leopold. *Der Mechaniker Ernst Schneider und sein Antisemitismus.* Vienna, 1886.

Hron, Karl. *Wiens antisemitische Bewegung.* Vienna, 1890.

Jacques, Heinrich. *Denkschrift über die Stellung der Juden in Oesterreich.* Vienna, 1859.

Kaizl, Josef. "Die Reform des Gewerberechts in Österreich im Jahre 1883." *JNS* 8 (1884).

Kalchberg, Josef von. *Mein politisches Glaubensbekenntniss.* Leipzig, 1881.

Kannengieser, Alphonse. *Juden und Katholiken in Österreich-Ungarn.* Trier, 1896.

Kautsky, Karl. *Aus der Frühzeit des Marxismus.* Prague, 1935.

———. *Das Erfurter Programm in seinem grundsätzlichen Theil.* Stuttgart, 1892.

Kielmansegg, Erich. *Kaiserhaus, Staatsmänner, und Politiker.* Ed. by Walter Goldinger. Vienna, 1965.

Klonkavius, M. *Die Wucherfrage.* Amberg, 1878.

Klopp, Wiard von. *Leben und Wirken des Sozialpolitikers Karl Freiherr von Vogelsang.* Vienna, 1930.

———. "Eine sozialpolitische Gesellschaft vor dreissig Jahren in der 'Goldenen Ente.'" *DNR* 9 (1926).

Klopp, Wiard von, ed. *Die socialen Lehren des Freiherrn Karl v Vogelsang.* St. Pölten, 1894.

Koch, Matthias. *Österreichs innere Politik.* Stuttgart, 1847.

Kordačs, Franz. "Franz Kordačs Briefe ins Germanikum." Ed. by Augustin K. Huber. *AKBMS* 1 (1967).

Kralik, Richard. *Karl Lueger und der christliche Sozialismus.* 2 vols. Vienna, 1923.

Kudlich, Hans. *Rückblicke und Erinnerungen.* 3 vols. Vienna and Leipzig, 1873.

Kunschak, Leopold. "Aus dem Werden der christlichen Arbeiterbewegung Österreichs." *VW* 14 (1923).

Kuppe, Rudolf. *Karl Lueger und seine Zeit.* Vienna, 1933.

———. *Pfarrer Eichhorn zur Arbeiterfrage.* Vienna, 1925.

Leb, Josef. *P. Heinrich Abel.* Innsbruck, 1926.

Lehmann's Allgemeiner Wohnungs-Anzeiger. Vienna, 1888–96.

Lehmkuhl, A. "Deutung oder Missdeutung der kirchlichen Vorschriften über Zins und Wucher." *SML* 28 (1885).

———. "Socialistische Aufstände und 'die treuen Söhne der katholischen Kirche.'" *SML* 30 (1886).

———. "Zins und Wucher vor dem Richterstuhle der Kirche und der Vernunft." *SML* 16 (1879).

———. "Zur Arbeiterfrage." *SML* 25 (1883).

———. "Zur Verständigung in der sozialen Frage." *SML* 25 (1883).

Leisching, Eduard. *Ein Leben für Kunst und Volksbildung, 1858–1938.* Ed. by Robert Kann and Peter Leisching. Vienna, 1978.

Lent, Carl. "Die deutsche und die österreichische Burschenschaft." *Burschenschaftliche Blätter* 5 (1890/91).

Liechtenstein, Alois. *Über Interessenvertretung im Staate mit besonderer Beziehung auf Österreich.* Vienna and Pest, 1977.

Martini, J. *Zur Congruafrage des katholischen Seelsorge Clerus in Österreich.* 2d ed. Graz, 1883.

Mayer, Sigmund. *Ein jüdischer Kaufmann, 1831 bis 1911.* Leipzig, 1911.

———. *Die Wiener Juden.* Vienna and Berlin, 1918.

Melcher, Richard. *Die Ursache des Niederganges der Kleingewerbe.* Vienna, 1889.

Menger, Carl. *Der Übergang zur Goldwährung.* Vienna, 1892.

Metschl, Karl. *Wiener Lehrlings-Elend.* Vienna, 1907.

Meyer, Rudolf H. *Hundert Jahre conservativer Politik und Literatur.* Vienna, 1895.

Mirbach-Sorquitten, Freiherr von. *Zur Währungs- und Wucherfrage.* Berlin, 1880.

Mises, Ludwig von. *Notes and Recollections.* South Holland, Ill., 1978.

Molisch, Paul, ed. *Briefe zur deutschen Politik in Österreich von 1848 bis 1918.* Vienna and Leipzig, 1934.

Müller, Franz. *Die Wahlkörper des Wiener Gemeinderathes.* Vienna, 1849.

Müller, Gustav. *Die Erhabenheit und Bedeutung des katholischen Priesterthums.* Vienna, 1890.

Naske, Alois. *Die gewerbepolitische Bewegung in Österreich und ihre Schlagworte.* Brünn, 1896.

Neupauer, Josef von. *Die Schäden und Gefahren der Valutaregulierung.* Vienna, 1892.

Neurath, Wilhelm. *Volkswirtschaftliche und Socialphilosophische Essays.* Vienna, 1880.

Pater Abel S. J. und die Wiener Männerfahrten nach Maria-Zell. Vienna, 1907.

Perthaler, Hans v. *Auserlesene Schriften.* Ed. by Ambros Mayr. 2 vols. Vienna, 1883.

Peukert, Josef. *Erinnerungen eines Proletariers aus der revolutionären Arbeiterbewegung.* Berlin, 1913.

Pichl, Eduard. *Georg Schönerer.* 6 vols. Oldenburg i. O., 1938.

Pieper, August. *Volksbildungsbestrebungen. Ihre Noth und ihr Mittel.* München-Gladbach, 1899.

Pipitz, F. E. *Verfall und Verjüngung. Studien über Oesterreich in den Jahren 1838–1848.* Zurich, 1848.

Piwonka, Wilhelm von. *Die Judenfrage und ihre Lösung.* Vienna, 1894.

———. *Wozu? Eine politische Studie.* Vienna, 1896.

Plener, Ernst von. *Erinnerungen.* 3 vols. Stuttgart and Leipzig, 1911–21.

Pollak, Heinrich. *Dreissig Jahre aus dem Leben eines Journalisten. Erinnerungen und Aufzeichnungen.* 3 vols. Vienna, 1894–98.

Popp, Adelheid. *Autobiography of a Working Woman.* Trans. by E. S. Harvey. Chicago, 1913.

Protokolle des VII. allgemeinen österreichischen Lehrertages. Vienna, 1879.

Der Prozess Msgr. Stojalowski in Krakau, 20–29 Juni 1893. Vienna, 1893.

Psenner, Ludwig. *Die neueste Gefahr für den österreichischen Mittelstand.* Vienna, 1895.

Renner, Karl. *An der Wende zweier Zeiten. Lebenserinnerungen von Karl Renner.* Vol. 1. 2d ed. Vienna, 1946.

————. *Österreich von der ersten zur zweiten Republik.* Vienna, 1953.

Reschauer, Heinrich. *Geschichte des Kampfes der Handwerkerzünfte und der Kaufmannsgremien mit der österreichischen Bureaukratie.* Vienna, 1882.

————. *Das Wort des Kaisers und die Bedürfnisse des Gewerbestandes.* Vienna, 1873.

Rieder, Franz. "Der katholische Klerus in Österreich und die Constitution." *TPQS* 1 (1848).

Rosegger, Peter. "Ein Reichsdeutscher über das katholische Leben in Österreich." *Heimgarten* 25 (1900).

Sänger und Prophet. Gedenkblätter zum 70. Geburtstage des Dichters Franz Eichert. Innsbruck, 1927.

Schaeffle, Albert. *Aus meinem Leben.* 2 vols. Berlin, 1905.

Scheicher, Joseph. *Arme Brüder.* Stuttgart, 1913.

————. *Der Clerus und die soziale Frage.* Innsbruck, 1884; 2d ed. St. Pölten, 1897.

————. *Der österreichische Clerustag.* Vienna, 1903.

————. *Erlebnisse und Erinnerungen.* 6 vols. Vienna, 1906–12.

————. *Sebastian Brunner. Ein Lebensbild.* Würzburg, 1888.

Schindler, Franz M. *Denkschrift über die sociale Frage, gerichtet an den hochwürdigsten Episcopat Westösterreichs.* Warnsdorf, 1888.

————. *Ist der reine Lohnvertrag an sich mit den Grundsätzen der christlichen Gerechtigkeit vereinbar?* Vienna, 1893.

————. *Ist der Staat nach dem Naturrecht und der christlichen Moral berechtigt, seine Unterthanen zu zwingen, sich zu versichern?* Warnsdorf, 1885.

————. "Das Kapitalzinsproblem." *Die Kultur* 4 (1902).

————. "Neun Jahre Entenabende." *VW* 14 (1923).

————. "Österreich." *Jahrbuch der Zeit- und Kulturgeschichte* 1 (1907).

————. *L'organisation corporative des professions libérales selon des Etats.* Fribourg, 1890.

————. "Organisation der Volksstände." *Austria Nova* 2 (1916).

————. *Die soziale Frage der Gegenwart.* Vienna, 1905.

Schindler, Franz M., ed. *Soziale Vorträge, gehalten bei dem Wiener socialen Vortrags-Curse, 1894.* Vienna, 1895.

Schirnding, Ferdinand Leopold, Graf v. *Österreich im Jahre 1840.* 4 vols. Leipzig, 1840–44.

Schmitz, Hans. "Aus P. Abels Erinnerungen an die christlichsoziale Frühzeit." *VW* 14 (1923).

Schneider, Ernst. *Beiträge zum Gewerbetag.* Vienna, 1881.

Schnitzler, Arthur. *Jugend in Wien.* Vienna, 1968.

Schöffel, Joseph. *Erinnerungen aus meinem Leben.* Vienna, 1905.

Schöpfer, Aemilian. "Katholizismus und Politik." In *Der Katholizismus in Österreich,* ed. by Alois Hudal. Innsbruck, Vienna, and Munich, 1931.

Schreiber, J. M. *Die 1. allgemeine österreichische Lehrerversammlung zu Wien.* Vienna, 1867.

Schuselka, Franz. *Deutsche Fahrten.* Vol. 2. *Während der Revolution.* Vienna, 1849.

Sieghart, Rudolf. *Die letzten Jahrzehnte einer Grossmacht.* Berlin, 1932.

Singer, Isidor. *Berlin, Wien, und der Antisemitismus.* Vienna, 1882.

Skedl, Arthur, ed. *Der politische Nachlass des Grafen Eduard Taaffe.* Vienna, 1922.

Sommeregger, Franz. "Die Wege und Ziele der österreichischen Agrarpolitik seit der Grundentlastung." In *Die soziale Woche* (qv).

Die soziale Woche. Bericht über den vom "Katholischen Volksbund für Österreich" unter dem Namen "Soziale Woche" veranstalteten sozialwissenschaftlichen Kursus vom 5. bis 10. September 1911. Vienna, 1911.

Spitzmüller, Alexander. *. . . und hat auch Ursach es zu Lieben.* Vienna, 1955.

Stauracz, Franz. *Dr. Karl Lueger. Zehn Jahre Bürgermeister.* Vienna, 1907.

———. *Die Entwicklung der christlich-socialen Partei und deren Hausfeinde.* Vienna, 1901.

———. *Der Schlachtengewinner Dittes und sein Generalstab, oder Ein Jammerbild österreichischer Schulzustände.* Vienna, 1889.

Stenographisches Protokoll der Versammlung vom 7. Jänner 1897 des Central Vereins der Wiener Lehrerschaft. Vienna, 1897.

Stenographische Protokolle über die Verhandlungen des VIII. allgemeinen österreichischen Lehrertages. Reichenberg, 1882.

Suess, Eduard. *Erinnerungen.* Leipzig, 1916.

Swoboda, August. *Statuten des Privat-Darlehen-Vereins.* Vienna, 1848.

Toniolo, Giuseppe. *Lettere.* Vol. 1. *1871–1895,* ed. by Guido Anichini and Nello Vian. Vatican City, 1952.

Uhl, Friedrich. *Aus meinem Leben.* Stuttgart and Berlin, 1908.

Vasily, Paul. *La Société de Vienne.* Paris, 1885.

Der Verein der Verfassungsfreunde im VII. Bezirke von 1873–1888. Eine Vereins-Chronik. Vienna, 1888.

Vergani, Ernst. *Die Judenfrage in Oesterreich.* Leipzig, 1892.

Verhandlungen der am 23., 24., 25, September 1897 in Köln abgehaltenen Generalversammlung des Vereins für Sozialpolitik. Leipzig, 1898.

Verhandlungen des Allgemeinen österreichischen Katholikentages. Vienna, 1877.

Verhandlungen des sechsten österreichischen Sozialdemokratischen Parteitages. Vienna, 1897.

Verhandlungen des II. Allgemeinen österreichischen Katholikentages. Vienna, 1889.

Vetter, Cornelius. *Nur für Mechaniker Schneider. Eine Erwiderung.* Vienna, 1886.

Violand, Ernst. *Die sociale Geschichte der Revolution in Österreich.* Leipzig, 1850.

Vogelsang, Karl, Freiherr von. *Gesammelte Aufsätze.* Augsburg, 1886.

———. *Die Grundbelastung und Entlastung.* Vienna, 1879.

———. *Das Ministerium Lasser, genannt "Auersperg." Eine zisleithanische Zeitstudie.* Amberg, 1877.

———. *Die Notwendigkeit einer neuen Grundentlastung.* Vienna, 1880.

———. *Ein offenes Wort an Herrn Justizminister Dr. Glaser.* Amberg, 1877.

———. *Zins und Wucher.* Vienna, 1884.

Vogelsang, Marie Freiin von. "Aus dem Leben des Sozialpolitikers Frh. Karl von Vogelsang." *DNR* 7 (1924).

Wagner, Josef. "Joseph Scheicher." *Hochland* 24 (1926–27).

Weiss, Albert M. *Lebensweg und Lebenswerk*. Freiburg i. B., 1925.

Wermuth, Adolf. *Ein Beamtenleben*. Berlin, 1922.

Die Wiener Oktober-Revolution. Aus dem Tagebuch des Dr. Schütte. Prague, 1848.

W-m-r, J. *Der Judenhass*. Vienna, 1873.

Zenker, Ernst Victor. *Kirche und Staat*. Leipzig and Vienna, 1909.

Zweig, Stefan. *Die Welt von Gestern*. Frankfurt a.m., 1952.

Secondary Sources

Adler, Emanuel. *Über die Lage des Handwerks in Österreich*. Freiburg i. B., 1898.

Adler, Georg. *Die Sozialreform und der Kaufmannsstand*. Munich, 1891.

Adler-Rudel, S. "Moritz Baron Hirsch." *LBY* 8 (1963).

Alexander, Edgar. "Church and Society in Germany." In *Church and Society: Catholic Social and Political Thought and Movements, 1789–1950*, ed. by J. N. Moody. New York, 1953.

Allmayer-Beck, Johann Christoph. *Vogelsang*. Vienna, 1952.

Almond, Gabriel, and Powell, G. B. *Comparative Politics: A Developmental Approach*. Boston, 1966.

Andreski, Stanislav. *The Uses of Comparative Sociology*. Berkeley, 1965.

Arkel, Dirk van. *Antisemitism in Austria*. Leiden, 1966.

Ascher, Arnold. "Das Schirmmachergewerbe in Wien." In *Untersuchungen über die Lage des Handwerks* (qv).

Atlas, Moshe. "Grosse jüdische Ärzte Wiens im neunzehnten und zwanzigsten Jahrhundert." In Josef Fraenkel, ed., *The Jews of Austria* (qv).

Bachem, Karl. *Vorgeschichte, Geschichte, und Politik der deutschen Zentrumspartei*. 9 vols. Cologne, 1927–32.

Baltzarek, Franz; Hoffmann, Alfred; and Stekl, Hannes. *Wirtschaft und Gesellschaft der Wiener Stadterweiterung*. Wiesbaden, 1975.

Battista, Ludwig. "Die pädagogische Entwicklung des Pflichtschulwesens und der Lehrerbildung in 1848–1948." *100 Jahre Unterrichts Ministerium, 1848–1948. Festschrift des Bundesministeriums für Unterricht*. Vienna, 1948.

Bauer, Clemens. "Wandlungen der sozialpolitischen Ideenwelt im deutschen Katholizismus des 19. Jahrhunderts." In *Die soziale Frage und der Katholizismus* (qv).

Bauer, Stephan. "Die Heimarbeit und ihre geplante Regelung in Österreich." *Das Leben* 1 (1897).

Beidtel, Ignaz. *Geschichte der österreichischen Staatsverwaltung, 1740–1848*. 2 vols. Innsbruck, 1896–98.

Benedikt, Heinrich, ed. *Geschichte der Republik Österreich*. Munich, 1954.

———. "Der Josephinismus vor Joseph II." In *Österreich und Europa* (qv).

———. *Die wirtschaftliche Entwicklung in der Franz-Joseph-Zeit*. Vienna and Munich, 1958.

Berdahl, Robert. "Prussian Aristocracy and Conservative Ideology: A Methodological Examination." *Social Science Information* 15 (1976).

Berelson, Bernard R.; Lazarsfeld, Paul F.; and McPhee, William N. *Voting: A Study of Opinion Formation in a Presidential Campaign.* Chicago, 1954.

Berg, Leopold. *Wien und die Vereinigung der Vororte.* Vienna, 1876.

Bernstein, Eduard. *Die Berliner Arbeiterbewegung von 1890 bis 1905.* Berlin, 1924.

Bibl, Victor. *Die niederösterreichischen Stände im Vormärz.* Vienna, 1911.

Bilinski, Leon. *Wspomnienia i dokumenty.* 2 vols. Warsaw, 1924–25.

Blasius, Dirk. "Bürgerliches Recht und bürgerliche Identität." In *Vom Staat des Ancien Régime zum modernen Parteienstaat. Festschrift für Theodor Schieder,* ed. by Helmut Berding et al. Munich and Vienna, 1978.

Bobek, Hans, and Lichtenberger, Elisabeth. *Wien. Bauliche Gestalt und Entwicklung seit der Mitte des 19. Jahrhunderts.* Graz, 1966.

Böhme, Helmut. *Deutschlands Weg zur Grossmacht. Studien zum Verhältnis von Wirtschaft und Staat während der Reichsgründungszeit, 1848–1881.* 2d ed. Cologne, 1972.

Bombiero-Kremanać, Julius. "Die Entwicklung der staatlichen Kongrua-gesetzgebung in Österreich." *ZSSR* 12 (1922).

Bosl, Karl, ed. *Der moderne Parlamentarismus und seine Grundlagen in der ständischen Repräsentation.* Berlin, 1977.

Botz, Gerhard. *Wohnungspolitik und Judendeportation in Wien, 1938 bis 1945.* Vienna, 1975.

Bowen, Ralph Henry. *German Theories of the Corporative State.* New York, 1947.

Boyer, John W. "Catholic Priests in Lower Austria: Anti-Liberalism, Occupational Anxiety, and Radical Political Action in Late Nineteenth Century Vienna." *PAPS* 118 (1974).

———. "Freud, Marriage, and Late Viennese Liberalism: A Commentary from 1905." *JMH* 50 (1978).

———. "Veränderungen im politischen Lebens Wiens. Gross Wien, der Radikalismus der Beamten und die Wahlen von 1891." *JVGSW,* forthcoming.

Brandl, Manfred. "Theologie im österreichischen Vormärz." In *Kirchen und Liberalismus im 19. Jahrhundert,* ed. by Martin Schmidt and Georg Schwaiger. Göttingen, 1976.

Brandt, Harm-Hinrich. *Der österreichische Neoabsolutismus. Staatsfinanzen und Politik, 1848–1860.* 2 vols. Göttingen, 1978.

Bratassevic, Eduard. "Die öffentliche Armenpflege in Österreich während der letzten zwanzig Jahre." *SM* 21 (1895).

Brauer, Theodor. "Der deutsche Katholizismus und die soziale Entwicklung des kapitalistischen Zeitalters." *ARWP* 24 (1930–31).

Braunthal, Julius. *Victor und Friedrich Adler.* Vienna, 1965.

Briefs, Goetz. "Die wirtschafts- und sozialpolitischen Ideen des Katholizismus." In *Die Wirtschaftswissenschaft nach dem Kriege. Festgabe für Lujo Brentano.* 2 vols. Berlin, 1925.

Brockhausen, Carl. *Die österreichische Gemeindeordnung.* Vienna, 1905.

Brooks, Robert C. "City Government by Taxpayers: The Three-Class Election System in Prussian Cities." *Municipal Affairs* 3 (1899).

Bruckmüller, Ernst. *Landwirtschaftliche Organisationen und gesellschaftliche Modernisierung. Vereine, Genossenschaften, und politische Mobilisierung der Landwirtschaft Österreichs vom Vormärz bis 1914*. Salzburg, 1977.

Brügel, Ludwig. *Geschichte der österreichischen Sozialdemokratie*. 5 vols. Vienna, 1922–25.

————. *Soziale Gesetzgebung in Österreich von 1848 bis 1918*. Vienna and Leipzig, 1919.

Brunner, Otto. "Staat und Gesellschaft im vormärzlichen Österreich, 1740–1848." In *Staat und Gesellschaft im deutschen Vormärz, 1815–1848*, ed. by Werner Conze. Stuttgart, 1962.

Brusatti, Alois. *Österreichische Wirtschaftspolitik vom Josephinismus zum Ständestaat*. Vienna, 1965.

————. "Die Staatsgüterveräusserungen in der Zeit von 1780–1848." *MÖSA* 11 (1958).

Byrnes, Robert. *Antisemitism in Modern France*. Vol. 1. New Brunswick, 1950.

Cappelli, Giampiero. *Romolo Murri. Contributo per una biografia*. Rome, 1965.

Cecchini, Francesco. *Murri e il murrismo*. Urbino, 1973.

Charmatz, Richard. *Adolf Fischhof. Das Lebensbild eines österreichischen Politikers*. Stuttgart and Berlin, 1910.

————. *Deutsch-österreichische Politik*. Leipzig, 1907.

————. "Franz Schuselka." *ÖRD* 28 (1911).

————. *Österreichs innere Geschichte*. 2 vols. Leipzig, 1909.

Cheml, Joseph. "Actenstücke zur Geschichte des österreichischen römisch-katholischen Kirchenwesens unter Kaiser Leopold II." *Archiv für Kunde österreichischer Geschichts-Quellen* 4 (1850).

Cohen, Gary B. "Jews in German Society: Prague, 1860–1914." *CEH* 10 (1977).

Conze, Werner, ed. *Sozialgeschichte der Familie in der Neuzeit Europas*. Stuttgart, 1976.

Cronbach, Else. "Zur Frage des landwirtschaftlichen Gross- und Kleinbetriebes." *ZVSV* 17 (1908).

Croon, Helmuth. *Die gesellschaftlichen Auswirkungen des Gemeindewahlrechts in den Gemeinden und Kreisen des Rheinlandes und Westfalens im 19. Jahrhundert*. Cologne, 1960.

Czedik, Alois von. *Zur Geschichte der k. k. österreichischen Ministerien, 1861–1916*. 4 vols. Teschen, Vienna, and Leipzig, 1917–20.

Czeike, Felix. *Liberale, Christlichsoziale, und Sozialdemokratische Kommunalpolitik (1861–1934)*. Vienna, 1962.

————. *Wien und seine Bürgermeister. Sieben Jahrhunderte Wiener Stadtgeschichte*. Vienna and Munich, 1974.

Czeike, Felix, and Lugsch, Walter. *Studien zur Sozialgeschichte von Ottakring und Hernals*. Vienna, 1955.

Dahl, Robert. *Who Governs? Democracy and Power in an American City*. New Haven and London, 1961.

Dahrendorf, Ralf. *Class and Class Conflict in Industrial Society*. Stanford, 1959.

————. *Society and Democracy in Germany*. New York, 1967.

Dansette, Adrien. *Religious History of Modern France*. 2 vols. New York, 1961.

Daum, Adolf. *Zur Reform der Wiener Gemeindeordnung.* Vienna, 1890.

Dempf, Alois. *Albert Ehrhard.* Kolmar, 1946.

——. "Die letzte Vollanthropologie. Dem Andenken Anton Günthers (1863)." *Wissenschaft und Weltbild* 15 (1962).

Deutsch, Julius. *Geschichte der österreichischen Gewerkschaftsbewegung.* Vienna, 1908.

Diamant, Alfred. *Austrian Catholics and the First Republic.* Princeton, 1960.

Eberstadt, Rudolf. *Neue Studien über Städtebau und Wohnungswesen.* Jena, 1912.

——. "Wiener Wohnverhältnisse." In idem, *Neue Studien* (qv).

Ebert, Kurt. *Die Anfänge der modernen Sozialpolitik in Österreich.* Vienna, 1975.

Eder, Karl. *Der Liberalismus in Altösterreich.* Vienna, 1955.

Eissert, Josef. "Die persönlichen Bezüge im Staatshaushalte Österreichs." *BZ* 21 (1890).

Endean, J. Russell. *The Public Education of Austria.* London, 1888.

Engel-Janosi, Friedrich. "Einleitung." In *Die Protokolle des österreichischen Ministerrates 1848–67.* VI. Abteilung. *Das Ministerium Belcredi.* Vol. 2. Vienna, 1973.

——. *Österreich und der Vatikan.* 2 vols. Graz, Vienna, and Cologne, 1958–60.

——. "Die Theorie vom Staat im deutschen Österreich 1815–48." *ZÖR* 2 (1921).

——. "Der Wiener juridisch-politische Leseverein." *MVGSW* 4 (1923).

Die Erbauung des Wiener städtischen Gaswerks. Vienna, 1901.

Evert, Geog. *Die Staats- und Gemeindewahlen im preussischen Staate.* *Zeitschrift des Königlich preussischen statistischen Bureaus,* 17th Ergänzungsheft. Berlin, 1895.

Feibelmann, Kurt. *Rudolf Meyer.* Jena, 1931.

Feldbauer, Peter. *Stadtwachstum und Wohnungsnot. Determinanten unzureichender Wohnungsversorgung in Wien, 1848 bis 1914.* Vienna, 1977.

——. "Die Wohnungsverhältnisse der Unterschichten im Franzisko-Josephinischen Wien. Thesen und Probleme." *JVGSW* 34 (1978).

Fellner, Fritz. "Das Februarpatent von 1861. Entstehung und Bedeutung." *MIÖG* 63 (1955).

——. "Kaiser Franz Joseph und das Parlament. Materialien zur Geschichte der Innenpolitik Österreichs in den Jahren 1867–1873." *MÖSA* 9 (1956).

——. "Kaiser Franz Josephs Haltung in der Krise des Bürgerministeriums. Nach Aufzeichnungen und Briefen Ignaz von Pleners." *MÖSA* 6 (1953).

Fest, Joachim. *Hitler.* Trans. by Richard and Clara Winston. New York, 1975.

Festschrift Franz Loidl zum 65. Geburtstag. Ed. by Victor Flieder. 3 vols. Vienna, 1970.

Fischer, Alfred. *Das österreichische Doktorat der Rechtswissenschaften und die Rechtsanwaltschaft.* Innsbruck and Munich, 1974.

Fournier, August. *Gerhard van Swieten als Censor.* Vienna, 1876.

Fraenkel, Josef, ed. *The Jews of Austria.* London, 1967.

Frank, Ferdinand. *Die österreichische Volksschule, 1848–1898.* Vienna, 1898.

Franke, F. "Der Säcular-Clerus Österreichs im Jahre 1875." *SM* 3 (1887).

Franz, Georg. *Liberalismus. Die deutschliberale Bewegung in der Habsburgischen Monarchie.* Munich, 1955.

Franz-Ferron, J. *Neu-Wien. Rückblick auf die Geschichte der am 21. December 1891 zur Commune Wien einverleibten Vororte-Gemeinden.* Korneuburg, 1892.

Frey, Friedrich, and Maresch, Rudolf. *Sammlung von Gutachten und Entscheidungen über den Umfang der Gewerberechte.* 2 vols. Vienna, 1894, 1897.

Friedjung, Heinrich. *Österreich von 1848 bis 1860.* 2 vols. Stuttgart and Berlin, 1912.

Fritsch, Benno. "Studien zum österreichischen Kongruagesetz vom 19. September 1898." *Österreichisches Verwaltungsarchiv* 1 (1904).

Fuchs, Albert. *Geistige Strömungen in Österreich.* Vienna, 1949.

Fuhrmann, Robert. *Die Beamten der Gemeinden mit Ausschluss der autonomen Städte.* Vienna, 1898.

Fürth, Emil von. *Die Einkommersteuer in Österreich und ihre Reform.* Leipzig, 1892.

Gall, Lothar, ed. *Liberalismus.* Cologne, 1976.

———. "Liberalismus und 'bürgerliche Gesellschaft.' Zu Charakter und Entwicklung der liberalen Bewegung in Deutschland." *HZ* 220 (1975).

Garver, Bruce M. *The Young Czech Party, 1874–1901, and the Emergence of a Multi-Party System.* New Haven and London, 1978.

Das Gemeindegesetz und das Heimatgesetz. Vienna, 1871.

Gerstel, Gustav. *Der Beitrieb der Wiener Stadtbahn.* Vienna, 1898.

Gierach, E., ed. *Sudetendeutsche Lebensbilder.* Reichenberg, 1930.

Gillis, John R. *The Prussian Bureaucracy in Crisis, 1840–1860.* Stanford, 1971.

Glettler, Monika. *Die Wiener Tschechen um 1900. Strukturanalyse einer nationalen Minderheit in der Grossstadt.* Munich and Vienna, 1972.

Gneist, Rudolf. "The Government of Berlin." *CR* 46 (1884).

Gold, Hugo. *Geschichte der Juden in Wien.* Tel Aviv, 1966.

Goldhammer, Leo. *Die Juden Wiens.* Vienna and Leipzig, 1927.

Goldinger, Walter. "Das Verhältnis von Staat und Kirche in Österreich nach Aufhebung des Konkordats von 1855." *Religion, Wissenschaft, Kultur* 8 (1957).

Gönner, Rudolf. *Die österreichische Lehrerbildung von der Normalschule bis zur Pädagogischen Akadamie.* Vienna, 1967.

Gratz, Alois. "Die österreichische Finanzpolitik von 1848 bis 1948." In Hans Mayer, ed., *Hundert Jahre österreichische Wirtschaftsentwicklung, 1848–1948.* Vienna, 1949.

Greenberg, Louis. *The Jews in Russia.* Ed. by Mark Wischnitzer. 2 vols. New Haven, 1944–51.

Greive, Hermann. "Die gesellschaftliche Bedeutung der christlich-jüdischen Differenz. Zur Situation im deutschen Katholizismus." In Werner E. Mosse, ed., *Juden im Wilhelminischen Deutschland* (qv).

Grunberger, Richard. "Jews in Austrian Journalism." In Josef Fraenkel, ed., *The Jews of Austria* (qv).

Grunwald, Kurt. "A Note on the Baron Hirsch Stiftung in Vienna." *LBY* 17 (1972).

Grunwald, Max. *Vienna*. Philadelphia, 1936.

Gugel, Michael. *Industrieller Aufstieg und bürgerliche Herrschaft*. Cologne, 1975.

Gutkas, Karl. *Geschichte des Landes Niederösterreich*. 3 vols. St. Pölten, 1955–59.

Hahn, Adalbert. *Die Berliner Revue. Ein Beitrag zur Geschichte der konservativen Partei zwischen 1855–1875*. Berlin, 1932.

Hamerow, Theodore S. *Restoration, Revolution, Reaction: Economics and Politics in Germany, 1815–1871*. Princeton, 1958.

Hanisch, Ernst. *Der kranke Mann an der Donau. Marx und Engels über Österreich*. Vienna, 1978.

Harrington-Müller, Diethild. *Der Fortschrittsklub im Abgeordnetenhaus des österreichischen Reichsrats, 1873–1910*. Vienna, Cologne, and Graz, 1972.

Häusler, Wolfgang. "Ernst von Violand (1818–1875). Der Lebensweg eines österreichischen Demokraten." *JIDG* 6 (1977).

———. "Hermann Jellinek (1823–1848). Ein Demokrat in der Wiener Revolution." *JIDG* 5 (1976).

———. "Hermann Jellinek im Vormärz. Seine Entwicklung zum revolutionären Demokraten." In *Beiträge zur neueren Geschichte Österreichs*, ed. Heinrich Fichtenau and Erich Zöllner. Vienna, 1974.

———. "Konfessionelle Probleme in der Wiener Revolution von 1848." In *Studia Judaica Austriaca*. Vol. 1. *Das Judentum im Revolutionsjahr 1848*. Vienna and Munich, 1974.

———. "'Orthodoxie' und 'Reform' im Wiener Judentum in der Epoche des Hochliberalismus." *Studia Judaica Austriaca* 6 (1978).

———. "Toleranz, Emanzipation, und Antisemitismus. Das österreichische Judentum des bürgerlichen Zeitalters (1782–1918)." In *Das österreichische Judentum*, ed. by Nikolaus Vielmetti. Vienna and Munich, 1974.

Havránek, J. "Diskussionsbeitrag." In *Die nationale Frage in der Österreichisch-Ungarischen Monarchie, 1900–1918*. Budapest, 1966.

Heffter, Heinrich. *Die deutsche Selbstverwaltung im 19. Jahrhundert*. Stuttgart, 1950.

Hegel, Eduard. "Die Situation der deutschen Priesterausbildung um Wende vom 18. zum 19. Jahrhundert." In *Kirche und Theologie im 19. Jahrhundert*, ed. by Georg Schwaiger. Göttingen, 1975.

Heindl, Waltraud. "Probleme der Edition." In *Die Protokolle des österreichischen Ministerrates 1848–1867*. III. Abteilung. *Das Ministerium Buol-Schauenstein*. Vol. 1. Vienna, 1975.

Heller, Victor. *Der Getreidehandel und seine Technik in Wien*. Tübingen, 1901.

Henning, Hansjoachim. *Das westdeutsche Bürgertum in der Epoche der Hochindustrialisierung, 1860–1914. Soziales Verhalten und Soziale Strukturen*. Wiesbaden, 1972.

Herkner, H. "Über Erhaltung und Verstärkung der Mittelclasse." *ZVSV* 2 (1893).

Herrdegen, J. "Das Pfaidlergewerbe in Wien." In *Untersuchungen über die Lage des Handwerks* (qv).

Herrfahrdt, Heinrich. *Das Problem der berufsständischen Vertretung von der französischen Revolution bis zur Gegenwart*. Stuttgart, 1921.

Hersche, Peter. "Erzbischof Migazzi und die Anfänge der jansenistischen Bewegung in Wien." *MÖSA* 24 (1971).

———. "Die österreichischen Jansenisten und die Unionsverhandlungen der Utrechter Kirche mit Rom." *ZKG* 82 (1971).

———. *Der Spätjansenismus in Österreich.* Vienna, 1977.

———. "War Maria Theresia eine Jansenistin?" *ÖGL* 15 (1971).

Herzfeld, Hans, ed. *Berlin und die Provinz Brandenburg im 19. und 20. Jahrhundert.* Berlin, 1968.

Hintze, Otto. "Die Entstehung der modernen Staatsministerien." In *Staat und Verfassung. Gesammelte Abhandlungen zur allgemeinen Verfassungsgeschichte,* ed. by Gerhard Oestreich. Göttingen, 1962.

———. "Der österreichische und der preussische Beamtenstaat im 17. und 18. Jahrhundert." In *Staat und Verfassung. Gesammelte Abhandlungen zur allgemeinen Verfassungsgeschichte,* ed. by Gerhard Oestreich. Göttingen, 1962.

Hirsch, P., and Lindemann, H. *Das Kommunale Wahlrecht.* Berlin, 1905.

Hoffmann, Alfred. "Bürokratie insbesondere in Österreich." In *Beiträge zur neueren Geschichte Österreichs,* ed. by Heinrich Fichtenau and Erich Zöllner. Vienna, Cologne, and Graz, 1974.

Hohorst, Gerd; Kocka, Jürgen; and Ritter, Gerhard A. *Sozialgeschichtliches Arbeitsbuch. Materialien zur Statistik des Kaiserreichs, 1870–1914.* Munich, 1975.

Holleis, Eva. *Die Sozialpolitische Partei.* Munich, 1978.

Hosp, Eduard. *Kirche im Sturmjahr. Erinnerungen an Johann Michael Häusle.* Vienna, 1953.

———. *Kirche Österreichs im Vormärz, 1814–1850.* Vienna and Munich, 1971.

———. *Zwischen Aufklärung und katholischer Reform. Jakob Frint, Bischof von St. Pölten.* Vienna and Munich, 1962.

Hubbard, William H. "Forschungen zur städtischen Haushaltsstruktur am Ende des 19. Jahrhunderts." In Werner Conze, ed., *Sozialgeschichte der Familie* (qv).

Huber, Augustin K. *Ambros Opitz, 1846–1907. Ein Bahnbrecher der katholischen Bewegung Altösterreichs.* Königstein, 1961.

Hussarek, Max von. "Die Krise und Lösung des Konkordates vom 18. August 1855." *AÖG* 112 (1932).

———. "Die Verhandlung des Konkordates vom 18. August 1855." *AÖG* 109 (1921).

Inama-Sternegg, Karl Theodor. *Die persönlichen Verhältnisse der Wiener Armen.* Vienna, 1891.

Jenks, William A. *Austria under the Iron Ring, 1879–1893.* Charlottesville, Va., 1965.

"The Jewish Background of Victor and Friedrich Adler." *LBY* 10 (1965).

Johnston, William M. *The Austrian Mind: An Intellectual and Social History, 1848–1938.* Berkeley and Los Angeles, 1972.

Jostock, Paul. *Der deutsche Katholizismus und die Überwindung des Kapitalismus.* Regensburg, 1932.

Die Juden in Österreich. Veröffentlichungen des Bureaus für Statistik der Juden, Heft 4. Berlin, 1908.

Judt, Tony. *Socialism in Provence.* Cambridge, 1978.

Juraschek, Franz von. "Der Besuch der österreichischen Universitäten in den Jahren 1861–1875." *SM* 2 (1876).

————. "Das Wachstum des Territoriums, der Bevölkerung, und des Verkehrs von Wien, 1857–1894." *SM* 22 (1896).

Kaizl, Josef. "Die Reform des Gewerberechts in Österreich vom Jahre 1883." *JNS* 42 (1884).

————. "Der Regierungsentwurf eines Gesetzes zur Abänderung und Ergänzung der Gewerbeordnung in Österreich." *JNS* 34 (1879).

Kann, Robert A. *The Multinational Empire.* 2 vols. New York, 1950.

————. *A Study in Austrian Intellectual History.* New York, 1960.

Kappelmann, H. "Die Verfassung und Verwaltungsorganisation der preussischen Städte nach der Städteordnung vom 30. Mai 1853." In *Verfassung und Verwaltungsorganisation der Städte. SVSP,* vol. 117. Leipzig, 1906.

Kienböck, Victor. "Die Gürtler und Bronzearbeiter in Wien." In *Untersuchungen über die Lage des Handwerks* (qv).

Klabouch, Jiři. *Die Gemeindeselbstverwaltung in Österreich, 1848–1918.* Vienna, 1968.

Klemperer, Klemens von. *Ignaz Seipel.* Princeton, 1972.

Klenner, Fritz. *Die österreichischen Gewerkschaften.* 2 vols. Vienna, 1951–53.

Klimburg, R. von. *Die Entwicklung des gewerblichen Unterrichtswesens in Österreich.* Tübingen and Leipzig, 1900.

Klingenstein, Grete. "Einige Überlegungen zum politischen System des aufgeklärten Absolutismus." In *Les Lumières en Hongrie, en Europe centrale, et en Europe orientale. Actes du Troisième Colloque de Matrafüred, 28 septembre–2 octobre 1975.* Budapest, 1978.

————. *Staatsverwaltung und kirchliche Autorität im 18. Jahrhundert.* Munich, 1970.

Klopp, Wiard von. "Vogelsangs Lehre über Zins und Wucher." *NO* 4 (1928).

Knauer, Oswald. *Das österreichische Parlament von 1848–1966.* Vienna, 1969.

Knoll, August. *Der soziale Gedanke im modernen Katholizismus.* Vienna, 1932.

Knoll, Reinhold. "Zur Früh- und Entwicklungsgeschichte der christlichsozialen Bewegung in Österreich bis 1907." *ÖGL* 16 (1972).

————. *Zur Tradition der Christlich-Sozialen Partei.* Vienna, 1973.

Kobatsch, Rudolf. "Das österreichische Gewerberecht und seine bevorstehende Reform." *JNS* 66 (1896).

————. "Wien und das übrige Niederösterreich." In *Untersuchungen über die Lage des Hausiergewerbes* (qv).

Kobler, Franz. "The Contribution of Austrian Jews to Jurisprudence." In Josef Fraenkel, ed., *The Jews of Austria* (qv).

Kocka, Jürgen. "Theorien in der Sozial- und Gesellschaftsgeschichte. Vorschläge zur historischen Schichtungsanalyse." *GG* 1 (1975).

————. *Unternehmensverwaltung und Angestelltenschaft am Beispiel Siemens.* Stuttgart, 1969.

Koestler, Hugo. "Die Wiener Stadtbahn." In *Geschichte der Eisenbahnen der oesterreichisch-ungarischen Monarchie.* 4 vols. Vienna, 1898–1919.

Köllmann, Wolfgang. *Bevölkerung in der industriellen Revolution. Studien zur Bevölkerungsgeschichte Deutschlands.* Göttingen, 1974.

Kolmer, Gustav. *Parlament und Verfassung in Österreich.* 8 vols. Vienna and Leipzig, 1902–14.

Koren, Stefan. "Die Industrialisierung Österreichs. Vom Protektionismus zur Integration." In *Österreichs Wirtschaftsstruktur,* ed. by Wilhelm Weber, vol. 1. Berlin, 1961.

Koselleck, Reinhart. *Preussen zwischen Reform und Revolution.* Stuttgart, 1967.

Kovács, Elizabeth. "Kirchliches Zeremoniell am Wiener Hof des 18. Jahrhunderts im Wandel von Mentalität und Gesellschaft." *MÖSA* 32 (1979).

———. *Ultramontanismus und Staatskirchentum im Theresianisch-Josephinischen Staat.* Vienna, 1975.

Krieger, Leonard. *The German Idea of Freedom.* Boston, 1957.

Kübl, Friedrich. *Geschichte der österreichischen Advokatur.* Graz, 1925.

Kühnert, Dr. "Die Einkommensbesteuerung in Österreich und in Preussen in den Jahren 1898 und 1899." *ZKSB* 40 (1900).

Lamp, Karl. *Das Problem der städtischen Selbstverwaltung nach österreichischem und preussischem Recht.* Leipzig, 1905.

Lange, Annemarie. *Das Wilhelminische Berlin.* Berlin, 1967.

Lasswell, Harold. *Power and Personality.* New York, 1948.

Lederer, Emil. "Die Bewegung der öffentlichen Beamten." *ASWSP* 31 (1919).

———. "Mittelstandsbewegung." *ASWSP* 31 (1910).

———. "Privatbeamtenbewegung." *ASWSP* 31 (1910).

———. "Ein Vorschlag zur Reform der Gebäudesteuer." *ZVSV* 18 (1909).

Leiter, Friedrich. "Die Männerkleider-Erzeugung in Wien." In *Untersuchungen über die Lage des Handwerks* (qv).

———. *Die Verteilung des Einkommens in Österreich.* Vienna, 1907.

Lemberger, Hedwig. *Die Wiener Wäscheindustrie.* Vienna, 1907.

Lentze, Hans. *Die Universitätsreform des Ministers Graf Leo Thun-Hohenstein.* Vienna, 1962.

Levy, Richard S. *The Downfall of the Anti-Semitic Political Parties in Imperial Germany.* New Haven, 1975.

Lewis, Gavin. *Kirche und Partei im politischen Katholizismus.* Salzburg, 1977.

Lexis, Wilhelm. "Handel." In *Handbuch der politischen Ökonomie,* ed. by Gustav Schönberg. 4th ed. 1898.

Lichtenberger, Elisabeth. *Wirtschaftsfunktion und Sozialstruktur der Wiener Ringstrasse.* Vienna, 1970.

Löwe, Johann Heinrich. *Johann Emanuel Veith. Eine Biographie.* Vienna, 1879.

Löwy, Wilhelm. *Das Unterrichtswesen in Wien.* Part 2. *Mittel- und Hochschulen.* Vienna, 1891.

Maass, Ferdinand. *Der Frühjosephinismus.* Vienna, 1969.

———. *Der Josephinismus. Quellen zu seiner Geschichte in Österreich.* 5 vols. Vienna, 1951–61.

Macartney, C. A. *The Habsburg Empire, 1790–1918.* London and New York, 1969.

März, Eduard. *Österreichische Industrie- und Bankpolitik in der Zeit Franz Josephs I.* Vienna, 1968.

Magraw, Roger. "The Conflict in the Villages." In *Conflicts in French Society:*

Anticlericalism, Education, and Morals in the Nineteenth Century, ed. by Theodore Zeldin. London, 1970.

Mann, Erwin. "Die philosophisch-theologische Schule Anton Günthers." In *Festschrift Franz Loidl* (qv).

Marquardt, Frederick D. "Sozialer Aufstieg, sozialer Abstieg, und die Entstehung der Berliner Arbeiterclasse, 1806–1848." *GG* 1 (1975).

Marx, Julius. *Die österreichische Zensur im Vormärz*. Vienna, 1959.

———. "Polizei und Studenten. Ein Beitrag zur Vorgeschichte des 13. März 1848 in Wien." *JVGSW* 19/20 (1963–64).

———. *Die wirtschaftlichen Ursachen der Revolution von 1848 in Österreich*. Vienna, 1965.

Mataja, Victor. "Die gewerblichen Genossenschaften in Österreich," *JNS* 66 (1896).

Matis, Herbert. *Österreichs Wirtschaft, 1848–1913*. Berlin, 1972.

Mayer, Hans, ed. *Hundert Jahre österreichische Wirtschaftsentwicklung 1848 bis 1948*. Vienna, 1949.

McGrath, William J. *Dionysian Art and Populist Politics in Austria*. New Haven and London, 1974.

Mentschl, Josef. "Rudolf von Arthaber, ein Textilgrosshändler und Verleger der Biedermeierzeit." *ÖGL* 13 (1969).

Meyer, Robert. "Die ersten Ergebnisse der Personaleinkommensteuer in Österreich." *ZVSV* 8 (1899).

Michels, Robert. *Political Parties: A Sociological Study of the Oligarchical Tendencies of Modern Democracy*. Trans. by Eden Paul and Cedar Paul. Glencoe, 1949.

Miersch, Klausjürgen. *Die Arbeiterpresse der Jahre 1869 bis 1889 als Kampfmittel der österreichischen Sozialdemokratie*. Vienna, 1969.

Miko, Norbert. "Zur Mission des Kardinals Schönborn, des Bischofs Bauer, und des Pater Albert Maria Weiss OP im Jahr 1895." *RHM* 5 (1961/62).

Mikoletzky, Lorenz. "Karl Freiherr von Krauss, 1789–1881." *ÖGL* 14 (1970).

Mitchell, Alan. "Bonapartism as a Model for Bismarckian Politics." *JMH* 49 (1977).

Mitterauer, Michael. "Auswirkungen von Urbanisierung und Frühindustrialisierung auf die Familienverfassung an Beispielen des österreichischen Raums." In Werner Conze, ed., *Sozialgeschichte der Familie* (qv).

Mitterauer, Michael, and Sieder, Reinhard. *Vom Patriarchat zur Partnerschaft. Zum Strukturwandel der Familie*. Munich, 1977.

Molisch, Paul. "Anton v Schmerling und der Liberalismus in Österreich." *AÖG* 116 (1943).

———. *Die deutschen Hochschulen in Oesterreich*. Munich, 1922.

———. *Geschichte der deutsch-nationalen Bewegung*. Jena, 1926.

———. "Die Stellung Wiens in der deutschösterreichischen Politik von 1848 bis 1918." *JVGSW* 3/4 (1942).

———. "Die Wiener Akademische Legion und ihr Anteil an den Verfassungskämpfen des Jahres 1848." *AÖG* 110 (1924).

Mommsen, Hans. *Arbeiterbewegung und Nationale Frage. Ausgewählte Aufsätze*. Göttingen, 1979.

————. *Die Sozialdemokratie und die Nationalitätenfrage im Habsburgischen Vielvölkerstaat. I. Das Ringen um die supranationale Integration der zisleithanischen Arbeiterbewegung (1867–1907).* Vienna, 1963.

Mommsen, Wolfgang J. "Der deutsche Liberalismus zwischen 'klassenloser Bürgergesellschaft' und 'Organisiertem Kapitalismus.' Zu einigen neueren Liberalismusinterpretationen." *GG* 4 (1978).

Mosse, Werner E., ed. *Juden im Wilhelminischen Deutschland, 1890–1914.* Tübingen, 1976.

————. "Die Juden in Wirtschaft und Gesellschaft." In Werner E. Mosse, ed., *Juden im Wilhelminischen Deutschland* (qv).

Most, Otto, ed. *Die deutsche Stadt und ihre Verwaltung.* 3 vols. Berlin, 1912.

Mourret, Fernand. *L'église contemporaine.* Vol. 9 Paris, 1925.

Müller, Franz. "Zur Beurteilung des Kapitalismus in der katholischen Publizistik des 19. Jahrhunderts." In *Der deutsche Katholizismus im Zeitalter des Kapitalismus.* Augsburg, 1932.

Müller, Josef. *Der pastoraldidaktische Ansatz in Franz Stephan Rautenstrauchs "Entwurf zur Einrichtung der Theologischen Studien."* Vienna, 1969.

————. "Zu den theologiegeschichtlichen Grundlagen der Studienreform Rautenstrauchs." *TQ* 146 (1966).

Munk, Leo. *Die Steuerbelastung der Reichshauptstädte Wien und Berlin in vergleichender Darstellung.* Vienna, 1889.

Myrbach, Franz von. "Die Reform der direkten Steuer in Österreich." *JGVV* 22 (1898).

Nemec, Ludwik. "The Czech Jednota, the Avant-Garde of Modern Clerical Progressivism and Unionism." *PAPS* 112 (1968).

Niethammer, Lutz, and Brüggemeier, Franz. "Wie wohnten Arbeiter im Kaiserreich?" In *Archiv für Sozialgeschichte* 16 (1976).

Nipperdey, Thomas. *Gesellschaft, Kultur, Theorie.* Göttingen, 1976.

————. "Die Organisation der bürgerlichen Parteien in Deutschland vor 1918." In idem, *Gesellschaft, Kultur, Theorie* (qv).

————. "Verein als soziale Struktur in Deutschland im späten 18. und frühen 19. Jahrhundert. Eine Fallstudie zur Modernisierung." In idem, *Gesellschaft, Kultur, Theorie* (qv).

Noonan, John T. *The Scholastic Analysis of Usury.* Cambridge, 1957.

O'Brien, Charles C. "Jansenists and Josephinism: 'Nouvelles ecclésiastiques' and Reform of the Church in Late Eighteenth Century Austria." *MÖSA* 32 (1979).

Oestreich, Gerhard. "Strukturprobleme des europäischen Absolutismus." *VSWG* 55 (1968).

Oppenheimer, Freiherr von. *Die Wiener Gemeindeverwaltung und der Fall des liberalen Regimes in Staat und Kommune.* Vienna, 1905.

Österreich und Europa. Festgabe für Hugo Hantsch zum 70. Geburtstag. Graz, 1965.

Österreichisches Staatswörterbuch. 4 vols. Vienna, 1905–9.

Otruba, Gustav. "Katholischer Klerus und 'Kirche' im Spiegel der Flugschriftenliteratur des Revolutionsjahres 1848." In *Festschrift Franz Loidl* (qv).

Otruba, Gustav, and Rutschka, L. S. "Die Herkunft der Wiener Bevölkerung in den letzten hundert Jahren." *JVGSW* 23 (1957/58).

Papanek, Ernst. *The Austrian School Reform.* New York, 1962.

Philippovich, Eugen von. "Organisation der Berufsinteressen." *ZVSV* 8 (1899).

———. "Referat." *Verhandlungen des Vereins für Sozialpolitik.* Leipzig, 1898.

———. "Wiener Wohnungsverhältnisse." *ASGSS* 7 (1894).

Pizzala, Josef. "Die Bauthätigkeit in und um Wien in den Jahren 1843–1881." *SM* 8 (1882).

———. "Der Consum Wiens in den Jahren 1871–1881." *SM* 7 (1881).

———. "Österreich-Ungarns Aussenhandel im Jahre 1891." *SM* 18 (1892).

———. "Der Verzehrungssteuer-Ertrag Wiens in den Jahren 1871–1880." *SM* 8 (1882).

Pollitzer, Johann. *Die Lage der Lehrlinge im Kleingewerbe in Wien.* Tübingen, 1900.

Popper, E. "Der Abänderungs-Entwurf zur österreichischen Gewerbeordnung." *JNS* 39 (1882).

Posch, Andreas. "Die deutschkatholische Gemeinde in Wien." in *Festschrift zur Feier des zweihundertjährigen Bestandes des Haus-, Hof-, und Staatsarchivs,* ed. by Leo Santifaller. 2 vols. Vienna, 1951.

Poulat, Emile. *Catholicisme, démocratie, et socialisme.* Paris, 1977.

Powell, G. Bingham. *Social Fragmentation and Political Hostility: An Austrian Case Study.* Stanford, 1970.

Préclin, Edmond. *Les Jansénistes du XVIIIᵉ siècle et la Constitution civile du clergé.* Paris, 1929.

Preradovich, Nikolaus von. *Die Führungsschichten in Österreich und Preussen, 1804–1918.* Wiesbaden, 1955.

Preuss, Hugo. *Die Entwicklung des deutschen Städtewesens.* Leipzig, 1906.

———. "Verwaltungsreform und Staatsreform in Österreich und Preussen." *ZP* 5 (1912).

Pritz, Joseph. "Anton Günther." In *Katholische Theologen Deutschlands im 19. Jahrhundert,* ed. by Heinrich Fries and Georg Schwaiger, vol. 1. Munich, 1975.

———. *Glauben und Wissen bei Anton Günther.* Vienna, 1963.

———. *Mensch als Mitte. Leben und Werk Carl Werners.* Vienna, 1968.

———. "Zur Lehre Anton Günthers von der Kirche." *Wiener Beiträge zur Theologie* 10 (1965).

Prochazka, J. *Die provisorische Gemeindeordnung für die Stadt Wien.* Vienna, 1850.

Pross, Helge. "Bürgerlich-konservative Kritik an der kapitalistischen Gesellschaft. Zur Theorie Lorenz von Steins." *KZSS* 18 (1966).

Pulzer, Peter G. J. "Die jüdische Beteiligung an der Politik." In Werner E. Mosse, ed., *Juden im Wilhelminischen Deutschland* (qv).

———. *The Rise of Political Antisemitism in Germany and Austria.* New York, 1965.

Rabinbach, Anson. "The Migration of Galician Jews to Vienna 1857–1880." *AHY* 11 (1975).

Rath, R. John. *The Viennese Revolution of 1848.* Austin, 1957.

Rauchberg, Heinrich. "Die Alters- und Familienstandsgliederung der Israeliten in den im Reichsrate vertretenen Königreichen und Ländern." *SM* 19 (1893).

————. *Die Bevölkerung Österreichs auf Grund der Ergebnisse der Volkszählung vom 31. Dezember 1890.* Vienna, 1895.

Redlich, Josef. "Lasser und Schmerling (nach ihren Briefen)." *ÖRD* 19 (1909).

————. *Das österreichische Staats- und Reichsproblem.* 2 vols. Leipzig, 1920–26.

————. *Schicksalsjahre Österreichs, 1908–1919. Das politische Tagebuch Josef Redlichs.* Ed. by Fritz Fellner. 2 vols. Graz and Cologne, 1953.

————. *Das Wesen der österreichischen Kommunalverfassung.* Leipzig, 1910.

Reinhardt, Rudolf. "Zur Kirchenreform in Österreich unter Maria Theresia." *ZKG* 77 (1966).

Rémond, René. *Les deux congrès ecclésiastiques de Reims et de Bourges, 1896–1900.* Paris, 1964.

Reschauer, Heinrich, and Smets, Moritz. *Das Jahr 1848. Geschichte der Wiener Revolution.* 2 vols. Vienna, 1876.

Ritter, Emil. *Die katholisch-soziale Bewegung Deutschlands im neunzehnten Jahrhundert und der Volksverein.* Cologne, 1954.

Ritter, Gerhard A., ed. *Die deutschen Parteien vor 1918.* Cologne, 1973.

Rizzi, Hans. "Karl, Freiherr von Vogelsang." *NÖB* 2 (1925).

Röhrig, Floridus. "Die Gründung der österreichischen Chorherren-Kongregation und ihre Vorgeschichte." In *Festschrift Franz Loidl,* vol. 2: (qv).

Rogge, Walter. *Oesterreich seit der Katastrophe Hohenwart-Beust.* 2 vols. Leipzig and Vienna, 1879.

————. *Oesterreich von Vilagos bis zur Gegenwart.* 3 vols. Leipzig, 1872–73.

Roschmann-Herburg, Julius von. "Die Viehzählung in Österreich vom 31. Dez. 1890." *SM* 19 (1893).

Rosenberg, Hans. *Grosse Depression und Bismarckzeit. Wirtschaftsablauf, Gesellschaft, und Politik.* Berlin, 1967.

Rothschild, Kurt. "Wurzeln und Triebkräfte der Entwicklung der österreichischen Wirtschaftsstruktur." In *Österreichs Wirtschaftsstruktur,* ed. by Wilhelm Weber, vol. 1. Berlin, 1961.

Rudolph, Richard. "The Pattern of Austrian Industrial Growth from the Eighteenth to the Early Twentieth Century." *AHY* 11 (1975).

Rürup, Reinhard. *Emanzipation und Antisemitismus. Studien zur "Judenfrage" der bürgerlichen Gesellschaft.* Göttingen, 1975.

————. "Emanzipation und Krise. Zur Geschichte der 'Judenfrage' in Deutschland vor 1890." In Werner E. Mosse, ed., *Juden im Wilhelminischen Deutschland* (qv).

Rumpler, Helmut. *Die Protokolle des österreichischen Ministerrates, 1848–1867. Einleitungsband: Ministerrat und Ministerratsprotokolle, 1848–1867.* Vienna, 1970.

Runciman, W. G. *Relative Deprivation and Social Justice.* Berkeley and Los Angeles, 1966.

Saurer, Edith. *Die politischen Aspekte der österreichischen Bischofsernennungen, 1867–1903.* Vienna, 1968.

Sax, Emil. "Die österreichische Gewerbenovelle von 1883." *JGVV* 7 (1883).

Schidl, Victor. "Die österreichische Staatsbeamtenorganisation. Ihre Ziele und Methoden." *Dokumente des Fortschritts* 4 (1911).

Schiff, Walter. "Die ältere Gewerbestatistik in Österreich und die Entstehung der Betriebszählung vom Jahre 1902." *SM* 33 (1907).

Schimmer, Gustav Adolf. *Die Bevölkerung von Wien und seiner Umgebung nach dem Beruf und der Beschäftigung.* Vienna, 1874.

———. "Die Juden in Österreich nach der Zählung vom 31. December 1880." *SM* 7 (1881).

———. "Vergleichende Statistik der direkten Reichsratswahlen in Österreich." *SM* 3 (1877).

Schmid, Ferdinand. *Finanzreform in Österreich.* Tübingen, 1911.

Schmid-Egger, Barbara. *Klerus und Politik in Böhmen um 1900.* Munich, 1974.

Schmidt, Georg. "Die Nationalliberalen—eine regierungsfähige Partei? Zur Problematik der inneren Reichsgründung, 1870–1878." In *Die deutschen Parteien vor 1918,* ed. by Gerhard A. Ritter. Cologne, 1973.

Schmoller, Gustav. *Zur Geschichte der deutschen Kleingewerbe im 19. Jahrhundert.* Halle, 1870.

Schnee, Heinrich. *Karl Lueger.* Berlin, 1960.

———. "Die politische Entwicklung des Wiener Bürgermeisters Dr. Karl Lueger." *Historisches Jahrbuch* 76 (1956).

Schnell, Hermann. *100 Jahre Pädagogisches Institut der Stadt Wien.* Vienna, 1968.

Schnierer, Friedrich. "Die Steigerung der Mietzinse in Wien, 1881–1907." *Mitteilungen der Zentralstelle für Wohnungsreform in Österreich,* no. 20 (Aug. 1911).

Schober, Richard. "Die Tiroler Konservativen in der Ära Taaffe." *MÖSA* 29 (1976).

Schorske, Carl E. "Politics in a New Key: An Austrian Triptych." *JMH* 39 (1967).

Schriften des Vereins für Sozialpolitik. Leipzig, 1875–1910.

Schroeder, Oskar. *Aufbruch und Missverständnis. Zur Geschichte der reformkatholischen Bewegung.* Graz and Vienna, 1969.

Schrutka von Rechtenstamm, Helmut. "Rechts- und Staatswissenschaftliche Facultät." In *Geschichte der Wiener Universität von 1848 bis 1898.* Vienna, 1898.

Schüller, Ludwig. "Die Wiener Enquête über Frauenarbeit." *ASGSS* 10 (1897).

Schüller, Richard. "Die österreichische Handwerkergesetzgebung." *ASGSS* 11 (1897).

———. "Die Schuhmacherei in Wien." In *Untersuchungen über die Lage des Handwerks* (qv).

Schullern-Schrattenhofen, Hermann von. "Die Bewegung der Getreidepreise in Österreich." *SM* 21 (1895).

Schulte, Friedrich von. "Bureaucracy and Its Operation in Germany and Austria-Hungary." *CR* 37 (1880).

Schütz, Friedrich. *Werden und Wirken des Bürgerministeriums.* Leipzig, 1909.

Schwalber, Josef. *Vogelsang und die moderne chrislich-soziale Politik.* Munich, 1927.

Schwarz, Paul. "Die Entwicklung der städtischen Grundrente in Wien." In *Neue Untersuchungen über die Wohnungsfrage in Deutschland und im Ausland. SVSP* 94 (1901).

Schwiedland, Eugen. "Die Entstehung der Hausindustrie mit Rücksicht auf Österreich." *ZVSV* 1 (1892).

————. "Die Heimarbeit und ihre staatliche Regelung." *Das Leben* 1 (1897).

————. *Kleingewerbe und Hausindustrie in Österreich.* 2 vols. Leipzig, 1894.

Schwingenschlögl, Rudolf. *Der erste allgemeine Beamten-Verein der österreichisch-ungarischen Monarchie. Geschichte seiner Gründung, Entstehung, und Tätigkeit während der ersten 25 Jahre seines Bestehens, 1865–1890.* Vienna, 1890.

Segall, Jakob. *Die beruflichen und sozialen Verhältnisse der Juden in Deutschland.* Berlin, 1912.

Sheehan, James J. *German Liberalism in the Nineteenth Century.* Chicago, 1978.

————. "Liberalism and the City in Nineteenth-Century Germany." *PP* 51 (1971).

————. "Liberalism and Society in Germany, 1815–1848." *JMH* 45 (1973).

————. "Liberalismus und Gesellschaft in Deutschland, 1815–1848." In *Liberalismus,* ed. by Lothar Gall. Cologne, 1976.

Siebertz, Paul. *Karl Fürst zu Löwenstein. Ein Bild seines Lebens und Wirkens.* Munich, 1924.

Sieghart, Rudolf. *Die letzten Jahrzehnte einer Grossmacht.* Berlin, 1932.

————. "The Reform of Direct Taxation in Austria." *Economic Journal* 8 (1898).

Silberbauer, Gerhard. *Österreichs Katholiken und die Arbeiterfrage.* Graz, Vienna, and Cologne, 1966.

Simmel, Georg. *Conflict* and *The Web of Group Affiliation.* Trans. by Kurt H. Wolff and Reinhard Bendix. Glencoe, 1955.

Simons, Thomas W. "Vienna's First Catholic Political Movement: The Güntherians, 1848–1857." *Catholic Historical Review* 55 (1969).

Skalnik, Kurt. *Dr. Karl Lueger.* Vienna, 1954.

Soderini, Eduardo. *Il Pontificato di Leone XIII.* Vol. 1. Milan, 1932.

Die soziale Frage und der Katholizismus. Festschrift zum 40. jährigen Jubiläum der Enzyklika "Rerum Novarum." Paderborn, 1931.

Spiegel, Ludwig. "Das Heimatrecht und die Gemeinden." In *Verfassung und Verwaltungsorganisation der Städte. SVSP* 122 (1907).

Springer, Anton. *Geschichte Oesterreichs seit dem Wiener Frieden, 1809.* 2 vols. Leipzig, 1863–65.

Springer, Rudolf. *Grundlagen und Entwicklungsziele der Österreichisch-Ungarischen Monarchie.* Vienna and Leipzig, 1906.

Die Stadt Cöln im ersten Jahrhundert unter preussischer Herrschaft, 1815–1915. 2 vols. Cologne, 1916.

Stegmann, Dirk. *Die Erben Bismarcks. Parteien und Verbände in der Spätphase des wilhelminischen Deutschlands.* Cologne and Berlin, 1970.

Steiner, Herbert. *Die Arbeiterbewegung Österreichs, 1867–1889.* Vienna, 1964.

Steiner, Kurt. *Politics in Austria.* Boston, 1972.

Stölzl, Christoph. *Die Ära Bach in Böhmen*. Munich and Vienna, 1971.

Stourzh, Gerald. "Die österreichische Dezemberverfassung von 1867." *ÖGL* 12 (1968).

Strakosch-Grassmann, Gustav. *Das allgemeine Wahlrecht in Österreich seit 1848.* Leipzig and Vienna, 1906.

———. *Geschichte des österreichischen Unterrichtswesens*. Vienna, 1905.

Stürmer, Michael. *Regierung und Reichstag im Bismarckstaat, 1871–1880. Cäsarismus oder Parlamentarismus*. Düsseldorf, 1974.

Sutter, Berthold. *Die Badenischen Sprachenverordnungen von 1897*. 2 vols. Graz and Cologne, 1960–65.

Swoboda, Heinrich. *Grossstadtseelsorge*. Regensburg, 1909.

Teml, Hubert. "Die Lehrerbildung nach dem Reichsvolksschulgesetz." *Österreichische Bildungs- und Schulgeschichte von der Aufklärung bis zum Liberalismus. Jahrbuch für österreichische Kulturgeschichte*, 4 (1974).

Theimer, Kamilla. *Frauenarbeit in Österreich*. Vienna, 1909.

Thienen-Adlerflycht, Christoph. *Graf Leo Thun im Vormärz*. Graz, 1967.

Till, Rudolf. "Die Anfänge der christlichen Volksbewegung in Österreich." *JLG* (1937).

———. *Geschichte der Wiener Stadtverwaltung in den letzten 200 Jahren*. Vienna, 1957.

———. *Hofbauer und sein Kreis*. Vienna, 1951.

———. "Die Mitglieder der ersten Wiener Gemeindevertretung im Jahre 1848." *WG* 5 (1950).

———. "Theologen in der Wiener Stadtverwaltung." *JVGSW* 13 (1957/58).

Trippen, Norbert. *Theologie und Lehramt im Konflikt*. Freiburg i. B., 1977.

Tur-Sinai, N. H. "Viennese Jewry." In Josef Fraenkel, ed., *The Jews of Austria* (qv).

Twardowski, Julius von. *Statistische Daten über Österreich*. Vienna, 1902.

Untersuchungen über die Lage des Handwerks in Österreich. SVSP 71 (1896).

Untersuchungen über die Lage des Hausiergewerbes in Österreich. SVSP 82 (1899).

Valentin, Hellwig. "Der Prozess Schönerer und seine Auswirkungen auf die parteipolitischen Verhältnisse in Österreich." *ÖGL* 16 (1972).

Valjavec, Fritz. *Der Josephinismus*. Brünn, 1944.

Vigener, Fritz. *Ketteler. Ein deutsches Bischofsleben des neunzehnten Jahrhunderts*. Munich and Berlin, 1924.

Vistalli, Francesco. "Il cardinale Antonio Agliardi." *La Scuola Cattolica* 43 (1915).

Vogelsang, Marie Freiin von. "Die Handlungsgehilfen in Österreich." *MCSR* 13 (1891).

Volcelka, Karl. *Verfassung oder Konkordat? Der publizistische und politische Kampf der österreichischen Liberalen um die Religionsgesetze des Jahres 1868*. Vienna, 1978.

Volkov, Shulamit. *The Rise of Popular Antimodernism in Germany: The Urban Master Artisans, 1873–1896*. Princeton, 1978.

Waentig, Heinrich. *Gewerbliche Mittelstandspolitik*. Leipzig, 1898.

Wagner, Hans. "Der Einfluss von Gallikanismus und Jansenismus auf die Kirche und den Staat der Aufklärung in Österreich." *ÖGL* 11 (1967).

Waldinger, Ernst. "Darstellung einer jüdischen Jugend in der Wiener Vorstadt." In Josef Fraenkel, ed., *The Jews of Austria* (qv).

Walf, Knut. *Das bischöfliche Amt in der Sicht Josephinischer Kirchenrechtler.* Cologne and Vienna, 1975.

Walker, Mack. *German Home Towns: Community, Estate, and General Estate, 1648–1871.* Ithaca and London, 1971.

Walter, Friedrich. *Die österreichische Zentralverwaltung.* II/1. 2. Halbband. 2. Teil. *Die Zeit Franz II. (I.) und Ferdinands I. (1792–1848).* Vienna, 1956.

———. *Die österreichische Zentralverwaltung.* III/3. *Die Geschichte der Ministerien vom Durchbruch des Absolutismus bis zum Ausgleich mit Ungarn und zur Konstitutionalisierung der österreichischen Länder 1852 bis 1867.* Vienna, 1970.

Walter, Friedrich, ed. *Die österreichische Zentralverwaltung.* II/4. *Die Zeit Josephs II. und Leopolds II.* Vienna, 1956.

Wangermann, Ernst. *From Joseph II to the Jacobin Trials.* 2d ed. Oxford, 1969.

Weber, Christoph. *Quellen und Studien zur Kurie und zur Vatikanischen Politik unter Leo XIII.* Tübingen, 1973.

Weber, Max. *Gesammelte politische Schriften.* Munich, 1921.

———. *Wirtschaft und Gesellschaft.* 4th ed. Tübingen, 1956.

Weber, Wilhelm, ed. *Österreichs Wirtschaftsstruktur.* 2 vols. Berlin, 1961.

Wehler, Hans-Ulrich. *Das Deutsche Kaiserreich, 1870–1918.* Göttingen, 1973.

Wehrl, Franz. "Der 'Neue Geist.' Eine Untersuchung der Geistesrichtungen des Klerus in Wien, 1750–1790." *MÖSA* 20 (1967).

Weiler, Rudolf. "Katholische Soziallehre unterwegs." In *Festschrift Franz Loidl,* vol. 2 (qv).

Weinzierl-Fischer, Erika. "Alois Prinz Liechtenstein." *NÖB* 14 (1961).

———. "Aus den Anfängen der christlich sozialen Bewegung in Österreich. Nach der Korrespondenz des Grafen Anton Pergen." *MÖSA* 14 (1961).

———. "Aus den Anfängen der 'Österreichischen Monatsschrift für Gesellschaftswissenschaft und christliche Sozialreform.'" In *Im Dienst der Sozialreform. Festschrift für Karl Kummer.* Vienna, 1965.

———. "Friedrich Gustav Piffl." *NÖB* 9 (1956).

———. "Die Kirchenfrage auf dem österreichischen Reichstag, 1848/49." *MÖSA* 8 (1955).

———. *Die österreichischen Konkordate von 1855 und 1933.* Vienna, 1960.

———. "Österreichs Clerus und die Arbeiterschaft." *WW* 10 (1957).

———. "On the Pathogenesis of the Anti-Semitism of Sebastian Brunner (1814–1893)." *Yad Vashem Studies* 10 (1974).

———. "Visitationsberichte österreichischer Bischöfe an Kaiser Franz I." *MÖSA* 6 (1953).

Weiskirchner, Richard. "Das Hutmachergewerbe in Wien." In *Untersuchungen über die Lage des Handwerks* (qv).

———. "Die Zuckerbäckerei und die mit derselben verwandten Gewerbe in Wien." In *Untersuchungen über die Lage des Handwerks* (qv).

Weiss, Karl. *Entwicklung der Gemeinde-Verfassung der Stadt Wien, 1221–1850.* Vienna, 1867.

———. *Rückblicke auf die Gemeindeverwaltung der Stadt Wien in den Jahren 1838–1848.* Vienna, 1875.

Wenzel, Paul. *Das wissenschaftliche Anliegen des Güntherianismus.* Essen, 1961.

Werner, Karl Heinz. "Österreichs Industrie- und Aussenhandelspolitik 1848 bis 1948." In *Hundert Jahre österreichische Wirtschaftsentwicklung, 1848–1948,* ed. by Hans Mayer. Vienna, 1949.

Whiteside, Andrew. *The Socialism of Fools.* Berkeley and Los Angeles, 1975.

Wieser, Friedrich von. *Die Ergebnisse und die Aussichten der Personaleinkommensteuer in Österreich.* Leipzig, 1901.

Windt, Berthold. "Die Juden an den Mittel- und Hochschulen Österreichs seit 1850." *SM* 7 (1881).

Winkler, Heinrich August. "Gesellschaftsreform und Aussenpolitik. Eine Theorie Lorenz von Steins in zeitgeschichtlicher Perspektive." *HZ* 214 (1972).

———. *Pluralismus oder Protektionismus? Verfassungspolitische Probleme des Verbandswesens im deutschen Kaiserreich.* Wiesbaden, 1972.

———. "Der rückversicherte Mittelstand. Die Interessenverbände von Handwerk und Kleinhandel im deutschen Kaiserreich." In *Zur soziologischen Theorie und Analyse des 19. Jahrhunderts,* ed. by Walter Rüegg and Otto Neuloh. Göttingen, 1971.

———. "Vom linken zum rechten Nationalismus. Der deutsche Liberalismus in der Krise von 1878/79." *GG* 4 (1978).

Winter, Eduard. *Bernard Bolzano und sein Kreis.* Leipzig, 1933.

———. "Differenzierungen in der katholischen Restauration in Österreich." *Historisches Jahrbuch* 52 (1932).

———. *Frühliberalismus in der Donaumonarchie.* Berlin, 1968.

———. *Die geistige Entwicklung Anton Günthers und seiner Schule.* Paderborn, 1931.

———. *Der Josephinismus.* Berlin, 1962.

———. "Die katholische Restauration in Österreich, 1808–1820. Ihre Entwicklung und Auswirkung." In *Katholischer Glaube und Deutsches Volkstum in Österreich.* Salzburg, 1933.

———. *Russland und das Papsttum.* 2 vols. Berlin, 1960–72.

———. *Russland und die slawischen Völker in der Diplomatie des Vatikans, 1878–1903.* Berlin, 1950.

———. *Wissenschaft und Religion im Vormärz. Der Briefwechsel B. Bolzanos mit M. J. Fesl, 1822–1848.* Berlin, 1965.

Winter, Eduard, and Winter, Maria. *Der Bolzanokreis, 1824–1833.* Vienna, 1970.

———. *Domprediger Johann Emanuel Veith und Kardinal Friedrich Schwarzenberg. Der Güntherprozess in unveröffentlichten Briefen und Akten.* Vienna, 1972.

Winter, Ernst Karl. "Abel." In *Staatslexikon,* vol. 1. Freiburg i. B., 1926.

———. "Anton Günther. Ein Beitrag zur Romantikforschung." *ZGSW* 88 (1930).

———. *Arbeiterschaft und Staat.* Vienna, 1934.

———. "Die beiden Schulen des mitteleuropäischen Katholizismus." *NO* 3 (1927).

Winter, Fritz. "Die Heimarbeit in der österreichischen Konfektionsindustrie." *ASGSS* 15 (1900).

Wirth, Max. "Volkswirtschaftliche Entwickelung der Stadt Wien." In *Wien, 1848–1888. Denkschrift zum 2. December 1888.* 2 vols. Vienna, 1888.

Wodka, Josef. *Kirche in Österreich.* Vienna, 1959.

Wolf, Gerson. *Geschichte der Juden in Wien.* Vienna, 1876.

Wolf, Mechthild. *Ignaz von Plener. Vom Schicksal eines Ministers unter Kaiser Franz Joseph.* Munich, 1975.

Wolfsgruber, Cölestin. *Friedrich Kardinal Schwarzenberg.* 3 vols. Vienna and Leipzig, 1906–17.

———. "Die Haltung des Wiener Klerus in den 'Märztagen' 1848." *JLN* 13 (1914–15).

———. *Joseph Othmar Cardinal Rauscher.* Freiburg i. B., 1888.

Zatschek, Heinz. *550 Jahre Jung sein. Die Geschichte eines Handwerks.* Vienna, 1958.

———. *Handwerk und Gewerbe in Wien.* Vienna, 1949.

Zauner, A. *Die Frage des Anschlusses der Vororte an die Gross Commune Wien.* Vienna, n.d.

Zenker, Ernst Victor. *Die Wiener Revolution 1848 in ihren socialen Voraussetzungen und Beziehungen.* Vienna and Leipzig, 1897.

Zoppi, Sergio. *Romolo Murri e la prima Democrazia cristiana.* Florence, 1968.

Zwiedeneck-Südenhorst, Otto von. "Die Bedeutung des Bedarfs für die Entwicklung der gewerblichen Betriebsysteme." *ZVSV* 7 (1898).

Unpublished Dissertations

Adelmaier, Werner. *Ernst Vergani.* University of Vienna, 1969.

Albertin, Lothar. *Nationalismus und Protestantismus in der österreichischen Los von Rom Bewegung um 1900.* University of Cologne, 1954.

Anheil, Ferdinand. *Caritative und soziale Unternehmungen in der Wiener Erzdiözese von 1802 bis 1918.* University of Vienna, 1968.

Bammer, Winfried. *Beiträge zur Sozialstruktur der Bevölkerung Wiens auf Grund der Verlassenschaftsakten des Jahres 1830.* University of Vienna, 1968.

Bischof, Ferdinand. *Kardinal Gruscha und die soziale Frage.* University of Vienna, 1959.

Burger, Erwin. *Die Frage der Bestätigung der Wahl Dr. Karl Luegers zum Bürgermeister von Wien.* University of Vienna, 1952.

Czaschka, Jürgen. *Sozialgeschichte der Wiener Gemeindebezirke Josefstadt und Hietzing von 1840–1910.* University of Vienna, 1967.

David, Hedwig. *Joseph Scheicher als Sozialpolitiker.* University of Vienna, 1946.

Deters, Fred. *The Role of the Suburbs in the Modernization of Vienna.* University of Chicago, 1974.

Fiala, Brigitte. *Der Wiener Gemeinderat in den Jahren 1879 bis 1883.* University of Vienna, 1974.

Frieben, Birgit. *Die Sozialstruktur Wiens am Anfang des Vormärz.* University of Vienna, 1966.

Ghelardoni, Paul. *Die feudalen Elemente in der österreichischen bürgerlichen Gesellschaft von 1803 bis 1914.* University of Vienna, 1961.

Gross, Nahum. *Industrialization in Austria in the Nineteenth Century.* University of California at Berkeley, 1966.

Hagenhofer, Johann. *Die soziale Lage der Wiener Arbeiter um die Jahrhundertwende.* University of Vienna, 1966.

Hahnkamper, Gertrude. *Der Wiener Gemeinderat Zwischen 1861 und 1864.* University of Vienna, 1973.

Harrer, Karl. *Dr. Richard Weiskirchner.* University of Vienna, 1950.

Hartel, Gertrude. *Graf Gustav Blome.* University of Vienna, 1952.

Hartmayer, Hans. *Die führenden Abgeordneten des Liberalismus in Österreich.* University of Vienna, 1949.

Hausner, Eduard. *Die Tätigkeit des Wiener Gemeinderates in den Jahren 1884–1888.* University of Vienna, 1974.

Helmbe, Martha. *Die Tätigkeit des Wiener Gemeinderates von 1889–1892.* University of Vienna, 1974.

Holzer, Heribert. *Dr. Josef Deckert.* University of Vienna, 1959.

Hummel, Elfriede. *Der Liberalismus in seiner Relation zur Wiener Presse mit besonderer Berücksichtigung der ideengeschichtlichen Entwicklung.* University of Vienna, 1953.

Kant, Friedrich. *Der niederösterreichische Landtag von 1902 bis 1908.* University of Vienna, 1949.

Kendl, Joseph. *Joseph Scheicher.* University of Salzburg, 1967.

Kraus, Therese. *Die Entstehung des 'Niederösterreichischen Bauernbundes.* University of Vienna, 1950.

Kretschmer, Helmut. *Dr. Julius Newald. Bürgermeister von Wien.* University of Vienna, 1971.

Kunze, Margot. *Dr. Karl Lueger als Gemeinderat von 1875–1896.* University of Vienna, 1968.

Ladinger, Peter. *Die soziale Stellung der Volksschullehrer vor und nach dem Reichsvolksschulgesetz.* University of Vienna, 1975.

Loibl, Alfred. *Die Stellung der "Konstitutionellen Vorstadt-Zeitung" zur sozialen Frage, 1855–1878.* University of Vienna, 1950.

Miko, Norbert. *Die Vereinigung der christlich-sozialen Reichspartei und des katholisch-konservativen Zentrums im Jahre 1907.* University of Vienna, 1949.

Moritz, Johannes. *Dr. Ludwig Psenner—von der antisemitischen Volksbewegung zur christlichsozialen Reform.* University of Vienna, 1962.

Ninkov, Benno. *Die politischen Anfänge Dr. Karl Luegers im Lichte der Wiener Presse.* University of Vienna, 1946.

Novotny, Friedrich. *Die Vorarbeiter der Enzyklika Rerum Novarum.* University of Vienna, 1954.

Ortner, Heidemarie. *Das Eindringen des Wiener Bürgertums und Geldadels in den landtäflichen Grundbesitz Niederösterreichs, 1815–1895.* University of Vienna, 1968.

Posch, Otto. *Anton Gruscha und der österreichische Katholizismus.* University of Vienna, 1949.

Prammer, Johann. *Konservative und christlichsoziale Politik im Viertel ob dem Wienerwald.* University of Vienna, 1973.

Richter, Josefa. *Die sozialen Verhältnisse der Wiener Arbeiter, 1867–1889.* University of Vienna, 1965.

Scheithauer, Erich. *Beiträge zur Sozialstruktur der Wiener Aussenbezirke. Entwicklung im Zeitraum 1850–1910 an Hand der Volkszählungsergebnisse.* University of Vienna, 1954.

Schmid, Johanna. *Der Wandel des Bildes Josephs II. in der österreichischen Historiographie von den Zeitgenossen bis zum Ende der Monarchie.* University of Vienna, 1972.

Schmitz, Gertrud. *Die Entwicklungsgeschichte der christlichen Volksbewegung in Österreich.* University of Vienna, 1938.

Stöger, Gertrud. *Die politischen Anfänge Luegers.* University of Vienna, 1941.

Stöger, Walter. *Das Verhältnis der Konservativen zur Christlichsozialen Partei.* University of Vienna, 1949.

Uhl, Elisabeth. *Eduard Uhl. Bürgermeister der Stadt Wien, 1882–1889.* University of Vienna, 1950.

Unterberger, Erhard. *Liberalismus in St. Pölten (1870–1918).* University of Vienna, 1966.

Weinberger, Dorit. *Die christliche Sozialreform Anton Orels.* University of Vienna, 1966.

Wodak, Erika. *Die Selbstverwaltung der Stadt Wien von 1848–1861.* University of Vienna, 1936.

Wymetal, Elisabeth. *Eduard Herbst, sein Werdegang und seine Persönlichkeit vornehmlich auf Grund seiner selbstbiographischen Aufzeichnungen.* University of Vienna, 1944.

Index

Abel, Heinrich: and origins of Christian Socialism, 224; popular revivalism of, 119–20; and religious antisemitism, 156; and Joseph Scheicher, 141

Adler, Emanuel, on Austrian craft industries, 52

Adler, Victor, 154, 318; and anti-Socialist law, 214; and Austrian bureaucracy, 410; and the clergy, 160; and the 1897 elections, 406, 408; and mass political aesthetics, 241, 318; and municipal politics, 232; and Socialist party in 1896, 382; and Vogelsang, 180

Agliardi, Antonio, 164, 348; role in Christian Social politics, 340–42, 346–48

Allgemeiner Stand. See Bürgertum

Almond, Gabriel, on communications subsystems in politics, 102

Angestellten: political behavior of, 371; political radicalism of, 306, 309–11; social status of, 308–10

Anticlericalism: in the 1870s, 137; in France and Austria, 31–32; Liberal use of, 30, 333, 353, 355; and the Progressive party, 30–31; in the school system, 152–53

Antisemitism: among the artisans, 70–76; and the economy, 80; origins before 1880, 76; racialism in, 78–79, 88, 92–93; and the *Reformverein*, 90–97; religion in, 113–21; role of elites and sub-elites in, 72–73; among university students, 89. *See also* Jews in Vienna

Anzengruber, Ludwig, and the portrait of the Viennese *Hausherren*, 393

Arbeiter-Zeitung: attacks on the *Hausherren*, 388, 402; municipal program of, 383

Artisans in Vienna: apprentices of, 51; conflicts with workers, 111–12; congresses in Vienna, 63, 64, 106–7; cooperative movement of, 55, 57, 101; cultural views of, 51, 67–68; demands for protectionism, 48, 54, 63; and depression of 1873, 44–45; economic basis of prosperity among, 68–69; economic decline of, 42–51; guild organizations for, 99–113; house industry among, 43, 45–46; Jewish integration into, 86–88; and *massnehmen*, 75; nonguild members among, 8; political organizations of, 49, 112–13; political profile before 1880, 41; professional training of, 50; and protectionism in Germany, 66; religious attitudes of, 113–17; role of the *Weiner Gewerbegenossenschaftstag* among, 59, 60, 67, 103–6, 112–13; surveys of contemporary opinion among, 57–58, 75–76

Associations, in politics, 71, 162, 238–40

Auersperg, Count Adolf: and Austrian Liberalism, 22; and the *Beamten* movement, 258

Auersperg, Count Carlos, and the Liberal *Beamten* movement, 258

Ausgleich of 1867, impact on Liberal politics, 35

Austerlitz, Friedrich, and the Social Democratic *Handlungsgehilfen* movement, 312

"Austriacus," and early Austrian antisemitism, 77

Axmann, Julius: and the elections of 1897, 407–8; as leader of the antisemitic *Handlungsgehilfen* movement, 75, 309–11

Bach, Alexander, and the 1849–50 negotiations for the Viennese *Gemeindeordnung*, 15–16, 275

Bacquehem, Oliver, Marquis de: in the ministry of 1893, 326; in the negotiations over Cilli, 329

Badeni, Count Casimir: and Karl Lueger, 320, 345, 373–77, 380–81; ministerial poli-